SPARKNOTES™

SAT & PSAT

2004 Edition

Editorial Director Justin Kestler

Executive Editor Ben Florman

Director of Technology Tammy Hepps

Series Editor John Crowther

Managing Editor Vincent Janoski

Illustrations Porter Mason

Cover Design Dan O. Williams

This edition published by Spark Publishing.

Spark Publishing
A Division of SparkNotes LLC
120 Fifth Avenue, 8th Floor
New York, NY 10011

Please submit all comments and questions or report errors to www.sparknotes.com/errors

Library of Congress information available upon request

Printed and bound in Canada

Standard edition: ISBN 1-58663-958-7
Deluxe edition: ISBN 1-58663-959-5

Orientation

SAT Verbal

SAT Vocabulary **91**

The 1000 Most Common SAT Words **97**

SAT Math

The PSAT

Practice Tests

Orientation

Introduction
to the SAT

Chapter Contents

EACH YEAR, MORE THAN A MILLION students spend three grueling hours taking the SAT (officially called the SAT I), a test that colleges and universities use to help them decide which students to admit. In addition to the time spent taking the test, most students also devote many hours preparing before the test to make sure they get the best score possible, and fruitless hours after the test worrying about whether they actually got that score.

Because it plays such an important role in the college admissions process, students often look upon the test with dread. This introduction is an attempt to cut through all the fear and hyperbole (a good SAT vocabulary word, by the way) by explaining what the SAT is, how it's scored, and why colleges use it to evaluate prospective students. We will also discuss the test's controversial flaws, the test preparation industry that has grown up around the SAT, and, most important, how you should approach the test to minimize your anxiety and maximize your score.

Content & Structure of the SAT

The SAT has two major sections: verbal and math. Using three different types of questions, the Verbal section seeks to test your facility with language, your ability to read and comprehend, and your critical thinking skills. The Math section also uses three different types of questions to gauge your skills in basic math and critical thinking.

Though the SAT is split into verbal and math divisions, the test is not presented in two big parts. Instead, it is divided into timed sections. Three of these sections cover verbal skills and three cover math. In this discussion of the content and structure of the SAT, we'll begin with the types of questions and then move to a description of the timed sections.

The Verbal Questions

The SAT contains a total of 78 verbal questions, divided into three types. All three types are multiple-choice.

- **Sentence completions** (19 questions). You are given a sentence with one or two blanks and must choose the best word or words to fill the blanks.

- **Analogies** (19). You are given two words that are related in some way and must choose the word pair that shares the same relation.

- **Reading comprehension** (40). These questions test your ability to read and understand facts and arguments based on a reading passage.

Sentence completion and analogy questions are organized according to difficulty. For example, in a group of sentence completions, the first third will be the easiest, the second third will be moderate, and the last third will be difficult. Reading comprehension passages and questions are not ordered by difficulty. This book gives each question type its own chapter, provides examples, and explains specific strategies.

The Math Questions

The 60 SAT math questions also come in three types. Once again, each of the question types is explained in much greater detail later in this book.

- **Regular multiple-choice** (35 questions). You are presented with a math question, and have to choose between five possible answer choices.

- **Quantitative comparisons** (15). These questions present you with two values and ask you to determine which of the two is larger, whether the two are equal, or whether it cannot be determined which is larger.

- **Grid-Ins** (10). Grid-ins are the only non multiple-choice questions on the test. For these questions you are given a math question and must produce an answer by filling out a special answer grid.

All math questions are roughly ordered by difficulty within a section. The first third is easy, the second third moderate, and the last third difficult.

Unlike verbal questions, math questions can also be broken down according to the subject they cover. In general, math questions on the SAT will test your knowledge of basic arithmetic, algebra, geometry, and a few miscellaneous topics. Within these areas, the SAT covers specific math topics:

Arithmetic

1. Basic Operations, Order of Operations, and Place Value
2. Odd and Even Numbers
3. Positive and Negative Numbers
4. Divisibility and Remainders
5. Multiples, Factors, and Primes
6. Fractions, Decimals, and Percents
7. Ratios and Proportions
8. Rates
9. Mean, Median, and Mode
10. Exponents and Square Roots
11. Combinations, Permutations, and Probability
12. Series
13. Sets

Miscellaneous Math

1. Charts and Graphs
2. Logical Reasoning
3. Problems with Unique Symbols

Algebra

1. Substitution
2. Building Expressions and Equations
3. Simplifying and Manipulating Expressions
4. Solving Linear Equations

5. Solving Systems of Equations

6. Solving Inequalities

7. Multiplying Binomials and Polynomials

Geometry

1. Angles and Lines

2. Triangles

3. Polygons

4. Circles

5. Solids

6. Coordinate Geometry

7. Geometric Visualization

Don't be overwhelmed by the size of the list. You probably already know how to handle most of these topics. In addition, this book covers all the math you need to know for the SAT in the chapters SAT Arithmetic, SAT Geometry, SAT Algebra, and Miscellaneous SAT Math. A particular SAT test will probably cover most of these 30 topics. No SAT test will ask questions about topics that don't appear on this list.

The Seven Timed Sections of the SAT

Every SAT organizes the three different types of math and verbal questions into timed sections. Each SAT has seven timed sections in total: three sections cover math, three cover verbal, and one experimental section may cover either math or verbal. The seven sections are as follows:

- 30-minute math section containing 25 multiple-choice questions.

- 30-minute verbal section containing 10 sentence completions, 13 analogies, and 12 reading comprehension questions.

- 30-minute math section containing 15 quantitative comparison questions and 10 grid-ins.

- 30-minute verbal section containing 9 sentence completions, 6 analogies, and 15 reading comprehension questions.

- 15-minute math section containing 10 multiple-choice questions.

- 15-minute verbal section containing 13 reading comprehension questions.

- 30-minute experimental section that may cover either verbal or math. (This section does not impact your score.)

No matter when you take the SAT, you will encounter these seven timed sections. The seven sections will not necessarily appear in the order presented here, however.

The Experimental Section

The test writers use the experimental section to try out new questions. The section also helps the writers measure the difficulty of the test from year to year. The experimental section on the test you take might be verbal or might be math. Either way, you won't be able to tell which of the sections is experimental, so you should treat all seven sections as if they are the real deal.

The practice tests in this book will not contain an experimental section.

Freedom to Move Within a Timed Section

Taking a timed section is like being locked in a room. You can't leave the room, but you can be anywhere in the room at any time. Similarly, you can answer the questions located in one section in any order you prefer. For example, if you were in one of the 30-minute verbal sections and discovered that you couldn't answer the last two sentence completions, you could skip them and move on to the analogies. If you use this freedom correctly and strategically, you will be able to control your pace and make sure that you answer as many questions as you can.

SAT Scoring

There are three important SAT scores, which are all actually different ways of describing the same score. The "raw score" is a simple measure of your right and wrong answers, similar to the grade you might receive on a normal test in school. The "percentile score" takes your raw score and compares it to the rest of the raw scores in the country, letting you (and colleges) know how you did in comparison to your peers. The "scaled score," which ranges from 400–1600 (200–800 for verbal and 200–800 for math), compares your score to the scores received by all students who have ever taken the SAT.

The Raw Score

You will never know what your raw score was on the SAT because the raw score is not included in the SAT score report. But you should understand how the raw score is calculated, since this knowledge can affect your test-taking strategy.

A student's raw score is based solely on the number of questions answered correctly, incorrectly, or left blank. A correct answer is worth one point; leaving a question blank yields no points; a wrong answer results in the loss of of ¼ of a point if the question had five answer choices or ⅓ of a point if it had four (quantitative comparisons). Getting a grid-in wrong will not negatively affect your raw score.

Calculating the raw score for the verbal section is easy. Just add up the number of questions you got right and the number of questions you got wrong. Then multiply the number you got wrong by ¼, and subtract this value from the number you got right:

$$\text{verbal raw score} = \text{correct answers} - \frac{1}{4}\text{ incorrect answers}$$

The math raw score is a little harder to calculate, since you have to account for the different values you can lose when you get different types of math questions wrong:

$$\text{math raw score} = \text{correct answers}$$
$$-\frac{1}{4}\text{ incorrect multiple-choice answers}$$
$$-\frac{1}{3}\text{ incorrect quantitative comparison}$$

In the chapter called **General SAT Strategies** (see page 17) we'll discuss how the rules for calculating a raw score affect strategies for guessing and leaving questions blank.

The Percentile

Your percentile is based on the percentage of the total test takers who received a lower raw score than you did. If, for example, James Joyce received a verbal score in the 99th percentile, that would mean he scored better on the verbal section than 99% of the other students who took the same test (it also means that 1% of the students taking that test scored as well or better).

The Scaled Score

The scaled score takes the raw score and uses a formula to place it onto the standard SAT scale of 200–800 for each section. The average scaled score on the SAT is a few points above 500, and more students receive 800s than 200s.

A more detailed scoring chart that will show you how to translate your raw score into a scaled score resides with the practice tests at the end of the book . Please note that because ETS, the company that produces the SAT, slightly adjusts the curve for each administration of the test, our chart will not always be precisely correct. But it will be generally correct—within 20 points.

Scaled Score	Math Percentile	Verbal Percentile
800	99	99
700	96	95
600	79	77
500	47	47
400	16	16
300	3	2

Why Colleges Use the SAT

More than 80 percent of all four-year colleges and universities require SAT scores as a part of a student's application for admission. Why?

Colleges and universities use SAT scores as an objective means to compare students attending different high schools. It's easiest to make this point using an example. Imagine a university admissions officer who is considering the applications of two students, Joe and Marshall. Both Joe and Marshall have strong A averages in their respective high schools, but Joe goes to a school that allows him to take lunch as a graded course, while Marshall's school makes its students take extremely difficult classes such as Advanced Chaos Theory and Apache Module Software Development. Suddenly, Joe's A and Marshall's A look very different.

But how is the university admissions officer supposed to know that Marshall's A was so much more difficult to attain than Joe's? That's where the SAT comes in. Since Marshall took much more difficult classes, he will have better verbal and math skills and will likely get a better score on the SAT. The SAT therefore serves as a consistent standard by which colleges can measure all students against each other.

How Colleges Use the SAT

There are two things you need to know about how colleges use the SAT in making their admissions decisions. First, 20 to 30 point differences on the SAT really don't matter. Colleges recognize that 20 points on the SAT might be a matter of a single lucky guess. So don't sweat 20 points. Differences in scores of more than 50 points will be significant to admissions officers, since it's unlikely that differences of that magnitude result from chance or luck.

Second, your SAT scores are not the only part of your application that an admissions officer considers. Colleges also scrutinize high-school grades and course load, extracurricular activities, college essays, and letters of recommendation, as well as subject-specific SAT II tests and Advanced Placement tests. Admissions officers are even interested in less quantifiable things, such as your leadership capacity, athletic ability, or musical talent. Mediocre SAT scores will not necessarily destroy your chances of attending the college of your choice if the other aspects of your application are strong. Similarly, excellent SAT scores might not assure you acceptance if you took easy classes and didn't participate in any extracurricular activities.

In other words, when you think about the SAT, think about it in context. The test is a very important part of your college application since it allows a college admissions officer to see you in relation to all of your peers on a national scale. Also, because an SAT score is quantifiable, it's often the first thing an admissions officer will notice about your application. But SAT scores are only one part of what an admissions officer will see. Colleges and universities are eager to create communities of engaged, interesting students who will inspire each other. An admissions officer is therefore more likely to admit an exciting, vibrant, well-rounded individual than a mope who scored 50 points higher on the SATs.

Finally, you should know that not all schools treat SATs in the same way. In general, larger universities often rely more heavily on the SATs than smaller ones do, simply because larger schools have to deal with so many more applications for admission.

Controversies About the SAT

The SAT is not a perfect test. There are all sorts of controversies surrounding it. Some critics argue that the test doesn't actually test any true knowledge. Others argue about whether the test is predictive of future success or simply a gauge of past achievement. Still others believe the test contains gender, racial, or socioeconomic biases.

What Does the SAT Test?

ETS, the company that writes the SAT, claims that the test gauges verbal, math, and critical-thinking skills, all of which are vital for success in college. Critics respond that the SAT emphasizes speed more than anything else, and actually penalizes students who try to understand the questions. Critics also claim that the verbal section places too much importance on simple vocabulary and does not significantly test a person's ability to read, write, or formulate arguments. Other critics argue that the SAT tests only your ability to take the SAT—and nothing more.

None of these perspectives is entirely correct. We agree that the SAT's emphasis on speed can hurt people who understand the material but who like to work problems out methodically. However, the emphasis on speed isn't entirely unfair: the people who best understand math will be able to take advantage of the shortcuts that can be used to solve many of the SAT math questions. We also agree with the critics who argue that the SAT places too much emphasis on vocabulary in the verbal sections. For the most part, the SAT verbal section doesn't test "verbal skills" much at all. The sentence completion and analogy sections, in particular, test vocabulary and critical-thinking skills. Still, there is some correlation between doing a lot of good reading and writing and receiving high scores on the verbal section.

As a final assessment, we would say that the SAT definitely has flaws. It's emphasis on speed rather than understanding is both troubling and unnecessary. But there is some real relationship between students' abilities in math and English and their scores in the math and verbal sections. The SAT is not just a sham.

Is the SAT Predictive?

ETS states that the SAT can predict how a student will perform in his or her first year of college. In fact, ETS's claim is true: outside experts agree that SAT scores show an 18 percent correlation with freshman-year grades. Sadly for ETS, however, those same experts are quick to point out that many things (such as high-school grades, whether your family eats dinner together, your height) also have an 18 percent correlation to freshman-year grades. Further, these experts also remind us that college lasts for four years. Who cares about freshman-year grades? Nobody claims that the SAT predicts grades beyond freshman year. For these reasons, don't think of the SAT as a predictive test: it isn't an excellent predictor of the things it claims to predict, and what it claims to predict isn't all that important.

Many people believe that the SAT measures your intelligence. This is absolutely untrue. The SAT doesn't test intelligence any more than it can predict grades through all of college. In fact, the most predictive thing about the SAT is that anyone who mentions his or her scores after freshman year can safely be predicted to be a loser.

The SAT and Gender Bias

The SAT's gender bias is well documented. Girls consistently score 40 points lower than guys on the SAT, even though girls' high school and college grades are usually better in both math and English classes. Most experts, including the College Board, the institution that employs ETS to write the SAT, agree that the gender bias results from the SAT's emphasis on speed and guessing rather than sustained reasoning. Girls just don't seem to use the strategies that work best on this test. Of course, 40 points on the SAT will not keep someone out of college, especially since universities across the nation recognize that the gender bias exists.

The SAT and Socioeconomic Bias

The SAT's socioeconomic bias, also well documented, is more prevalent and damaging than the gender bias. But the common understanding of the socioeconomic bias is incorrect. According to this misconception, the SAT favors the affluent because it asks questions using words or situations with which people of a certain background are more likely to be familiar. Though this might once have been the case, it is no longer true: ETS is extremely sensitive to such bias, in part because of the anger and antagonism that would arise if the tests were found to be unfair.

The actual socioeconomic bias of the SAT results from the simple fact that doing well on the SAT is largely affected by scholastic background. Students from better schools will generally score higher than students who attend schools that are overcrowded, understaffed, or otherwise under-equipped. And there is no question that students of higher socioeconomic status usually have access to better schools. Similarly, those students are more likely to have the time and money to spend on some sort of test preparation course, further skewing the results in their favor. Sadly, the socioeconomic bias seems to be more a fault of our society than of the test.

The SAT and Racial Bias

The racial bias of the SAT, though widely touted, actually seems to be the product of other biases rather than a factor unto itself. Minority SAT averages are generally lower because of the high correlation between socioeconomic status and race. Those scores are further lowered because the speed element of the SAT is unfavorable to non-native English speakers, most of whom belong to minority groups.

The Future of the SAT

There are some signs that the SAT might be losing favor among universities across the nation. University admissions officers and other administrators have voiced a desire to lessen the importance of the SAT, or even to do without it altogether. However, while some university officials dislike the test, many more still see it as a helpful tool for comparing students across the nation. No matter what the long-term outcome of this debate, it is certain that at least for the next five years, the SAT will remain a fact of high school life. Unless you're reading this book as a sixth grader, you'd better get prepared.

Can the SAT Be Coached?

ETS and the major SAT test preparation companies are engaged in an endless debate. The test prep companies claim that the SAT can be coached: they say that they can teach you, or anyone, how to "psych out" the test and choose correct answers without even knowing the subject matter. ETS responds that the SAT is absolutely resistant to coaching; that the only way to improve your chances on the SAT is to take good math and English courses and read lots of books.

Neither side is being entirely honest, but the reasons underlying each group's arguments are quite clear.

It is very important to ETS that people perceive the SAT as a completely objective test. If the test were not seen as objective, colleges would cease to use it, and ETS would lose the millions of dollars the SAT makes for them every year.

Test prep companies claim that the SAT is *completely* coachable, and that the SAT tests your ability to take the SAT rather than your math or verbal skills. However, this statement is untrue and self-serving. The test prep companies want you to think that the only way for you to do well on the SAT is to learn the "secret" test-taking techniques. The companies argue that the SAT doesn't actually test any sort of real knowledge or skill because they want to be the only source for you to learn the "tricks" the companies profess to teach. As part of their efforts to attract students to their courses, test prep companies portray ETS as an evil entity and themselves as saviors who simply want to help you out. Keep in mind, however, that the test prep companies *love* the SAT (and every other standardized test). The SAT gets these companies their slice of the billion-dollar test prep industry. The test prep companies are as much a part of the SAT system as the SAT itself.

So if neither ETS nor the test prep companies are being entirely honest, what does that say about the SAT's coachability? The test prep companies claim that you can become better at taking the SAT, and you can. There *are* strategic ways to think about every multiple-choice test that will help you work more quickly and get more answers right. In particular, there are ways to think about the SAT that can help you earn a higher score. At the same time, the SAT absolutely does test your knowledge of math, some reading and writing skills, and your general critical-thinking skills.

What you probably don't realize is that it's a *good* thing for you that the SAT tests real knowledge. A test that covers knowledge is a test for which you can study and prepare (without the costly aid of a test prep company). And because the SAT tests the knowledge it covers in standard, similar ways from test date to test date, you can prepare not only by acquiring the knowledge, but also by learning how the SAT normally tests that knowledge.

Approaching the SAT

Instead of seeing the SAT as some sort of monster, approach it as if it were a tool, a means to an end—getting into college. Don't worry about your score in relation to 1600. Your score is only important in relation to the scores of other people applying to the colleges to which you are applying.

Therefore, the first part of your SAT preparation should have nothing to do with filling in multiple-choice grids. Instead, you should do some research to figure out, given your grades and extracurricular activities, the colleges you have a realistic chance of getting into and, of those colleges, which you might want to attend. Talk to your guidance counselor. Go to the bookstore and thumb through a guide on colleges. If you have an older sibling or siblings in college, talk to them. If you have a friend with an older sibling or siblings in college, try to talk to them. If you have a friend with an extremely attractive older sibling in college, try very hard to talk to them. It'll be worth it, even if you don't learn a thing.

While getting a sense of the college scene and where you see yourself within it, you should also get a sense of what SAT scores you'll need to get into the schools you're considering. Most guides on college admissions publish the average SAT scores of incoming freshmen.

If the average SAT scores of incoming freshmen at the schools you want to attend range from 1100–1200, you should set a target score of 1260 (a good target is something a little higher than the average of the schools that appeal to you). Once you have a target score, forget about 1600. Your target score becomes the only important number.

SparkNotes Test Prep

The SAT is not a perfect test. And to compound the pain, SAT test prep companies charge huge amounts of money to teach you "secret tricks" of test taking that are really not much more than critical-thinking skills. But if you want to prepare for the SAT, what else can you do but take a course?

SparkNotes Test Prep gives you another alternative. Unlike the books produced by test prep companies that are designed to hook you into their expensive courses, we want to teach you the skills that will enable you to avoid the courses. This guide will teach you the critical-thinking techniques you need to help you figure out how to attack and beat the test. At the same time, it will also providing in-depth discussion of all the different sorts of skills and knowledge that the SAT tests. We've also included three full-length diagnostic SAT tests and explains the study methods that will let you use those tests to pinpoint your strengths and weaknesses as well as any course could do.

A Final Note Before Getting Started

Often, test prep companies give the impression that if you pay them a lot of money, preparing for the SATs will be easy. They imply that they will just show you how to approach the test and you'll ace it. The truth, however, is not so rosy: to prepare for the

SAT, you really do have to put in a good amount of time and effort. Whether you like it or not, the SATs are important, and you should treat them as such. We can advise you to study and will provide you with the tools, information, and strategies that will make your preparation as fruitful as possible. As for the actual studying—that's up to you.

Introduction to the SAT

General SAT Strategies

Chapter Contents

THE SAT IS A MULTIPLE-CHOICE TEST. It has six timed sections, three of which cover math and three that cover verbal skills. Two of the math sections contain only multiple-choice questions, while the third is made up of quantitative comparison questions and grid-in questions. One of the verbal sections contains only reading comprehension questions, while the other two contain separate groups of sentence completions, analogies, and reading comprehension questions. In general, questions increase in difficulty as you progress through a group of same-type questions. All questions are worth the same number of points, and for all questions except grid-ins, there are penalties for wrong answers. In this chapter, we will show you that the structure of the SAT is very important to your success.

Imagine two children playing tag in the forest. Who will win—the girl who never stumbles because she knows the placement of every tree and all the twists, turns, and hiding spots, or the kid who keeps falling down and tripping over roots because he does not pay any attention to the landscape? The answer is obvious. Even if the other kid is faster and more athletic, the girl will still win because she knows how to navigate the landscape and use it to her advantage.

This example of tag in the forest is extreme, but it illustrates the point. The structure of the SAT is the forest. Taking the test is the game of tag.

17

Basic Rules

You should observe the following rules in every section of the SAT. Essentially, they are just common sense guidelines, but if you follow them, you will save time and cut down on careless errors.

Know the instructions for each section.

The SAT is a timed test, and you will definitely need every second. Don't waste time reading the instructions. Make sure you know the instructions so that you don't even have to glance at them on test day.

Use your test booklet as scratch paper.

Some students feel as though they must keep their test booklets clean and pretty. There's no truth to that. When you finish with your test booklet, it just gets thrown away. Plus, writing on your test booklet can benefit you. If you need to write down a sentence or an equation to help you think through a problem, why not do it right next to the question? If you come to a question you want to skip and come back to later, mark it. (Do not make unnecessary marks on your answer sheet—it is definitely not scratch paper!)

Answer easy questions before hard questions.

All questions are worth the same number of points regardless of difficulty, so it makes sense to answer the questions you find easy and less time-consuming first and the more difficult questions later. This way you'll be sure to accumulate as many points as possible. The structure of the test helps you to identify easy and difficult questions, as is explained in the "Order of Difficulty" section. And remember, you can skip around within a timed section. If you wanted to, you could answer all the easy sentence completions in a 30-minute verbal section, then skip over to the easy analogies, then go back to the moderate sentence completions, and so on.

Don't get bogged down.

While taking seven minutes to solve a particularly difficult question may feel like a moral victory, it's quite possible that you could have used that same time to answer three other questions. Do not be scared to skip a question if it's giving you a lot of trouble—you can come back to it if you have time at the end.

Know when to guess.

We will cover the specific strategies for guessing later.

Avoid carelessness.

There are two types of carelessness, and both will cost you points. The first type of carelessness results from moving too fast. In speeding through the test, you make yourself vulnerable to misinterpreting the question, failing to see that the question contains some subtlety or extra nuance, overlooking one of the answer choices, or simply making a mathematical or logical mistake. So don't speed through the test. Make sure that you are moving quickly, but not so quickly that you become reckless.

The second type of carelessness results from lack of confidence. Do not simply assume out of frustration that you will not be able to answer a question without even looking at it. You should at least glance at every question to see if it's something you can answer. Skipping a question you could have answered is almost as bad as answering incorrectly a question you should have gotten right.

Be careful gridding in your answers.

The scoring computer is unintelligent and unmerciful. If you answered a question correctly, but somehow made a mistake in marking your answer grid, the computer will mark that question wrong. If, somehow, you skipped question 5, but put the answer to question 6 in row 5, and the answer to question 7 in row 6, and so on, thereby throwing off your answers for an entire section . . . well, that would not be good.

Be very careful when filling out your answer grid. Many people will tell you many different ways that are the "best" way to fill out the sheet. We don't care how you do it as long as you're careful. We will give one piece of advice: talk to yourself. As you fill in the answer sheet, say to yourself: "number 23, B; number 24, E; number 25, A." Seriously. Talking to yourself will force you to look at the details and will increase your accuracy.

Answering SAT Multiple-Choice Questions

By now, you know that the SAT is a multiple-choice test. What you may not know is how the multiple-choice structure should affect your approach to answering the questions. Lucky for you, we're going to explain how.

Only the Answer Matters

A machine, not a person, will score your SAT. The scoring machine does not care how you came to your answers; it cares only whether your answers are correct and readable in little oval form. The test booklet in which you worked out your answers gets thrown in the garbage, or, if your proctor is conscientious, into a recycling bin.

The SAT has no partial credit, and no one looks at your work. If you get a question right, it doesn't matter if you did pristine work. In fact, it doesn't even matter whether you knew the answer or guessed. The multiple-choice structure of the test is a message to you from ETS: we only care about your answers. Remember, the SAT is your tool to get into college, so treat it as a tool. It wants right answers. Give it right answers, as many as possible, using whatever strategies you can.

Multiple-Choice and Scratch Work

Because the SAT is a timed test, and since your work doesn't matter, there's no reason to do more work than necessary to solve a problem. Speed matters on the SAT, so don't try to impress the test with excellent work. Do only what you have to do to ensure that you get the right answer and aren't working carelessly.

Multiple-Choice: You've Already Got the Answers

Here's an example of a simple multiple-choice math problem:

$2 + 2 = ?$

(A)   1
(B)   8
(C)   22
(D)   154
(E)   8006

It's immediately obvious that this is a bad question: all of the answers are wrong. You will never see a question like this on the SAT. Every SAT multiple-choice question will have exactly one correct answer. Again, obvious, but let's look at the implications of this fact.

When you look at any SAT multiple-choice question, the answer is already right there in front of you. Of course, ETS doesn't just give you the correct answer; they hide it among a bunch of incorrect answer choices. Your job on each question is to find the right answer. The important thing to realize is that a multiple-choice question is vulnerable to two separate methods :

- Find the **right answer**.

- Look at the answer choices and **eliminate wrong answers** until there's only one answer left—in other words, work backward.

Both methods have their advantages: you are better off using one in some situations. In a perfect scenario, when you are sure how to answer a question, the first method is clearly better than the second. Coming to a conclusion about a problem and then picking the single correct choice is a much simpler process than going through every answer choice and discarding the four that are wrong. However, when you are unsure how to solve the problem, the second method becomes more attractive: you should focus on eliminating the incorrect answer choices rather than trying to pick out the right answer.

You might be able to use the answer choices to lead you in the right direction, or to solve the problem through trial and error. You also might be able to eliminate answer choices through a variety of strategies (these strategies vary by question type; we'll cover them in the chapters dedicated to each specific type of question). In some cases, you might be able to eliminate all the wrong answers. In others, you might be able to eliminate only one, which will still improve your odds when you attempt to guess.

Part of your task in preparing for the SAT will be to get some sense of when to use the correct strategy. Using the right strategy can increase your speed without affecting your accuracy, giving you more time to work on and answer as many questions as possible.

Guessing on the SAT

Should you guess on the SAT? We'll begin to answer this question by posing another SAT question:

> Ben is holding five cards, numbered 1–5. Without telling you, he has selected one of the numbers as the "correct" card. If you pick a single card, what is the probability that you will choose the "correct" one?

Okay, this isn't really an SAT question, and the answer choices aren't that important, though the answer is $\frac{1}{5}$. But the question does precisely describe the situation you're in when you guess blindly on any SAT question with five answer choices. If you were to guess on five multiple-choice questions with five answer choices, you would probably get one question right for every five guesses you made.

ETS took these probabilities into account when devising its system to calculate raw scores. As described in the introduction, for every right answer on the SAT, you get one point added to your raw score. For each answer left blank, you get zero points. For each incorrect multiple-choice answer you lose some fraction of a point:

- $\frac{1}{4}$ for incorrect five-choice questions
- $\frac{1}{3}$ for incorrect four-choice questions (quantitative comparisons)
- 0 points for incorrectly answering a grid-in question.

It's easy to figure out why ETS chose the wrong-answer penalties that it did. Let's look at each type of question and examine what its penalty value means.

Five-choice.

If you guess blindly on these questions, probability dictates that you will get one question right for every four wrong. Since you get 1 point for your right answer and lose $\frac{1}{4}$

point for each wrong answer, you're left with $1 - 4 \times \frac{1}{4} = 0$ points. Guessing blindly for five-choice questions is a waste of time.

Quantitative comparisons.

If you guess blindly on these questions, probability says that you will get one question right for every three wrong. Since you get 1 point for your right answer, and lose $\frac{1}{3}$ point for each wrong answer, you're left with $1 - 3 \times \frac{1}{3} = 0$ points. Guessing blindly for four-choice questions is, once again, a waste of time.

Grid-ins.

These are not multiple-choice questions. There are so many possible answers that guessing the answer is immensely improbable. If you have even a vague idea of what the answer might be, you might as well guess, though, since there's no penalty.

Intelligent Guessing

The numbers above show that the wrong-answer penalty renders any sort of blind guessing pointless. But what if your guessing isn't blind? Let's say you're answering the following sentence completion question:

In Greek mythology, Hades, the realm of the dead, is guarded by ---- dog.

    (A)   an anthropomorphic
    (B)   a protean
    (C)   a sesquipedalian
    (D)   a delicious
    (E)   a sanguinary

It seems likely that you don't know the meanings of the words **anthropomorphic, protean, sesquipedalian,** or **sanguinary** since we purposely chose words that were more obscure than the vocabulary that appears on the SAT. But you probably do know the meaning of **delicious,** and can tell immediately that it does not fit correctly into the sentence (a delicious dog?). Once you've eliminated delicious as a possible answer, you only have to guess between four rather than five choices. Is it now worth it to guess? If you guess among four choices, you will get one question right for every three you get wrong. For that one correct answer you'll get 1 point, and for the three incorrect answers you'll lose a total of $\frac{3}{4}$ of a point. $1 - \frac{3}{4} = \frac{1}{4}$, meaning that if you can eliminate one answer, then the odds of guessing turn in your favor: you become more likely to gain points than lose points.

The rule for guessing, therefore, is simple: if you can eliminate even one answer choice on a question, you should definitely guess. The only time you should ever leave a question blank is if you cannot eliminate any of the answer choices.

Guessing as Partial Credit

Some students feel that guessing correctly should not be rewarded with full credit. But instead of looking at guessing as an attempt to gain undeserved points, you should look at it as a form of partial credit. Let's use the example of the sentence completion about the dog guarding Hades. Most people taking the test will only know the word delicious, and will only be able to throw out that word as a possible answer, leaving them with a 1 in 4 chance of guessing correctly. But let's say that you knew that protean means "able to change shape," and that the dog guarding Hades was not protean. When you look at this question, you can throw out both "delicious" and "protean" as answer choices, leaving you with a 1 in 3 chance of getting the question right if you guess. Your extra knowledge gives you better odds of getting this question right.

Order of Difficulty

SAT questions are divided into groups. For example, in one of the 30 minute verbal sections, the 10 sentence completions are grouped together as questions 1–10, the 13 analogies are listed together as questions 11–23, and the 12 reading comprehension questions make up questions 24–35. Math questions are similarly organized by groups: regular multiple choice, quantitative comparisons, and grid-ins are all listed separately from each other. Except for reading comprehension questions, all of these groups of questions are arranged by difficulty, from easiest to most difficult.

Making Decisions Based on the Order of Difficulty

Imagine that you are taking a test that consists of two questions. After your teacher hands out the test, and before you set to work, a helpful little gnome whispers to you from the corner, "The first problem is very simple, the second is much harder." Would the gnome's statement affect the way you approach the two problems? The answer, of course, is yes. For a "very simple" question, it seems likely that you should be able to answer it quickly and without much, or any, agonized second-guessing. On a "much harder" question, you will probably have to spend much more time, both to come up with an answer and to check your work to make sure you didn't make an error somewhere along the way.

And what about all the other students who didn't hear the gnome? They might labor over the first easy question, exhaustively checking their work and wasting time that they'll need for the tricky second problem. Then, when those other students do get to the second problem, they might not check their work or be wary of traps, since they have no idea that the problem is so difficult.

Because SAT questions are ordered by difficulty, it's as if you have that helpful little gnome sitting next to you for the entire test. The simple knowledge of question difficulty can help you in a variety of ways.

Knowing Where to Spend Your Time

As discussed earlier, you should try to avoid getting bogged down, and you don't have to answer questions in numerical order. In fact, in some situations it can be a good idea to skip an occasional question. Think about it: every question on the SAT is worth the same number of raw points, so what matters most on the test is answering as many questions correctly as possible. If skipping a question that's giving you trouble allows you the time to answer three other questions, then it's a good bargain.

How many questions you should skip depends entirely on your target score. If you have a target score of 1400 or higher, you need to answer every question, so there isn't much of a reason to skip around. But if, for example, your target score is an 1100, you can afford to skip 2–3 questions in every group. In this case, if you encounter a sentence completion you just can't answer, don't spend a ton of time trying to figure it out. Skip it and move on to the next. If the sentence completions you find difficult happen to be the last one or two in the group, don't worry about leaving them behind, and move on to the analogies.

Please note that we are *not* suggesting that you skip all the questions in a group as soon as you hit one that you find difficult. Don't just assume that all questions appearing after a question that you find hard will be too hard for you. Sometimes, for whatever reason, a question will be hard for you even if the question after it is easy. The location of a question is a clue about its difficulty, but you shouldn't let the test dictate what you can and cannot answer simply based on its location. If you have a sense of how difficult a question probably is, and a similar sense of how many questions you can afford to skip, you should be able to make an informed decision about whether to skip a question or not. But make sure that your decision is informed: at least try to glance at every question in a group to see if you might be able to answer it.

Knowing When to Be Wary

Most students answer the easy SAT questions correctly. Only some students get moderately difficult questions right. Very few students get difficult questions right. What does this mean to you? It means that when you are going through the test, you can often trust your first instincts on an easy question. With difficult questions, however, you should be much more cautious. There is a reason most people get these questions wrong: not only are they more difficult, containing more sophisticated vocabulary or mathematical concepts, they are also often tricky, full of enticing wrong answers that seem as if they must be correct. But because the SAT orders its questions by difficulty, the test tips you off about when to take a few extra seconds to make sure you haven't been fooled by an answer that only *seems* right.

Pacing

The SAT presents you with a lot of questions and not that much time to answer them. As you take the test, you will probably feel some pressure to answer quickly. As we've already discussed, getting bogged down on a single question is not a good thing. But rushing too quickly isn't any good either. In the end, there's no real difference between answering very few questions and answering lots of questions incorrectly: both will lead to low scores. What you have to do is find a happy medium, a groove, a speed at which you can be both accurate and efficient and get the score you want.

Setting a Target Score

The previous paragraph sure makes it sound easy. But how do you actually go about finding a good speed? First, before anything else, you should recognize that you absolutely do not have to answer every question on the test. Remember, the SAT is your tool to help you get into one of the schools of your choice, and it probably won't take a perfect score to get you there. You should set a target score, and your efforts should be directed toward gaining that score—not necessarily a 1600.

In setting a target score, the first rule is always this: be honest and realistic. Base your target score on the schools you want to go to and have a realistic chance of getting into. Talking to a college counselor can help you gauge how reasonable your choices are. You can also gauge your expectations by your first practice test. If you score a 450 on the math section of the first practice test, it's foolish to set your target score at 750. Instead, your target should be about 50–100 points higher on each section than your score on your first practice test. That's a total of 100–200 points higher for the whole test.

If you reach your target score during preparation, give yourself a cookie or some other treat and take a break from working. But just because you hit your target score doesn't mean you should stop working altogether. In fact, you should view reaching your target score as a clue that you can do better than that score: set a new target 50–100 points above your original, pick up your pace a little bit, and skip fewer questions. By working to improve in manageable increments, you can slowly work up to your top speed, integrating your new knowledge of how to take the test and the subjects the test covers without overwhelming yourself by trying to take on too much too soon. If you can handle working just a little faster without

General SAT Strategies

becoming careless and losing points, your score will certainly go up. If you meet your new target score again, repeat the process.

Your Target Score Determines Your Overall Strategy

Your target score can, and should, deeply affect your strategy. If you want to get a 1000 on the test, your strategy will differ significantly from that of someone aiming for a 1400. A person who wants a 1400 must work fast and try to answer almost every question. He or she must be able to work very quickly without carelessness. A person looking to score a 1000 does not have to answer every question. In fact, that person probably shouldn't try to answer every question. So, what's the moral? Adjust your pacing to the score you want. The chart below shows the approximate raw scores necessary to achieve certain scaled target scores on each section of the SAT.

Math		Verbal	
Target Score	Raw Score	Target Score	Raw Score
800	60	800	78
750	56	750	72
700	53	700	66
650	49	650	59
600	43	600	51
550	35	550	42
500	29	500	34
450	22	450	27
400	15	400	20

If your target score is a 1000 (a 500 on math and a 500 on verbal) you need a raw score of 63 (29 + 34). Think about what this means. There are a total of 138 possible raw points on the SAT. To get a 1000, you need to get a little less than half of those points. In other words, you need to answer a little less than half of the questions cor rectly (assuming you don't answer any questions wrong). If we take into account that you probably will answer at least a few questions incorrectly, then you know that you need to get a few more than half of the questions right. Even so, a little over half only constitutes the easy and moderate questions on the test. You could probably get a 1000 without answering a single difficult question—this realization should help you pace yourself accordingly. Instead of rushing to answer as many questions as possible, spend the time you need to avoid errors and make sure you'll hit your target.

Knowing the Clock

When you take both your practice tests and the real SAT, you should be aware of the clock. You should not become obsessed with the clock and lose time by constantly glancing at those terrible ticking seconds, but you should have a sense of the time to keep yourself on proper pace.

We recommend that you always take practice tests with the clock. Since your proctor will enforce the time on the real SAT strictly, you should do the same on your practice tests. By using the clock on practice tests, you will learn to manage your time and become more familiar with taking the test as the clock ticks down to zero.

Luck

If you have lucky clothes, or any other lucky items, you might as well wear them, carry them, twirl them over your head and dance beneath them: do whatever works. A little luck never hurt anyone.

General SAT Strategies

The Verbal SAT

The Verbal SAT

THE THREE VERBAL SECTIONS OF THE SAT contain 78 questions in total:

- 19 Sentence completions

- 19 Analogies

- 40 Reading comprehension

The following three chapters are devoted to analyzing, breaking down, and explaining the strategies that will help you do your best on each of these three question types.

Before getting to the specifics, though, it is best to discuss the verbal section as a whole. This chapter focuses on the general skills and strategies you need to succeed on the verbal section.

Vocabulary and the Verbal SAT

The verbal SAT claims to test your facility with language. This is sort of true: the analogies, sentence completions, and reading comprehension questions gauge your ability to form relationships between individual words, to understand words in context, and to comprehend written passages. Even so, these questions test your vocabulary far more extensively than they do any other verbal or literary skill. All of the analogy and sentence completion questions test vocabulary, and about one fifth of reading comprehension questions do too. If you know the vocabulary used in a particular question, not only will you have a better chance of answering the question correctly, your speed will also increase, allowing you to answer more questions and spend more time focusing on difficult questions. On the SAT, knowing your vocabulary can pay off in a big way.

The SAT's emphasis on vocabulary makes it a rather poor test of verbal or literary skills, but that doesn't mean that the stress on vocabulary makes those sections more difficult. After all, it's easier to learn vocabulary words than it is to develop your critical-reading skills. Furthermore, the SAT often reuses words from test to test. As part of this guide, we have included a list of the 1000 most common words to appear on recent SATs. Study the list. When you go through a practice test and come upon a word you don't know, write the word down and learn it.

It's unlikely that you'll be able to remember the exact meaning of every single word you try to learn, but it isn't so improbable that you'll get a sense of all those words. For example, even if all you can remember about a word is that it expresses something negative, that information can go a long way toward helping you get the right answer.

General Verbal SAT Strategies

The verbal half of the SAT is made up of three sections. Two of those sections are 30 minutes long and include analogies, sentence completions, and reading comprehension questions. The other section is 15 minutes long and contains one reading comprehension passage and its corresponding questions. The analogies and sentence completions are roughly organized from easiest to most difficult, but reading comprehension questions are not ordered by difficulty.

The only thing that's important on the SAT is getting as many answers correct as you possibly can. Getting the hard questions right earns no more points than correctly answering the easy questions. And answering the easy questions is much easier than answering difficult ones. Given this, it seems wise to devise a strategy that ensures that you get to see, and answer, all of the easier questions.

Answer Easy Questions First

Let's say you're in the 30-minute verbal section that has 10 sentence completions followed by 13 analogies, and a reading comprehension passage. Answer the sentence completions first. When you hit a question that's too difficult, skip it and move on to the next question. Do *not* skip out of the sentence completion section entirely. On this first run through, at least look at every question to see whether you think you can answer it. If you do skip a question, mark it in some way so that you can go back to it. Once you've gone through the sentence completions, skipping where necessary, move on to the analogies and do the same thing. After the analogies, turn to the reading comprehension, read the passage, and answer every question you can. Finally, go back to the questions you've skipped and see if you can figure out the answers or eliminate some answer choices and put yourself in a good position to guess.

Know Your Strengths

If you take a couple of practice tests before the test date, you'll start to get a feel for your SAT verbal strengths. If you're best at analogies, go back to the analogy group and give the hard ones another shot. If you are least good at sentence completion questions, return to those last. By refusing to follow the order in which the test presents itself and instead making certain you answer all the questions you can, you tailor the SAT to your strengths. And the closer the test fits your strengths, the better you'll do.

The Verbal SAT

Sentence Completions

T HE SAT INCLUDES 19 SENTENCE COM- PLETIONS, broken into two groups—one of 9 questions and one of 10. The two groups of sentence completions will appear on the two 30-minute verbal sections. In each case, the sentence completions will appear first, before the analogies and reading comprehension.

Sentence Completion Instructions

You should be comfortable with the test instructions before you arrive on test day. Here are the instructions for the sentence completions. Learn them.

> Each sentence below has one or two blanks, each blank indicating that something has been omitted. Beneath the sentence are five words or sets of words labeled A through E. Choose the word or set of words that, when inserted in the sentence, best fits the meaning of the sentence as a whole.

Example:

Medieval kingdoms did not become constitutional republics overnight; on the contrary, the change was ----.

(A)   unpopular
(B)   unexpected
(C)   advantageous
(D)   sufficient
(E)   gradual

Correct Answer: (E)

Anatomy of a Sentence Completion

As described in the instructions you just read (if you didn't, go read them!), every sentence completion includes a sentence with one or two blank spaces and five possible answer choices that have either one or two words. Below are examples of each.

One-Word Completion

Bel Biv Devoe was a terrible rap and R&B group in the early '90s; its music was dull and its lyrics ----.

(A)   excellent
(B)   new
(C)   poor
(D)   loud
(E)   fresh

Two-Word Completion

Though out of water seals lumber around and look ---- , within the sea they move smoothly and ---- .

(A)   cute..wonderfully
(B)   sleek..purposefully
(C)   ungainly..slowly
(D)   cruel..quickly
(E)   awkward..gracefully

While looking at the structure and format of SAT sentence completions, you should recognize two important facts:

1. The sentences are logical and contain all the information necessary to define the word that fits in the blank.

2. All of the answer choices are grammatically correct. The correct choice will be the word that makes the most sense. In other words, don't be fooled into picking an answer simply because it makes grammatical sense.

These two guidelines are important. The first makes it clear that you should almost always be able to figure out the gist of the missing word or words. If you understand the vocabulary in the sentence, you should be able to deduce if a missing word should have a positive or negative connotation and what it should probably mean. The second fact just tells you that all the words in the answer choices will sound right, since they are all grammatically correct. Choose your answers by meaning, not by sound.

Decoding Sentence Completions

Sentence completions are not just pure vocabulary tests. To figure out the right answer, you have to decode the sentence to understand how it's functioning. "Decoding a sentence" might sound difficult, but it's something you do every day. For example, when you a hear a sentence such as "Usually I am happy, but . . ." you immediately know that the second half of the sentence will go something like "I am not happy right now." On hearing the word "but" in relation to the initial statement, you realize that the second half will contradict the first half. This intuitive thought process is what we mean by decoding the sentence.

Let's apply the decoding technique to the two examples above. In the one-word example about Bel Biv Devoe, there are no words like "but," so the first and second part of the sentence must agree—if Bel Biv Devoe is a terrible singing group, then their lyrics must be *poor.* For the two-word example sentence about seals, you can decode it by realizing that the initial word, "though," implies that the two halves of the sentence will oppose each other. In other words, what is true in the first half will be the opposite in the second half: though seals might lumber and look *awkward* on land, they move smoothly and *gracefully* in the water.

Sentence Flow and Hinge Words

Think of a simple sentence. Actually, forget it. We'll give you a simple sentence:

> The scientists' research confirmed their theories.

This sentence has a single flow or direction: it expresses a single idea from the beginning to the end. Now consider a variation of this sentence:

> Though the scientists' research confirmed their theories, many people refused to believe them.

In this second sentence, there are two flows: the half of the sentence before the comma states a fact, and the half of the sentence after the comma states a different fact that is *in opposition* to the first. The flow of the sentence changed.

Now let's say that the second sentence was an SAT sentence completion with, for the sake of simplicity, only two possible answers:

> Though the scientists' research confirmed their theories, many people ---- to believe them.

(A) began
(B) refused

We already know that the answer is *refused,* but pretend for a moment that you don't. How could you figure out the answer? We'll answer this question by writing out a sentence in which *began* actually would make sense:

> The scientists' research confirmed their theories, and many people ---- to believe them.

These two sentences differ by only two words: the first sentence begins with "though," while the second sentence replaces the "though" with an "and" in the middle. The addition or subtraction of the "though" and the "and" completely change how the sentence functions. We call such words "hinge words" because, just as a hinge determines whether a door is open or closed, hinge words determine the flow of the sentence. The sentence about the scientists with the hinge word "though" is a contrasted sentence—there is a change of direction between the first and second halves. The second sentence with the hinge word "and" is a straight or direct sentence with a single flow.

As you can see, being able to identify hinge words is a vital part of decoding a sentence. You should also notice that there are two types of hinge words: those such as "and" that signal a sentence will continue in the same direction, and those like "though," which signal that a sentence will change direction.

Hinge words that signal a direct flow in a sentence:

and	because	since	so	thus	therefore

Hinge words that change the flow of a sentence:

but	though	although	while	rather	instead
unless	despite	however	nevertheless	notwithstanding	

Identifying hinge words to help you determine the flow of the sentence is one of the best methods for answering sentence completions. Learning to identify hinge words should be one of your first tasks in preparing for the sentence-completion portion of the SATs.

Answering Sentence Completions

The process for answering one-blank and two-blank sentence completions is quite similar, but there are some important differences. We will therefore treat the two types separately.

Answering One-Word Sentence Completions

There is a definite process you should follow when answering one-blank sentence completions.

1.   Read the question (without looking at the answers).

In this initial reading, you should try to get a sense of the sentence. Look for hinge words and identify the sentence's flow. You might want to circle or otherwise mark the hinge words. Locate where the blanks fit into the sentence's flow. Does the blank fit into the single flow of the sentence? Is the blank set against the flow of the rest of the sentence by a hinge word? Let's look at the example about Bel Biv Devoe:

> Bel Biv Devoe was a terrible rap and R&B group in the early '90s; its music was dull and its lyrics ---- .

In this sentence, there are no obvious hinge words. Still, the second half of the sentence seems to flow directly from the first. The first half of the sentence says Bel Biv Devoe was "terrible" and the second half says that its music was "dull." The two halves of the sentence agree. The blank fits into a flowing sentence.

Next, figure out *what* the blank is referring to or describing within the sentence, and then *how* the sentence refers to or describes that thing. In the sentence about Bel Biv Devoe, the blank refers to Bel Biv Devoe's lyrics. The sentence also gives you the information that Bel Biv Devoe was a bad group with bad music. Since the sentence contained no change-of-direction hinge word, it seems safe to assume that BBD's lyrics will also be described negatively.

2.   Read the question again (still without looking at the answers).

Once you've decoded the sentence, read through it again and try to come up with your own answer to fill in the blanks. This answer can be either a single word or a description of the meaning of the word that should fill the blank. By anticipating what type of word will fill the blank before looking at any of the answers, you are making sure that you don't fall for any of ETS's tricky wrong answers.

> Bel Biv Devoe was a terrible rap and R&B group in the early '90s; its music was dull and its lyrics ----.

In reading this sentence through the second time, after decoding it and realizing that the two halves of the sentence agree, you could come up with the following:

> Bel Biv Devoe was a terrible rap and R&B group in the early '90s; its music was dull and its lyrics *bad*.

By inserting "bad" into the blank, you certainly haven't generated the word that *is* the correct answer (bad isn't even one of the answer choices), but you have come up with a word that defines, explains, or provides a synonym for the right answer.

If the sentence is difficult and you can't come up with a distinct word or phrase, at least try to determine whether each blank is positive or negative. Often, even that much information can show you the correct answer or help you to eliminate wrong answers.

3. Look through the answers and pick one.

Now that you have a good sense of what kind of word should fill the blank, go through the answers. Find the answer that fits with the word or idea you've decided should fill the blank.

> Bel Biv Devoe was a terrible rap and R&B group in the early '90s; its music was dull and its lyrics *bad*.
>
> (A) excellent
> (B) new
> (C) poor
> (D) loud
> (E) fresh

Obviously, the only answer with a meaning similar to "bad" is **(C) poor.**

4. Try the answer out in the sentence.

Once you've chosen a word, plug it into the sentence and try it out. If it works, you're set. If it doesn't, go back to the sentence and check to see that you decoded it correctly.

5. Guessing.

If you cannot come to a decisive correct answer, you can still guess, which you should do if you can eliminate at least one answer choice. When you've gotten to this point in the process, you should at least have a sense of whether the word that fills a blank should have a positive or negative connotation. Use this information to eliminate answer choices.

Though the method described above seems extensive, once you're comfortable with the process, you should be able to fly through each step in a few seconds.

Answering Two-Word Sentence Completions

Two-word sentence completions are probably somewhat more intimidating to you than the one-word variety, since you have two blanks to fill. However, the process you follow to solve them should not be all that different.

1. Read the question (without looking at the answers).

Just as with one-blank sentence completions, read through the sentence, identify the hinge word if there is one, and determine how the blanks fit in the sentence and what each refers to.

2. Read the question again (still without looking at the answers).

Again, just as with one-blank sentences, try to anticipate the connotation of the words that will fit in the blanks.

3.   Look through the answers and pick one.

This step might actually be easier in two-blank sentences than one-blank sentences because you can eliminate an answer choice if just one of the words in the pair doesn't fit. In other words, two-blank questions offer you twice as many opportunities to eliminate an answer choice.

4.   Try the answer out in the sentence.

Same as with one-word sentence completions.

5.   Guessing.

Same as with one-word sentence completions.

When dealing with two blanks, you are more likely to be tempted to choose words based on what they mean in a vacuum rather than on their function within the sentence. In other words, you should not focus on the relationship between the two words in the answer pairs. You should focus on how each word needs to function in the sentence. If you come to the conclusion that a sentence contrasts, you might be tempted to choose words that are antonyms, or one word that has a positive connotation and one that has a negative connotation. But that could lead you to the wrong answer. Instead of choosing two words that contrast each other, you should choose words that make the *entire sentence* change direction.

> Tired of war and finally becoming hopeful that a(n) ---- might be a real possibility, the two factions redoubled their efforts to hammer out a settlement that would end their years of ----.

After reading this sentence carefully, you should realize a few things:

The first half and the second half of the sentence are *directly* related: the hope of *something* in the first half of the sentence is exactly what pushed the two sides to try to create a settlement that will end *something*. There is no hinge word or situation that might make the two sides of the sentence contrast.

Once you realize that the sentence is direct, you can infer the following:

- Both factions are tired of war (meaning both want to end the war).

- They each see the possibility of accomplishing *something* that is related to being "tired of war."

- Because they are tired of war, the two sides "redouble their efforts to hammer out a settlement" that ends their *something*.

With this information, you should have a good sense of how to answer the question:

Sentence Completions

- Since both sides are tired of war and want it to end, what would they be "hopeful" about? The prospect of peace, most likely.

- In order to bring about this peace, the two sides try to create a settlement that will end their years of *something*. If the two factions have been fighting, what might characterize their last few years? Something angry and violent.

Plug these words into the sentence:

> Tired of war and finally becoming hopeful that a(n) *something peaceful* might be a real possibility, the two factions redoubled their efforts to hammer out a settlement that would end their years of *something angry and violent.*
>
> (A) battle..enmity
> (B) chamber..lawfulness
> (C) agreement..friendship
> (D) truce..hatred
> (E) tryst..romance

As you scan the answers and try to match them with the words or phrases that you think define the right answers, you can quickly throw out (A) because a battle isn't peaceful; (B) because a chamber makes no sense in this sentence; (C) because the two sides would not have had years of friendship if they were at war; and (E) because tryst and romance are words to describe a love affair, not the hope of ending a war. That leaves choice **(D)**, and if you plug in the answers, you'll see that it is an effective practice. Notice, however, that to create this direct sentence, we used two words that are themselves opposite: **truce** and **hatred.** It's not the relation between the words themselves that matters, but how those words function in the sentence. In this example, we needed to find the two words that would fit the direct flow of the sentence in which the hope of peace led to the end of anger and violence. Remember, sentence completions are about vocabulary in context. Your job is to find the words that make the sentence work.

The Five Types of Sentence Completions

The better you are at identifying and decoding a sentence, the more quickly and accurately you will be able to answer sentence completions. We have compiled a list that describes the five main types of sentence completions.

1. One-Word Direct Sentences

One-word direct questions are the simplest kind of sentence completion, and are also the most common. About 6 of the 19 sentence completions on the SAT will be of this type. In one-word direct sentences, the sentence has a single flow of argument, and the word you choose to fill the blank must fit within that flow. One-word direct sentences come in two variations, each just as common as the other. The first type of one-word direct is just a simple sentence with a word left out. The second type of one-word direct involves two clauses set off from each other by a semicolon, colon, or comma. Usually, the first half of the sentence contains the blank, and the second half describes the word that goes in the blank.

Simple Sentence

The first type of one-word direct is just a simple sentence with a word left out:

> The ---- undergrowth of the jungle made it difficult for the explorers to remain on a straight path without using their machetes.
>
> (A) slight
> (B) limp
> (C) dense
> (D) standard
> (E) green

The correct answer is **dense**; the undergrowth made it difficult for the explorers to stay on the path, meaning the undergrowth was impenetrable or dense.

This example was fairly easy. The more difficult sentences of this type usually involve harder vocabulary and describe more sophisticated concepts, but the structure of the sentence is rarely more complicated.

Semicolon

> Big John Stud was a ---- wrestler; all of the other wrestlers in the WWF were hesitant to pit themselves against his great might.
>
> (A) minor
> (B) troubled
> (C) fearsome
> (D) tall
> (E) serviceable

In this sentence, the phrase "all of the other wrestlers in the WWF were hesitant to pit themselves against his great might" makes it clear that Big John Stud must be super-tough or **fearsome.** Note that this kind of sentence is particularly easy to decode. Your job is to figure out what kind of wrestler Big John Stud is, and the second half of the sentence gives evidence that describes precisely what kind of wrestler Big John Stud is. The example above used a semicolon; below you'll find examples of this type of question using commas and colons.

Colon

Listeners were constantly amazed by the president's ---- speeches: he seemed unable to put together a coherent sentence.

- (A) excellent
- (B) lengthy
- (C) inarticulate
- (D) dogged
- (E) efficient

If the president is "unable to put together a coherent sentence," then his speeches must be very bad, or **inarticulate.**

Comma

Many sports fans considered the 1998 Yankees to be a(n) ---- team, one unbeatable by any other team in the league.

- (A) middling
- (B) destructive
- (C) artistic
- (D) quiescent
- (E) invincible

An "unbeatable" team is **invincible.**

In rare instances, the structure of this type of sentence might be flipped, with the blank appearing after the semicolon, colon, or comma. In that case, the clause before the semicolon, colon, or comma provides the description or definition of the word needed to fill the answer blank.

2. One-Word Contrast Sentences

On average, SAT tests include about four one-word contrast sentences. In this type of sentence completion, the single blank stands in contrast to some other clause in the sentence. There are two types of one-word contrast sentences: those that include hinge words and those that don't. We will give examples of each.

One-Word Contrast with a Hinge Word

If you are familiar with hinge words and can identify them when necessary, this type of sentence should be easy to recognize. Once you've identified the sentence as a one-word, hinged contrast, you know immediately that the word that fits in the blank must somehow stand in opposition to another part of the sentence. All you have to do then is determine which phrase or idea the blank contrasts.

Carlita thought her pranks were ----, but her former friends found her actions annoying and juvenile.

(A) hilarious
(B) angry
(C) colossal
(D) trite
(E) new

Here, the hinge word, "but," clearly sets the feelings of Carlita's former friends against her own sentiments. Therefore, if Carlita's former friends find her pranks annoying and juvenile, you should, without even looking at the answer choices, know that Carlita finds her pranks good, or funny, or something similar. The correct answer is **hilarious.**

Although the radical youth of the '60s saw rock music as embodying the desire for peace and love, many conservatives saw the music as a threat that ---- the moral values of America.

(A) embraced
(B) revitalized
(C) undermined
(D) justified
(E) displayed

Clearly the vocabulary in this sentence is more difficult than that in the easy question about Carlita. The sentence also deals with concepts and issues that are more sophisticated than those in the easy sentence. Even after you recognize "although" as a hinge word and see that the second half of the sentence must oppose the first half, it still might take a little effort to figure out what the opposition to "embodying the desire for peace and love rather than war" might be.

In attempting to answer this question, the first thing you should realize is that the "desire for peace and love rather than war" is a positive thing, and so the radical youth of the '60s saw rock music as a good thing. Once you recognize this, it should be simple, given the hinge word "although," that the conservatives saw rock music differently—as a negative thing, a "threat."

With this knowledge, you are ready to look at the answer choices. Embrace, answer (A), means to support and show love, which is clearly not what the conservatives feared rock music might do to American moral values. Similarly, conservatives would have been happy with rock music if they saw it as revitalizing (renewing or giving strength to) or displaying American moral values, but the conservatives described in the sentence are not happy. The word justified (meaning "demonstrated to be correct or valid") doesn't fit well within the sentence; the conservatives might see the existence of rock music as a justification for increased stress on morals, but they wouldn't see rock music itself as justifying morals. That leaves only **undermined,** which creates the proper negative connotation needed in the second half of the sentence to stand in contrast to the first half.

Of the five answer choices in the question we just answered, the correct answer was the only word that had a *negative* connotation. To embrace, revitalize, display, or justify are all either positive or neutral actions. Undermining someone or something, in contrast, is a negative action. That we picked the sole negative word in order to get the proper negative sense might seem perfectly correct and logical, but you must be cautious here. Remember that your goal is not to pick an individual word whose connotation opposes the first half of the sentence, but to pick a word that will make the *entire* second half contrast the first. For example, what if the sentence above had been:

> Although the radical youth of the sixties saw rock music as embodying the desire for peace and love, many conservatives saw the music as ---- anarchy and the overthrow of the American government.

In the previous example, the conservatives saw music as threatening something that they loved: moral values. The music therefore had to be doing something negative to those values. But in this example, the second half of the sentence discusses things the conservatives feared: "anarchy and the overthrow of the American government." In order for it to make sense that the conservatives dislike rock music in this sentence, the rock music must be doing something *positive* for "anarchy and the overthrow of American government." But it's not as simple as, "The conservatives hate rock music, therefore rock music must be doing something negative." You must always examine the word in the context of the sentences in which it appears.

One-Word Contrast Without a Hinge Word

Some sentences can create a contrast relationship without using hinge words. Without such an identifying marker, these contrast sentences are harder to identify. For example:

> Once a(n) ---- theory, the notion that the earth revolves around the sun is now accepted by virtually everyone.
>
> (A) terrific
> (B) pleasant
> (C) esteemed
> (D) beloved
> (E) controversial

The sentence describes two different reactions to the "theory" at different times: at one time the world reacted a certain way, and now it reacts another way. Together, "once" and "now" describe a change through time that necessitates a contrast between the two halves of the sentence. In this example, the contrast to everyone accepting the theory could be that either no one believes in the theory or that many people dispute it. The only answer that works is **controversial.**

In general, when a sentence describes more than one point in time, it is usually a contrast sentence.

3. Two-Word Direct Sentences

Two-word direct sentence completions contain two blanks that fit into the same flow of argument. About three of the sentence completions on the SAT will be two-word direct.

A good clue that a two-blank sentence is a direct sentence is the presence of same-direction hinge words such as *and, because, since, so,* and *therefore.* Another good way to determine if a sentence is direct is to ask yourself, "Does one part of the sentence happen because of another part of the sentence?" If the answer is yes, the sentence is probably direct. If the answer is no, if one part of the sentence happened *despite* the situation or facts described in the other part of the sentence, then the sentence as a whole is probably a contrast. Two-word direct sentences can come in a few forms:

Simple Statements

Creating a hypothesis involves ---- a great deal of data and identifying ---- that explain the data's distribution.

(A)   studying..patterns
(B)   defying..issues
(C)   seeing..plateaus
(D)   raising..structures
(E)   encountering..plans

Simple statements define a single thing, in this case the creation of a hypothesis; the two words you use must make that definition correct. In this case the answer is **studying . . patterns** because creating a hypothesis demands studying data and interpreting the patterns that the data form.

Blanks Appearing Near Each Other

The ---- conditions ---- even the intrepid explorer, who never again ventured out into the tundra.

(A)   destructive..angered
(B)   gorgeous..moved
(C)   harsh..terrified
(D)   appalling..enveloped
(E)   serene..pleased

The answer is **harsh . . terrified.** In looking at the question, you should see that the two blanks help define a situation that directly caused the intrepid explorer never to venture into the tundra again.

Distant Blanks

> Well known as a man who was ---- even when under the heaviest fire, the general was as ----
> as a person could be.
>
> (A)   composed..tremulous
> (B)   helpless..efficient
> (C)   frigid..warlike
> (D)   serene..unflappable
> (E)   grave..humorous

As you can see in this example, many two-word direct sentences of this form actually use one blank as the key to understanding the other. In this sentence, the clause before the comma describes the general when under fire. The second half of the sentence then uses the first half to justify an assertion about the general's character. In other words, there's no way we can come to an understanding of the general's character if we don't know how the general acted under heavy fire, and the word that describes the general's behavior under fire is a blank!

Frustrating, right? Not really. If the first blank describes behavior generally characteristic of the general, then the two words you choose must go together. You can immediately throw out *composed . . tremulous, helpless . . efficient,* and *grave . . humorous* because all three contain words that are antonyms. *Frigid . . warlike* just doesn't make much sense together or in the sentence, so you can throw that choice out too, leaving you with **serene . . unflappable,** the correct answer.

Sentences in which one blank actually contains the word crucial to knowing what should fill the other blank are not particularly difficult. But in those first moments they might scare you a little, since the key word seems to be hidden. Simply knowing that these types of questions exist will help you answer them with ease.

4. Two-Word Contrast Sentences

Like one-word contrast sentence completions, two-word contrast sentences have some sort of internal shift in direction, where one side of the sentence is set against the other. These contrasts are usually marked by change-of-direction hinge words. In some instances, the contrast is created by progression in which what was true *back then* is no longer the case *now.* Below are examples of hinge word and non-hinge word two-word contrast sentence completions.

About five of the sentence completions on the SAT will be of this type.

Two-Word Contrasts with a Hinge Word

We'll give examples of an easy and a difficult hinge-word question. Notice that difficult questions have more advanced vocabulary *and* more sophisticated ideas.

Although the lives of the highest officials of the oppressive government are filled with luxury and ----, the general populace lives in terrible ----.

(A)   pain..joy
(B)   splendor..poverty
(C)   love..friendship
(D)   comfort..cruelty
(E)   anger..corruption

With the obvious hinge word of "Although," this sentence clearly sets the living experience of the "highest officials" against that of the "general populace." The word "luxury," used in reference to the life of the high officials, functions as a clue and makes it clear that their life is good and filled with riches—the general populace must be poor and unfortunate. As you go through the answers, the only one that fits is **splendor . . poverty.**

Faulkner's use of intense, adjective-filled language in his novels is now accepted as an essential aspect of his style and a product of his literary ----; but when his fiction was first published, many critics often ---- his style as needlessly ornate.

(A)   proclivities..extolled
(B)   descrimination..praised
(C)   abilities..examined
(D)   genius..decried
(E)   bombast..enlightened

Obviously, this sentence is slightly longer, a little more grammatically complex, and involves more sophisticated vocabulary and concepts than the previous example did. However, the basic method for finding an answer is the same. The presence of the word "but" in the sentence should tell you that this is a contrast sentence, and you should then realize that the response of the early critics to Faulkner's work is very different from the modern response. Further, the words "essential aspect of his style" in the clause about the modern response and the words "needlessly ornate" in the clause about the early critics should give you the sense that the modern response is positive while many early critics responded negatively to Faulkner's style.

Therefore, the word that fills the first blank must allow the first clause to be positive, while the word for the second blank should make the second clause negative. You can eliminate *proclivities . . extolled* and *descrimination . . praised* because "extolled" and "praised" are positive actions in which critics who saw flaws in Faulkner's work would not engage. *Bombast . . enlightened* can also be thrown out since its words just don't make sense in the sentence. That leaves (C), *abilities . . examined*, and **(D), genius . . decried.** (D) is a much better choice, since "examined" in (C) doesn't fit the context of the sentence.

Sentence Completions

Two-Word Contrasts Without a Hinge Word

Non-hinge contrast sentences are much less common than hinged ones. Those that you do come across will almost always be difficult. Such non-hinged sentences usually focus on time and how things have changed through time.

> The student found it ironic that the medieval belief that bathing was bad for one's ----
> actually helped to create the ---- conditions that resulted in plagues and epidemics.
>
> (A) behavior..superb
> (B) relations..specific
> (C) development..ideal
> (D) standards..unfortunate
> (E) well-being..unsanitary

The word "irony" as it is used in this sentence should function as a clue that the way people acted or thought actually had the opposite effect than the one they expected. You should also have a good idea that the first blank discusses issues of disease or health since the second half of the sentence says that beliefs about *something* "ironically" brought about "plagues and epidemics." With that knowledge, you should quickly be able to pick out **well-being . . unsanitary** as the correct answer, since only this choice deals with issues of health or well-being, while also logically filling the second blank with the word "unsanitary."

5. Other Types of Sentence Completions

There are some types of sentence completions that do not fit into any of these categories. Luckily, these "other" sentence completions aren't all that common: almost 90 percent of all sentence completions will fit into the categories we've described above. Also, you can be sure that only two-word completions make up the "other" category. All one-word completions will either be direct or contrast.

Because they can vary quite widely, there is no way to provide you with examples of *all* of these other sentence completions. But rest assured that these other sentences are just as decodable as the sentences we've just covered. If you follow the standard procedure, paying attention to hinge words and tracking the flow of a sentence, you should be able to figure out how the two blanks function and relate within the sentence. Once you've done that, you'll be able to choose the words that correctly fill the blanks, or, if the vocabulary gives you trouble, you'll at least be able to eliminate answers that are obviously wrong and guess from among the remaining choices.

Don't Know the Vocabulary? There's Still Hope

There may be some questions for which you simply don't know some of the vocabulary included in the answer choices or in the sentence. While this can be frustrating, you should not immediately write off these questions as unanswerable. First, even if you don't know the precise meaning of a vocabulary word, you may have a sense of whether it has a positive or negative connotation. In that case, you might very well be able to go through the sentence and figure out what type of word (positive or negative) needs to be used to fill the blank. It's quite possible that only one word out of all the answer choices might fit the type of word you need. More likely, though, you'll be able to eliminate some of the answer choices based on the criteria of positive or negative connotation, which will put you in a strong position to guess.

If the sentence completion is simply too hard, or if you think that it will take you a tremendous amount of time to eliminate even a few answer choices, then you should skip the question, marking it as one you might want to return to. The time you spend answering that question would be better used answering several easy and moderate analogy or reading comprehension questions.

Sentence Completions

Analogies

THE SAT INCLUDES 19 ANALOGIES, broken into two groups—one of 6 questions and one of 13. The two groups of analogies will appear on the two 30-minute verbal sections. In each case, the analogies will appear after the sentence completions and before the reading comprehension questions.

Analogy Instructions

Don't waste time reading the analogy instructions during the test. Instead, learn them now. Here are the instructions, as they appear on the SAT:

Each question below consists of a related pair of words or phrases, followed by five pairs of words or phrases labeled A through E. Select the pair that best expresses a relationship similar to that expressed in the original pair.

Example:

CRUMB : BREAD ::

(A)   ounce : unit
(B)   splinter : wood
(C)   water : bucket
(D)   twine : rope
(E)   cream : butter

Correct Answer: (B)

Format and Structure of an Analogy

The idea behind analogies is simple. ETS gives you two capitalized words that are related in some way, but you have to figure out their relationship. Then you have to go through a list of five other pairs of words and find the pair that has the same relationship as the capitalized pair. Every analogy will have the same format as the example below:

HAPPY : SMILE : :

(A)   friendly : milk
(B)   angry : lawnmower
(C)   loving : elevator
(D)   sad : frown
(E)   smart : intelligence

HAPPY : SMILE :: is the original pair of words, what we will call the "stem pair" from here on. The colon between the words means, "is related to." The double colon after the stem words means, "in the same way as." When you read the analogy above, you should read it as "HAPPY is related to SMILE in the same way as . . .", or you can shorten the sentence and just say, "HAPPY is to SMILE as . . ." Working through the analogy: "HAPPY is to SMILE as **sad** is to **frown**."

There are two structural issues of analogies that can affect the answer: the order of words in a stem or answer pair; and the parts of speech used in the analogies.

Word Order

In SAT analogies, the order of words in a pair is important. Let's say, for example, that the question above actually looked like this, with the answer pair in (D) flipped around:

HAPPY : SMILE ::

(A)   friendly : milk
(B)   angry : lawnmower
(C)   loving : elevator
(D)   frown : sad
(E)   smart : intelligence

Answer (D) was the correct answer in the last example, but is it now? Is HAPPY related to SMILE in the same way as *frown* is related to *sad*? No. When you look for the correct answer to an analogy, the answer you choose must not only contain words that relate to each other in the same way as the stem pair, but the two words of the answer pair must also follow the same *order* as the stem pair. In the example above, therefore, there is no correct answer (don't worry, every real SAT analogy will have a correct answer).

The SAT will definitely try to use word order to trick you during the test. Often the test will provide an answer pair that has the same association as the stem pair, except the answer pair will be flipped in the wrong direction. Be careful.

Parts of Speech

The parts of speech found in a stem pair will always be mirrored in the answer pairs. If, for example, both of the stem words are nouns, then every answer pair will be made up of two nouns. If the stem pair has a noun and a verb, then the answer pairs will always be a noun and a verb:

	NOUN : NOUN ::			NOUN : VERB ::
(A)	noun : noun		(A)	noun : verb
(B)	noun : noun		(B)	noun : verb
(C)	noun : noun		(C)	noun : verb
(D)	noun : noun		(D)	noun : verb
(E)	noun : noun		(E)	noun : verb

Knowing this facet of analogy structure can help you on more difficult questions. ETS occasionally includes words that can function as more than one part of speech. Take a look at the following example:

COMPOUND : BUILDING ::

(A)	heart : life
(B)	trial : jury
(C)	forest : tree
(D)	tennis : ball
(E)	razor : hair

The word "compound" is most commonly used as a verb meaning "to combine," and your instinct will probably be to try to make a relation between the verb compound and the noun "building." If you were to do so, you wouldn't find an answer that fits among the answer choices. Instead, you should notice that all of the answer pairs follow the format NOUN : NOUN, meaning the stem pair must also be NOUN : NOUN. As a noun, compound means a group of buildings protected by a wall. The answer is **(C)**: just as a COMPOUND is composed of many BUILDINGS, so is a **forest** composed of many **trees.**

Answering Analogies: Making Sentences

Everyone from the test preparation companies to the College Board agrees: making a sentence that defines the specific relationship between the stem words is the single best way to answer an analogy. Once you have the sentence, you can easily test an answer choice by replacing each stem word with the corresponding word from the answer pair. Let's go back to the first example:

HAPPY : SMILE ::

(A)   owl : milk
(B)   lawnmower : anger
(C)   love : elevator
(D)   sad : frown
(E)   college : intelligence

A good sentence for this analogy is, "When people are happy, they smile." If you look at each of the answer choices, the only one that fits is **(D)**, "When people are sad, they frown."

Few of the analogies on the SAT will be quite this easy. Let's try one that's harder:

LIMB : BODY ::

(A)   eyes : view
(B)   cast : bone
(C)   branch : tree
(D)   surgery : injury
(E)   blade : grass

A sentence for this analogy is: a LIMB is part of a BODY. If you try out each of the answer pairs, you'll quickly see that only one fits your sentence: a **branch** is part of a **tree.**

Write the Most Specific Sentence Possible

The truth is, while the sentence "a limb is part of a body" turned out to be good enough for the last example, it wasn't actually the *best possible* sentence. The best possible sentence would have been more specific: "a limb is part of a body that extends from the main trunk."

As you'll see in the next example, having the most specific possible sentence can at times be very important:

METER : DISTANCE ::

(A)   runner : race
(B)   mile : exhaustion
(C)   hourglass : time
(D)   quart : volume
(E)   summer : heat

You might be tempted to make the following sentence for this analogy: A METER measures DISTANCE. As you searched for the answers you would come upon, "An **hourglass** measures **time**," fitting your sentence perfectly. And if you then happily put down (C) as your answer, you'd have gotten the question wrong. Woe is you! If you had only chosen a better, more specific sentence, none of this would have happened. For instance, if you came up with the more specific sentence: A METER is a single unit of DISTANCE measurement," then *hourglass* : *time* doesn't fit, since an hourglass isn't a unit of time. But **quart** : **volume** does fit perfectly, since a quart is a single unit of volume measurement.

Knowing When Your Sentence Is Good Enough

There's a simple way to determine whether the sentence you've created is specific enough: go through every answer pair. If more than one answer pair fits with your sentence, then go back and modify the sentence so that it's more specific.

In the case of LIMB : BODY, the sentence was good enough even though it wasn't very specific; you were still able to whittle down the answer choices to one possibility. For METER : DISTANCE, you had to make the sentence more specific.

In other words, don't sweat it. Come up with a sentence and try it out. If multiple answer choices fit the sentence, go back and make your sentence more specific. If no answer choices fit the sentence, check to see if you made it too specific, or if you somehow misjudged the relation between the stem words. You should definitely not waste time trying to come up with the perfect sentence.

As you practice analogies, don't just focus on getting them right. Think about the process of getting them right. Did you come up with a good enough sentence the first time? Did you have to try a number of sentences, meaning the questions took you more time? If you pay some attention to the sentences you come up with for each question you encounter, you will train yourself to create better sentences in the future.

Types of Analogies

There are a variety of ways in which words can be related. Luckily for you, the SAT seems only partially aware of this fact: a few relationships appear on the test much more frequently than others. Creating a sentence to define a relationship becomes easier when you recognize an analogy as a particular *kind* of analogy—becoming familiar with the different sorts of analogies is therefore a very good idea.

The following table outlines, in order of frequency, the twelve most common types of analogies found on the SAT:

Analogies

Type	Example
Function / Purpose	CHAINSAW : TREE *the function of a chainsaw is to cut a tree*
Part / Whole	PETAL : FLOWER *a petal is part of a flower*
Characteristic Action	DOCTOR : SURGERY *a doctor characteristically performs surgery*
Relative Size & Degree	DRY : ARID *an arid place is very dry*
Type	CANAL : WATERWAY *a canal is a type of waterway*
Characteristic Location	CAR : GARAGE *a car is typically parked in a garage*
Attribute	NOVICE : EXPERIENCE *lack of experience defines a novice*
Descriptive Pair	TEXTURE : ROUGH *a texture feels rough*
Cause & Effect	CAST : MOVEMENT *the effect of a cast is to stop movement*
Lack	PAUPER : MONEY *a pauper lacks money*
Characteristic Use	FISHERMAN : ROD *a fisherman uses a rod*
Other	About $\frac{1}{6}$ of SAT analogies fall into this category.

Though we've given you this list, we have to be honest—the science of categorizing SAT analogies is not perfect. Some categories do overlap slightly. However, if you become comfortable with these categories and are able to identify whether a particular analogy fits into one of them, it will usually make creating a sentence much simpler. And the better you are at creating a good sentence, the faster and more accurately you will be able to move through the two analogy sections.

1. Function / Purpose

Function analogies relate an object and the purpose for which it is used. A very simple example would be CHAINSAW : TREE—the purpose of a chainsaw is to cut down trees. Almost all function analogies follow the model of CHAINSAW : TREE, in which the analogy is NOUN : NOUN and the sentence you produce includes a verb that describes how one noun functions by acting upon the other. In the CHAINSAW : TREE example, the verb you have to supply is "cut down." However, we've found a few instances of NOUN : VERB function analogies, such as CHAINSAW : CUT. In these instances, the sentence you produce would be something more general, such as, "The purpose of a chainsaw is to cut."

NOUN : NOUN Example

LAMP : LIGHT ::

(A)   elevator : skyscraper
(B)   lever : machine
(C)   microphone : amplifier
(D)   mentor : guidance
(E)   honey : food

The correct answer is **(D).** The function of a LAMP is to provide LIGHT, just as the function of a **mentor** is to provide **guidance.**

NOUN : VERB Example

LIE : DECEIVE ::

(A)   truth : cheat
(B)   speech : communicate
(C)   payment : save
(D)   hand : sort
(E)   eye : glance

The correct answer is **(B).** The function of a LIE is to DECEIVE, just as the function of **speech** is to **communicate.** The only answer choice that should have given you trouble here is (E). But while an eye can glance, glancing is not the function of an eye; seeing is the eye's function.

2. Part / Whole

There are three types of part/whole analogies, all of which are related. The first involves a particular thing and a larger structure or entity completely composed of a number of the original things. Consider an example like SOLDIER : ARMY—an army is made up of many soldiers. The second involves a thing and a larger structure of which that thing is a part, though that larger entity is not composed entirely of the original thing. For example, TOE : FOOT. The third is very similar to the second, but it involves a further spatial dimension. For example, ROOF : HOUSE—a roof is the part of a house *located at the top of the house.*

Type 1 Example

TREE : FOREST ::

- (A) broccoli : vegetable
- (B) album : music
- (C) actor : troupe
- (D) forum : speaker
- (E) inquisitor : question

The correct answer is **(C)**. A FOREST is made up of many TREES, just as a **troupe** is made up of many **actors**.

Type 2 Example

PETAL : FLOWER ::

- (A) eyes : view
- (B) nose : head
- (C) seedling : plant
- (D) surgery : injury
- (E) blade : grass

The correct answer is **(B)**. A PETAL is part of a FLOWER (though the flower is not made up entirely of petals), just as **nose** is a part of the **head**.

Type 3 Example

ROOF : HOUSE ::

- (A) plateau : landscape
- (B) door : entrance
- (C) status : hierarchy
- (D) summit : mountain
- (E) surfeit : resources

The correct answer is **(D)**. The ROOF is the highest part of a HOUSE, just as the **summit** is the highest part of a **mountain**.

3. Characteristic Action

Characteristic action analogies in the form NOUN : NOUN relate something and what that thing (or being) typically does. In the examples below, note that not only is the vocabulary harder for the difficult example, the relation between the stem words is also more sophisticated.

Easy Example

NOVELIST : BOOK ::

(A)   house : roof
(B)   tailor : needle
(C)   weaver : cloth
(D)   unicorn : horn
(E)   scientist : laboratory

The correct answer is **(C)**. A NOVELIST makes a BOOK, just as a **weaver** makes **cloth.**

Difficult Example

ICONOCLAST : CONVENTION ::

(A)   tailor : robe
(B)   sycophant : love
(C)   pariah : friendship
(D)   anarchist : government
(E)   fireman : safety

The correct answer is **(D)**. An ICONOCLAST dislikes and fights against CONVEN-TION, just as an **anarchist** dislikes and opposes **government.**

Sometimes you might see characteristic action analogies in the form ADJECTIVE : VERB. In these cases, the adjective describes a person or thing, and the verb is something that person or thing characteristically does.

DISSATISFIED : COMPLAIN

(A)   pleased : tolerate
(B)   ungrateful : enliven
(C)   friendly : ridicule
(D)   curious : inquire
(E)   generous : pacify

The correct answer is **(D)**. A DISSATISFIED person COMPLAINS, just as a **curious** person **inquires.**

4. Relative Size and Degree

This type of analogy describes a thing or state of being and a second thing or state of being that is similar but smaller or larger in size or degree.

Analogies

Easy Example

POKE : PUNCH ::

(A)   murmur : shout
(B)   crouch : smack
(C)   lose : win
(D)   groan : hurt
(E)   stink : smell

The correct answer is **(A).** A POKE is a much weaker touch than a PUNCH, just as a **murmur** is much weaker sound than a **shout.** You might have been tempted by the answer choice *stink : smell,* but that choice is not best answer because the relationship between stink and smell is one of type, not degree. A stink is a bad smell.

Difficult Example

LUDICROUS : SILLY ::

(A)   monstrous : skyscraper
(B)   brackish : messy
(C)   conscientious : moralistic
(D)   spurious : rotten
(E)   emaciated : thin

The correct answer is **(E).** To be LUDICROUS is to be extremely SILLY, just as to be **emaciated** is to be extremely **thin**.

5. Type

In type analogies, one stem word names a category into which the other typically fits. For the moderately difficult type questions, the relation between the two words may be a little more complicated. For example, in the stem pair NIGHTMARE : DREAM, a nightmare is a bad or ominous kind of dream. The SAT almost never includes difficult type analogies.

Easy Example

BANANA : FRUIT ::

(A)   lung : organ
(B)   grape : raisin
(C)   crab : lobster
(D)   ocean : land
(E)   slope : mountain

The correct answer is **(A).** A BANANA is a type of FRUIT, just as a **lung** is a type of **organ.**

Moderate Example

EMOTION: ANGUISH ::

(A)   fascination : frenetic
(B)   dossier : categorized
(C)   cabbage : vegetative
(D)   sensation : burning
(E)   compensation : financial

The correct answer is **(D).** ANGUISH is an intense and unpleasant type of EMO-TION, just as **burning** is an intense and unpleasant type of **sensation.**

6. Characteristic Location or Event

In this type of analogy, one of the stem pair words describes a typical location or event at which the other word can be found. These analogies are generally simple. Only rarely will you find one in the difficult last third of an analogy group.

HORSE : STABLE ::

(A)   rider : saddle
(B)   heart : blood
(C)   street : lamp
(D)   view : window
(E)   guest : hotel

The correct answer is **(E).** A HORSE stays in a STABLE, just as a **guest** stays in a **hotel.**

7. Attribute

In attribute analogies, one word describes an integral characteristic of the other word. Attribute analogies often involve difficult vocabulary and can be quite subtle.

DICTATOR : POWER ::

(A)   priest : congregation
(B)   mathematician : energy
(C)   neophyte : inexperience
(D)   tyrant : wrath
(E)   creator : benevolence

The correct answer is **(C).** An attribute of a DICTATOR is POWER, just as an attribute of a **neophyte** is **inexperience.** Another way to write this sentence would be, "A dictator could not be a dictator if he did not have power, just as a neophyte could not be a neophyte if he was not inexperienced."

Analogies

8. Descriptive Pair

Description analogies are unlike any other type. Description analogies come in the form ADJECTIVE : NOUN, in which the adjective modifies or describes the noun in some specific way. The answer pair must contain an adjective that modifies a noun in a similar way. Note that this type of analogy isn't so much about a relation between the words—it's more about the suitability of the adjective as a descriptor of the noun.

GUTTURAL : SOUND ::

(A)   economical : money
(B)   bombastic : speech
(C)   scattered : pilgrims
(D)   coarse : texture
(E)   gradual : slope

The correct answer is **(D)**. A GUTTURAL SOUND is rough, just as a **coarse texture** is rough.

9. Cause and Effect

In cause and effect analogies, one word is an action, result, or situation that the other word creates or stops. Such analogies can follow one of three forms: NOUN : NOUN; VERB : NOUN; or VERB : ADJECTIVE.

In NOUN : NOUN cause and effect analogies, one of the nouns is an object that causes or stops the second noun:

BANDAGE : BLOOD ::

(A)   cable : bridge
(B)   cast : injury
(C)   fort : army
(D)   dam : river
(E)   pacemaker : heart

The correct answer is **(D)**. A BANDAGE stops the flow of BLOOD, just as a **dam** stops the flow of a **river.**

In VERB : NOUN cause and effect analogies, the verb describes an action committed upon the noun, somehow causing the noun to be changed:

SHEAR : SHEEP ::

(A)   grade : paper
(B)   peel : apple
(C)   herd : cattle
(D)   punish : law
(E)   emancipate : freedom

The correct answer is **(B).** To SHEAR a SHEEP is to remove its outer covering, just as to **peel** an **apple** is to remove its outer covering.

In VERB : ADJECTIVE cause and effect analogies, the verb describes an action, and the adjective describes the effect of the verb:

EXPAND : LARGE ::

(A)   abridge : short
(B)   spread : slim
(C)   answer : correct
(D)   destroy : miniscule
(E)   garble : clear

The correct answer is **(A).** When you EXPAND something, you make it LARGER, just as when you **abridge** something you make it **shorter.**

10. Lack

Lack analogies follow two basic forms: NOUN : NOUN or ADJECTIVE : NOUN. In NOUN : NOUN lack analogies, one noun describes something that the other noun, by definition, lacks:

DROUGHT : WATER ::

(A)   gully : river
(B)   tornado : wind
(C)   plague : health
(D)   store : goods
(E)   vestibule : hangars

The correct answer is **(C).** A DROUGHT involves a lack of WATER, just as a **plague** involves a lack of **health.**

In ADJECTIVE : NOUN lack analogies, the adjective describes a state of being, and the noun describes what is lacking in order to make that state of being a reality. ADJECTIVE : NOUN lack analogies are usually a little harder than NOUN : NOUN lack analogies because the ADJECTIVE : NOUN versions tend to use somewhat harder vocabulary:

LISTLESS : ENERGY ::

(A)   devout : prayer
(B)   frigid : warmth
(C)   potent : power
(D)   distant : location
(E)   somber : gravity

The correct answer is **(B).** To be LISTLESS is to lack ENERGY, just as to be **frigid** is to lack **warmth.**

11. Characteristic Use

In this type of analogy, one word is a person or thing and the other is what that person or thing uses. Characteristic use analogies are always NOUN : NOUN. Often one of the nouns is a tool used by the other, such as CAMERA : PHOTOGRAPHER. These analogies are usually either easy or moderately difficult.

> PALETTE : PAINTER ::
>
> (A)　　trial : jury
> (B)　　barber : scissors
> (C)　　sandwich : restaurant
> (D)　　saddle : jockey
> (E)　　tapestry : weaver

The correct answer is **(D)**. A PAINTER uses a PALETTE as part of his job, just as a **jockey** uses a **saddle** as part of his job. (Note that *barber : scissors* is a trick, since its order is flipped.)

12. Other

About ⅙ of the analogies you will encounter on practice SATs—and on the real thing—will not fit into any of the 11 categories we have defined. If you come upon an analogy that doesn't seem to fit, don't worry. The process you should follow is exactly the same. Create a sentence that defines the relationship between the stem words, and then apply that sentence to the answer choices.

Analogy Tricks the SAT Likes to Pull

The SAT embeds certain tricks in its analogy questions to trip up the careless and to lure the confused. Such tricks are most common among difficult questions, which can be particularly troublesome since tricks work most effectively when you are already a little confused. All of the tricks used by ETS on analogy questions are designed to make a wrong answer look like the right one. When you have little time and desperately want to find the right answer, those "attractive" wrong answers become very enticing.

If you know the tricks are lurking out there, you will be much less likely to fall into their diabolical clutches. Plus, if you learn to identify an answer choice as a trick, you can use that knowledge to eliminate it. After all, if an answer choice is a trick, it can't be the right answer.

Bogus Associations

One kind of SAT analogy trickery involves the use of an answer pair in which one of the words is somehow associated with one of the words in the stem pair. Take a look at the example:

BANDAGE : BLOOD ::

(A)   cable : bridge
(B)   cast : injury
(C)   fort : army
(D)   dam : river
(E)   pacemaker : heart

The correct answer for this question is **(D) dam : river,** since a dam stops the flow of a river in the same way that a BANDAGE stops the flow of BLOOD. However, let's say you didn't immediately see the answer and had to scour through the answer choices. BANDAGE : BLOOD conjures images of pain and injury, as does the answer choice *cast : injury.* Because the words in this answer pair are related to those in the stem pair, you might be tempted to think it is the correct answer. Don't be. The relation between *cast* and *injury* is very different from that between BANDAGE and BLOOD. (In fact, the relation between a cast and an injury isn't clear; an injury is too general a term to have any real relation to a cast, which is used to immobilize broken bones but is unrelated to injuries like burns.)

To avoid the SAT trap of bogus associations, you should make sure to focus on the relation between the words in the analogies rather than on the words themselves. Also, when you see a word in an answer pair that is similar or closely associated with a word in the stem pair, be suspicious. Now that you are aware that this type of trap exists on the SAT, you should be able to avoid it.

Flipped Answers

As discussed earlier in this section, word order is extremely important in analogies. EYE : VISION cannot be related to HEARING : EAR because the two relations are flipped. The SAT will sometimes give you questions with the answers flipped, such as:

PALETTE : PAINTER ::

(A)   trial : jury
(B)   barber : scissors
(C)   sandwich : restaurant
(D)   saddle : jockey
(E)   tapestry : weaver

Analogies

In this example, a barber uses scissors for his job, just as a PAINTER uses his PAL-ETTE, but the order of the two word pairs is reversed. *Barber : scissors* cannot be the answer. (The correct answer is **saddle : jockey**). When you pick an answer, be sure that its words are in the same order as those in the stem pair. You might want to touch each word with your pencil when you insert it into your sentence to remind you to check for the correct word order.

When Vocabulary Is Difficult

On harder analogies, you will often come across difficult vocabulary, some of which you might not know. So how can you possibly form a sentence to relate two words you don't know? And if you can't form a sentence, how can you even try to answer the question?

There are a few strategies to help you come to an answer if you don't know the vocabulary of one or even both words in the stem pair. Using these strategies may occasionally enable you to come to a single answer. More likely, the strategies will help you to eliminate two or three of the answer pairs, putting you in a good position to guess.

If You Don't Know One of the Stem Words

If you can't form a relational sentence because you don't know one of the stem words in an analogy, you obviously won't be able to identify an answer immediately. However, that doesn't mean all is lost. Remember, because SAT questions are multiple-choice, the answer is always right there in front of you. So if you can't pick it out of the crowd, perhaps you can eliminate the crowd around it.

There's a handy two-step method that will help you to eliminate incorrect analogy answer choices.

1. Go through the answer pairs and try to make defining sentences.

Often, the words in an answer pair will not be very well related. If that is the case, you can eliminate that answer pair. Stem words always have a strong relation to each other, so the words in the correct answer pair will too. Here's the strategy in action:

???????? : GOVERNMENT ::

(A)   leader : office
(B)   claimant : throne
(C)   soldier : platoon
(D)   attorney : trial
(E)   boss : business

Answer choices (B), (C), (D), and (E) all have fairly good relations. A *claimant* desires to ascend to the *throne*, a *soldier* is a member of a *platoon*, an *attorney* works at a *trial*, and a *boss* heads a *business*. However, *leader* : *office* does not have a very good relation—a leader might work in an office, but he or she certainly doesn't have to. Therefore, you can eliminate (A) as a possible answer. Now you're down to four choices, shifting the odds in your favor.

2. Find the relation for each answer pair, and see if the word you know in the stem pair can possibly fit.

We'll use the same example we did before. Remember, (A) has already been eliminated. In (B), a *claimant* desires to ascend to the *throne*. Can you imagine the unknown word means "someone who wants to ascend to government"? Seems unlikely, so you can eliminate (B). In (C), a *soldier* is a member of a *platoon*. Could the unknown word mean "member of a government"? Possibly. Keep it. In (D), an *attorney* works at a *trial*. Is there a name for a person who "works in government"? Seems likely, though you might notice that an attorney working at a trial is not quite the same thing as a bureaucrat working in a government. This relation is possible, but it's not as good as (C). If guessing, you probably shouldn't choose this one. In (E), a *boss* heads a *business*. Could the word mean "head of the government"? Possibly. Keep this one too.

The Results of the Process

After employing the two-step process, we were able to eliminate two answer pairs. Further, while we weren't willing to entirely eliminate (D), we did have the sense that it wasn't as good as the other two we kept. So we have to guess between (C) and (E), which leaves our odds for getting the question right at 50 percent. Not bad for an analogy in which we didn't even know the meaning of one of the words.

If You Don't Know Either of the Stem Words

If you don't know either of the stem words in an analogy, you can still look through the answers to see if any of the pairs has a bad internal relation. If you can eliminate even one possibility this way, it's in your favor to guess. If you can't eliminate any, you should move on to another question.

Reading Comprehension

O F THE 78 QUESTIONS IN THE VERBAL half of the SAT, 40 are reading comprehension. That's more than half. In other words, to do well on the verbal SAT, you have to do well on reading comprehension.

Regrettably, studying for reading comprehension is not as easy as preparing for the other verbal sections. Reading comprehension questions don't come in one basic form, and there aren't always tricks for eliminating answers (though you will often be able to eliminate an answer choice). The best way to study for the reading comprehension section is to read newspapers, magazines, or books, and to question yourself about what you read, both while you do it and after you've finished. Through this sort of practice, you can build up your ability to read and understand quickly.

Location of Reading Comprehension

The SAT includes four sets of reading comprehension passages and questions. One of these four sets is actually a dual passage, involving two passages and subsequent questions. Of the four, two are located at the end of one of the 30-minute verbal sections, one will be at the end of the other 30-minute verbal section, and one will take up the entire final 15-minute verbal section. Usually the dual passage will be found in the 15-minute verbal section, but that is not always the case.

Order of Difficulty

Reading comprehension questions are organized by what part of the passage they test, not by difficulty. The early questions on each passage test the early portions of the passage; the later ones test the end of it. This organizational pattern provides no clue for determining question difficulty within each passage. In an analogy group, you can determine the difficulty of a question based on its location. However, in reading comprehension groups, you can make those decisions only after you've looked at the questions. Since the goal is to answer as many questions as possible, you may want to skip those that immediately strike you as difficult. Of course, how many questions you want to skip depends on your target score. Even so, you should be aware of how the unique organizational scheme for reading comprehension affects your strategy for answering these questions.

Reading Comprehension Instructions

Here are the instructions for reading comprehension, as they appear on the SAT.

> Each passage below is followed by questions based on its content. Answer the questions following each passage on the basis of what is stated or implied in that passage and in any introductory material that may be provided.

Have you read them? Read them again. Do you understand them? Will you remember them tomorrow? Good. Let's move on.

Format and Structure

Reading comprehension sections follow a fairly standard format. Preceding each passage is an italicized introductory blurb that offers some contextual information. *Read this introduction.* Knowing the context it provides will help you understand the passage. Below the introduction is the passage, which can range from 450 to 900 words. The four reading passages on each SAT generally fit into one of the following categories:

- Science

- Art

- Literary criticism

- History or historical criticism

- Fiction or nonfiction narrative

Some passages might overlap categories, as when an artist provides a narrative about his or her experience with art. A few passages might not fit into any of these categories well. There will be at least one science and one narrative passage on every SAT.

Anywhere from 5 to 13 questions accompany each passage. These questions test your comprehension of general themes, points, or tone; your ability to comprehend and breakdown arguments; your ability to interpret implied and explicit information; and your understanding of vocabulary words in context. We cover each of these types of questions later in this section. In addition to the types of questions mentioned above, dual passages include questions that ask you to relate the two passages.

To simplify a bit, reading comprehension questions ask about two things: general understanding and specific information. Questions about general understanding focus on themes, tone, and techniques of writing. Questions on specific information will pinpoint a specific section in the passage and then ask about the meaning of some implied or explicit information in that section, or the meaning of a specific word in context. It is important to note that the questions that ask for specific information will tell you where that information is located. We'll explain how this should affect your reading strategy in the aptly named "Strategic Approaches" section, below.

Of the four reading comprehension passages, one will usually be around 500 words long with 5 questions, one around 700 words with 10 questions, and two around 900 words with 12 or 13 questions. The dual passage will be one of the 900-word passages.

Strategic Approaches

To do well on reading comprehension, you must learn to find the proper balance between time spent reading the passage and time spent answering the questions. There's no use laboring over the passage and making sure you understand everything if you run out of time before getting to the questions. Similarly, there's no use flying through the passage and understanding nothing, since that will obviously make it difficult to answer the questions.

In the following paragraphs, we will provide some strategies to help you balance your time between reading the passages and answering the questions. These strategies will certainly help, but to put your time and effort to best use, you must also practice and learn how quickly you can read without sacrificing understanding. Some test preparation companies promote the use of speed-reading techniques, but in our opinion, these techniques are dubious and often don't result in a very good understanding of the material you read.

Knowing that reading comprehension questions will test your understanding of both general and specific information probably makes you think that when you read the passage, you'll have to spend time focusing on the big themes and the small details.

But that's not really true. A single passage contains one general tone and one general theme, and it will have a particular point. That same passage will have numerous pieces of specific information. At most, you will have to answer 13 questions about a passage, and while those 13 might be able to cover most of the general themes, there's simply no way they can test *all* of the specific information. The strategy we propose for approaching reading comprehension passages will minimize wasted time and effort. It will allow you to get a general sense of the passage and a contextual understanding that will make answering questions about specific information that much easier.

Passage First, Questions After

In this method, you read the passage first and pay no attention to the questions until after you've finished reading. You should read the passage quickly and lightly. Do not dwell on details, but make sure you get a general understanding of what is going on in the passage. Pay active attention to what's going on, but don't get bogged down trying to completely assimilate every fact. This doesn't mean you should ignore the core of every paragraph and focus only on the topic sentence. It means that you should read the passage and see the lay of the land. You should read so that you understand the themes of the passage and the reason the passage was written.

The specific facts are a part of the author's effort to achieve his or her goals, but as you read, you should be more concerned with the cumulative effect of the specific facts than with the specific facts themselves. The only time you should slow down and go back is if you lose the flow of the passage and end up lost. Read the passage with an awareness of the general questions the SAT might ask you. What is the author's goal in writing the passage? What are the tone, themes, and major points? When you finish a passage, you should be able to answer these questions and also have a sense of the passage's structure and of where things lie within it.

When you finish the passage, go to the questions. You should be able to answer general questions without needing to look at the passage. Questions on specific information will indicate the lines in the passage to which they refer. Before going back to the paragraph, articulate to yourself exactly what the question is asking, but don't look at the answers (this will help you avoid being influenced by "trick" answers). Then go to the specified area in the passage and read a few lines before and after it to get a sense of the context. Come up with your own answer to the question, then go back and find the answer that best matches yours.

The Merits of the Passage-First Strategy

Some test-prep courses or books advise you to skim over the questions before reading the passage so you know what to look for. In theory it sounds like a good idea, but in the end we think it will just make your life confusing. Holding 13 questions in your head isn't easy, and some are bound to get mixed up. Also, to answer the specific questions swarming in your head you would have to concentrate on the small facts of the passage to make sure you don't miss anything. That concentration is likely to limit your speed, lessen your understanding of the passage as a whole, and perhaps even affect your memory of the questions you skimmed. It's more effective to take a top-down approach and understand the passage as a whole before trying to fill in the specific blanks, questions by question.

Concentration Strategies for Reading Comprehension

Many students have trouble with reading comprehension passages because they find it hard to maintain focus for the entire passage. To combat the devastating loss-of-focus disease, we've provided some practical advice.

Paragraph-by-Paragraph Analysis

If you have a tendency to drift, to suddenly realize that you have read a hundred words but have no idea what they said, you could take a brief moment—and we mean brief—and think about each paragraph once you've finished. Think about what the paragraph said, what it was about, and how it fit into the overall passage. By stopping after each paragraph, you give yourself a structure that will help you concentrate and better understand what's happening in the passage.

Underline and Circle

Another way to help you focus and remember things when you have to go back to the passage is to underline or circle key arguments, sentences, and facts—anything relating to general themes and ideas, the main idea of each paragraph, or other aspects of the passage that strike you as important. This will reinforce what you read and give you a sort of map for when you go back to the passage to answer specific questions.

Special Strategy for Dual Passages

Dual passages are exactly what their name implies: two passages that deal with the same subject. Because of the way the passages and the questions that follow them are organized, however, your approach to them should be different.

As you look at the dual passage section, you will first see a single introductory blurb that puts both passages into context. The two passages follow the blurb, one after the other. The two passages might differ in length relative to each other, but together they will take up 80–100 lines. Either 12 or 13 questions accompany the dual passages. As with the questions for single passages, dual-passage questions are organized according to line number. Those questions dealing with passage 1 will therefore be first, followed by the questions asking about passage 2. The last few questions will ask you to relate the two passages.

When you come to the dual passage, read the introductory paragraph and passage 1, using the techniques outlined earlier. After you've finished passage 1, go to the questions, starting with the first. Answer the questions that ask about passage 1, skipping and marking for later those that seem as if they'll take too much time. When you reach the first question about passage 2, go back and read passage two. Ask yourself while you're reading how this second passage relates to the first. Does it agree? Disagree? Does it do both at different times? Mark places where the second passage seems to intersect most with the first, whether in disagreement or agreement. After reading passage 2, return to the questions and begin answering where you left off. Eventually you'll reach the questions that relate the two passages. By this point, you'll not only have read both passages, you'll also have a better understanding of each because of the questions you've already answered.

Types of Reading Passages

As we said earlier, the reading passages on the SAT usually fit into one of five categories: science, art, literary criticism, history or historical criticism, and fiction or nonfiction narrative. Every SAT has at least one passage on science and one narrative. The other two passages on each test can come from any of the five categories. On rare occasions, ETS chooses a passage that doesn't really fit into any of the five categories. If that happens on a test you're taking, don't worry—these passages don't test any skills that are different from those tested by the five categories with which you will soon be familiar.

We can give you some idea about the content you can expect within each passage type and what kinds of questions are usually asked about each. Note, however, that when we say that the questions about a certain type of passage *usually* focus on one thing, we are not saying that you'll *never* be asked anything else about that type of passage. For example, though the questions about fiction or nonfiction narratives often focus on the writer's technique, that doesn't mean that you can't be asked about the writer's intentions.

Science Passages

Science passages range from discussions or debates about science to descriptions of historical scientific events. Students tend to be a little frightened by these passages simply because they cover science, and students think that they have to do a lot of studying to understand science and scientific topics. Do not be intimidated by these passages. No SAT passage will ever require advanced scientific knowledge. The scientific claims these passages make are always general. For example, one thesis in a scientific passage might be "genetics affect decisions about where people build their cities." In those instances when the test wants you to understand scientific arguments, the actual science will be fairly simple. If the passage uses a technical term, it will define that term for you, so don't panic when you see a word or words you don't immediately recognize. Look at the surrounding sentences, and find the term's explanation.

There may be some passages that do discuss more advanced science, but in those instances the passages will focus on the history of a discovery rather than on the science behind the discovery. In these passages, the science is rather unimportant compared to the history or the argument that the writer is making about the history. Questions about science passages will focus on how well you understand the arguments that have been made, on specific information, and on your ability to comprehend words in context. There will be at least one science passage on every SAT.

Fiction or Nonfiction Narratives

The content of fiction or nonfiction narratives is not so easy to pinpoint. Often a narrative will focus on a description of a particular person. You will have to intuit information from that description. Sometimes the narratives describe a coming-of-age anecdote or an important experience. As you read these narratives, you should think about why the author is choosing to write what he or she is writing. Why does the writer choose the metaphors used in the passage? What is the tone? Why are some details explored and others barely acknowledged? The writers of these narratives make artistic choices to mold an overall sense of their stories. Pay attention to these aspects of the passage as you read. The questions will likely ask you about them.

The questions for fiction or nonfiction narratives tend to cover quite a bit, with emphasis on words in context, understanding arguments or points, the writer's technique, and both implied and explicit information.

History Passages

The history passages are either passages taken from history—such as a historical address about an event or situation in society—or passages in which historians write about and interpret history. In either case, these passages usually contain a lot of argumentation, with the use of examples or facts as support. Often, the writer will refer to other writers or thinkers, either to agree with or to refute what the other writer has said.

Questions about history passages focus on your ability to understand the arguments being made, your understanding of specific and implied information, and, to some extent, your comprehension of words in context.

Literary Criticism Passages

Like the history passages, literary-criticism articles are also quite heavy on argument. In these passages, a critic or writer discusses a particular book or writer, a literary movement or trend, or some literary idea. As you read these passages, you should make sure that you understand the arguments the writer is making about the subject in question. You probably don't have to worry very much about the subject itself. For example, if the passage is on *Robinson Crusoe,* you will see questions such as, "How does the writer of the passage feel about Crusoe's religious conversion?" You will *not* see questions like, "At what point in the book does Robinson Crusoe begin to dedicate himself completely to God?"

Questions following literary-criticism passages focus mostly on your ability to understand the arguments being made and your comprehension of words in context.

Art Passages

Art passages discuss specific pieces of art (painting, architecture, or music) or particular artists. The passages might involve the artist speaking about his or her own work, the artist speaking about his field in general, a critic discussing a specific work or artist, or a description of some controversy in the art world. Like history and literary-criticism passages, art passages are often centered on arguments, since they are often about interpreting or explaining the subject they address.

Questions on art passages focus on your ability to understand arguments, specific information, and words in context.

Types of Reading Comprehension Questions

ETS has created eight basic types of questions to test reading comprehension skills.

1. Main Theme, Idea, or Point

2. Author's Attitude or Tone

3. Specific Information

4. Implied Information

5. Understanding Themes and Arguments

6. Structure and Technique

7. Understanding Words in Context

8. Relating Two Passages

Below, we describe each of these eight question types and provide examples of each. The examples should familiarize you with the most common ways that ETS phrases its questions, and get you thinking about what sort of understanding each question tests.

1. Main Theme, Idea, or Point Questions

Main theme, idea, or point questions—which we'll call main idea questions—test your understanding of the entire passage. The questions do not provide line numbers or specific quotations to focus your search. Instead, they ask broad questions that focus on the passage's primary issues. It is unlikely that you'll see more than three main idea questions for a given passage. Often, though not always, main idea questions will be among the first few you encounter.

Main idea questions come in a variety of forms. Below are examples of the most common ones. We include answer choices with each example to give you a better idea of what the question will look like. You shouldn't be able to answer these questions, since you haven't seen the reading passage on which they are based. Don't worry about that. Just study the questions and figure out what they're asking and how you would have to read the unknown passage from which they came to answer them. If while reading the passage you remain alert to the sorts of general questions that the SAT is likely to ask, you probably won't have to go back to the passage to answer such questions when you encounter them, thereby saving valuable time.

Examples

The primary purpose of the passage is to

(A)   describe the day to day life of inmates in American insane asylums in the early twentieth century
(B)   raise concerns about the inhumane treatment of the clinically insane in America today
(C)   prompt psychiatrists to be more diligent when they diagnose someone as insane
(D)   examine the benefits and detriments of the insane asylum to those it is meant to treat
(E)   demand an alternative method of housing and treating the insane

The passage as a whole suggests that the author disagrees with his parents about

(A)   the wisdom of moving from their homeland to the United States
(B)   his parents' unwavering belief in the benefits of American capitalism
(C)   his parents' decision to wear traditional clothes on the cultural holidays of their homeland
(D)   the importance of maintaining a connection with their roots
(E)   his parents' adoption of Christmas as a special holiday though they did not celebrate it in their own country

Which of the following titles best summarizes the passage?

(A)   Lost Land: the Tragedy of Native Americans
(B)   Native Americans and Oral History
(C)   The Importance of Oral History in Contemporary Native American Literature
(D)   The Cultural Legacy of Native American Creation Myths
(E)   Coping with Loss: The Native American Effort to Reappropriate Land Through Literature

2. Author's Attitude or Tone Questions

This type of question tests whether you understand how the author views the subject about which he or she writes. Attitude and tone questions will ask you for a description of the author's feelings about the subject. As you read these kinds of passages, think to yourself about whether the argument the writer is making seems to support or attack his subject. Also pay attention to the language the author uses, which will help you to determine tone.

As you will see in the examples, the differences between the answer choices are sometimes slight. For example, you might have to choose between "anger" and "disapproval." Both of these words imply that the author has negative sentiments about what the passage is discussing, so to answer this question correctly you have to determine the intensity of the author's negative perspective. Is the author enraged, mildly disturbed, or strongly disapproving? If you have one answer choice that describes the author as feeling positive about his subject and one as feeling negative, then you know one must be wrong. If you are unable to figure out the definitive answer to this type of question, you may still have a good chance of eliminating some answers so that you can guess.

Examples

The author's attitude toward those who believe that better technology is the only measure of progress is one of

(A)   disgust
(B)   amazement
(C)   amusement
(D)   agreement
(E)   disbelief

In this question, if you know that the author's attitude toward these people is not negative, you can immediately throw out (A) *disgust* as a possible answer, and possibly also (E) *disbelief.*

The tone of the passage might best be described as

(A) gently mocking
(B) bitterly angry
(C) emphatically approving
(D) cautiously ambivalent
(E) powerfully optimistic

In this example, the negative answer choices (A) and (B) are direct opposites of the positive (C) and (E). You should definitely be able to eliminate at least two choices simply by determining whether the passage's tone is positive or negative.

3. Specific Information Questions

Questions on specific information ask you to find precisely that: specific information. The questions will indicate a section of the passage, usually through the use of line numbers, and ask a question about the information presented within that specific area. The specific information that these questions ask about varies widely, making it difficult to provide you with representative examples covering all possible forms. However, we will provide you with a few sample questions to help you get a feel for the type of information these questions are after.

Examples

Lines 15–18 suggest that the attempted restoration of the paintings actually served to reveal

(A) that the supposed originals were forgeries
(B) the impressive skill of medieval artists
(C) some of the techniques, hitherto unknown, employed by medieval painters
(D) that the paintings were themselves restorations of earlier works
(E) that modern, polluted air contains chemicals that react with medieval paints, dramatically dulling them

The author claims which of the following about the "fops" (line 65)?

(A) They were more concerned about personal glory than justice.
(B) They were an important part of the political structure of the royal courts.
(C) Their relations were dependent on their success at the royal court.
(D) They cared only about luxury and influence and were willing to stoop to political fawning of all kinds to achieve their goals.
(E) They were excellent equestrians.

Reading Comprehension

The claim that "everyone is always wrong" (line 78) is presented by the passage as the opinion of

(A)   Jacques
(B)   Robertson
(C)   Crane
(D)   Minstrel
(E)   Kramer

Because these questions test specific information, you can eliminate an answer only if you know that the information it states is wrong. Sometimes you might be able to eliminate an answer simply because it seems rather flimsy. In the case of the first question, it seems unlikely that a restoration of a painting would suddenly illuminate the great skill of medieval painters, so (B) seems weak as an answer choice. Otherwise, there is no easy strategy for eliminating answers. However, because the answer choices state facts, you should be able to compare what they say with the facts discussed in the indicated section of the passage.

4. Implied Information Questions

Questions on implied information are quite similar in form to those on specific information. Just as in specific information questions, these questions will identify and inquire about a particular section of the passage. However, whereas specific information questions ask about concrete information contained in the text, implied information questions ask about the less obvious information contained "between the lines" of the text. Often, you will be able to identify these questions through the use of words such as "inferred," "implied," "indicated," or "suggested."

Examples

The author's use of the phrase "irreconcilable tragedy" (line 18) in reference to the bombing of Hiroshima suggests that

(A)   the devastating effects of the bombing cannot be lessened even if the reasons for the bombing were noble
(B)   there are many different interpretations of why the US dropped the bomb
(C)   the US dropped the bomb on Hiroshima for the wrong reasons
(D)   the dropping of the bomb was justified if you consider the historical context
(E)   the dropping of the bomb changed the world

In the context of the passage, lines 80–82 imply that the author

(A)   saw himself as the embodiment of a mythical savior
(B)   believed that only he could lead his people to independence
(C)   felt burdened by his birthright
(D)   hated the inequality created by the caste system
(E)   never wanted to be involved in politics

It can be inferred that "early architects" (line 47) did their work with little concern for

(A)   aesthetic values
(B)   structural integrity
(C)   geography
(D)   materials
(E)   functionality

Each of these examples asks you to discern information that is vital to the passage but that is not offered outright. As you might imagine, questions on implied information are therefore fairly uncommon in science passages, in which the author's main goal is to be clear and specific. But in passages where the author tries to create a picture or portrait of something, information is often implied, since a straight retelling of facts can be boring.

As with questions on specific information, there is no distinct strategy to help you answer question choices. Some answer choices might simply seem weak to you, but that is a gut instinct more than a strategy. Your best bet is to go back to the passage and see how each answer fits with what the passage says.

5. Understanding Themes and Arguments Questions

These questions test your ability to look at particular lines in the text and identify the underlying assumptions. Alternatively, you might look at these questions as testing your ability to understand how particular lines fit into the larger arguments or themes in the passage. Argument questions are very common, so it pays to be ready for them. Because these questions are so dependent on passages, they vary widely. We will provide you with a number of examples to give you a sense of the types of issues these questions tend to address. Be aware that these examples give a glimpse rather than an exhaustive survey of this type of question.

Examples

The discussion of sculpture (lines 51–57) illuminates the author's assumption that

(A)   sculpture in the classical period is far superior to modern sculpture
(B)   good sculpture must involve the human form
(C)   sculpture is superior to painting as an art form
(D)   the best sculptors often move into sculpture from another field
(E)   modern sculpture places too little emphasis on the craft of building

Which of the following most clearly expresses what the author means by claiming to be "adept at the smaller forms of communication" (lines 33–34)?

(A)   He is capable of adapting to whatever situation in which he finds himself.
(B)   He speaks eloquently and concisely.
(C)   He can intuit others' thoughts by observing their body language.
(D)   He likes to engage in deep conversations.
(E)   He is shy with his feelings.

The comment by the shopkeeper in lines 79–81 serves primarily to

(A)   illustrate the extent to which the town loves football
(B)   indicate how Coach Lombardi's lessons on the football field also helped his players become terrific businessmen
(C)   demonstrate the affection the players felt for Coach Lombardi
(D)   describe how football can be seen as a metaphor for the United States
(E)   explain how Coach Lombardi's success helped save football in the United States

Each of these examples asks you to look at information within the context of the passage and synthesize it into some paraphrased form that allows you to answer the question. The ability to paraphrase is an important skill in reading comprehension—the better you are at paraphrasing, the better you will be at answering these questions.

6. Structure and Technique Questions

Technique questions test your understanding of the nuts and bolts of writing. These questions will ask about how everything from parenthetical statements to full paragraphs function in the passage. These questions might also ask you about the overall structure of the passage.

As you should be able to see from these three examples, structure and technique questions ask about the function of very small units in the paragraph, such as a single word or simple parenthetical statement, as well as larger units, such as the relation between entire paragraphs. Again, other than going back to look at the passage as you answer, there are no easy strategies for eliminating answers. The best way to study for this type of question—and for most reading comprehension questions—is to read widely, question yourself about what you read, and take a lot of practice tests to get the hang of it.

Examples

In what way is the second paragraph related to the first?

(A)   It provides examples to support the claims made in the first paragraph.
(B)   It focuses the broad claims of the first paragraph.
(C)   It uses the information in the first paragraph.
(D)   It refutes the statements made in the first paragraph.
(E)   It extends the arguments made in the first paragraph to their logical limit.

The parenthetical statement in lines 31–32 serves to

(A)   provide support for the author's earlier arguments through citation of other authorities
(B)   allow the author to comment critically on his own theories
(C)   distance the author from the controversial claims made by his contemporaries
(D)   undercut all disagreeing theories
(E)   tell an amusing anecdote

The author uses the word "cacophonous" (line 54) to

(A) describe the confusion apparent in scientific debate
(B) illustrate the excitement created by new discoveries
(C) describe the rancor that can emerge between scientists promoting competing theories
(D) indicate the chaos that emerges when science proves insufficient
(E) emphasize the view that science cannot answer every question

7. Words-in-Context Questions

Words-in-context questions follow a very standard form. These questions will provide you with a line number and a word or short phrase in quotes and ask you about the meaning of that word in the context of the passage.

The majority of words-in-context questions look like this:

The word "content" (line 34) most nearly means

(A) destitute
(B) satisfied
(C) subject
(D) matter
(E) technical

Unlike most other reading comprehension questions, you can approach these questions in a strategic way that will—at the very least—help you eliminate choices. When you see a words-in-context question, before looking at the answer choices, go to the line number of the passage indicated by the question. Then, turn the question into a sentence completion. Read the sentence that contains the word on which you're being tested, but ignore the word itself. Come up with a different word or phrase to fill that space. Once you have your synonym in mind, go back to the question and compare your synonym to the answers. When you've found a match, you have your answer. In effect, you are building a sort of synonym bridge between the word in the passage and the correct word in the answer choices.

Using this bridge-building method is important because it can help you avoid the tricks embedded in the answer choices. Often, the answer choices will include words that are correct secondary meanings of the tested word. For instance, in the example above, *satisfied* and *subject* are both correct meanings of the word *content*. Remember that these questions are testing the word *in context*. By going back to the passage and approaching the sentence as if it were a sentence completion, you can take the context into account and make sure that you aren't distracted by tricky answer choices. Also, by approaching the question as a sentence completion, you can use the sentence completion strategies you already know for eliminating answer choices even if you cannot come up with a definite answer.

Some words in context questions take different forms. The two most common are:

Which of the following best captures the meaning of the word "traitorous" in line 65?

The phrase "subliminal influence" (line 18) refers to

These modified forms should not affect your strategy for tackling the question. Be aware, however, that the answers may be phrases rather than words.

8. Questions Relating Two Passages

The final questions for the dual passage test your ability to understand the passages in relation to each other. The three most common types of question are:

Relating Main Ideas.

Which statement best describes a disparity between the two passages?

Relating Arguments.

How would the author of passage 2 react to the concept of "responsibilities of brotherhood" (line 65) described in passage 1?

Relating Specific Information.

Which piece of information in passage 2 provides the best support for the "value of friendship and cooperation" (line 80) referred to in passage 1?

While thinking about these questions, you can often uncover a clue to the answers by thinking of the general relation between the passages. For example, if you know the passages disagree completely, you can use that knowledge to assume that the author of passage 2 will feel negatively about the "illicit codes of honor" described in passage 1.

Sample Passage and Questions

In the following pages, we provide an entire sample passage and accompanying questions with explanations. Use the passage and questions to focus your strategies for reading comprehension. The type of question is identified at the end of each explanation.

The following passage discusses the scientific life of Galileo Galilei in reference to the political, religious, artistic, and scientific movements of the age.

Galileo Galilei was born in 1564 into a Europe wracked by cultural ferment and religious divisions. The popes of the Roman Catholic Church, powerful in their roles as both religious and secular leaders, had proven vulnerable to the worldly and decadent spirit of the age, and

5 their personal immorality brought the reputation of the papacy to historic lows. In 1517, Martin Luther, a former monk, attacked Catholicism for having become too worldly and politically corrupt and for obscuring the fundamentals of Christianity with pagan elements. His reforming zeal, which appealed to a notion of an original,

10 "purified" Christianity, set in motion the Protestant Reformation and split European Christianity in two. In response, Roman Catholicism steeled itself for battle and launched the Counter-Reformation, which emphasized orthodoxy and fidelity to the true Church.

The Counter-Reformation reinvigorated the Church and, to some

15 extent, eliminated its excesses. Unfortunately, the Counter-Reformation also contributed to the decline of the Italian Renaissance, a revival of arts and letters that sought to recover and rework the classical art and philosophy of ancient Greece and Rome. The popes had once been great patrons of Renaissance arts and sciences, but the

20 Counter-Reformation put an end to the Church's liberality and leniency in these areas. Further, the Church's new emphasis on religious orthodoxy would soon clash with the emerging scientific revolution.

Galileo, with his study of astronomy, found himself at the center of

25 this clash. Conservative astronomers of Galileo's time, working without telescopes, ascribed without deviation to the ancient theory of geocentricity. This theory of astronomy held that the earth ("geo," as in "geography" or "geology") lay at the center of the solar system, orbited by both the sun and the other planets. Indeed, to the casual

30 observer, it seemed common sense that since the sun "rose" in the morning and "set" at night, it must have circled around the earth. Ancient authorities like Aristotle and the Roman astronomer Ptolemy had championed this viewpoint, and the notion also coincided with the Catholic Church's view of the universe, which placed mankind, God's

35 principal creation, at the center of the cosmos. Buttressed by common sense, the ancient philosophers, and the Church, the geocentric model of the universe seemed secure in its authority.

The Ptolemaic theory, however, was not impervious to attack. In the 16th century, astronomers strained to make modern observations fit

40 Ptolemy's geocentric model of the universe. Increasingly complex mathematical systems were necessary to reconcile these new observations with Ptolemy's system of interlocking orbits. Nicholas Copernicus, a Polish astronomer, openly questioned the Ptolemaic system and proposed a heliocentric system in which the planets—

45 including earth— orbited the sun ("helios"). This more mathematically satisfying way of arranging the solar system did not attract many supporters at first, since the available data did not yet support a

wholesale abandonment of Ptolemy's system. By the end of the 16th
century, however, astronomers like Johannes Kepler (1571–1630) had
50   also begun to embrace Copernicus's theory.

Once Galileo began to observe the heavens through his telescope,
the fate of the Ptolemaic system was sealed. But so too was Galileo's
fate. The Catholic Church, desperately trying to hold the Protestant
heresy at bay, could not accept a scientific assault on its own theories
55   of the universe. The pressures of the age set in motion a historic
confrontation between religion and science, one which would
culminate in 1633 when the Church put Galileo on trial, forced him to
recant his stated and published scientific beliefs, and put him under
permanent house arrest.

Sample Questions

1. The term "ferment" in line 2 most closely means

(A)   alienation
(B)   turmoil
(C)   consolidation of social institutions
(D)   anachronisms in the Church
(E)   stagnation

2. Which of the following was *not* a reason for Martin Luther's attack on the Catholic Church (lines 6–8)?

(A)   pagan elements in its practices
(B)   the amorality of its leadership
(C)   its excessive attention to piety
(D)   its corruption and worldliness
(E)   the political involvement of the popes

3. According to this passage, the Catholic Church started the Counter-Reformation primarily to

(A)   fight scientific heresy
(B)   clean out its own ranks
(C)   reinvigorate artists and intellectuals
(D)   elect a new pope
(E)   counter Protestant challenges

4. Which of the following is *not* part of the meaning of the term "conservative" in line 25?

(A)   reverent of ancient thinkers
(B)   old-fashioned
(C)   religiously orthodox
(D)   technologically limited
(E)   simple-minded

Reading Comprehension

5. The development of the heliocentric model of the solar system, as discussed in this passage, suggests that observations of the natural world

(A) are often dependent on technology
(B) are never to be trusted
(C) should fit with common sense
(D) can always be explained mathematically
(E) can only be made by scientists

6. Which of the following best states the underlying theme of the passage?

(A) Science always conflicts with religion.
(B) Science is vulnerable to outside social forces.
(C) Ideally, scientific theories should reinforce religious doctrine.
(D) Science operates in a vacuum.
(E) Advanced technology is the only route to good scientific theories.

Answers and Explanations

1.   (B)

To answer this word-in-context question, you should first go back to the specified line and read the sentence in which the word is contained and the surrounding sentences. In this case, the sentence refers to "cultural ferment and religious divisions," and the following sentences go on to describe a Europe in the midst of religious and political strife. The word "ferment," therefore, must describe this division and strife. *Turmoil* is the only word to come close to filling this need. Try substituting the answer choices into the passage if you are unsure.

2.   (C)

This specific information question is a little tricky, since it asks you which of the answer choices did *not* cause Martin Luther's attack. If you missed that *not*, then you very well might have looked at the first answer choice, seen that it caused Martin Luther's attack on the Catholic Church, and chosen that as the correct answer. So be careful when reading the question.

To answer this question correctly, you must simply go back to the indicated area and read. Since this is a *not* question, all of the wrong answers must be stated as reasons for Martin Luther's hatred of the church in the text. So the best way to go about answering this question is to eliminate answers until you're left with one. The indicated lines clearly state that Luther hated what he saw as the church's worldliness and corruption. That throws out answer choice (D). It also throws out answer choices (B) and (E), since those are both aspects of the Church's corruption and worldliness. The text also clearly states that Luther felt the Church was incorporating pagan instruments, so you can throw out answer (B). That leaves you with (C), the right answer.

3. **(E)**

This question tests whether you can follow the flow of argument within the text. More specifically, it tests your ability to differentiate between the causes and effects of the Counter-Reformation. Answers (A), (B), and (C) refer to effects of the Counter-Reformation. Answer (D) has absolutely no basis in the text. Only answer choice (E) refers to the cause of the Counter-Reformation as defined by the passage.

4. **(E)**

Most of the answers to this words in context question can be eliminated by carefully rereading the section of the passage that contains the word "conservative." This section explains that "conservative" astronomers were technologically limited (they worked without telescopes), relied on ancient authorities, and did not challenge common beliefs—this lets us eliminate answers (A), (B), (C), and (D). The passage does not, however, suggest that these individuals were of limited intelligence, so (E) is the best answer to this question.

5. **(A)**

This question tests your general understanding of the passage. You shouldn't have to go back to the passage to answer the question. This question gives you a good gauge of whether you understood enough during your read-through. This question also teaches an important lesson. The right answer on reading comprehension questions will almost never be absolute or all-encompassing answers such as "Science can only be proven mathematically." If you see an answer choice that includes the words always, only, never, or any other word that implies a definitive statement lasting through all eternity, beware. For this question, you can throw out all the absolute answers: (B), (D), and (E). Answer (C) is not mentioned anywhere in the text, so (A) is the right answer.

6. **(B)**

This question also tests your general understanding of the passage. Once again, you'll see some absolute statements within the answer choices ("science always conflicts with religion") that should immediately make you suspicious. With some thought you should be able to eliminate answers (A) and (E). Also, nowhere does the passage espouse the idea that science should only reinforce religion, so you can knock out (C). Answer (D) is proven wrong by the example of Galileo, so you can throw that out also, leaving you with the right answer, (B).

SAT Vocabulary

I T'S IMPOSSIBLE TO DENY: DOING WELL ON the verbal section of the SAT is largely a matter of knowing vocabulary. For that reason, a significant part of your preparation time for the SAT should be spent increasing your vocabulary and learning how to guess the meanings of unfamiliar words.

Building Vocabulary

Building your vocabulary for the SAT can take quite some time and effort. But there are a number of study methods that can help speed your progress. These methods range from ways to manage your preparation time to learning how to study vocabulary specifically for the SAT.

Remembering Words

In the next few pages, we will discuss some study methods that will make your efforts to learn SAT vocabulary as efficient as possible. First off, you can't learn SAT vocabulary words by memorizing them all in one night. The best way to hammer a word into your mind is to *use* it. Try to use every SAT word that you learn at least twice in actual conversations. Instead of being a dead memorized object in your brain, the word will be a living thing that you have made your own.

SAT Vocabulary

How to Study

When we talk about how to study words, we aren't discussing whether you use flashcards or word lists. We're talking about how you should be thinking while studying vocabulary. Most importantly, you must study. So if using flashcards gets you to study words, do that. If setting a strict schedule of learning 20 words a night gets you going, then do that. Just manage your time so that you spend time studying vocabulary, and make an effort to use the words you learn.

Read

Reading is probably the best way to learn vocabulary, but it is a long-term solution. So if you're reading this paragraph three weeks before taking the SAT, it probably won't help you that much to start reading several novels right now. But if you have a few months, start reading books, good magazines, and newspapers. When you run into a word that you don't immediately know, see if you can guess what it means from its context. Then look it up in the dictionary and find out if you were right. If you knew the word: terrific. If you didn't, try to make a sentence using the word so that you remember it. By reading, you will increase your vocabulary, and also become skillful at figuring out words in context, an important skill for reading comprehension passages.

Build Associations

Making up odd associations between a word and its meaning will almost always help you remember new vocabulary. For example, if you cannot remember that "archaic" means "old-fashioned or outmoded," you might build an association in your head between archaic and Noah's Ark, which is also very old. This system is not very precise or sophisticated, but once you get the association in your head, you'll probably never have to look the word up again.

Take Advantage of the Way the SAT Tests Vocabulary

The SAT verbal section is primarily a vocabulary test. But that isn't a very specific description. To study well for the SAT vocabulary, you should have some understanding of what *kind* of vocabulary test the SAT is.

So what kind of vocabulary is the SAT? Not a very good one. When you take a vocabulary test in school, you probably have to know the definition of the words precisely. For the SAT, you don't have to know the meaning of the words to the same specificity. SAT questions do not ask you to produce the dictionary definition of a word. You need only have a rough understanding of a word. Take, for example, the words "acclaim" and "accolade," both of which appear on the SparkNotes list of 1000 SAT vocabulary words.

acclaim high praise

accolade special distinction, an award

Both acclaim and accolade generally refer to honors given to excellent people or things. The words do differ slightly, however. Acclaim is like praise or applause, given by a multitude to an individual. An accolade more often involves special distinction from one person to another. An accolade is more of a *thing* than acclaim is. So there is a difference between the two words.

Why did we tell you this? Because you should ignore these differences for the SAT. The SAT will *never* require you to make a decision based on a sentence or analogy that acclaim is more correct than accolade, or vice versa. On the SAT, these words would be treated as absolutely identical and interchangeable. For example, you won't see a sentence completion like this:

> Upon returning home after single-handedly convincing all of mankind that war is useless and everyone should just love each other, Albert received special ---- from the President of the United States.

> (A)   hatred
> (B)   deliberations
> (C)   accolades
> (D)   torment
> (E)   acclaim

We could make a pretty good case that *accolades* is the better choice here, but many people might argue with us. The SAT wants to avoid arguments and controversy. It will never put two words in the sentence completion answer choices that are so similar and force you to decide which one is better.

However, for analogies, the SAT probably *will* include two answer choices with similar meanings:

> DISAPPROVAL : CONDEMNATION

> (A)   distrust : acclaim
> (B)   trauma : evolution
> (C)   distinction : accolade
> (D)   respite : lull
> (E)   rhetoric : decision

In analogies, remember, the important thing is the relation between words, not the words themselves. So while acclaim and accolade are equivalent words, in this question only *distinction : accolade* embodies the relation of degree found in DISAPPROVAL : CONDEMNATION (condemnation is an extreme form of disapproval, just as an accolade is an extreme form of distinction).

SAT Vocabulary

All You Need to Know: General Meaning and Degree

You don't have to know all the particulars about the words you study. All you have to know is their general meaning and degree. All you need to know about acclaim and accolade is that both mean an extreme sort of praise. As long as you know that approval, appreciation, and praise mean the same thing to a lesser degree, you're pretty much set.

In the end, the fact that you only have to know the general meaning of a word and its general degree can shorten your study time. For the SAT, don't try to learn every nuance about a word. Don't even try to memorize the exact definitions we provide. Just get a good understanding of what the word means in simple terms. In fact, figuring out how to define a word in your own simple terms is probably the best way to ensure that you'll remember its definition.

Don't Always Study Words in the Same Order

Have you ever had the experience while listening to a CD that you know what the next song on an album is, even though you would never be able to recite the order of songs on the album if you weren't listening to it? Studying words is similar. If you learn words only in the pattern in which you study them, you might not be able to remember them out of that context. Try to break up the pattern of the words as you study—make flashcards that you can mix up instead of just using a static list.

Decoding Unfamiliar Words

In this section, we provide you with a list of the 1000 most common vocabulary words that appear on the SAT. But we wouldn't be able to provide a list that is sure to cover cover every word that might appear on the SAT, even if we gave you a list of 5000 words. There are just too many words out there in the world. When you take the SAT, the likelihood is that you will come across a few words that you haven't studied. Don't panic: it is possible to figure out the meanings of words you don't know.

Go with Your Gut—and Use Word Charge

Even if you don't know what a word means, you may have some feeling about the word's "charge." Is the word a good thing or a bad thing? Is it neutral? Does it refer to something extreme, or to something slight? Use these gut feelings—they usually come from somewhere. And since the SAT is such an imprecise vocabulary test, knowing that a word is positive, negative, or of a certain degree can often allow you to make a decision on whether a word might work as a possible answer choice. Even if using your gut feeling about a word's charge doesn't bring you to a definite answer on a question, word charge probably will help you eliminate answers and put yourself into a good position to guess.

Word Roots and What We Think of Them

Some test preparation companies suggest that you study word roots as part of your vocabulary building strategy. It's easy to see why. Words are often made up of subunits derived from Latin or Greek. These subunits have meanings, and often you can get a good sense of the meaning of the word if you recognize its subunits. For example, if you encounter the word "antebellum" and don't know what it means, you can get clues about its meaning if you know something about its roots. Ante means "before," and bellum means "war" (think belligerent or rebellion), so you might think that ante-bellum means "before the war." If you did, you'd be right. Even if you only knew what the root "ante" meant, you would at least have the sense that that word is used to set a time frame, which might be all you need to know to answer the question.

However, just as often as they can help you, word roots can lead you astray. Say you saw the word "precept" and knew that the root "pre" means "before" and the root "cept" means "to take." Precept must then mean "before taking" or something like that, right? Well, here's the actual definition of the word:

precept a rule defining conduct or behavior

Word roots pretty much hosed you there, didn't they? In our opinion, roots are as much trouble as they are helpful. Because the positives and negatives they provide cancel each other out, it seems you'd be better off avoiding the word roots strategy.

Use Your Knowledge of Foreign Languages

Most English words come from Latin or Greek, but any romance language (French, Spanish, Italian) takes enough words from Latin that trying to guess based on a cognate (a word related to one from another language) is almost always a good idea. If you know that *simpatico* is a common word for "nice" in Spanish, you might deduce that sympathetic means something similar in English, which it does ("sympathetic" means "able to understand the feelings of others").

Vocabulary and Life

We've said a few times already that when you study for the SAT, you aren't really learning anything new. You're refreshing your math skills, perhaps, but really, studying for the test often feels like studying material that is specifically designed not to apply to the rest of your life. Learning vocabulary is different. Clearly, sitting there with a list of words is not the most entertaining or exciting thing you could be doing. But it might help you to realize that studying vocabulary for the SAT expands the vocabulary you will use throughout your life.

Okay, enough. Here's the word list.

SAT Vocabulary

The 1000 Most Common SAT Words

A

abase *(v.)* to humiliate, degrade *(After being overthrown and abased, the deposed leader offered to bow down to his conqueror.)*

abate *(v.)* to reduce, lessen *(The rain poured down for a while, then abated.)*

abdicate *(v.)* to give up a position, usually one of leadership *(When he realized that the revolutionaries would surely win, the king abdicated his throne.)*

abduct *(v.)* to kidnap, take by force *(The evildoers abducted the fairy princess from her happy home.)*

aberration *(n.)* something that differs from the norm *(In 1918, the Boston Red Sox won the World Series, but the success turned out to be an aberration, and the Red Sox have not won a World Series since.)*

abet *(v.)* to aid, help, encourage *(The spy succeeded only because he had a friend on the inside to abet him.)*

abhor *(v.)* to hate, detest *(Because he always wound up kicking himself in the head when he tried to play soccer, Oswald began to abhor the sport.)*

abide 1. *(v.)* to put up with *(Though he did not agree with the decision, Chuck decided to abide by it.)* 2. *(v.)* to remain *(Despite the beating they've taken from the weather throughout the millennia, the mountains abide.)*

abject *(adj.)* wretched, pitiful *(After losing all her money, falling into a puddle, and breaking her ankle, Eloise was abject.)*

abjure *(v.)* to reject, renounce *(To prove his honesty, the President abjured the evil policies of his wicked predecessor.)*

abnegation *(n.)* denial of comfort to oneself *(The holy man slept on the floor, took only cold showers, and generally followed other practices of abnegation.)*

abort *(v.)* to give up on a half-finished project or effort *(After they ran out of food, the men, attempting to jump rope around the world, had to abort and go home.)*

abridge 1. *(v.)* to cut down, shorten *(The publisher thought the dictionary was too long and abridged it.)* 2. *(adj.)* shortened *(Moby-Dick is such a long book that even the abridged version is longer than most normal books.)*

abrogate *(v.)* to abolish, usually by authority *(The Bill of Rights assures that the government cannot abrogate our right to a free press.)*

abscond *(v.)* to sneak away and hide *(In the confusion, the super-spy absconded into the night with the secret plans.)*

absolution *(n.)* freedom from blame, guilt, sin *(Once all the facts were known, the jury gave Angela absolution by giving a verdict of not guilty.)*

abstain *(v.)* to freely choose not to commit an action *(Everyone demanded that Angus put on the kilt, but he did not want to do it and abstained.)*

abstruse *(adj.)* hard to comprehend *(Everyone else in the class understood geometry easily, but John found the subject abstruse.)*

accede *(v.)* to agree *(When the class asked the teacher whether they could play baseball instead of learn grammar they expected him to refuse, but instead he acceded to their request.)*

accentuate *(v.)* to stress, highlight *(Psychologists agree that those people who are happiest accentuate the positive in life.)*

accessible *(adj.)* obtainable, reachable *(After studying with SparkNotes and getting a great score on the SAT, Marlena happily realized that her goal of getting into an Ivy-League college was accessible.)*

acclaim *(n.)* high praise *(Greg's excellent poem won the acclaim of his friends.)*

accolade *(n.)* high praise, special distinction *(Everyone offered accolades to Sam after he won the Noble Prize.)*

accommodating *(adj.)* helpful, obliging, polite *(Though the apartment was not big enough for three people, Arnold, Mark, and Zebulon were all friends and were accommodating to each other.)*

accord *(n.)* an agreement *(After much negotiating, England and Iceland finally came to a mutually beneficial accord about fishing rights off the cost of Greenland.)*

accost *(v.)* to confront verbally *(Though Antoinette was normally quite calm, when the waiter spilled soup on her for the fourth time in 15 minutes she stood up and accosted the man.)*

accretion *(n.)* slow growth in size or amount *(Stalactites are formed by the accretion of minerals from the roofs of caves.)*

acerbic *(adj.)* biting, bitter in tone or taste *(Jill became extremely acerbic and began to cruelly make fun of all her friends.)*

acquiesce *(v.)* to agree without protesting *(Though Mr. Correlli wanted to stay outside and work in his garage, when his wife told him that he had better come in to dinner, he acquiesced to her demands.)*

acrimony *(n.)* bitterness, discord *(Though they vowed that no girl would ever come between them, Biff and Trevor could not keep acrimony from overwhelming their friendship after they both fell in love with the lovely Teresa.)*

acumen *(n.)* keen insight *(Because of his mathematical acumen, Larry was able to figure out in minutes problems that took other students hours.)*

acute 1. *(adj.)* sharp, severe *(Arnold could not walk because the pain in his foot was so acute.)* 2. *(adj.)* having keen insight *(Because she was so acute, Libby instantly figured out how the magician pulled off his "magic.")*

adamant *(adj.)* impervious, immovable, unyielding *(Though public pressure was intense, the President remained adamant about his proposal.)*

adept *(adj.)* extremely skilled *(Tarzan was adept at jumping from tree to tree like a monkey.)*

adhere 1. *(n.)* to stick to something *(We <u>adhered</u> the poster to the wall with tape.)* 2. *(n.)* to follow devoutly *(He <u>adhered</u> to the dictates of his religion without question.)*

admonish *(v.)* to caution, criticize, reprove *(Joe's mother <u>admonished</u> him not to ruin his appetite by eating cookies before dinner.)*

adorn *(v.)* to decorate *(We <u>adorned</u> the tree with ornaments.)*

adroit *(adj.)* skillful, dexterous *(The <u>adroit</u> thief could pick someone's pocket without attracting notice.)*

adulation *(n.)* extreme praise *(Though the book was pretty good, Marcy did not believe it deserved the <u>adulation</u> it received.)*

adumbrate *(v.)* to sketch out in a vague way *(The coach <u>adumbrated</u> a game plan, but none of the players knew precisely what to do.)*

adverse *(adj.)* antagonistic, unfavorable, dangerous *(Because of <u>adverse</u> conditions, the hikers decided to give up trying to climb the mountain.)*

advocate 1. *(v.)* to argue in favor of something *(Arnold <u>advocated</u> turning left at the stop sign, even though everyone else thought we should turn right.)* 2. *(n.)* a person who argues in favor of something *(In addition to wanting to turn left at every stop sign, Arnold was also a great <u>advocate</u> of increasing national defense spending.)*

aerial *(adj.)* somehow related to the air *(We watched as the fighter planes conducted <u>aerial</u> maneuvers.)*

aesthetic *(adj.)* artistic, related to the appreciation of beauty *(We hired Susan as our interior decorator because she has such a fine <u>aesthetic</u> sense.)*

affable *(adj.)* friendly, amiable *(People like to be around George because he is so <u>affable</u> and good-natured.)*

affinity *(n.)* a spontaneous feeling of closeness *(Jerry didn't know why, but he felt an incredible <u>affinity</u> for Kramer the first time they met.)*

affluent *(adj.)* rich, wealthy *(Mrs. Grebelski was <u>affluent</u>, owning a huge house, three cars, and an island near Maine.)*

affront *(n.)* an insult *(Bernardo was very touchy, and took any slight as an <u>affront</u> to his honor.)*

aggrandize *(v.)* to increase or make greater *(Joseph always dropped the names of the famous people his father knew as a way to <u>aggrandize</u> his personal stature.)*

aggregate 1. *(n.)* a whole or total *(The three branches of the U.S. Government form an aggregate much more powerful than its individual parts.)* 2. *(v.)* to gather into a mass *(The dictator tried to aggregate as many people into his army as he possibly could.)*

aggrieved *(adj.)* distressed, wronged, injured *(The foreman mercilessly overworked his aggrieved employees.)*

agile *(adj.)* quick, nimble *(The dogs were too slow to catch the agile rabbit.)*

agnostic *(adj.)* believing that the existence of God cannot be proven or disproven *(Joey's parents are very religious, but he is agnostic.)*

agriculture *(n.)* farming *(It was a huge step in the progress of civilization when tribes left hunting and gathering and began to develop more sustainable methods of obtaining food, such as agriculture.)*

aisle *(n.)* a passageway between rows of seats *(Once we got inside the stadium we walked down the aisle to our seats.)*

alacrity *(n.)* eagerness, speed *(For some reason, Chuck loved to help his mother whenever he could, so when his mother asked him to set the table he did so with alacrity.)*

alias *(n.)* a false name or identity *(He snuck past the guards by using an alias and fake ID.)*

allay *(v.)* to soothe, ease *(The chairman of the Federal Reserve gave a speech to try to allay investors' fears about an economic downturn.)*

allege *(v.)* to assert, usually without proof *(The policeman had alleged that Marshall committed the crime, but after the investigation turned up no evidence, Marshall was set free.)*

alleviate *(v.)* to relieve, make more bearable *(This drug will alleviate the symptoms of the terrible disease, but only for a while.)*

allocate *(v.)* to distribute, set aside *(The Mayor allocated 30 percent of the funds for improving the town's schools.)*

aloof *(adj.)* reserved, distant *(The scientist could sometimes seem aloof, as if he didn't care about his friends or family, but really he was just thinking about quantum mechanics.)*

altercation *(n.)* a dispute, fight *(Jason and Lionel blamed one another for the car accident, leading to an altercation.)*

amalgamate *(v.)* to bring together, unite *(Because of his great charisma, the presidential candidate was able to amalgamate all democrats and republicans under his banner.)*

ambiguous *(adj.)* uncertain, variably interpretable *(Some people think Caesar married Cleopatra for her power, others believe he was charmed by her beauty. His actual reasons are ambiguous.)*

ambivalent *(adj.)* having opposing feelings *(My feelings about Calvin are ambivalent because on one hand he is a loyal friend, but on the other, he is a cruel and vicious thief.)*

ameliorate *(v.)* to improve *(The tense situation was ameliorated when Sam proposed a solution everyone could agree upon.)*

amenable *(adj.)* willing, compliant *(Our father was amenable when we asked him to drive us to the farm so we could go apple picking.)*

amenity *(n.)* an item that increases comfort *(Bill Gates's house is stocked with so many amenities, he never has to do anything for himself.)*

amiable *(adj.)* friendly *(An amiable fellow, Harry got along with just about everyone.)*

amicable *(adj.)* friendly *(Claudia and Jimmy got divorced, but amicably and without hard feelings.)*

amorous *(adj.)* showing love, particularly sexual *(Whenever Albert saw Mariah wear her slinky red dress, he began to feel quite amorous.)*

amorphous *(adj.)* without definite shape or type *(The effort was doomed from the start, because the reasons behind it were so amorphous and hard to pin down.)*

anachronistic *(adj.)* being out of correct chronological order *(In this book you're writing, you say that the Pyramids were built after the Titanic sank, which is anachronistic.)*

analgesic *(n.)* something that reduces pain *(Put this analgesic on the wound so that the poor man at least feels a little better.)*

analogous *(adj.)* similar to, so that an analogy can be drawn *(Though they are unrelated genetically, the bone structure of whales and fish is quite analogous.)*

anarchist *(n.)* one who wants to eliminate all government *(An anarchist, Carmine wanted to dissolve every government everywhere.)*

anathema *(n.)* a cursed, detested person *(I never want to see that murderer. He is an anathema to me.)*

anecdote *(n.)* a short, humorous account *(After dinner, Marlon told an <u>anecdote</u> about the time he got his nose stuck in a toaster.)*

anesthesia *(n.)* loss of sensation *(When the nerves in his spine were damaged, Mr. Hollins suffered <u>anesthesia</u> in his legs.)*

anguish *(n.)* extreme sadness, torment *(Angelos suffered terrible <u>anguish</u> when he learned that Buffy had died while combating a strange mystical force of evil.)*

animated *(adj.)* lively *(When he begins to talk about drama, which is his true passion, he becomes very <u>animated</u>.)*

annex 1. *(v.)* to incorporate territory or space *(After defeating them in battle, the Russians <u>annexed</u> Poland.)* 2. *(n.)* a room attached to a larger room or space *(He likes to do his studying in a little <u>annex</u> attached to the main reading room in the library.)*

annul *(v.)* to make void or invalid *(After seeing its unforeseen and catastrophic effects, Congress sought to <u>annul</u> the law.)*

anomaly *(n.)* something that does not fit into the normal order *("That rip in the space-time continuum is certainly a spatial <u>anomaly</u>," said Spock to Captain Kirk.)*

anonymous *(adj.)* being unknown, unrecognized *(Mary received a love poem from an <u>anonymous</u> admirer.)*

antagonism *(n.)* hostility *(Superman and Bizarro Superman shared a mutual <u>antagonism</u>, and often fought.)*

antecedent *(n.)* something that came before *(The great tradition of Western culture had its <u>antecedent</u> in the culture of Ancient Greece.)*

antediluvian *(adj.)* ancient *(The <u>antediluvian</u> man still believed that Eisenhower was president of the United States and that hot dogs cost a nickel.)*

anthology *(n.)* a selected collection of writings, songs, etc. *(The new <u>anthology</u> of Bob Dylan songs contains all his greatest hits and a few songs that you might never have heard before.)*

antipathy *(n.)* a strong dislike, repugnance *(I know you love me, but because you are a liar and a thief, I feel nothing but <u>antipathy</u> for you.)*

antiquated *(adj.)* old, out of date *(That <u>antiquated</u> car has none of the features, like power windows and steering, that make modern cars so great.)*

antiseptic *(adj.)* clean, sterile *(The <u>antiseptic</u> hospital was very bare, but its cleanliness helped to keep patients healthy.)*

antithesis *(n.)* the absolute opposite *(Your values, which hold war and violence in the highest esteem, are the <u>antithesis</u> of my pacifist beliefs.)*

anxiety *(n.)* intense uneasiness *(When he heard about the car crash, he felt <u>anxiety</u> because he knew that his girlfriend had been driving on the road where the accident occurred.)*

apathetic *(adj.)* lacking concern, emotion *(Uninterested in politics, Bruno was <u>apathetic</u> about whether he lived under a capitalist or communist regime.)*

apocryphal *(adj.)* fictitious, false, wrong *(Because I am standing before you, it seems obvious that the stories circulating about my demise were <u>apocryphal</u>.)*

appalling *(adj.)* inspiring shock, horror, disgust *(The judge found the murderer's crimes and lack of remorse <u>appalling</u>.)*

appease *(v.)* to calm, satisfy *(When the child cries, the mother gives him candy to <u>appease</u> him.)*

appraise *(v.)* to assess the worth or value of *(A realtor will come over tonight to <u>appraise</u> our house.)*

apprehend 1. *(v.)* to seize, arrest *(The criminal was <u>apprehended</u> at the scene.)* 2. *(v.)* to perceive, understand, grasp *(The student has trouble <u>apprehending</u> concepts in math and science.)*

approbation *(n.)* praise *(The crowd welcomed the heroes with <u>approbation</u>.)*

appropriate *(v.)* to take, make use of *(The government <u>appropriated</u> the farmer's land without justification.)*

aquatic *(adj.)* relating to water *(The marine biologist studies starfish and other <u>aquatic</u> creatures.)*

arable *(adj.)* suitable for growing crops *(The farmer purchased a plot of <u>arable</u> land on which he will grow corn and sprouts.)*

arbiter *(n.)* one who can resolve a dispute, make a decision *(The divorce court judge will serve as the <u>arbiter</u> between the estranged husband and wife.)*

arbitrary *(adj.)* based on factors that appear random *(The boy's decision to choose one college over another seems <u>arbitrary</u>.)*

arbitration *(n.)* the process or act of resolving a dispute *(The employee sought official <u>arbitration</u> when he could not resolve a disagreement with his supervisor.)*

arboreal *(adj.)* of or relating to trees *(Leaves, roots, and bark are a few <u>arboreal</u> traits.)*

arcane *(adj.)* obscure, secret, known only by a few *(The professor is an expert in arcane Lithuanian literature.)*

archaic *(adj.)* of or relating to an earlier period in time, outdated *(In a few select regions of Western Mongolian, an archaic Chinese dialect is still spoken.)*

archetypal *(adj.)* the most representative or typical example of something *(Some believe George Washington, with his flowing white hair and commanding stature, was the archetypal politician.)*

ardor *(n.)* extreme vigor, energy, enthusiasm *(The soldiers conveyed their ardor with impassioned battle cries.)*

arid *(adj.)* excessively dry *(Little other than palm trees and cacti grow successfully in arid environments.)*

arrogate *(v.)* to take without justification *(The king arrogated the right to order executions to himself exclusively.)*

artifact *(n.)* a remaining piece from an extinct culture or place *(The scientists spent all day searching the cave for artifacts from the ancient Mayan civilization.)*

artisan *(n.)* a craftsman *(The artisan uses wood to make walking sticks.)*

ascertain *(v.)* to perceive, learn *(With a bit of research, the student ascertained that some plants can live for weeks without water.)*

ascetic *(adj.)* practicing restraint as a means of self-discipline, usually religious *(The priest lives an ascetic life devoid of television, savory foods, and other pleasures.)*

ascribe *(v.)* to assign, credit, attribute to *(Some ascribe the invention of fireworks and dynamite to the Chinese.)*

aspersion *(n.)* a curse, expression of ill-will *(The rival politicians repeatedly cast aspersions on each others' integrity.)*

aspire *(v.)* to long for, aim toward *(The young poet aspires to publish a book of verse someday.)*

assail *(v.)* to attack *(At dawn, the war planes assailed the boats in the harbor.)*

assess *(v.)* to evaluate *(A crew arrived to assess the damage after the crash.)*

assiduous *(adj.)* hard-working, diligent *(The construction workers erected the skyscraper during two years of assiduous labor.)*

assuage *(v.)* to ease, pacify *(The mother held the baby to assuage its fears.)*

SAT Vocabulary

astute *(adj.)* very clever, crafty *(Much of Roger's success in politics results from his ability to provide astute answers to reporters' questions.)*

asylum 1. *(n.)* a place of refuge, protection, a sanctuary *(For Thoreau, the forest served as an asylum from the pressures of urban life.)* 2. *(n.)* an institution in which the insane are kept *(Once diagnosed by a certified psychiatrist, the man was put in an asylum.)*

atone *(v.)* to repent, make amends *(The man atoned for forgetting his wife's birthday by buying her five dozen roses.)*

atrophy *(v.)* to wither away, decay *(If muscles do not receive enough blood, they will soon atrophy and die.)*

attain *(v.)* to achieve, arrive at *(The athletes strived to attain their best times in competition.)*

attribute 1. *(v.)* to credit, assign *(He attributes all of his success to his mother's undying encouragement.)* 2. *(n.)* a facet or trait *(Among the beetle's most peculiar attributes is its thorny protruding eyes.)*

atypical *(adj.)* not typical, unusual *(Screaming and crying is atypical adult behavior.)*

audacious *(adj.)* excessively bold *(The security guard was shocked by the fan's audacious attempt to offer him a bribe.)*

audible *(adj.)* able to be heard *(The missing person's shouts were unfortunately not audible.)*

augment *(v.)* to add to, expand *(The eager student seeks to augment his knowledge of French vocabulary by reading French literature.)*

auspicious *(adj.)* favorable, indicative of good things *(The tennis player considered the sunny forecast an auspicious sign that she would win her match.)*

austere *(adj.)* very bare, bleak *(The austere furniture inside the abandoned house made the place feel haunted.)*

avarice *(n.)* excessive greed *(The banker's avarice led him to amass a tremendous personal fortune.)*

avenge *(v.)* to seek revenge *(The victims will take justice into their own hands and strive to avenge themselves against the men who robbed them.)*

aversion *(n.)* a particular dislike for something *(Because he's from Hawaii, Ben has an aversion to autumn, winter, and cold climates in general.)*

SAT Vocabulary

B

balk *(v.)* to stop, block abruptly *(Edna's boss balked at her request for another raise.)*

ballad *(n.)* a love song *(Greta's boyfriend played her a ballad on the guitar during their walk through the dark woods.)*

banal *(adj.)* dull, commonplace *(The client rejected our proposal because they found our presentation banal and unimpressive.)*

bane *(n.)* a burden *(Advanced physics is the bane of many students' academic lives.)*

bard *(n.)* a poet, often a singer as well *(Shakespeare is often considered the greatest bard in the history of the English language.)*

bashful *(adj.)* shy, excessively timid *(Frankie's mother told him not to be bashful when he refused to attend the birthday party.)*

battery 1.*(n.)* a device that supplies power *(Most cars run on a combination of power from a battery and gasoline.)* 2. *(n.)*assault, beating *(Her husband was accused of assault and battery after he attacked a man on the sidewalk.)*

beguile *(v.)* to trick, deceive *(The thief beguiled his partners into surrendering all of their money to him.)*

behemoth *(n.)* something of tremendous power or size *(The new aircraft carrier is among several behemoths that the Air Force has added to its fleet.)*

benevolent *(adj.)* marked by goodness or doing good *(Police officers should be commended for their benevolent service to the community.)*

benign *(adj.)* favorable, not threatening, mild *(We were all relieved to hear that the medical tests determined her tumor to be benign.)*

bequeath *(v.)* to pass on, give *(Jon's father bequeathed his entire estate to his mother.)*

berate *(v.)* to scold vehemently *(The angry boss berated his employees for failing to meet their deadline.)*

bereft *(adj.)* devoid of, without *(His family was bereft of food and shelter following the tornado.)*

beseech *(v.)* to beg, plead, implore *(The servant beseeched the king for food to feed his starving family.)*

bias *(n.)* a tendency, inclination, prejudice *(The judge's hidden bias against smokers led him to make an unfair decision.)*

bilk (v.) cheat, defraud (*The lawyer discovered that this firm had bilked several clients out of thousands of dollars.*)

blandish (v.) to coax by using flattery (*Rachel's assistant tried to blandish her into accepting the deal.*)

blemish (n.) an imperfection, flaw (*The dealer agreed to lower the price because of the many blemishes on the surface of the wooden furniture.*)

blight 1. (n.) a plague, disease (*The potato blight destroyed the harvest and bankrupted many families.*) 2. (n.) something that destroys hope (*His bad morale is a blight upon this entire operation.*)

boisterous (adj.) loud and full of energy (*The candidate won the vote after giving several boisterous speeches on television.*)

bombastic (adj.) excessively confident, pompous (*The singer's bombastic performance disgusted the crowd.*)

boon (n.) a gift or blessing (*The good weather has been a boon for many businesses located near the beach.*)

bourgeois (n.) a middle-class person, capitalist (*Many businessmen receive criticism for their bourgeois approach to life.*)

brazen (adj.) excessively bold, brash (*Critics condemned the novelist's brazen attempt to plagiarize Hemingway's story.*)

brusque (adj.) short, abrupt, dismissive (*The captain's brusque manner offended the passengers.*)

buffet 1. (v.) to strike with force (*The strong winds buffeted the ships, threatening to capsize them.*) 2. (n.) an arrangement of food set out on a table (*Rather than sitting around a table, the guests took food from our buffet and ate standing up.*)

burnish (v.) to polish, shine (*His mother asked him to burnish the silverware before setting the table.*)

buttress 1. (v.) to support, hold up (*The column buttresses the roof above the statue.*) 2. (n.) something that offers support (*The buttress supports the roof above the statues.*)

C

cacophony (n.) tremendous noise, disharmonious sound (*The elementary school orchestra created a cacophony at the recital.*)

cadence (*n.*) a rhythm, progression of sound (*The pianist used the foot pedal to emphasize the cadence of the sonata.*)

cajole (*v.*) to urge, coax (*Fred's buddies cajoled him into attending the bachelor party.*)

calamity (*n.*) an event with disastrous consequences (*The earthquake in San Francisco was a calamity worse than any other natural disaster in history.*)

calibrate (*v.*) to set, standardize (*The mechanic calibrated the car's transmission to make the motor run most efficiently.*)

callous (*adj.*) harsh, cold, unfeeling (*The murderer's callous lack of remorse shocked the jury.*)

calumny (*n.*) an attempt to spoil someone else's reputation by spreading lies (*The local official's calumny ended up ruining his opponent's prospect of winning the election.*)

camaraderie (*n.*) brotherhood, jovial unity (*Camaraderie among employees usually leads to success in business.*)

candor (*n.*) honesty, frankness (*We were surprised by the candor of the mayor's speech because he is usually rather evasive.*)

canny (*adj.*) shrewd, careful (*The canny runner hung at the back of the pack through much of the race to watch the other runners, and then sprinted past them at the end.*)

canvas 1. (*n.*) a piece of cloth on which an artist paints (*Picasso liked to work on canvas rather than on bare cement.*) 2. (*v.*) to cover, inspect (*We canvassed the neighborhood looking for clues.*)

capacious (*adj.*) very spacious (*The workers delighted in their new capacious office space.*)

capitulate (*v.*) to surrender (*The army finally capitulated after fighting a long costly battle.*)

capricious (*adj.*) subject to whim, fickle (*The young girl's capricious tendencies made it difficult for her to focus on achieving her goals.*)

captivate (*v.*) to get the attention of, hold (*The fireworks captivated the young boy, who had never seen such things before.*)

carouse (*v.*) to party, celebrate (*We caroused all night after getting married.*)

carp (*v.*) to annoy, pester (*The husband divorced his wife after listening to her carping voice for decades.*)

catalog 1. *(v.)* to list, enter into a list *(The judge cataloged the victim's injuries before calculating how much money he would award.)* 2. *(n.)* a list or collection *(We received a catalog from J. Crew that displayed all of their new items.)*

catalyze *(v.)* to charge, inspire *(The president's speech catalyzed the nation and resuscitated the economy.)*

caucus *(n.)* a meeting usually held by people working toward the same goal *(The ironworkers held a caucus to determine how much of a pay increase they would request.)*

caustic *(adj.)* bitter, biting, acidic *(The politicians exchanged caustic insults for over an hour during the debate.)*

cavort *(v.)* to leap about, behave boisterously *(The adults ate their dinners on the patio, while the children cavorted around the pool.)*

censure 1. *(n.)* harsh criticism *(The frustrated teenager could not put up with anymore of her critical mother's censure.)* 2. *(v.)* to rebuke formally *(The principal censured the head of the English Department for forcing students to learn esoteric vocabulary.)*

cerebral *(adj.)* related to the intellect *(The books we read in this class are too cerebral— they don't engage my emotions at all.)*

chaos *(n.)* absolute disorder *(Mr. Thornton's sudden departure for the lavatory plunged his classroom into chaos.)*

chastise *(v.)* to criticize severely *(After being chastised by her peers for mimicking Britney Spears, Miranda dyed her hair black and affected a Gothic style.)*

cherish *(v.)* to feel or show affection toward something *(She continued to cherish her red plaid trousers, even though they had gone out of style and no longer fit her.)*

chide *(v.)* to voice disapproval *(Lucy chided Russell for his vulgar habits and sloppy appearance.)*

choreography *(n.)* the arrangement of dances *(The plot of the musical was banal, but the choreography was stunning.)*

chronicle 1. *(n.)* a written history *(The library featured the newly updated chronicle of World War II.)* 2. *(v.)* to write a history *(Albert's diary chronicled the day-to-day growth of his obsession with Cynthia.)*

chronological *(adj.)* arranged in order of time *(Lionel carefully arranged the snapshots of his former girlfriends in chronological order, and then set fire to them.)*

circuitous *(adj.)* roundabout *(The bus's <u>circuitous</u> route took us through numerous outlying suburbs.)*

circumlocution *(n.)* indirect and wordy language *(The professor's habit of speaking in <u>circumlocutions</u> made it difficult to follow his lectures.)*

circumscribed *(adj.)* marked off, bounded *(The children were permitted to play tag only within a carefully <u>circumscribed</u> area of the lawn.)*

circumspect *(adj.)* cautious *(Though I promised Rachel's father I would bring her home promptly by midnight, it would have been more <u>circumspect</u> not to have specified a time.)*

circumvent *(v.)* to get around *(The school's dress code forbidding navel-baring jeans was <u>circumvented</u> by the determined students, who were careful to cover up with long coats when administrators were nearby.)*

clairvoyant *(adj.)* able to perceive things that normal people cannot *(Zelda's uncanny ability to detect my lies was nothing short of <u>clairvoyant</u>.)*

clamor 1. *(n.)* loud noise *(Each morning the birds outside my window make such a <u>clamor</u> that they wake me up.)* 2. *(v.)* to loudly insist *(Neville's fans <u>clamored</u> for him to appear on stage, but he had passed out on the floor of his dressing room.)*

clandestine *(adj.)* secret *(Announcing to her boyfriend that she was going to the gym, Sophie actually went to meet Joseph for a <u>clandestine</u> liaison.)*

cleave 1. *(v.)* to divide into parts *(Following the scandalous disgrace of their leader, the entire political party <u>cleaved</u> into warring factions.)* 2. *(v.)* to stick together firmly *(After resolving their marital problems, Junior and Rosa <u>cleaved</u> to one another all the more tightly.)*

clemency *(n.)* mercy *(After he forgot their anniversary, Martin could only beg Maria for <u>clemency</u>.)*

clergy *(n.)* members of Christian holy orders *(Though the villagers viewed the church rectory as quaint and charming, the <u>clergy</u> who lived there regarded it as a mildewy and dusty place that aggravated their allergies.)*

cloying *(adj.)* sickeningly sweet *(Though Ronald was physically attractive, Maud found his constant compliments and solicitous remarks <u>cloying</u>.)*

coagulate *(v.)* to thicken, clot *(The top layer of the pudding had <u>coagulated</u> into a thick skin.)*

coalesce *(v.)* to fuse into a whole *(Gordon's ensemble of thrift-shop garments coalesced into a surprisingly handsome outfit.)*

cobbler *(n.)* a person who makes or repairs shoes *(I had my neighborhood cobbler replace my worn-out leather soles with new ones.)*

coerce *(v.)* to make somebody do something by force or threat *(The court decided that Vanilla Ice did not have to honor the contract because he had been coerced into signing it.)*

cogent *(adj.)* intellectually convincing *(Irene's arguments in favor of abstinence were so cogent that I could not resist them.)*

cognizant *(adj.)* aware, mindful *(Jake avoided speaking to women in bars because he was cognizant of the fact that drinking impairs his judgment.)*

coherent *(adj.)* logically consistent, intelligible *(Renee could not figure out what Monroe had seen because he was too distraught to deliver a coherent statement.)*

collateral 1. *(adj.)* secondary *(Divorcing my wife had the collateral effect of making me poor, as she was the only one of us with a job or money.)* 2. *(n.)* security for a debt *(Jacob left his watch as collateral for the $500 loan.)*

colloquial *(adj.)* characteristic of informal conversation *(Adam's essay on sexual response in primates was marked down because it contained too many colloquial expressions.)*

collusion *(n.)* secret agreement, conspiracy *(The three law students worked in collusion to steal the final exam.)*

colossus *(n.)* a gigantic statue or thing *(For 56 years, the ancient city of Rhodes featured a colossus standing astride its harbor.)*

combustion *(n.)* the act or process of burning *(The unexpected combustion of the prosecution's evidence forced the judge to dismiss the case against Ramirez.)*

commendation *(n.)* a notice of approval or recognition *(Jared received a commendation from Linda, his supervisor, for his stellar performance.)*

commensurate *(adj.)* corresponding in size or amount *(Ahab selected a very long roll and proceeded to prepare a tuna salad sandwich commensurate with his enormous appetite.)*

commodious *(adj.)* roomy *(Holden invited the three women to join him in the back seat of the taxicab, assuring them that the car was quite commodious.)*

compelling (*adj.*) forceful, demanding attention (*Eliot's speech was so* <u>compelling</u> *that Lenore accepted his proposal on the spot.*)

compensate (*v.*) to make an appropriate payment for something (*Reginald bought Sharona a new dress to* <u>compensate</u> *her for the one he'd spilled his ice cream on.*)

complacency (*n.*) self-satisfied ignorance of danger (*Colin tried to shock his friends out of their* <u>complacency</u> *by painting a frightening picture of what might happen to them.*)

complement (*v.*) to complete, make perfect (*Ann's scarf* <u>complements</u> *her blouse beautifully, making her seem fully dressed even though she isn't wearing a coat.*)

compliant (*adj.*) ready to adapt oneself to another's wishes (*Sue had very strong opinions about what to do on a first date, and Ted was absolutely* <u>compliant</u>.)

complicit (*adj.*) being an accomplice in a wrongful act (*By keeping her daughter's affair a secret, Maddie became* <u>complicit</u> *in it.*)

compliment (*n.*) an expression of esteem or approval (*I blushed crimson when Emma gave me a* <u>compliment</u> *on my new haircut.*)

compound 1. (*v.*) to combine parts (*The difficulty of finding a fire escape amid the smoke was* <u>compounded</u> *with the dangers posed by the panicking crowds.*) 2. (*n.*) a combination of different parts (*My attraction to Donna was a* <u>compound</u> *of curiosity about the unknown, physical desire, and intellectual admiration.*) 3. (*n.*) a walled area containing a group of buildings (*When the fighting started, Joseph rushed into the family* <u>compound</u> *because it was safe and well defended.*)

comprehensive (*adj.*) including everything (*She sent me a* <u>comprehensive</u> *list of the ingredients needed to cook rabbit soufflé.*)

compress (*v.*) to apply pressure, squeeze together (*Lynn* <u>compressed</u> *her lips into a frown.*)

compunction (*n.*) distress caused by feeling guilty (*He felt* <u>compunction</u> *for the shabby way he'd treated her.*)

concede (*v.*) to accept as valid (*Andrew had to* <u>concede</u> *that what his mother said about Diana made sense.*)

conciliatory (*adj.*) friendly, agreeable (*I took Amanda's invitation to dinner as a very* <u>conciliatory</u> *gesture.*)

SAT Vocabulary

concise *(adj.)* brief and direct in expression *(Gordon did not like to waste time, and his instructions to Brenda were nothing if not concise.)*

concoct *(v.)* to fabricate, make up *(She concocted the most ridiculous story to explain her absence.)*

concomitant *(adj.)* accompanying in a subordinate fashion *(His dislike of hard work carried with it a concomitant lack of funds.)*

concord *(n.)* harmonious agreement *(Julie and Harold began the evening with a disagreement, but ended it in a state of perfect concord.)*

condolence *(n.)* an expression of sympathy in sorrow *(Brian lamely offered his condolences on the loss of his sister's roommate's cat.)*

condone *(v.)* to pardon, deliberately overlook *(He refused to condone his brother's crime.)*

conduit *(n.)* a pipe or channel through which something passes *(The water flowed through the conduit into the container.)*

confection *(n.)* a sweet, fancy food *(We went to the mall food court and purchased a delicious confection.)*

confidant *(n.)* a person entrusted with secrets *(Shortly after we met, she became my chief confidant.)*

conflagration *(n.)* great fire *(The conflagration consumed the entire building.)*

confluence *(n.)* a gathering together *(A confluence of different factors made tonight the perfect night.)*

conformist *(n.)* one who behaves the same as others *(Julian was such a conformist that he had to wait and see if his friends would do something before he would commit.)*

confound *(v.)* to frustrate, confuse *(MacGuyver confounded the policemen pursuing him by covering his tracks.)*

congeal *(v.)* to thicken into a solid *(The sauce had congealed into a thick paste.)*

congenial *(adj.)* pleasantly agreeable *(His congenial manner made him popular wherever he went.)*

congregation *(n.)* a gathering of people, especially for religious services *(The priest told the congregation that he would be retiring.)*

congruity *(n.)* the quality of being in agreement *(Bill and Veronica achieved a perfect congruity of opinion.)*

connive (v.) to plot, scheme (She _connived_ to get me to give up my vacation plans.)

consecrate (v.) to dedicate something to a holy purpose (Arvin _consecrated_ his spare bedroom as a shrine to Christina.)

consensus (n.) an agreement of opinion (The jury was able to reach a _consensus_ only after days of deliberation.)

consign (v.) to give something over to another's care (Unwillingly, he _consigned_ his mother to a nursing home.)

consolation (n.) an act of comforting (Darren found Alexandra's presence to be a _consolation_ for his suffering.)

consonant (adj.) in harmony (The singers' _consonant_ voices were beautiful.)

constituent (n.) an essential part (The most important _constituent_ of her perfume is something called ambergris.)

constrain (v.) to forcibly restrict (His belief in nonviolence _constrained_ him from taking revenge on his attackers.)

construe (v.) to interpret (He _construed_ her throwing his clothes out the window as a signal that she wanted him to leave.)

consummate (v.) to complete a deal; to complete a marriage ceremony through sexual intercourse (Erica and Donald _consummated_ their agreement in the executive boardroom.)

consumption (n.) the act of consuming (_Consumption_ of intoxicating beverages is not permitted on these premises.)

contemporaneous (adj.) existing during the same time (Though her novels do not feature the themes of Romanticism, Jane Austen's work was _contemporaneous_ with that of Wordsworth and Byron.)

contentious (adj.) having a tendency to quarrel or dispute (George's _contentious_ personality made him unpopular with his classmates.)

contravene (v.) to contradict, oppose, violate (Edwidge _contravened_ his landlady's rule against overnight guests.)

contrite (adj.) penitent, eager to be forgiven (Blake's _contrite_ behavior made it impossible to stay angry at him.)

contusion (n.) bruise, injury (The _contusions_ on his face suggested he'd been in a fight.)

conundrum (n.) puzzle, problem (*Interpreting Jane's behavior was a constant* <u>*conundrum*</u>.)

convene (v.) to call together (*Jason* <u>*convened*</u> *his entire extended family for a discussion.*)

convention 1. (n.) an assembly of people (*The hotel was full because of the cattle-ranchers'* <u>*convention*</u>.) 2. (n.) a rule, custom (*The cattle-ranchers have a* <u>*convention*</u> *that you take off your boots before entering their houses.*)

convivial (adj.) characterized by feasting, drinking, merriment (*The restaurant's* <u>*convivial*</u> *atmosphere put me immediately at ease.*)

convoluted (adj.) intricate, complicated (*Grace's story was so* <u>*convoluted*</u> *that I couldn't follow it.*)

copious (adj.) profuse, abundant (<u>*Copious*</u> *amounts of Snapple were imbibed in the cafeteria.*)

cordial (adj.) warm, affectionate (*His* <u>*cordial*</u> *greeting melted my anger at once.*)

coronation (n.) the act of crowning (*The new king's* <u>*coronation*</u> *occurred the day after his father's death.*)

corpulence (adj.) extreme fatness (*Henry's* <u>*corpulence*</u> *did not make him any less attractive to his charming, svelte wife.*)

corroborate (v.) to support with evidence (*Luke's seemingly outrageous claim was* <u>*corroborated*</u> *by witnesses.*)

corrosive (adj.) having the tendency to erode or eat away (*The effect of the chemical was highly* <u>*corrosive*</u>.)

cosmopolitan (adj.) sophisticated, worldly (*Lloyd's education and upbringing were* <u>*cosmopolitan*</u>, *so he felt right at home among the powerful and learned.*)

counteract (v.) to neutralize, make ineffective (*The antidote* <u>*counteracted*</u> *the effect of the poison.*)

coup 1. (n.) a brilliant, unexpected act (*Alexander pulled off an amazing* <u>*coup*</u> *when he got a date with Cynthia by purposely getting hit by her car.*) 2. (n.) the overthrow of a government and assumption of authority (*In their* <u>*coup*</u> *attempt, the army officers stormed the Parliament and took all the legislators hostage.*)

covet (v.) to desire enviously (*I* <u>*coveted*</u> *Moses's house, wife, and car.*)

covert *(adj.)* secretly engaged in *(Nerwin waged a <u>covert</u> campaign against his enemies, while outwardly appearing to remain friendly.)*

credulity *(n.)* readiness to believe *(His <u>credulity</u> made him an easy target for con men.)*

crescendo *(n.)* a steady increase in intensity or volume *(The <u>crescendo</u> of the brass instruments gave the piece a patriotic feel.)*

criteria *(n.)* standards by which something is judged *(Among Mrs. Fields's <u>criteria</u> for good cookies are that they be moist and chewy.)*

culmination *(n.)* the climax toward which something progresses *(The <u>culmination</u> of the couple's argument was the decision to divorce.)*

culpable *(adj.)* deserving blame *(He was <u>culpable</u> of the crime, and was sentenced to perform community service for 75 years.)*

cultivate *(v.)* to nurture, improve, refine *(At the library, she <u>cultivated</u> her interest in spy novels.)*

cumulative *(adj.)* increasing, building upon itself *(The <u>cumulative</u> effect of hours spent in the sun was a deep tan.)*

cunning *(adj.)* sly, clever at being deceitful *(The general devised a <u>cunning</u> plan to surprise the enemy.)*

cupidity *(n.)* greed, strong desire *(His <u>cupidity</u> made him enter the abandoned gold mine despite the obvious dangers.)*

cursory *(adj.)* brief to the point of being superficial *(Late for the meeting, she cast a <u>cursory</u> glance at the agenda.)*

curt *(adj.)* abruptly and rudely short *(Her <u>curt</u> reply to my question made me realize that she was upset at me.)*

curtail *(v.)* to lessen, reduce *(Since losing his job, he had to <u>curtail</u> his spending.)*

D

daunting *(adj.)* intimidating, causing one to lose courage *(He kept delaying the <u>daunting</u> act of asking for a promotion.)*

dearth *(n.)* a lack, scarcity *(An eager reader, she was dismayed by the <u>dearth</u> of classic books at the library.)*

debacle *(n.)* a disastrous failure, disruption *(The elaborately designed fireworks show turned into a <u>debacle</u> when the fireworks started firing in random directions.)*

debase (v.) to lower the quality or esteem of something (*The large raise that he gave himself debased his motives for running the charity.*)

debauch (v.) to corrupt by means of sensual pleasures (*An endless amount of good wine and cheese debauched the traveler.*)

debunk (v.) to expose the falseness of something (*He debunked her claim to be the world's greatest chess player by defeating her in 18 consecutive matches.*)

decorous (adj.) socially proper, appropriate (*The appreciative guest displayed decorous behavior toward his host.*)

decry (v.) to criticize openly (*The kind video rental clerk decried the policy of charging customers late fees.*)

deface (v.) to ruin or injure something's appearance (*The brothers used eggs and shaving cream to deface their neighbor's mailbox.*)

defamatory (adj.) harmful toward another's reputation (*The defamatory gossip spreading about the actor made the public less willing to see the actor's new movie.*)

defer (v.) to postpone something; to yield to another's wisdom (*Ron deferred to Diane, the expert on musical instruments, when he was asked about buying a piano.*)

deferential (adj.) showing respect for another's authority (*His deferential attitude toward her made her more confident in her ability to run the company.*)

defile (v.) to make unclean, impure (*She defiled the calm of the religious building by playing her banjo.*)

deft (adj.) skillful, capable (*Having worked in a bakery for many years, Marcus was a deft bread maker.*)

defunct (adj.) no longer used or existing (*They planned to turn the defunct schoolhouse into a community center.*)

delegate (v.) to hand over responsibility for something (*The dean delegated the task of finding a new professor to a special hiring committee.*)

deleterious (adj.) harmful (*She experienced the deleterious effects of running a marathon without stretching her muscles enough beforehand.*)

deliberate (adj.) intentional, reflecting careful consideration (*Though Mary was quite upset, her actions to resolve the dispute were deliberate.*)

delineate (v.) to describe, outline, shed light on (*She neatly delineated her reasons for canceling the project's funding.*)

demagogue *(n.)* a leader who appeals to a people's prejudices *(The demagogue strengthened his hold over his people by blaming immigrants for the lack of jobs.)*

demarcation *(n.)* the marking of boundaries or categories *(Different cultures have different demarcations of good and evil.)*

demean *(v.)* to lower the status or stature of something *(She refused to demean her secretary by making him order her lunch.)*

demure *(adj.)* quiet, modest, reserved *(Though everyone else at the party was dancing and going crazy, she remained demure.)*

denigrate *(v.)* to belittle, diminish the opinion of *(The company decided that its advertisements would no longer denigrate the company's competitors.)*

denounce *(v.)* to criticize publicly *(The senator denounced her opponent as a greedy politician.)*

deplore *(v.)* to feel or express sorrow, disapproval *(We all deplored the miserable working conditions in the factory.)*

depravity *(n.)* wickedness *(Rumors of the ogre's depravity made the children afraid to enter the forest.)*

deprecate *(v.)* to belittle, depreciate *(Always over-modest, he deprecated his contribution to the local charity.)*

derelict *(adj.)* abandoned, run-down *(Even though it was dangerous, the children enjoyed going to the deserted lot and playing in the derelict house.)*

deride *(v.)* to laugh at mockingly, scorn *(The bullies derided the foreign student's accent.)*

derivative *(adj.)* taken directly from a source, unoriginal *(She was bored by his music because she felt that it was derivative and that she had heard it before.)*

desecrate *(v.)* to violate the sacredness of a thing or place *(They feared that the construction of a golf course would desecrate the preserved wilderness.)*

desiccated *(adj.)* dried up, dehydrated *(The skin of the desiccated mummy looked like old paper.)*

desolate *(adj.)* deserted, dreary, lifeless *(She found the desolate landscape quite a contrast to the hustle and bustle of the overcrowded city.)*

SAT Vocabulary

despondent *(adj.)* feeling depressed, discouraged, hopeless *(Having failed the first math test, the <u>despondent</u> child saw no use in studying for the next and failed that one too.)*

despot *(n.)* one who has total power and rules brutally *(The <u>despot</u> issued a death sentence for anyone who disobeyed his laws.)*

destitute *(adj.)* impoverished, utterly lacking *(The hurricane destroyed many homes and left many families <u>destitute</u>.)*

deter *(v.)* to discourage, prevent from doing *(Bob's description of scary snakes couldn't <u>deter</u> Marcia from traveling in the rainforests.)*

devious *(adj.)* not straightforward, deceitful *(Not wanting to be punished, the <u>devious</u> girl blamed the broken vase on the cat.)*

dialect *(n.)* a variation of a language *(In the country's remote, mountainous regions, the inhabitants spoke a <u>dialect</u> that the country's other inhabitants had difficulty understanding.)*

diaphanous *(adj.)* light, airy, transparent *(Sunlight poured in through the <u>diaphanous</u> curtains, brightening the room.)*

didactic 1. *(adj.)* intended to instruct *(She wrote up a <u>didactic</u> document showing new employees how to handle the company's customers.)* 2. *(adj.)* overly moralistic *(His <u>didactic</u> style of teaching made it seem like he wanted to persuade his students not to understand history fully, but to understand it from only one point of view.)*

diffident *(adj.)* shy, quiet, modest *(While eating dinner with the adults, the <u>diffident</u> youth did not speak for fear of seeming presumptuous.)*

diffuse 1. *(v.)* to scatter, thin out, break up *(He <u>diffused</u> the tension in the room by making in a joke.)* 2. *(adj.)* not concentrated, scattered, disorganized *(In her writings, she tried unsuccessfully to make others understand her <u>diffuse</u> thoughts.)*

dilatory *(adj.)* tending to delay, causing delay *(The general's <u>dilatory</u> strategy enabled the enemy to regroup.)*

diligent *(adj.)* showing care in doing one's work *(The <u>diligent</u> researcher made sure to check her measurements multiple times.)*

diminutive *(adj.)* small or miniature *(The bullies, tall and strong, picked on the <u>diminutive</u> child.)*

dirge *(n.)* a mournful song, especially for a funeral *(The bagpipers played a <u>dirge</u> as the casket was carried to the cemetery.)*

disaffected (*adj.*) rebellious, resentful of authority (*Dismayed by Bobby's poor behavior, the parents sent their disaffected son to a military academy to be disciplined.*)

disavow (*v.*) to deny knowledge of or responsibility for (*Not wanting others to criticize her, she disavowed any involvement in the company's hiring scandal.*)

discern (*v.*) to perceive, detect (*Though he hid his emotions, she discerned from his body language that he was angry.*)

disclose (*v.*) to reveal, make public (*The CEO disclosed to the press that the company would have to fire several employees.*)

discomfit (*v.*) to thwart, baffle (*The normally cheery and playful children's sudden misery discomfited the teacher.*)

discordant (*adj.*) not agreeing, not in harmony with (*The girls' sobs were a discordant sound amid the general laughter that filled the restaurant.*)

discrepancy (*n.*) difference, failure of things to correspond (*He was troubled by the discrepancy between what he remembered paying for the appliance and what his receipt showed he paid for it.*)

discretion (*n.*) the quality of being reserved in speech or action; good judgment (*Not wanting her patient to get overly anxious, the doctor used discretion in deciding how much to tell the patient about his condition.*)

discursive (*adj.*) rambling, lacking order (*The professor's discursive lectures seemed to be about every subject except the one initially described.*)

disdain 1. (*v.*) to scorn, hold in low esteem (*Insecure about their jobs, the older employees disdained the recently hired ones, who were young and capable.*) 2. (*n.*) scorn, low esteem (*After learning of his immoral actions, Justine held Lawrence in disdain.*)

disgruntled (*adj.*) upset, not content (*The child believed that his parents had unjustly grounded him, and remained disgruntled for a week.*)

disheartened (*adj.*) feeling a loss of spirit or morale (*The team was disheartened after losing in the finals of the tournament.*)

disparage (*v.*) to criticize or speak ill of (*The saleswoman disparaged the competitor's products to persuade her customers to buy what she was selling.*)

disparate (*adj.*) sharply differing, containing sharply contrasting elements (*Having widely varying interests, the students had disparate responses toward the novel.*)

SAT Vocabulary

dispatch *(v.)* to send off to accomplish a duty *(The carpenter dispatched his assistant to fetch wood.)*

dispel *(v.)* to drive away, scatter *(She entered the office as usual on Monday, dispelling the rumor that she had been fired.)*

disperse *(v.)* to scatter, cause to scatter *(When the rain began to pour, the crowd at the baseball game quickly dispersed.)*

disrepute *(n.)* a state of being held in low regard *(The officer fell into disrepute after it was learned that he had disobeyed the orders he had given to his own soldiers.)*

dissemble *(v.)* to conceal, fake *(Not wanting to appear heartlessly greedy, she dissembled and hid her intention to sell her ailing father's stamp collection.)*

disseminate *(v.)* to spread widely *(The politician disseminated his ideas across the town before the election.)*

dissent 1. *(v.)* to disagree *(The principal argued that the child should repeat the fourth grade, but the unhappy parents dissented.)* 2. *(n.)* the act of disagreeing *(Unconvinced that the defendant was guilty, the last juror voiced his dissent with the rest of the jury.)*

dissipate 1. *(v.)* to disappear, cause to disappear *(The sun finally came out and dissipated the haze.)* 2. *(v.)* to waste *(She dissipated her fortune on a series of bad investments.)*

dissonance *(n.)* lack of harmony or consistency *(Though the president of the company often spoke of the company as reliant solely upon its workers, her decision to increase her own salary rather than reward her employees revealed a striking dissonance between her alleged beliefs and her actions.)*

dissuade *(v.)* to persuade someone not to do something *(Worried that he would catch a cold, she tried to dissuade him from going out on winter nights.)*

distend *(v.)* to swell out *(Years of drinking beer caused his stomach to distend.)*

dither *(v.)* to be indecisive *(Not wanting to offend either friend, he dithered about which of the two birthday parties he should attend.)*

divine *(adj.)* godly, exceedingly wonderful *(Terribly fond of desserts, she found the rich chocolate cake to be divine.)*

divisive *(adj.)* causing dissent, discord *(Her divisive tactics turned her two friends against each other.)*

divulge (v.) to reveal something secret (*Pressured by the press, the government finally divulged the previously unknown information.*)

docile (adj.) easily taught or trained (*She successfully taught the docile puppy several tricks.*)

dogmatic (adj.) aggressively and arrogantly certain about unproved principles (*His dogmatic claim that men were better than women at fixing appliances angered everyone.*)

dormant (adj.) sleeping, temporarily inactive (*Though she pretended everything was fine, her anger lay dormant throughout the dinner party and exploded in screams of rage after everyone had left.*)

dour (adj.) stern, joyless (*The children feared their dour neighbor because the old man would take their toys if he believed they were being too loud.*)

dubious (adj.) doubtful, of uncertain quality (*Suspicious that he was only trying to get a raise, she found his praise dubious.*)

duplicity (n.) crafty dishonesty (*His duplicity involved convincing his employees to let him lower their salaries and increase their stock options, and then to steal the money he saved and run the company into the ground.*)

duress (n.) hardship, threat (*It was only under intense duress that he, who was normally against killing, fired his gun.*)

dynamic (adj.) actively changing (*The parents found it hard to keep up with the dynamic music scene with which their children had become very familiar.*)

E

ebullient (adj.) extremely lively, enthusiastic (*She became ebullient upon receiving an acceptance letter from her first-choice college.*)

eclectic (adj.) consisting of a diverse variety of elements (*That bar attracts an eclectic crowd: lawyers, artists, circus clowns, and investment bankers.*)

ecstatic (adj.) intensely and overpoweringly happy (*The couple was ecstatic when they learned that they had won the lottery.*)

edict (n.) an order, decree (*The ruler issued an edict requiring all of his subjects to bow down before him.*)

efface *(v.)* to wipe out, obliterate, rub away *(The husband was so angry at his wife for leaving him that he efface all evidence of her presence; he threw out pictures of her and gave away all her belongings.)*

effervescent *(adj.)* bubbly, lively *(My friend is so effervescent that she makes everyone smile.)*

efficacious *(adj.)* effective *(My doctor promised me that the cold medicine was efficacious, but I'm still sniffling.)*

effrontery *(n.)* impudence, nerve, insolence *(When I told my aunt that she was boring, my mother scolded me for my effrontery.)*

effulgent *(adj.)* radiant, splendorous *(The golden palace was effulgent.)*

egregious *(adj.)* extremely bad *(The student who threw sloppy joes across the cafeteria was punished for his egregious behavior.)*

elaborate *(adj.)* complex, detailed, intricate *(Dan always beats me at chess because he develops such an elaborate game plan that I can never predict his next move.)*

elated *(adj.)* overjoyed, thrilled *(When she found out she had won the lottery, the writer was elated.)*

elegy *(n.)* a speech given in honor of a dead person *(At the funeral, the widow gave a moving elegy describing her love for her husband.)*

elicit *(v.)* to bring forth, draw out, evoke *(Although I asked several times where the exit was, I elicited no response from the stone-faced policeman.)*

eloquent *(adj.)* expressive, articulate, moving *(The priest gave such an eloquent sermon that most churchgoers were crying.)*

elucidate *(v.)* to clarify, explain *(I didn't understand why my friend was so angry with me, so I asked Janine to elucidate her feelings.)*

elude *(v.)* to evade, escape *(Despite an intense search, the robber continues to elude the police.)*

emaciated *(adj.)* very thin, enfeebled looking *(My sister eats a lot of pastries and chocolate but still looks emaciated.)*

embellish 1. *(v.)* to decorate, adorn *(My mom embellished the living room by adding lace curtains.)* 2. *(v.)* to add details to, enhance *(When Harry told me that he had "done stuff" on his vacation, I asked him to embellish upon his account.)*

embezzle *(v.)* to steal money by falsifying records *(The accountant was fired for embezzling $10,000 of the company's funds.)*

emend *(v.)* to correct or revise a written text *(If my sentence is incorrect, the editor will emend what I have written.)*

eminent 1. *(adj.)* distinguished, prominent, famous *(Mr. Phillips is such an eminent scholar that every professor on campus has come to hear him lecture.)* 2. *(adj.)* conspicuous *(There is an eminent stain on that shirt.)*

emollient *(adj.)* soothing *(This emollient cream makes my skin very smooth.)*

emote *(v.)* to express emotion *(The director told the actor he had to emote, or else the audience would have no idea what his character was going through.)*

empathy *(n.)* sensitivity to another's feelings as if they were one's own *(I feel such empathy for my sister when she's in pain that I cry too.)*

empirical 1. *(adj.)* based on observation or experience *(The scientist gathered empirical data on the growth rate of dandelions by studying the dandelions behind his house.)* 2. *(adj.)* capable of being proved or disproved by experiment *(That all cats hate getting wet is an empirical statement: I can test it by bathing my cat, Trinket.)*

emulate *(v.)* to imitate *(I idolize Britney Spears so much that I emulate everything she does: I wear her outfits, sing along to her songs, and date a boy named Justin.)*

enamor *(v.)* to fill with love, fascinate, usually used in passive form followed by "of" or "with" *(I grew enamored of that boy when he quoted my favorite love poem.)*

encore *(n.)* the audience's demand for a repeat performance; also the artist's performance in response to that demand *(At the end of the concert, all the fans yelled, "Encore! Encore!" but the band did not come out to play again.)*

encumber *(v.)* to weigh down, burden *(At the airport, my friend was encumbered by her luggage, so I offered to carry two of her bags.)*

enervate *(v.)* to weaken, exhaust *(Writing these sentences enervates me so much that I will have to take a nap after I finish.)*

enfranchise *(v.)* to grant the vote to *(The Nineteenth Amendment enfranchised women.)*

engender *(v.)* to bring about, create, generate *(During the Olympics, the victories of U.S. athletes engender a patriotic spirit among Americans.)*

enigmatic *(adj.)* mystifying, cryptic *(That man wearing the dark suit and dark glasses is so enigmatic that no one even knows his name.)*

SAT Vocabulary

enmity *(n.)* ill will, hatred, hostility *(Mark and Andy have clearly not forgiven each other, because the* <u>enmity</u> *between them is obvious to anyone in their presence.)*

ennui *(n.)* boredom, weariness *(I feel such* <u>ennui</u> *that I don't look forward to anything, not even my birthday party.)*

entail *(v.)* to include as a necessary step *(Building a new fence* <u>entails</u> *tearing down the old one.)*

enthrall *(v.)* to charm, hold spellbound *(The sailor's stories of fighting off sharks and finding ancient treasures* <u>enthralled</u> *his young son.)*

ephemeral *(adj.)* short-lived, fleeting *(She promised she'd love me forever, but her "forever" was only* <u>ephemeral</u>*: she left me after one week.)*

epistolary *(adj.)* relating to or contained in letters *(Some people call me "Auntie's boy," because my aunt and I have such a close* <u>epistolary</u> *relationship that we write each other every day.)*

epitome *(n.)* a perfect example, embodiment *(My mother, the* <u>epitome</u> *of good taste, always dresses more elegantly than I do.)*

equanimity *(n.)* composure *(Even though he had just been fired, Mr. Simms showed great* <u>equanimity</u> *by neatly packing up his desk and wishing everyone in the office well.)*

equivocal *(adj.)* ambiguous, uncertain, undecided *(His intentions were so* <u>equivocal</u> *that I didn't know whether he was being chivalrous or sleazy.)*

erudite *(adj.)* learned *(My Latin teacher is such an* <u>erudite</u> *scholar that he has translated some of the most difficult and abstruse ancient poetry.)*

eschew *(v.)* to shun, avoid *(George hates the color green so much that he* <u>eschews</u> *all green food.)*

esoteric *(adj.)* understood by only a select few *(Even the most advanced students cannot understand the physicist's* <u>esoteric</u> *theories.)*

espouse *(v.)* to take up as a cause, support *(I love animals so much that I* <u>espouse</u> *animal rights.)*

ethereal *(adj.)* heavenly, exceptionally delicate or refined *(In her flowing silk gown and lace veil, the bride looked* <u>ethereal</u>*.)*

etymology *(n.)* the history of words, their origin and development *(From the study of* <u>etymology</u>*, I know that the word "quixotic" derives from Don Quixote and the word "gaudy" refers to the Spanish architect Gaudí.)*

euphoric (*adj.*) elated, uplifted (*I was euphoric when I found out that my sister had given birth to twins.*)

evanescent (*adj.*) fleeting, momentary (*My joy at getting promoted was evanescent because I discovered that I would have to work much longer hours in a less friendly office.*)

evince (*v.*) to show, reveal (*Christopher's hand-wringing and nail-biting evince how nervous he is about the upcoming English test.*)

exacerbate (*v.*) to make more violent, intense (*The gruesome and scary movie I saw last night exacerbated my fears of the dark.*)

exalt (*v.*) to glorify, praise (*Michael Jordan is the figure in basketball we exalt the most.*)

exasperate (*v.*) to irritate, irk (*George's endless complaints exasperated his roomate.*)

excavate (*v.*) to dig out of the ground and remove (*The pharaoh's treasures were excavated by archeologists in Egypt.*)

exculpate (*v.*) to free from guilt or blame, exonerate (*My discovery of the ring behind the dresser exculpated me from the charge of having stolen it.*)

excursion (*n.*) a trip or outing (*After taking an excursion to the Bronx Zoo, I dreamed about pandas and monkeys.*)

execrable (*adj.*) loathsome, detestable (*Her pudding is so execrable that it makes me sick.*)

exhort (*v.*) to urge, prod, spur (*Henry exhorted his colleagues to join him in protesting against the university's hiring policies.*)

exigent (*adj.*) urgent, critical (*The patient has an exigent need for medication, or else he will lose his sight.*)

exonerate (*v.*) to free from guilt or blame, exculpate (*The true thief's confession exonerated the man who had been held in custody for the crime.*)

exorbitant (*adj.*) excessive (*Her exorbitant praise made me blush and squirm in my seat.*)

expedient (*adj.*) advisable, advantageous, serving one's self-interest (*In his bid for reelection, the governor made an expedient move by tabling all controversial legislation.*)

expiate (*v.*) to make amends for, atone (*To expiate my selfishness, I gave all my profits to charity.*)

expunge (v.) to obliterate, eradicate (*Fearful of an IRS investigation, Paul tried to expunge all incriminating evidence from his tax files.*)

expurgate (v.) to remove offensive or incorrect parts, usually of a book (*The history editors expurgated from the text all disparaging and inflammatory comments about the Republican Party.*)

extant (adj.) existing, not destroyed or lost (*My mother's extant love letters to my father are in the attic trunk.*)

extol (v.) to praise, revere (*Violet extolled the virtues of a vegetarian diet to her meat-loving brother.*)

extraneous (adj.) irrelevant, extra, not necessary (*Personal political ambitions should always remain extraneous to legislative policy, but, unfortunately, they rarely are.*)

extricate (v.) to disentangle (*Instead of trying to mediate between my brother and sister, I extricated myself from the family tension entirely and left the house for the day.*)

exult (v.) to rejoice (*When she found out she won the literature prize, Mary exulted by dancing and singing through the school's halls.*)

F

fabricate (v.) to make up, invent (*When I arrived an hour late to class, I fabricated some excuse about my car breaking down on the way to school.*)

façade 1. (n.) the wall of a building (*Meet me in front of the museum's main façade.*) 2. (n.) a deceptive appearance or attitude (*Despite my smiling façade, I am feeling melancholy.*)

facile 1. (adj.) easy, requiring little effort (*This game is so facile that even a four-year-old can master it.*) 2. (adj.) superficial, achieved with minimal thought or care, insincere (*The business was in such shambles that any solution seemed facile at best; nothing could really help it in the long-run.*)

fallacious (adj.) incorrect, misleading (*Emily offered me cigarettes on the fallacious assumption that I smoked.*)

fastidious (adj.) meticulous, demanding, having high and often unattainable standards (*Mark is so fastidious that he is never able to finish a project because it always seems imperfect to him.*)

fathom (v.) to understand, comprehend (*I cannot fathom why you like that crabby and mean-spirited neighbor of ours.*)

fatuous *(adj.)* silly, foolish *(He considers himself a serious poet, but in truth, he only writes fatuous limericks.)*

fecund *(adj.)* fruitful, fertile *(The fecund tree bore enough apples to last us through the entire season.)*

felicitous 1. *(adj.)* well suited, apt *(While his comments were idiotic and rambling, mine were felicitous and helpful.)* 2. *(adj.)* delightful, pleasing *(I spent a felicitous afternoon visiting old friends.)*

feral *(adj.)* wild, savage *(That beast looks so feral that I would fear being alone with it.)*

fervent *(adj.)* ardent, passionate *(The fervent protestors chained themselves to the building and shouted all night long.)*

fetid *(adj.)* having a foul odor *(I can tell from the fetid smell in your refrigerator that your milk has spoiled.)*

fetter *(v.)* to chain, restrain *(The dog was fettered to the parking meter.)*

fickle *(adj.)* shifting in character, inconstant *(In Greek dramas, the fickle gods help Achilles one day, and then harm him the next.)*

fidelity *(n.)* loyalty, devotion *(Guard dogs are known for the great fidelity they show toward their masters.)*

figurative *(adj.)* symbolic *(Using figurative language, Jane likened the storm to an angry bull.)*

flabbergasted *(adj.)* astounded *(Whenever I read an Agatha Christie mystery novel, I am always flabbergasted when I learn the identity of the murderer.)*

flaccid *(adj.)* limp, not firm or strong *(If a plant is not watered enough, its leaves become droopy and flaccid.)*

flagrant *(adj.)* offensive, egregious *(The judge's decision to set the man free simply because that man was his brother was a flagrant abuse of power.)*

florid *(adj.)* flowery, ornate *(The writer's florid prose belongs on a sentimental Hallmark card.)*

flout *(v.)* to disregard or disobey openly *(I flouted the school's dress code by wearing a tie-dyed tank top and a pair of cut-off jeans.)*

foil *(v.)* to thwart, frustrate, defeat *(Inspector Wilkens foiled the thieves by locking them in the bank along with their stolen money.)*

SAT Vocabulary

forage (*v.*) to graze, rummage for food (*When we got lost on our hiking trip, we* <u>foraged</u> *for berries and nuts in order to survive.*)

forbearance (*n.*) patience, restraint, toleration (*The doctor showed great* <u>forbearance</u> *in calming down the angry patient who shouted insults at him.*)

forestall (*v.*) to prevent, thwart, delay (*I* <u>forestalled</u> *the cold I was getting by taking plenty of vitamin C pills and wearing a scarf.*)

forlorn (*adj.*) lonely, abandoned, hopeless (*Even though I had the flu, my family decided to go skiing for the weekend and leave me home alone, feeling feverish and* <u>forlorn</u>.)

forsake (*v.*) to give up, renounce (*My New Year's resolution is to* <u>forsake</u> *smoking and drinking.*)

fortitude (*n.*) strength, guts (*Achilles'* <u>fortitude</u> *in battle is legendary.*)

fortuitous (*adj.*) happening by chance, often lucky or fortunate (*After looking for Manuel and not finding him at home, Harriet had a* <u>fortuitous</u> *encounter with him at the post office.*)

forum (*n.*) a medium for lecture or discussion (*Some radio talk-shows provide a good* <u>forum</u> *for political debate.*)

foster (*v.*) to stimulate, promote, encourage (*To* <u>foster</u> *good health in the city, the mayor started a "Get out and exercise!" campaign.*)

fractious (*adj.*) troublesome or irritable (*Although the child insisted he wasn't tired, his* <u>fractious</u> *behavior—especially his decision to crush his cheese and crackers all over the floor—convinced everyone present that it was time to put him to bed.*)

fraught (*adj.*) (usually used with "with") filled or accompanied with (*Her glances in his direction were* <u>fraught</u> *with meaning, though precisely what meaning remained unclear.*)

frenetic (*adj.*) frenzied, hectic, frantic (*In the hours between night and morning, the* <u>frenetic</u> *pace of city life slows to a lull.*)

frivolous (*adj.*) of little importance, trifling (*Someday, all that anxiety about whether your zit will disappear before the prom will seem totally* <u>frivolous</u>.)

frugal (*adj.*) thrifty, economical (*Richard is so* <u>frugal</u> *that his diet consists almost exclusively of catfish and chicken liver—the two most inexpensive foods in the store.*)

furtive *(adj.)* secretive, sly *(Jane's placement of her drugs in her sock drawer was not as furtive as she thought, as the sock drawer is the first place most parents look.)*

G

garish *(adj.)* gaudy, in bad taste *(Mrs. Watson has poor taste and covers every object in her house with a garish gold lamé.)*

garrulous *(adj.)* talkative, wordy *(Some talk show hosts are so garrulous that their guests can't get a word in edgewise.)*

genial *(adj.)* friendly, affable *(Although he's been known to behave like a real jerk, I would say that my brother is an overall genial guy.)*

gluttony *(n.)* overindulgence in food or drink *(Ada's fried chicken tastes so divine, I don't know how anyone can call gluttony a sin.)*

goad *(v.)* to urge, spur, incite to action *(Jim may think he's not going to fight Billy, but Billy will goad Jim on with insults until he throws a punch.)*

gourmand *(n.)* someone fond of eating and drinking *(My parents, who used to eat little more than crackers and salad, have become real gourmands in their old age.)*

grandiloquence *(n.)* lofty, pompous language *(The student thought her grandiloquence would make her sound smart, but neither the class nor the teacher bought it.)*

grandiose *(adj.)* on a magnificent or exaggerated scale *(Margaret planned a grandiose party, replete with elephants, trapeze artists, and clowns.)*

gratuitous *(adj.)* uncalled for, unwarranted *(Every morning the guy at the donut shop gives me a gratuitous helping of ketchup packets.)*

gregarious *(adj.)* drawn to the company of others, sociable *(Well, if you're not gregarious, I don't know why you would want to go to a singles party!)*

grievous *(adj.)* injurious, hurtful; serious or grave in nature *(Electrocuting the inmate without being sure of his guilt would be a truly grievous mistake.)*

guile *(n.)* deceitful, cunning, sly behavior *(Because of his great guile, the politician was able to survive scandal after scandal.)*

H

hackneyed *(adj.)* unoriginal, trite *(A girl can only hear "I love you" so many times before it begins to sound hackneyed and meaningless.)*

hallowed (*adj.*) revered, consecrated (*In the hallowed corridors of the cathedral, the disturbed professor felt himself to be at peace.*)

hapless (*adj.*) unlucky (*My poor, hapless family never seems to pick a sunny week to go on vacation.*)

harangue 1. (*n.*) a ranting speech (*Everyone had heard the teacher's harangue about gum chewing in class before.*) 2. (*v.*) to give such a speech (*But this time the teacher harangued the class about the importance of brushing your teeth after chewing gum.*)

hardy (*adj.*) robust, capable of surviving through adverse conditions (*I too would have expected the plants to be dead by mid-November, but apparently they're very hardy.*)

harrowing (*adj.*) greatly distressing, vexing (*The car crash was a harrowing experience, but I have a feeling that the increase in my insurance premiums will be even more upsetting.*)

haughty (*adj.*) disdainfully proud (*The superstar's haughty dismissal of her costars will backfire on her someday.*)

hedonist (*n.*) one who believes pleasure should be the primary pursuit of humans (*Because he's such a hedonist, I knew Murray would appreciate the 11 cases of wine I bought him for his birthday.*)

hegemony (*n.*) domination over others (*Britain's hegemony over its colonies was threatened once nationalist sentiment began to spread around the world.*)

heinous (*adj.*) shockingly wicked, repugnant (*The killings were made all the more heinous by the fact that the murderer first tortured his victims for three days.*)

heterogeneous (*adj.*) varied, diverse in character (*I hate having only one flavor so I always buy the swirled, or should I say heterogeneous, type of ice cream.*)

hiatus (*n.*) a break or gap in duration or continuity (*The hiatus in service should last two or three months—until the cable lines are repaired.*)

hierarchy (*n.*) a system with ranked groups, usually according to social, economic, or professional class (*Women found it very difficult to break into the upper ranks of the department's hierarchy.*)

hypocrisy (*n.*) pretending to believe what one does not (*Once the politician began passing legislation that contradicted his campaign promises, his hypocrisy became apparent.*)

hypothetical *(adj.)* supposed or assumed true, but unproven *(Even though it has been celebrated by seven major newspapers, that the drug will be a success when tested in humans is still hypothetical.)*

I

iconoclast *(n.)* one who attacks common beliefs or institutions *(Jane goes to one protest after another, but she seems to be an iconoclast rather than an activist with a progressive agenda.)*

idiosyncratic *(adj.)* peculiar to one person; highly individualized *(I know you had trouble with the last test, but because your mistakes were highly idiosyncratic, I'm going to deny your request that the class be given a new test.)*

idolatrous *(adj.)* excessively worshipping one object or person *(Xena's idolatrous fawning over the band—following them on tour, starting their fan club, filming their documentary—is really beginning to get on my nerves.)*

ignominious *(adj.)* humiliating, disgracing *(It was really ignominious to be kicked out of the dorm for having an illegal gas stove in my room.)*

illicit *(adj.)* forbidden, not permitted *(The fourth-grader learned many illicit words from a pamphlet that was being passed around school.)*

immerse *(v.)* to absorb, deeply involve, engross *(After breaking up with her boyfriend, Nancy decided to immerse herself in her work in order to avoid crying.)*

immutable *(adj.)* not changeable *(The laws of physics are immutable and constant.)*

impassive *(adj.)* stoic, not susceptible to suffering *(Stop being so impassive; it's healthy to cry every now and then.)*

impeccable *(adj.)* exemplary, flawless *(If your grades were as impeccable as your sister's, then you too would receive a car for a graduation present.)*

impecunious *(adj.)* poor *("I fear he's too impecunious to take me out tonight," the bratty girl whined.)*

imperative 1. *(adj.)* necessary, pressing *(It is imperative that you have these folders organized by midday.)* 2. *(n.)* a rule, command, or order *(Her imperative to have the folders organized by midday was perceived as ridiculous by the others.)*

imperious *(adj.)* commanding, domineering *(The imperious nature of your manner led me to dislike you at once.)*

SAT Vocabulary

impertinent *(adj.)* rude, insolent *(Most of your comments are so impertinent that I don't wish to dignify them with an answer.)*

impervious *(adj.)* impenetrable, incapable of being affected *(Because of their thick layer of fur, many seals are almost impervious to the cold.)*

impetuous *(adj.)* rash; hastily done *(Hilda's hasty slaying of the king was an impetuous, thoughtless action.)*

impinge 1. *(v.)* to impact, affect, make an impression *(The hail impinged the roof, leaving large dents.)* 2. *(v.)* to encroach, infringe *(I apologize for impinging upon you like this, but I really need to use your bathroom. Now.)*

implacable *(adj.)* incapable of being appeased or mitigated *(Watch out: once you shun Grandma's cooking, she is totally implacable.)*

implement 1. *(n.)* an instrument, utensil, tool *(Do you have a knife or some other sort of implement that I could use to pry the lid off of this jar?)* 2. *(v.)* to put into effect, to institute *(After the first town curfew failed to stop the graffiti problem, the mayor implemented a new policy to use security cameras to catch perpetrators in the act.)*

implicate *(v.)* to involve in an incriminating way, incriminate *(Even though Tom wasn't present at the time of the shooting, he was implicated by the evidence suggesting that he had supplied the shooters with guns.)*

implicit *(adj.)* understood but not outwardly obvious, implied *(I know Professor Smith didn't actually say not to write from personal experience, but I think such a message was implicit in her instruction to use scholarly sources.)*

impregnable *(adj.)* resistant to capture or penetration *(Though the invaders used battering rams, catapults, and rain dances, the fortress proved impregnable and resisted all attacks.)*

impudent *(adj.)* casually rude, insolent, impertinent *(The impudent young man looked the princess up and down and told her she was hot even though she hadn't asked him.)*

impute *(v.)* to ascribe, blame *(The CEO imputed the many typos in the letter to his lazy secretary.)*

inane *(adj.)* silly and meaningless *(Some films are so inane that the psychology of the characters makes absolutely no sense.)*

inarticulate *(adj.)* incapable of expressing oneself clearly through speech *(Though he spoke for over an hour, the lecturer was completely inarticulate and the students had no idea what he was talking about.)*

incarnate 1. *(adj.)* existing in the flesh, embodied *(In the church pageant, I play the role of greed incarnate.)* 2. *(v.)* to give human form to *(The alien evaded detection by incarnating himself in a human form.)*

incendiary 1. *(n.)* a person who agitates *(If we catch the incendiary who screamed "bomb" in the middle of the soccer match, we're going to put him in jail.)* 2. *(adj.)* inflammatory, causing combustion *(Gas and lighter fluid are incendiary materials that should be kept out of hot storage areas.)*

incessant *(adj.)* unending *(We wanted to go outside and play, but the incessant rain kept us indoors for two days.)*

inchoate *(adj.)* unformed or formless, in a beginning stage *(The country's government is still inchoate and, because it has no great tradition, quite unstable.)*

incisive *(adj.)* clear, sharp, direct *(The discussion wasn't going anywhere until her incisive comment allowed everyone to see what the true issues were.)*

inclination *(n.)* a tendency, propensity *(Sarah has an inclination to see every foreign film she hears about, even when she's sure that she won't like it.)*

incontrovertible *(adj.)* indisputable *(Only stubborn Tina would attempt to disprove the incontrovertible laws of physics.)*

incorrigible *(adj.)* incapable of correction, delinquent *(You can buy Grandma nicotine gum all you want, but I think that after sixty-five years of smoking she's incorrigible.)*

increment *(n.)* an enlargement; the process of increasing *(The workmen made the wall longer, increment by increment.)*

incumbent 1. *(n.)* one who holds an office *(The incumbent senator is already serving his fifth term.)* 2. *(adj.)* obligatory *(It is incumbent upon this organization to offer aid to all who seek it.)*

indefatigable *(adj.)* incapable of defeat, failure, decay *(Even after traveling 62 miles, the indefatigable runner kept on moving.)*

indigenous *(adj.)* originating in a region *(Some fear that these plants, which are not indigenous to the region, may choke out the vegetation that is native to the area.)*

indigent *(adj.)* very poor, impoverished *(I would rather donate money to help the indigent population than to the park sculpture fund.)*

indignation *(n.)* anger sparked by something unjust or unfair *(I resigned from the sorority because of my indignation at its hazing of new members.)*

indolent (*adj.*) lazy (*Why should my <u>indolent</u> children, who can't even pick themselves up off the couch to pour their own juice, be rewarded with a trip to the mall?*)

indomitable (*adj.*) not capable of being conquered (*To be honest, Jim, my <u>indomitable</u> nature means I could never take orders from anyone, and especially not from a jerk like you.*)

induce (*v.*) to bring about, stimulate (*Who knew that our decision to boycott school lunch would <u>induce</u> a huge riot?*)

ineffable (*adj.*) unspeakable, incapable of being expressed through words (*It is said that the experience of playing with a dolphin is <u>ineffable</u> and can only be understood through direct encounter.*)

inept (*adj.*) not suitable or capable, unqualified (*She proved how <u>inept</u> she was when she forgot three orders and spilled a beer in a customer's lap.*)

inexorable (*adj.*) incapable of being persuaded or placated (*Although I begged for hours, Mom was <u>inexorable</u> and refused to let me stay out all night after the prom.*)

inextricable (*adj.*) hopelessly tangled or entangled (*Unless I look at the solution manual, I have no way of solving this <u>inextricable</u> problem.*)

infamy (*n.*) notoriety, extreme ill repute (*The <u>infamy</u> of his crime will not lessen as the decades pass.*)

infusion (*n.*) an injection of one substance into another; the permeation of one substance by another (*The <u>infusion</u> of Eastern religion into Western philosophy created interesting new schools of thought.*)

ingenious (*adj.*) clever, resourceful (*Her <u>ingenious</u> use of walnuts instead of the peanuts called for by the recipe was lauded by the other garden club members who found her cake delicious.*)

ingenuous (*adj.*) not devious; innocent and candid (*He must have writers, but his speeches seem so <u>ingenuous</u> it's hard to believe he's not speaking from his own heart.*)

inhibit (*v.*) to prevent, restrain, stop (*When I told you I needed the car last night, I certainly never meant to <u>inhibit</u> you from going out.*)

inimical (*adj.*) hostile, enemylike (*I don't see how I could ever work for a company that was so cold and <u>inimical</u> to me during my interviews.*)

iniquity (*n.*) wickedness or sin (*"Your <u>iniquity</u>," said the priest to the practical jokester, "will be forgiven."*)

injunction (*n.*) an order of official warning (*After his house was toilet-papered for the fifth time, the mayor issued an <u>injunction</u> against anyone younger than 21 buying toilet paper.*)

innate (*adj.*) inborn, native, inherent (*His incredible athletic talent is <u>innate</u>, he never trains, lifts weights, or practices.*)

innocuous (*adj.*) harmless, inoffensive (*In spite of their <u>innocuous</u> appearance, these mushrooms are actually quite poisonous.*)

innovate (*v.*) to do something in an unprecedented way (*Because of the stiff competition, the company knew it needed to pour a lot of energy into <u>innovating</u> new and better products.*)

innuendo (*n.*) an insinuation (*During the debate, the politician made several <u>innuendos</u> about the sexual activities of his opponent.*)

inoculate (*v.*) to introduce a microorganism, serum, or vaccine into an organism in order to increase immunity to illness; to vaccinate (*I've feared needles ever since I was <u>inoculated</u> against 37 diseases at age one; but I have also never been sick.*)

inquisitor (*n.*) one who inquires, especially in a hostile manner (*The <u>inquisitor</u> was instructed to knock on every door in town in order to find the fugitive.*)

insatiable (*adj.*) incapable of being satisfied (*My <u>insatiable</u> appetite for melons can be a real problem in the winter.*)

insidious (*adj.*) appealing but imperceptibly harmful, seductive (*Lisa's <u>insidious</u> chocolate cake tastes so good but makes you feel so sick later on!*)

insinuate (*v.*) to suggest indirectly or subtly (*I wish Luke and Spencer would stop <u>insinuating</u> that my perfect report card is the result of anything other than my superior intelligence and good work habits.*)

insipid (*adj.*) dull, boring (*The play was so <u>insipid</u>, I fell asleep halfway through.*)

insolent (*adj.*) rude, arrogant, overbearing (*That celebrity is so <u>insolent</u>, making fun of his fans right to their faces.*)

instigate (*v.*) to urge, goad (*The demagogue <u>instigated</u> the crowd into a fury by telling them that they had been cheated by the federal government.*)

insular (*adj.*) separated and narrow-minded; tight-knit, closed off (*Because of the sensitive nature of their jobs, those who work for the CIA must remain <u>insular</u> and generally only spend time with each other.*)

SAT Vocabulary

insurgent (n.) one who rebels (*The insurgent snuck into and defaced a different classroom each night until the administration agreed to meet his demands.*)

integral (adj.) necessary for completeness (*Without the integral ingredient of flour, you wouldn't be able to make bread.*)

interject (v.) to insert between other things (*During our conversation, the cab driver occasionally interjected his opinion.*)

interlocutor (n.) someone who participates in a dialogue or conversation (*When the officials could not come to an agreement over the correct cover of the flags, the prime minister acted as an interlocutor.*)

interminable (adj.) without possibility of end (*The fact that biology lectures came just before lunch made them seem interminable.*)

intimation (n.) an indirect suggestion (*Mr. Brinford's intimation that he would soon pass away occurred when he began to discuss how to distribute his belongings among his children.*)

intractable (adj.) difficult to manipulate, unmanageable (*There was no end in sight to the intractable conflict between the warring countries.*)

intransigent (adj.) refusing to compromise, often on an extreme opinion (*The intransigent child said he would have 12 scoops of ice cream, or he would bang his head against the wall until his mother fainted from fear.*)

intrepid (adj.) brave in the face of danger (*After scaling a live volcano prior to its eruption, the explorer was praised for his intrepid attitude.*)

inundate (v.) to flood with abundance (*Because I am the star of a new sitcom, my fans are sure to inundate me with fan mail and praise.*)

inure (v.) to cause someone or something to become accustomed to a situation (*Twenty years in the salt mines inured the man to the discomforts of dirt and grime.*)

invective (n.) an angry verbal attack (*My mother's irrational invective against the way I dress only made me decide to dye my hair green.*)

inveterate (adj.) stubbornly established by habit (*I'm the first to admit that I'm an inveterate coffee drinker—I drink four cups a day.*)

inviolable (adj.) secure from assault (*Nobody was ever able to break into Batman's inviolable Batcave.*)

irascible (adj.) easily angered (*At the smallest provocation, my irascible cat will begin scratching and clawing.*)

iridescent (*adj.*) showing rainbow colors (*The bride's large diamond ring was iridescent in the afternoon sun.*)

irreverence (*n.*) disrespect (*The irreverence displayed by the band that marched through the chapel disturbed many churchgoers.*)

irrevocable (*adj.*) incapable of being taken back (*The Bill of Rights is an irrevocable part of American law.*)

J

jubilant (*adj.*) extremely joyful, happy (*The crowd was jubilant when the firefighter carried the woman from the flaming building.*)

judicious (*adj.*) having or exercising sound judgment (*When the judicious king decided to compromise rather than send his army to its certain death, he was applauded.*)

juxtaposition (*n.*) the act of placing two things next to each other for implicit comparison (*The interior designer admired my juxtaposition of the yellow couch and green table.*)

K

knell (*n.*) the solemn sound of a bell, often indicating a death (*Echoing throughout our village, the funeral knell made the stormy day even more grim.*)

kudos (*n.*) praise for an achievement (*After the performance, the reviewers gave the opera singer kudos for a job well done.*)

L

laceration (*n.*) a cut, tear (*Because he fell off his bike into a rosebush, the paperboy's skin was covered with lacerations.*)

laconic (*adj.*) terse in speech or writing (*The author's laconic style has won him many followers who dislike wordiness.*)

languid (*adj.*) sluggish from fatigue or weakness (*In the summer months, the great heat makes people languid and lazy.*)

larceny (*n.*) obtaining another's property by theft or trickery (*When my car was not where I had left it, I realized that I was a victim of larceny.*)

largess (*n.*) the generous giving of lavish gifts (*My boss demonstrated great largess by giving me a new car.*)

latent *(adj.)* hidden, but capable of being exposed (*Sigmund's dream represented his latent paranoid obsession with other people's shoes.*)

laudatory *(adj.)* expressing admiration or praise (*Such laudatory comments are unusual from someone who is usually so reserved in his opinions.*)

lavish 1. *(adj.)* given without limits (*Because they had worked very hard, the performers appreciated the critic's lavish praise.*) 2. *(v.)* to give without limits (*Because the performers had worked hard, they deserved the praise that the critic lavished on them.*)

legerdemain *(n.)* deception, slight-of-hand (*Smuggling the French plants through customs by claiming that they were fake was a remarkable bit of legerdemain.*)

lenient *(adj.)* demonstrating tolerance or gentleness (*Because Professor Oglethorpe allowed his students to choose their final grades, the other teachers believed that he was excessively lenient.*)

lethargic *(adj.)* in a state of sluggishness or apathy (*When Jean Claude explained to his boss that he was lethargic and didn't feel like working that day, the boss fired him.*)

liability 1. *(n.)* something for which one is legally responsible, usually involving a disadvantage or risk (*The bungee-jumping tower was a great liability for the owners of the carnival.*) 2. *(n.)* a handicap, burden (*Because she often lost her concentration and didn't play defense, Marcy was a liability to the team.*)

libertarian *(adj.)* advocating principles of liberty and free will (*The dissatisfied subjects overthrew the monarch and replaced him with a libertarian ruler who respected their democratic principles.*)

licentious *(adj.)* displaying a lack of moral or legal restraints (*Marilee has always been fascinated by the licentious private lives of politicians.*)

limpid *(adj.)* clear, transparent (*Mr. Johnson's limpid writing style greatly pleased readers who disliked complicated novels.*)

linchpin *(n.)* something that holds separate parts together (*The linchpin in the prosecution's case was the hair from the defendant's head, which was found at the scene of the crime.*)

lithe *(adj.)* graceful, flexible, supple (*Although the dancers were all outstanding, Jae Sun's control of her lithe body was particularly impressive.*)

litigant *(n.)* someone engaged in a lawsuit (*When the litigants began screaming at each other, Judge Koch ordered them to be silent.*)

lucid *(adj.)* clear, easily understandable (*Because Guenevere's essay was so <u>lucid</u>, I only had to read it once to understand her reasoning.*)

luminous *(adj.)* brightly shining (*The light of the <u>luminous</u> moon graced the shoulders of the beautiful maiden.*)

lurid *(adj.)* ghastly, sensational (*Gideon's story, in which he described a character torturing his sister's dolls, was judged too <u>lurid</u> to be printed in the school's literary magazine.*)

M

maelstrom *(n.)* a destructive whirlpool which rapidly sucks in objects (*Little did the explorers know that as they turned the next bend of the calm river a vicious <u>maelstrom</u> would catch their boat.*)

magnanimous *(adj.)* noble, generous (*Although I had already broken most of her dishes, Jacqueline was <u>magnanimous</u> enough to continue letting me use them.*)

malediction *(n.)* a curse (*When I was arrested for speeding, I screamed <u>maledictions</u> against the policeman and the entire police department.*)

malevolent *(adj.)* wanting harm to befall others (*The <u>malevolent</u> old man sat in the park all day, tripping unsuspecting passersby with his cane.*)

malleable *(adj.)* capable of being shaped or transformed (*Maximillian's political opinions were so <u>malleable</u> that anyone he talked to was able to change his mind instantly.*)

mandate *(n.)* an authoritative command (*In the Old Testament, God <u>mandates</u> that no one should steal.*)

manifest 1. *(adj.)* easily understandable, obvious (*When I wrote the wrong sum on the chalkboard, my mistake was so <u>manifest</u> that the entire class burst into laughter.*) 2. *(v.)* to show plainly (*His illness first <u>manifested</u> itself with particularly violent hiccups.*)

manifold *(adj.)* diverse, varied (*The popularity of Dante's Inferno is partly due to the fact that the work allows for <u>manifold</u> interpretations.*)

maudlin *(adj.)* weakly sentimental (*Although many people enjoy romantic comedies, I usually find them <u>maudlin</u> and shallow.*)

maverick *(n.)* an independent, nonconformist person (*Andreas is a real <u>maverick</u> and always does things his own way.*)

mawkish (adj.) characterized by sick sentimentality (Although some nineteenth-century critics viewed Dickens's writing as mawkish, contemporary readers have found great emotional depth in his works.)

maxim (n.) a common saying expressing a principle of conduct (Miss Manners's etiquette maxims are both entertaining and instructional.)

meager (adj.) deficient in size or quality (My meager portion of food did nothing to satisfy my appetite.)

medley (n.) a mixture of differing things (Susannah's wardrobe contained an astonishing medley of colors, from olive green to fluorescent pink.)

mendacious (adj.) having a lying, false character (The mendacious content of the tabloid magazines is at least entertaining.)

mercurial (adj.) characterized by rapid change or temperamentality (Though he was widely respected for his mathematical proofs, the mercurial genius was impossible to live with.)

meritorious (adj.) worthy of esteem or reward (Manfred was given the congressional medal of honor for his meritorious actions.)

metamorphosis (n.) the change of form, shape, substance (Winnifred went to the gym every day for a year and underwent a metamorphosis from a waiflike girl to an athletic woman.)

meticulous (adj.) extremely careful with details (The ornate needlework in the bride's gown was a product of meticulous handiwork.)

mitigate (v.) to make less violent, alleviate (When I had an awful sore throat, only warm tea would mitigate the pain.)

moderate 1. (adj.) not extreme (Luckily, the restaurant we chose had moderate prices; none of us have any money.) 2. (n.) one who expresses moderate opinions (Because he found both the liberal and conservative proposals too excessive, Mr. Park sided with the moderates.)

modicum (n.) a small amount of something (Refusing to display even a modicum of sensitivity, Henrietta announced her boss's affair in front of the entire office.)

modulate (v.) to pass from one state to another, especially in music (The composer wrote a piece that modulated between minor and major keys.)

mollify (v.) to soften in temper (The police officer mollified the angry woman by giving her a warning instead of a ticket.)

morass *(n.)* a wet swampy bog; figuratively, something that traps and confuses *(When Theresa lost her job, she could not get out of her financial morass.)*

mores *(n.)* the moral attitudes and fixed customs of a group of people. *(Mores change over time; many things that were tolerated in 1975 are no longer seen as being socially acceptable.)*

morose *(adj.)* gloomy or sullen *(Jason's morose nature made him very unpleasant to talk to.)*

multifarious *(adj.)* having great diversity or variety *(This Swiss Army knife has multifarious functions and capabilities. Among other things, it can act as a knife, a saw, a toothpick, and a slingshot.)*

mundane *(adj.)* concerned with the world rather than with heaven, commonplace *(He is more concerned with the mundane issues of day-to-day life than with spiritual topics.)*

munificence *(n.)* generosity in giving *(The royal family's munificence made everyone else in their country rich.)*

mutable *(adj.)* able to change *(Because fashion is so mutable, what is trendy today will look outdated in five years.)*

myriad *(adj.)* consisting of a very great number *(It was difficult to decide what to do Friday night because the city presented us with myriad possibilities for fun.)*

N

nadir *(n.)* the lowest point of something *(My day was boring, but the nadir came when I accidentally spilled a bowl of spaghetti on my head.)*

nascent *(adj.)* in the process of being born or coming into existence *(Unfortunately, my brilliant paper was only in its nascent form on the morning that it was due.)*

nebulous *(adj.)* vaguely defined, cloudy *(The transition between governments meant that who was actually in charge was a nebulous matter.)*

nefarious *(adj.)* heinously villainous *(Although Dr. Meanman's nefarious plot to melt the polar icecaps was terrifying, it was so impractical that nobody really worried about it.)*

negligent *(adj.)* habitually careless, neglectful *(Jessie's grandfather called me a negligent fool after I left the door to his apartment unlocked even though there had been a recent string of robberies.)*

neophyte (*n.*) someone who is young or inexperienced (*As a neophyte in the literary world, Malik had trouble finding a publisher for his first novel.*)

nocturnal (*adj.*) relating to or occurring during the night (*Jackie was a nocturnal person; she would study until dawn and sleep until the evening.*)

noisome (*adj.*) unpleasant, offensive, especially to the sense of smell (*Nobody would enter the stalls until the horse's noisome leavings were taken away.*)

nomadic (*adj.*) wandering from place to place (*In the first six months after college, Jose led a nomadic life, living in New York, California, and Idaho.*)

nominal (*adj.*) trifling, insignificant (*Because he was moving the following week and needed to get rid of his furniture more than he needed money, Jordan sold everything for a nominal fee.*)

nonchalant (*adj.*) having a lack of concern, indifference (*Although deep down she was very angry, Marsha acted in a nonchalant manner when she found out that her best friend had used her clothing without asking.*)

nondescript (*adj.*) lacking a distinctive character (*I was surprised when I saw the movie star in person because she looked nondescript.*)

notorious (*adj.*) widely and unfavorably known (*Jacob was notorious for always arriving late at parties.*)

novice (*n.*) a beginner, someone without training or experience (*Because we were all novices at yoga, our instructor decided to begin with the basics.*)

noxious (*adj.*) harmful, unwholesome (*Environmentalists showed that the noxious weeds were destroying the insects' natural habitats.*)

nuance (*n.*) a slight variation in meaning, tone, expression (*The nuances of the poem were not obvious to the casual reader, but the professor was able to point them out.*)

nurture (*v.*) to assist the development of (*Although Serena had never watered the plant, which was about to die, Javier was able to nurture it back to life.*)

O

obdurate (*adj.*) unyielding to persuasion or moral influences (*The obdurate old man refused to take pity on the kittens.*)

obfuscate (*v.*) to render incomprehensible (*The detective did want to answer the newspaperman's questions, so he obfuscated the truth.*)

oblique *(adj.)* diverging from a straight line or course, not straightforward *(Martin's oblique language confused those who listened to him.)*

oblivious *(adj.)* lacking consciousness or awareness of something *(Oblivious to the burning smell emanating from the kitchen, my father did not notice that the rolls in the oven were burned until much too late.)*

obscure *(adj.)* unclear, partially hidden *(Because he was standing in the shadows, his features were obscure.)*

obsequious *(adj.)* excessively compliant or submissive *(Mark acted like Janet's servant, obeying her every request in an obsequious manner.)*

obsolete *(adj.)* no longer used, out of date *(With the inventions of tape decks and CDs, which both have better sound and are easier to use, eight-track players are now entirely obsolete.)*

obstinate *(adj.)* not yielding easily, stubborn *(The obstinate child refused to leave the store until his mother bought him a candy bar.)*

obstreperous *(adj.)* noisy, unruly *(Billy's obstreperous behavior prompted the librarian to ask him to leave the reading room.)*

obtuse *(adj.)* lacking quickness of sensibility or intellect *(Political opponents warned that the prime minister's obtuse approach to foreign policy would embroil the nation in mindless war.)*

odious *(adj.)* instilling hatred or intense displeasure *(Mark was assigned the odious task of cleaning the cat's litter box.)*

officious *(adj.)* offering one's services when they are neither wanted nor needed *(Brenda resented Allan's officious behavior when he selected colors that might best improve her artwork.)*

ominous *(adj.)* foreboding or foreshadowing evil *(The fortuneteller's ominous words flashed through my mind as the hooded figure approached me in the alley.)*

onerous *(adj.)* burdensome *(My parents lamented that the pleasures of living in a beautiful country estate no longer outweighed the onerous mortgage payments.)*

opulent *(adj.)* characterized by rich abundance verging on ostentation *(The opulent furnishings of the dictator's private compound contrasted harshly with the meager accommodations of her subjects.)*

oration (*n.*) a speech delivered in a formal or ceremonious manner (*The prime minister was visibly shaken when the unruly parliament interrupted his oration about failed domestic policies.*)

ornate (*adj.*) highly elaborate, excessively decorated (*The ornate styling of the new model of luxury car could not compensate for the poor quality of its motor.*)

orthodox (*adj.*) conventional, conforming to established protocol (*The company's profits dwindled because the management pursued orthodox business policies that were incompatible with new industrial trends.*)

oscillate (*v.*) to sway from one side to the other (*My uncle oscillated between buying a station wagon to transport his family and buying a sports car to satisfy his boyhood fantasies.*)

ostensible (*adj.*) appearing as such, seemingly (*Jack's ostensible reason for driving was that airfare was too expensive, but in reality, he was afraid of flying.*)

ostentatious (*adj.*) excessively showy, glitzy (*On the palace tour, the guide focused on the ostentatious decorations and spoke little of the royal family's history.*)

ostracism (*n.*) exclusion from a group (*Beth risked ostracism if her roommates discovered her flatulence.*)

P

pacific (*adj.*) soothing (*The chemistry professor's pacific demeanor helped the class remain calm after the experiment exploded.*)

palatable (*adj.*) agreeable to the taste or sensibilities (*Despite the unpleasant smell, the exotic cheese was quite palatable.*)

palette (*adj.*) a range of colors or qualities (*The palette of colors utilized in the painting was equaled only by the range of intense emotions the piece evoked.*)

palliate (*v.*) to reduce the severity of (*The doctor trusted that the new medication would palliate her patient's discomfort.*)

pallid (*adj.*) lacking color (*Dr. Van Helsing feared that Lucy's pallid complexion was due to an unexplained loss of blood.*)

panacea (*n.*) a remedy for all ills or difficulties (*Doctors wish there was a single panacea for every disease, but sadly there is not.*)

paradigm (*n.*) an example that is a perfect pattern or model (*Because the new SUV was so popular, it became the paradigm upon which all others were modeled.*)

paradox *(n.)* an apparently contradictory statement that is perhaps true *(The diplomat refused to acknowledge the paradox that negotiating a peace treaty would demand more resources than waging war.)*

paragon *(n.)* a model of excellence or perfection *(The mythical Helen of Troy was considered a paragon of female beauty.)*

paramount *(adj.)* greatest in importance, rank, character *(It was paramount that the bomb squad disconnect the blue wire before removing the fuse.)*

pariah *(n.)* an outcast *(Following the discovery of his plagiarism, Professor Hurley was made a pariah in all academic circles.)*

parody *(n.)* a satirical imitation *(A hush fell over the classroom when the teacher returned to find Deborah acting out a parody of his teaching style.)*

parsimony *(n.)* frugality, stinginess *(Many relatives believed that my aunt's wealth resulted from her parsimony.)*

partisan *(n.)* a follower, adherent *(The king did not believe that his rival could round up enough partisans to overthrow the monarchy.)*

patent *(adj.)* readily seen or understood, clear *(The reason for Jim's abdominal pain was made patent after the doctor performed a sonogram.)*

pathology *(n.)* a deviation from the normal *(Dr. Hastings had difficulty identifying the precise nature of Brian's pathology.)*

pathos *(n.)* an emotion of sympathy *(Martha filled with pathos upon discovering the scrawny, shivering kitten at her door.)*

paucity *(adj.)* small in quantity *(Gilbert lamented the paucity of twentieth century literature courses available at the college.)*

pejorative *(adj.)* derogatory, uncomplimentary *(The evening's headline news covered an international scandal caused by a pejorative statement the famous senator had made in reference to a foreign leader.)*

pellucid *(adj.)* easily intelligible, clear *(Wishing his book to be pellucid to the common man, Albert Camus avoided using complicated grammar when composing The Stranger.)*

penchant *(n.)* a tendency, partiality, preference *(Jill's dinner parties quickly became monotonous on account of her penchant for Mexican dishes.)*

penitent *(adj.)* remorseful, regretful *(The jury's verdict may have been more lenient if the criminal had appeared penitent for his gruesome crimes.)*

penultimate (*adj.*) next to last (*Having smoked the* penultimate *cigarette remaining in the pack, Cybil discarded the last cigarette and resolved to quit smoking.*)

penurious (*adj.*) miserly, stingy (*Stella complained that her husband's* penurious *ways made it impossible to live the lifestyle she felt she deserved.*)

perfidious (*adj.*) disloyal, unfaithful (*After the official was caught selling government secrets to enemy agents, he was executed for his* perfidious *ways.*)

perfunctory (*adj.*) showing little interest or enthusiasm (*The radio broadcaster announced the news of the massacre in a surprisingly* perfunctory *manner.*)

permeate (*v.*) to spread throughout, saturate (*Mrs. Huxtable was annoyed that the wet dog's odor had* permeated *the furniture's upholstery.*)

pernicious (*adj.*) extremely destructive or harmful (*The new government feared that the Communist sympathizers would have a* pernicious *influence on the nation's stability.*)

perplex (*v.*) to confuse (*Brad was* perplexed *by his girlfriend's suddenly distant manner.*)

perspicacity (*adj.*) shrewdness, perceptiveness (*The detective was too humble to acknowledge that his* perspicacity *was the reason for his professional success.*)

pert (*adj.*) flippant, bold (*My parents forgave Sandra's* pert *humor at the dinner table because it had been so long since they had last seen her.*)

pertinacious (*adj.*) stubbornly persistent (*Harry's parents were frustrated with his* pertinacious *insistence that a monster lived in his closet. Then they opened the closet door and were eaten.*)

perusal (*n.*) a careful examination, review (*The actor agreed to accept the role after a two-month* perusal *of the movie script.*)

pervasive (*adj.*) having the tendency to spread throughout (*Stepping off the plane in Havana, I recognized the* pervasive *odor of sugar cane fields on fire.*)

petulance (*n.*) rudeness, irritability (*The Nanny resigned after she could no longer tolerate the child's* petulance*.*)

philanthropic (*adj.*) charitable, giving (*Many people felt that the billionaire's decision to donate her fortune to house the homeless was the ultimate* philanthropic *act.*)

phlegmatic (*adj.*) uninterested, unresponsive (*Monique feared her dog was ill after the animal's* phlegmatic *response to his favorite chew toy.*)

SAT Vocabulary

pillage (*v.*) to seize or plunder, especially in war (*Invading enemy soldiers pillaged the homes scattered along the country's border.*)

pinnacle (*n.*) the highest point (*Book reviewers declared that the author's new novel was extraordinary and probably the pinnacle of Western literature.*)

pithy (*adj.*) concisely meaningful (*My father's long-winded explanation was a stark contrast to his usually pithy statements.*)

pittance (*n.*) a very small amount, especially relating to money (*Josh complained that he was paid a pittance for the great amount of work he did at the firm.*)

placate (*v.*) to ease the anger of, soothe (*The man purchased a lollipop to placate his irritable son.*)

placid (*adj.*) calm, peaceful (*The placid lake surface was as smooth as glass.*)

platitude (*n.*) an uninspired remark, cliché (*After reading over her paper, Helene concluded that what she thought were profound insights were actually just platitudes.*)

plaudits (*n.*) enthusiastic approval, applause (*The controversial new film received plaudits from even the harshest critics.*)

plausible (*adj.*) believable, reasonable (*He studied all the data and then came up with a plausible theory that took all factors into account.*)

plenitude (*n.*) an abundance (*My grandmother was overwhelmed by the plenitude of tomatoes her garden yielded this season.*)

plethora (*n.*) an abundance, excess (*The wedding banquet included a plethora of oysters piled almost three feet high.*)

pliable (*adj.*) flexible (*Aircraft wings are designed to be somewhat pliable so they do not break in heavy turbulence.*)

poignant (*adj.*) deeply affecting, moving (*My teacher actually cried after reading to us the poignant final chapter of the novel.*)

polemic (*n.*) an aggressive argument against a specific opinion (*My brother launched into a polemic against my arguments that capitalism was an unjust economic system.*)

portent (*n.*) an omen (*When a black cat crossed my sister's path while she was walking to school, she took it as a portent that she would do badly on her spelling test.*)

SAT Vocabulary

potable (*adj.*) suitable for drinking (*During sea voyages it is essential that ships carry a supply of* <u>potable</u> *water because salty ocean water makes anyone who drinks it sick.*)

potentate (*n.*) one who has great power, a ruler (*All the villagers stood along the town's main road to observe as the* <u>potentate's</u> *procession headed towards the capital.*)

pragmatic (*adj.*) practical (*The politician argued that while increased security measures might not fit with the lofty ideals of the nation, they were a* <u>pragmatic</u> *necessity to ensure everyone's safety.*)

precipice (*n.*) the face of a cliff, a steep or overhanging place (*The mountain climber hung from a* <u>precipice</u> *before finding a handhold and pulling himself up.*)

preclude (*v.*) to prevent (*My grandfather's large and vicious guard dog* <u>precluded</u> *anyone from entering the yard.*)

precocious (*adj.*) advanced, developing ahead of time (*Derek was so academically* <u>precocious</u> *that by the time he was 10 years old, he was already in the ninth grade.*)

predilection (*n.*) a preference or inclination for something (*Francois has a* <u>predilection</u> *for eating scrambled eggs with ketchup, though I prefer to eat eggs without any condiments.*)

preponderance (*adj.*) superiority in importance or quantity (*Britain's* <u>preponderance</u> *of naval might secured the nation's role as a military power.*)

prepossessing (*adj.*) occupying the mind to the exclusion of other thoughts or feelings (*His* <u>prepossessing</u> *appearance made it impossible for me to think of anything else.*)

presage (*n.*) an omen (*When my uncle's old war injury ached, he interpreted it as a* <u>presage</u> *of bad weather approaching.*)

prescient (*adj.*) to have foreknowledge of events (*Questioning the fortune cookie's prediction, Ray went in search of the old hermit who was rumored to be* <u>prescient</u>.*)

prescribe (*v.*) to lay down a rule (*The duke* <u>prescribed</u> *that from this point further all of the peasants living on his lands would have to pay higher taxes.*)

presumptuous (*adj.*) disrespectfully bold (*The princess grew angry after the* <u>presumptuous</u> *noble tried to kiss her, even though he was far below her in social status.*)

pretense *(n.)* an appearance or action intended to deceive *(Though he actually wanted to use his parents' car to go on a date, Nick borrowed his parents' car under the pretense of attending a group study session.)*

primeval *(adj.)* original, ancient *(The first primates to walk on two legs, called Australopithecus, were the primeval descendants of modern man.)*

privation *(n.)* lacking basic necessities *(After decades of rule by an oppressive government that saw nothing wrong with stealing from its citizens, the recent drought only increased the people's privation.)*

probity *(n.)* virtue, integrity *(Because he was never viewed as a man of great probity, no one was surprised by Mr. Samson's immoral behavior.)*

proclivity *(n.)* a strong inclination toward something *(In a sick twist of fate, Harold's childhood proclivity for torturing small animals grew into a desire to become a surgeon.)*

procure *(v.)* to obtain, acquire *(The FBI was unable to procure sufficient evidence to charge the gangster with racketeering.)*

profane *(adj.)* lewd, indecent *(Jacob's profane act of dumping frogs in the holy water in the chapel at his boarding school resulted in his dismissal.)*

profligate *(adj.)* dissolute, extravagant *(The profligate gambler loved to drink, spend money, steal, cheat, and hang out with prostitutes.)*

profuse *(adj.)* plentiful, abundant *(The fans were profuse in their cheers for the star basketball player.)*

promulgate *(v.)* to proclaim, make known *(The film professor promulgated that both in terms of sex appeal and political intrigue, Sean Connery's James Bond was superior to Roger Moore's.)*

propagate *(v.)* to multiply, spread out *(Rumors of Paul McCartney's demise propagated like wildfire throughout the world.)*

propensity *(n.)* an inclination, preference *(Dermit has a propensity for dangerous activities such as bungee jumping.)*

propitious *(adj.)* favorable *(The dark storm clouds visible on the horizon suggested that the weather would not be propitious for sailing.)*

propriety *(n.)* the quality or state of being proper, decent *(Erma's old-fashioned parents believed that her mini-skirt lacked the propriety expected of a "nice" girl.)*

prosaic (*adj.*) plain, lacking liveliness (*Heather's prosaic recital of the poem bored the audience.*)

proscribe (*v.*) to condemn, outlaw (*The town council voted to proscribe the sale of alcohol on weekends.*)

protean (*adj.*) able to change shape; displaying great variety (*Among Nigel's protean talents was his ability to touch the tip of his nose with his tongue.*)

prowess (*n.*) extraordinary ability (*The musician had never taken a guitar lesson in his life, making his prowess with the instrument even more incredible.*)

prudence (*n.*) cautious, circumspect (*After losing a fortune in a stock market crash, my father vowed to practice greater prudence in future investments.*)

prurient (*adj.*) eliciting or possessing an extraordinary interest in sex (*David's mother was shocked by the discovery of prurient reading material hidden beneath her son's mattress.*)

puerile (*adj.*) juvenile, immature (*The judge demanded order after the lawyer's puerile attempt to object by stomping his feet on the courtroom floor.*)

pugnacious (*adj.*) quarrelsome, combative (*Aaron's pugnacious nature led him to start several barroom brawls each month.*)

pulchritude (*n.*) physical beauty (*Several of Shakespeare's sonnets explore the pulchritude of a lovely young man.*)

punctilious (*adj.*) eager to follow rules or conventions (*Punctilious Bobby, hall monitor extraordinaire, insisted that his peers follow the rules.*)

pungent (*adj.*) having a pointed, sharp quality—often used to describe smells (*The pungent odor in the classroom made Joseph lose his concentration during the test.*)

punitive (*adj.*) involving punishment (*If caught smoking in the boys' room, the punitive result is immediate expulsion from school.*)

putrid (*adj.*) rotten, foul (*Those rotten eggs smell putrid.*)

Q

quagmire (*n.*) a difficult situation (*We'd all like to avoid the kind of military quagmire characterized by the Vietnam War.*)

quaint (*adj.*) charmingly old-fashioned (*Hilda was delighted by the quaint bonnets she saw in Amish country.*)

quandary *(n.)* a perplexed, unresolvable state *(Carlos found himself in a quandary: should he choose mint chocolate chip or cookie dough?)*

quell *(v.)* to control or diffuse a potentially explosive situation *(The skilled leader deftly quelled the rebellion.)*

querulous *(adj.)* whiny, complaining *(If deprived of his pacifier, young Brendan becomes querulous.)*

quixotic *(adj.)* idealistic, impractical *(Edward entertained a quixotic desire to fall in love at first sight in a laundromat.)*

quotidian *(adj.)* daily *(Ambika's quotidian routines include drinking two cups of coffee in the morning.)*

R

rail *(v.)* to scold, protest *(The professor railed against the injustice of the college's tenure policy.)*

rancid *(adj.)* having a terrible taste or smell *(Rob was double-dog-dared to eat the rancid egg salad sandwich.)*

rancor *(n.)* deep, bitter resentment *(When Eileen challenged me to a fight, I could see the rancor in her eyes.)*

rapport *(n.)* mutual understanding and harmony *(When Margaret met her paramour, they felt an instant rapport.)*

rash *(adj.)* hasty, incautious *(It's best to think things over calmly and thoroughly, rather than make rash decisions.)*

raucous *(adj.)* loud, boisterous *(Sarah's neighbors called the cops when her house party got too raucous.)*

raze *(v.)* to demolish, level *(The old tenement house was razed to make room for the large chain store.)*

rebuke *(v.)* to scold, criticize *(When the cops showed up at Sarah's party, they rebuked her for disturbing the peace.)*

recalcitrant *(adj.)* defiant, unapologetic *(Even when scolded, the recalcitrant young girl simply stomped her foot and refused to finish her lima beans.)*

recapitulate *(v.)* to sum up, repeat *(Before the final exam, the teacher recapitulated the semester's material.)*

SAT Vocabulary

reciprocate (v.) to give in return (*When Steve gave Samantha a sweater for Christmas, she reciprocated by giving him a kiss.*)

reclusive (adj.) solitary, shunning society (*Reclusive authors such as J.D. Salinger do not relish media attention and sometimes even enjoy holing up in remote cabins in the woods.*)

reconcile 1. (v.) to return to harmony (*The feuding neighbors finally reconciled when one brought the other a delicious tuna noodle casserole.*) 2. (v.) to make consistent with existing ideas (*Alou had to reconcile his skepticism about the existence of aliens with the fact that he was looking at a flying saucer.*)

rectitude (n.) uprightness, extreme morality (*The priest's rectitude gave him the moral authority to counsel his parishioners.*)

redoubtable 1. (adj.) formidable (*The fortress looked redoubtable set against a stormy sky.*) 2. (adj.) commanding respect (*The audience greeted the redoubtable speaker with a standing ovation.*)

refract (v.) to distort, change (*The light was refracted as it passed through the prism.*)

refurbish (v.) to restore, clean up (*The dingy old chair, after being refurbished, commanded the handsome price of $200.*)

refute (v.) to prove wrong (*Maria refuted the president's argument as she yelled and gesticulated at the TV.*)

regurgitate 1. (v.) to vomit (*Feeling sick, Chuck regurgitated his dinner.*) 2. (v.) to throw back exactly (*Margaret rushed through the test, regurgitating all of the facts she'd memorized an hour earlier.*)

relegate 1. (v.) to assign to the proper place (*At the astrology conference, Simon was relegated to the Scorpio room.*) 2. (v.) to assign to an inferior place (*After spilling a drink on a customer's shirt, the waiter found himself relegated to the least lucrative shift.*)

relish (v.) to enjoy (*Pete always relished his bedtime snack.*)

remedial (adj.) intended to repair gaps in students' basic knowledge (*After his teacher discovered he couldn't read, Alex was forced to enroll in remedial English.*)

remiss (adj.) negligent, failing to take care (*The burglar gained entrance because the security guard, remiss in his duties, forgot to lock the door.*)

renovate 1. (*v.*) restore, return to original state (*The renovated antique candelabra looked as good as new.*) 2. (*v.*) to enlarge and make prettier, especially a house (*After getting renovated, the house was twice as big and much more attractive.*)

renown (*n.*) honor, acclaim (*The young writer earned international renown by winning the Pulitzer Prize.*)

renunciation (*n.*) to reject (*Fiona's renunciation of red meat resulted in weight loss, but confused those people who thought she'd been a vegetarian for years.*)

repentant (*adj.*) penitent, sorry (*The repentant Dennis apologized profusely for breaking his mother's vase.*)

replete (*adj.*) full, abundant (*The unedited version was replete with naughty words.*)

repose (*v.*) to rest, lie down (*The cat, after eating an entire can of tuna fish, reposed in the sun and took a long nap.*)

reprehensible (*adj.*) deserving rebuke (*Jean's cruel and reprehensible attempt to dump her boyfriend on his birthday led to tears and recriminations.*)

reprieve (*n.*) a temporary delay of punishment (*Because the governor woke up in a particularly good mood, he granted hundreds of reprieves to prisoners.*)

reproach (*v.*) to scold, disapprove (*Brian reproached the customer for failing to rewind the video he had rented.*)

reprobate (*adj.*) evil, unprincipled (*The reprobate criminal sat sneering in the cell.*)

reprove (*v.*) to scold, rebuke (*Lara reproved her son for sticking each and every one of his fingers into the strawberry pie.*)

repudiate (*v.*) to reject, refuse to accept (*Kwame made a strong case for an extension of his curfew, but his mother repudiated it with a few biting words.*)

repulse 1. (*v.*) to disgust (*Antisocial Annie tried to repulse people by neglecting to brush her teeth.*) 2. (*v.*) to push back (*With a deft movement of her wrist and a punch to the stomach, Lacy repulsed Jack's attempt to kiss her.*)

reputable (*adj.*) of good reputation (*After the most reputable critic in the industry gave the novel a glowing review, sales took off.*)

requisition (*n.*) a demand for goods, usually made by an authority (*During the war, the government made a requisition of supplies.*)

rescind (*v.*) to take back, repeal (*The company rescinded its offer of employment after discovering that Jane's resume was full of lies.*)

reservoir 1. *(n.)* reserves, large supply *(Igor the Indomitable had quite a reservoir of strengh and could lift ten tons, even after running 700 miles, jumping over three mountains, and swimming across an ocean.)* 2. *(n.)* a body of water used for storing water *(After graduation, the more rebellious members of the senior class jumped into the town reservoir used for drinking water.)*

resilient *(adj.)* able to recover from misfortune; able to withstand adversity *(The resilient ballplayer quickly recovered from his wrist injury.)*

resolute *(adj.)* firm, determined *(With a resolute glint in her eye, Catherine announced that she was set on going to college in New York City even though she was a little frightened of tall buildings.)*

resolve 1. *(v.)* to find a solution *(Sarah and Emma resolved their differences and shook hands.)* 2. *(v.)* to firmly decide *(Lady Macbeth resolved to whip her husband into shape.)*

respite *(n.)* a break, rest *(Justin left the pub to gain a brief respite from the smoke and noise.)*

resplendent *(adj.)* shiny, glowing *(The partygoers were resplendent in diamonds and fancy dress.)*

restitution *(n.)* restoration to the rightful owner *(Many people feel that descendants of slaves should receive restitution for the sufferings of their ancestors.)*

restive *(adj.)* resistant, stubborn, impatient *(The restive audience pelted the band with mud and yelled nasty comments.)*

retract *(v.)* withdraw *(As the media worked itself into a frenzy, the publicist hurriedly retracted his client's sexist statement.)*

revel *(v.)* to enjoy intensely *(Theodore reveled in his new status as Big Man on Campus.)*

revere *(v.)* to esteem, show deference, venerate *(The doctor saved countless lives with his combination of expertise and kindness and became universally revered.)*

revoke *(v.)* to take back *(After missing the curfew set by the court for eight nights in a row, Marcel's freedom of movement was revoked.)*

rhapsodize *(v.)* to engage in excessive enthusiasm *(The critic rhapsodized about the movie, calling it an instant classic.)*

ribald *(adj.)* coarsely, crudely humorous *(While some giggled at the ribald joke involving a parson's daughter, most sighed and rolled their eyes.)*

rife *(adj.)* abundant *(Surprisingly, the famous novelist's writing was rife with spelling errors.)*

ruminate *(v.)* to contemplate, reflect *(Terry liked to ruminate while sitting on the banks of the river, staring pensively into the water.)*

ruse *(n.)* a trick *(Oliver concocted an elaborate ruse for sneaking out of the house to meet his girlfriend while simultaneously giving his mother the impression that he was asleep in bed.)*

S

saccharine *(adj.)* sickeningly sweet *(Tom's saccharine manner, although intended to make him popular, actually repelled his classmates.)*

sacrosanct *(adj.)* holy, something that should not be criticized *(In the United States, the Constitution is often thought of as a sacrosanct document.)*

sagacity *(n.)* shrewdness, soundness of perspective *(With remarkable sagacity, the wise old man predicted and thwarted his children's plan to ship him off to a nursing home.)*

salient *(adj.)* significant, conspicuous *(One of the salient differences between Alison and Nancy is that Alison is a foot taller.)*

salutation *(n.)* a greeting *(Andrew regularly began letters with the bizarre salutation "Ahoy ahoy.")*

salve *(n.)* a soothing balm *(After Tony applied a salve to his brilliant red sunburn, he soon felt a little better.)*

sanctimonious *(adj.)* giving a hypocritical appearance of piety *(The sanctimonious Bertrand delivered stern lectures on the Ten Commandments to anyone who would listen, but thought nothing of stealing cars to make some cash on the side.)*

sanguine *(adj.)* optimistic, cheery *(Polly reacted to any bad news with a sanguine smile and the chirpy cry, "When life hands you lemons, make lemonade!")*

satiate *(v.)* to satisfy excessively *(Satiated after eating far too much turkey and stuffing, Liza lay on the couch watching football and suffering from stomach pains.)*

scathing *(adj.)* sharp, critical, hurtful *(Two hours after breaking up with Russell, Suzanne thought of the perfect scathing retort to his accusations.)*

scintillating (*adj.*) sparkling (*The ice skater's scintillating rhinestone costume nearly blinded the judges.*)

scrupulous (*adj.*) painstaking, careful (*With scrupulous care, Sam cut a snowflake out of white paper.*)

scurrilous (*adj.*) vulgar, coarse (*When Bruno heard the scurrilous accusation being made about him, he could not believe it because he always tried to be nice to everyone.*)

sedentary (*adj.*) sitting, settled (*The sedentary cat did little but loll in the sun.*)

semaphore (*n.*) a visual signal (*Anne and Diana communicated with a semaphore involving candles and window shades.*)

seminal (*adj.*) original, important, creating a field (*Stephen Greenblatt's essays on Shakespeare proved to be seminal, because they initiated the critical school of New Historicism.*)

sensual (*adj.*) involving sensory gratification, usually related to sex (*With a coy smile, the guest on the blind-date show announced that he considered himself a very sensual person.*)

sensuous (*adj.*) involving sensory gratification (*Paul found drinking Coke, with all the little bubbles bursting on his tongue, a very sensuous experience.*)

serendipity (*n.*) luck, finding good things without looking for them (*In an amazing bit of serendipity, penniless Paula found a $20 bill in the subway station.*)

serene (*adj.*) calm, untroubled (*Louise stood in front of the Mona Lisa, puzzling over the famous woman's serene smile.*)

servile (*adj.*) subservient (*The servile porter crept around the hotel lobby, bowing and quaking before the guests.*)

sinuous (*adj.*) lithe, serpentine (*With the sinuous movements of her arms, the dancer mimicked the motion of a snake.*)

sobriety (*n.*) sedate, calm (*Jason believed that maintaining his sobriety in times of crisis was the key to success in life.*)

solicitous (*adj.*) concerned, attentive (*Jim, laid up in bed with a nasty virus, enjoyed the solicitous attentions of his mother, who brought him soup and extra blankets.*)

solipsistic (*adj.*) believing that oneself is all that exists (*Colette's solipsistic attitude completely ignored the plight of the homeless people on the street.*)

soluble *(adj.)* able to dissolve *(The plot of the spy film revolved around an untraceable and water-soluble poison.)*

solvent 1. *(n.)* a substance that can dissolve other substances *(Water is sometimes called the universal solvent because almost all other substances can dissolve into it.)* 2. *(adj.)* able to pay debts *(Upon receiving an unexpected check from her aunt, Annabelle found herself suddenly solvent.)*

somnolent *(adj.)* sleepy, drowsy *(The somnolent student kept falling asleep and waking up with a jerk.)*

sophomoric *(adj.)* immature, uninformed *(The mature senior rolled her eyes at the sophomoric gross-out humor of the underclassman.)*

sovereign *(adj.)* having absolute authority in a certain realm *(The sovereign queen, with steely resolve, ordered that the traitorous nobleman be killed.)*

speculative *(adj.)* not based in fact *(Sadly, Tessa was convicted on merely speculative evidence.)*

spurious *(adj.)* false but designed to seem plausible *(Using a spurious argument, John convinced the others that he had won the board game on a technicality.)*

stagnate *(v.)* to become or remain inactive, not develop, not flow *(With no room for advancement, the waiter's career stagnated.)*

staid *(adj.)* sedate, serious, self-restrained *(The staid butler never changed his expression no matter what happened.)*

stingy *(adj.)* not generous, not inclined to spend or give *(Scrooge's stingy habits did not fit with the generous, giving spirit of Christmas.)*

stoic *(adj.)* unaffected by passion or feeling *(Penelope's faithfulness to Odysseus required that she be stoic and put off her many suitors.)*

stolid *(adj.)* expressing little sensibility, unemotional *(Charles's stolid reaction to his wife's funeral differed from the passion he showed at the time of her death.)*

strenuous *(adj.)* requiring tremendous energy or stamina *(Running a marathon is quite a strenuous task. So is watching an entire Star Trek marathon.)*

strident *(adj.)* harsh, loud *(A strident man, Captain Von Trapp yelled at his daughter and made her cry.)*

stupefy *(v.)* to astonish, make insensible *(Veronica's audacity and ungratefulness stupefied her best friend, Heather.)*

subjugate *(v.)* to bring under control, subdue *(The invading force captured and subjugated the natives of that place.)*

sublime *(adj.)* lofty, grand, exalted *(The homeless man sadly pondered his former wealth and once sublime existence.)*

submissive *(adj.)* easily yielding to authority *(In some cultures, wives are supposed to be submissive and support their husbands in all matters.)*

succinct *(adj.)* marked by compact precision *(The governor's succinct speech energized the crowd while the mayor's rambled on and on.)*

superfluous *(adj.)* exceeding what is necessary *(Tracy had already won the campaign so her constant flattery of others was superfluous.)*

surfeit *(n.)* an overabundant supply or indulgence *(After partaking of the surfeit of tacos and tamales at the All-You-Can-Eat Taco Tamale Lunch Special, Beth felt rather sick.)*

surmise *(v.)* to infer with little evidence *(After speaking to only one of the students, the teacher was able to surmise what had caused the fight.)*

surreptitious *(adj.)* stealthy *(The surreptitious CIA agents were able to get in and out of the house without anyone noticing.)*

surrogate *(n.)* one acting in place of another *(The surrogate carried the child to term for its biological parents.)*

swarthy *(adj.)* of dark color or complexion *(When he got drunk, Robinson's white skin became rather swarthy.)*

sycophant *(n.)* one who flatters for self-gain *(Some see the people in the cabinet as the president's closest advisors, but others see them as sycophants.)*

T

tacit *(adj.)* expressed without words *(I interpreted my parents' refusal to talk as a tacit acceptance of my request.)*

taciturn *(adj.)* not inclined to talk *(Though Jane never seems to stop talking, her brother is quite taciturn.)*

tangential *(adj.)* incidental, peripheral, divergent *(I tried to discuss my salary, but the boss kept veering off into tangential topics.)*

tantamount *(adj.)* equivalent in value or significance *(When it comes to sports, fearing your opponent is tantamount to losing.)*

tedious (*adj.*) dull, boring (*As time passed and the history professor continued to drone on and on, the lecture became increasingly tedious.*)

temerity (*n.*) audacity, recklessness (*Tom and Huck entered the scary cave armed with nothing but their own temerity.*)

temperance (*n.*) moderation in action or thought (*Maintaining temperance will ensure that you are able to think rationally and objectively.*)

tenable (*adj.*) able to be defended or maintained (*The department heads tore down the arguments in other people's theses, but Johari's work proved to be quite tenable.*)

tenuous (*adj.*) having little substance or strength (*Your argument is very tenuous, since it relies so much on speculation and hearsay.*)

terrestrial (*adj.*) relating to the land (*Elephants are terrestrial animals.*)

timorous (*adj.*) timid, fearful (*When dealing with the unknown, timorous Tallulah almost always broke into tears.*)

tirade (*n.*) a long speech marked by harsh or biting language (*Every time Jessica was late, her boyfriend went into a long tirade about punctuality.*)

toady (*n.*) one who flatters in the hope of gaining favors (*The other kids referred to the teacher's pet as the Tenth Grade Toady.*)

tome (*n.*) a large book (*In college, I used to carry around an anatomy book that was the heaviest tome in my bag.*)

torpid (*adj.*) lethargic, dormant, lacking motion (*The torpid whale floated, wallowing in the water for hours.*)

torrid (*adj.*) giving off intense heat, passionate (*I didn't want to witness the neighbor's torrid affair through the window.*)

tortuous (*adj.*) winding (*The scary thing about driving in mountains are the narrow, tortuous roads.*)

tractable (*adj.*) easily controlled (*The horse was so tractable, Myra didn't even need a bridle.*)

tranquil (*adj.*) calm (*There is a time of night when nothing moves and everything is tranquil.*)

transgress (*v.*) to violate, go over a limit (*The criminal's actions transgressed morality and human decency.*)

SAT Vocabulary

transient *(adj.)* passing through briefly; passing into and out of existence *(Because virtually everyone in Palm Beach is a tourist, the population of the town is quite transient.)*

transmute *(v.)* to change or alter in form *(Ancient alchemists believed that it was possible to transmute lead into gold.)*

travesty *(n.)* a grossly inferior imitation *(According to the school newspaper's merciless theater critic, Pacific Coast High's rendition of the musical Oklahoma was a travesty of the original.)*

tremulous *(adj.)* fearful *(I always feel a trifle tremulous when walking through a graveyard.)*

trenchant *(adj.)* effective, articulate, clear-cut *(The directions that accompanied my new cell phone were trenchant and easy to follow.)*

trepidation *(n.)* fear, apprehension *(Feeling great trepidation, Anya refused to jump into the pool because she thought she saw a shark in it.)*

trite *(adj.)* not original, overused *(Keith thought of himself as being very learned, but everyone else thought he was trite because his observations about the world were always the same as David Letterman's.)*

truculent *(adj.)* ready to fight, cruel *(This club doesn't really attract the dangerous types, so why was that bouncer being so truculent?)*

truncate *(v.)* to shorten by cutting off *(After winning the derby, the jockey truncated the long speech he had planned and thanked only his mom and his horse.)*

turgid *(adj.)* swollen, excessively embellished in style or language *(The haughty writer did not realize how we all really felt about his turgid prose.)*

turpitude *(n.)* depravity, moral corruption *(Sir Marcus's chivalry often contrasted with the turpitude he exhibited with the ladies at the tavern.)*

U

ubiquitous *(adj.)* existing everywhere, widespread *(It seems that everyone in the United States has a television. The technology is ubiquitous here.)*

umbrage *(n.)* resentment, offense *(He called me a lily-livered coward, and I took umbrage at the insult.)*

uncanny *(adj.)* of supernatural character or origin *(Luka had an <u>uncanny</u> ability to know exactly what other people were thinking. She also had an <u>uncanny</u> ability to shoot fireballs from her hands.)*

unctuous *(adj.)* smooth or greasy in texture, appearance, manner *(The <u>unctuous</u> receptionist seemed untrustworthy, as if she was only being helpful because she thought we might give her a big tip.)*

undulate *(v.)* to move in waves *(As the storm began to brew, the placid ocean began to <u>undulate</u> to an increasing degree.)*

upbraid *(v.)* to criticize or scold severely *(The last thing Lindsay wanted was for Lisa to <u>upbraid</u> her again about missing the rent payment.)*

usurp *(v.)* to seize by force, take possession of without right *(The rogue army general tried to <u>usurp</u> control of the government, but he failed because most of the army backed the legally elected president.)*

utilitarian *(adj.)* relating to or aiming at usefulness *(The beautiful, fragile vase couldn't hold flowers or serve any other <u>utilitarian</u> purpose.)*

utopia *(n.)* an imaginary and remote place of perfection *(Everyone in the world wants to live in a <u>utopia</u>, but no one can agree how to go about building one.)*

V

vacillate *(v.)* to fluctuate, hesitate *(I prefer a definite answer, but my boss kept <u>vacillating</u> between the distinct options available to us.)*

vacuous *(adj.)* lack of content or ideas, stupid *(Beyonce realized that the lyrics she had just penned were completely <u>vacuous</u> and tried to add more substance.)*

validate *(v.)* to confirm, support, corroborate *(Yoko's chemistry lab partner was asleep during the experiment and could not <u>validate</u> the accuracy of her methods.)*

vapid *(adj.)* lacking liveliness, dull *(The professor's comments about the poem were surprisingly <u>vapid</u> and dull.)*

variegated *(adj.)* diversified, distinctly marked *(Each wire in the engineering exam was <u>variegated</u> by color so that the students could figure out which one was which.)*

vehemently *(adv.)* marked by intense force or emotion *(The candidate <u>vehemently</u> opposed cutting back on Social Security funding.)*

SAT Vocabulary

veneer (*n.*) a superficial or deceptively attractive appearance, façade (*Thanks to her Chanel makeup, Shannen was able to maintain a veneer of perfection that hid the flaws underneath.*)

venerable (*adj.*) deserving of respect because of age or achievement (*The venerable Supreme Court justice had made several key rulings in landmark cases throughout the years.*)

venerate (*v.*) to regard with respect or to honor (*The tribute to John Lennon sought to venerate his music, his words, and his legend.*)

veracity (*n.*) truthfulness, accuracy (*With several agencies regulating the reports, it was difficult for Latifah to argue against its veracity.*)

verbose (*adj.*) wordy, impaired by wordiness (*It took the verbose teacher two hours to explain the topic, while it should have taken only fifteen minutes.*)

verdant (*adj.*) green in tint or color (*The verdant leaves on the trees made the world look emerald.*)

vestige (*n.*) a mark or trace of something lost or vanished (*Do you know if the Mexican tortilla is a vestige of some form of Aztec corn-based flat bread?*)

vex (*v.*) to confuse or annoy (*My little brother vexes me by poking me in the ribs for hours on end.*)

vicarious (*adj.*) experiencing through another (*All of my lame friends learned to be social through vicarious involvement in my amazing experiences.*)

vicissitude (*n.*) event that occurs by chance (*The vicissitudes of daily life prevent me from predicting what might happen from one day to the next.*)

vigilant (*adj.*) watchful, alert (*The guards remained vigilant throughout the night, but the enemy never launched the expected attack.*)

vilify (*v.*) to lower in importance, defame (*After the Watergate scandal, almost any story written about President Nixon sought to vilify him and criticize his behavior.*)

vindicate (*v.*) to avenge; to free from allegation; to set free (*The attorney had no chance of vindicating the defendant with all of the strong evidence presented by the state.*)

vindictive (*adj.*) vengeful (*The vindictive madman seeks to exact vengeance for any insult that he perceives is directed at him, no matter how small.*)

virtuoso (*n.*) one who excels in an art; a highly skilled musical performer (*Even though Lydia has studied piano for many years, she's only average at it. She's no virtuoso, that's for sure.*)

viscous *(adj.)* not free flowing, syrupy *(The viscous syrup took three minutes to pour out of the bottle.)*

vitriolic *(adj.)* having a caustic quality *(When angry, the woman would spew vitriolic insults.)*

vituperate *(v.)* to berate *(Jack ran away as soon as his father found out, knowing he would be vituperated for his unseemly behavior.)*

vivacious *(adj.)* lively, sprightly *(The vivacious clown makes all of the children laugh and giggle with his friendly antics.)*

vocation *(n.)* the work in which someone is employed, profession *(After growing tired of the superficial world of high-fashion, Edwina decided to devote herself to a new vocation: social work.)*

vociferous *(adj.)* loud, boisterous *(I'm tired of his vociferous whining so I'm breaking up with him.)*

W

wallow *(v.)* to roll oneself indolently; to become or remain helpless *(My roommate can't get over her breakup with her boyfriend and now just wallows in self-pity.)*

wane *(v.)* to decrease in size, dwindle *(Don't be so afraid of his wrath because his influence with the president is already beginning to wane.)*

wanton *(adj.)* undisciplined, lewd, lustful *(Vicky's wanton demeanor often made the frat guys next door very excited.)*

whimsical *(adj.)* fanciful, full of whims *(The whimsical little girl liked to pretend that she was an elvin princess.)*

wily *(adj.)* crafty, sly *(Though they were not the strongest of the Thundercats, wily Kit and Kat were definitely the most clever and full of tricks.)*

winsome *(adj.)* charming, pleasing *(After such a long, frustrating day, I was grateful for Chris's winsome attitude and childish naivete.)*

wistful *(adj.)* full of yearning; musingly sad *(Since her pet rabbit died, Edda missed it terribly and sat around wistful all day long.)*

wizened *(adj.)* dry, shrunken, wrinkled *(Agatha's grandmother, Stephanie, had the most wizened countenance, full of leathery wrinkles.)*

wrath *(n.)* vengeful anger, punishment *(Did you really want to incur her wrath when she is known for inflicting the worst punishments legally possible?)*

Y

yoke *(v.)* to join, link *(We yoked together the logs by tying a string around them.)*

Z

zealous *(adj.)* fervent, filled with eagerness in pursuit of something *(If he were any more zealous about getting his promotion, he'd practically live at the office.)*

zenith *(n.)* the highest point, culminating point *(I was too nice to tell Nelly that she had reached the absolute zenith of her career with that one hit of hers.)*

zephyr *(n.)* a gentle breeze *(If not for the zephyrs that were blowing and cooling us, our room would've been unbearably hot.)*

The Math SAT

The Math SAT

THE MATH HALF OF THE SAT SPANS three timed sections, three different question types, and a total of 60 questions. The three types of math questions are quite different from each other. For now, we will just name them, but we will cover each type in more detail later. On the test, you will find:

- 35 multiple-choice questions (MC)

- 15 quantitative comparisons (QC)

- 10 grid-ins (GI)

These three question types are always divided into the following sections.

- A 30-minute section containing 25 MCs

- A 30-minute section containing 15 QCs and 10 GIs

- A 15-minute section containing 10 MCs

The questions in these timed sections are ordered by difficulty. The first third of the questions will generally be easy, the second third moderate, and the last third difficult.

Knowing Math Fundamentals

Many test prep companies state that the SAT only tests your ability to take the SAT and doesn't actually test any real learning or knowledge. This statement is misleading, especially in reference to the Math SAT. Someone who has studied and understands the math topics on this test will do better than someone who only studied the SAT tricks. Knowing the tricks can be helpful, of course, but it will only augment your math knowledge. We'll state it again, just because we are so annoyed at the test prep companies who self-servingly deny this fact: if you understand math, you will do better on the Math SAT than someone who knows little math, no matter which of you knows more tricks.

This does not mean you should study *all* of high-school math, and neither does it mean you should *avoid* learning the strategies and tricks. It means you should study the right topics in math—the math covered on the SAT, all of which is covered in the following chapters. It also means that you should learn and think about strategic ways to approach questions as a way to enhance your skill, speed, and accuracy, not as a replacement.

General Math Strategies

Knowing math is the most important ingredient to doing well on the Math SAT. Knowing how to approach math questions strategically can make your math skill shine. This section discusses math strategy, explaining how you can maximize your time and give yourself the opportunity to earn the most points you possibly can.

Know What's in the Reference Area

Each math section comes with a reference area that provides you with basic geometric formulas and information.

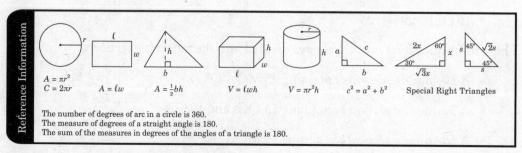

You should know all of these formulas without needing the reference. The reference area should only be used as a last resort. If you can avoid flipping through your test book to remember formulas, you will save time.

Move through the Sections Strategically

We mentioned this strategy in the verbal section: know where you are in the order of difficulty, and use that knowledge to help you strategize for particular problems as well as the entire section. For instance, in the 30-minute section with QCs and GIs, each group of questions is ordered by difficulty: first the QCs will progress from easiest to hardest, then the GIs will do the same. Remember to use the order of difficulty to your advantage: there is no sense struggling with a difficult QC when a number of easy GIs are ripe for the plucking.

Don't get bogged down on a hard question if there are easier questions left to answer. When a question seems like it's too difficult, either mark it as something to return to, or eliminate whatever answers you can and guess.

Write All Over Your Test Booklet

Draw diagrams or write out equations to help you think. Mark up graphs or charts as necessary. Cross out answers that can't be right. Basically, the test booklet is yours to write on, and writing can often help clarify things so that you can work more quickly with fewer mistakes.

Remember that the SAT Rewards Answers, Not Work

Now that we've told you to write in your test book, we're going to qualify that advice. Doing math scratchwork can definitely help you avoid careless errors, but doing pristine work, or more work than necessary, can be worthlessly consuming. You must find a balance between speed and accuracy. You need to be able to follow and understand your work, but other people don't. Nobody will look at or reward your work, so don't write it out as if you're being judged.

Avoid Carelessness

Carelessness is the worst, leading to lost points and lost dreams. Here are two ways to avoid being careless on the math section of the test.

Don't get tricked by the test.

Do not look at the answer choices immediately after reading a question. Instead, you should first take a second to process the question, making sure you understand what the question is asking and what method you think you should use to solve it. Then come up with your own answer. Only then should you look at answers. This way, you won't get bamboozled by tricks in the question or distractor answers.

Don't get tricked by yourself.

After you come to an answer, quickly plug the answer back into the question. Take a few seconds to make sure you haven't made a careless mistake.

Know When to Guess

Guessing on the math section is a little different from guessing on the verbal. For the regular MC and QC questions, you should guess if you can eliminate one possible answer choice. But be careful: just because QC questions have only four possible answer choices, don't assume you should automatically guess. The guessing penalty for QC questions is slightly higher than it is for the MCs, so you still have to eliminate an answer to make guessing beneficial. There is no guessing penalty for GIs, but that's because it's incredibly unlikely that you will be able to guess correctly. There's no real point to blind guessing on GIs, but since there's no penalty, if you come up with an answer, *any* answer, you should grid it in.

Calculators and the SAT

You are allowed to use calculators during the SAT, and statistics show that those who use calculators often do a little better on the math section than those who do not. If you are careful entering data, calculators can help you avoid careless computational errors.

Here are the rules for calculators on the SAT. The actual rules are those that you'll see in the test instructions. The practical rules are the common-sense rules that the actual rules don't tell you.

Actual

- If you want to use a calculator, you must bring your own calculator to the test center.

- Your calculator can be a normal, everyday calculator, a scientific calculator, or a graphing calculator.

- Your calculator cannot be a pocket organizer, a minicomputer, anything that has a typewriter-style keypad, anything that uses paper or a printer, anything that makes noise, or anything that needs to connect to a wall outlet.

Practical

- Know your calculator before the test. Be comfortable and familiar with it so you don't waste time searching for buttons during the test, or—heaven forbid!—make a mistake by hitting the wrong button.

- Don't assume a calculator will allow you to breeze through the math. A calculator is a tool; it can't answer anything for you if you have no idea what direction to go in.

- Don't automatically reach for your calculator. A calculator can increase your speed, but there will be math questions on the SAT that you might be able to answer more quickly *without* the calculator. Also, if using a calculator replaces scratchwork, it can be harder to check your computations .

- Make sure your batteries are in good shape. We understand that giving this advice makes us sound like your mother, but who wants to be the fool whose batteries run out in the middle of the test?

SAT Math Trickiness

ETS is a pretty big company, but it can also be a tricky little sucker. In the math sections, the test writers attempt to separate the elite math students from the average ones by using enticing wrong answers to lure the unwary.

Difficult SAT math questions are made more difficult by the inclusion of possible answer choices that *seem* like the right answers because they are answers you would get if you were to make a mistake while working on the problem. For example, let's say you're flying through the test and have to multiply $6 \times 8 \times 3$. So you quickly multiply 6 and 8 to get 42 and then multiply 42 by 3 to get 126. You look down at the answers and there's 126! That's the answer you came to, and there it is among the answer choices like a little stamp of approval, so you mark it down as your answer. Of course, you'd be wrong ($6 \times 8 = 48$ not 42, making the correct answer 144).

Just because the answer you got is among the answer choices *does not* mean you definitely have it right. The SAT is designed to punish those who make careless errors. Don't be one of them. After you get an answer, quickly plug the answer back into the question.

Math Questions and Time

There are often several ways to answer an SAT math question: you can use trial and error; you can set up and solve an equation: for some questions, you might be able to answer the question quickly, intuitively, and elegantly, if you can just spot how. These different approaches to answering questions vary in the amount of time they take. Trial and error generally takes the longest, while the elegant method of relying on an intuitive understanding of conceptual knowledge takes the least amount of time.

Take, for example, the following problem:

> Which has a greater area, a square with sides measuring 4 cm or a circle with a radius of the same length?

The most obvious way to solve this problem is by plugging 4 into the formula for the area of a square and then the area of a circle. Area of a square $= s^2$, so the area of this

The Math SAT

square = 4^2 = 16. Area of a circle = πr^2, so the area of this circle must be $\pi 4^2$ = 16π. 16π is obviously bigger than 16, so the circle must have a larger area than the square. But a faster approach would have been to draw a quick to-scale diagram with the square and circle superimposed.

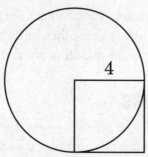

An even quicker way would have been to understand the area equations for squares and circles so well that it was just *obvious* that the circle was bigger, since the equation for the circle will square the 4 and multiply it by π, whereas the equation for the square will only square the 4.

While you may not be able to become a math whiz and just *know* the answer, you can learn to look for a quicker route, such as choosing to draw a diagram instead of working out the equation. As with the example above, a quicker route is not necessarily a less accurate one. Making such choices comes down to practice, an awareness that other routes are out there, and basic mathematical ability.

The value of time-saving strategies is obvious: less time spent on some questions allows you to devote more time to difficult problems. It is this issue of time that separates the students who score high on the math section from those who merely do well. Whether or not the ability to find accurate shortcuts is an actual measure of mathematical prowess is not for us to say (though we can think of arguments on either side), but the ability to find those shortcuts absolutely matters on this test.

Shortcuts Are Really Math Intuition

To some extent, through practice, you can teach yourself to recognize when a question might contain a shortcut. For example, from the problem above, you know that there will probably be a shortcut for all those questions that give you the dimensions of two shapes and ask you to compare them: you can just draw a diagram. A smart test-taker would see the information given and then seize on the simplest route and work out the equations.

You shouldn't go into every question searching for a shortcut. In some questions, a shorcut may not exist. In others, for whatever reason, you may not find one that does exist. If you have to search and search for a shortcut, it might end up taking *longer* than the first route to solving the problem that came into your mind. Rather than searching for shortcuts, you should be aware of them. Just knowing shortcuts exist can help you find them; don't get so focused and frantic about getting a question right that you miss the possibility that a shortcut exists.

Finally, the fact that we advocate using shortcuts doesn't mean you shouldn't focus on learning how to work a problem out. In fact, we can guarantee that you're not going to find a shortcut for a problem *unless* you know how to work it out the "long" way. After all, a shortcut is just using your knowledge to see a faster way to answer the question. To put it another way, while we've been using the term *math shortcut*, we could just as easily have used the term *math intuition*. If you don't have that knowledge base to work from, you're not going to have anything on which to base your intuition. In contrast, you might be able to figure out an answer by trial and error, even if you don't see exactly how to answer the problem.

Strategy = Target Score

Your strategy in the math section, and particularly the extent of your efforts to find shortcuts, should be based on your target score. If you're looking to get a 550 or lower on the Math SAT, there simply is no need to go looking for shortcuts. You can get a 550, or even a 600, without answering quite a number of questions, so there's no need to race through the test. You should focus on getting questions right. Of course, you should remain aware that shortcuts exist and use them when you see them, but don't get upset or worried if you're not unearthing a shortcut in every other question.

Students looking to score a 650 or above on the Math SAT, though, should not be working out every question. Finding quicker ways to answer questions *must* be part of your strategy, because it is only through these faster methods that you will give yourself the time to answer the last few difficult questions in the math section that can make all the difference. On these last few questions, even the best students might have to guess their way through using trial and error, which takes a bit of time. So you must give yourself time by moving quickly through the earlier stages of the test.

Be wary: this advice does *not* imply that you should simply work faster. It recommends that you look for the shorter but *just as accurate* route to the answer. Do not sacrifice accuracy to speed. If you can find the short but accurate route, great. Otherwise, it's better to make sure you answer the question correctly, not that you find the wrong answer super-fast.

The Math SAT

Types of Questions on the Math SAT

As you know by now, there are three types of math questions on the SAT: 35 regular multiple-choice, 15 quantitative comparisons, and 10 grid-ins. This section looks in detail at all three question types, explaining strategies specific to each one.

General Math Instructions

Before looking at each particular type of math question, it's a good idea to look at SAT math questions in general. All three types of math questions come with a standard core of directions. For the regular MCs, these core instructions are the only directions you'll need. QCs and GIs come with additional instructions that we'll cover later. Now, without further ado, here are the general math instructions:

> In this section solve each problem, using any available space on the page for scratchwork. Then decide which is the best of the choices given and fill in the corresponding oval on the answer sheet.

> Notes:

> 1. The use of a calculator is permitted. All numbers are real numbers.
> 2. Figures that accompany problems in this test are intended to provide information useful in solving the problems. They are drawn as accurately as possible EXCEPT when it is stated in a specific problem that the figure is not drawn to scale. All figures lie in a plane unless otherwise indicated.

The first note tells you the reassuring news that you will only have to deal with real numbers. If you've done some high school math, you should know that real numbers constitute all integers and all the fractions that exist between those integers.

The second note tells you two things. First, for all normal diagrams, if one angle looks bigger than another, it truly will be bigger: you can trust the diagrams and use them to help you. Second, this statement warns you to check if a diagram is marked "This figure is not drawn to scale." If a diagram is marked in that way, you know to be careful and to trust your knowledge of geometry rather than the given figure. You also might want to draw your own figure that *is* to scale.

Approaching Multiple-Choice Questions

MC questions are the most common type of math question on the test. These problems involve a mathematical statement or question that you need to solve, followed by five answer choices. Sometimes the problem will include a chart, graph, or geometric diagram. Your job, obviously, is to choose the right answer.

The MCs are split into two groups: 25 in one of the 30-minute math sections and 10 in the 15-minute section. Both groups are organized according to difficulty, so you know the first questions of each group will be easier while the last will be harder.

The procedure to follow for answering individual MCs is not that different from the one we described for answering sentence completions and analogies.

1. Read the question without looking at the answers. Determine what the question is asking and come to some conclusion about how to solve it. Do not look at the answers unless you decide that using the process of elimination is the best way to go (we describe how to use the process of elimination below).

2. If you think you can solve the problem, go ahead. Once you've derived an answer—and only then— see if your answer matches one among the choices.

3. Once you've decided on an answer, test it out to make sure it's correct and move on.

Working Backward: The Process of Elimination

If you run into difficulty while trying to solve an MC, you might want to try the process of elimination. On every question, the answer is right in front of you, hidden among those five answer choices. So if you can't solve the problem directly, you might be able to plug each answer into the question to see which one works.

Not only can this process help you when you can't figure out a question, there are times when it can actually be faster than setting up an equation, especially if you work strategically. Take the following example:

> A classroom contains 31 chairs, some which have arms and some of which do not. If the room contains 5 more armchairs than chairs without arms, how many armchairs does it contain?
>
> (A) 10
> (B) 13
> (C) 16
> (D) 18
> (E) 21

Given this question, you could build the equations:

$$\text{total chairs } (31) = \text{armchairs } (x) + \text{normal chairs } (y)$$
$$\text{normal chairs } (y) = \text{armchairs } (x) - 5$$

Then, since $y = x - 5$, you can make the equation:

$$31 = x + (x - 5)$$
$$31 = 2x - 5$$
$$36 = 2x$$
$$x = 18$$

This approach of building and working out the equations will produce the right answer, but it takes a long time. What if you strategically plugged in the answers instead? Since the numbers ascend in value, let's choose the one in the middle: (C) 16. This is a smart strategic move because if we plug in 16 and discover that it was too small a number to satisfy the equation, we can eliminate (A) and (B) along with (C). Alternatively, if 16 is too big, we can eliminate (D) and (E) along with (C).

So our strategy is in place. Now let's work it out. If you have 16 armchairs, then you would have 11 normal chairs and the room would contain 27 total chairs. We needed the total numbers of chairs to equal 31, so clearly (C) is not the right answer. But because the total number of chairs was too small, you can also eliminate (A) and (B), the answer choices indicating fewer numbers of armchairs. If you then plug in **(D)** 18, you have 13 normal chairs and 31 total chairs. There's your answer. In this instance, plugging in the answers takes less time and in general just seems easier.

Notice that the last sentence began with the phrase "in this instance." Working backward and plugging in is *not* always the best method. For the SAT, you will need to build up a sense of when working backward can help you most. A good rule of thumb for deciding whether to work backward is:

Work backward when the question describes an equation of some sort and the answer choices are all rather simple numbers.

If the answer choices contain variables, working backward will often be quite difficult— more difficult than working out the problem would be. If the answer choices are complicated, containing hard fractions or radicals, plugging in might prove so complex that the process will be a waste of time.

Substituting Numbers

Substituting numbers is a lot like working backward, except the numbers you plug into the equation *aren't* in the answer choices. Instead, you have to strategically decide on numbers to substitute to take the place of variables. For example, take the question:

> If p and q are odd integers, then which of the following must be odd?
>
> (A) $p + q$
> (B) $p - q$
> (C) $p^2 + q^2$
> (D) $p^2 \times q^2$
> (E) $p + q^2$

It might be hard to conceptualize how the two variables in this problem interact. But what if you chose two odd numbers, let's say 5 and 3, to represent the two variables? Once you begin this substitution it quickly becomes clear that:

> (A) $p + q = 5 + 3 = 8$
> (B) $p - q = 5 - 3 = 2$
> (C) $p^2 + q^2 = 25 + 9 = 34$
> (D) $p^2 \times q^2 = 25 \times 9 = 225$
> (E) $p + q^2 = 5 + 9 = 14$

By picking two numbers that fit the definition of the variables provided by the question, it becomes clear that the answer has to be **(D)** $p^2 \times q^2$ since the equation equals 225. (By the way, you could have answered this question without doing the multiplication since two odd numbers, such as 9 and 25, when multiplied, will always result in an odd number.)

Substituting numbers can help you transform problems from the abstract into the concrete. However, you have to remember to keep the substitution consistent. If you're using a 5 to represent p, don't suddenly start using 3. Also, when picking numbers to use as substitutes, pick wisely. Choose numbers that are easy to work with and that fit the definitions provided by the question.

Quantitative Comparisons

The 15 QC questions appear before the 10 grid-ins in one of the two 30-minute math sections. The QCs are arranged by order of difficulty, from least to most difficult.

QC Instructions

In addition to the directions provided above in general math instructions, Quantitative Comparisons have their own special instructions:

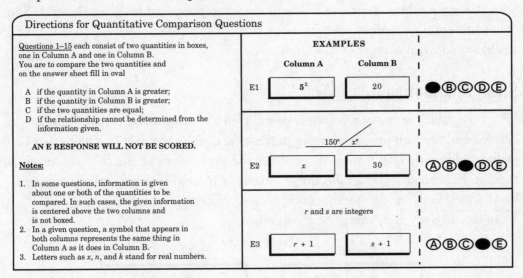

Note that though QC questions have only four possible answer choices while the grid has five answer spaces. Know the instructions!

QC questions ask you to look at two expressions or mathematical statements and choose which is of greater value. For example:

Column A	Column B
2	4

Answering (A) means you think that the expression in Column A is bigger. Answering (B) means you think that the expression in Column B is bigger. If the two expressions are equal, answer (C). If the relative size of the two expressions can't be determined, then answer (D). The answer in the easy example above is (B), since 4 is bigger than 2.

In the example above, the values in Columns A and B were expressed by actual numbers. The columns might also contain:

	Column A	Column B
Expressions	$1 + \frac{1}{2}$	$\frac{1}{3} - \frac{1}{16} + \frac{1}{8}$
Simple Variables	x	y
Algebraic Expressions	$x + y$	$x - y$
Word problems	Jimmy's age	Mary's age
Geometric figures	Area of $ABCD$	Area of $EFGH$

Sometimes the values in the two columns will be represented in different ways. You may come upon a quantitative comparison that has an algebraic expression in Column A and a simple real number in Column B.

Given Information

When the values in the two columns contain variables, algebraic expressions, values derived from a word problem, or geometric information, the problem will often also include additional information that defines the expressions in the columns or gives them some context. For example, the statement "All variables represent positive numbers" would limit and define what numbers a variable can represent.

In fact, let's say you came upon the question:

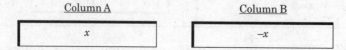

The answer to this question would have to be **(D),** because if $x = 0$, then the two columns would be equal; if $x = 1$, then Column A would be greater; if $x = -1$, then Column B would be greater. But what if the question also included the following information?

All variables represent positive numbers.

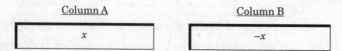

From the information provided, you know that in this problem x can never equal 0 or any negative number. Instead, x must always be positive, which means that Column A will always be greater than Column B, making the answer to the question **(A).** Make sure to look at and understand the given information because it will always affect the outcome of the question.

The Difference Among A, B, C, and D

If you answer a quantitative comparison with choice (A), (B), or (C), you are implicitly stating that the value of the expressions in each column can be determined in some relative way. After all, you can only claim that one column is greater than the other or that the two columns are equal if you know the relative values of two columns *under every circumstance*. In contrast, if you select answer choice (D) you are claiming that there is no possible way to know the value of at least one of the columns under every circumstance.

This difference among (A), (B), (C), and (D) has two important ramifications.

- (D) can only possibly be an answer if you have a variable in one of the columns. If both columns hold numbers, you can't answer (D) because the value of each column is constant. (This won't happen much—it lets you get an answer too easily.)

- If you are able to show that it is possible for two different relationships to exist between the columns, the answer must be (D).

Column A	Column B
$x + y$	$x - y$

At first glance, you might think that of course Column A is bigger than Column B because Column A involves addition while B uses subtraction. But what if y represents a negative number? Then everything gets flipped and Column B will be bigger than Column A. Depending on which number you plug into the variables, you will receive difference answers, so the answer must be **(D)**.

Note, however, that just showing that the value of one column *can* vary does not necessarily prove that the relative relationship between the two columns *must* vary. For example, let's say you can prove that Column A can be either 3 or 7 (and nothing else), while Column B will always be 2. Even though Column A changes in value, its relative value will still always be greater than Column B, and so the answer will be **(A)**.

Answering Quantitative Comparisons

Your job on QCs is to compare the relative size of the two columns, not the exact value of each column. While there will be many times when you do compute exact values to find the relative sizes, sometimes you won't have to do any calculations at all. Always remember your QC priorities: do enough work so that you can successfully compare the two columns but no more. Of course, you must make sure you do enough work to compare the two expressions in *every* possible circumstance. Below are some techniques to help you in your efforts.

Element by Element Comparison

Working out a problem can take quite a bit of time and often isn't necessary, as we just said. Take the following example:

Column A	Column B
$\frac{1}{2} + \frac{3}{8} + \frac{1}{4}$	$\frac{9}{16} + \frac{1}{2} + \frac{7}{8}$

To find the value of each of these expressions, you first would have to find a common denominator for each and then carry out the necessary steps. None of that is needed however, to quickly and accurately answer this question.

Since the only process in each expression is addition, you should automatically recognize that the column that contains bigger pieces will have the greater sum. Look at the pieces, and see if they can be easily compared. Both Column A and Column B have a $\frac{1}{2}$, so at this point the columns are equal. The $\frac{7}{8}$ in Column B is greater than the $\frac{3}{8}$ in Column A. It is possible to then quickly calculate that the $\frac{1}{4}$ in Column A is equal to $\frac{4}{16}$, and then see that the $\frac{9}{16}$ in Column B is larger. The fractions in Column B are all either larger or equal to their counterparts in Column A, so the value of Column B as a whole must also be larger. There's the answer, and without having to do any math more complicated than converting $\frac{1}{4}$ to $\frac{4}{16}$.

Perform the Same Operation on Each Column

In fact, the last problem could have been made even simpler. Instead of immediately comparing the two expressions, it would have been better to simplify the two columns by subtracting $\frac{1}{2}$ from each side. Then you would only have to deal with two fractions on each side.

Column A	Column B
$\frac{3}{8} + \frac{1}{4}$	$\frac{9}{16} + \frac{7}{8}$

The simpler the expression, the more likely you are to see how to compare them quickly.

Make sure that when you employ this technique you do so evenly on each column. If you inadvertently perform an operation on only one column, you will not preserve the relative values of the two columns and you will get the question wrong.

Transform Apples and Oranges into Pears and Pears

As the cliché goes, you can't compare apples and oranges. But there are times in QCs comparisons when it seems as if you're being asked to do just that. In such situations, don't panic: these questions are designed so that by applying some knowledge of math you will be able to make the columns comparable. For example:

Column A	Column B
$(x)(x + a)$	$x^2 + ax$

At first glance, these two columns look very different, and as if they can't be compared. But if you simply multiply out the first column, it will resemble the second:

Column A	Column B
$x^2 + ax$	$x^2 + ax$

Whenever you get into a situation in which you don't know how to compare the two columns, see if there might be a way for you to make the two columns similar.

Substituting Numbers QC Style

Sometimes the best way to compare two columns that have variables is to choose substitute numbers for those variables. Choosing the proper substitute numbers takes some skill and practice. First, you should try to use numbers that are easy to calculate. Second, you must make sure that the numbers you choose to substitute represent all possible circumstances. Remember, when you are answering QCs you are not trying to figure out a single answer. You must also figure out if you can arrive at a definitive answer. Take the following example:

$$p > q$$

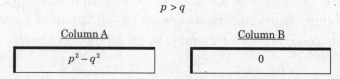

Column A	Column B
$p^2 - q^2$	0

Let's plug in two easy-to-use numbers that fit the definition in the given information; how about 3 for p (which makes $p^2 = 9$) and 2 for q (making $q^2 = 4$)? Plugging the numbers into Column A, we get $9 - 4 = 5$. Column A is greater than Column B.

Before we congratulate ourselves, it's necessary to make sure that Column A is always larger than Column B, not just in this single instance with these particular numbers. Let's try negative numbers (remember, p has to be larger than q, meaning p has to be *less* negative than q). A good move is to take your original numbers and make them negative. In this case, we also have to remember to keep p greater than q, so we must also switch the numerical values of the two variables: $p = -2$ and $q = -3$. If we plug these new numbers into Column A we get $(-2)^2 - (-3)^2 = 4 - 9 = (-5)$. In this instance, Column A is *smaller* than Column B. In other words, Column A can be larger than Column B in some instances and smaller in others, meaning that there is no definite answer and the answer must be **(D)**.

Whenever you plug in numbers for QCs, you must be aware that it is possible that other numbers might yield a different result. So, any time you plug in numbers, you must make certain to try all of the different possible numbers. Therefore, each time you plug in numbers make sure to:

- Use a number larger than 1.

- Use the number 1.

- Use a fraction.

- Use 0.

- Use a negative number.

If any of these options yields a comparative result different from the others, your answer should be **(D)**.

Guessing on QCs

Because QCs have four rather than five multiple-choice possibilities, ETS adjusted the guessing penalty so that you lose $1/3$ of a point rather than $1/4$ of a point for a wrong answer. This means that you still have to eliminate at least one possibility on a QC in order to make guessing worthwhile.

Sometimes eliminating an answer choice is easier than it looks. Remember that for the answer to be (D), you must not be able to find the exact value of either side. Therefore, if you know that each side has an exact value, even if you don't know how to determine what those values are, you *do* know that (D) cannot be the answer. At that point, the guessing odds are in your favor. Take the following example:

Column A	Column B
$\dfrac{17}{49}$	$\dfrac{22}{51}$

This is a pretty easy problem, but let's say that you didn't have enough time to cross-multiply and figure out that column (B) is greater. Even so, from looking at these two columns you should *instantaneously* know that their respective values are set in stone, meaning (D) cannot be the answer.

Time Management and QCs

The 15 QCs are found in the same 30-minute section as the 10 GIs. As you already know, both of these question-type groups are organized by difficulty. Depending on your target score, you can manage your time by skipping over questions that you just can't figure out. Remember, you should make sure to take a look at every problem in a section to see if you can answer it or put yourself in position to guess, but don't struggle to answer questions that are too difficult. You should use the location of a question as a hint of its probable difficulty, but you shouldn't just skip a question without ever looking at it. If you get to the end of the QCs and haven't answered a few questions, don't worry. Just move on to the GIs and answer what you can. If time allows, when you've answered everything you definitely can, then come back to the questions you skipped and give them another try.

Grid-Ins

Like the other types of SAT math questions, the 10 GIs are ordered from easiest to most difficult. Unlike every other type of question on the test, the 10 GIs are not multiple-choice. Instead, you have to generate your own answer and express this answer to the machine grading the test by filling in a special grid.

Directions for Student-Produced Response Questions

Each of the remaining 10 questions (16–25) requires you to solve the problem and enter your answer by marking the ovals in the special grid, as shown in the examples below.

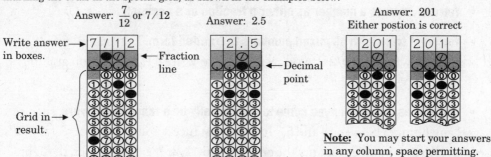

Answer: $\frac{7}{12}$ or 7/12   Answer: 2.5   Answer: 201 Either position is correct

Write answer in boxes. ← Fraction line ← Decimal point

Grid in result.

Note: You may start your answers in any column, space permitting. Columns not needed should be left blank.

- Mark no more than one oval in any column.

- Because the answer sheet will be machine-scored, **you will receive credit only if the ovals are filled in completely.**

- Although not required, it is suggested that you write your answer in the boxes at the top of the columns to help you fill in the ovals accurately.

- Some problems may have more than one correct answer. In such cases, grid only one answer

- No question has a negative answer.

- **Mixed numbers** such as $2\frac{1}{2}$ must be gridded as 2.5 of 5/2. If [2 1 / 2] is gridded, it will be interpreted as $\frac{21}{2}$, not $2\frac{1}{2}$.)

- **Decimal Accuracy:** If you obtain a decimal answer, **enter the most accurate value the grid will accommodate.** For example, if you obtain an answer such as 0.6666 . . . , you should record the result as .666 or .667. **Less accurate values such as .66 or .67 are not acceptable.** Acceptable ways to grid $\frac{2}{3}$ = .666 . . .

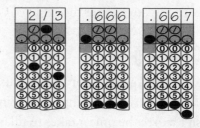

Grid-In Instructions: The Grid

ETS provides extensive instructions that describe how to fill in the grid. As always, memorize these instructions before you take the test. As you look at the instructions, note that for some questions you will be able to write your answer in more than one form.

Those directions are a little intense. Here's a summary:

- **The computer that grades the test can't read anything but the ovals.** You don't actually have to write anything in the spaces at the top as long as you fill in the ovals correctly. However, filling in the spaces at the top might help you to avoid making careless mistakes. We recommend that you do write out your answers in the spaces: the increased accuracy is worth that extra bit of time. Whether you decide to write out your answers or not, make sure you don't forget to fill in the ovals!

- **The grid cannot accommodate any number longer than four digits or any decimal or fraction that includes more than three numbers.** The grid also cannot indicate a negative sign. If the answer you come up with can't fit into the grid or if your answer is negative, then your answer is incorrect.

- **You can express a number as either a fraction or a decimal.**

- **You must transform all mixed numbers to fraction form.** For example, $4\frac{1}{2}$ must be written as $9/2$. If you were to try to write $41/2$ the dumb grading machine would read it as $\frac{41}{2}$.

- **Sometimes the answer you come to will actually be a range of answers,** such as "any number between 4 and 5." In those instances, you will be correct if you oval in any number that fits the criteria; 4.6, 4.2, $9/2$. Remember, though: no mixed numbers.

No Tricks

Because GIs aren't multiple choice, there really aren't any strategies we can offer you to help you come to an answer on a particular question. Taking practice tests will help you to get comfortable with answering GIs in general, and studying those tests will help you learn how to answer the types of GI questions typically asked.

Grid-in Guessing

There's no guessing penalty for GIs because the likelihood of a person guessing correctly on a question is shockingly, amazingly, incredibly small. In most situations, guessing isn't worth the time it takes to fill out the ovals in the grid. However, if you're low on time and you've worked on a question and come to an answer that fits in the grid, it wouldn't hurt to fill in the grid.

SAT Arithmetic

$\mathbf{A}$LMOST HALF OF THE 60 MATH questions on the SAT test basic arithmetic. The SAT does not cover *all* of arithmetic, however. In fact, the test covers only thirteen arithmetic topics, as you can see in the table of contents to the right. The SAT usually covers these 13 topics in very similar ways. Because the SAT is so focused in what it tests, we are too. We don't cover arithmetic. We explain *SAT arithmetic*, covering only the topics the SAT will test and explaining how the SAT will test those topics.

Chapter Contents

Order of Operations

The SAT does not often directly test the order of operations, but you must know the order in which mathematical operations should be performed in order to deal with many of the questions on the test. The best way to remember which operation gets performed before another is the acronym PEMDAS, which stands for:

Parentheses
Exponents
Multiplication
Division
Addition
Subtraction

If you come across an equation that contains any or all of these elements, you should carry out the math within the parentheses first, then work out the exponents, then do the multiplication, then the division, and finally the subtraction. Given the expression:

$$\frac{(18 - 3) \times 2^2}{5} - 7 + (6 \times 3 - 1)$$

You would first work out the math in the parentheses (following PEMDAS even within the parentheses, meaning do multiplication before subtraction):

$$\frac{15 \times 2^2}{5} - 7 + 17$$

Then work out the exponents:

$$\frac{15 \times 4}{5} - 7 + 17$$

Then do the multiplication:

$$\frac{60}{5} - 7 + 17$$

Then the division:

$$12 - 7 + 17$$

Then the addition:

$$12 - 24$$

Then the subtraction:

$$-12$$

Odd and Even Numbers

Again, you should already know about odd and even numbers and the difference between them. For this topic, however, we will provide a very quick review.

Even Numbers

Even numbers are numbers that are divisible by 2 with no remainder. Remember that 0 is included within this definition.

$$\ldots, -6, -4, -2, 0, 2, 4, 6, \ldots$$

Odd Numbers

Odd numbers are numbers that, when divided by 2, will leave a remainder of 1.

$$\ldots, -5, -3, -1, 1, 3, 5, \ldots$$

Operations and Odd and Even Numbers

There are a number of rules regarding operations and odd and even numbers that you should know instinctively.

Addition	Subtraction	Multiplication
Even + Even = Even	Even – Even = Even	Even × Even = Even
Odd + Odd = Even	Odd – Odd = Even	Odd × Odd = Odd
Even + Odd = Odd	Even – Odd = Odd	Even × Odd = Even

When the SAT tests your knowledge of odd and even numbers, which happens about once or twice a test, it will usually test your knowledge of these rules.

Signed Numbers

The term "signed numbers" refers to numbers that include either a positive or negative sign, and are therefore marked as being either greater than 0 (positive) or less than 0 (negative). Zero has no sign. For our purposes, the term usually refers to negative numbers, since you already know instinctively how to think about positive numbers.

Here's a look at negative numbers on a number line:

$$\ldots, -5, -4, -3, -2, -1, \ldots$$

Students who are comfortable with positive numbers sometimes get confused when dealing with negative numbers. For example, while positive numbers become larger as they move farther away from 0, negative numbers become smaller: −10 is a smaller number than −1. When dealing with negative numbers, be careful not to see the 10 in −10 and just assume that it is a larger number than −1.

Negative Numbers and Operations

Negative numbers behave differently from positive numbers when you perform various operations on them. In terms of addition and subtraction, negative numbers invert the operations.

Adding Signed Numbers

When a negative number is added to another number, the sum will be a smaller number. In fact, adding a negative number is the same as subtracting a positive number of the same value.

$$3 + -2 = 1, \text{ just as } 3 - 2 = 1$$

Subtracting Signed Numbers

When a negative number is subtracted from another number, the difference will be a *larger* number. In fact, subtracting a negative number is the same as adding the inverse positive number.

$$3 - (-2) = 5, \text{ just as } 3 + 2 = 5$$

Negative numbers also follow different rules when you multiply or divide them.

Multiplying and Dividing with Negative Numbers

Negative numbers also follow different rules when you include them in multiplication or division.

Multiplying with Negative Numbers	Dividing with Negative Numbers
Positive × Positive = Positive	Positive ÷ Positive = Positive
Negative × Negative = Positive	Negative ÷ Negative = Positive
Positive × Negative = Negative	Positive ÷ Negative = Negative

Negative Numbers and Quantitative Comparisons

Because negative numbers act in such different ways from positive numbers, whenever you plug a positive number into a QC question to try to determine which of the two columns is bigger, you must also plug in a negative number. Often, you'll discover that positive and negative numbers will yield different answers, meaning that the relative size of the columns cannot be determined.

Divisibility and Remainders

A number (x) is divisible by another number (y) if, when x is divided by y, the answer is a whole number. For example, 6 is divisible by 3 because $6 \div 3 = 2$, and 2 is a whole number. 6 is not divisible by 4, because $6 \div 4 = 1\,^2/_4 = 1\,^1/_2$, which is not a whole number. Another way of describing $6 \div 4$ is to say that you can make one complete division with a remainder of 2.

The SAT will sometimes test whether you can determine if one number is divisible by another. To check divisibility, you can always do the division by hand and see if the result is a whole number. However, if the number you have to divide is large, working out the problem by hand can be quite difficult. There are some divisibility rules that make this task much easier—these rules allow us to determine whether a number is divisible by another number without having to carry out the division.

Divisibility Rules

1. All whole numbers are divisible by 1.

2. All numbers with a ones digit of 0, 2, 4, 6, or 8 are divisible by 2.

3. A number is divisible by 3 if its digits add up to a number divisible by 3. For example, 6,711 is divisible by 3 because $6 + 7 + 1 + 1 = 15$, and 15 is divisible by 3.

4. A number is divisible by 4 if its last two digits are divisible by 4. For example, 780, 52, and 80,744 are divisible by 4, but 7,850 is not.

5. A number is divisible by 5 if it ends in 0 or 5.

6. A number is divisible by 6 if it is even and also divisible by 3.

7. Sorry. There are no rules for 7.

SAT Arithmetic

8. A number is divisible by 8 if its last three digits are divisible by 8. For example, 905,256 is divisible by 8 because 256 is divisible by 8. 74,513 is not divisible by 8 because 513 is not divisible by 8.

9. A number is divisible by 9 if its digits add up to a number divisible by 9. For example, 1,458 is divisible by 9 because 1 + 4 + 5 + 8 = 18 and 18 is divisible by 9.

10. A number is divisible by 10 if it ends in 0.

Two Notes:

(1) Because a number divided by itself always yields 1, a number is always divisible by itself. For example, 7 is divisible by 7, and 8,374 is divisible by 8,374. **(2)** No number is divisible by a number greater than itself.

Multiples, Factors, and Primes

SAT questions on multiples, factors, and primes can be difficult simply because of all the terminology they so freely throw around. Below, we give you the definition for these three mathematical concepts. You don't have to love them, but you should know them.

Multiples

The multiple of a number is the product generated when that number is multiplied by an integer. The first five multiples of 7 are 7, 14, 21, 28, and 35 since $7 \times 1 = 7$; $7 \times 2 = 14$; $7 \times 3 = 21$; $7 \times 4 = 28$; $7 \times 5 = 35$.

The Least Common Multiple

The least common multiple (LCM) is the name given to the lowest multiple that two particular numbers share. For example, the multiples of 6 and 8 are:

Multiples of 6:

$$6, 12, 18, 24, 30, 36, 42, 48, 54, \ldots$$

Multiples of 8:

$$8, 16, 24, 32, 40, 48, 56, 64, 72, \ldots$$

As the two lists show, 6 and 8 both have 24 and 48 as multiples (they also share many other multiples, such as 72, 96, . . .) Because 24 is the lowest in value of these shared multiples, it is the least common multiple of 6 and 8.

Being able to figure out the least common multiple of two numbers can prove quite handy on the SAT, especially for questions in which you have to add or subtract two fractions with unlike denominators, which we'll explain later in this chapter.

Factors

A factor of a number is the quotient produced when that number is divided by an integer. For example, 2, 3, 4, and 6 are all factors of 12 because $12 \div 6 = 2$; $12 \div 4 = 3$; $12 \div 3 = 4$; and $12 \div 2 = 6$. Factors, then, are related to multiples. A given number is a multiple of all its factors: 2 and 6 are factors of 12, so 12 is a multiple of both 2 and 6.

The Greatest Common Factor

The Greatest Common Factor (GCF) of two numbers is the largest factor that the two numbers share. For example, the GCF of 18 and 24 is 6, since 6 is the largest number that is a factor for both 18 and 24.

Primes

A prime number is divisible by only 1 and itself (the number 1 itself is not considered prime). For example, 17 is prime because it is divisible by only 1 and 17. The first few primes, in increasing order, are:

$$2, 3, 5, 7, 11, 13, 17, 19, 23, 29, 31, 37, 41, 43, 47, 53, \ldots$$

Let's say the SAT asks you whether 91 is prime. You should try to answer this question by showing that 91 is not prime. You can do this pretty quickly if you understand the rules above. Here is the strategic way to check whether 91 is prime:

1. Is 91 divisible by 2? No, it does not end with an even number.

2. Is 91 divisible by 3? No, $9 + 1 = 10$, which is not divisible by 3. You don't have to check if 91 is divisible by 4, because you already know that is isn't divisible by 2. No number that isn't divisible by 2 will be divisible by 4.

3. Is 91 divisible by 5? No, 91 does not end with 0 or 5. You don't have to check if 91 is divisible by 6, because you already know that is isn't divisible by 2 or 3.

4. Is 91 divisible by 7? Yes! $^{91}/_7 = 13$.

Therefore, 91 is not prime.

Fractions, Decimals, and Percents

The SAT focuses far more closely on fractions, decimals, and percents than on any other arithmetic topic. In fact, almost 14 percent of all SAT math questions require some knowledge of fractions, decimals, or percents. On a single SAT, 7 to 8 questions will deal with this topic. Because fractions encompass such a large part of the test, knowing your stuff here can really help your final score.

Fractions

A fraction describes a part of a whole. The number on the bottom of the fraction is called the denominator, and it denotes the number of equal parts into which the whole is divided. The number on the top of the fraction is called the numerator, and denotes how many of those equal parts the fraction has. For example, the fraction $^3/_4$ denotes "3 of 4 equal parts," 3 being the numerator and 4 being the denominator.

You can also think of fractions as similar to division. In fact, $^3/_4$ means the same thing as $3 \div 4$.

Equivalent Fractions

Two fractions are equivalent if there is a number by which both the numerator and the denominator of one fraction can be multiplied or divided to yield the other fraction. For example, $^2/_3$ is equivalent to $^4/_6$ because if you multiply the numerator and denominator of $^2/_3$ by 2, you get $^4/_6$:

$$\frac{2 \times 2}{2 \times 3} = \frac{4}{6}$$

Equivalent fractions are equivalent in value. When you multiply or divide both the numerator and denominator of a fraction by the same number, *you will not change the overall value of the fraction.* Because fractions represent a part of a whole, if you increase both the part and whole by the same multiple, you will not change the relationship between the part and the whole. See how $^1/_3$ of a pizza is exactly the same as $^3/_9$?

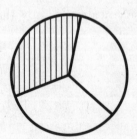 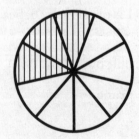

Reducing Fractions

On the SAT, you will sometimes encounter fractions involving large, unwieldy numbers, such as $18/102$. It would probably be hard (and time consuming) for you to work with $18/102$, just because the numbers in the numerator and denominator are so big. When faced with such cases, it is always a good idea to see if the fraction can be reduced, or simplified.

The fastest way to simplify a fraction is to divide both the numerator and denominator by their Greatest Common Factor (GCF). In the case of $18/102$, the GCF of 18 and 102 is 6, leaving you with $3/17$. With your knowledge of divisibility rules, you should be able to see that both the numerator and denominator are divisible by 6. Had you not immediately seen that 6 was the GCF, you could have divided both numbers by 2 and gotten $9/51$. From there, it would have been pretty obvious that both numerator and denominator are also divisible by 3, yielding $3/17$.

On the SAT, when you encounter a fraction that involves big numbers, very often that fraction can be reduced. And because the SAT is in part a test of speed, any knowledge you have that lessens the time it takes to answer a question is very important. You need to get skilled not only at reducing fractions, but also at recognizing when a fraction can be reduced.

Comparing Fractions

Particularly on quantitative comparison questions, you may be asked to compare two fractions. If either the denominators or the numerators of the two fractions are the same, that comparison is easy. $8/9$ is obviously greater than $5/9$, and $5/9$ is greater than $5/17$. Just remember, if the denominators are the same, the fraction with the larger numerator is bigger. If the numerators of the two fractions are the same, the fraction with the smaller denominator is bigger.

If the two fractions don't lend themselves to immediate easy comparison, don't fret. There is a trick that allows you to compare fractions: cross-multiplication. To cross-multiply, multiply the numerator of each fraction by the denominator of the other. Write the product of each multiplication next to the numerator you used to get it. The greater product will be next to the greater fraction. For example:

$$32 = \frac{4}{7} \searrow \times \swarrow \frac{5}{8} = 35$$

35, the greater product, is next to the fraction $5/8$, so that is the greater fraction.

Adding and Subtracting Fractions

There are two different types of fractions that the SAT might ask you to add or subtract. It might ask you to work with two fractions that have the same denominator. Or it might ask you to handle two fractions with different denominators.

If fractions have the same denominator, adding them is extremely easy. All you have to do is add up the numerators:

$$\frac{1}{20} + \frac{3}{20} + \frac{13}{20} = \frac{17}{20}$$

Subtraction works similarly. If the denominators of the fractions are equal, then you simply subtract one numerator from the other:

$$\frac{13}{20} - \frac{2}{20} = \frac{11}{20}$$

If the fractions do not have equal denominators, the process is somewhat more involved. The first step is to make the denominators the same. To set the denominators of two fractions equal, find the Least Common Denominator (LCD), which is simply the Least Common Multiple (LCM) of the two denominators. For example, 18 is the LCD of $\frac{1}{6}$ and $\frac{4}{9}$, since 18 is the smallest multiple of both 6 and 9.

Setting the denominators of two fractions equal to each other is a two-step process. First, find the LCD. Second, write each fraction as an equivalent fraction with the LCD as the new denominator, remembering to multiply the numerator by the same multiple as the denominator. For example, if you wanted to add $\frac{5}{12}$ and $\frac{4}{9}$, you would do the following:

I. Find the LCD

1. Factor the denominators. $12 = 2 \times 2 \times 3$ and $9 = 3 \times 3$.

2. Find the LCM of the denominators. $2 \times 2 \times 3 \times 3 = 36$.

3. The LCD is 36.

II. Write each fraction as an equivalent fraction with the LCD as the new denominator.

1. Multiply the denominator and numerator of the first fraction by the LCD.

$$\text{denominator} = 12 \times 3 = 36$$
$$\text{numerator} = 5 \times 3 = 15$$

The new fraction is, therefore, $\frac{15}{36}$.

2. Multiply the denominator and numerator of the second fraction by the LCD.

$$\text{denominator} = 9 \times 4 = 36$$
$$\text{numerator} = 4 \times 4 = 16$$

The new fraction is $^{16}/_{36}$.

Now that the fractions have the same denominator, you can quickly add the numerators to get the final answer. $15 + 16 = 31$, so the answer is $^{31}/_{36}$.

If you think it will take you too long to figure out the LCD, you can always multiply the denominators together to get a common denominator that isn't the least common denominator. For example, if the two denominators are 6 and 8, you can use 48 as your common denominator just as easily as 24 (the LCD). There are two drawbacks to not using the LCD. First, you will have to work with larger numbers. Second, because the answer choices will appear as reduced fractions, you will have to reduce your answer at the end.

Multiplying Fractions

Multiplying fractions is quite easy. Simply multiply the numerators together and the denominators together, as seen in the example below.

$$\frac{4}{5} \times \frac{2}{7} \times \frac{1}{3} = \frac{4 \times 2 \times 1}{5 \times 7 \times 3} = \frac{8}{105}$$

Canceling Out

You can often make multiplying fractions even easier by canceling out. If the numerator and denominator of any of the fractions you need to multiply share a common factor, you can divide by the common factor to reduce both numerator and denominator. For example, the fraction:

$$\frac{4}{5} \times \frac{1}{8} \times \frac{10}{11}$$

can be rewritten, after canceling out the 4, 8, 5, and 10, as:

$$\frac{\cancel{4}^1}{\cancel{5}^1} \times \frac{1}{\cancel{8}^2} \times \frac{\cancel{10}^2}{11} = \frac{1}{1} \times \frac{1}{2} \times \frac{2}{11}$$

then, canceling the 2's, you get:

$$\frac{1}{1} \times \frac{1}{\cancel{2}^{1}} \times \frac{\cancel{2}^{1}}{11} = \frac{1}{1} \times \frac{1}{1} \times \frac{1}{11}$$

Though multiplying fractions is fairly easy mechanically, it is a little tricky intuitively. You are probably used to the product of multiplication being bigger than the numbers that are being multiplied. But when dealing with a fraction, the product of two numbers is *smaller*. Note that this phenomenon only occurs in reference to fractions smaller than one, in which the numerator is smaller than the denominator.

Dividing Fractions

Multiplication and division are inverse operations. It makes sense, then, that to perform division with fractions, all you have to do is invert (flip over) the dividing fraction and then multiply.

$$\frac{\frac{1}{4}}{\frac{5}{8}} = \frac{1}{4} \times \frac{8}{5}$$

Also note that just as multiplication of fractions that are smaller than one results in an even smaller product, division of fractions smaller than one results in a *larger* product.

Converting Mixed Numbers to Fractions

A mixed number is composed of a whole number and a fraction: $6\frac{2}{3}$, for example, is a mixed number because 6 is a whole number and $\frac{2}{3}$ is a fraction. For the SAT, it is very important that you be able to convert a mixed number into a fraction. Whenever you are asked to perform an operation of any sort on a mixed number, you will first have to convert it to fraction form. Also, for GI questions you will have to convert any mixed numbers to fractions before gridding them in.

To convert a mixed number into a fraction, multiply the whole number by the denominator and add the result to the numerator. Do not change the denominator.

For example, $6\frac{2}{3}$ can be converted into a fraction in the following way: multiply the whole number, 6, by the denominator, 3, and then add the yielded product to the original numerator, 2.　$(6 \times 3) + 2 = 20$.　The denominator remains the same, so the answer is $\frac{20}{3}$.

Decimals

Decimals are simply another way to express fractions. To get a decimal, divide the numerator of a fraction by the denominator. For example, if you take the fraction $\frac{2}{5}$ and divide 2 by 5 you would get .4.

Place Value and Decimals

Normally, numbers get bigger when they involve more numerals. The number 4000, for example, is obviously bigger than 4. However, with decimals, more zeros often means less: .4 is larger than .004. If you remember that decimals are just another way to express fractions, the reason for this difference in size is easy to see. .4 is equivalent to the $^4/_{10}$, while .004 is equivalent to $^4/_{1000}$.

The SAT will occasionally try to trip you up by asking you to compare a decimal such as .002 with the decimal .0008. Because you aren't so used to looking at decimals and 8 is obviously a larger integer than 2, you may be tempted to overlook that the second decimal includes an additional 0 and choose it as the larger decimal. To avoid such mistakes, all you have to do is be careful. One way to insure that you're being careful is to line up the decimal points of the two decimals. While .0008 might seem larger than .002,

> .0008 will always seem smaller than
> .002

To make the situation even more obvious, you can add an extra zero to the bottom decimal to make it just as long as the upper

> .0008
> .0020

Now you are comparing $^8/_{1000}$ to $^{20}/_{1000}$, and $^{20}/_{1000}$ is clearly the bigger of those two numbers. If numbers are being added to the right of the decimal number, then it's a different story.

> .0008 is smaller than
> .000819

Operations, Decimals, and Calculators

The processes of addition, subtraction, multiplication, and division for decimal numbers are quite similar to the rules of those same operations for integers. However, we're not going to delve into the specifics of those rules right now for a very simple reason: when dealing with the addition, subtraction, multiplication, or subtraction of decimals, it is almost always faster and more accurate to use a calculator. If you type in the correct decimals to begin with, your calculator will always come out with the right answer.

Percents

Percents are just another way to talk about a specific type of fraction (which also means that percents are also just another way to talk about a specific type of decimal). *Percent* literally means "of 100" in Latin, so when you have 25 percent of all the money in the world, that means you have $^{25}/_{100}$ (or .25) of the world's money.

But, sadly, you don't have that much money, and you have to take the SAT. So let's look at an example question: 4 is what percent of 20? This question presents you with a whole, 20, and then asks you to determine how much of that whole 4 represents in percentage form. To come to the answer, you have to set up an equation that sets the fraction $^4/_{20}$ to $^x/_{100}$:

$$\frac{4}{20} = \frac{x}{100}$$

if you then cross-multiply to solve for x, you get $20x = 400$, meaning $x = 20$. Therefore, 4 is 20% of 20. You also might realize that instead of working out all this cross multiplication, you could simply cancel out the 20 and the 100 to get

$$\frac{4}{20} \times 100 = 4 \times 5 = 20$$

Converting Percents into Fractions or Decimals

Converting percents into fractions and decimals will almost surely come up on the SAT. To convert from a percent to a fraction, all you have to do is take the percentage number and place it as a numerator over the denominator 100. If you have 88 percent of something, then you can quickly convert it into the fraction $^{88}/_{100}$.

To convert from a percent to a decimal, you must take a decimal point and insert it into the percent number two spaces from the right. 79% therefore becomes .79, while 350% becomes 3.5.

To convert from either a fraction or decimal back to a percent, perform the processes in reverse: multiply the fraction by 100 or move the decimal point two spaces to the left.

To save time while taking the SAT, you should memorize some of the conversions between common fractions, decimals, and percents.

$$\frac{1}{2} = 50\% = .5$$

$$\frac{1}{4} = 25\% = .25$$

$$\frac{1}{5} = 20\% = .2$$

$$\frac{1}{10} = 10\% = .1$$

$$\frac{1}{20} = 5\% = .05$$

$$\frac{1}{25} = 4\% = .04$$

Part Versus Whole Problems

Percentage problems on the SAT can often be hard but not because the math they use is confusing. Instead, it is the words the problems use that can cause difficulties. To combat this verbal nastiness, we're going to look at a sample question and explain where and why it is tricky.

What percent of 2 is 5?

When you see a percentage question, your first goal should always be to determine which number represents the whole and which the part. Intuitively, when you see the question above, you will probably think that 2 is the part, since 2 is smaller than 5, and how can you have a part that's bigger than the whole? But you can calculate the percentage when the part is bigger than the whole: the answer will simply be bigger than 100%. Now, let's break down the question. What percent of 2 is 5? This question could be written: 5 is what percent of 2? Once we've reorganized the question, it should be obvious that the "of 2" marks the 2 as the whole and the 5 as the part. We can then set up the fraction $5/2 \times 100 = 250\%$.

Remember the most important lesson of percents: before beginning a problem, always identify which number represents the whole and which represents the part.

Important Percent Terms

Percent terminology can be a little tricky, so here is a very short dictionary of terms:

- Percent more—if Max has 50% more children than Chris does, then Max has the same number of children as Chris *plus* an additional 50%.

- Percent increase—percent increase means the same thing as percent more. If the price of a $10 shirt increases 10%, the new price is the original $10 plus 10% of the $10 original.

- Percent decrease—the opposite of percent increase. This term means you subtract the specified percent of the original value from the original value.

Sometimes students see these terms and figure out what the 10% increase or decrease is, but then forget to carry out the necessary addition or subtraction. The SAT writers know about this tendency and will try to use it to trick you:

A shirt originally cost $20, but during a sale its price was reduced by 15%. What is the current price of the shirt?

(A) $3
(B) $5
(C) $13
(D) $17
(E) $23

To answer this question, you should multiply $20 by .15 to see what the change in price was:

$$\$20 \times .15 = \$3$$

Once you know that price change, then you need to subtract it from the original price, since the question asks you to find the *reduced* price of the shirt:

$$\$20 - \$3 = \$17$$

The answer is **(C)**. But if you only finished the first part of this question and looked at the answers, you might see the $3 at answer (A) like a big affirmation of correctness and be tempted to choose it without finishing the calculation.

Double Percents

Some SAT questions will ask you to determine a percent of a percent. For example, take the question:

The original price of a banana in a store is $2. During a sale, the store reduces the price by 25% and Joe buys the banana. Joe then meets his friend Sam who is faint with hunger. Seeing an opportunity, Joe raises the price of the banana 10% from the price at which he bought it and sells it to Sam. How much does Sam pay for the banana?

In this question, you are being asked to determine the cumulative effect of two percent changes. The key to solving this type of problem is to realize that each percentage change is dependent on the last. In other words, you have to work out the effect of the first percentage change, come up with a value, and then use that value to determine the effect of the second percentage change. When you are working on a percentage problem that involves a series of percentage changes, you should follow the same basic procedure that we explained for one percentage change, except in this case you should follow the procedure twice. For the first percentage change, figure out what is the whole, calculate the percentage of the whole, make sure to perform addition or subtraction if necessary, then take the new value and put it through these same steps for the second percentage change.

To answer the problem, you should first find 25% of the original price:

$$\frac{25}{100} \times \$2 = \frac{50}{100} = \$.50$$

Now subtract that .50 from the original price:

$$\$2 - \$.5 = \$1.50$$

Then we use $1.50 and increase it by 10%:

$$\frac{10}{100} \times \$1.50 = \frac{15}{100} = \$.15$$

Therefore, Sam buys the banana at a price of $1.50 + $.15 = $1.65.

When dealing with double-percent questions, some students are tempted to simply combine the two percentage changes. But you *cannot* simply add or subtract the two percent changes and then find that percent of the original value. If you tried to answer the question above by reasoning that the first percentage change lowered the price 25% and the second raised the price 10%, meaning that the total change was −15%, you would get the question wrong:

$$\frac{15}{100} \times \$2 = \frac{30}{100} = \$.30$$

Now subtract that .30 from the original price:

$$\$2 - \$.30 = \$1.70$$

We *promise* you that when the SAT gives you a double-percent problem they will include this sort of wrong answer among the choices as a distraction. Don't fall for the trick. Don't give them the satisfaction.

Ratios

Ratios can look a lot like fractions, and they are related to fractions, but they differ in important ways. Whereas a fraction describes a part out of a whole, a ratio compares two separate parts of the same whole.

A ratio can be written in a variety of ways. Mathematically it can appear as $\frac{3}{1}$ or as 3:1. In words, it would be written out as the ratio of 3 to 1. Each of these three forms of the ratio 3:1 mean the same thing, that there are three of one thing for every one of another. If you have three red marbles and one blue marble, then you would have a ratio of 3:1 for red marbles to blue marbles. For the SAT, you must remember that ratios compare *parts to parts,* rather than parts to a whole. The SAT will ask you questions like this:

Of every 40 games a baseball team plays, it loses 12 games. What is the ratio of the team's losses to wins?

(A)   3:10
(B)   7:10
(C)   3:7
(D)   7:3
(E)   10:3

The key to this sort of ratio question is to see that the question is stated in terms of a whole to a part but asks for a part to part answer. The questions tells you the team loses 12 of every 40 games, but it asks you for the ratio of losses : *wins* not losses : *games.* So the first thing you have to do is find out how many games the team wins in 40 games:

$$40 - 12 = 28$$

The team wins 28 games for every 40. So for every 12 losses, the team wins 28 games or 12:28. You can reduce this ratio by dividing both sides by 4 to get 3 losses for every 7 wins, or 3:7. Answer **(C)** is correct. If you didn't realize that the losses to games was a part to whole, you might have just reduced the ratio 12:40 to 3:10, and then chose answer (A). You can bet that on this sort of ratio problem the SAT will include the incorrect *part:whole* answer to try to trip you up.

Proportions

If you have a ratio of 3 red marbles to 1 blue, that doesn't necessarily mean that you have exactly 3 red marbles and 1 blue one. It could also mean that you have 6 red and 2 blue marbles or that you have 240 red and 80 blue marbles. In other words, ratios compare only *relative* size. In order to know how many of each color marble you actually have, in addition to knowing the ratios, you also need to know how many total marbles there are.

The SAT will often ask questions testing your ability to figure out a quantity based on the given information of a ratio between items and the total number of all items. For example:

> You have red, blue, and green marbles in the ratio of 5:4:3, and you have a total of 36 marbles. How many blue marbles do you have?

The information given states that for each group of 5 red marbles, you have a corresponding group of 4 blue marbles, and a group of 3 green marbles. The ratio therefore tells you that out of every 12 marbles (since 5 + 4 + 3 = 12) 4 of them will be blue. The question also tells you that you have 36 total marbles.

Since the ratio of blue marbles will not change no matter how many marbles you have, we can solve this problem by setting up a proportion, which is an equation that states that two ratios are equal. In this case, we are going to set equal 4:12 and x:36, with x being the number of blue marbles that we would have if we had 36 total marbles. To do math with proportions, it is most useful to set up proportions in fraction form:

$$\frac{4}{12} = \frac{x}{36}$$

Now you just need to isolate x by cross-multiplying, and then you can solve.

$$12x = 4 \times 36$$
$$12x = 144$$
$$x = 12$$

When you are dealing with ratio questions of this sort, you should always set up an equation of equivalent fractions and cross-multiply.

Rates

Rates are a special kind of ratio that deal with related quantities that have different units. The relationship between these two different quantities is defined by a rate:

$$\frac{\text{quantity 1 (measured in } x \text{ units)} \times \text{rate (measured in } \frac{y}{x} \text{ units)}}{\text{quantity 2 (measured in } y \text{ units)}}$$

That equation might seem a little complicated, but it will seem much simpler once we give some concrete examples. The most common rate questions on the SAT deal with speed, work, or price, so we'll use those.

Speed

In rate questions dealing with speed, you will usually find the first quantity measured in time, the second measured in distance, and the rate in distance covered per second, minute, or hour, a unit known as speed. If you traveled for 7 hours at 30 miles per hour, then:

$$7 \text{ hours} \times 30 \, \frac{\text{miles}}{\text{hour}} = 210 \text{ miles}$$

Notice how the units of "hour" canceled out, since the hour in the rate is at the bottom of the fraction, while the unit for the time is a normal number (meaning it could also be written as $7 \, {}^{\text{hours}}/_1$).

Work

In rate questions dealing with work, you will usually find the first quantity measured in time, the second quantity measured in work done, and the rate in measured in work done per time. If you worked for 5 hours and dug 3 ditches an hour, then:

$$5 \text{ hours} \times 3 \frac{\text{ditches}}{\text{hour}} = 15 \text{ ditches}$$

Notice how the "hour" units canceled out.

Price

In rate questions dealing with price, you will usually find the first quantity measured in numbers of items, the second measured in price, and the rate in price per item. Let's say you had 6 cucumbers, and you knew that cucumbers cost $.50 each.

$$6 \text{ cucumbers} \times \$0.50 \text{ rate } \frac{\text{price}}{\text{cucumber}} = 3 \text{ price}$$

Notice how the units of "cucumber" canceled out.

Simple Rate Problems

Simple SAT rate problems might test your ability to solve for any one of the three aspects of a rate equation: quantity 1, quantity 2, or the rate. The key to solving any rate problem is determining which values fit into which of the categories. Once you've figured out which information the question is giving you, all you have to do is plug in the numbers and work out the equation.

Take a look at the following example of a simple rate problem:

> A car salesmen sells cars at the rate of .3 per hour. How many cars will the salesmen sell in 15 days if he works 8 hours a day?

To answer this question let's first define what we know:

- **Quantity 1:** 15 days, since that is how much time the salesmen puts into his work in this problem.

- **Rate:** .3 cars sold per hour.

- **Quantity 2:** x cars sold?

First off, this problem contains a little trick. Did you notice that the units of time in the rate and input are not the same? The question states that the salesman sells .3 cars per *hour*, while asking you to figure out how many cars he will sell in 15 *days*. We included this trick in this sample problem because it is one that the SAT occasionally likes to play. So when you see rate questions dealing with time, be careful.

Before beginning to solve the problem, you must equalize the time units of hours and days. Since the salesman works 8 hours a day:

$$15 \text{ days} \times \frac{8 \text{ hours}}{\text{day}} = 120 \text{ hours}$$

Now that the units are equalized, the problem can be answered using the rate equation:

$$\text{quantity } 1 \times \text{rate} = \text{quantity } 2$$

so

$$120 \text{ hours} \times \frac{0.3 \text{ cars}}{\text{hour}} = 36 \text{ cars}$$

The salesmen sold 36 cars. Notice that in this problem, the hours unit for quantity 1 cancels with the cars/hours unit in the rate, yielding the proper unit of cars. If the units do not work out when you get your answer, you've probably made a mistake.

Complicated Rate Problems

Complicated SAT rate problems can involve more than one rate. Such problems might ask you to compare in some way two different objects moving at a different rate or to determine the distance traveled by an object going at two different rates. There is no way for us to cover every single example of a complicated rate problem in this section. We will provide one good example here, but you should also pay attention to these rate problems when you come upon them in practice tests.

> It took Griselda 5 hours to walk from her house to the supermarket and then back to her house by the same route. While going to the store, she walked at a rate of 3 kilometers per hour. Returning home, she was carrying heavy groceries, so her speed was reduced to 2 kilometers per hour. How many miles was the supermarket from Griselda's house?

We know Griselda traveled at a rate of 3 km/hr on the way to the store and 2 km/hr back from the store. We also know it took her a total of 5 hours to make the trip. Finally, since the distance between the store and Griselda's house remained constant for the trip there and back, we know that she must have spent a different amount of time traveling to the store and back. In fact, we know precisely the ratio between the time she spent walking to the store and the time she spent walking back. Since Griselda walked ½ as fast on the way to the store as she did on the way back, we know (because she traveled the same distance on each trip) that she must have spent only ⅔ as much time walking to the store as she spent walking back. Therefore, since we know she spent a total of 5 hours walking to and from the store, we can set up the equation:

$$y + \frac{2}{3}y = 5$$

where y stands for the number of hours Griselda spent walking home from the store. Now, to solve the equation for y

$$y + \frac{2}{3}y = 5$$
$$\frac{3y}{3} + \frac{2y}{3} = 5$$
$$\frac{5y}{3} = 5$$
$$5y = 15$$

We now know Griselda spent 3 hours walking home from the store. If we plug that 3 into the equation for her walk home we get:

$$3 \text{ hr} \times 2\frac{\text{km}}{\text{hr}} = \text{distance between store and house}$$
$$6 \text{ km} = \text{distance between store and house}$$

You can check this answer by looking back at the original question and making sure that the distance of 6 km works out. We know Griselda was walking at the speed of 3 km/hr to the store, and that the distance to the store was 6 km. Therefore, it took her 2 hours to walk to the store. We also know Griselda walked at the speed of 2 km/hr back from the store. Since the distance was 6 kilometers, it must have taken her 3 hours to walk back. In sum, then, it took her 5 hours to walk to and from the store, which fits the question perfectly.

Rate Problems with Variables

The SAT will occasionally ask rate problems using variables rather than numbers. These questions can be difficult because the variables can make it hard for you to figure out what refers to quantity 1, quantity 2, and the rate, and also because they can cause some confusion about what the question is asking you to do.

> A company produces soap at the rate of b bars in h hours. If the company can sell each bar of soap for 3 dollars, how many dollars worth of soap does it produce in x hours?

(A) $3b/h$
(B) $bx/3h$
(C) $3h/bx$
(D) $3bx/h$
(E) $3bh/x$

Many test-prep books recommend that you try to answer this question by substituting in numbers for the variables and then working out all the answer choices to see which one works. This method will work, but it's slow and laborious, and if you have a good understanding of rates, you would be better off just dealing with the variables directly. We'll cover both methods here.

Dealing Directly with the Variables

The key to answering this question is figuring out what the question wants and then figuring out how to give it what it wants. Looking at this question, we can see that the question is asking for the total value of the soap produced in x hours. Now, since we know that each bar of soap is worth 3 dollars, you know that the total value of soap produced in x hours is equal to:

$$\text{total worth} = 3 \times \text{the number of bars of soap produced}$$

Now all you have to do is figure out how many bars of soap are produced in x hours and multiply that expression by 3. To figure out the expression for soap produced in hours, you just need to identify what all those variables mean. Since the rate equation is:

$$\text{quantity 1} \times \text{rate} = \text{quantity 2}$$

we just have to figure out what variables go where. This is pretty easy. The question explicitly says that the rate is "b bars in h hours," which means that the rate is b/h. Also, since you know you are looking for bars of soap produced, you can substitute the variable for hours worked, x, in for quantity 1.

$$x \times \frac{b}{h} = \text{soap produced}$$

You already know that $\text{total worth} = 3 \times \text{soap produced},$ so you just have to substitute to get:

$$\text{total worth} = 3 \times \text{soap produced}$$
$$\text{total worth} = 3 \times \frac{xb}{h}$$
$$\text{total worth} = \frac{3xb}{h}$$

(D) is the right answer. Now, all that looks like a lot of work, but please note that we explained every possible step to teach you how to answer this question. If you were really good at rates, you probably could have done many of those steps in your head and just written this:

$$\text{soap produced} = \frac{bx}{h}$$
$$\text{value of soap} = 3 \times \text{soap produced}$$

and then substituted to get:

$$\text{soap produced} = \frac{3bx}{h}$$

See? Very quick.

Answering By Plugging In

If you aren't so comfortable with rates, your best bet is to substitute numbers in for the variables and then try to work out the question. We'll make $b = 4$, $h = 2$, and $x = 5$. So the question that once read:

> A company produces soap at the rate of b bars in h hours. If the company can sell each bar of soap for 3 dollars, how many dollars worth of soap does it produce in x hours?

now reads as:

> A company produces soap at the rate of 4 bars in 2 hours. If the company can sell each bar of soap for 3 dollars, how many dollars worth of soap does it produce in 5 hours?

With the variables gone, the question immediately becomes much less difficult to comprehend. You can see that the rate is $4/2 = 2$ bars per hour. And you can see that to find out the total numbers of bars produced, you just have to multiply the rate by the hours given:

$$\text{Soap produced} = 2 \text{ bars per hour} \times 5 \text{ hours} = 10$$

Then just multiply those 10 bars by the \$3 charged per bar, and you get \$30. To find the answer, you need to substitute the numbers into the answer choices and see which works out to \$30:

- (A) $3b/h = {}^{3 \times 4}/_2 = {}^{12}/_2 = 6$

- (B) $bx/3h = {}^{4 \times 5}/_{3 \times 2} = {}^{20}/_6 = 3^1/_3$

- (C) $3h/bx = {}^{3 \times 2}/_{4 \times 5} = {}^6/_{20} = {}^3/_{10}$

- (D) $3bx/h = {}^{3 \times 4 \times 5}/_2 = {}^{60}/_2 = 30$

- (E) $3bh/x = {}^{3 \times 4 \times 2}/_5 = {}^{24}/_5$

(D) is still the right answer. This method is conceptually easier than the last, but you must do all the math to use this method, which makes it take quite some time.

Arithmetic Mean, Median, and Mode

The arithmetic mean, median, and mode are all different ways to describe a group or set of numbers. The three concepts are related, and some questions on the SAT will test your knowledge of two or even three of them in conjunction. Here, we will cover each individually and then look at how they overlap.

Arithmetic Mean, a.k.a Average

The arithmetic mean, which also goes by the names *average* and *mean*, is the most important and most commonly tested of these three mathematical concepts. The basic rules of finding an average are not very complicated. To find an average of a set of *n* numbers, you need to find the sum of all the numbers and divide that sum by *n*.

For example, the average of the set 9, 8, 13, 10 is equal to the sum of those four numbers divided by 4:

$$\frac{9 + 8 + 13 + 10}{4} = \frac{40}{4} = 10$$

Occasionally, the SAT will test your knowledge of averages in a straightforward manner, giving you a bunch of numbers and asking you to find their average. More often, the SAT will find some roundabout way to test your knowledge of averages. The SAT might give you three numbers of a four-number set, the average of that set, and then ask you to find the fourth number in the set:

> If the average of four numbers is 22, and three of the numbers are 7, 11, and 18, then what is the fourth number?

There are two ways to solve this type of problem, and both are fairly simple. To use the first method, you have to realize that if you know the average of a group and also know how many numbers are in the group, you can calculate the sum of the numbers in the group. In the question asked above, you know that the average of the numbers is 22 and that there are four numbers. The four numbers, when added together, must equal $4 \times 22 = 88$. From the information given in the problem and our own calculations, we know three of the four numbers in the set, and the total sum of the numbers in the set:

$$7 + 11 + 18 + \text{unknown number} = 88$$

Solving for the unknown number is easy. All you have to do is subtract the sum of 7, 11, and 18 from 88: $\quad x = 88 - (7 + 11 + 18) = (88 - 36) = 52.$

All average problems on the SAT cover these, and basically only these, fundamental points. Difficult problems simply cover them in a trickier manner.

For example:

> The average of a set of 7 numbers is 54. The average of three of those seven numbers is 38. What is the average of the other four numbers?

This question seems really tough, since it keeps splitting apart this theoretical set of seven numbers and you have no idea what the numbers in the set are. Often, when students can't say exactly what numbers are in a set, they panic. But for this problem you don't have to know the exact numbers in the set. All you have to know is how averages work. So let's solve the problem.

There are 7 numbers in the entire set and the average of those numbers is 54. The sum of the seven numbers in the set is therefore: $7 \times 54 = 378$. Now, as the problem states, if we take three particular numbers from the set, their average is 38. We can calculate that the the sum of those three numbers is: $3 \times 38 = 114$. Suddenly, we can calculate the sum of the four remaining numbers, since that value must be the total sum of the set of seven minus the sum of the mini-set of three, $378 - 114 = 264$. Now, since we know the total sum of the four numbers, to get the average of those numbers, all we have to do is divide that by 4: $264 \div 4 = 66$.

Median

The median is the number whose value is in the middle of the numbers in a particular set. Take the set: $\{6, 19, 3, 11, 7\}$. If we arrange the numbers in order of value, we get:

$$\{3, 6, 7, 11, 19\}$$

When we list the numbers in this order, it becomes clear that the middle number in this group is 7, making 7 the median.

The set we just looked at contained an odd number of items, but in a set with an even number of items it's impossible to isolate a single number as the median. Let's add one number to the set from the previous example:

$$\{3, 6, 7, 11, 19. 20\}$$

In this case, we find the median by taking the two most middle numbers and finding their average. The two middle numbers in this set are 7 and 11, so the median of the set is $^{(7+11)}/_2 = 9$.

Mean and Median on the SAT

As we said earlier, some SAT questions might test your knowledge of mean and median in conjunction. For example, a question might show you five sets and ask you to pick the set in which the average is greater than the median. For these questions, there are a few things you should know:

1. The median and mean of a set do not have to be equal. In fact, they very seldom will be equal. The median might be larger or smaller than the mean in any set with more than two numbers. For example, take a set of three numbers where the mean is 10. The numbers could be {9, 10, 11}, which means the median and mean would be equal. The set could be {7, 8, 15}, which means the mean is larger than the median. Finally, the set could be {1, 14, 15}, and the median would be larger than the mean.

2. If you have a set of consecutive numbers, then the median and the mean will always be equal. This rule is true no matter how many numbers are in the set. In a set with five consecutive numbers, such as {7, 8, 9, 10, 11}, both mean and median are 9. In a set with four consecutive numbers, such as {7, 8, 9, 10}, both mean and median are 8.5. This rule comes up in questions fairly regularly on the SAT.

Mode

The mode is the number within a set that appears most frequently. In the set {10, 11, 13, 11, 20}, the mode is 11 since it appears twice and all the others appear just once. In a set where more than one number appears at the same highest frequency, there can be more than one mode: the set {2, 2, 3, 4, 4} has modes of 2 and 4. In a set such as {1, 2, 3, 4, 5}, where all of the numbers appear an equal number of times, there is no mode.

Exponents

Exponents are a shorthand method of describing how many times a particular number is being multiplied by itself. To write $3 \times 3 \times 3 \times 3 \times 3$ in exponent form, we would simply count out how many 3s were being multiplied together (in this case five), and then write 3^5. In written or verbal form, 3^5 is stated as: "three to the fifth power."

There are a number of exponent terms that are important to know. The SAT will not directly test you on this knowledge, but you should know these terms if you are going to discuss or learn about exponents.

- **Base.** The base refers to the 3 in 3^5. In other words, the base is the number that is being multiplied by itself, however many times specified by the exponent.

- **Exponent.** The exponent is the 5 in 3^5. In other words, the exponent tells how many times the base is to be multiplied with itself.

- **Squared.** Saying that a number is squared is a common code word to say that it has been raised to the second power, i.e., that it has an exponent of 2. In the expression 6^2, 6 has been squared.

- **Cubed.** Saying that a number is cubed is a common code word to say that it has been raised to the third power, i.e., that it has an exponent of 3. In the expression 4^3, 4 has been cubed.

When you take the SAT, you should already know the squares of numbers 1 through about 15. Memorizing this little chart can save you a lot of time on the test.

Number	Square	Number	Square
1	1	9	81
2	4	10	100
3	9	11	121
4	16	12	144
5	25	13	169
6	36	14	196
7	49	15	225
8	64		

You should also know that 2 cubed (2^3) = 8 and that $3^3 = 27$, and—just to be safe—that $4^3 = 64$ and $5^3 = 125$.

Adding and Subtracting Numbers with Exponents

Actually, you can't add or subtract numbers with exponents. Instead, you have to work out each exponent to find its value and then add the two numbers. For example, to add $3^3 + 4^2$, you must work out the exponents to get $(3 \times 3 \times 3) + (4 \times 4)$ and then calculate $27 + 16 = 43$. (You probably don't need to write out the whole first step when doing a problem like this one. We included it just to be complete.) Often, you can work out exponents on your calculator, so figure out how to use your calculator's exponent functions before the test. It can save you time and increase your accuracy.

Multiply and Dividing Numbers with Exponents

To multiply two base exponential numbers that have the same base, all you have to do is add the exponents together:

$$3^6 \times 3^2 = 3^{(6+2)} = 3^8$$

To divide two same-base exponential numbers, just subtract the exponents.

$$\frac{3^6}{3^2} = 3^{(6-2)} = 3^4$$

If you need to multiply or divide two exponential numbers that do not have the same base or exponent, you'll just have to do your work the old-fashioned way: multiply the exponential numbers out and multiply or divide them accordingly.

Raising an Exponent to an Exponent

Occasionally you might see an exponent raised to another exponent, as seen in the following format $(3^2)^4$. In such cases, multiply the exponents:

$$(3^2)^4 = 3^{(2 \times 4)} = 3^8$$

Exponents and Fractions

To raise a fraction to an exponent, raise both the numerator and denominator to that exponent:

$$(\frac{1}{3})^3 = \frac{1}{27}$$

Exponents and Negative Numbers

When you multiply a negative number by a negative number, you get a positive number, and when you multiply a negative number by a positive number, you get a negative number. These rules affect how negative numbers function in reference to exponents.

- **A negative number raised to an even-number exponent results in a positive number.** For example $(-2)^4 = 16$. To see why this is so, let's break down the example. $(-2)^4$ means $(-2) \times (-2) \times (-2) \times (-2)$. When you multiply the first two –2s together, you get positive 4 because you are multiplying two negative numbers. Then when you multiply the (+4) by the next (–2), you get (–8), since you are multiplying a positive number by a negative number. Finally, you multiply the (–8) by the last (–2) and get (+16), since you're once again multiplying two negative numbers.

- **A negative number raised to an odd power results in a negative number.** To prove this to yourself all you have to do is look at the example above and stop the process at (–8), which equals $(-2)^3$.

Square Roots

The square root of a number is the number that, when squared (multiplied by itself), is equal to the given number. For example, the square root of 16 is 4, because $4^2 = 4 \times 4 = 16$. A perfect square is a number whose square root is an integer.

The sign denoting a square root is $\sqrt{\ }$. To use the previous example, $\sqrt{16} = 4$. As with exponents, you need to know how to multiply and divide square roots.

Multiplication and Square Roots

$$\sqrt{4}\sqrt{6} = \sqrt{24}$$

As the example shows, to multiply two square roots, you should multiply the numbers within each individual square root and place the product under a single square root.

This rule also works in reverse, so you can take a number within a $\sqrt{\ }$ and factor it into perfect squares.

$$\sqrt{48} = \sqrt{16}\sqrt{3} = 4\sqrt{3}$$

Notice in this example that once we separated out 16 from 48, we could change the $\sqrt{16}$ into 4. This skill is important for the SAT. When dealing with square roots, you may get an answer that looks quite different from any of the answer choices. In such situations, you probably have just neglected to reduce the number within the square-root sign.

Division and Square Roots

Just as when you multiply square roots, when you divide them, you can divide the numbers and place them under a single square root.

$$\frac{\sqrt{20}}{\sqrt{16}} = \sqrt{\frac{20}{16}} = \sqrt{\frac{5}{4}}$$

Fractions and Square Roots

To find the square root of a fraction, take the square root of both the numerator and the denominator. For example, $\sqrt{1/16} = 1/4$. In some instances, either the numerator or denominator might not be a perfect square. In these instances, you won't be able to get rid of the $\sqrt{}$ sign. For example, $\sqrt{4/17} = 2/\sqrt{17}$.

Probability

Usually, about two questions on each SAT cover the topic of probability. To begin to deal with these questions you first have to understand what probability is:

$$\frac{\text{chance of a particular outcome}}{\text{total number of possible outcomes}}$$

For example, let's say you're on a game show and are shown three doors. Behind one door there is a prize while behind the other two doors are big piles of nothing. The probability that you will choose the door with the prize is $1/3$, because out of the three possibilities, there is one chance that you will pick the correct door.

How about a more detailed example?

Joe has 3 green marbles, 2 red marbles, and 5 blue marbles, and if all the marbles are dropped into a dark bag, what is the probability that Joe will pick out a green marble?

There are 3 ways for Joe to pick a green marble (since there are 3 different green marbles), but there are 10 total possible outcomes (one for each marble in the bag). Therefore the probability of picking a green marble is

$$\begin{aligned} \text{Probability} &= \frac{\text{particular outcomes}}{\text{total outcomes}} \\ &= \frac{\text{green marbles}}{\text{total marbles}} \\ &= \frac{3}{10} \end{aligned}$$

When you calculate probability, always be careful to divide by the total number of chances. In the last example, you may have been tempted to leave out the three chances of picking a green marble from the total possibilities, yielding the incorrect equation P = 3/7.

Backward Probability

The SAT might also ask you a "backward" probability question. For example, if you have a bag holding twenty marbles, and you have a $1/5$ chance of picking a blue marble, how many blue marbles are in the bag? All you have to do is set up the proper equation, following the model of $P = {}^m/n$:

$$\frac{1}{5} = \frac{x}{20}$$

and x is the variable denoting the number of blue marbles. Cross-multiplying through the equation, you get $5x = 20$, which reduces to $x = 4$.

Combinations

Combination questions are more rarely found on the SAT than probability questions. Still, they do occasionally show up, so we cover them here. You can think of combination problems as half-probability problems. These questions give you a situation and ask you to figure out the total number of outcomes that can arise from that situation. Whereas for probability questions you have to figure out the likelihood of one outcome in comparison to the total outcomes, in combination problems you only have to figure out the total number of outcomes. For example:

> Imagine a man (or, if you want, a woman). To make things interesting, let's make him a naked man who wants to put on a pair of pants and a shirt. He has 6 pairs of pants and 3 shirts. How many different outfits does he have to choose from?

To answer this question you have to figure out how many different combinations of shirts and pants the man can make. To do this, multiply the total number of object 1 (6 pants) by the total number of object 2 (3 shirts). Total outfits = $3 \times 6 = 18$.

If the man also had 4 hats, to calculate the total number of outfits he could make you would multiply $3 \times 6 \times 4 = 72$ total outfits—that's over two months of outfits!

Series

A series is a sequence of numbers that proceed one after another according to some pattern. Usually the SAT will give you a few numbers in a series and ask you to specify what number should come next. For example,

$$-1, 2, -4, 8, -16$$

is a series. Can you figure out which number should come after the –16? Well, in this series, each number is multiplied by –2 to yield the next number. Therefore, 32 is the number in the series after –16. These types of questions ask you to be able to recognize patterns and then apply them. Learning to recognize the patterns is key. When you look at a pattern, try to think whether it is changing by addition or subtraction, multiplication or division, or by exponents. There isn't one tried-and-true way to find a pattern. Just think critically, and use your intuition and trial and error.

Series Problems that Seem Harder than They Are

Sometimes the SAT might show you a series and ask you to identify the 50th number in the series or to calculate the sum of the first 24 numbers in the series. These questions seem difficult and time-consuming, so many students skip them. Other students write out the series and do the math, which does take a bit of time. Whenever you see such a question, you should assume that there is some shortcut to the answer. For example, on a question that asks for the 50th term in the series, see if the series begins to repeat itself. Take the following problem:

> The first two numbers of a series are 1 and 2. All the numbers in the series after that are produced by subtracting from the previous term the term before that. What is the fiftieth term in the sequence?

To answer this question, start writing out the sequence

$$1, 2, 1, -1, -2, -1, 1, 2, 1, \ldots$$

By this time you should see that the pattern has begun to repeat itself: the 1st term is the same as the 7th, the 2nd is the same as the 8th . . . Since you know the sequence repeats, you can extrapolate into the future. If the 1st term is the same as the 7th, it will also be the same as the 14th, 21st, 28th, 35th, 42nd, and 49th. This repetion means that the second term must be equal to the 50th term, so the answer is 2.

If you were given the same question but asked to figure out the sum of the first 35 terms, you would do basically the same thing. Once you discovered that the sequence repeats every seven terms, you would know that the value of the first 24 terms is equal to   4 × the sum of the first six   terms, since terms 1–6, 7–12, 13–18, and 19–24 will all be identical. The sum of the first 6 terms is:

$$1 + 2 + 1 + (-1) + (-2) + (-1) = 0$$

So the sum of the first 24 terms is equal to 0.

Sets

Sets are discrete groups of items. For example, the number of people who received a B in Mr. Japlonski's chemistry class can be considered a set. A set contains only those things that can fit its definitions. If a student got an A in Mr. Japlonski's class, he cannot be in the set of students who got Bs. If you have a set that is defined as $(1, 2, \sqrt{7})$, then the only things that can be in that set are $(1, 2, \sqrt{7})$. Really, on the SAT, sets don't get much more complicated than that.

The One Exception

That is, set questions don't get more complicated except for one specific type of question. In this question, the SAT will describe two sets and a few people who fit into both sets. Then it will ask how many total people are in the two sets. For example:

> Of the lions at the zoo, 13 eat zebra meat, 11 eat giraffe meat, and 7 eat both. How many total lions are there in the zoo?

When you read it, this question just feels like it's going to be very hard. A lot of students will therefore not even try to answer it. So what does that mean to you? It's a chance for you to gain points in comparison to other students. Luckily, this type of question is actually quite simple to answer, as long as you know and use the following formula:

Total = number in set 1 + number in set 2 – number common to set 1 and 2

To answer the question about the lions, write:

Total lions = 13 zebra eaters + 11 giraffe eaters – 7 eaters of both
Total lions = 17

Once you know the formula, all you have to do is figure out which numbers in the word problem define set 1, which define set 2, and which define the overlap set. After that, you just have to plug in the numbers and do some simple addition and subtraction.

SAT Algebra

Chapter Contents

Almost a third of the questions on the math portion of the SAT deal with algebra. This news strikes fear into the hearts of many students who associate algebra with intense and difficult math. But take heart: the algebra tested on the SAT is not very difficult. The equations on the test are fairly simple, and the questions asked about particular topics of algebra are often quite similar.

In this section we will cover the seven major algebraic topics covered by the SAT: substitution, building expressions and equations, simplifying and manipulating expressions, solving linear equations, solving systems of equations, solving inequalities, and multiplying binomials and polynomials

Before covering these topics, however, we will address a question brought up by the teachings of some other test prep companies.

To Algebra or Not to Algebra

There are many ways to answer most algebra problems. You can use algebra—setting up and working out equations. You can plug numbers into equations to try and avoid using algebra. In some cases, you might even be able to solve a question by being a particularly intuitive genius and finding a magnificent shortcut.

We want to stress that none of these methods is necessarily better than another. Which method is best for you relies on your math ability and your target score. Trying to solve problems with algebra is more conceptually demanding, but can take less time. Plugging in numbers makes questions easier to understand but will likely take more time. In general, if you are uncomfortable with algebra, you should generally try to use plugging in. If you are comfortable with algebra, using it is probably the best way to go. Still, these suggestions are not hard and fast rules. If you are generally comfortable with algebra but come upon a question that is stumping you, try plugging in answers. If you usually prefer plugging in answers but come upon a question you can solve using algebra, then use algebra. When you study your practice tests, while looking at the algebra questions you got wrong, you should think about the method you employed. Did you plug in when you should have used algebra? Did you use algebra when you should have plugged in? As for being an intuitive math genius, it can't just be taught—though we will show you how one might think.

Here's an example algebra question:

A man flipped a coin 162 times. The coin landed with heads side up 62 more times than it landed with tails up. How many times did the coin land heads?

(A)   100
(B)   104
(C)   108
(D)   112
(E)   116

Solving by Algebra

If you answer this question with algebra, you realize that if heads are represented by the variable x, then tails are represented by $(x - 62)$. Therefore,

$$x + (x - 62) = 162$$
$$2x - 62 = 162$$
$$2x = 224$$
$$x = 112$$

As you can see, there's simply less math to do for this problem when you use algebra. Using algebra will only take you longer than plugging in if you have trouble coming up with the equation $x + (x - 62) = 162$.

Therefore, if you can quickly come up with the necessary equation, then use algebra to solve algebra problems. If you have the sense that it will take you a while to figure out the correct equation, then plug in.

Solving by Plugging In

If you were to answer this problem by plugging in, you would pick (C) 108 as the first number to try, since if it does not happen to be the answer, you can still discard either the numbers smaller than it or larger than it. So, if the coin came up heads 108 times, then how many times did it land tails? It landed tails 162 − 108 = 54. Is 108 heads landings 62 more than 54 tails landings? No, 108 − 54 = 54. In order for the problem to work out you need more head landings. You can eliminate (A) and (B) as possibilities. Let's say we choose (D) 112 as our next plug in number. 162 − 112 = 50. Does 112 − 50 = 62? Yes. **(D)** is the answer.

Solving by Being an Amazing Genius

It is quite possible that you just looked at this problem and said to yourself, "Other than the 62 more heads, all the other flips were equally heads and tails. So: if you take the 62 out of the total of 162, then you know that the other 100 flips were 50 heads and 50 tails. Now I can just add 62 + 50 = 112. Man, I am an amazing genius!"

The Bottom Line on Using Algebra

Hopefully, our example has convinced you that there isn't any "right way" to answer a question dealing with algebra. There are faster ways and slower ways, and it always benefits you to use the faster way if you can, but the most important thing is getting the question right. Therefore, when you come to a question, don't insist on using only one method to try to answer it. Just do what you have to in order to answer the question correctly in as little time as possible.

Now we'll cover the topics of algebra tested by the SAT.

Substitution

Substitution questions are some of the simplest algebra questions on the SAT. These questions provide you with an algebraic expression and give you the value of one of the variables within the equation. For example:

> If $2y + 8x = 11$, what is the value of $3(2y + 8x)$?

You might see this equation filled with variables and panic. You shouldn't. The problem is immensely simple. Since $2y + 8x = 11$, all you have to do is substitute 11 in for $2y + 8x$ in the expression $3(2y + 8x)$, and you get $3(11) = 33$.

Some substitution questions are a tad more complicated. For these, you might have to do some simple math either before or after the substitution.

Math Before Substitution

> If $3x − 7 = 8$, then $23 − 3x =$

SAT Algebra

In this problem you have to find what $3x$ equals before you can substitute that value into the expression $23 - 3x$. To find $3x$, simply take

$$3x - 7 = 8$$

and add 7 to both sides, giving:

$$3x = 15$$

Now we can substitute that 15 into $23 - 3x$:

$$23 - 15 = 8$$

Math After Substitution

If $a + b = 7$ and $b = 3$, then $4a = ?$

Here we first have to solve for a by substituting 3 for b:

$$a + b = 7$$
$$a + 3 = 7$$
$$a = 4$$

Once you know that $a = 4$, just substitute into $4a$:

$$4 \times 4 = 16$$

Building Expressions and Equations

Occasionally the SAT will ask a word problem, and you will have to write out an expression that describes the word problem, and perhaps simplify it. For example:

Mary poured g cups of water into a bucket, leaving the bucket with a total of f cups in it. Mary then removed $(g - 3)$ cups of water from the bucket. How many cups of water remain in the bucket?

To answer this question, you have to interpret the word problem. In other words, you have to figure out what is important in the word problem and how it fits into the expression you need to build. In this question, you are asked to generate an expression that describes how many cups of water there are in the bucket after Mary removes $(g - 3)$ cups. It doesn't matter what g actually equals, because we don't care how much water was in the bucket before Mary added g cups. The question only includes that detail to trick you. As far as we're concerned the problem might as well have been:

> There were f cups of water in a bucket. Mary then removed $(g - 3)$ cups of water from the bucket. How many cups of water remain in the bucket?

To work out the equation, we take the number of cups in the bucket and subtract what was removed:

$$f - (g - 3) = f - g + 3$$

The equation to state how many cups of water are in the bucket is: total cups $= f - g + 3$.

ETS often deliberately writes equations less clearly than it could. Instead of writing:

> Mark collects worms, frogs, and toasters. He has 6 more toasters than frogs, and 3 times as many frogs as worms.

ETS would probably write:

> Mark collects worms, frogs, and toasters. The number of toasters he has is 6 more than the number of frogs, and the number of frogs is 3 times as large as the number of worms.

The ETS writers do this simply to confuse you, which seems rather juvenile of them. But you should still be ready for it.

These types of questions usually appear in the last, difficult third of SAT math sections. If you are looking to score above a 600, you should definitely make sure that you know how to answer them.

Simplifying and Manipulating Expressions

Simplifying Algebraic Expressions

Often the SAT will ask a question about an equation that seems impossibly complicated. In such cases, simplifying the equation can often reveal the answer more clearly or make calculating the answer a less harrowing task. There are two primary ways to simplify an equation, factoring and combining like terms.

Factoring and Expansion

Factoring an algebraic expression means finding factors common to all the terms in an expression and dividing them out. For example, to factor $3a + 3b$, divide out the three to get $3(a + b)$. Factoring is merely reversing the distributive property of multiplication. Below are some examples of factoring:

$$6y + 8x = 2(3y + 4x)$$
$$8b + 24 = 8(b + 3)$$
$$3(x + y) + 4(x + y) = (3 + 4)(x + y) = 7(x + y)$$
$$\frac{2x + y}{x} = \frac{2x}{x} + \frac{y}{x} = 2 + \frac{y}{x}$$

Expansion involves taking a factored expression, such as $8(b + 3)$, and distributing one term to the other(s) by multiplying them: $8b + 24$.

Combining Similar Terms

If an expression contains like terms you can combine those terms and simplify the equation. Like terms are identical variables that have the same exponential value.

$$x^2 + 8x^2 = 9x^2$$
$$y^{13} + 754y^{13} = 755y^{13}$$
$$m^3 + m^3 = 2m^3$$

As long as two terms have the same variable and the same exponential value, you can combine them. Note that when you combine like terms, the variable doesn't change.

Variables that have different exponential values are not like terms and cannot be combined. Two terms that do not share a variable are also not like terms, and cannot be combined regardless of their exponential value.

$$\text{You can't combine: } x^4 + x^2 =$$
$$y^2 + x^2 =$$

Manipulating Equations

A number of SAT questions will provide you with an equation such as $x = yz$ and then ask you to show what that equation looks like in terms of y. The secret to answering such questions is a simple rule: you can perform any operation on one side of the equation as long as you perform the same operation on the other side of the equation. For the question described above, you need to isolate y from the other two variables. To do so, all you have to do is divide both sides of the equation by z.

$$x = yz$$
$$\frac{x}{z} = y$$

A more difficult SAT question might ask:

If $x - 2 = z$ and $y = 7$, then $xy = ?$

To answer this question, you have to isolate x, multiply both sides of the new equation by y, and then substitute 7 for y on the right side.

$$x - 2 = z$$
$$x = z + 2$$
$$xy = y(z + 2)$$
$$xy = 7(z + 2)$$
$$xy = 7z + 14$$

Solving Linear Equations

You can always solve linear equations on the SAT by isolating the variable whose value you are trying to determine on one side of the equation. However, if you stay alert, you can often find shortcuts that will save you time without affecting your accuracy. Let's look at an easy example:

If $6p + 2 = 20$, then $6p - 3 = ?$

This is an easy problem to solve through the normal algebraic method. First solve for p:

$$6p + 2 = 20$$
$$6p = 18$$
$$p = 3$$

and then we plug 3 into the second equation:

$$6p - 3 =$$
$$6(3) - 3 =$$
$$18 - 3 = 15$$

But it's possible to answer this question much more quickly. The secret to this question is that you don't have to solve for p at all. Instead, you have to notice that both equations contain $6p$ and that the value of $6p$ will not change. Therefore, all you have to do in the first equation is solve for $6p$. And as you can see above, that simply means subtracting 2 from 20 to get 18. Once you know $6p$ is 18, you can plug 18 in for $6p$ in the second equation and get your answer of 15.

When you come upon an algebra question asking you to solve an equation, you should always take a moment to look for shortcuts. Look for equations that not only have the same variables, but the same coefficients attached to that variable (such as $6p$ and $6p$). ETS puts these shortcuts into their questions on purpose. They believe that if you're knowledgeable enough about math to see shortcuts, then you deserve the extra time those shortcuts will give you on the test. Since you now know that the shortcuts are there, you might as well take advantage of them.

Solving Systems of Equations

Occasionally the SAT will give you two equations and ask you to determine the value of a particular variable or some other equation or expression. For example, the SAT might ask :

If $3x + 4y = 32$ and $2y - x = 6$, then $x - y = ?$

The best way to answer this type of question is to use a type of substitution method: solve for one variable and then substitute that value into the other equation. Since the x in the second equation has no coefficient next to it, it will be easier to solve for that variable. All it takes is a little reorganizing:

$$2y - x = 6$$
$$2y - 6 = x$$
$$x = 2y - 6$$

Now, all we have to do is plug $2y - 6$ into the value for x in the first equation:

$$3(2y - 6) + 4y = 32$$

Now, we have only one variable to deal with in the equation, and we can easily solve for it:

$$6y - 18 + 4y = 32$$
$$10y = 50$$
$$y = 5$$

Once we know the value of y, we can plug that value into either equation to solve for x.

$$x = 2y - 6$$
$$x = 2(5) - 6$$
$$x = 4$$

Since $y = 5$ and $x = 4$, $x - y = 4 - 5 = -1$.

When you solve problems that deal with systems of equations, always be careful of two things.

- Make sure you solve for the first variable in its lowest form (solve for x rather than $2x$).

- Answer the question the SAT asks. For example, in the sample above, the question asked for the value of x − y. But it's certainly possible that after doing all the work and figuring out that x = 4, you might forget to carry out the final simple operation 4 − 5 = −1 and think that the answer is 4. You can be sure that the test will try to trick you by including 4 as one of its answer choices.

Solving Inequalities

An equation states that the values on either side of the = sign are of the same value. An inequality states that one side of the equation is greater than the other: $a < b$ states that a is less than b, while $a > b$ states that a is greater than b. $a \le b$ means that a is less than or equal to b, while $a \ge b$ means that a is greater than or equal to b.

Solving an inequality is basically the same as solving a normal equation: all the rules of simplification still apply, as does the rule stipulating that whatever you do to one side of the equation you must also do to the other side. The one rule that does differ for inequalities comes when you multiply both sides by a negative. If you do so, you must flip the greater than or less than sign: if $x > y$, then $-x < -y$.

Inequalities often appear in QC questions.

$$2 \le 2y - 3 \le 4$$

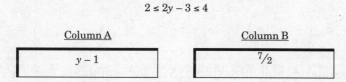

Column A	Column B
$y - 1$	$^7/_2$

The fastest way to answer this question is to substitute $^7/_2$ into the inequality $2 < 2y - 3 < 9$ to see if it is a possible value for y. If you did this, you'd see that $2(^7/_2) - 3 = 4$, making $^7/_2$ a possible value for y. Also, because when $^7/_2$ is plugged into the expression it gives you the value of 4, which is the highest possible allowed value of the expression as stated by $2y - 3 \le 4$, you know that y can never be bigger than $^7/_2$. And since the expression in column A is $y - 1$, you know that Column B must be bigger than Column A.

Multiplying Binomials and Polynomials

Multiplying binomials or polynomials can look like a daunting task, but it really isn't. It's actually pretty mindless. The most important thing is to be careful that you haven't forgotten a term somewhere.

Binomials

Problems that require you to multiply binomials are pretty common on the SAT. This is not a difficult task if you remember the acronym FOIL, which stands for First Outer Inner Last. For example, if you must multiply the binomials $(x + 1)(x + 3)$ you start by multiplying the first number in each polynomial $(x)(x)$, then the outer numbers $(x)(3)$, then the inner numbers $(1)(x)$, and finally the last numbers $(1)(3)$ and you get:

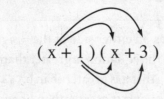

$$x^2 + 3x + 1x + 3 = x^2 + 4x + 3$$

The only tricky part to following FOIL is remembering to pay attention to signs. For instance, if you have the polynomials $(x + 1)(x - 3)$, then the -3 comes to play an important role. You always add up the products of FOIL, but look what happens when there's a negative number involved:

$$(x + 1)(x - 3) = x^2 + 1x + (-3x) + (-3) = x^2 + 1x - 3x - 3 = x^2 - 2x - 3$$

There are a few standard binomials that ETS includes in almost every SAT. You should memorize how to multiply these binomials:

$$(x + y)(x - y) = x^2 - y^2$$
$$(x + y)(x + y) = x^2 + 2xy + y^2$$
$$(x - y)(x - y) = x^2 - 2xy + y^2$$

Polynomials

On extremely rare occasions, a question on the SAT might ask you to multiply polynomials. For example, you might be asked to multiply the polynomial $(a + b + c)$ by the binomial $(d + e)$. To carry out this multiplication, you should treat the larger polynomial as a single term and distribute the smaller one across it:

$$(d + e)(a + b + c) = d(a + b + c) + e(a + b + c) = da + db + dc + ea + eb + ec$$

To multiply $(2x + 3)(x^2 + 4x + 7)$:

$$2x(x^2 + 4x + 7) + 3(x^2 + 4x + 7) = 2x^3 + 8x^2 + 14x + 3x^2 + 12x + 21$$

Then combine like terms to get your final answer:

$$= 2x^3 + 11x^2 + 26x + 21$$

SAT Algebra

SAT Geometry

A BOUT A THIRD OF THE MATH questions on the SAT deal with topics of basic geometry. The geometry tested on the SAT is less complicated than the geometry taught in high school. For the test, you will have to know about lines, angles, triangles, circles, polygons and other shapes, but you will not have to write out a proof or prove a geometric theorem. The SAT contains no trigonometry.

There are seven main categories of geometry tested on the SAT, as you can see in the table of contents on this page. In addition to covering these seven topics, we also provide a brief run-through of the basics of geometry so that you're fresh on the concepts and terminology.

Geometry Basics

We've included this first little review of geometry basics because you need to understand certain terms and ideas before you can discuss the geometry topics tested on the SAT.

Points

A point is a way to describe a specific location in space. Below is pictured the point *B*.

B.

A point has no length or width. Though in the picture point *B* is a black dot, in real life, points take up no space and are not tangible. Points are useful for identifying specific locations but are not objects in themselves. They only appear so when drawn on a page.

Lines

A line is an infinite set of points arrayed in a straight formation, named by any two points in that set. A line has no thickness but is infinitely long in both directions. To form a line, take any two points, A and B, and draw a straight line through them. The resulting line is a called line AB.

A line can be drawn through any two points.

Line Segments

A line segment is the portion of a line that lies between two points on that line—in this example, points A and B. Whereas a line has infinite length, a line segment has a finite length. A line segment is named by the two points it lies between

A line segment can be drawn between any two points.

Rays

A ray is a cross between a line and a line segment. It extends without bound in one direction but not the other. Below is a figure of a ray:

A ray is named by its endpoint and another point that it passes through.

Okay, now we've covered the basics. All of the following topics are tested directly by the SAT.

Angles and Lines

An angle is a geometric figure consisting of two lines, rays, or line segments with a common endpoint:

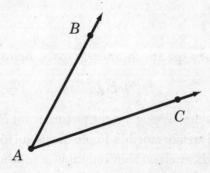

The endpoint of the angle is called the vertex. In the angle pictured above, the vertex is point *A*. The angle can be called either angle *CAB* or angle *BAC*. When naming an angle in this way, the only rule is that the vertex must be the middle "initial" of the angle. The SAT will also refer to angles using symbols: ∠A.

Measuring Angles

Angles are measured in degrees, sometimes denoted by the symbol °. There are 360° in a complete rotation around a point; a circle therefore has 360°. There are some other ways to measure angles, such as radians. You may not have learned about radians in high school. Well, don't worry about them. For the SAT, you only have to be familiar with degrees.

Take two intersecting lines. The intersection of these lines produces four angles.

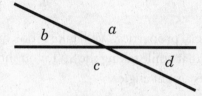

From the diagram below, you should see that the four angles together encompass one full revolution around the two lines' point of intersection. Therefore, the four angles produced by two intersection lines total 360°; angle $a + b + c + d = 360°$.

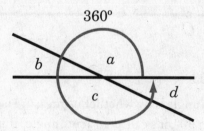

Types of Angles

There are different types of angles, categorized by the number of degrees they have.

Zero Angles

An angle with a measure of 0° is called a zero angle. If this is hard to visualize, consider two lines that form some angle greater than 0°. Then picture one of the lines rotating toward the other until they both fall on the same line. The angle they create has been shrunk from its original measure to 0°, forming a zero angle:

Right Angles

An angle with a measure of 90° is called a right angle. Notice that a right angle is symbolized with a square drawn in the corner of the angle. Whenever you see that little square, you know that you are dealing with a right angle.

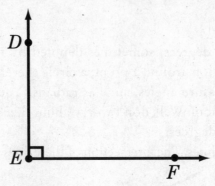

Right angles often have special properties. We'll take a look at these properties later on. For now, it's enough to say that while taking the SAT, you should be on the lookout for the little square that denotes a right angle.

Straight Angle

An angle with a measure of 180° is called a straight angle. It looks just like a line. Don't confuse straight angles with zero angles, which look like a single ray.

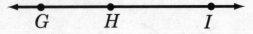

Acute and Obtuse Angles

Another way to classify an angle is by whether its measure is greater or less than 90°. If an angle measures less than 90°, it's called an acute angle. If it measures more than 90°, it's called an obtuse angle. Right angles are neither acute nor obtuse. They're just right.

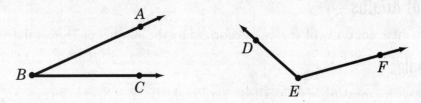

In the picture below, ∠ABC is acute while ∠DEF is obtuse.

Complementary and Supplementary Angles

Special names are given to pairs of angles whose sums equal either 90° or 180°. Angles whose sum is 90° are called complementary angles. If two angles sum to 180°, they're called supplementary angles.

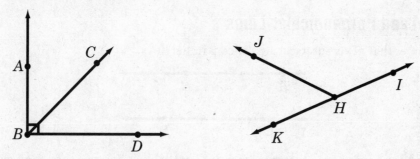

In the picture above ∠ABC and ∠CBD are complementary, since together they make up a right angle. Angle ∠JHK and ∠JHI are supplementary, since they make up a straight line.

On the SAT, you will often have to use the rules of complementary and supplementary angles to figure out the degree measure of an angle. For instance, let's say you are given the following diagram and are told that *AC* is a line:

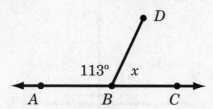

The picture tells you that ∠ABD is 113°, but how many degrees is ∠DBC? Well, since you know that AC is a line, you know that ∠ABC is a straight angle and equals 180°. You also know that ∠ABD and ∠DBC are supplementary angles that add up to 180°. Therefore, to find out the value of ∠DBC, you can simply take 180° and subtract 113°, which tells you that ∠DBC = 67°.

Vertical Angles

When two lines (or line segments) intersect, the angles that lie opposite each other, called vertical angles, are always equal.

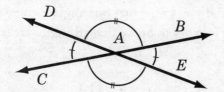

Angle ∠DAC and ∠BAE are vertical angles and are therefore equal to each other. Angle ∠DAB and ∠CAE are also vertical (and equal) angles. This is very important knowledge for the SAT. At some point during the test, you will likely be asked to figure out the degree of an angle, and knowing this rule will help you immensely.

Parallel and Perpendicular Lines

Pairs of lines that never intersect are called parallel lines.

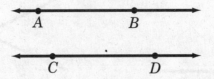

On the SAT, never assume that two lines are parallel just because they look as if they are. If the lines are parallel, the SAT will tell you.

Lines (or segments) are called perpendicular if their intersection forms a right angle. Notice that if one of the angles formed by the intersection of two lines or segments is a right angle, then all four angles created will also be right angles (incidentally illustrating our point that the four angles formed by two intersecting lines will equal 360°, since 90° + 90° + 90° + 90° = 360°).

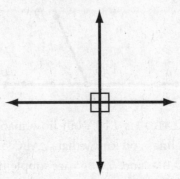

As with parallel lines, don't assume that lines on the SAT are perpendicular unless the SAT states that they are. The SAT will alert you to perpendicular lines either by stating that two lines are perpendicular or by using the little box to indicate that the angles are 90°.

Also, you should note that if you see two lines that intersect and you know that the two lines form one right angle, but you don't explicitly know the value of the other three angles, you still know that the two lines are perpendicular and that all four angles equal 90°. Think about it. If you know that one angle is equal to 90°, then you can use the rules of supplementary angles to prove that all angles are equal to 90°.

Parallel Lines Cut by a Transversal

When two parallel lines are cut by a third straight line, the third line, known as a transversal, will intersect with each of the parallel lines. The eight angles created by these two intersections have special relationships with one another.

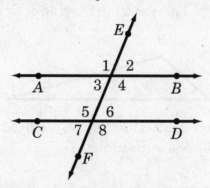

Angles 1, 4, 5, and 8 are all equal to each other. So are angles 2, 3, 6, and 7. Also, the sums of any two adjacent angles, such as 1 and 2 or 7 and 8 equal 180°. From these rules, you can make justified claims about seemingly unrelated angles. For example, since angles 1 and 2 sum to 180° — and since angle 2 and 7 are equal — the sum of angle 1 and 7 also equals 180°. The SAT likes to test this topic. When you see parallel lines cut by a transversal, you should immediately know how the angles are related. If you just know that angle 2 and angle 7 are equal, you will be able to answer the question a lot more quickly than if you have to work out the question by using the rules of supplementary and complementary angles.

Triangles

Triangles are closed figures containing three angles and three sides. The sum of the three angles in a triangle will always equal 180°. This is a very important fact. You *must* know it. There are two other important rules of triangles that you should know for the SAT.

1. The longest side of a triangle is always opposite the largest angle; the second longest side is always opposite the second largest angle; and the shortest side of the triangle is opposite the smallest angle. The reverse is also true: the largest angle will stand opposite the longest side, etc.

2. No side of a triangle can be as large as the sum of the other two sides. If you know that a triangle has sides of length 4 and 6, you know the third side is smaller than 10 (6 + 4) and bigger than 2 (6 − 4). This can help you eliminate possible answer choices on MC questions.

There are a number of specialized types of triangles. Each of these types of triangles have special properties. The SAT will definitely test your understanding of these properties.

Scalene Triangles

A scalene triangle has no equal sides and, therefore, no equal angles.

The special property of this triangle is that it doesn't really have any special properties. SAT questions don't usually deal with scalenes.

Isosceles Triangles

Isosceles triangles have two equal sides, in this case sides a and b (the little marks in those two sides mark the sides as being congruent or equal in length). The angles opposite the congruent sides are also equal, in this case the angles marked by $x°$ and $y°$.

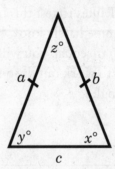

Because two of the angles of the isosceles triangle are equal and all triangles contain exactly 180°, if you know the value of one of the two equal angles, you can figure out the value of all the angles in the triangle. For example, if you know the value of $\angle x$, you know the value of $\angle y$, since $\angle x$ and $\angle y$ are equal. Angle z is equal to $180° - 2x$ (since x and y are equal, $x + y = 2x$). If you know the measure of $\angle z$, you can figure out the measures of $\angle x$ and $\angle y$, since each equals $^{180 - x}/_2$.

The SAT will test your knowledge of isosceles triangles. It might give you the length of a side and ask you the length of the other side to test your understanding of congruence. It might give you the value of an angle and ask you to figure out the value of another angle. It might ask you something else a little more indirect. But if you know these rules and remember them each time you see an isosceles triangle, you'll do fine.

Equilateral Triangles

An equilateral triangle is a triangle in which all the sides and all angles are equal. Since the angles of a triangle must total 180°, the measure of each angle of an equilateral triangle must be 60°.

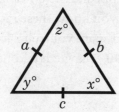

Right Triangles

A triangle with a right angle (90°) is called a right triangle. Because the angles of a triangle must total 180°, the non-right angles ($\angle x$ and $\angle y$ in the diagram below) in a right triangle must add up to 90°. The side opposite the right angle (side c in the diagram below) is called the hypotenuse.

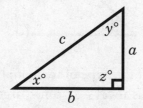

There are many different types of right triangles, but two are particularly important for the SAT.

30-60-90 Triangle

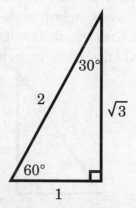

A 30-60-90 triangle is true to its name: it has angles of 30°, 60°, and 90°. A 30-60-90 triangle is actually half of an equilateral triangle. If you imagine an equilateral triangle and then cut it down the middle, you'll end up with a 30-60-90 (knowing this fact can often help you on SAT problems).

As the diagram shows, the ratio between the three sides of a 30-60-90 triangle is always the same. The side opposite the 90° angle is always twice as long as the side opposite the 30° angle. The side opposite the 60° angle is always $\sqrt{3}$ times as long as the side opposite the 30° angle. If you know these ratios and come across a 30-60-90 triangle during the SAT, you could spare yourself a lot of calculation. Note that these side lengths are *ratios*. A 30-60-90 triangle could have sides that measure 3, 6, and $3\sqrt{3}$ or 50, 100, and $50\sqrt{3}$.

45-45-90 Triangle

A 45-45-90 triangle lives a double life: it is both an isosceles triangle and a right triangle.

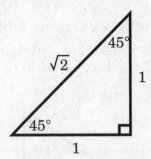

As the figure shows, the sides of this type of triangle always adhere to the same ratio. The side opposite the 90° angle is always $\sqrt{2}$ times larger than the two equal sides that sit opposite the 45° angles.

The Pythagorean Theorem

The Pythagorean theorem defines the vital relationship between the sides of every right triangle (and that means every right triangle, not just the special ones we've already talked about). The theorem states that the length of the hypotenuse squared is equal to the sum of the squares of the lengths of the legs.

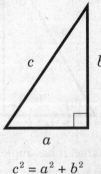

$$c^2 = a^2 + b^2$$

If a triangle is a right triangle, this formula will always hold. Conversely, if the formula holds for a particular triangle, you know that triangle is a right triangle. If you are given any two sides of a right triangle, you can use this formula to calculate the length of the third side.

Certain groups of three *integers* can be the lengths of a right triangle. Such groups of integers are called Pythagorean triples. Some common Pythagorean triples include {3, 4, 5}, {5, 12, 13}, {8, 15, 17}, {7, 24, 25}, and {9, 40, 41}. Any multiple of one of these groups of numbers also can be a Pythagorean triple. For example, {9, 12, 15} = 3{3, 4, 5}. If you know these basic Pythagorean triples, they might help you quickly determine, without calculation, the length of a side of a right triangle in a problem that gave you the length of the other two sides.

Similarity of Triangles

In reference to triangles, the word similar means "of the same shape." Two triangles are similar if their corresponding angles are equal. If this is the case, then the lengths of corresponding sides will be proportional to each other. For example, if ∆ABC and ∆DEF are similar, then sides *AB* and *DE* correspond to each other, as do *BC* and *EF*, and *CA* and *FE*.

That corresponding sides are proportional means that *AB/DE = BC/EF = CA/FD*.

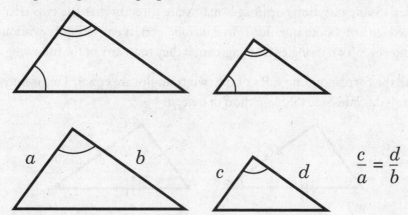

$$\frac{c}{a} = \frac{d}{b}$$

Similarity can be very helpful on the SAT. For example, let's say you come across the following question:

Triangles *ABC* and *DEC* are similar, and line *l* is parallel to segment *AB*. What is the length of *CE*?

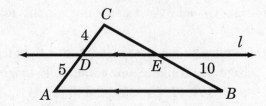

If you know the rule of similarity, then you can see that the ratio of *CD:CA* is 4:9, and know that *CE:CB* must obey the same ratio. Since *EB* is equal to 10, the only possible length of *CE* is 8, since 8:18 is equivalent to 4:9.

Trickier questions on the SAT might not tell you whether two triangles are similar. However, they will include information that will allow you to see that the two triangles are similar. If two pairs of corresponding angles are equal or if one pair of angles is equal and the two pairs of adjacent sides are proportional, then you know that two triangles are similar.

Congruence

Congruence is another helpful rule of triangles. Congruence means that two triangles are identical. Some questions or images may state directly that the two triangles pictured are congruent. Some questions may include congruent triangles without explicit mention, however. Two triangles are congruent if they meet any of the following criteria:

- All the corresponding sides of the two triangles are equal. This is known as the Side-Side-Side (SSS) method of determ

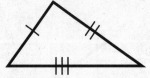 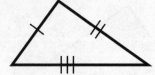

- ining congruency.

- The corresponding sides of each triangle are equal, and the mutual angles between those corresponding sides are also equal. This is known as the Side-Angle-Side (SAS) method of determining congruency.

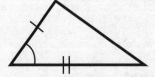 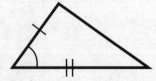

- The two triangles share two equal corresponding angles, and also share any pair of corresponding sides. This is known as the Angle-Side-Angle (ASA) method of determining congruency.

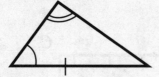 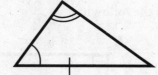

Perimeter of a Triangle

The perimeter of a triangle is equal to the sum of the lengths of the triangle's three sides. If a triangle has sides of lengths 4, 6, and 9, then its perimeter is 4 + 6 + 9 = 19.

Area of a Triangle

The area of a triangle is equal to $\frac{1}{2}$ the base of the triangle times the height: $A = \frac{1}{2}bh$. For example, given the following triangle,

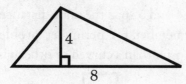

in which $b = 8$ and $h = 4$:

the area equals $\frac{1}{2}bh = \frac{1}{2}$ $(8 \times 4) = 16$. The height of the triangle must be perpendicular to the base. You will almost definitely have to calculate the area of a triangle for the SAT. Know this formula.

Polygons

By definition, a polygon is a two-dimensional figure with three or more straight sides. Under that definition, triangles are a type of polygon. However, since triangles are such an important part of the SAT, we gave them their own section. This section will deal with polygons of four sides or more.

There are a number of properties common to all polygons.

Perimeter of Polygons

As with triangles, the perimeter of a polygon is equal to the sum of the length of its sides. The SAT occasionally makes up fancy perimeter questions in which they create diagrams such as the following:

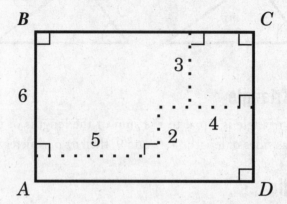

Such a figure looks more complicated than it is. It's actually just a little puzzle where all the information is given to you. You can figure out that the lengths of AD and BC are 9 since the dotted lines of 4 and 5 span the same distance as AD and BC.

Another good rule to remember for perimeter problems on the SAT is that a straight line will always be shorter than a curved or otherwise non-straight line.

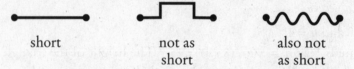

| short | not as short | also not as short |

Polygons and the Number of Degrees They Hold

Just as the angles of triangles always add up to 180 degrees, the angles in various polygons will also add up to the same number. The formula that defines the sum of the angles of all polygons is $180° \times (n - 2)$, where n equals the number of sides of the polygon. Take a look at the table below.

Triangle	3	$180° \times (1)$	180°
Rectangle	4	$180° \times (2)$	360°
Pentagon	5	$180° \times (3)$	540°
Hexagon	6	$180° \times (4)$	720°
Septagon	7	$180° \times (5)$	900°

If you come upon any questions on the SAT in which you are shown a polygon and the angle values of all of the vertices but one are given, you can always find the lone missing value by using this formula to calculate the total angle value and subtracting the value of each angle you know.

Parallelograms

The word "parallelogram" refers to a great number of different geometric figures. The parallelogram is the most general; the rectangle, rhombus, and square are all parallelograms with certain special features.

Parallelogram

A parallelogram is a four sided figure (a quadrilateral) whose opposite sides are parallel.

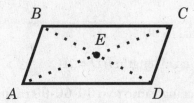

In a parallelogram:

- Opposite sides are equal in length: $BC = AD$ and $AB = DC$

- Opposite angles are equal: $\angle ABC = \angle ADC$ and $\angle BAD = \angle BCD$

- Adjacent angles are supplementary: $\angle ABC + \angle BCD = 180°$

- The diagonals bisect each other: $BE = ED$ and $AE = EC$

- One diagonal splits a parallelogram into two congruent triangles: $\triangle ABD = \triangle BCD$

- Two diagonals split a parallelogram into two pairs of congruent triangles: $\triangle AEB = \triangle DEC$ and $\triangle BEC = \triangle AED$.

Rectangle

A rectangle is a parallelogram whose angles all equal 90°. All of the rules that hold for a parallelogram also hold for a rectangle. A rectangle has further properties, however, that you should also know.

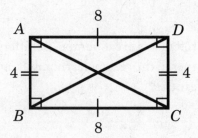

In a rectangle:

- The angles are all equal to 90°.

- The diagonals are equal in length: $BD = AC$

- A diagonal splits a rectangle into two 30-60-90 triangles: triangle BAD and BCD are 30-60-90 triangles.

- The area of a triangle is equal to length multiplied by width: $A = lw$. In the case of the rectangle pictured above, the area equals $8 \times 4 = 32$ square units.

Rhombus

A rhombus is a specialized parallelogram in which all four sides are of equal length.

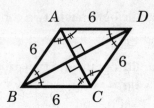

In a rhombus:

- All four sides are equal: $AD = DC = CB = BA$

- The diagonals bisect each other and form perpendicular lines (but note that the diagonals are not equal in length).

- The diagonals bisect the vertex angles
  ($\angle ADB = \angle CDB$, $\angle DCA = \angle BCA$)

Square

A square combines the special features of the rectangle and rhombus: all its angles are 90°, and all four sides are equal in length.

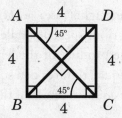

The square has many, many additional special qualities. In a square:

- All sides are of equal length: $AD = DC = CB = BA$

- All angles = 90°

- Diagonals bisect each other at right angles.

- Diagonals bisect the vertex angles to create 45° angles. (This means that the two diagonals break the square into four 45-45-90 triangles.)

- Diagonals are equal in length.

- Area equals one side times another. Since any two sides are equal, $A = s^2$. In the case of the square above, the area is $A = 4^2 = 16$.

Area of a Parallelogram

To calculate the area of a parallelogram, we must introduce a new term: altitude. The altitude of a parallelogram is the line segment perpendicular to a pair of opposite sides with one endpoint on each. The dotted lines show the altitudes of various parallelograms.

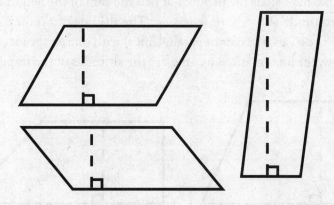

The area of a parallelogram is the product of the length of its altitude and the length of a side that contains an endpoint of the altitude. This side is called the base of the parallelogram. Any side can become a base of a given parallelogram: all you need to do is draw an altitude from it to the opposite side. A common way to describe the area of a parallelogram is the base times the height (base × height), where the height is the altitude.

The formulas for the area of various special parallelograms are even simpler.

For a rectangle, the area is the product of the lengths of any two adjacent sides. Because the sides of a square are equal, the area of a square is the length of any one side squared. The area of a rhombus is equal to one-half the product of its diagonals.

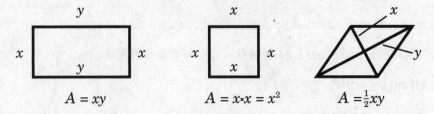

$$A = xy \qquad A = x \cdot x = x^2 \qquad A = \tfrac{1}{2}xy$$

Trapezoid

Trapezoids are four-sided figures but not parallelograms. In a trapezoid, one pair of sides is parallel while the other is not.

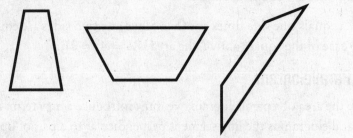

Area of a Trapezoid

The area of a trapezoid equals the product of half the sum of the length of its bases and the height of the altitude: $A = \tfrac{1}{2}\,(b_1 + b_2) \times h$. The altitude of a trapezoid is a segment perpendicular to the bases (the pair of parallel lines) with one endpoint on each base. In the images, below, the lines marked by an a are the altitudes of the trapezoids:

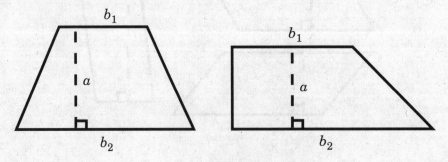

If you were presented with the trapezoid pictured below, you can just plug the numbers from the trapezoid into the trapezoid area formula.

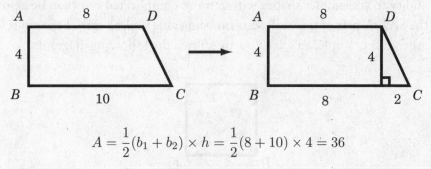

$$A = \frac{1}{2}(b_1 + b_2) \times h = \frac{1}{2}(8 + 10) \times 4 = 36$$

It is also sometimes possible to solve for the area of a trapezoid by transforming the trapezoid into a rectangle and a triangle. In the picture above, the area of the trapezoid *ABCD* is equal to the area of the rectangle (4×8) plus the area of the triangle $(\frac{1}{2} \times 4 \times 2)$, which means the total area is $32 + 4 = 36$.

Polygons with More than Four Sides

The SAT will sometimes include polygons that have more than four sides. The most important rule to remember for dealing with these many-sided polygons is one we already covered: the sum of the angles of a many-sided polygon is equal to $180°$ ($n -$ 2), where n is the number of sides the polygon has.

Many of the polygons you encounter on the SAT will be regular polygons, meaning that the angles and sides of the polygon will be equal. Since all the angles of a regular polygon are equal, you can easily calculate the value of every angle within that polygon. All you have to do is calculate the sum of the angles and divide by the number of angles.

Therefore, the value of an angle in a regular polygon is $\frac{180°(n-2)}{n}$.

Sum of angles = $180°(n - 2)$
= $180°(8 - 2)$
= $180°(6)$
= $1140°$

Degree of a single angle = $\dfrac{1140°}{8} = 142.5°$

The Last Word on SAT Polygons

If you are working with polygons, especially if you are trying to find the area of an irregular polygon, it is often a good idea to try to cut the polygon down into more manageable parts. For example, you might be able to cut a trapezoid into two triangles and a square rather than have to deal with it as a trapezoid at all.

The ability to see simpler shapes within more complicated ones can be a powerful tool on the SAT. A part of this skill rests on being able to deal with shapes in reference to each other. For example, let's say you are shown the following diagram:

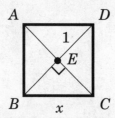

This figure asks you to determine the value of *x* based only on the information that *DE* equals 1. The question might seem impossible, but if you have some knowledge of squares and triangles, it's extremely easy. If you remember, the diagonals of a square bisect each other, so just as *ED* = 1, so too do *EB* and *EC*.

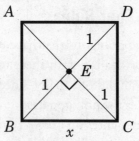

You should also know that two diagonals cut a square into four 45-45-90 triangles. DC is the hypotenuse of one of these triangles, since it is opposite the right angle. And, as you should know from the section on triangles, the ratio of sides to hypotenuse in a 45-45-90 triangle is always 1: $\sqrt{2}$.

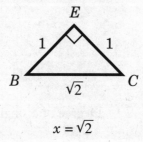

$$x = \sqrt{2}$$

We solved this problem simply by knowing about the attributes of squares and 45-45-90 triangles and without having to do any time-consuming math.

Circles

A circle is the set of all points equidistant from a given point. The point from which all the points on a circle are equidistant is called the center, and the distance from that point to the circle is called the radius.

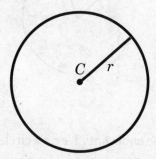

The circle above has its center at point C and a radius of length r. All circles also have a diameter. The diameter of a circle is a segment that contains the center and whose endpoints are both on the circle. The length of the diameter is twice that of the radius.

Circumference of a Circle

It is almost certain that you will encounter an SAT question or two that will in some way test your ability to find the circumference of a circle. The formula to find the circumference of a circle is $2\pi r$, where r stands for the length of the radius. Because two times the radius is also equal to a circle's diameter, the formula for the circumference of a circle can also be written as πd.

This is one of the equations found in the reference section of every math SAT section. You should memorize it, but if you do forget it, you've got back up.

Area of a Circle

The area of a circle is the square of the radius multiplied by π: πr^2. Again, this formula can be found in the reference bar at the top of each SAT math section, but you should memorize it for the sake of efficiency, and because we told you to.

Arcs

An arc of a circle consists of two points on the circle and of the points on the circle that lie between those two points. It's like a line segment that has been wrapped partway around a circle. An arc is measured not by its length (although it can be, of course) but most often by the measure of the angle whose vertex is the center of the circle and whose rays intercept the endpoints of the arc. Hence, an arc can be anywhere from 0 to 360 degrees.

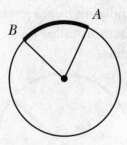

Chords

A chord is a line segment whose endpoints are on a circle. A diameter is a special chord that includes the center, but note that a chord does not have to include the center.

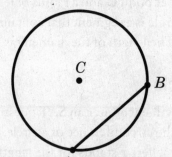

A chord and two radii, each extending from one endpoint of the chord to the center of the circle, form an isosceles triangle.

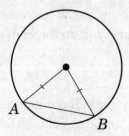

Solids

Solids refer to three-dimensional shapes. On the SAT, the only solids you will have to deal with are cubes, rectangular solids, and right cylinders. For these shapes, you will have to know how to calculate surface area and volume.

Cubes and Rectangular Solids

A rectangular solid is a six-sided shape in which all angles are 90°. It has length, depth, and height.

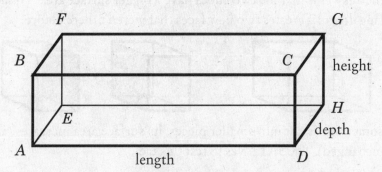

Just as squares are specialized rectangles, so are cubes specialized rectangular solids. For a cube, the length, depth, and height are all equal.

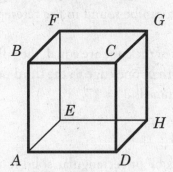

Surface Area of a Rectangular Solid

The surface area of a solid is the area of its outermost skin. A cardboard box, for example, is made up of a bunch of rectangles fastened together. The sum of the areas of those rectangles is the surface area of the cardboard box.

To calculate the surface area of a rectangular solid, all you have to do is find the area of each of the sides and add them together. In fact, your job is even easier than that. The six sides of a rectangular solid can be divided into three pairs of two. If you look at the rectangular solid diagramed above, you should see that panel $ABFE = DCGH$, $BCDA = FGHE$, and $BCGF = ADHE$. Therefore, you only have to calculate the areas of one of each of the three pairs, sum those areas, and multiply that answer by 2.

With a cube, finding the surface area is even easier. By definition, each side of a cube will always be the same, so to calculate the surface area, find the area of one side, and multiply it by 6.

Finally, there is one property of surface area of which you should be aware. Pictured below is a rectangular solid that has a length of 8, a depth of 4, and a height of 4.

Then a giant cleaver comes down and cuts the solid into two cubes, each of which have lengths, widths, and heights of 4. Do the two cubes have a bigger combined surface area? A smaller combined surface area? Or a combined surface area equal to the original solid? The answer is that the two cubes have a bigger surface area. Think about the cleaver coming down: it creates two new faces that weren't there before.

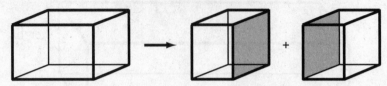

Whenever something is cut into smaller pieces, its surface area increases (although its volume is unchanged). The SAT loves to test this fact.

Volume of a Rectangular Solid

The volume of a rectangular solid can be found by multiplying the length × width × height ($V = lwh$; this formula can be found in the reference area at the beginning of each math SAT section).

Because all the dimensions of the cube are equal, the volume of a cube is even easier to calculate: just raise the length of one edge to the third power. If a cube has a length, width, and height of 3, the volume is $3^3 = 27$.

Right Circular Cylinders

You probably know what a cube or rectangular solid looks like, but you might not know what a right circular cylinder looks like. Here's a picture of one:

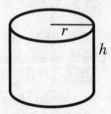

Surface Area of a Right Circular Cylinder

You will never have to calculate the surface area of a right circular cylinder on the SAT.

Volume of a Right Circular Cylinder

It's perfectly likely that you will have to calculate the volume of a right circular cylinder. Luckily, the formula isn't so hard, and it's available in the reference bar at the beginning of every SAT math section. Of course, as we say every time, you should still memorize the formula. The formula is: Volume = $\pi r^2 h$. Like all other volumes, to get the volume of a right cylinder, you have to find the area of a base (in this case a circle) and then multiply it by the height.

Solids and Word Problems

Often, the SAT will pose its problems on solids as word problems. It will say something like: what is the total surface area of two boxes, each with dimensions of $3 \times 4 \times 5$? Often, the best approach to these word problems is to draw a sketch:

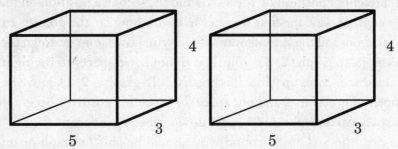

Once you see the drawing, you should see that you have four panels of 3×5, four of 4×5, and four of 3×4, meaning that the total area is $4(15) + 4(20) + 4(12) = 60 + 80 + 48 = 188$.

Whenever you see a word problem, it's a good idea to draw a sketch.

Coordinate Geometry

Coordinate geometry questions test your ability to interpret and deal with geometric figures on an xy-graph.

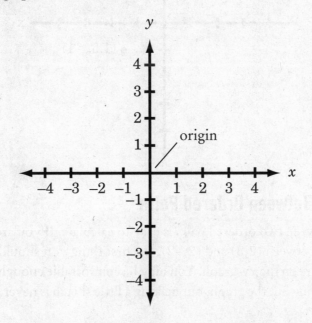

The point at which the x and y axes meet is called the origin. As you go to the right on the x-axis, you move into positive numbers, and as you go to the left, you move into negative numbers. Likewise, as you go up on the y-axis, you move into positive numbers, while moving down brings you into negative numbers (xy-graphs on the SAT will not have their intervals as clearly marked as this diagram does).

To specify a particular point on any xy-graph, you must use ordered pairs. Ordered pairs are two numbers put in parentheses and separated by commas: (x,y). The first number represents a position on the x-axis and the second a position on the y-axis. To think of it another way, the first number tells you how far the point is to the left or right of the origin, and the second number tells you how far up or down the point is.

For example, to graph $(2, 3)$, you should move two spaces to the right (since 2 is positive) and three spaces up (since 3 is positive). To graph $(-2, 1)$, move two spaces to the left (since -2 is negative) and one space up (since 1 is positive). To graph $(1.5, -1)$, move 1.5 spaces to the right, and 1 space down (since -1 is negative).

By the time the SAT rolls around, you should be able to graph or interpret any ordered pairs that you might see. You should know how to calculate the distance between two pairs and be able to state what the mirror of an ordered pair might be.

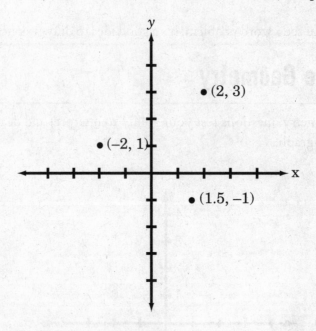

The Distance Between Ordered Pairs

The distance between two ordered pairs is easy to calculate. If you are asked to calculate the distance between $(2,3)$ and $(2,-2)$, the first thing you should do is figure out where each appears on the xy-graph. You may be comfortable enough to do this without actually drawing out the graph, but making a little sketch is never a bad idea.

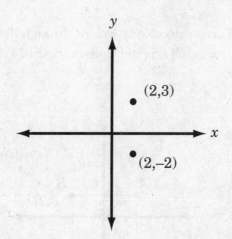

As the ordered pairs indicate, there is no difference between the two pairs in reference to the *x*-axis: both points are the same number of spaces to the right. But the points are not equal in reference to the *y*-axis. One is positive 3, and so it is three spaces up, while the other is –2, meaning it is two spaces down. Therefore, to get from one to the other, you would have to move a total of five spaces, mathematically $(3 - (-2)) = 5$.

In working out this example we've come to a rule about finding the distance between two ordered pairs: if the pairs have one coordinate in common, then the distance between the two pairs is the absolute value or difference between the dissimilar coordinates. For example, the distance between: (4,6) and (2,6) is 4–2 = 2. The distance between the points (–2, 7) and (–2, –1) is 7 – (–1) = 8.

For the SAT, you will not have to calculate the length between two ordered pairs with different coordinates in each place. You will not, for instance, have to calculate the distance between (1,6) and (–4,2).

Reflected Points

Points can be reflected across the x- or y-axis or through the origin. Pairs of reflected points are equidistant from each axis and from the origin. Take a look at the following problem:

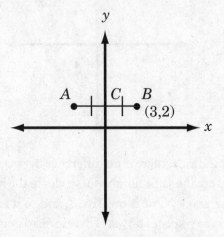

Because AC = BC, this drawing tells you that point A is the same distance to the left of the y-axis as B is to the right of it. It also tells you that line AB is parallel to the x-axis, which means that the y coordinate for each ordered pair will be the same. Immediately we know that the coordinates of A are $(x,2)$. To find x, all we need is a little common sense. If the coordinates of point B are $(3,2)$ and A is just as far from the y-axis but on the opposite side, then the size of the x coordinate of point A must be the same as the x-coordinate for point B. Only the sign must be different. Therefore, the coordinates of A must be $(-3,2)$.

Points that reflect through the origin are only slightly more difficult to deal with:

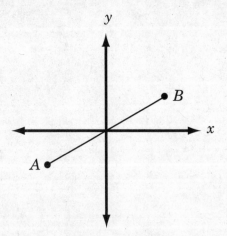

Here, the signs of the coordinates will be opposite, but their values will be the same. For example, in the diagram above, if point A were $(-4,-1)$, point B would have to be $(4,1)$.

Slope

In addition to its familiar meaning, the word "slope" has a precise mathematical definition. The slope of a line is known as the "rise over run," or the change in y divided by the change in x. To find the slope of a line, pick any two points on that line. Then subtract their y-coordinates and their x-coordinates, in the same order, and divide the difference of the y-coordinates by the difference of the x-coordinates. For example, to find the slope of the line which passes through the points $(2, 5)$ and $(0, 1)$:

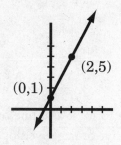

$$m = \frac{5 - 1}{2 - 0} = \frac{4}{2} = 2$$

A slope of 2 means that for each unit x increases anywhere on the line, y increases by 2 units; whenever x decreases by 1, y decreases by 2.

Positive and Negative Slope

The sign, positive or negative, of a slope indicates how the line moves away from the origin. Since slope is the measure of "rise over run"—the change in y divided by the change in x—the slope of a line will be positive when the change in y is positive and the change in x is positive, or when both are negative. This is true because of the division rules we covered earlier: both a positive number divided by a positive number and a negative number divided by a negative number will result in positive quotients.

$$\frac{+ \text{ change in } y}{+ \text{ change in } x} = + \text{slope} \qquad \frac{- \text{ change in } y}{- \text{ change in } x} = + \text{slope}$$

Alternatively, if the change in y and the change in x have different signs, meaning one is positive and one is negative, the slope of the line will be negative.

$$\frac{- \text{ change in } y}{+ \text{ change in } x} = - \text{slope} \qquad \frac{+ \text{ change in } y}{- \text{ change in } x} = - \text{slope}$$

For the SAT, you should be able to look at two sets of coordinate points located on a line, such as $(2, 3)$ and $(4, 1)$, and be able to tell if the slope of that line is positive or negative. In the case of these two points, you can see that the x-coordinate is increasing from 2 to 4 while the y-coordinate is decreasing from 3 to 1, meaning that the slope must be negative.

A line with positive slope on a graph will rise moving from left to right. A line with negative slope will lower moving from left to right.

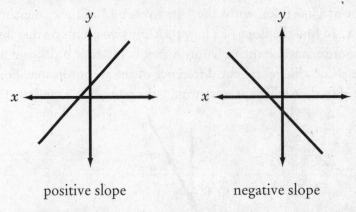

positive slope   negative slope

For the SAT, you should be able to look at a line on a coordinate graph and know immediately whether it has a positive or negative slope.

Slopes of Horizontal and Vertical Lines

Horizontal and vertical lines have special slope values. Horizontal lines always have the same y-coordinate. There is no rise over run.

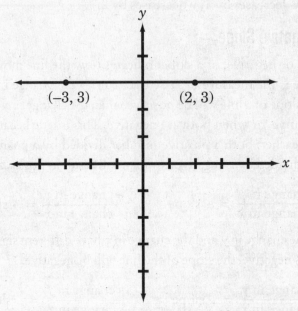

The slope of this line is: $m = {}^{3-3}/_{2-(-3)} = {}^{0}/_{5} = 0$. The slope of any horizontal line is 0, indicating that as x increases or decreases, y does not change.

For vertical lines, x remains constant as y increases or decreases:

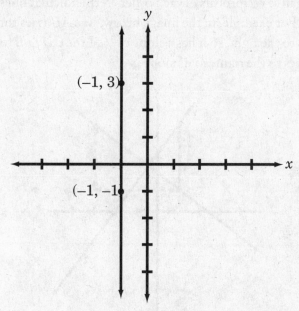

Vertical lines have no "run," so the change in x is 0. Yet the slope equation demands that you divide by the change in x. Division by 0 is impossible and makes the slope undefined: $m = {}^{3-(-1)}/_{-1-(-1)} = {}^4/_0 =$ undefined. Since it is impossible to divide a number by zero, the slope of any vertical line is undefined.

Slope and Parallel and Perpendicular Lines

Two lines are parallel if they have the same slope. Parallel lines, when extended, do not intersect at any point because they have the exact same rise over run, so one line can never get closer to another. In the image below, lines AB and CD have the same slope, so they are parallel.

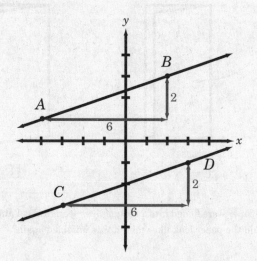

Perpendicular lines intersect each other at right angles. Two lines are perpendicular if their slopes are negative reciprocals of each other. Perpendicular lines have exact opposite rise over runs. For example, in the image below, line *AB* rises three units for every four units it moves to the right, so it has a slope of ¾. Line *CD falls* four spaces for each three spaces it moves to the right, so its slope is −⁴⁄₃.

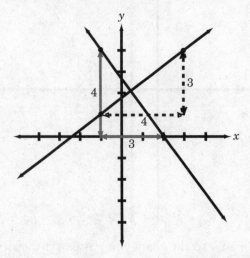

Not all lines have fractional slopes, of course. To find the perpendicular slope for a line with a whole number slope, for example a line with a slope of 2, just think of the whole number as if it was a fraction ²⁄₁ and take the negative reciprocal: −½

Geometric Visualizations

Geometric-visualization questions test your ability to twist and flip in your mind an image presented to you on paper. For example, look at the problem below:

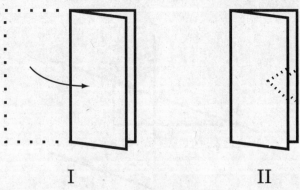

I   II

If a square piece of paper were folded into a rectangle as seen in Fig. I and then cut, as seen in Fig. II, what would the paper look like when it was unfolded again?

There isn't any good way for us to teach you how to do this problem other than to tell you that you should always draw a sketch before looking at the answers on this type of problem. The only thing that can make you better on geometric visualizations is practice, so pay attention when you see them in practice tests.

The answer, incidentally, is:

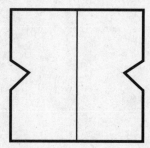

So there you have it. That's SAT geometry.

Special SAT Math: Charts, Logic, Symbols

Special SAT Math

I N THE SECTIONS ON ARITHMETIC, GEOMETRY, AND ALGEBRA WE COVERED the vast majority of the math topics tested by the SAT. But there are three math topics that often pop up in the SAT that do not fit into any of those standard math categories. These three topics are charts and graphs, logical reasoning, and weird symbols questions.. As in the arithmetic, geometry, and algebra sections, we will go through each topic, break it down, and explain the best ways to approach each type of question.

Charts and Graphs

There are two varieties of SAT questions on charts and graphs. The first type asks you to look at data organized in a chart or graph and interpret it. The second type asks you to perform some type of operation on data found in a chart or graph, such as calculating a mean or a percent.

Reading Charts and Graphs

Reading charts and graphs questions are pretty simple: the question will show you a chart or graph and then ask you about the data presented.

In the following bar graph, between what two months was the greatest change in the net income of Joe's Lemonade Stand?

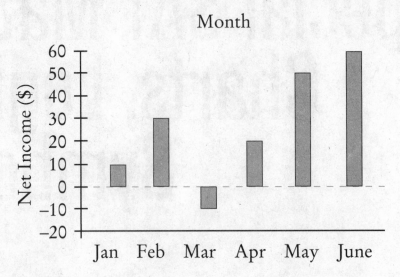

It may be that you look at this question and realize that you don't know what the term "net income" means. *That doesn't matter.* The graph tells you that the bars represent net income, so all you have to do is interpret the bars to figure out between which months the net income differed most. This is a key fact about SAT charts: you don't have to completely understand the terms that describe the data in the chart, you just have to be able to figure out how the data is related. In the case of this chart describing net income, it is only important that you see that the net income changes from month to month.

To figure out the two months between which Joe's net income changed most, you need to determine which two bars on the graph represent the two numbers that are most different in size. For this graph, the two biggest differences in terms of net income per month are obviously between April and May, and between February and March. The net income in April was $20 and the net income in May was $50, making the April-May difference $30. The net income in February was $30 and the net income in March was –$10, so the February-March difference was $40. The answer, therefore, is February to March. This question throws a tiny trick at you by including negative numbers as net income. If you don't realize that March is negative, then you might choose the April–May difference. When dealing with graphs and charts, be sure to pay attention to negative and positive values.

Performing Operations on Charts and Graphs

This second type of charts and graphs question asks you to do more than just interpret a graph or chart. You must also use the data and perform some operation on it in order to get the right answer. For instance, you may be asked to figure out the mean of the data shown in a graph. You might also be asked to look at a bar graph like the one shown previously and then to calculate the percentage change in net income between two of the months. Here's a question involving that same graph from before:

What was the percent increase in the net income from April to May?

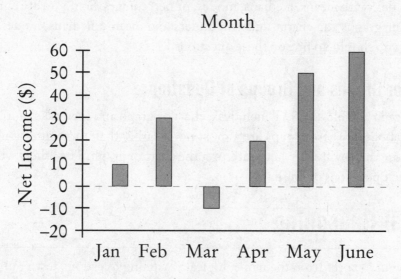

To answer this question, you first have to make sure you understand what it is asking. First, the question mentions percent increase. This means that the question is asking you to find out how much the net income increased between April and May and then to compare that increase to the original net income in April. The difference between the net incomes from April to May is the increase in income. The percent increase of net income can only be found if you look at that increase in relation to the original income. (You should know what percent increase means from our discussion of percents starting on page 202.)

Once you've figured out what the question is asking for, working out the math is easy. The difference in net income between April and May is:

May net income ($50) − April net income ($20) = $30

Now, to calculate the percent increase, you have to divide the change in net income by the original income in April:

$$\frac{30}{20} = 1.5$$

Here's the final trick in the question. The answer is *not* 1.5% change. Remember, to get percents, you must multiply by a hundred. The answer is therefore $1.5 × 100 = 150\%$.   But you can be sure that in this sort of question the SAT will include 1.5% as one of its answer choices to try to fool you.

This example is just one of the ways that the SAT might test your ability to work with graphs. There's no way for us to prepare you for all the different varieties of hybrid charts and graphs questions that might appear. However, the majority of these questions deal with means, medians, modes, or percentages. So if you are comfortable interpreting graphs and charts, and you understand means, medians, modes, and percentages, you should do fine on these questions.

Charts or Graphs and Groups of Questions

Every once in a while, the SAT includes a chart or graph and then asks more than one question about it. These groups are almost never larger than three questions. One or two of those three will ask you to interpret the chart or graph. The others will ask you to perform operations on the data.

Logical Reasoning

As you would expect from the name, logical reasoning questions test your ability to reason logically. There probably won't be more than two logic problems on any SAT test you take. There are two types of logic problems you might encounter: chart problems and word problems.

Chart Logic Problems

Chart logic problems present you with a partially filled in chart or table and ask you to fill it in completely given either the information in the chart, or some information given by the question. For example,

8		y
x		
4	9	2

In the figure above, each of the nine boxes must be filled by an integer from 1 to 9, so that each row and diagonal is equal. No integer may be repeated. What is the value of $x + y$?

To answer these problems, you need only rely on your common sense. For this problem, you should see that the bottom row is equal to 15. Since the question states that each row is of equal value, you should see that:

$$8 + x + 4 = 15$$
$$x = 15 - 8 - 4$$
$$x = 3$$

The question also states that each box must be filled with a number from 1 and 9 and that each number can only be used once. The numbers 2, 3, 4, 8, and 9 have already been used, leaving you with 1, 5, 6, and 7 to fill in the remaining boxes. You should see immediately that the 7 can't go in the same row or diagonal with the 8, because that would add up to 15 for just two boxes in a row, and the *entire* row must add up to fifteen. The seven therefore must go here:

8		y
x		7
4	9	2

Now you can see that:

$$y + 7 + 2 = 15$$
$$y = 15 - 7 - 2$$
$$y = 6$$

Since the problem asks you for the value of $x + y$, add $3 + 6 = 9$.

Word Logic Problems

Word logic problems are less common than chart logic problems. A word logic problem on the SAT will involve some initial statements of fact and will ask you to determine which statement logically follows from the initial facts. For example:

Carlos traveled to City X, which is accessible only by sea or air. Which of the following must be true?

(A)   Carlos traveled by boat.
(B)   Carlos traveled by airplane.
(C)   Carlos did not travel by bus.
(D)   Carlos did not travel to City X.
(E)   Carlos did not fly first class.

To answer questions of this kind, you have to understand the conditions set up by the initial statement and the question asked about the initial statement. In regard to this specific question, the conditions are as follows: 1) the city can be reached only through the air or by sea (implicitly this means City X *cannot* be reached by land); and 2) the answer you choose *must* be true. In other words, there must not be any situation within the given conditions in which the statement could be untrue. Now let's go through the answer choices and see how they fit within these conditions:

Carlos traveled by boat.

The city is accessible by boat, so Carlos could have traveled there by boat. Therefore this could be the correct answer, right? Well, actually this choice is a bit of a trick. Carlos could have traveled to the city by boat, but he didn't *have to* travel there by boat. He could have flown. This statement therefore doesn't fulfill the condition set up by the question when it said the answer must be true.

Carlos traveled by plane.

This statement does not fit the given conditions for the same reasons we just covered above. Carlos might have traveled to City X by plane, but he might also have traveled by boat.

Carlos did not travel by bus.

Given the conditions stated by the question, is there any way Carlos could have traveled to City X by bus? Well, the city is accessible only by sea or air. Can buses float or fly? No. So Carlos *must* not have traveled to the city by bus. This statement must be true.

Carlos did not travel to City X.

The question clearly stated that Carlos did go to City X. This statement is definitely false.

Carlos did not fly first class.

We know that Carlos might have taken a plane to City X, and if he took a plane, there's certainly the possibility that he flew first class. This statement will not *always* be true, so it can't be the answer.

The answer is **(C)**. Carlos did not travel by bus. See, just a little logic bit of logic lets you figure out this question pretty easily.

Weird Symbols Questions (Algebra in Disguise)

The writers of the SAT seem to get a wacky thrill from creating odd symbols and then defining those symbols as mathematical functions. For example, a typical easy symbol SAT question might say:

Let $a @ b$ be defined as a^2/b, where $b \neq 0$. What is the value of 4 @ 2?

To answer this question, simply take the given numbers and plug them into the appropriate parts of the function assigned to $a @ b$. In other words, symbol questions are often just a glorified type of algebraic substitution question: you look at the formula with its variables and plug in the given numbers. In this specific problem,

$$4 @ 2 = \frac{4^2}{2} = \frac{16}{2} = 8$$

Some students get frazzled when they see the odd symbols in their test booklet, which is exactly what the SAT wants. The test-makers figure that if you get nervous and can't get the answer right, then you can't be all that good or comfortable with math. But if you know that you shouldn't be frightened of these problems, you can answer them easily because they really aren't all that hard.

More Difficult Symbol Questions

Having said that symbol questions aren't all that hard, we must admit that the SAT does throw out some more difficult variations. For example, the SAT might "stack" a symbol question, asking you to perform the operation defined by the symbol twice.

Let $a\#b\#c\#d$ be defined for all numbers by $a\#b\#c\#d = ab - cd$. If $x = 6\#3\#5\#4$, then what is the value of $7\#x\#3\#11$?

Here you have a question with strange symbols all over the place, and, furthermore, the question is asking you to calculate the value of a strange symbol with a variable in it! Again, many students will see this question and be overwhelmed. But you shouldn't be. To answer this question, you have to do two things:

1. Calculate the value of x.

2. Calculate the value of $7\#x\#3\#11$ (which won't be very hard, since by that time you'll know exactly what x equals).

Since

$$a\#b\#c\#d = ab - cd$$
$$x = 6\#3\#5\#4 = (6)(3) - (5)(4) = 18 - 20 = -2$$
$$x = -2$$

Now that it is clear that $x = -2$, you can easily calculate the value of $7\#x\#3\#11$:

$$7\#x\#3\#11 = 7\# - 2\#3\#11 = (7)(-2) - (3)(11) = -14 - 33 = -47$$

You should see from this example that the difficult symbol questions are simply more intricate versions of the simpler symbol questions. In both cases, you have to substitute numbers into the function with which the symbol is associated. It's just that in the difficult questions, you have to substitute into the function more than once.

The key to answering symbol questions is to avoid getting bogged down in the symbol at all. Whenever you see the symbol, you should immediately think of the associated function. To make sure you don't get confused by symbols, it is always a good idea to write in the function above the symbol each time it appears in the question.

The PSAT

The PSAT

THE REAL NAME OF THE PSAT IS THE PSAT/NMSQT, which stands for the Preliminary SAT/National Merit Scholarship Qualifying Test. The PSAT is very similar in format and content to the SAT (with one big difference that we will explain) and is administered each year to high-school juniors who will soon take the SAT. Colleges do not directly consider PSAT scores when making acceptance decisions.

At this point, you should be asking, "So why should I take the PSAT, if colleges don't care about it." We're glad you asked.

Why Take the PSAT?

There are two main reasons to take the PSAT:

- It is the best practice for the SAT.

- The National Merit Scholarship Corporation uses the PSAT to decide which high-school students will be distinguished as National Merit Commendations, Semi-Finalists, Finalists, and Scholars. Colleges take the National Merit Scholarships very seriously. Some National Merit Finalists will also receive up to $2500. In addition to the money, these awards and distinctions will enhance your college application.

The PSAT as Wonderful Practice

Taking the PSAT is probably the best preparation for taking the SAT. This may seem curious since we've already told you that the format is not exactly the same, but it's true. Taking the PSAT feels like taking the SAT in a way that no practice test can simulate. You have to take it on a specified morning, it's proctored, and, most important, you're probably going to be a little nervous because something is actually at stake.

The other great thing about the PSAT is that while doing very well can help you, doing poorly can't work against you. Colleges don't look closely at your PSAT scores. They are much more interested in whether you received a Merit Scholarship than in what your score was. So if you don't do as well as you would have liked, it's not the end of the world.

In sum, taking the PSAT will give you a good idea of how you will do on the real SAT and will make you more comfortable in the test-taking environment. You may not enjoy it while you're doing it, but preparing for and taking the PSAT will pay off in the very near future.

The PSAT as the Road to Riches

The PSAT can be good for you. And when we say "be good for you," we mean "get you academic glory and, maybe, money." Glory and riches don't come easily though. Over one million students take the PSAT each year, and only those who score among the top 5% receive National Merit Commendations. Even fewer students, just 15,000, are recognized as National Merit Semi-Finalists. And of those 15,000, only about 14 percent receive scholarship awards. In other words, the National Merit Scholarship awards are given to the top performers on the PSAT. That's why receiving a Letter of Commendation or any higher distinction from the National Merit Scholarship Corporation can so greatly help your college application move from the "Maybe" into the "Yes" pile.

You may be wondering how the National Merit Scholarship Corporation chooses its award recipients. Letters of Commendation and Semi-Finalist status are doled out according to your "selection index," which is a fancy name for your total score. No other criteria are considered. Interestingly enough, however, the "National" in "National Merit Scholarship" is a little inaccurate. In actuality, you're only competing with students in your state, so a given selection index might be good enough for Semi-Finalist status in one state but only merit a Letter of Commendation in another.

A Semi-Finalist who wants to become a Finalist must fill out an application form and meet academic and other requirements. About 14,000 of 15,000 Semi-Finalists become Finalists. After that, the National Merit Scholarship Corporation selects its scholarship winners. Two thousand of those finalists will receive $2,500 scholarships funded by the Corporation. Some other winners might receive scholarships from other corporations or money straight from the university they will attend. It's not clear how the award winners are picked, so we can't tell you how to beat that system. But at least it should be clear now that the PSAT is something you should take seriously.

Content and Structure

The content and structure of the PSAT and SAT are quite similar. Yet there is one big difference between the tests and a number of minor differences. The biggest difference between the tests is the presence of a Writing Skills section in the PSAT. This section appears at the end of the test, and, unlike the verbal section, it focuses largely on grammar rather than vocabulary.

Questions

The PSAT contains 52 verbal, 40 math, and 39 writing skills questions. Of the 52 verbal questions, 13 are sentence completions, 13 are analogies, and 26 are reading comprehension: just as on the SAT verbal, reading comprehension weighs twice as heavily as the other types of verbal questions. The math section is broken down into 20 regular multiple-choice, 12 quantitative comparison, and 8 grid-ins. Finally, the writing skills section has 19 sentence error identifications, 14 sentence improvements, and 6 paragraph improvements. We'll discuss each of the three types of writing skills questions in this chapter.

The Five Timed Sections

The PSAT is a shorter test than the SAT, lasting just two hours and ten minutes. These two hours and ten minutes of mad PSAT excitement are divided into five different timed sections. Here's a look at how the sections are organized and how the questions are placed within each section:

- one 25-minute verbal section with 6 or 7 sentence completions, 6 or 7 analogies and 13 reading comprehension questions

- one 25-minute math section of 20 regular multiple choice

- one 25-minute verbal section with 6 or 7 sentence completions, 6 or 7 analogies and 13 reading comprehension questions

- one 25-minute math section with 12 quantitative comparisons and 8 grid-ins

- one 30-minute writing skills section with all 39 writing skills questions

The five sections will always appear in this order. There are no experimental questions.

The PSAT

Scoring the PSAT

A raw PSAT score is calculated the same way as a raw SAT score. For each section (verbal, math, or writing skills), you get one point for a correct answer, but you lose $1/4$ of a point for an incorrect regular multiple-choice answer. In the math section, you lose $1/3$ of a point for each incorrect quantitative comparison answer; there is no penalty for incorrectly answering a grid-in. There is also no penalty for skipped questions.

The first difference between the scoring of the tests comes in the scaled score. On the PSAT, scaled scores range from 20 to 80 (not 200 to 800, as on the SAT). Luckily, verbal and math PSAT scaled scores directly correspond to SAT scaled scores. For example, a combined math and verbal PSAT score of 110 means the same thing as a 1100 on the SAT. To use your PSAT as a gauge of what you might score on the SAT, just take your math and verbal scores, add them together, and multiply them by ten.

For each of your scaled scores, you will also receive a percentile that tells you where your score stands in comparison to the national average. This score can be important, since it is probably the first time that you've been ranked against most other students nationwide in your age group.

Selection Index

The inclusion of a selection index score is the most important difference between the score report you will receive for the PSAT and the one you will receive for the SAT. The selection index is just a fancy name for the sum of your verbal, math, and writing skills scaled scores. This score can range from 60 to 240. The selection index is the number that the National Merit Scholarship Corporation uses to select scholarship recipients.

The Writing Skills Section

It seems as if it would be very difficult to measure someone's writing skills without a writing sample, but ETS apparently feels up to the challenge. The writing skills section only includes multiple-choice questions. Luckily, it is much easier to prepare for these kinds of questions than it would be to improve your writing. In fact, preparation for this section is largely a matter of knowing a few key grammar rules and trusting your good instincts about what "sounds" right.

The three different types of questions on the Writing Skills section generally test different types of grammar errors. We'll cover each particular type of grammar error while discussing the question type in which the error most often occurs.

Sentence Error Identification Questions

The first 19 questions in the writing skills section give you a sentence with four under-lined words or phrases and ask you to choose which word or phrase, if any, contains an error. Here are the precise instructions, including an example question:

The following sentences test your knowledge of grammar, usage, word choice, and idiom.

Some sentences are correct.

No sentence contains more than one error.

You will find that the error, if there is one, is underlined and lettered. Elements of the sentence that are not underlined will not be changed. In choosing answers, follow the requirements of standard written English. If there is an error, select the one underlined part that must be changed to make the sentence correct and fill in the corresponding oval on your answer sheet.

If there is no error, fill in oval (E).

Example:

The other delegates and him immediately accepted the resolution drafted by the neutral
   A   B   C   D
states. No error
         E

There are several things that you should notice about these instructions. First of all, they are long and fairly involved. Make sure you know what they say before you arrive on test day. Having to read over them to refresh your memory is a waste of a good 40 seconds. Second, notice that you are only allowed to consider making changes to the underlined answer choices. If changing an answer choice would fix the sentence only if you also made changes to another part of the sentence, it is not the correct answer. Finally, you should notice that some sentences do not have errors. In fact, ETS tries to make all the answer choices occur an equal number of times (so random guessing really is random). This equal distribution of answers means that in a 19-question section, answer (E), which means no error, should be the answer three or four times. So if you really don't think there's an error in a sentence, you don't need to nitpick to find one. Answer (E) and move on.

Common Sentence Identification Errors

The grammar tested on the PSAT is not very complicated. You don't have to know how or why something is grammatically incorrect, just that it is, so don't worry about technical terms. In addition, you will often be able to "hear" the error in many of the sentences. If you feel yourself wince a little when you hit an underlined word, you know you've probably found your error. Of course, sometimes the test writers arrange a sentence so that the error is harder to find. To help you out when that happens, we've broken down the kinds of grammatical errors the PSAT most often tests .

Nouns

If the error in a sentence is a noun, it is almost definitely because the noun does not agree in number with some other part of the sentence. For example:

The women's <u>temper</u> flared after they <u>learned</u> <u>someone</u> had stolen their <u>money</u>. <u>No error</u>
         A   B   C   D   E

The sentence clearly refers to a number of people through the words: "women," "they," and "their." But a group of people cannot share a single temper. **(A)** is the correct answer because "temper" should be plural.

Verbs

Verbs can be incorrect if they are in the wrong person or are in the wrong tense.

Verbs in the Wrong Person. Verbs in the wrong person don't agree with their subjects, which you'll immediately recognize as long as the subject and verb are close together in the sentence. Frequently, however, a long phrase or clause will come between the subject and the verb, making it harder to identify the problem. For example:

The brother and sister of my <u>very favorite</u> baseball player <u>does</u> not <u>grant interviews to</u> the
                               A   B   C

press on a <u>regular</u> basis. <u>No error</u>
         D   E

This sentence tries to trick you by inserting the prepositional phrase "of my very favorite professional baseball player" between the subject of the sentence and its verb. The subjects of this sentence are "the brother and sister." Plural subjects should take a plural verb. *Does* cannot take a plural subject, so the correct answer is **(B)**. When you see prepositional phrases on the writing skills section, you should be wary. Always remember to check for agreement, not with the noun that happens to come just before the verb but with the verb's actual subject.

Verb agreement can be especially confusing if the subject is a collective noun or a pronoun. For example, the sentence "Our group of friends are going out together tonight," is incorrect even though it might sound fine to your ear. If you find yourself in doubt, read the subject and verb without the intervening phrases and see how it sounds: "Our group are going out," is clearly incorrect, and should be "Our group *is* going out."

Verbs in the Wrong Tense. To know a verb is in the wrong person, you need to look at its subject. You can decide if a verb is in the wrong tense by looking at another verb in the sentence. If two verbs are in different tenses for no apparent reason, the underlined one is probably in the wrong tense. For example:

My mother always <u>had</u> a friendly smile <u>on her face</u>, but she wears <u>too much</u> lipstick,
                  A   B   C

<u>ruining</u> the effect. <u>No error</u>
  D   E

Here, you know that the whole sentence should be in the present tense because "wears" is in the present and isn't underlined. For that reason, *had,* which is in the past tense, is incorrect, and **(A)** is the right answer.

Another way to check for tense is to find words or phrases that put the sentence in a certain time period. "Yesterday" indicates that the sentence should be in the past tense, while "in the year 2045" tells you that the sentence should be in the future tense. Use these clues to your advantage whenever the test writers offer them.

Pronouns

The PSAT tests pronoun errors in three ways. A pronoun will either not agree with its antecedent, be in the wrong case, or will not be sufficiently specific. Since there are so many issues to consider, pronouns can be pretty tricky. If you have a sentence with no obvious error and one of the answer choices is a pronoun, you should take extra care to make sure the pronoun is being used correctly.

Pronoun Agreement. To check for pronoun agreement, you must correctly identify the antecedent, the noun that the pronoun replaces. Once you know what the pronoun is supposed to replace, it's fairly simple to see whether it's the correct pronoun to use. For example:

Jonathon and Michael bought a <u>newly</u> refurbished car <u>for</u> Susan, who <u>felt</u> deep gratitude
                                 A   B   C

for <u>his</u> generosity. <u>No error</u>
  D   E

In this sentence, the pronoun "his" refers back to "Jonathon and Michael," but "their" is the correct possessive pronoun to replace both people. **(D)** is the correct answer.

The slightly sneakier way of making a pronoun disagree is to switch pronouns mid-sentence. For example:

If one has the opportunity, you should really go to the opera.

In this sentence, the pronoun changes from "one" to "you"—from the third person to the second—causing a disagreement.

Another kind of improper pronoun shift occurs when two pronouns disagree in number:

A powerful person should use their influence for good rather than for evil.

"Their" is plural, but its antecedent, "a powerful person," is singular. The correct pronoun in place of "their" should be "his" or "his or her." These rules may seem confusing, but as long as you remember that pronouns must agree with their antecedents and be consistent within the sentence, you should not have trouble finding pronoun errors.

Pronouns in the Wrong Case. You may not have formally studied cases in school, but if you've ever deliberated about whether to use "who" or "whom" or "I" or "me," you are familiar with the issue. A pronoun's case is determined by whether it functions in the sentence as a subject or an object. A pronoun is a subject if there is some verb that it is the subject of (*She* called), and it is an object if something is being done to it (Call *her*) or if it is the object of a preposition (He called out to *her*). Here is a basic pronoun case error:

> I <u>asked</u> my <u>twin brother</u> and his friend to save two seats near <u>them</u> on the bus for you and
> A   B   C
> I. <u>No error</u>
> D E

In this sentence, **(D)** is the correct answer because "I" is the object of the preposition "for," so it should be in the objective case, which is "me." If you read the sentence without the "you and," "save two seats for I" just *sounds* wrong. In fact, case errors often involve two pronouns like this because the first acts like a buffer and makes the sentence sound more correct. So when you see two pronouns together, you should make sure that they are in the correct case.

Below is a sentence with a very sneaky case error:

> I am a better golfer than him.

At first it seems like "him" would be the correct pronoun to use since it is not acting as the subject of any verb in the sentence. This sentence "sounds" correct to most people's ears. But it is wrong because when you make a comparison between two things, they must be equivalent to each other. Therefore, "I" must have a first-person equivalent, which is "he." As it stands now, this sentence literally reads:

> I am a better golfer than him is.

Pronoun Specificity. Pronouns replace nouns. But for a pronoun to be grammatically correct, it must be clear which noun a pronoun is replacing. In other words, the pronoun must be specific, referring only to a single noun in the sentence. Determining whether a pronoun is specific is not very difficult. Simply ask yourself if you can tell what or whom the pronoun is replacing. Here is an example of vague pronoun use:

> Sarah and Hannah have been very close <u>since</u> junior <u>high school</u>, so <u>she</u> did not mind
>   A   B   C
> meeting her friend <u>at</u> the airport last week. <u>No error</u>
>   D   E

"She" is clearly the pronoun in this sentence. But to whom does "she" refer? Who is picking whom up from the airport? The sentence gives you no clues as to whether "she" is Sarah or Hannah, so you know that the pronoun has been used incorrectly. This sort of error is fairly easy to spot once you know to look for it. The trick is remembering to check in the first place. Unlike most other grammatical errors, vague pronouns don't make the sentence sound wrong on the first read, so they are easy to miss. Remember, whenever you see a sentence about two men, two women, or two groups, be on the lookout for a vague pronoun.

Modifiers—Adjectives and Adverbs

Adjectives are words that describe nouns. Adverbs are words that describe everything else (verbs, adjectives, other adverbs). If you see a modifier and can't tell whether it is an adverb or an adjective, ask yourself some questions. Is the word adding some detail to a noun? If so, the word is an adjective.

> The blue bird sang.

Bird is a noun. Blue is an adjective because it describes how the bird is.

Is the word providing added detail to a verb, or is it describing the degree to which an adjective is describing a noun?

> The blue bird sang loudly.

> The extremely blue bird sang.

"Loudly" and "extremely" are adverbs. "Loudly" describes the verb "sang," while "extremely" explains the degree to which the bird was blue.

You can also often tell adverbs and adjectives apart from their endings: adverbs generally end in the letters "–ly." Adjectives will never end in those letters. Some adverbs, such as the word "very," do not end in "–ly," though, so this method is not foolproof.

Interchanged Adjectives and Adverbs.
Sometimes the PSAT will present you with a sentence in which a word that should be an adjective is written in adverb form or vice versa. Want an example? You got it.

> The snow fell <u>light</u> around the cabin the first night we <u>were</u> there, but it got <u>stronger</u> later
> in the week. <u>No error</u>

"Light" is being used in this sentence to describe the verb "fell," so it should be in adverb form: "lightly." This type of error is not conceptually difficult to understand, but it can be hard to hear the error as you read through the sentence. So if you get a sentence with no obvious error and a modifier as an answer choice, take a second to make sure the modifier is in the correct form.

When a sentence contains a linking verb (a linking verb is a verb that does not express action) such as "is," "seems," "feels," or "tastes," it can be trickier to figure out whether a modifier should be an adjective or adverb. For example, consider this sentence:

> This fish tastes oddly.

This sentence looks and sounds correct. The modifier is next to the verb and seems to be modifying the verb, so it is correct that it should be an adverb, right? Well, no. Let's define what this sentence is trying to say: "this fish does not have the flavor that it is expected a fish should have." The modifier, therefore, shouldn't describe the verb. It should describe the noun. It is the fish that seems odd, not the actual tasting of the fish. (If the person were trying to taste the fish by putting the fish in his ear, *then* the tasting of fish would be odd.) One good way to test out whether a sentence with a linking verb has the correct modifier is to replace the linking verb with the verb "is."

> This fish is oddly.

Now it's clear that the modifier is incorrect and the sentence should be "This fish is odd" or "This fish tastes odd." However, there is an extra complication. Let's go back to the example of the fish sentence.

> This fish tastes oddly.

What if the three sentences before this sentence described how the fish tasted things by putting those things in its ear? Then, as the context indicates, the fish actually goes about tasting things oddly: the fish tastes oddly. In this instance, because of the context of the surrounding sentences, "tastes" functions as an action verb rather than a linking verb. Here's another example. It is correct to say "My horse does not smell good" and "My horse does not smell well," if you are referring in the first case to its odor and in the second to its inability to distinguish scents. When you see a sentence of this sort, you have to use the context of the sentence to decide if the verb somehow names an action or if it acts like an "is" between the subject and the modifier.

Determining whether a verb is acting as an action verb or a linking verb can sometimes be tricky, which means that figuring out whether a modifier should be an adjective or an adverb can also be tricky. The key is to figure out what the sentence means and then to decide if that meaning necessitates that the noun be modified or the verb be modified. Also, the PSAT does not test linking verbs very often.

Double Negatives Another type of modifier error is the double negative, the kind of rule that people intuitively understand but often cannot explain well. Why, these people wonder, is it fine to say, "I never said that you were not tall enough," but not "I never not said what you think I said"? The answer is this: it's not wrong to have two negating words in a sentence *as long as they modify different verbs.* In the first sentence "never" modifies the word "said," while "not" modifies the word "were." In the second sentence, both "never" and "not" modify the verb "said."

Here's an example of how the PSAT might test your knowledge of double negatives:

> <u>Yesterday</u>, the bus driver <u>barely</u> did not have <u>enough</u> gas to get us to school <u>on time</u>.
>   A   B   C   D
>
> <u>No error</u>
>   E

This sentence is tricky because you might not immediately recognize "barely" as a negative, but it is, as are "hardly" and "scarcely." Because "barely" and "not" modify the same verb, the sentence has a double negative. Do not worry about whether removing or changing barely would change the meaning of the sentence (whatever it means in the first place); you only need to know that removing or changing it would make the sentence grammatically correct.

Parallel Structure

The last major area of grammar that you need to check for in these sentences is parallel structure. For example, if a sentence contains several verbs in a series, they should all be conjugated in the same form. Look at this example of a nonparallel series:

> Last night, my mother asked <u>me</u> to clean my room, take out <u>last night's</u> trash, finish my
>   A   B
>
> homework <u>before</u> 10:00, and <u>to</u> send a letter to my grandmother. <u>No error</u>
>   C   D   E

The error in this sentence is subtle. All the verbs in the series are controlled by the "to" that comes immediately before "clean," so the "to" before "send" is unnecessary and incorrect. The sentence as written actually reads:

> Last night, my mother asked me to clean my room, to take out last night's trash, to finish my homework before 10:00, and to to send a letter to my grandmother.

Obviously that double "to to" before "send a letter to my grandmother" is a problem.

Often sentence errors involving nonparallel structure will be more obvious than in this example because the verb form in the series will change from an infinitive (to walk) to a gerund (running).

> Mary called and <u>asked</u> Jane to find out if it was supposed to rain, bring some chips
>   A
>
> <u>to the party</u>, and <u>calling</u> Gary to make sure he knew he was <u>invited</u>. <u>No error</u>
>   B   C   D   E

In this sentence, "calling Gary" should stick out at you like a sore thumb. The first two parts of the series involve infinitive verbs, while the third is a gerund.

Usage Errors

We'll use the term "usage" for all language questions that are not settled by general rules of grammar. Often these errors are really just a matter of word choice—using the correct preposition or not confusing two words that sound very similar.

Here are the three most common types of usage errors tested by the PSAT.

Preposition Use

A given context requires using one preposition over another without a steadfast rule, and the PSAT likes to capitalize on the confusion this can cause. Try this example:

> <u>Your</u> very <u>sensible</u> mother and I think you should try discussing <u>of</u> it with her when she
> A   B   C
>
> visits <u>you</u> next week. <u>No error</u>
>   D   E

In this sentence, the correct answer choice is **(C).** The verb "to discuss" should not be followed by any preposition, so "of" is used incorrectly here.

Hopefully you can just hear this kind of error when you read a sentence. If you can't, look for other errors in the sentence. If you can decide that either the sentence is correct or the preposition is wrong, you are in a very good position to guess.

Number Versus Amount

Discrete nouns are used for things that can be counted (cars, people, dollars). "Fewer" and "many" are good examples of discrete terms. Mass nouns are appropriate when the thing cannot be counted (soup, snow, praise). "Less" and "much" are typical mass nouns. To illustrate, the following example contains an error of number or amount terms:

> <u>Although</u> he has <u>less</u> children than Jim, Bob has <u>many</u> more grandchildren <u>than</u> his
>   A   B   C   D
>
> brother. <u>No error</u>
>   E

(B) is the correct answer choice for this question. Children can certainly be counted, so the sentence should read that Bob has "fewer" children than Jim. These kinds of questions can be tricky because lots of people confuse these parts of speech in everyday usage. But if you remember the rule, you should be fine. Just remember to be on the lookout when one of these words is an underlined choice.

Commonly Confused Words

Every so often, by using a word that sounds like a word that would be correct, the test writers will create a sentence error that you almost certainly will not hear. For example:

The <u>turbulent</u> political climate <u>deeply</u> <u>effected</u> Carol's <u>otherwise</u> idyllic childhood. <u>No error</u>
     A   B   C   D   E

The correct answer choice for this question is **(C).** When used as a verb, "effect" means to achieve, which clearly makes this sentence meaningless. The word that should be used is "affect," which means to alter or influence. Other commonly confused words pairs include accept/except, then/than, insure/ensure, conscious/conscience, and patients/patience.

You will almost always know what both words of a confused word pair mean. The key to not missing these errors is reading the sentence slowly and being suspicious of any possible word confusion if you do not find other errors.

Sentence Improvement Questions

After the sentence error identification questions, you will find 14 sentence improvement questions. In these questions, all or part of the sentence will be underlined, and you must choose the best rewording of that portion based on rules of grammar and usage. Here are the exact instructions given for these questions:

> Select the choice that best expresses the meaning of the original sentences. If the original sentence is better than any of the alternative phrasings, choose A; otherwise, select one of the alternatives.

> To the surprise of the school's staff, the new freshman class at Ravenswood High <u>being larger than last year's</u>.

   (A)   being larger than last year's class
   (B)   is large more so than last year
   (C)   which is larger than the one last year
   (D)   is larger than last year's
   (E)   by far larger than the last

Notice that answer choice (A) is always identical to the original sentence. It is the equivalent of answer choice (E) on the sentence error identification questions. Something else you might learn from the sample question they provide is that by the time you get to the correct answer (in this case **(D)** is the right choice), you may have forgotten what you are looking for. It's a good idea to try to fix the sentence in your mind *before* you look at the answer choices. It can also be helpful to write down a key word or two. In this case, you might have written "is" to remind you that you need a conjugated verb at the beginning of your answer. Finally, make sure you read an answer choice all the way through before choosing it. Sometimes an answer choice will fix the error in the sentence but introduce a new one, just like (B) in this example.

The kinds of errors you will find in this type of question usually involve sentence structure. You might also encounter and need to correct the kinds of grammatical errors that we discussed in the previous section, but those errors will occur in addition to the structural problem. In this section, we isolate seven kinds of structural problems and show you how to deal with each one.

Sentence Fragments

Sentence fragments are incomplete sentences. A sentence fragment can fail as a sentence in one of two ways. It might not contain a subject, or it might not contain a properly conjugated verb. To correct this kind of error, typically you will just have to change a clause into an independent sentence. For example:

The advertising agency, which is composed of several divisions that work together to conceive, develop, and implement marketing strategies for major corporations.

(A)   The advertising agency, which is composed of several divisions.
(B)   The advertising agency, composed of several divisions.
(C)   The advertising agency is composed of several divisions.
(D)   The advertising agency, although it is composed of several divisions.
(E)   The advertising agency is composed by several divisions.

Note that the sentence fragment is the *entire* supposed sentence, from "The advertising agency" to "for major corporations." You can fix the sentence fragment by changing the underlined portion of the sentence. This particular sentence is incorrect in its original form because there is no verb that corresponds to "The advertising agency." The only answer choice that fixes this problem without introducing a new error is **(C)**. Answer (C) eliminates the clause that begins with "which" and connects the subject—the advertising agency—to its characteristics in a single correct sentence.

Run-on Sentences

Run-on sentences try to say too much. There are two effective ways to fix a run-on sentence. Either you can split the sentence into two sentences by using a period or semi-colon, or you can connect the two disparate ideas in the sentence through the use of a conjunction such as "and."

Government spending is on the rise again this year, agricultural subsidies have almost doubled.

(A)   Government spending is on the rise again this year, agricultural subsidies have almost doubled.
(B)   Government spending rising again this year, and agricultural subsidies having almost doubled.
(C)   Government spending is rising again this year, being that agricultural subsidies having almost doubled.
(D)   Government spending is on the rise again this year; agricultural subsidies having almost doubled.
(E)   Government spending is on the rise again this year, with agricultural subsidies having almost doubled.

The answer choices in this example hint at the many ways you can fix a run-on sentence. In (B), the answer choices are linked by "and," which would have worked had the independent sentences not been changed into dependent clauses through the inclusion of the comma. Answer choice (D) tries to use a semi-colon to join the thoughts, but again, one of the sentences has been changed into a dependent clause because the verb "have" is incorrectly conjugated. **(E)** is the correct answer since it successfully makes the second part of the sentence dependent upon the first.

Nonparallel Comparisons

When making comparisons, it is important to use the same kind of things. You can compare oranges and apples or an orange's color to an apple's color but you can't compare an orange's color to an apple. If this kind of error appears in a sentence, only one object of comparison will be underlined, so it is your job to find the answer choice that includes an appropriate second object of comparison. Look at the following example:

Mrs. Morrison has always thought that Picasso's use of color <u>was superior to Matisse</u>.

(A) was superior to Matisse
(B) was better than Matisse
(C) was superior to Matisse's
(D) bettered Matisse
(E) was super to Matisse

The original sentence compares Picasso's technique to Matisse himself, which is not a legitimate comparison. The answer choice must change the comparison so that it refers to Matisse's use of color. Only answer **(C)** accomplishes this task. The best way to approach this kind of question is to decide before looking at the answer choices how you would change the sentence.

Misplaced Modifiers

In the section on sentence error identification, we explained how the PSAT might use single word modifiers (adjectives and adverbs) incorrectly. In sentence improvement questions, with their focus on structural issues, the test might misplace an entire modifying clause so that it no longer describes what was intended. Modifying clauses must immediately precede or follow the noun that they describe. For example:

Flying high in the sky, <u>Martin was thrilled by the new kite his mother had given him</u>.

(A) Martin was thrilled by the new kite his mother had given him
(B) the new kite, which his mother had given him, thrilled Martin
(C) Martin was thrilled with the new kite his mother gave him
(D) Martin's mother, who had given him a new kite, thrilled him
(E) the new kite, which his mother had given him, was thrilled by Martin

The modifying phrase "flying high in the sky" is clearly meant to describe the kite, since boys do not typically fly. The grammar of the original sentence, however, implies that Martin is the one flying. The correct answer fixes this problem without changing the original intended meaning of the sentence. Both (B) and (E) structure the sentence so that the participial phrase describes the kite, but (E) changes the meaning by making the kite be thrilled by Martin instead of the other way around. Therefore, **(B)** is your correct answer.

Awkwardness

Sometimes the original sentence in a question will not contain any specific error, but it will be worded so poorly that it needs to be changed. You might think that this sort of error is unfair because it requires you to make a judgment call. But don't worry: the original sentence will be so awful and the improved one will be so clearly better that these questions turn out to be quite easy. Take a look at this example to see what we mean:

> <u>Before the growing heat made them start sweating because the power had gone out,</u>
> <u>sixteen people in the fantastically cold office shivered.</u>

     (A) Before the growing heat made them start sweating because the power had gone out,

         sixteen people in the fantastically cold office shivered.

  (B)   The power went out, and the growing heat made them start sweating. Until that happened, sixteen people shivered in the fantastically cold office.

  (C)   In what had once been a fantastically cold office that made all sixteen people shiver, the power went out, and the heat grew, and everybody started sweating.

  (D)   Sixteen people shivered in the fantastically cold office until the power went out and they began to sweat in the growing heat.

  (E)   Sweating from the growing heat, the once fantastically cold office that had made people shiver lost its power.

Hopefully, you know just by reading the answer choices that the correct answer is **(D)**—all the other choices are hopelessly awkard. If, however, you didn't think the answer was really clear, you could at least eliminate some answer choices for other reasons. The pronoun "them" in choice (B) does not clearly refer to anything until the second sentence, which is really too late. The modifying phrase at the beginning of choice (E) is misplaced and refers to the office instead of the people, so you can eliminate that option as well. This leaves you with three answer choices before you even have to start evaluating the awkwardness of each sentence.

Paragraph Improvement Questions

The last six questions in the writing skills section are called paragraph improvement. For these questions, you will be asked to read a single passage and answer questions about how to improve its clarity, organization, and grammar. Below are the instructions for this section. Learn them.

> The following passage is an early draft of an essay. Some parts of the passage need to be rewritten. Read the passage and select the best answers for the questions that follow. Some questions are about particular sentences or parts of sentences and ask you to improve sentence structure and word choice. Other questions refer to parts of the essay or the entire essay and ask you to consider organization and development. In making your decisions, follow the rules of standard written English. After you have chosen your answer, fill in the corresponding oval on your answer sheet.

Based on the instructions, you should realize that the questions can touch on a pretty broad range of issues. Basically, everything covered in the sentence error identification section and the sentence improvement section is fair game, as are questions about organization and content. You should know that "an early draft of an essay" is code for "a badly written essay," and that when we say "badly written," we mean "awful." There will be many more problems with the essay than can be addressed in six questions. For that reason, your initial read of the passage should be quick, just enough to get the main idea. Do not try to start improving the paragraph before you've looked at the questions—that would take way too long.

Here is a sample passage. Look it over. The sample questions that we use in the rest of this section will always refer to this passage:

(1) *The First Amendment to the Constitution protects several fundamental individual rights.* (2) *The right to freedom of speech, the right to freedom of religion, and the right to freedom of assembly are the rights protected by the First Amendment.* (3) *Individuals get to do things that other people or the government might find offensive.* (4) *Protesting outside a business that does unethical policies is an example of how people can exercise their rights to free speech and assembly.* (5) *Some people think that this is the most important part of the Bill of Rights because it provides a check on the government, business, and other individuals.* (6) *I agree.*

(7) *Not all speech is protected under the First Amendment.* (8) *If one yells, "Fire!" in a crowded theater, for example, you can be arrested for putting people's lives in danger because it might cause a dangerous charge for the door.* (9) *If there is not really a fire, that is.* (10) *Another limit on free speech is that you also cannot spread lies about people in newspapers or magazines.* (11) *That is called "libel."* (12) *If you commit libel, you might have to publish a retraction and paying damages to the person you lied about.*

(13) *There are also limits to the other rights protected by the First Amendment.* (14) *You cannot assemble on other people's private property without their consent, and you cannot do lots of otherwise illegal things in the name of religion.* (15) *The Supreme Court has the final say on whether an act or speech is protected under the First Amendment.* (16) *It is sometimes hard to weigh public interest against individual rights.* (17) *The Supreme Court has made lots of important decisions about free speech in many different contexts.*

You should have a grasp of the general idea of the passage—it's about the First Amendment and its limits. You probably also noticed that there are several big grammatical mistakes throughout the passage. Don't let those distract you—you will probably only have to answer questions about some of them.

Sentence Revision

The simplest kind of improving paragraphs question will ask you to revise a particular sentence, given its context in the passage. You should try to improve the diction and flow of the sentence, and also make sure that the answer you choose fits into the passage well. For example:

Which of the following best replaces the underlined portion of sentence (3), reproduced below?

<u>Individuals get to</u> do things that other people or the government might find offensive.

(A)   That individuals get to
(B)   However, individuals can still
(C)   These protections ensure that individuals may
(D)   No one appreciates it when individuals get to
(E)   Individual rights says that people can

When approaching this question, you should immediately eliminate any ungrammatical answers. (A) makes the sentence a fragment, and (E) contains a verb that does not agree with its subject, so you can throw these out without even considering their meaning. Now you are left with (B), (C), and (D). To choose among these answer choices, go back to the passage and reread sentences (2) and (3). You will see that sentence (3) further explains what is said in sentence (2). Only choice **(C)** creates an appropriate link between the two sentences, so it is the correct answer.

Not all questions will require going back and looking at the context of the passage. Sometimes the question will really be a sentence improvement question like the ones we discussed in the previous section. For example:

Which of the following is the best way to improve sentence (8), reproduced below?

If one yells, "Fire!" in a crowded theater, for example, you can be arrested for putting people's lives in danger because it might cause a dangerous charge for the door.

(A)   Yelling, "Fire!" in a crowded theater, for example, can get one arrested for putting people's lives in danger because you might cause a dangerous charge for the door.
(B)   For example, if one yells, "Fire!" in a crowded theater, you can be arrested because a dangerous charge for the door might put people's lives in danger.
(C)   One can be arrested, for example, for putting people's lives in danger if you yell, "Fire!" in a crowded theater and cause a danger charge for the door.
(D)   Putting people's lives in danger and causing a dangerous charge for the door by yelling "Fire!" in a crowded theater, for example, is something you can be arrested for.
(E)   For example, one can be arrested for yelling, "Fire!" in a crowded theater because such an action might cause a dangerous charge for the door.

Since context is irrelevant, you do not have to keep referring back to the passage. Since it can be difficult to know just by looking at the question whether the context is important, you should always check out the grammar first. If you don't need context, you will be able to eliminate all the incorrect answer choices immediately. If you do need context, you can at least eliminate the grammatically incorrect answer choices before deciding which one also fits well in the passage. The answer to this question, by the way, is **(E).**

Combining Sentences

Combining sentences is a lot like revising them, except that you have to take two independent thoughts and combine them. The sentences are almost always closely related, so it should be fairly easy to combine them. Take a look at this sample question:

Which of the following is the best way to revise and combine sentences (5) and (6)?

(A) I agree that some people think that this is the most important part of the Bill of Rights because it provides a check on the government, business, and other individuals.

(B) Some people think that this is the most important part of the Bill of Rights because it provides a check on the government, business, and other individuals, and I agree with them.

(C) Some people and I think the First Amendment is the most important part of the Bill of Rights because it provides a check on the government, business, and other individuals.

(D) Because it provides a check on the government, business, and other individuals, some people, this writer included, think that this is the most important part of the Bill of Rights.

(E) I agree with those who think that the First Amendment is the most important part of the Bill of Rights since it provides a check on the government, business, and other individuals.

To answer this question, you need to decide how the two sentences are related and should be combined. You can eliminate (A) because it misconstrues the relationship between the sentences: the writer does not agree that people have a particular opinion; he or she agrees with the people who hold that opinion. Next, you should decide if there are any grammatical problems with the remaining answer choices. (B) and (D) retain the word "this," which does not have a clear antecedent. You can eliminate those answer choices. Finally, (C) is worded awkwardly, which leaves you only with **(E),** the correct answer.

These kinds of questions ask you to deal with several different issues and to read rather lengthy answer choices. If you think that you will not be able to answer every question in the writing skills section, you might consider skipping these without really even trying them.

Content

The final type of question in the writing skills section asks you to make decisions about the content of the passage. In some ways, these questions are like reading comprehension, except that you have to think more about what is *missing* than about what is actually there. Some content questions will ask you about what should come immediately before or after the passage. For example:

> Which of the following would be the most appropriate topic for the next paragraph in this essay?
>
> (A) An example of a Supreme Court case involving First Amendment rights
> (B) The Second Amendment
> (C) Other limits on First Amendment rights
> (D) Countries that do not protect freedom of speech
> (E) A personal example about a time when the writer exercised his or her right to free assembly

Because the passage ends by discussing the "many different contexts" in which the Supreme Court has evaluated First Amendment rights, the next logical topic would be to discuss a particular example. For that reason, **(A)** is the correct answer. Any of the other choices would cause an abrupt change in the flow of the passage.

Other content questions will ask you how the argument made by the passage could be strengthened:

> Which of the following, if added, would most strengthen the writer's claim that the First Amendment is the most important part of the Bill of Rights?
>
> (A) Quotations from several famous thinkers about the importance of the First Amendment
> (B) A sentence about why other Amendments are not very important
> (C) An explanation of why a check on government, business, and other individuals allows people to protect all their other rights
> (D) A description of a time when First Amendment rights were not protected
> (E) A discussion of the historical context surrounding the writing of the Bill of Rights

(B) and (C) are the two answer choices that seem to make the claim more strong. But if you think about it, showing that other rights are not very important does not demonstrate that First Amendment rights have more relative importance. On the other hand, if First Amendment rights are the basis for protecting other rights, then the writer's claim seems harder to attack. **(C)** is the correct answer.

Strategies for the Writing Skills Section

The math and verbal sections of the PSAT follow the same order of difficulty as the SAT—the questions get harder as you move through a group, with the exception of the reading comprehension groups. Unfortunately, the writing skills section is not ordered by difficulty. Still, there are ways to use the structure of the writing skills section to your advantage.

You will probably find that you perform better on one type of writing skills question than on others. No matter where those questions are in the section, start with them and rack up some points right off the bat. Then, of the remaining two groups, move to the one about which you feel more confident. Also, keep in mind that you should not give up on a group just because you hit one hard question. Unlike other sections, you do not know if the next question will be as difficult, so a tough question might be followed by a very simple one. Otherwise, you should follow the same general strategies as you would on any other section of the test. Remember not to get bogged down: do not be afraid to skip a question if you have no idea, and guess if you can eliminate even one answer choice. On the error identification and sentence improvement groups, eliminating an answer should be fairly easy. If you sense that the sentence has an error, even if you cannot decide what it is, you can eliminate (E) or (A), respectively, and guess from there.

The biggest tip we can give you for this section is to trust your instincts. If something doesn't sound right, it probably isn't. Remember that you do not have to be able to explain your answer, so listening to your gut can get you as many points as being able to explicate complicated grammar rules. Of course, that doesn't mean you shouldn't prepare for this section. If you are going to trust your gut, you need to make sure that your gut is trustworthy in the first place.

The PSAT

Practice Tests

Practice Tests Are Your Best Friends

Most test preparation books and courses treat practice tests in similar ways. After a brief introduction, the test prep guys ask you to take an initial practice test called a "diagnostic" test that diagnoses your strengths and weaknesses under test-like conditions. When you get your results for the test, you get more information than simply your scores in the math and verbal sections. The test prepsters chart your diagnostic test to see how well you do on sentence completions, analogies, and reading comprehension on the verbal section, and how you do on multiple choice questions, qualitative comparisons, and grid-ins on the math. The diagnostic test also usually identifies your strengths or weaknesses in arithmetic, algebra, and geometry. After the diagnostic test, your test prep tutor will likely recommend that you take a number of additional practice tests to become more comfortable with the SAT and to gauge your progress as you try to reach your target score.

As you take practice tests, you do become more familiar with the test, and being familiar with the test will make the actual SAT much less stressful. Taking practice tests also gives you a sense of how fast you can work. Take enough practice tests, and you will learn to avoid getting bogged down, find easy points, maximize your time, and employ the various methods available to you to navigate a multiple-choice test.

Most test-prep companies give you just one diagnostic test at the beginning of the class. But *every* practice test you take should be treated with the same scrutiny as the first diagnostic test. In fact, if used correctly, practice tests can be an extremely targeted study tool that will precisely pinpoint the areas in which you are weakest and then help you to learn how to combat and overcome those weaknesses.

Practice Tests

If a smarmy test prep guru were writing this, he or she would tell you that these are the secret study skills that will unlock your full SAT potential. We're not going to say that. Instead, we're just going to show you how and why practice tests can be your best friend when it comes to preparing for the SAT.

The Theory Behind Using Practice Tests

This section will explain why practice tests can be such beneficial study tools in your preparation for the SAT. The following section will explain more concretely how you should go about implementing the theory.

SAT Similarity

The SAT tests specific subjects in specific ways. Since 1994, when the format of the test slightly changed, every SAT verbal section has included 19 analogies, 19 sentence completions, and 40 reading comprehension questions. These questions always test the same general skills. Similarly, the math section every year consists of 25 five-choice multiple-choice questions, 15 quantitative comparison questions, and 10 grid-ins. These three types of math questions all ask questions testing the same fundamental math knowledge, spanning specific (and easily definable) topics in basic arithmetic, algebra, and geometry.

SAT tests stay similar from year to year for obvious reasons. First, to make sweeping changes to the test each year would cost ETS tremendous amounts of money. Second—and probably more important—to change the test every year would destroy one of the factors of the SAT that ETS very much wants to maintain: the consistency of the scores over time. The SAT is designed to objectively measure a test taker not only against his peers but also against those people who have taken the test before. This way, a college looking at an SAT score can place the test-taker into a historical context. If the SAT were to change from time to time, that valuable aspect of SAT scores would disappear. Because the SAT tests the same specific subjects with the same types of questions, the questions on one test resemble the questions on another test. The words used on vocabulary questions (whether analogies or sentence completions) often overlap from test to test, and questions on triangles on one test are often quite similar to questions on triangles on another.

Using SAT Similarity for Personal Gain: A Case Study

A girl named Molly Bloom takes a practice test and (because it makes this example much simpler) gets only one question wrong. Molly checks her answers and then jumps from her chair and does a little dance that would be embarrassing if anyone else saw her. After her euphoria passes, Molly begins to wonder which question she got wrong and returns to her chair. She discovers that the question dealt with triangles and the Pythagorean theorem. She soon realizes that she answered the question wrong because she thought the formula for the Pythagorean theorem was $a = b + c$, when really it's $a^2 = b^2 + c^2$. Molly doesn't know where or when she became confused about the Pythagorean Theorem, but as she studies the question and learns how and why she got it wrong, she knows that she'll never make that mistake again.

Analyzing Molly Bloom

Molly's actions here seem like a minor thing. All she did was study a question she got wrong until she understood why she got it wrong and what she should have done to get it right. But think about the implications. Molly got that question wrong because she didn't know how to answer it correctly, and the practice test pointed out her mistaken understanding in the most noticeable way possible: she got the question wrong. After doing her admittedly goofy little dance, Molly wasn't content simply to see what the correct answer was and get on with her day—she wanted to see *how* and *why* she got the question wrong and what she should have done to get it right. So, with a look of determination, telling herself, "I will figure out why I got this question wrong, yes I will, yes," she spent five to ten minutes studying the question, discovered her mistaken understanding of the Pythagorean theorem, and learned the correct Pythagorean theorem. If Molly were to take that same test again, she would not get that question wrong.

"But she never will take that test again, so she's never going to see that particular question again," some poor sap who hasn't read this guide might sputter. "She wasted her precious time. What a dork!"

Why That Poor Sap Really Is a Poor Sap

In some sense, that poor sap is correct: Molly will never take that exact practice test again. But the poor sap is wrong to call Molly a dork because we know that the SAT is remarkably similar from year to year, both in the topics it covers and in the way it asks questions about those topics. Therefore, when Molly taught herself how to answer that one question about the Pythagorean Theorem, she actually learned how to answer the questions dealing with the Pythagorean theorem that will appear on every future practice test she takes and on the real SAT.

In studying the results of her practice test—in figuring out exactly why she got her one question wrong and what she should have known and done to get it right—Molly has targeted a weakness and overcome it. She'll be ready for future questions about triangles and the Pythagorean theorem on the SAT.

Molly and You

What if you take a practice test and get 30 questions wrong, and your errors span a large number of different topics, from analogies to ratios? Well, you should do exactly what Molly did. Take your test and *study it*. Identify every question you got wrong, figure out why you got it wrong, and then teach yourself what you should have done to get the question right. If you can't figure out your error, ask someone who can.

Think about it. What does an incorrect answer mean? That wrong answer identifies a weakness in your test taking, whether that weakness is an lack of familiarity with a particular topic, a tendency to be careless, or a vulnerability for those enticing, "tricky" wrong answers that ETS often includes among the answer choices. If you got 30 questions wrong on a practice test, then each of those thirty questions identifies a weakness in your ability to take the SAT or your knowledge about the topics the SAT tests. But as you study each question you got wrong and figure out why you answered incorrectly, you are actually learning how to answer the similar questions that will *undoubtedly* appear in similar form on your real SAT. You are discovering your exact SAT weaknesses and addressing them, and you are learning to understand not just the knowledge required to answer a particular question, but the way that ETS asks all its questions. As we said in the introduction to this guide book, both ETS and the test prep companies are correct: the SAT is a test of knowledge, and it is a test of tricks. In using practice tests to study, you tackle both aspects of the test at once.

This method becomes more powerful the more you employ it. As you move through a series of practice tests, studying your mistakes and learning how to get those questions right, you will encounter and learn to answer an increasing variety of questions on the specific topics covered by the test. You will thereby increase your ability to recognize and handle whatever the SAT throws at you.

The Practice of Using Practice Tests

Practice tests are valuable study tools for the SAT because they help you pinpoint and address your weaknesses. But how can you you use practice tests to the best effect? Glad you asked.

Taking a Practice Test

When taking a practice test, you should try to approximate the conditions you will face in the real SAT as closely as possible. You should also approach the test as if it were the real SAT.

Take the tests timed.

Don't give yourself extra time on any sections. Be stricter with yourself than the meanest proctor you can imagine. If you can, don't give yourself time off for bathroom breaks. If you have to go to the bathroom, let the clock keep running—that's what will happen on the real SAT.

Take the test in a single sitting.

The only reason not to take the test in a single block of time is if you don't have three spare hours. You will have to take the real SAT in one sitting, so training yourself to endure that much test taking is part of your preparation.

Find a place to take the test that offers no distractions.

Don't take the practice test in a room with lots of people walking through it. Go to a library, your bedroom, or a well-lit closet—anywhere without distractions.

These are the rules for controlling your test-taking environment. If you follow these rules, you will be better able to concentrate and will more quickly progress toward your target score.

However, here's another rule: if you can't make yourself study because all the rules above make it too boring, you can bend a couple. Do what you have to do in order to make your SAT preparation experience as productive as possible. If following all the rules makes studying excruciating, find little ways to bend them that won't interfere with your concentration too much. Listen to music, or call a friend between sections to tell him or her how bored you are. Imperfect studying, while inherently not ideal, is still better than not studying at all.

Practice Test Strategy

A practice test should simulate the real SAT as closely as possible: aim for your target score when you take it. Resist the temptation to be more daring on practice tests than you would be on the actual test. Similarly, don't be less vigilant about making careless mistakes. The more closely your attitude and strategies on the practice test reflect those you'll employ on the actual test, the more helpful the practice test will be in predicting what particular types of questions you tend to get wrong.

Scoring Your Practice Test

After you take your practice test, you'll want to score it and see how you did. When you do your scoring, don't just write down how many questions you answered correctly. You should also keep a list of every question you got wrong and every question you skipped. This list will be your guide when you study your test.

Studying Your . . . No, Wait, Go Take a Break

You know how to have fun. Go do that for a while. Come back when you're refreshed and ready to continue.

Practice Tests

Studying Your Practice Test

After grading your test, you should have a list of the questions you answered incorrectly or skipped. Studying your test involves examining each question on this list to help you understand why you got the question wrong, why the correct answer is the right one, and what you could have done to get the question right. Do not move on from any question you are studying until you can confidently answer all three of these questions.

Why Did You Get the Question Wrong?

There are four reasons why you might have gotten a question wrong:

1. **You thought you understood the topic or question perfectly,** but you were wrong.

2. **You were unsure about the topic** a question covered or didn't understand the specific question, yet you still managed to eliminate an answer or two and take a guess. You guessed incorrectly.

3. **You understood the topic and the question** but made a careless mistake.

4. **You got tricked by one of the enticing wrong answers** that ETS loves to include in SAT questions.

Reasons (1) and (2) for getting a wrong answer are similar: each results from you not knowing a topic or not understanding how that topic was being tested. In the second case, you made the correct strategic maneuver, while in the first you had a misguided sense of your own knowledge. In either case, you know that you have a weakness in the topic that the question covers. Reasons (3) and (4) are also similar: in each, you made some sort of mistake. In the first, you made some error all on your own. In the second, you fell for a trap set by the test. If you answered a question incorrectly for either of these reasons, you should *not* just say to yourself, "Oh I made a careless error, I won't do that again." Make *sure* you don't do it again. Reenact your thought process on the problem and see where and how your error took place. Did you rush? Did you skip a mathematical operation? Know your error, look it in the eye, and then promise yourself not to make that mistake again. If the test tricked you, figure out exactly how it tricked you and run through how you should have approached the problem to avoid the trick—a future test will definitely try to trick you in the same way.

Why Is the Correct Answer the Correct Answer?

If you got a question wrong because you were careless or tricked, it will probably not be all that difficult for you to understand why the correct answer is correct. If you got a question wrong because you didn't understand the topic it covered or the way the question tested that topic, then this is a very important step. In order to figure out why the correct answer is the correct answer, you must understand the question and the subject the question tests. In other words, by learning why the right answer is the right answer, you learn the knowledge the question is based on and how that specific SAT question tests that knowledge.

What Could You Have Done to Get the Question Right?

Once you understand why an answer is the right one, don't just assume that you will be able to arrive at the right answer so easily. It is easy to get confused when you're in the middle of a question, even if you theoretically know the right answer. Work the question out. Make sure that you not only know the right answer but that you can derive the right answer on your own.

If you left the question blank, the steps for determining what you could have done better are somewhat different. Leaving a question blank can result from one of three things:

You didn't understand the question in any way.

If you left a question blank because you simply had no idea how to deal with it and couldn't eliminate even one answer, then clearly you need to go back to that topic and do some studying.

You were familiar with the topic but were unable to eliminate any answers.

If this was the case, you should spend some time learning about how to eliminate answers. Go through the question again and see how you might have been able to eliminate some answer choices.

A lack of time.

If you left a question blank simply because you didn't even have time to look at it, look over the question to see whether you could have answered it. If you definitely could, then you know that you are probably working too slowly and throwing away points. If you couldn't have answered the question, then study the topic the question covered.

The Secret Weapon: Talking to Yourself

Yeah, it's embarrassing. Yeah, you'll look dumb. But talking to yourself is perhaps the best way to pound something into your brain. As you go through the steps of studying a question, you should talk them out. When you verbalize something to yourself, it makes it much harder to delude yourself into thinking that you're working if you're really not.

This is just a suggestion. We can't enforce it. But it is a nice little study trick. And it will help you.

SAT Practice Test 1

SAT PRACTICE TEST 1 ANSWER SHEET

MATH SECTION 1	VERBAL SECTION 1	MATH SECTION 2	VERBAL SECTION 2
1. Ⓐ Ⓑ Ⓒ Ⓓ Ⓔ	8. Ⓐ Ⓑ Ⓒ Ⓓ Ⓔ	10. Ⓐ Ⓑ Ⓒ Ⓓ Ⓔ	22. Ⓐ Ⓑ Ⓒ Ⓓ Ⓔ
2. Ⓐ Ⓑ Ⓒ Ⓓ Ⓔ	9. Ⓐ Ⓑ Ⓒ Ⓓ Ⓔ	11. Ⓐ Ⓑ Ⓒ Ⓓ Ⓔ	23. Ⓐ Ⓑ Ⓒ Ⓓ Ⓔ
3. Ⓐ Ⓑ Ⓒ Ⓓ Ⓔ	10. Ⓐ Ⓑ Ⓒ Ⓓ Ⓔ	12. Ⓐ Ⓑ Ⓒ Ⓓ Ⓔ	24. Ⓐ Ⓑ Ⓒ Ⓓ Ⓔ
4. Ⓐ Ⓑ Ⓒ Ⓓ Ⓔ	11. Ⓐ Ⓑ Ⓒ Ⓓ Ⓔ	13. Ⓐ Ⓑ Ⓒ Ⓓ Ⓔ	25. Ⓐ Ⓑ Ⓒ Ⓓ Ⓔ
5. Ⓐ Ⓑ Ⓒ Ⓓ Ⓔ	12. Ⓐ Ⓑ Ⓒ Ⓓ Ⓔ	14. Ⓐ Ⓑ Ⓒ Ⓓ Ⓔ	26. Ⓐ Ⓑ Ⓒ Ⓓ Ⓔ
6. Ⓐ Ⓑ Ⓒ Ⓓ Ⓔ	13. Ⓐ Ⓑ Ⓒ Ⓓ Ⓔ	15. Ⓐ Ⓑ Ⓒ Ⓓ Ⓔ	27. Ⓐ Ⓑ Ⓒ Ⓓ Ⓔ
7. Ⓐ Ⓑ Ⓒ Ⓓ Ⓔ	14. Ⓐ Ⓑ Ⓒ Ⓓ Ⓔ	16. Ⓐ Ⓑ Ⓒ Ⓓ Ⓔ	28. Ⓐ Ⓑ Ⓒ Ⓓ Ⓔ
8. Ⓐ Ⓑ Ⓒ Ⓓ Ⓔ	15. Ⓐ Ⓑ Ⓒ Ⓓ Ⓔ	17. Ⓐ Ⓑ Ⓒ Ⓓ Ⓔ	29. Ⓐ Ⓑ Ⓒ Ⓓ Ⓔ
9. Ⓐ Ⓑ Ⓒ Ⓓ Ⓔ	16. Ⓐ Ⓑ Ⓒ Ⓓ Ⓔ	18. Ⓐ Ⓑ Ⓒ Ⓓ Ⓔ	30. Ⓐ Ⓑ Ⓒ Ⓓ Ⓔ
10. Ⓐ Ⓑ Ⓒ Ⓓ Ⓔ	17. Ⓐ Ⓑ Ⓒ Ⓓ Ⓔ	19. Ⓐ Ⓑ Ⓒ Ⓓ Ⓔ	31. Ⓐ Ⓑ Ⓒ Ⓓ Ⓔ
11. Ⓐ Ⓑ Ⓒ Ⓓ Ⓔ	18. Ⓐ Ⓑ Ⓒ Ⓓ Ⓔ	20. Ⓐ Ⓑ Ⓒ Ⓓ Ⓔ	32. Ⓐ Ⓑ Ⓒ Ⓓ Ⓔ
12. Ⓐ Ⓑ Ⓒ Ⓓ Ⓔ	19. Ⓐ Ⓑ Ⓒ Ⓓ Ⓔ	21. Ⓐ Ⓑ Ⓒ Ⓓ Ⓔ	33. Ⓐ Ⓑ Ⓒ Ⓓ Ⓔ
13. Ⓐ Ⓑ Ⓒ Ⓓ Ⓔ	20. Ⓐ Ⓑ Ⓒ Ⓓ Ⓔ	22. Ⓐ Ⓑ Ⓒ Ⓓ Ⓔ	34. Ⓐ Ⓑ Ⓒ Ⓓ Ⓔ
14. Ⓐ Ⓑ Ⓒ Ⓓ Ⓔ	21. Ⓐ Ⓑ Ⓒ Ⓓ Ⓔ	23. Ⓐ Ⓑ Ⓒ Ⓓ Ⓔ	35. Ⓐ Ⓑ Ⓒ Ⓓ Ⓔ
15. Ⓐ Ⓑ Ⓒ Ⓓ Ⓔ	22. Ⓐ Ⓑ Ⓒ Ⓓ Ⓔ	24. Ⓐ Ⓑ Ⓒ Ⓓ Ⓔ	**MATH SECTION 3**
16. Ⓐ Ⓑ Ⓒ Ⓓ Ⓔ	23. Ⓐ Ⓑ Ⓒ Ⓓ Ⓔ	25. Ⓐ Ⓑ Ⓒ Ⓓ Ⓔ	1. Ⓐ Ⓑ Ⓒ Ⓓ Ⓔ
17. Ⓐ Ⓑ Ⓒ Ⓓ Ⓔ	24. Ⓐ Ⓑ Ⓒ Ⓓ Ⓔ	**VERBAL SECTION 2**	2. Ⓐ Ⓑ Ⓒ Ⓓ Ⓔ
18. Ⓐ Ⓑ Ⓒ Ⓓ Ⓔ	25. Ⓐ Ⓑ Ⓒ Ⓓ Ⓔ	1. Ⓐ Ⓑ Ⓒ Ⓓ Ⓔ	3. Ⓐ Ⓑ Ⓒ Ⓓ Ⓔ
19. Ⓐ Ⓑ Ⓒ Ⓓ Ⓔ	26. Ⓐ Ⓑ Ⓒ Ⓓ Ⓔ	2. Ⓐ Ⓑ Ⓒ Ⓓ Ⓔ	4. Ⓐ Ⓑ Ⓒ Ⓓ Ⓔ
20. Ⓐ Ⓑ Ⓒ Ⓓ Ⓔ	27. Ⓐ Ⓑ Ⓒ Ⓓ Ⓔ	3. Ⓐ Ⓑ Ⓒ Ⓓ Ⓔ	5. Ⓐ Ⓑ Ⓒ Ⓓ Ⓔ
21. Ⓐ Ⓑ Ⓒ Ⓓ Ⓔ	28. Ⓐ Ⓑ Ⓒ Ⓓ Ⓔ	4. Ⓐ Ⓑ Ⓒ Ⓓ Ⓔ	6. Ⓐ Ⓑ Ⓒ Ⓓ Ⓔ
22. Ⓐ Ⓑ Ⓒ Ⓓ Ⓔ	29. Ⓐ Ⓑ Ⓒ Ⓓ Ⓔ	5. Ⓐ Ⓑ Ⓒ Ⓓ Ⓔ	7. Ⓐ Ⓑ Ⓒ Ⓓ Ⓔ
23. Ⓐ Ⓑ Ⓒ Ⓓ Ⓔ	30. Ⓐ Ⓑ Ⓒ Ⓓ Ⓔ	6. Ⓐ Ⓑ Ⓒ Ⓓ Ⓔ	8. Ⓐ Ⓑ Ⓒ Ⓓ Ⓔ
24. Ⓐ Ⓑ Ⓒ Ⓓ Ⓔ	31. Ⓐ Ⓑ Ⓒ Ⓓ Ⓔ	7. Ⓐ Ⓑ Ⓒ Ⓓ Ⓔ	9. Ⓐ Ⓑ Ⓒ Ⓓ Ⓔ
25. Ⓐ Ⓑ Ⓒ Ⓓ Ⓔ	32. Ⓐ Ⓑ Ⓒ Ⓓ Ⓔ	8. Ⓐ Ⓑ Ⓒ Ⓓ Ⓔ	10. Ⓐ Ⓑ Ⓒ Ⓓ Ⓔ
26. Ⓐ Ⓑ Ⓒ Ⓓ Ⓔ	33. Ⓐ Ⓑ Ⓒ Ⓓ Ⓔ	9. Ⓐ Ⓑ Ⓒ Ⓓ Ⓔ	**VERBAL SECTION 3**
27. Ⓐ Ⓑ Ⓒ Ⓓ Ⓔ	34. Ⓐ Ⓑ Ⓒ Ⓓ Ⓔ	10. Ⓐ Ⓑ Ⓒ Ⓓ Ⓔ	1. Ⓐ Ⓑ Ⓒ Ⓓ Ⓔ
28. Ⓐ Ⓑ Ⓒ Ⓓ Ⓔ	35. Ⓐ Ⓑ Ⓒ Ⓓ Ⓔ	11. Ⓐ Ⓑ Ⓒ Ⓓ Ⓔ	2. Ⓐ Ⓑ Ⓒ Ⓓ Ⓔ
29. Ⓐ Ⓑ Ⓒ Ⓓ Ⓔ	**MATH SECTION 2**	12. Ⓐ Ⓑ Ⓒ Ⓓ Ⓔ	3. Ⓐ Ⓑ Ⓒ Ⓓ Ⓔ
30. Ⓐ Ⓑ Ⓒ Ⓓ Ⓔ	1. Ⓐ Ⓑ Ⓒ Ⓓ Ⓔ	13. Ⓐ Ⓑ Ⓒ Ⓓ Ⓔ	4. Ⓐ Ⓑ Ⓒ Ⓓ Ⓔ
VERBAL SECTION 1	2. Ⓐ Ⓑ Ⓒ Ⓓ Ⓔ	14. Ⓐ Ⓑ Ⓒ Ⓓ Ⓔ	5. Ⓐ Ⓑ Ⓒ Ⓓ Ⓔ
1. Ⓐ Ⓑ Ⓒ Ⓓ Ⓔ	3. Ⓐ Ⓑ Ⓒ Ⓓ Ⓔ	15. Ⓐ Ⓑ Ⓒ Ⓓ Ⓔ	6. Ⓐ Ⓑ Ⓒ Ⓓ Ⓔ
2. Ⓐ Ⓑ Ⓒ Ⓓ Ⓔ	4. Ⓐ Ⓑ Ⓒ Ⓓ Ⓔ	16. Ⓐ Ⓑ Ⓒ Ⓓ Ⓔ	7. Ⓐ Ⓑ Ⓒ Ⓓ Ⓔ
3. Ⓐ Ⓑ Ⓒ Ⓓ Ⓔ	5. Ⓐ Ⓑ Ⓒ Ⓓ Ⓔ	17. Ⓐ Ⓑ Ⓒ Ⓓ Ⓔ	8. Ⓐ Ⓑ Ⓒ Ⓓ Ⓔ
4. Ⓐ Ⓑ Ⓒ Ⓓ Ⓔ	6. Ⓐ Ⓑ Ⓒ Ⓓ Ⓔ	18. Ⓐ Ⓑ Ⓒ Ⓓ Ⓔ	9. Ⓐ Ⓑ Ⓒ Ⓓ Ⓔ
5. Ⓐ Ⓑ Ⓒ Ⓓ Ⓔ	7. Ⓐ Ⓑ Ⓒ Ⓓ Ⓔ	19. Ⓐ Ⓑ Ⓒ Ⓓ Ⓔ	10. Ⓐ Ⓑ Ⓒ Ⓓ Ⓔ
6. Ⓐ Ⓑ Ⓒ Ⓓ Ⓔ	8. Ⓐ Ⓑ Ⓒ Ⓓ Ⓔ	20. Ⓐ Ⓑ Ⓒ Ⓓ Ⓔ	11. Ⓐ Ⓑ Ⓒ Ⓓ Ⓔ
7. Ⓐ Ⓑ Ⓒ Ⓓ Ⓔ	9. Ⓐ Ⓑ Ⓒ Ⓓ Ⓔ	21. Ⓐ Ⓑ Ⓒ Ⓓ Ⓔ	12. Ⓐ Ⓑ Ⓒ Ⓓ Ⓔ
			13. Ⓐ Ⓑ Ⓒ Ⓓ Ⓔ

SAT TEST

Time—30 Minutes
25 Questions

In this section solve each problem, using any available space on the page for scratchwork. Then decide which is the best of the choices given and fill in the corresponding oval on the answer sheet.

Notes:

1.   The use of a calculator is permitted. All numbers used are real numbers.

2.   Figures that accompany problems in this test are intended to provide information useful in solving the problems. They are drawn as accurately as possible EXCEPT when it is stated in a specific problem that the figure is not drawn to scale. All figures lie in a plane unless otherwise indicated.

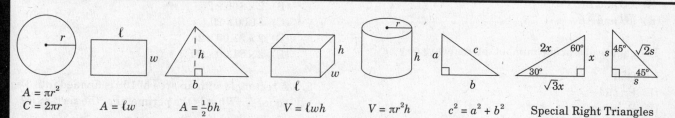

$A = \pi r^2$
$C = 2\pi r$

$A = \ell w$

$A = \frac{1}{2}bh$

$V = \ell w h$

$V = \pi r^2 h$

$c^2 = a^2 + b^2$

Special Right Triangles

Reference Information

The number of degrees of arc in a circle is 360.
The measure in degrees of a straight angle is 180.
The sum of the measures in degrees of the angles of a triangle is 180.

---

1.   If it takes a runner 6 minutes to complete a lap around a park, what fraction of a lap has the runner run in 4 minutes, assuming she runs at a constant pace?

(A) $\frac{1}{24}$

(B) $\frac{1}{6}$

(C) $\frac{1}{4}$

(D) $\frac{1}{2}$

(E) $\frac{2}{3}$

2.   If Mark is older than Judy, and Judy is older than Brian but younger than Lisa, then which of the following statements must be true?

(A) Mark is older than Lisa.
(B) Lisa is older than Mark.
(C) Brian is older than Lisa.
(D) Brian is younger than Mark.
(E) Lisa is younger than Brian.

3.   If $xy = x$ and $x \neq 0$, then what is the value of yz?

(A) 0
(B) 1
(C) x
(D) y
(E) z

GO ON TO THE NEXT PAGE

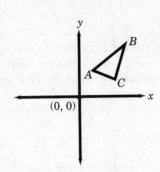

4. Which side(s) of the triangle have negative slope?

   (A) $\overline{AB}$
   (B) $\overline{BC}$
   (C) $\overline{AC}$
   (D) $\overline{AB}$ and $\overline{BC}$
   (E) $\overline{AC}$ and $\overline{AB}$

5. The square of a prime number must always be what?

   I.   Odd
   II. Prime
   III. Positive

   (A) I only
   (B) II only
   (C) III only
   (D) II and III only
   (E) I, II, and III

6. What is $\frac{1}{3} \times \frac{3}{2}$ divided by $\frac{3}{8}$?

   (A) $\frac{1}{12}$

   (B) $\frac{1}{2}$

   (C) $\frac{3}{4}$

   (D) $\frac{4}{3}$

   (E) 3

7. Which of the following numbers is greater than $\frac{5}{8}$ and less than $\frac{3}{4}$?

   (A) 0.25
   (B) 0.5
   (C) 0.7
   (D) 0.8
   (E) 0.9

8. If a one-way bus ride costs $.90, and John rides to and from school in the bus every school day, which is the best estimate of how much John will spend on bus rides in the month of February? Assume that there are 21 school days in the month of February.

   (A) $.50 × 20
   (B) 2 × $50 × 25
   (C) $1.00 × 20
   (D) 2 × $1.00 × 25
   (E) 2 × $1.00 × 20

9. A rectangle with an area of 108 is divided into 3 equal squares. What is the perimeter of the rectangle?

   (A) 18
   (B) $12\sqrt{3}$
   (C) 36
   (D) 48
   (E) 72

10. Donna is the head of the school recycling drive. It takes her 15 minutes to crush the aluminum cans in one trash bag. If the school collected 180 trash bags full of cans, and there are 3 hours to crush cans, how many people does she need to recruit to help her? Assume that everyone crushes cans at the same rate, and that Donna is working too.

    (A) 4
    (B) 11
    (C) 12
    (D) 14
    (E) 15

GO ON TO THE NEXT PAGE

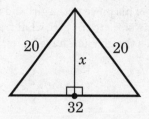

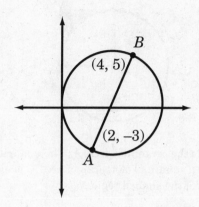

11. If $\overline{AB}$ is a diameter of the circle, what are the coordinates of the center of the circle?

    (A) (0,0)
    (B) (2,2)
    (C) (3,1)
    (D) (6,2)
    (E) (6,8)

12. There is a large cookie jar filled with 45 cookies. If the cookies are distributed in a 2:3:4 ratio among three children, what is the greatest number of cookies that any one child receives?

    (A) 2
    (B) 4
    (C) 15
    (D) 20
    (E) 36

13. What is the least common multiple of the prime factors of 36?

    (A) 1
    (B) 2
    (C) 3
    (D) 6
    (E) 36

14. What percent of 4 is 16?

    (A) 20%
    (B) 25%
    (C) 75%
    (D) 200%
    (E) 400%

15. What is the value of x?

    (A) $\sqrt{624}$
    (B) 20
    (C) 16
    (D) 12
    (E) 10

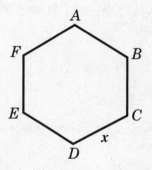

16. If $x = 4$, what is the area of equilateral hexagon *ABCDEF*?

    (A) 36
    (B) $24\sqrt{3}$
    (C) 48
    (D) 64
    (E) $48\sqrt{3}$

GO ON TO THE NEXT PAGE

17. Two boys and one girl evenly split one apple pie. If one boy gives 1/2 of his piece to the girl and the other boy gives 3/4 of his piece to the girl, what fraction of the entire pie does the girl now have?

    (A) $\dfrac{1}{4}$

    (B) $\dfrac{1}{3}$

    (C) $\dfrac{5}{12}$

    (D) $\dfrac{1}{2}$

    (E) $\dfrac{3}{4}$

18. Points $A, B, C, D,$ and E are on line segment $\overline{AE}$. $\overline{BC}$ is twice as long as $\overline{AB}$. $\overline{CD}$ is twice as long as $\overline{BC}$. $\overline{DE}$ is twice as long as $\overline{CD}$. What is the shortest possible length of $\overline{CD}$, such that the length of each of the segments $\overline{AB}$, $\overline{BC}$, $\overline{CD}$, and $\overline{DE}$ is a whole number?

    (A) 1
    (B) 2
    (C) 3
    (D) 4
    (E) 8

19. How many of the first 200 positive integers contain the digit 1 exactly once?

    (A) 36
    (B) 37
    (C) 99
    (D) 100
    (E) 121

20. A local pet store sells dogs and cats and no other animals. For every d dogs in the store at a given time, there are c cats. One day there are 30 animals in the store. How many dogs are there?

    (A) $\dfrac{30d}{d+c}$

    (B) $\dfrac{30}{d+c}$

    (C) $\dfrac{c}{29}$

    (D) $30 - c$

    (E) $\dfrac{30(d+c)}{d}$

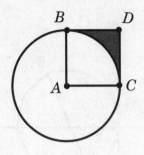

21. Point A is the center of Circle A. The quadrilateral $ABCD$ is a square. The length of arc BC is 4π. What is the area of the shaded region?

    (A) $64 - 64\pi$
    (B) $16 - 16\pi$
    (C) $64 - 16\pi$
    (D) $64\pi - 16$
    (E) $64\pi - 64$

22. Starting with the second term, the even terms of a sequence are consecutive powers of two, such that the second term is 2^1, the fourth term is 2^2, etc. The odd terms, starting with the third term, are the averages of the terms immediately preceding them and the terms immediately following them. For example, the third term is the average of the second and fourth term. The first term is 3/2. What is the sum of the third, fifth, and seventh terms of this sequence?

    (A) 11
    (B) 14
    (C) 15
    (D) 18
    (E) 21

23. p is a prime number. How many factors does p^n have?

    (A) p
    (B) n
    (C) pn
    (D) $n + p$
    (E) $n + 1$

GO ON TO THE NEXT PAGE

24. If the mean of 3, 4, and r is the same as the mean of 4, 6 and s, what is the difference between r and s?

    (A) 1
    (B) 2
    (C) 3
    (D) 4
    (E) 5

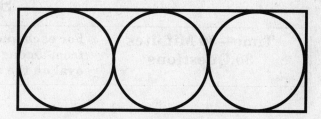

25. The circumference of each of the three identical circles is 10π. What is the perimeter of the rectangle?

    (A) 20
    (B) 30
    (C) 40
    (D) 60
    (E) 80

S T O P

IF YOU FINISH BEFORE TIME IS CALLED, YOU MAY CHECK YOUR WORK IN THIS SECTION ONLY.
DO NOT TURN TO ANY OTHER SECTION IN THE TEST.

SAT TEST

Time—30 Minutes
30 Questions

For each question in this section, select the best answer from among the choices given and fill in the corresponding oval on the answer sheet.

Each sentence below has one or two blanks, each blank indicating that something has been omitted. Beneath the sentence are five words or sets of words labeled A through E. Choose the word or set of words that, when inserted in the sentence, <u>best</u> fits the meaning of the sentence as a whole.

Example:
   Medieval kingdoms did not become constitutional republics overnight; on the contrary, the change was ----.

   (A) unpopular
   (B) unexpected
   (C) advantageous
   (D) sufficient
   (E) gradual

1. Unable to grasp the question in front of her, Karen seemed ----.

    (A) furious
    (B) abstinent
    (C) perplexed
    (D) prepared
    (E) earnest

2. Understanding the United States tax code is a ---- undertaking; nevertheless, many people continue to rush through their taxes as though it were an ---- task.

    (A) formidable . . undemanding
    (B) noble . . exceptional
    (C) rewarding . . enriching
    (D) civic . . irresponsible
    (E) miniscule . . straightforward

3. Despite years of intermittent ----, politicians in the Middle East continue to offer the hope of ----.

    (A) disagreement . . hatred
    (B) war . . religion
    (C) prosperity . . starvation
    (D) bloodshed . . peace
    (E) turmoil . . supremacy

4. Though he was ----, the young entrepreneur tried ---- to come out ahead at the negotiating table.

    (A) terrified . . valiantly
    (B) unnerved . . timidly
    (C) egomaniacal . . doggedly
    (D) amoral . . shrewdly
    (E) wealthy . . desperately

5. Unlike the signing of the Magna Carta in 1215, which guaranteed the rights of only a limited group of elite English nobles, the signing of the United States Constitution was intended to guarantee the rights of the ---- as well.

    (A) administration
    (B) bourgeoisie
    (C) gentry
    (D) clergy
    (E) oligarchy

6. Knowing that her controversial findings were likely to be heavily scrutinized, Yolanda ---- documented every aspect of her research.

    (A) callously
    (B) dexterously
    (C) meticulously
    (D) passively
    (E) undeniably

GO ON TO THE NEXT PAGE

7. Her colleagues showered Berenice with ---- after she solved the conundrum that had ---- theorists for more than a decade.

   (A) commendations . . benefited
   (B) accolades . . confounded
   (C) disparagement . . calibrated
   (D) contempt . . flabbergasted
   (E) tribute . . denigrated

8. Born ----, baby howler monkeys will explore every inch of their surroundings without any sense of fear, since they are not ---- of the possibility of danger at such a young age.

   (A) inquisitive . . cognizant
   (B) malleable . . perspicacious
   (C) pugnacious . . wary
   (D) adventurous . . imprudent
   (E) timorous . . apprehensive

9. The doctor suspected that her patient had leukemia, but until she could know ----, she kept her diagnosis to herself.

   (A) medically
   (B) unequivocally
   (C) reputably
   (D) precariously
   (E) ambiguously

GO ON TO THE NEXT PAGE

Each question below consists of a related pair of words or phrases, followed by five pairs of words or phrases labeled A through E. Select the pair that <u>best</u> expresses a relationship similar to that expressed in the original pair.

Example:

CRUMB : BREAD ::

(A) ounce : unit
(B) splinter : wood
(C) water : bucket
(D) twine : rope
(E) cream : butter

10. SUGAR : SWEETENER ::

(A) milk : cookies
(B) politics : governor
(C) judge : verdict
(D) gasoline : fuel
(E) cat : kitten

11. PRESIDENT : NATION ::

(A) principal : school
(B) soldier : army
(C) senator : congress
(D) judge : jury
(E) waiter : restaurant

12. CAPTAIN : SHIP ::

(A) soldier : war
(B) store : grain
(C) clerk : office
(D) pupil : teacher
(E) judge : court

13. INAUGURATION : COMMENCE ::

(A) summary : elaborate
(B) gesture : agitate
(C) epilogue : conclude
(D) explanation : bewilder
(E) demagogue : ameliorate

14. CULTIVATE : CROP ::

(A) mail : letter
(B) conceive : mother
(C) nurture : infant
(D) nourish : food
(E) converse : words

15. PREAMBLE : DOCUMENT ::

(A) prologue : novel
(B) appendix : treatise
(C) digression : plot
(D) fugue : music
(E) abbreviation : term

GO ON TO THE NEXT PAGE

SAT TEST

The passage below is followed by questions based on its content. Answer the questions on the basis of what is <u>stated</u> or <u>implied</u> in the passage and in any introductory material that may be provided.

Questions 16–20 are based on the following passage.

The excerpt below is from a memoir written by the composer Igor Stravinsky, a native Russian who spent much of his life away from his homeland.

My profound emotion on reading news of war, which aroused patriotic feelings and a sense of sadness at being so distant from my country, found some alleviation in the
Line delight with which I steeped myself in Russian folk poems.
5   What fascinated me in this verse was not so much the stories, which were often crude, or the pictures and metaphors, always so deliciously unexpected, as the sequence of the words and syllables, and the cadence they create, which produces an effect on one's sensibilities very closely
10 akin to that of music. For I consider that music is, by its very nature, essentially powerless to *express* anything at all, whether a feeling, an attitude of mind, a psychological mood, a phenomenon of nature, etc. . . . *statement* has never been an inherent property of music. That is by no means the purpose
15 of its existence. If, as is nearly always the case, music appears to express something, this is only an illusion and not a reality. It is simply an additional attribute which, by tacit agreement, we have lent it, thrust upon it, as a label, a convention – in short, an aspect that unconsciously or by
20 force of habit we have come to confuse with its essential being.
    Music is the sole domain in which man realizes the present. By the imperfection of his nature, man is doomed to submit to the passage of time—to its categories of past and
25 future—without ever being able to give substance, and therefore stability, to the category of the present.
    The phenomenon of music is given to us with the sole purpose of establishing an order in things, including, and particularly, the coordination between *man* and *time*. To be
30 put into practice, its indispensable and single requirement is construction. Construction once completed, this order has been attained, and there is nothing more to be said. It would be futile to look for, or expect anything else from it. It is precisely this construction, this achieved order, which
35 produces in us a unique emotion having nothing in common with our ordinary sensations and our responses to the impressions of daily life. One could not better define the sensation produced by music than by saying that it is identical with that evoked by contemplation of the interplay
40 of architectural forms. Goethe thoroughly understood that when he called architecture petrified music.

16. In the first paragraph of the passage, Stravinsky says that he began to read Russian folk poems because:

(A) he wanted to translate them.
(B) he wanted to write literary criticism about them.
(C) he was writing poetry of his own.
(D) he wanted to compare them to music.
(E) he was homesick for Russia.

17. Music, according to Stravinsky, best expresses:

(A) metaphors.
(B) the present moment in time.
(C) mood.
(D) images of nature.
(E) narratives and folk tales.

18. In line 23, which of the following is closest to what Stravinsky means by "the imperfection of [man's] nature"?

(A) Man's stupidity
(B) Man's mortality
(C) Man's ugliness
(D) Man's tendency to live in cities
(E) Man's inability to appreciate music

19. By comparing music to architecture in lines 37–41, Stravinsky suggests all of the following except:

(A) music is best compared to non-narrative forms
(B) both depend on manipulations of time
(C) both require careful contemplation
(D) there are both emotional and intellectual components to music and architecture
(E) neither music nor architecture is a real art form

20. The main point of this passage is to:

(A) describe Stravinsky's homesickness for Russia.
(B) provide a justification for Stravinsky's own musical style.
(C) consider philosophically the function of music.
(D) compare music to architecture.
(E) examine the Russian character.

GO ON TO THE NEXT PAGE

The passage below is followed by questions based on its content. Answer the questions on the basis of what is <u>stated</u> or <u>implied</u> in the passage and in any introductory material that may be provided.

Questions 21–30 are based on the following passage.

In the following passage, the writer, a woman, discusses a transition in the role of women in American society that occurred in the early years of the twentieth century.

When one set of people see that another set of people are taking from them that which they very much want to have, the intelligent procedure is to find the reasons behind the shift. The housewives of this country are seeing the great body of girls and women on whom they have always depended for household service turn their backs on them and accept employment in thousands of different kinds of shops and factories. They see the girl that they think they ought to secure as a waitress much preferring to go into a candy factory. They find the woman that they think would make an admirable cook possibly making munitions, if she lives in Dayton, Ohio, for instance. This shift from the house to the factory is not local and sporadic. It is general and permanent.

There are, of course, reasons. Now what are the reasons? What the household employers in this country ought to do is to study carefully why the manufacturers can attract labor when they cannot. The factory has no way of compelling girls and women to come to it. They go, it is obvious, because they prefer it. Why do they prefer it?

Most housewives have traditional notions of the factory as something cruel, dark, distressing. They are appalled that any woman should prefer to go into these places, of which they have such horror. But is their notion correct? Take the woman who might be the cook. Why does she go to a factory? It is not at all because she does not want to cook. It is because she does want a regular day of a fixed number of hours. It is because she does want her Sundays and holidays. It is because she wants a fixed task, which she can perform without the hourly fussing and intrusion of a person, who because she is in authority, is unwilling to let her whom she hires go ahead and do her work in her own way. It is because she can have a home, a place which is her own, to which she can give her personal stamp, where she can be more independent, more cheerful, more of a person than she can in the home that is provided by the housewife.

The woman prefers the factory, too, because she finds that her employer and those who are immediately over her show her and her work more respect than the housewife ordinarily does. She can weave or spin. She can run a lathe or feed a machine, and the policeman on the beat will not look down on her, as he so often does if she is in a kitchen. She keeps caste in the factory, as she cannot keep it in the house.

The women of this country are never going to be able to hold household workers until they offer the same physical and social advantages that the factory does. There never was a clearer demonstration that money has less influence with the mass of people than opportunities for a free life and for social standing. The woman makes more money in the average household. Her weekly wage may not be quite as large as that of the factory, but what she saves brings the earnings up considerably above that of the highest paid factory workers. It is with her a question of self-respect, a question of freedom, a question of opportunity to advance, to take and make a place for herself in the community.

Socially and economically speaking, the housewives of the United States are back in the eighteenth century, and not the eighteenth century of the revolutionary France and revolutionary America, but the feudal eighteenth century. They see this thing from an aristocratic point of view, not from the democratic. Until they purge themselves of the class spirit, until they go out and study why the manufacturer is able to hold the labor which he wants, and are willing to transform their spirit and their methods, and are ready to adopt his spirit and his methods, they are not going to be able to stabilize and dignify the great industry which they control. They can learn what it is necessary to do from the factory.

21. According to the passage, women generally prefer factory work to domestic household work because:

(A) Factory work allows women to save money.
(B) Housewives are typically very cruel employers.
(C) Factory work is new and exciting, while household work is familiar and dull.
(D) Factory work provides employees with more stability, independence, and social status.
(E) Factory work is more challenging and more interesting.

22. In line 13, the word "sporadic" is used to mean:

(A) temporary.
(B) involuntary.
(C) irregular.
(D) based on economic circumstance.
(E) troubling.

GO ON TO THE NEXT PAGE

23. Which statement best characterizes the housewives' impression of factory work, according to lines 20–21?

    (A) It is extremely difficult.
    (B) It involves an undesirable and uncomfortable working environment.
    (C) It threatens to disrupt traditional labor patterns.
    (D) It is a far preferable alternative for women who might otherwise become domestic help.
    (E) It is very dull and dreary compared to domestic labor.

24. In line 28, the word "fixed" is used to mean:

    (A) stable and unchanging
    (B) repaired or put back together
    (C) unfairly rigged
    (D) in a dire or desperate situation
    (E) determined to accomplish a particular goal

25. The author uses the example of the "policeman on the beat" (line 40) to:

    (A) indicate the thin line separating the law-abiding working girl from the criminal woman of the streets
    (B) paint a vivid portrait of life in the American industrial landscape
    (C) draw a connection between the power of the law and the power of the factory owner
    (D) hint at the respect young women in the workplace feel for the men who protect them from danger
    (E) illustrate the difference in treatment of factory workers and domestic workers by an individual in a position of authority

26. In lines 46–49, the author says that money:

    (A) is easier to come by in a factory than in a home
    (B) is the main problem with factory work, as women are criminally underpaid
    (C) is more relevant to the domestic laborer than to the factory worker
    (D) is less important to women than independence and self-respect
    (E) is necessary to ensure one's place in the community

27. What is the author's general idea about how housewives can keep their domestic laborers?

    (A) They must offer working women a more democratic environment.
    (B) They must understand why working women would prefer to work in factories, then model their employment practices on the lessons they have learned.
    (C) They must undercut the factories by offering more money for less work.
    (D) They must work to strengthen the social status of the traditional home and family, putting a stop to the progressive new strain in American society.
    (E) They must accept a lower standard of employee.

28. What two perspectives does the author contrast in lines 56–61?

    (A) the domestic worker's and the factory worker's
    (B) the housewife's and the working girl's
    (C) the progressive and the conservative
    (D) the housewife's and the factory employee's
    (E) the aristocratic and the democratic

29. In order to deal with the prevalent social assumptions of her day, the author addresses this passage to the

    (A) working girl
    (B) average citizen
    (C) housewife
    (D) factory owner
    (E) domestic employee

30. The overall tone of this passage is

    (A) wry and humorous
    (B) disinterested and academic
    (C) passionate
    (D) critical and moralizing
    (E) objective and sympathetic

S T O P

IF YOU FINISH BEFORE TIME IS CALLED, YOU MAY CHECK YOUR WORK IN THIS SECTION ONLY.
DO NOT TURN TO ANY OTHER SECTION IN THE TEST.

SAT TEST

Time—30 Minutes
25 Questions

In this section solve each problem, using any available space on the page for scratchwork. Then decide which is the best of the choices given and fill in the corresponding oval on the answer sheet.

<u>Notes:</u>

1. The use of a calculator is permitted. All numbers used are real numbers.

2. Figures that accompany problems in this test are intended to provide information useful in solving the problems. They are drawn as accurately as possible EXCEPT when it is stated in a specific problem that the figure is not drawn to scale. All figures lie in a plane unless otherwise indicated.

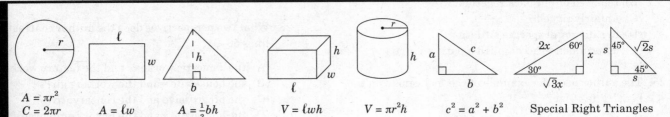

Reference Information

$A = \pi r^2$
$C = 2\pi r$

$A = \ell w$

$A = \frac{1}{2}bh$

$V = \ell wh$

$V = \pi r^2 h$

$c^2 = a^2 + b^2$

Special Right Triangles

The number of degrees of arc in a circle is 360.
The measure in degrees of a straight angle is 180.
The sum of the measures in degrees of the angles of a triangle is 180.

Directions for Quantitative Comparison Questions

<u>Questions 1–15</u> each consist of two quantities in boxes, one in Column A and one in Column B.
You are to compare the two quantities and on the answer sheet fill in oval

A if the quantity in Column A is greater;
B if the quantity in Column B is greater;
C if the two quantities are equal;
D if the relationship cannot be determined from the information given.

AN E RESPONSE WILL NOT BE SCORED.

<u>Notes:</u>

1. In some questions, information is given about one or both of the quantities to be compared. In such cases, the given information is centered above the two columns and is not boxed.
2. In a given question, a symbol that appears in both columns represents the same thing in Column A as it does in Column B.
3. Letters such as x, n, and k stand for real numbers.

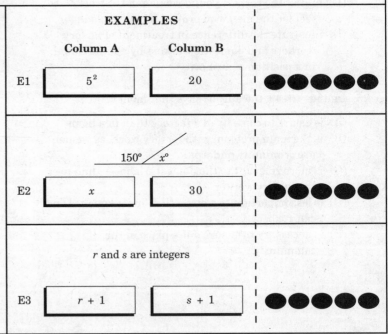

EXAMPLES

Column A	Column B

E1 | 5^2 | 20

E2 | x | 30 (150° / x°)

r and s are integers

E3 | $r + 1$ | $s + 1$

Column A	Column B

1.

| 300% of 5 | 50% of 30 |

$a \times b = 1$

2.

| $a \times \dfrac{1}{b}$ | a^2 |

$a = bc$

3.

| $\dfrac{2a}{bc}$ | $\dfrac{3bc}{a}$ |

$f > g$

4.

| $f - g$ | $g - f$ |

$x, y \geq 1$ and $2x \geq 20 + 8y$

5.

| x | 8 |

Column A	Column B

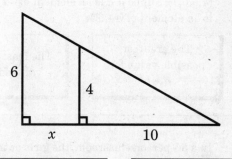

6.

| Area of *ABCDEFG* | 40 |

7.

| $\dfrac{1}{2} - \dfrac{1}{6}$ | $\dfrac{3}{4} - \dfrac{1}{3}$ |

8.

| x | 6 |

GO ON TO THE NEXT PAGE

Column A	Column B

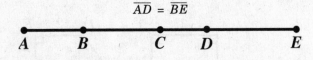

$\overline{AD} = \overline{BE}$

9. $\overline{AC}$ | $\overline{CE}$

The math club has 18 members. The rugby club has 25 members. All the students in a particular class are members of at least one club, and exactly 6 people are in both clubs.

10. The number of people in this particular class | 37

Let @x,y@ be defined as the set of all integers between x and y, inclusive. For example, @4,7@ = {4,5,6,7}. Suppose a is an element of @2,4@ and b is an element of @4,6@.

11. The greatest possible value for $a + b$ | The least possible value for $a + b$

In a 30-person classroom, the girls outnumber the boys. Also, there are more girls with straight hair than there are girls with curly hair.

12. The greatest possible number of girls with curly hair | 12

$x + y + z = 100$ and $x + y + 2z = 130$

13. z | 30

Column A	Column B

The first term of a sequence is 12.

14. The second term of the sequence | The third term of the sequence

---

Vehicle Type	Gasoline	Diesel	Total
Cars	80		100
Trucks			
Total	85	35	

The vehicles on a particular highway during a given period of time are classified as either cars or trucks and as either gasoline-fueled or diesel-fueled. The chart with this data is incomplete, though.

15. The ratio of trucks to gasoline-fueled cars | The ratio of diesel-fueled vehicles to total vehicles

GO ON TO THE NEXT PAGE ▶

SAT TEST

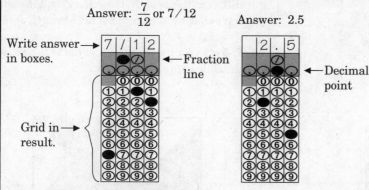
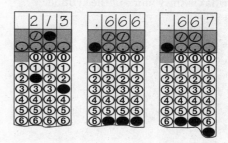
16. A public health study found that in a certain town, 30% of the citizens are overweight. If that town has a population of 1320, how many of its citizens are overweight?

17. Maria has 6 blue balls, 4 red balls, and 8 black balls. What fraction of the total number of balls aren't black?

18. If $2^x = 4^y = 16^z$, what is $\frac{x}{y} + \frac{x}{z}$?

GO ON TO THE NEXT PAGE

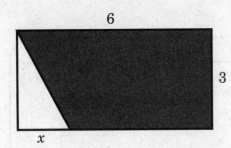

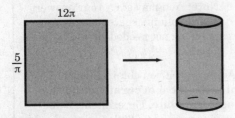

19. If $x = 2$, what is the area of the shaded region?

20. If $2^x \times 2^y = 256$, what is the value of $x + y$?

21. If the rectangle in the figure is rolled into a cylinder according to the figure above (so that the edges of length 5/π touch), what is the volume of the cylinder?

22. Each ticket in a certain lottery has 3 digits written on it, in a specific order. The lottery pays \$1 for having one matching digit, \$3 for two matching digits, and \$10 for three matching digits (in order to "match," the digit(s) must be in the right place). If the winning digits are 233, in that order, and John knows that his ticket has 3 different digits on it, how many combinations could he have that would make his ticket worth at least \$3?

23. If $5 \le x + 3y \le 8$, and $z \le 5$, what is the greatest possible value of $2x + 6y + z$?

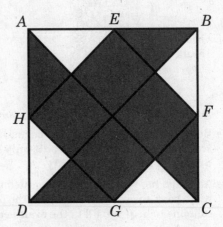

24. In square $ABCD$, points E, F, G, and H are the midpoints of their respective sides. What is the area of the shaded portion if $\overline{AB} = 4$?

25. A jar holds 3 black marbles and 2 white marbles. Two marbles are taken out at the same time. What is the probability that one is black and one is white?

S T O P

IF YOU FINISH BEFORE TIME IS CALLED, YOU MAY CHECK YOUR WORK IN THIS SECTION ONLY.
DO NOT TURN TO ANY OTHER SECTION IN THE TEST.

SAT TEST

For each question in this section, select the best answer from among the choices given and fill in the corresponding oval on the answer sheet.

Each sentence below has one or two blanks, each blank indicating that something has been omitted. Beneath the sentence are five words or sets of words labeled A through E. Choose the word or set of words that, when inserted in the sentence, <u>best</u> fits the meaning of the sentence as a whole.

Example:
   Medieval kingdoms did not become constitutional republics overnight; on the contrary, the change was ----.

   (A) unpopular
   (B) unexpected
   (C) advantageous
   (D) sufficient
   (E) gradual

1. In retrospect many historians consider the Tet Offensive during the Vietnam War to have been downright ----, since it culminated in so many casualties and so few gains.

    (A) punctual
    (B) foolhardy
    (C) fickle
    (D) bold
    (E) admirable

2. He is often hailed as a ---- writer, but Mark Twain's later work often probes unsettling and ---- truths.

    (A) troubling .. funny
    (B) disturbing .. bothersome
    (C) hilarious .. disorganized
    (D) patriotic .. regional
    (E) comic .. serious

3. Known for their ---- and ---- waters, Florida's beaches are a favored vacation destination throughout the year.

    (A) opaque .. unsanitary
    (B) calming .. abrupt
    (C) unsoiled .. pellucid
    (D) picturesque .. inaccessible
    (E) residual .. posterior

4. While not having been a direct participant in the ----, Cindy did admit that she encouraged the two boys to fight for the right to take her to the junior prom.

    (A) altercation
    (B) selection
    (C) dalliance
    (D) artifice
    (E) reconciliation

5. In general, an Ice Age, a period in which the average temperature of the planet ---- significantly, develops gradually; ice and cold do not ---- appear out of nowhere.

    (A) grows .. swiftly
    (B) decreases .. dramatically
    (C) changes .. indirectly
    (D) lessens .. slowly
    (E) extends .. merely

6. While he may have once hoped to ---- Europe from the system of monarchy, Napoleon quickly became a ----, consolidating his power at the expense of his subjects' freedom.

    (A) free .. hero
    (B) salvage .. warrior
    (C) dominate .. tyrant
    (D) administrate .. thug
    (E) liberate .. despot

GO ON TO THE NEXT PAGE

7. Although *The New Yorker* is often regarded as an ----
publication, it is actually very ----, with one of the
largest circulations of any magazine in the country.

  (A) outdated . . superficial
  (B) elitist . . popular
  (C) irrelevant . . well-written
  (D) enjoyable . . demeaning
  (E) estimable . . notorious

8. In prehistoric North and South America, some ground
sloths were ----, much larger than modern-day tree
sloths.

  (A) feral
  (B) gargantuan
  (C) amorphous
  (D) anthropocentric
  (E) docile

9. Louisa's ---- of historical matters was ---- by the
erroneous comments she made regarding the events
leading up to the American Revolution.

  (A) mastery . . highlighted
  (B) ignorance . . epitomized
  (C) love . . evidenced
  (D) negligence . . eviscerated
  (E) obstruction . . articulated

10. Professor Lopez asked his students to present their
own arguments and opinions in their terms papers,
rather than just ---- what he had said in lecture.

  (A) promulgate
  (B) juxtapose
  (C) enfranchise
  (D) mitigate
  (E) regurgitate

GO ON TO THE NEXT PAGE ➤

Each question below consists of a related pair of words or phrases, followed by five pairs of words or phrases labeled A through E. Select the pair that best expresses a relationship similar to that expressed in the original pair.

Example:
CRUMB : BREAD ::

(A) ounce : unit
(B) splinter : wood
(C) water : bucket
(D) twine : rope
(E) cream : butter   Ⓐ ● Ⓒ Ⓓ Ⓔ

11. BAKER : OVEN ::

(A) radio : station
(B) hammer : nail
(C) teacher : desk
(D) scientist : microscope
(E) reporter : story

12. FERTILIZER : PLANT ::

(A) root : harvest
(B) yeast : dough
(C) candle : cake
(D) leaf : canopy
(E) fury : wound

13. UNLIKELY : IMPOSSIBLE ::

(A) probable : doubtful
(B) ugly : hideous
(C) fair : unjust
(D) fickle : pleased
(E) sorrowful : sunny

14. SECOND : TIME ::

(A) foot : height
(B) minute : hour
(C) length : endurance
(D) velocity : speed
(E) pint : gallon

15. PHOTOGRAPH : NEGATIVE ::

(A) film : video
(B) dress : pattern
(C) computer : program
(D) novel : plot
(E) telephone : call

16. COVERT : SURREPTITIOUSLY ::

(A) passive : strongly
(B) outdated : currently
(C) sociable : affably
(D) secret : obviously
(E) casual : remorsefully

17. AMPLIFIER : SOUND ::

(A) binoculars : vision
(B) museum : art
(C) stereo : music
(D) perfume : scent
(E) movie : screen

18. PAINTER : STUDIO ::

(A) monkey : zoo
(B) farmhouse : landscape
(C) legislature : amendment
(D) conductor : locomotive
(E) violin : auditorium

19. ALBUM : SONGS ::

(A) book : index
(B) freeway : road
(C) compass : direction
(D) play : scenes
(E) fixture : animation

20. EXULTANT : HAPPY ::

(A) delusional : confused
(B) repudiated : proved
(C) considerate : disingenuous
(D) wretched : horrendous
(E) perspicacity : genius

21. LUBRICATE : FRICTION ::

(A) irrigate : hydration
(B) venerate : partisan
(C) permeate : dissonance
(D) embellish : enunciation
(E) illuminate : darkness

GO ON TO THE NEXT PAGE ➤

22. HEINOUS : CRIME ::

    (A) tasty : food
    (B) garish : decoration
    (C) garbled : larceny
    (D) hazardous : risk
    (E) authentic : forgery

23. PERFIDY : STEADFAST ::

    (A) jubilance : melancholy
    (B) functionality : active
    (C) homestead : domestic
    (D) worthiness : penitent
    (E) impudence : snubbed

GO ON TO THE NEXT PAGE

The passage below is followed by questions based on its content. Answer the questions on the basis of what is <u>stated</u> or <u>implied</u> in the passage and in any introductory material that may be provided.

Questions 24–35 are based on the following passage.

The following passage is adapted from a book about the human fascination with flight. This section deals with the famous Renaissance artist Leonardo da Vinci and his contributions to the field.

The modern world knows da Vinci as an artist; his age knew him as an architect, engineer, artist, and as a scientist during a time when science was a single study comprising all knowledge from mathematics to medicine. His range of knowledge and observation was so vast, a number of his compatriots, perhaps in jest, claimed that he had some compact with the devil. Da Vinci anticipated modern knowledge as Plato anticipated modern thought. His observations and deductions about human flight in particular were strikingly prophetic of advancements made in the field only some three centuries after his death. Regrettably, because da Vinci's *Treatise on the Flight of Birds*, which contained much of his insight into the matter, was lost soon after his death, the principles he observed and described had to be discovered as if for the first time by future generations when the treatise was rediscovered.

Still, the theories da Vinci put forward are of the greatest interest; they prove him a patient and keen student of the principles of flight, and show that his numerous activities in various fields did not render his work slipshod or shallow. His observations of birds in flight are lengthy in scope and singularly original for his time.

"A bird," da Vinci says in his Treatise, "is an instrument that works according to mathematical law, and, further, an instrument which it is within the capacity of man to reproduce in all its movements, though not with a corresponding ability to maintain equilibrium. We may say, therefore, that such an instrument constructed by man is lacking in nothing except the life of the bird, and this life must be supplied from that of man. Since we see that the bird is equipped for many apparent varieties of movement, we are able from this experience to deduce that the most simple of these movements will be capable of being comprehended." This comment shows not just da Vinci's profound belief that man is capable of flight, but also a far more definite statement of the principles by which flight might be achieved than any that had preceded it—and for that matter, than many that have succeeded it.

But the examples given do not begin to exhaust the range of da Vinci's observations and deductions. With regard to bird flight, he noticed that so long as a bird keeps its wings outspread it cannot fall directly to earth, but must glide down at an angle to alight—a small thing, now that the principle of the plane in opposition to the air is generally grasped, but da Vinci had to discover it. From observation he gathered how a bird checks its own speed by opposing tail and wing surface to the direction of flight, and thus alights at the proper "landing speed." Recognizing a bird's ability to take flight from a level plane through only the use of outstretched and motionless wings, da Vinci surmised the existence of upward air currents. Unlike those before who were so enamored of the feather, da Vinci wisely proposed that the wings of any flying device more closely resemble bat wings—a material quite similar to the fabric used to form the wings of the earliest airplanes. Finally, da Vinci recommended that experiments in flight be conducted at a good height from the ground, since, if equilibrium were to become lost for any reason, the height would provide time to regain it. This recommendation, by the way, received ample support in the training regimens of war pilots.

In the realm of practical contributions, da Vinci also made his presence felt. Apart from numerous drawings that still have value, da Vinci invented the principles behind the rotor of the helicopter and the parachute. The former he made and proved effective in model form. As to the parachute, the idea was doubtless inspired by observation of the effect a bird produced by pressure of its wings against the direction of flight.

Da Vinci's conclusions, and his experiments, were overlooked by most of his contemporaries and their descendants; his *Treatise* lay forgotten for nearly four centuries, overshadowed, perhaps, by his other work. But his contribution and genius endure nonetheless.

24. According to this passage, da Vinci participated in all of the following disciplines *except*:

   (A) engineering
   (B) politics
   (C) art
   (D) science
   (E) architecture

GO ON TO THE NEXT PAGE

25. The phrase "modern knowledge" in lines 7–8 refers to:

    (A) twentieth-century philosophy
    (B) avian biology and behavior
    (C) modern geographical awareness of the world
    (D) an up-to-date assemblage of facts
    (E) general science and technical understanding

26. The phrase "the life of the bird" (line 29) refers to which necessary component in the development of flying machines?

    (A) The energy needed to power flight
    (B) The divine intervention needed for success
    (C) The experience necessary to fly an airplane
    (D) The growth of the machine to a reasonable size
    (E) The environment in which an airplane can operate

27. The term "exhaust" in line 39 most nearly means:

    (A) to ventilate
    (B) to cover
    (C) to disprove
    (D) to minimalize
    (E) to appear outdated

28. Lines 40–45 respond to which of the following implied criticisms of da Vinci's work?

    (A) His work is wrong.
    (B) He may have come up with the ideas, but he didn't build the machines.
    (C) Da Vinci could have figured out more if he understood opposing planes.
    (D) Birds are the wrong model for human flight.
    (E) Da Vinci's work states only obvious principles.

29. Of the following, the best synonym for the term "gathered" in line 45 would be:

    (A) demonstrated
    (B) brought together
    (C) learned
    (D) bunched up
    (E) collected

30. Which of the following was *not* a recommendation da Vinci made concerning the development of flying machines?

    (A) Birds should be used to power human flight.
    (B) Bat wings are the best model for wing design.
    (C) Pilots should fly at a high altitude.
    (D) Flying machines should land at an angle.
    (E) The tail and wing surfaces should be used to control speed.

31. The reference to war pilots in line 60 is used to suggest that:

    (A) Da Vinci's ideas led to war machines.
    (B) Fewer pilots would die if more of da Vinci's ideas were used.
    (C) There have been no new ideas since da Vinci's time.
    (D) Da Vinci's ideas anticipated a wide range of modern machines and practices.
    (E) Da Vinci's ideas should be re-examined.

32. Which of the following is *not* an invention attributed to Leonardo?

    (A) the helicopter
    (B) the airplane
    (C) landing gear
    (D) the parachute
    (E) the airplane wing

33. This passage emphasizes da Vinci's:

    (A) creativity
    (B) use of experiments and models
    (C) observational skills
    (D) scientific writing skills
    (E) artistic ability

GO ON TO THE NEXT PAGE

34. The author of this passage seems to be interested in da Vinci's work on flight primarily because:

    (A) he is impressed that da Vinci could work so unscientifically
    (B) Da Vinci's work led to changes in the scientific method
    (C) he is interested in the role of observation in science
    (D) it shows the wide-ranging capabilities of the famous man
    (E) the work was important in the development of the airplane

35. Of the following, which would make the best title for the passage?

    (A) How da Vinci Reworked the Ideas of Others
    (B) Da Vinci's Little-Known Flight Engineering Career
    (C) Birds of the Renaissance
    (D) How Airplanes Work
    (E) Leonardo: Misunderstood Artist

S T O P

IF YOU FINISH BEFORE TIME IS CALLED, YOU MAY CHECK YOUR WORK IN THIS SECTION ONLY.
DO NOT TURN TO ANY OTHER SECTION IN THE TEST.

SAT TEST

<table>
<tr><td>Time—15 Minutes
10 Questions</td><td>In this section solve each problem, using any available space on the page for scratchwork. Then decide which is the best of the choices given and fill in the corresponding oval on the answer sheet.</td></tr>
</table>

Notes:

1. The use of a calculator is permitted. All numbers used are real numbers.

2. Figures that accompany problems in this test are intended to provide information useful in solving the problems. They are drawn as accurately as possible EXCEPT when it is stated in a specific problem that the figure is not drawn to scale. All figures lie in a plane unless otherwise indicated.

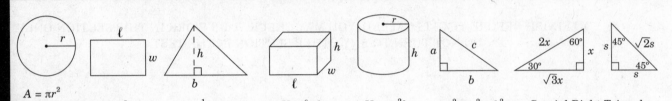

Reference Information

$A = \pi r^2$
$C = 2\pi r$

$A = \ell w$

$A = \frac{1}{2}bh$

$V = \ell w h$

$V = \pi r^2 h$

$c^2 = a^2 + b^2$

Special Right Triangles

The number of degrees of arc in a circle is 360.
The measure in degrees of a straight angle is 180.
The sum of the measures in degrees of the angles of a triangle is 180.

1. 30 of a building's windows have shades. If 2 of every 5 windows are shaded, then how many windows does the building have?

   (A) 12
   (B) 15
   (C) 30
   (D) 75
   (E) 150

2. What is the product of the remainder that you get from dividing 28 by 5 and the remainder you get when you divide 30 by 7?

   (A) 2
   (B) 3
   (C) 5
   (D) 6
   (E) 35

3. If a car travels at a constant rate of 66 miles per hour, how many miles does it travel in 20 minutes?

   (A) 20
   (B) 22
   (C) 46
   (D) 66
   (E) 1320

GO ON TO THE NEXT PAGE

4. A company produces boxes. It incurs a fixed cost prior to producing any boxes, and a unit cost for each box it produces. Which of the following graphs could represent the company's cost function?

(A)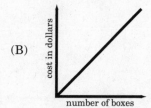

(B)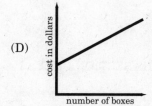

(C)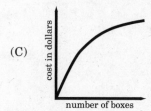

(D)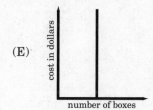

(E)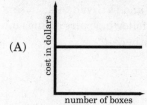

5. If $k = j$ and $x = y$, and $k, j, x, y \neq 0$, which of the following expressions is the equivalent of $k^2 y^2$?

(A) $y j^3$
(B) $k^2 j j$
(C) $(j + y)^2$
(D) $k j y^2$
(E) $y^2 j x$

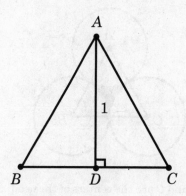

6. ABC is an equilateral triangle. $\overline{AD} = 1$. What is the length of $\overline{AC}$?

(A) $\dfrac{1}{2}$

(B) $\dfrac{\sqrt{3}}{2}$

(C) $\dfrac{2}{\sqrt{3}}$

(D) $\sqrt{2}$

(E) 1.5

7. If the mean of a and b is 10 and the mean of c and d is 12, what is the mean of $\{a, b, c, d, 26\}$?

(A) 13
(B) 14
(C) 15
(D) 16
(E) 17

8. A palindrome is a number that has the same value when the order of its digits is reversed. For example, 2772 and 101 are palindromes. Which of the following choices is NOT equal to a palindrome times 2.

(A) 44
(B) 132
(C) 252
(D) 1010
(E) 1454

GO ON TO THE NEXT PAGE

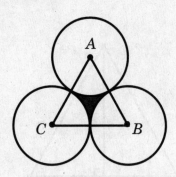

9. Points A, B, and C are the centers of three adjacent circles. ABC is an equilateral triangle. What is the area of the shaded region if the diameter of one circle is 6?

    (A) $9\sqrt{3} - \dfrac{9\pi}{2}$

    (B) $9\sqrt{3} - 9\pi$

    (C) $18 - \dfrac{9\pi}{2}$

    (D) $9(\sqrt{3} - 2\pi)$

    (E) $18(2 - \pi)$

10. Points A, B, C, D, E, and F lie on the same plane. Points A, B, and C lie on one line. A line connecting points B and D is perpendicular to a line connecting points A and C. A line connecting points C, E, and F is parallel to a line connecting points B and D. Given this information, which of the following pairs of lines must be perpendicular to each other?

    (A) $\overline{AB}$ and $\overline{CF}$
    (B) $\overline{BD}$ and $\overline{CF}$
    (C) $\overline{AD}$ and $\overline{EC}$
    (D) $\overline{AB}$ and $\overline{BC}$
    (E) $\overline{BD}$ and $\overline{EC}$

S T O P

IF YOU FINISH BEFORE TIME IS CALLED, YOU MAY CHECK YOUR WORK IN THIS SECTION ONLY.
DO NOT TURN TO ANY OTHER SECTION IN THE TEST.

SAT TEST

Time—15 Minutes
13 Questions

For each question in this section, select the best answer from among the choices given and fill in the corresponding oval on the answer sheet.

The two passages below are followed by questions based on their content and the relationship between the passages. Answer the questions on the basis of what is <u>stated</u> or <u>implied</u> in the passages and in any introductory material that may be provided.

Questions 1–13 are based on the following passages.

The following passages were adapted from articles published in two New York newspapers, the Herald *and the* Times, *around 1870. Both articles discuss the sport of baseball, which was just becoming popular at the time.*

Passage 1

Some few years ago there was no manly outdoor sport in which the youth of the country could indulge and which could be claimed as national. The game baseball in a crude form
Line was practiced among others and by a few gentlemen was
5 being systematized and perfected. The *Herald,* observing that in the game were all the elements which could commend it as a favorite pastime, styled it the National Game, and from that time to the present the young men—and many of the old men—of the country have adopted it as a means of
10 recreation, amusement, and physical development. That the game possesses the requisites for affording recreation and relaxation from daily labor is plainly shown by the thousands who flock to witness contests between any of the leading organizations. That it promotes the physical development is
15 attested beyond a doubt by the improved physiques of those who practice with the bat and ball. Every portion of the physical system is brought into action, while the mind is subjected, at the same time, to a recreative course of treatment. The eye is trained to take in at once the entire
20 situation; the hearing is quickened, to enable the players to note the slightest click of "tip" and to understand the call of the umpire or the order of the captains when the other faculties are intent on some other point; the judgment is exercised so as to enable the player to decide instantly on the
25 best course of action to benefit his party, and the muscular strength is developed by the running, throwing, pitching, and batting in which all take part during the contest.

The game has now been reduced to a science, and the objection which was formerly made to it, on the ground that,
30 compared to cricket, it was child's play, can no longer be raised. It was considered by some as being too dangerous; fingers were broken and the players were otherwise wounded, while in cricket the men could pad themselves so that they would not be hurt. Is it an objection to swimming
35 that people are drowned sometimes? Or to skating that people are hurt by collisions or falls on the ice? Besides, the fact that the players at baseball unflinchingly face the dangers shows the inherent bravery of the American people and their determination to obtain even amusement at the
40 risk of danger.

Aside from these considerations, the formation of clubs and state and national associations presents an advantage to the youth of this country. In these associations the members
Line are almost unconsciously trained in the system of legislation.
45 Business is conducted on the same plan as the legislative and corporate bodies throughout the country, and the members of the club become fitted for the proper performance of their duties as sovereigns. There is still another advantage to be derived from the associations which may be formed in the
50 leading amateur organizations, such as the Empire, Knickerbocker and Eagle clubs of New York, Excelsior and Star of Brooklyn, Eureka of Newark, and National of Albany; for in them gentlemen of the highest standing in business and social circles may be found, aiding by their presence and their
55 influence the progress and permanency of the national game.

Passage 2

The game of baseball is, in many respects, worthy of encouragement. In a community by far too much given to sedentary occupations and dyspepsia, it furnishes an incentive
Line to active open-air exercise, and we should be glad to see it even
5 more resorted to than it is, among the class who would profit most by its benefits. Our merchants and lawyers and over-worked clerks, after their day of harassing mental labor, would derive more advantage from a brisk game of baseball than from the favorite drive on the road with its accompaniments of
10 dust and dissipation. To be sure we do not share the opinion of some of its more enthusiastic advocates, that skill in our national pastime implies an exercise of the moral virtues, and we have taken occasion to express our dissent from the views of the president of a Western club, who appears to rank the
15 science of ball playing with the learned professions. Moderately used, however, in its legitimate sphere as an amusement, baseball is certainly a wholesome and invigorating sport.

It is one of the defects of our national characters, however,
20 that no sooner do we get hold of a good thing of this sort, than we proceed to make it hurtful by excess. Baseball as a recreation was well enough, but baseball established as a business calls upon us to revise our notions of its usefulness. Nor is professional baseball, as at present practiced entitled to
25 the only praise that might be urged in its favor; it is not even a healthy physical exercise. On the contrary, it is so dangerous to life and limb, that in insurance language it would be labeled extra hazardous. Fatal accidents on the ballfield have been so common of late as hardly to excite remark, and maiming is the
30 rule and not the exception among members of the first-class

clubs. One of the best players of the Red Stockings was so injured in a recent match that he is unable to walk without crutches. In fact, a veteran baseball player, whose teeth have not been knocked out, or whose bones have not been repeatedly broken, is a lucky rarity. The moral aspect of our national game is even less reassuring. At its best, it is an excuse for gambling; at its worst, a device for viler "jockeying" and swindling than ever disgraced the turf.

1. In Passage 1, line 7, "styled" most nearly means:

   (A) deemed
   (B) coiffed
   (C) arranged
   (D) decorated
   (E) annulled

2. In lines 1–27, the author notes that baseball serves as a venue for all of the following EXCEPT:

   (A) relaxation
   (B) reflex training
   (C) physical exercise
   (D) entertainment
   (E) financial gain

3. In lines 34–36, the author mentions the dangers involved in swimming and skating so as to:

   (A) discourage his audience from swimming and skating
   (B) highlight the dangers of baseball
   (C) encourage his audience to skate or swim rather than play baseball
   (D) downplay the dangers of baseball
   (E) encourage his audience to play baseball instead of swimming or skating

4. The author's tone in lines 28–40 could most accurately be characterized as

   (A) patriotic
   (B) xenophobic
   (C) anticlerical
   (D) wrathful
   (E) soothing

5. In lines 45–48, the author of Passage 1 suggests that the participation of important businessmen

   (A) corrupts the moral foundations of baseball
   (B) causes instability in the game
   (C) reflects baseball's ability to promote products through advertising
   (D) solidifies baseball as a national institution
   (E) demonstrates how baseball players are simply looking to make a quick buck

6. In Passage 2, line 7, "harassing" most closely means:

   (A) haranguing
   (B) tiring
   (C) molesting
   (D) pesky
   (E) facile

7. The author of Passage 2 argues that baseball

   (A) is a useful expression of social precepts
   (B) should serve exclusively as a means of gaining exercise and relaxation
   (C) functions as a unifying force for the American nation
   (D) encourages the development of interstate trade
   (E) induces religious piety in its spectators

8. In lines 26–28, the author characterizes baseball as:

   (A) innocuous
   (B) scientific
   (C) perilous
   (D) bellicose
   (E) reassuring

9. The "Red Stockings" (line 31) most likely refers to a

   (A) political party
   (B) corporation
   (C) baseball team
   (D) business venture
   (E) umpires' union

GO ON TO THE NEXT PAGE

10. In lines 36–37, the author asserts that "[a]t its best, [baseball] is an excuse for gambling" in order to

    (A) encourage the development of sports-related gambling
    (B) excuse his personal gambling habits
    (C) argue for the expansion of baseball in the West
    (D) highlight the fact that baseball encourages the development of immoral practices
    (E) reassure his readers that baseball is not dangerous

11. Both passages applaud baseball's usefulness as a forum for:

    (A) recreation
    (B) injury
    (C) business opportunities
    (D) patriotism
    (E) spirituality

12. Reading the phrase "it is so dangerous to life and limb, that in insurance language it would be labeled extra hazardous" (Passage 2, lines 26–28), the author of Passage 1 would most likely

    (A) strongly agree
    (B) strongly disagree
    (C) claim that baseball is safer than swimming
    (D) contend that more study must be done to before baseball can be called either safe or dangerous
    (E) argue that it is good that baseball is dangerous

13. Which of the following issues is NOT explicitly discussed in either passage?

    (A) sports injuries
    (B) patriotism
    (C) the moral implications of baseball
    (D) the funding of baseball teams
    (E) spectatorship

S T O P

IF YOU FINISH BEFORE TIME IS CALLED, YOU MAY CHECK YOUR WORK IN THIS SECTION ONLY.
DO NOT TURN TO ANY OTHER SECTION IN THE TEST.

SAT Practice Test 1 Explanations

Answers to SAT Practice Test 1

Question Number	Correct Answer	Right	Wrong	Question Number	Correct Answer	Right	Wrong	Question Number	Correct Answer	Right	Wrong
Math Section 1				**Verbal Section 1**				**Verbal Section 2**			
1.	E	—	—	24.	A	—	—	14.	A	—	—
2.	D	—	—	25.	E	—	—	15.	B	—	—
3.	E	—	—	26.	D	—	—	16.	C	—	—
4.	C	—	—	27.	B	—	—	17.	A	—	—
5.	C	—	—	28.	E	—	—	18.	D	—	—
6.	D	—	—	29.	C	—	—	19.	D	—	—
7.	C	—	—	30.	E	—	—	20.	A	—	—
8.	E	—	—					21.	E	—	—
9.	D	—	—	**Math Section 2**				22.	B	—	—
10.	D	—	—					23.	A	—	—
11.	C	—	—	1.	C	—	—	24.	B	—	—
12.	D	—	—	2.	C	—	—	25.	E	—	—
13.	D	—	—	3.	B	—	—	26.	A	—	—
14.	E	—	—	4.	A	—	—	27.	B	—	—
15.	D	—	—	5.	A	—	—	28.	E	—	—
16.	B	—	—	6.	A	—	—	29.	C	—	—
17.	E	—	—	7.	B	—	—	30.	A	—	—
18.	D	—	—	8.	B	—	—	31.	D	—	—
19.	C	—	—	9.	D	—	—	32.	C	—	—
20.	A	—	—	10.	C	—	—	33.	C	—	—
21.	C	—	—	11.	A	—	—	34.	D	—	—
22.	E	—	—	12.	A	—	—	35.	B	—	—
23.	E	—	—	13.	C	—	—				
24.	C	—	—	14.	D	—	—	**Math Section 3**			
25.	E	—	—	15.	B	—	—	1.	D	—	—
				16.	396	—	—	2.	D	—	—
Verbal Section 1				17.	5/9	—	—	3.	B	—	—
				18.	6	—	—	4.	D	—	—
1.	C	—	—	19.	15	—	—	5.	D	—	—
2.	A	—	—	20.	8	—	—	6.	C	—	—
3.	D	—	—	21.	180	—	—	7.	B	—	—
4.	A	—	—	22.	16	—	—	8.	C	—	—
5.	B	—	—	23.	21	—	—	9.	A	—	—
6.	C	—	—	24.	12	—	—	10.	A	—	—
7.	B	—	—	25.	3/5	—	—				
8.	A	—	—								
9.	B	—	—	**Verbal Section 2**				**Verbal Section 3**			
10.	D	—	—	1.	B	—	—	1.	A	—	—
11.	A	—	—	2.	E	—	—	2.	E	—	—
12.	E	—	—	3.	C	—	—	3.	D	—	—
13.	C	—	—	4.	A	—	—	4.	A	—	—
14.	C	—	—	5.	B	—	—	5.	D	—	—
15.	A	—	—	6.	E	—	—	6.	B	—	—
16.	E	—	—	7.	B	—	—	7.	B	—	—
17.	B	—	—	8.	B	—	—	8.	C	—	—
18.	B	—	—	9.	B	—	—	9.	C	—	—
19.	E	—	—	10.	E	—	—	10.	D	—	—
20.	C	—	—	11.	D	—	—	11.	A	—	—
21.	D	—	—	12.	B	—	—	12.	E	—	—
22.	A	—	—	13.	B	—	—	13.	D	—	—
23.	B	—	—								

Calculating Your SAT Score

Your raw score for SAT is a composite of your verbal and math raw scores. The raw scores of each section translate into a scaled score from 200 to 800. You can find your scaled scores for both verbal and math by checking the conversion table on page 350.

Your total SAT scaled score is the sum or your scaled math and verbal scores.

To Calculate Your Verbal Raw Score

The number of sentence completions, analogies, and reading comprehension questions you answered

$$\underset{\text{Correctly}}{\underline{\hspace{3cm}}} - (\tfrac{1}{4} \times \underset{\text{Incorrectly}}{\underline{\hspace{3cm}}}) = \underset{\text{A}}{\underline{\hspace{3cm}}}$$

Round the number in field A. This is your verbal raw score: $\underset{\text{B}}{\underline{\hspace{2cm}}}$

To Calculate Your Math Raw Score

The number of normal multiple-choice questions you answered

$$\underset{\text{Correctly}}{\underline{\hspace{3cm}}} - (\tfrac{1}{4} \times \underset{\text{Incorrectly}}{\underline{\hspace{3cm}}}) = \underset{\text{C}}{\underline{\hspace{3cm}}}$$

The number of quantitative comparisons you answered

$$\underset{\text{Correctly}}{\underline{\hspace{3cm}}} - (\tfrac{1}{4} \times \underset{\text{Incorrectly}}{\underline{\hspace{3cm}}}) = \underset{\text{D}}{\underline{\hspace{3cm}}}$$

The number of grid-ins you answered

$$\underset{\text{Correctly}}{\underline{\hspace{3cm}}} = \underset{\text{E}}{\underline{\hspace{3cm}}}$$

Add the numbers in fields C, D, and E = $\underset{\text{F}}{\underline{\hspace{3cm}}}$

Round the number in field F. This is your math raw score: $\underset{\text{G}}{\underline{\hspace{3cm}}}$

Converting Your Raw Scores

Raw Score	Scaled Verbal Score	Scaled Math Score	Raw Score	Scaled Verbal Score	Scaled Math Score
78	800		37	530	570
77	800		36	520	560
76	800		35	520	550
75	800		34	510	540
74	790		33	510	530
73	780		32	500	530
72	770		31	490	520
71	770		30	490	510
70	760		29	480	500
69	750		28	470	500
68	740		27	470	490
67	730		26	460	490
66	720		25	450	480
65	710		24	450	470
64	700		23	440	460
63	700		22	430	450
62	690		21	430	440
61	680		20	420	440
60	680	800	19	410	430
59	670	790	18	400	430
58	660	780	17	400	420
57	660	770	16	390	410
56	650	750	15	380	400
55	640	740	14	370	400
54	640	730	13	370	390
53	630	710	12	360	380
52	620	700	11	350	360
51	620	690	10	340	350
50	620	670	9	330	350
49	610	660	8	320	340
48	600	650	7	300	320
47	590	640	6	300	310
46	590	630	5	280	300
45	580	630	4	280	290
44	580	620	3	270	270
43	570	610	2	270	250
42	570	600	1	260	240
41	560	590	0	260	220
40	550	580	−1	250	210
39	550	580	−2	230	200
38	540	570	−3	230	200

Math Section 1

1. **(E)** Arithmetic: Rates   Difficulty: low

The runner's rate is ⅙ of a lap per minute. Thus, in 4 minutes, she will run
⅙ × 4 = ⁴⁄₆ = ⅔ laps.

2. **(D)** Miscellaneous Math: Logical Reasoning   Difficulty: low

This question is not difficult if you are able to organize information correctly. A good
way to keep track of the information is to write the names vertically in your test booklet
as we learn about each person. First we are told that Mark is older than Judy, so we can
write his name above hers:

Mark

Judy

We also know that Judy is older than Brian but younger than Lisa. Brain's name will go
under Judy's, so we just need to figure out where Lisa's name goes. We don't know
anything about how her age compares with Mark's, so we'll list them next to each other
(though we are not saying that they are equal!):

Mark / Lisa

Judy

Brian

Answers (A) and (B) could be true, but looking at our chart, neither one is above the
other. Choices (C) and (E) are definitely not true based on the relationships we depicted
above. Answer (D) is true because Mark is clearly listed above Brian.

3. **(E)** Algebra: Simplifying and Manipulating Expressions   Difficulty: low

A number is equal to itself when it is multiplied by 1, so we know that y must equal 1.
We could also solve for that directly:

$$xy = x$$
$$y = \frac{x}{x}$$
$$y = 1$$

Substituting $y = 1$ into the second equation, we see that $1 \times z = z$.

4. **(C)** Geometry: Coordinate Geometry   Difficulty: low
The slope of a line segment is defined as the change in y / change in x, where the x and y coordinates are the points on the segment. So, for example, on a line segment with positive slope, y increases as x increases and y decreases as x decreases. On a line segment with negative slope, however, y decreases as x increases and vice-versa.

More graphically, you can see that a line with positive slope goes upward as you trace it from left to right, while a line with negative slope goes down as you trace it from left to right. The only side of the triangle that has a negative slope is $\overline{AC}$.

5. **(C)** Arithmetic: Exponents and Square Roots   Difficulty: low
We should immediately see that statement III is true since the square of any non-zero number is positive. We can immediately eliminate answers (A) and (B) since they exclude III. We can then eliminate II, since by definition, any perfect square has its square root as a factor and is therefore non-prime. Since we know that 2 is an even prime, and its square (4) is also even, I can also be eliminated.

6. **(D)** Arithmetic: Fractions, Decimals, and Percents   Difficulty: low
The arithmetic is not too difficult; just remember that division by a fraction is calculated by multiplying by the fraction's reciprocal. The expression we are trying to solve, therefore, can be written and worked through like this:

$$\left(\frac{1}{3}\right)\left(\frac{3}{2}\right)\left(\frac{8}{3}\right) = \frac{24}{18} = \frac{4}{3}$$

7. **(C)** Arithmetic: Fractions, Decimals, and Percents   .   Difficulty: low
This question is easily solved if you remember that $\frac{5}{8} = 0.625$ and $\frac{3}{4} = 0.75$. Even if you don't know the decimal equivalent of $\frac{5}{8}$, it is clearly greater than 0.5 or $\frac{4}{8}$. 0.7 is the only possible answer.

8. **(E)** Arithmetic: Basic   Difficulty: low
When constructing an estimate, you want to find the nearest number that is easy to manipulate. $1.00 is a good round number that is pretty close to $.90, and 20 is a good round number near 21. Since John rides the bus two times each day (once to school and once home), you should multiply your estimate by 2. Thus, the best estimate among the possible choices is $2 \times \$1.00 \times 20$.

9. **(D)** Geometry: Geometric Visualization   Difficulty: medium
This question tests your understanding of area and visualization. We must first find the area of each of the squares. The rectangle's area is 108, so each of the three squares has area $\frac{108}{3} = 36$. A square of area 36 has a side of length $\sqrt{36} = 6$. These three squares must be aligned end-to-end in order to form an 18×6 rectangle, so the perimeter is $2l + 2w = 2(18) + 2(6) = 48$.

10. **(D)** Arithmetic: Rates   Difficulty: low

The key to this problem is to figure out how many hours of crushing need to be done. Since bags of cans can be crushed at the rate of 1 bag every ¼ hour, the total amount of work to be done is ¼ × 180 = 45 hours. We can set up an equation to solve for the number of workers needed: $3x = 45$. Since $x = 15$, Donna needs to recruit 14 more people to help her.

11. **(C)** Geometry: Coordinate Geometry   Difficulty: low

Given that line segment $\overline{AB}$ is a diameter of the circle all we have to do to find the center of the circle is find the midpoint of $\overline{AB}$. The x-coordinate of the midpoint is $\frac{4+2}{2} = 3$ (i.e. the average of the two given x-coordinates). The y-coordinate of the midpoint is $\frac{5+(-3)}{2} = 1$. So the midpoint and the center of the circle is (3, 1).

12. **(D)** Arithmetic: Ratios and Proportions   Difficulty: medium

Given a 2:3:4 ratio, you can set up the equation $2x + 3x + 4x = 45$, where x is a common multiplier, to find exactly how the 45 cookies are divided. We can solve the equation to see that $x = 5$. One child receives $2x$ cookies, one receives $3x$, and the last receives $4x$, or 10, 15, and 20 cookies, respectively. The greatest number of cookies that any one child receives is 20 cookies.

13. **(D)** Arithmetic: Multiples, Factors, and Primes   Difficulty: medium

First, we need to find the prime factors of 36: 36 = 2 × 2 × 3 × 3. Thus, the prime factors of 36 are 2 and 3. Now we must find their least common multiple, which is the smallest number that is evenly divided by both 2 and 3. The least common multiple of 2 and 3 is 6, the correct answer.

14. **(E)** Arithmetic: Fractions, Decimals, and Percents   Difficulty: medium

16 divided by 4 is 4. In order to determine the percentage, we simply need to multiply by 100: 4 × 100 = 400%. You could also solve this algebraically by setting up an equation:

$$\frac{x}{100} \times 4 = 16$$
$$\frac{4x}{100} = 16$$
$$\frac{x}{25} = 16$$
$$x = 16 \times 25$$
$$x = 400$$

15. **(D)** Geometry: Triangles   Difficulty: medium

The figure shows an isosceles triangle divided by a vertical line segment. This segment divides the base into two equal lines of length $^{32}\!/_2 = 16$. Now we have two right triangles, with hypotenuse 20, and with one leg of length 16. Use the Pythagorean theorem to find x:

$$x^2 + 16^2 = 20^2$$
$$x^2 + 256 = 400$$
$$x^2 = 144$$
$$x = 12$$

You might also recognize that this triangle is similar to the common 3:4:5 right triangle.

16. **(B)** Geometry: Polygons   Difficulty: high

Because $ABCDEF$ is an equilateral hexagon, we know that it is made up of six identical equilateral triangles, each with sides of length x. To find the area of the hexagon, we must find the area of one of these triangles and multiply by 6. Since we already have the length of one side, x, we just need the height (h) of a triangle to find the area. If we bisect an equilateral triangle, we end up with two right triangles, each with a hypotenuse of length x, a short leg of length $^x\!/_2$, and a long leg that is the height of the equilateral triangle.

According to the Pythagorean theorem, in a right triangle, $a^2 + b^2 = c^2$, and so $(x/2)^2 + h^2 = x^2$. Plug in 4 for x, and you get $2^2 + h^2 = 4^2$, or $h^2 = 12$. This means $h = 2\sqrt{3}$, and the area of one of the equilateral triangles is $(1/2)(4)(2\sqrt{3}) = 4\sqrt{3}$. The area of the hexagon, therefore, is $6(4\sqrt{3}) = 24\sqrt{3}$.

17. **(E)** Arithmetic: Fractions, Decimals, and Percents   Difficulty: high

Since the pie was originally split evenly among the three children, each child starts with $^1\!/_3$ of the pie. The first boy gave the girl $^1\!/_2$ of his share, or $^1\!/_2 \times ^1\!/_3 = ^1\!/_6$. The second boy gave the girl $^3\!/_4$ of his share, or $^3\!/_4 \times ^1\!/_3 = ^1\!/_4$. Therefore, the amount of pie the girl has is $^1\!/_3 + ^1\!/_6 + ^1\!/_4$. The least common multiple of the 3 denominators is 12. We can add the fractions by converting them to a common denominator:

$$\frac{4}{12} + \frac{2}{12} + \frac{3}{12} = \frac{9}{12}$$
$$\frac{9}{12} = \frac{3}{4}$$

18. **(D)** Geometry: Angles and Lines   Difficulty: high

The smallest whole number is 1, so we can minimize the length of the line by assigning a length of 1 to $\overline{AB}$, the shortest segment. Once the length of $\overline{AB}$ is set to 1, then $\overline{BC}$ is 2, $\overline{CD}$ is 4, and $\overline{DE}$ is 8, so the correct answer is (D). If $\overline{AB}$ were any shorter, its length wouldn't be a whole number, and if it were any longer, it wouldn't generate the shortest possible length, as required by the problem.

19. **(C)** Arithmetic: Series   Difficulty: high

This question requires that we determine how many of the first 200 positive integers contain the digit 1 exactly once. To do this as efficiently as possible, break the range into two groups: 1–100 and 101–200. Now we can imagine lining our two groups one over the other so that we see 1 and 101 together and 2 and 102 together:

1	2	3	4	5	6	7	8	9	10	11	12	13
101	102	103	104	105	106	107	108	109	110	111	112	113

Depicting the numbers in this manner helps us see that each number in the 101–200 group contains the digit 1 one more time than the corresponding number in the 1–100 group (with the exception of 100 and 200). So, in the first group, there are 11 numbers that contain the digit 1 exactly once: {1, 10, 21, 31, 41, 51, 61, 71, 81, 91, 100}. The corresponding numbers in the 100–200 will each contain the digit twice (with the exception of 200, which does not contain a 1), so these 11 numbers will count in the first 100, but their corresponding numbers will not count in the second group. Note that the number 11 is the only number between 1 and 100 that contains the digit 1 more than once, and its corresponding number, 111, contains it 3 times. So, of the second 100 numbers, 10 contain the digit 1 twice, 1 contains the digit 1 three times, and one does not contain it at all. The other $100 - 10 - 1 - 1 = 88$ numbers all contain the digit 1 once. $11 + 88 = 99$, the correct answer.

20. **(A)** Arithmetic: Ratios and Proportions   Difficulty: high

The expression that describes this problem is $dx + cx = 30$. dx is the number of dogs in the store, cx is the number of cats in the store, and x is a common multiple. To solve for x, factor out the x and then divide both sides by $(d + c)$. Now we have $x = 30/(d + c)$. Remember, we are looking for the number of dogs, dx, so we must multiply both sides by d. Now we see that the number of dogs, dx, equals $30d/(d + c)$.

Another way to attack a this type of ratio problem is to find the fraction of the animals that are dogs: $d/(d + c)$. Thus, the number of dogs among 30 animals is this fraction multiplied by 30, or $30d/(d + c)$.

21. **(C)** Geometry: Circles   Difficulty: high

The area of the shaded region is simply the difference in areas between the square and the part of the circle inside the square. We know that the arc length is 4π. From this we can find the radius, which will allow us to calculate the area of the square. The length of arc BC is ¼ the circumference of the circle because the angle that creates the arc is a 90° angle, and 90° is ¼ of 360°.

The formula for the circumference of a circle is $2\pi r$, where r is the radius of the circle. We can set up an equation to solve for r:

$$\frac{1}{4}(2)(\pi)(r) = 4\pi$$
$$r = 8$$

We know the length of the sides of square $ABCD$, so the area is $8^2 = 64$. The area of the circle segment inside square $ABCD$ is ¼ the area of the whole circle. This area is given by πr^2, which in this case equals 64π, so the circle segment in question has area ¼$(64)\pi$ $= 16\pi$. The area of the shaded region is $64 - 16\pi$.

22. **(E)** Arithmetic: Series   Difficulty: high

To find the third, fifth, and seventh terms of the sequence, we need to find the second, fourth, sixth, and eighth terms. This isn't too hard. These four terms are {2, 4, 8, 16}. Thus, the third, fifth, and seventh terms are 3, 6, and 12, respectively. Their sum is 21.

23. **(E)** Arithmetic: Multiples, Factors, and Primes   Difficulty: high

A factor of a number k is any number m that evenly divides that number. This means that k/m is an integer. A prime number is a number whose only factors are itself and one, so the factors of p are 1 and p. The factors of p^2 are $1, p$, and p^2. The factors of p^3 are $1, p, p^2$, and p^3. The pattern is clear: the number of factors is one more than the exponent of p. p^n has $n + 1$ factors.

24. **(C)** Arithmetic: Mean; Algebra: Simplifying Expressions   Difficulty: high

In order for the means of two sets of numbers (with the same number of elements) to be the same, the sum of the elements of each set must be the same as well. Using this fact, we can determine the relationship between r and s.

$$3 + 4 + r = 4 + 6 + s$$
$$7 + r = 10 + s$$
$$r - s = 10 - 7$$
$$r - s = 3$$

25. **(E)**   Geometry: Circles   Difficulty: high

The circumference of each circle is 10π, so the diameter of each must be 10. This means the height of the rectangle is 10, and since the rectangle is three diameters across, its length must be 30. Therefore, the perimeter of the rectangle is $10 + 10 + 30 + 30 = 80$.

Verbal Section 1

Sentence Completions

1.   **(C)**   One Word Direct   Difficulty: low

The blank in the sentence describes a way that "Karen seemed," and because the sentence has no hinge words to indicate a contrast, it should be obvious that Karen seems this way because she was "unable to grasp (or understand) the question in front of her." Immediately, you can eliminate prepared, because if she were prepared then Karen would understand the question. You should also be able to rule out earnest and abstinent, since neither makes any sense in reference to understanding a question. That leaves furious and perplexed. While you could make a case that Karen might be furious that she didn't understand the question, perplexed is clearly a better answer since it fits perfectly with the idea of not understanding present in the first half of the sentence.

2.   **(A)**   Two Word Contrast   Difficulty: medium

The hinge word in this sentence is "nevertheless," which signals us that we should look for words that will make the two parts of the sentence contrast. The words we use to fill the blanks should result in a sentence that describes the difference between the difficulty of learning the U.S. tax code and the attitude most people have about doing their taxes. Rewarding . . enriching and miniscule . . straightforward can be immediately discarded, because the words reinforce one another rather than contrast. Noble . . exceptional do not seem to relate in any definite way. Of the remaining two answer choices, civic . . irresponsible may look extremely tempting—to learn the tax code is a civic undertaking, and it is irresponsible to rush through one's taxes. But remember to plug the words into the sentence before making up your mind. In this case, the answer choice does not make sense, because of the phrase "an irresponsible task." The person might be irresponsible, but a task cannot be.

The only answer choice to make sense, then, is "formidable . . undemanding." It is a formidable task, but most people rush through it as though it were undemanding. "Formidable" and "undemanding" make the two parts of the sentence contrast, and they also make sense when plugged into the blanks.

3. **(D)** Two Word Contrast   Difficulty: low

The hinge word in this sentence is "despite," which signals us that the two halves of this sentence will contrast with one another—the politicians will offer something different from what the state of the Middle East has been for years. Disagreement . . hatred can be immediately discarded, as the words do not contrast. War . . religion do not relate directly enough to make sense in the sentence (though you might be tempted by this pair since religion has been an important part of the conflict in the Middle East). The same goes for turmoil . . supremacy. Prosperity . . starvation are contrasting words, but they do not make sense when applied to the sentence: no one would *hope* for starvation after years of prosperity.

The only answer that fits is bloodshed . . peace, which offers two contrasting words that make sense when plugged into the sentence. Additionally, as anyone with even a basic understanding of the political situation in the Middle East will see, the words seem to make the sentence *true*. While it is not necessary to know anything about the situation described in the sentence in order to answer it correctly—the clues are all there—it never hurts to apply what one does know.

4. **(A)** Two Word Contrast   Difficulty: medium

The hinge word in this sentence is "though," which indicates that the two parts of the sentence will contrast: whatever is true of the young entrepreneur as he sits down at the negotiating table, something about his effort to come out ahead seems to conflict with it. For that reason, we can discard unnerved . . timidly, egomaniacal . . doggedly, and amoral . . shrewdly right away: they each might describe a young entrepreneur, but they fail to capture a condition of contrast. Wealthy . . desperately is also incorrect, since if the young entrepreneur were already wealthy, he would not be desperate to win the negotiation. But terrified . . valiantly obviously make much more immediate sense when plugged into the sentence: the young entrepreneur was afraid, but he tried bravely to do well anyway. This choice fits the sentence's requirement for contrast and makes sense when you plug the terms into the blanks, which is ultimately the best test of any answer choice.

5. **(B)** One Word Contrast   Difficulty: high

The hinge word in this sentence is "unlike," which implies that the direction of the sentence will change after the comma. Because of the "unlike," we know that the sentence is asking us to find a word that contrasts with the idea of "a limited group of elite English nobles." We are presumably looking for a word that implies a broader group of common people.

Aristocracy is the easiest word to dismiss, since it means just the opposite of the common people. Gentry, though a harder vocabulary word, is usually used in a similar sense to refer to wealthy landowners. Clergy refers to religious officers, and so it too can be thrown out. Oligarchy is the most difficult word of the bunch. It means a government by a few powerful individuals or families, and is therefore wrong.

The only word remaining is bourgeoisie, which is the correct choice. Meaning the social order of the middle class, the bourgeoisie is an opposite of elite nobles, and fits the sense of the sentence.

Even if you didn't know the words oligarchy or bourgeoisie, you still should have been able to eliminate at least a few of the other words and put yourself in a position to guess.

6. **(C)** One Word Direct   Difficulty: medium

This sentence contains no hinge words, and you should be able to see that the way in which Yolanda documented her research is directly related to her knowledge that her "controversial findings were likely to be scrutinized." Since we know that her findings would be closely examined, we can assume that Yolanda was careful to record her data consistently and accurately. The word we need to fill in the blank must be something like "carefully," since Yolanda wants to be so careful that all the scrutinizers won't find any errors in her work. Meticulously is the only word that means "carefully."

7. **(B)** Two Word Direct   Difficulty: high

This sentence contains no hinge word or change of direction, and so we know that Berenice's colleagues' treatment ("showered her with ----") will result directly from the way that the conundrum affected the theorists for more than a decade. Therefore, if the conundrum had caused anguish or some pain to the theorists, then it seems likely they would treat Berenice well. Alternatively, if the status of the conundrum as unsolved somehow helps the theorists, then it seems likely they would be less pleased with Berenice. Now, if you have some understanding of theorists, you probably know that they are more likely to be happy when a conundrum is solved.

Right away, you should be able to discard disparagement . . calibrated and tribute . . denigrated, since conundrums can neither calibrate nor denigrate. You can also eliminate commendations . . benefited, since the theorists would not commend Bernice for solving a conundrum that had benefited them. You might think that contempt . . flabbergasted is a good choice, since her colleagues might be jealous of Bernice after she solved a conundrum that had long flabbergasted (confused) them. However, when plugged into the sentence, this choice gives us the phrase, "showered with contempt," which does not make much sense. That leaves the only satisfactory answer, accolades . . confounded, since the theorists will give Berenice accolades for solving a conundrum that had confounded them. Even if you didn't know the word denigrated, accolades . . confounded fits the sentence so well that it is clearly the best choice.

8. **(A)** Other   Difficulty: high

This question fits into the "other" category because the two blanks really share no relationship of direction. Instead, each blank fits individually with its own part of the sentence. In this question, the first blank is a word that must agree with the description of baby howler monkeys as "exploring every inch of their surroundings." The second blank explains why those monkeys explore "without any sense of fear." The first word must therefore be something like "curious," while the second must be something like "aware," so that the statement reads, "Since they are not aware of the possibility of danger at such a young age."

Once we know what types of words you need to fill the blanks, we can take a look at the possible answer pairs. Malleable . . perspicacious should be easy to discard, since neither word fits into its associated blank. In pugnacious . . wary, wary fits rather well into the second blank, but pugnacious means confrontational, and the sense of this sentence is not that the baby howler monkeys are trying to pick a fight. In adventurous . . imprudent, imprudent does not make sense in terms of its meaning, "reckless," and when placed in the sentence it forms the ungrammatical phrase "imprudent of." Timorous . . apprehensive will not work because the baby monkeys are certainly not timorous, which means "timid." This leaves only inquisitive . . cognizant, which fits perfectly as inquisitive means "curious" and cognizant means "aware."

9. **(B)** One Word Contrast   Difficulty: high
The hinge word in this sentence is "but," which changes the direction of the thought in the second clause. Because of the "but," we know that the sentence is asking us to find a word that contrasts with the idea of suspicion: the doctor is looking for a greater degree of conviction before she shares her diagnosis with her patient. The word we are looking for then, must imply certainty and accuracy.

Medically is a word simply thrown in to create a brief moment of confusion; it is tied to the sentence because the sentence describes a medical problem, but it obviously does not indicate a degree of conviction. Reputably indicates a certain measure of reliability and trust, but again, it does not indicate a degree of conviction—there is no way to know, based on reputation alone, whether or not a patient has leukemia. Precariously implies a certain kind of imbalance, and therefore fails to meet the needs of the sentence. Ambiguously implies even more uncertainty and should be easy to reject unless one misreads the sentence.

The only answer choice remaining is unequivocally, which means without any qualification or doubt. To know something unequivocally is to know it without doubt; her search for unequivocal knowledge explains the doctor's desire to keep her diagnosis to herself and correctly completes the sentence.

Analogies

10. **(D)** Type   Difficulty: low
The best sentence you can make for the two stem words is: SUGAR is a type of SWEETENER. Applying this sentence to the possible answers, the only pair that fits is gasoline : fuel. None of the other answer choices describes a type relationship.

11. **(A)** Characteristic Action   Difficulty: low

A PRESIDENT leads a NATION is the best sentence you could make with this pair of stem words. A principal leads a school in the same way, so principal : school is the best answer pair. None of the other answers involve a leader : group relationship.

12. **(E)** Characteristic Location   Difficulty: low

A CAPTAIN directs the action on a SHIP. Similarly, a judge determines the proceedings in a court. To answer the question correctly you have to realize that a CAPTAIN not only works on a SHIP, but also holds the highest position of command on the ship, just as a judge does in a court. If you do realize this, then you can avoid the two tricky wrong answer choices: soldier : war and clerk : office. Soldier : war might attract your attention because it is associated with war, as is CAPTAIN : SHIP. However, a soldier holds no command authority. Clerk : office might also seem like a nice choice since a clerk does work in an office, but a clerk does not hold command over an office in the way a captain does over a ship or a judge over a court.

13. **(C)** Function   Difficulty: high

"The function of an INAUGURATION is to COMMENCE something" is the best and most specific answer you could make with this stem pair. Similarly, the function of an epilogue is to conclude something. If you know the vocabulary, you should be able to eliminate summary : elaborate and explanation : bewilder rather easily, since in each case the function of the first word is actually the opposite of the second word; a summary simplifies rather than elaborates, while an explanation clarifies rather than bewilders. Finally, gesture : agitate and demagogue : ameliorate don't have good internal relationships at all and can be discarded for that reason.

14. **(C)** Other   Difficulty: medium

To CULTIVATE a CROP is to care for and raise it, just as to nurture an infant is to care for it and raise it. Of the other answer choices, you may be tempted by nourish : food because the word nourish is strongly associated with the idea of caring and raising in the relation between the stem pair. However, food cannot be nourished; it is a form of nourishment. The incorrectness of nourish : food should be apparent to you if you try to fit it into the sentence you created for CULTIVATE : CROP.

15. **(A)**   Part/Whole   Difficulty: high

"A PREAMBLE serves to introduce the DOCUMENT of which it is a part" is the best and most specific sentence you can make to relate the stem pair. A prologue fulfills a similar role in a novel. None of the other pairs has the same relationship. Appendix : treatise might be appealing because an appendix could be a part of a treatise, but it is by definition found at the end of the treatise (it is appended, or "added on"). If your original sentence was just "a PREAMBLE is a part of a DOCUMENT" you might think that appendix : treatise is the correct answer.

Although the vocabulary in both the stem pair and the answer pairs is difficult, one way to approach this question is to recognize that the prefixes "pre-" and "pro-" both refer to something that comes at the beginning of or precedes something else. The second words in each of those pairs—document and novel—are not difficult vocabulary. By recognizing the related prefixes, you can then answer the question without knowing precisely what a preamble is.

Reading Comprehension

16. **(E)**   Specific Information   Difficulty: low

This question can be answered quickly by glancing back at the first paragraph. There he discusses being sad because he could not be in Russia. Clearly, then, the answer is (E).

17. **(B)**   Specific Information   Difficulty: low

This question is very simple and most of the answers can be quickly eliminated, particularly because Stravinsky gives a list within the passage itself of several examples of what music cannot express, some of which appear in the answer choices. The main point of the passage is that music is only able to express man's relation to time, particularly his existence in the present. Therefore (B) is the correct answer.

18. **(B)**   Words in Context   Difficulty: high

This question asks you to interpret a fairly vague phrase. The best way to answer this question is by looking at the phrase in context. The sentence in which it appears refers to the necessity of man to "submit to the passage of time." This reference to time, coupled with the author's use of the word "doomed" in the same sentence, should suggest to you the idea of mortality.

19. **(E)**   Understanding Themes and Arguments   Difficulty: medium

While some of these answer choices involve subtle interpretations of the text that may be difficult to comprehend, this question is actually fairly easy to answer: the wrong statement, which is the right answer, is easy to spot. Stravinsky never suggests that music and architecture are not true art forms. Answer (E) can be identified as the wrong statement, and therefore the right answer.

20. **(C)**   Main Theme or Idea   Difficulty: medium

Several of these answers can be eliminated quickly. First, answer (E) has nothing to do with the passage. Answers (A) and (D) refer to points made in the passage, but these points are secondary, not central to the passage's meaning. Answer (B) refers to something that may be one of the underlying, unstated reasons for this passage, but this question does not ask you to speculate on the author's intent. Answer (C) is the correct answer.

21. **(D)**   Main Theme or Idea   Difficulty: medium

This question requires you to formulate a very general statement of the overall theme of the question. Reading through the passage makes it very clear that (D) is the correct answer. The writer cites the greater stability of factory work (it allows women to have their nights and weekends to themselves, and to perform a set number of tasks), the greater independence it affords (they are free from the meddling of the housewife), and the greater social status it grants them (people such as the "policeman on the beat" treat factory workers with respect, while looking down on domestic servants). The other answers should be fairly easy to discard—nowhere in the passage does the writer say that factory work is more lucrative, that housewives are cruel, that factory work is exciting, or that factory work is more challenging than domestic work. The main challenge in answering this question is compressing the main theme of this long passage into a brief statement.

22. **(A)**   Words in Context   Difficulty: low

Looking at the sentence in which this word is located makes it very easy to see why (A) is the best answer choice. In the sentence, the writer says that the migration of women to factories is not "local and sporadic" but rather "general and permanent." The impression is that "local and sporadic" mean the opposite of "general and permanent." "Local," obviously, is the opposite of "general," so it follows contextually that "sporadic" is used here to contrast with "permanent." Thus, though it is usually used to mean "infrequent," the general meaning of the word in this sentence is "temporary," and the answer is (A).

23. **(B)**   Specific Information   Difficulty: medium

The main challenge here lies in separating the various attitudes expressed in the passage as a whole from the small section referred to in the question, and correctly isolating the attitude of the housewives as expressed therein. The writer of the passage sees factory work as a legitimate occupation, and sees factories as disrupting traditional labor patterns. However, the question doesn't ask you what the writer thinks. It asks you what the housewives think. Looking at the specific passage in question, we see that housewives feel that the factory is "cruel, dark, distressing." This conjures an image of women laboring in factories under dungeon-like working conditions—making (B) the best answer choice.

24. **(A)** Words in Context   Difficulty: low

This vocabulary question is extremely simple. The passage describes the woman's desire for a "fixed task" which will start and end at the same time every day, and which will not be interrupted by the caprice of her employer. This indicates the use of "fixed" as in "fixed income"—a stable or unchanging quantity. The answer, then, is obviously (A).

25. **(E)** Understanding Themes and Arguments   Difficulty: high

Each of the answer choices suggests a fairly complex possible use of the figure of the beat-walking policeman. As with most reading comprehension questions, the only real way to sort through the complexity is to look at the passage and compare it to the statements in the answer choices. The author states that the woman keeps "caste" in a factory, that she is able to perform work that earns her the respect of others. As a result, the policeman on the beat does not look down on her, even though he does look down on the cook, her domestic counterpart. The policeman is used as a symbol for the person just above the working woman in the social hierarchy—he is in a position either to approve or disapprove of her, to take her seriously or to treat her as a joke. Choice (E) is therefore the best answer choice.

26. **(D)** Specific Information   Difficulty: medium

In the lines referred to in the question, the author says that it is easier to make money as a domestic laborer than as a factory worker. So (A) can be discarded. But she does not imply that women in factories are underpaid, so (B) can also be discarded. She says that women who choose to work in factories are motivated by a desire for self-respect and a respected place in the community—(D), then, must be the correct choice. It is certainly more applicable than (E), which runs counter to the idea of the passage, or (C), which is simply irrelevant to the theme under discussion. Domestic workers may make more than factory workers, but the passage does not state that they value money more, or are motivated by a desire for money. (D) seems to be the only true statement, and is the only choice that fits the passage.

27. **(B)** Main Theme or Idea   Difficulty: high

This question is somewhat difficult because it requires you to develop a general idea about the author's position based on several small pieces of evidence in the passage. To begin with, we can discard (E); the author never discusses "standards" of employees or of people. After a close reading of the passage, we can also disregard (D); the position of the author is too broad and sympathetic for her to take such a staunch position on the "progressive new strain" in American society. The author does mention that domestic workers make more money than factory workers, a point which she follows up by stating that money matters less to factory workers than self-respect; so we can disregard (C) as well.

Of the remaining choices, (A) might seem tempting, because the author does argue that housewives must adopt a more democratic perspective. But she does so in the context of a larger point that housewives must understand what factories have to offer young working women and model their own employment practices on the factories. She specifically states that they "can learn what is necessary to do from a factory." Therefore, (A) is an incomplete answer; only (B) takes in the whole spirit of the passage.

28. **(E)** Specific Information
Difficulty: low

Each of the answer choices conveys a perspective that appears in this passage and that could be contrasted within it. Looking at the lines specifically, however, we see that the author refers to the "aristocratic" and the "democratic" perspectives, making (E) the obvious choice. This is the easiest sort of reading comprehension question—the wording of the answer choice is matched by the wording of the lines referred to in the question.

29. **(C)** Author's Technique
Difficulty: high

To answer this question, we must notice that in the passage the author seems as if she is writing to an audience of housewives wondering why their domestic employees are leaving them to take jobs in factories. She makes it clear from the beginning that she is attempting to answer a question about the migration of working girls to factories ("What are the reasons? . . . Why do they prefer it?"). Additionally, she speculates that the person to whom these questions will have occurred is most likely to be the wealthy housewife who has lost her domestic workers to the lure of the factory. "When one set of people see that another set of people are taking from them that which they very much want to have, the intelligent procedure is to find the reasons behind the shift." In other words, the housewife, who "very much want[s] to have" her domestic help, sees factories "taking" it, and must "find the reasons behind the shift."

For the rest of the passage, the author periodically offers advice to housewives about the best ways to lure their workers back to them, and explains how they will have to change their mindsets in order to do so. Though it is not specifically addressed to housewives, the author subtly assumes the perspective of an inquisitive housewife. As a result, the correct answer is (C).

30. **(E)** Author's Attitude or Tone
Difficulty: high

This question is fairly difficult because it requires you to form an abstract conclusion about the author's attitude toward her subject. The best way to answer a question such as this is to try to characterize the author's attitude for yourself: how does she feel about her subject? Does she advance a particular argument or take sides in her presentation of a conflict, or is she more even-handed? Is she trying to convince the reader of something, or simply imparting information? In this case, the writer seems to understand the perspectives of both the housewives and the working women. She does not take sides between them. Nor does she advance a particular social argument beyond the fairly bland advice she offers to the housewives. She does not seem to have an agenda beyond imparting information, and though she is not in a rhetorical frenzy about her subject, she is not bored by it or overly intellectual about it, either. She certainly takes it seriously. As a result, the best answer choice must be (E), "objective and sympathetic." The author presents the merits of the working women's case and the understandable concerns of the housewives with equal tact.

Math Section 2

Quantitative Comparisons

1. **(C)** Arithmetic: Fractions, Decimals, and Percents   Difficulty: low
We can just solve this question by directly calculating each of the two quantities. 300% of 5 is $3 \times 5 = 15$. 50% of 30 is $0.5 \times 30 = 15$. The two quantities are equal.

2. **(C)** Algebra: Simplifying and Manipulating Expressions   Difficulty: low
Using the equation given to us, we can simplify the first expression. Because $ab = 1$, we can divide both sides by b to see that $a = 1/b$. So $a \times 1/b = a \times a = a^2$; thus the two quantities are equal.

3. **(B)** Algebra: Simplifying and Manipulating Expressions   Difficulty: low
Let's substitute bc for a in both equations. In column A:

$$\frac{2a}{bc} =$$
$$\frac{2bc}{bc} = 2$$

In column B :

$$\frac{3bc}{a} =$$
$$\frac{3bc}{bc} = 3$$

All that's left is to see that $3 > 2$.

4. **(A)** Algebra: Substitution   Difficulty: medium

Since f is larger than g, $f - g$ will always be positive and $g - f$ will always be negative. These quantities are, in fact, opposites, so one will always be greater than zero, and the other will always be less than zero. You could also solve this problem by plugging in values for f and g that satisfy the given constraint.

5. **(A)** Algebra: Solving Inequalities   Difficulty: medium

To solve this problem, we first divide each side of the second inequality by 2. The new inequality is $x \geq 10 + 4y$. Now, since $y \geq 0$ (from the first inequality), the smallest x can be is 10. Any value of y greater than 0 will cause x to be greater than 10. Regardless of the value of y, $x \geq 10$ always holds, so x is always greater than 8.

6. **(A)** Geometry: Polygons   Difficulty: medium

The figure $ABCDEFG$ is comprised of a rectangle, $AEFG$, with a right triangle, BCD, taken out. Thus, the area of $ABCDEFG$ is equal to the difference between the area of $AEFG$ and the area of BCD. To solve this problem, we need to know the length of the (imaginary) line segment $\overline{BD}$. With this information, we can find the areas of the rectangle and the triangle.

The triangle is a classic 3:4:5 right triangle, so the missing side must be 3. Now we know that the length of the rectangle is $3 + 3 + 2 = 8$, and the area of the rectangle, therefore, is $6 \times 8 = 48$. The area of the triangle is $\frac{1}{2}bh$, where b is the length of the base and h is the height. In the case of triangle BCD, we can set $b = 3$ and $h = 4$. So the area of the polygon $ABCDEFG$ is $48 - \frac{1}{2}(3)(4) = 48 - 6 = 42$. $42 > 40$, so the answer must be (A).

7. **(B)** Arithmetic: Fractions, Decimals, and Percents   Difficulty: low

To find the value of each quantity, we must simply subtract the fractions by first finding their common denominators. We can simplify the expression in each column:

$$\frac{1}{2} - \frac{1}{6} =$$

$$\frac{3}{6} - \frac{1}{6} =$$

$$\frac{2}{6} = \frac{1}{3}$$

And,

$$\frac{3}{4} - \frac{1}{3} =$$

$$\frac{9}{12} - \frac{4}{12} = \frac{5}{12}$$

$\frac{1}{3}$ is equal to $\frac{4}{12}$ which is less than the column B value of $\frac{5}{12}$.

8. **(B)** Geometry: Triangles   Difficulty: medium

The important thing to realize about this figure is that the small triangle is similar to the large one. If two triangles are similar, their corresponding sides are proportional to one another and their angles are congruent. We can set up the following proportion

$$\frac{6}{10 + x} = \frac{4}{10}$$

and solve for x by cross multiplication:

$$40 + 4x = 60$$
$$4x = 20$$
$$x = 5$$

Obviously $5 < 6$, so (B) is the correct choice.

9. **(D)** Geometry: Angles and Lines   Difficulty: high

We know that the length of $\overline{AD}$ is the same as the length of $\overline{BE}$, but we do not know where on the line C is placed. From the given information, we can determine that $\overline{AB} = \overline{DE}$. This information doesn't help us answer the question, though. If C were very close to B, then the length of $\overline{AC}$ would be less than that of $\overline{CE}$. If it were closer to D, then the length of $\overline{AC}$ would be greater than the length of $\overline{CE}$. Because more than one relationship between $\overline{AC}$ and $\overline{CE}$ is possible, the answer must be (D).

10. **(C)** Arithmetic: Sets   Difficulty: medium

In this class, 6 people are in both the math club and rugby club. If the rest of the people in the class are in one of the clubs, but not both, then $18 - 6 = 12$ of them are in just the math club, and $25 - 6 = 19$ of them are in just the rugby club. So the total number of students in the class is the sum of the number of people in both clubs, the number of people in only the rugby club, and the number of people in only the math club: $6 + 19 + 12 = 37$.

11. **(A)** Arithmetic: Sets   Difficulty: high

First, note that a can take on the values 2, 3, or 4, and b can take on the values 4, 5, or 6. The greatest possible value of $a + b$ would be the sum of the greatest possible a and the greatest possible b, which are 4 and 6, respectively. Their sum is $4 + 6 = 10$.

The least possible product ab would be the product of the least possible a and the least possible b. (Note: this would not be the case if both sets contained negative numbers.) 2 and 4 are the least possible values and $2 \times 4 = 8$, which is less than 10.

12. **(A)** Arithmetic: Sets   Difficulty: high

In order to maximize the number of curly-haired girls in the classroom, we need to maximize the total number of girls, since a portion of all girls are curly-haired girls. If there are 30 people in the class and girls outnumber the boys, the greatest possible number of girls is 30 (with 0 boys). In order to have more girls with straight hair than girls with curly hair, more than half (or 15) of the girls must have straight hair. The fewest number of straight-haired girls that is greater than 15 is 16, leaving 30 – 16 = 14 girls with curly hair.

13. **(C)** Algebra: Solving Systems of Equations   Difficulty: high

Whenever you are given more variables than equations and asked to find a numerical solution you should look for a shortcut. In this case, you should notice that each equation contains an $x + y$ term, so we can subtract one equation from the other (when subtracting equations from one another, subtract the left side of one equation from the left side of the other and the right side of one equation from the right side of the other):

$$
\begin{aligned}
x + y + 2z &= 130 \\
-\qquad x + y + z &= 100 \\
\hline
(x + y + 2z) - (x + y + z) &= 130 - 100 \\
z &= 30
\end{aligned}
$$

14. **(D)** Arithmetic: Series   Difficulty: medium

This question requires no calculation whatsoever, just an understanding that the terms in a sequence are not necessarily in ascending or descending order. Of course, the relationship between the terms is impossible to know without more information. Some sequences increase, some decrease, and others oscillate. The third term of this particular sequence could be greater than the second term, less than the second term, or equal to the second term, so the answer is (D).

15. **(B)** Miscellaneous Math: Charts; Arithmetic: Ratios   Difficulty: high

The first step in this problem is to complete the chart. We can determine the number of gasoline-fueled trucks by subtracting the number of gasoline-fueled cars from the total number of gasoline-fueled vehicles: 85 – 80 = 5. Similarly, the number of diesel cars is the difference between the total number of cars and the gasoline-fueled cars: 100 – 80 = 20. The number of diesel-fueled trucks is then the total number of diesel vehicles less the number of diesel cars: 35 – 20 = 15. The total column can be completed by addition.

It is now straightforward to calculate the ratios. The quantity in column A, the ratio of trucks to gasoline-fueled cars, is $^{20}\!/_{80} = \frac{1}{4}$. The quantity in column B, the ratio of diesel-fueled vehicles to total vehicles, is $^{35}\!/_{120}$, which is greater than $\frac{1}{4} = {}^{30}\!/_{120}$, so the correct answer is (B).

Grid-Ins

16. **396** Arithmetic: Fractions, Decimals, and Percents   Difficulty: low
30% of 1320 equals $0.30 \times 1320 = 396$ overweight citizens.

17. **5/9** Arithmetic: Fractions, Decimals, and Percents   Difficulty: medium
The total number of balls is $6 + 4 + 8 = 18$. The total number of balls that are not black is $6 + 4 = 10$. The fraction of the total number of balls that are not black is $^{10}/_{18} = ^5/_9$.

18. **6** Arithmetic: Exponents and Square Roots   Difficulty: medium
The first step of this problem is to recognize that each base is a power of 2 and can therefore be rewritten with as 2^n. The equation

$$2^x = 4^y = 16^z$$

can be rewritten as

$$2^x = (2^2)^y = (2^4)^z$$

or as

$$2^x = 2^{2y} = 2^{4z}$$

With all bases equal, we can equate the exponents to solve for the three variables: $x = 2y = 4z$. We can simply calculate that $^x/_y = 2$ and $^x/_z = 4$. The addition of these quotients yields the final answer of 6.

19. **15** Geometry: Triangles   Difficulty: medium
The area of the shaded region is the difference of the areas of the rectangle and the triangle. The area of the rectangle is $6 \times 3 = 18$. The area of the triangle is $\frac{1}{2}(\text{base})(\text{height}) = \frac{1}{2}(2)(3) = 3$. The difference of the areas is therefore $18 - 3 = 15$.

20. **8** Arithmetic: Exponents and Square Roots   Difficulty: medium
The first property you must know to solve this problem is that $x^a \times x^b = x^{a+b}$. Applying this property, we see that $2^{x+y} = 256$. As long as you know that $256 = 2^8$, you will also know that $x + y = 8$. If you don't know this off the top of your head, you could easily write out the powers of 2 up to 256.

21. **180** Geometry: Solids   Difficulty: medium

The volume of a right circular cylinder with radius r and height h is $\pi r^2 h$. This is simply the area of the circular base multiplied by the height of the cylinder. We can see that $h = {}^5\!/_\pi$ and we need to solve for r from the given information. The side of the rectangle that has length 12π becomes the circumference of the base of the cylinder when the rectangle is rolled as shown. The formula for the circumference of a circle is $2(\pi)(r)$. From this formula, we know that $12\pi = 2\pi r$ and after dividing each side by 2π, we know that $r = 6$. These values allow us to solve for the volume of the cylinder:

$$\begin{aligned} \text{Volume} &= \pi r^2 h \\ &= 36\pi \frac{5}{\pi} \\ &= 36 \times 5 = 180 \end{aligned}$$

22. **16** Arithmetic: Combinations and Probability   Difficulty: high

In order for John's ticket to be worth at least $3, it needs to have at least 2 matching digits. To approach this problem systematically, consider how John might be able to have two matching digits. If m represents a matching digit and x represents a non-matching digit, then there are four possible combinations that would be worth at least $3: $mmx, mxm, xmm,$ and mmm.

Because we know that John's ticket has three different digits, it cannot match with the last two digits of the winning ticket, 33, since having 2 of the same number prevents him from having three different numbers. xmm and mmm are therefore impossible.

In the mmx case, we know that the first two digits match, so his ticket begins with 23. Since we must have 3 different numbers, the last numbers must be one of the eight other digits: 0, 1, 4, 5, 6, 7, 8, or 9. The same logic holds true for the mxm case, so the total number of ways John's ticket can be worth at least $3 is $8 + 8 = 16$.

23. **21** Algebra: Solving Inequalities   Difficulty: high

To get the highest possible value of $2x + 6y + z$, we have to find the highest possible value of the quantity $2x + 6y$ and the variable z. From the information given, we know that the highest z can be is 5. If we multiply the first inequality by 2, we get $10 \le 2x + 6y \le 16$, so the highest possible value of $2x + 6y$ is 16. $16 + 5 = 21$ is the highest possible value of the expression.

24. **12** Geometry: Polygons   Difficulty: high

Let O be the center of the square $ABCD$ (the intersection of $\overline{AC}$ and $\overline{DB}$. Consider the four identical squares $AEOH$, $EBFO$, $OFCG$, and $HOGD$ that make up $ABCD$. $AEOH$ has diagonals $\overline{AO}$ and $\overline{EH}$, each of which divides the square $AEOH$ into halves. Together, $\overline{AO}$ and $\overline{EH}$ divide $AEOH$ into quarters. Three of these quarters are shaded and one is not shaded. Thus three-fourths of the square *AEOH* is shaded and the same holds true for each of the squares *EBFO*, *OFCG*, and *HOGD*. Since three-fourths of each of these squares is shaded, we can conclude that three-fourths of the entire square *ABCD* is shaded.

Each side of *ABCD* has length 4, so the area of *ABCD* is $4^2 = 16$. The area of the shaded region is three-fourths the that area: ¾ × 16 = 12.

25. **3/5** Arithmetic: Combinations and Probability   Difficulty: high
Drawing 2 marbles simultaneously is the equivalent of drawing 1 marble out and then drawing another one out of the remaining marbles, also known as drawing without replacement. We need to determine how many different ways we could end up with 1 black marble and 1 white marble. The black marble could be selected first, and then the white one or vice versa.

In the first case, the probability of drawing the black marble first is ⅗; the probably of drawing the white marble second after drawing a black marble is ²⁄₄. The probability of both happening is the product of their individual probabilities: ⅗ × ²⁄₄ = ⁶⁄₂₀ = ³⁄₁₀.

In the second case, the probability of drawing the white marble first is ⅖; the probably of drawing the black marble second after drawing a white marble is ¾. The probability of both happening is the product of their individual probabilities: ⅖ × ¾ = ⁶⁄₂₀ = ³⁄₁₀.

Since both outcomes satisfy the problem, we must add the likelihood that each event occurs: ³⁄₁₀ + ³⁄₁₀ = ⁶⁄₁₀ = ⅗.

Verbal Section 2

Sentence Completions

1. **(B)** One Word Direct   Difficulty: low
In this question, the blank word describes "the Tet Offensive" and the comma introduces a second clause, which clarifies the concept established in the first clause. In other words, the two sides of the sentence provide information about a single idea. We must find the word that describes the Tet Offensive in such a way that it means virtually the same thing as "culminating in many casualties and few gains."

Punctual and fickle fit poorly in the sentence because they both typically describe a person, not an abstract noun. Furthermore, when plugged into the sentence, their meanings do not suggest the content that will follow after the comma.

Because of its negative connotation and since it goes well with the emphatic adverb "downright," foolhardy is a good choice. The offensive was a mistake of fools, since many people died for so little gain.

Bold and admirable might seem like good answers, since any offensive in a war must contain at least some boldness, which would be admirable. But the second half of the sentence, in which the offensive is described as resulting in many deaths and few gains, suggests that the missing word should have a negative connotation, which neither bold nor admirable has.

2.   **(E)**   Two Word Contrast   Difficulty: low
The hinge word in this sentence is "but," which signals us to look for two contrasting words describing a difference between Mark Twain's reputation and his later themes. A further clue is the word "unsettling" in the second half of the sentence—this signals us that the word in this second clause must match the gravity of "unsettling," while the word in the first clause must contrast with "unsettling."

   With these ideas in mind, we can immediately discard troubling . . funny. Even though the two words contrast, it does not make sense to say that Mark Twain is hailed as a troubling writer, but his later works explore unsettling and funny truths. Disturbing . . bothersome are synonyms, not contrasting words, and hilarious . . disorganized do not seem to relate at all. Patriotic and regional don't contrast strongly, and the two words just don't fit well in this sentence. The only convincing choice, then, is the last one: Mark Twain is hailed as a comic writer, but his later work explores unsettling and serious truths. Comic . . serious offers the necessary contrast and fits the shape of the sentence as determined by the word "unsettling."

3.   **(C)**   Two Word Direct   Difficulty: low
Since the second half of the sentence tells us that Florida's beaches are a desirable locale, we know that we are looking for two adjectives with fairly positive attributes. This clearly rules out opaque . . unsanitary, calming . . abrupt, and picturesque . . inaccessible. Finally, residual and posterior are both irrelevant to the sentence. The answer is therefore unsoiled . . pellucid.

4.   **(A)**   One Word Contrast   Difficulty: medium
The question is looking for a noun associated with the verb "to fight." The logical answer to the question is altercation. If you didn't know the word altercation, you should still be able to work backwards. Depending on whether you know the vocabulary, you should be able to throw out the words selection, reconciliation, and artifice, none of which have anything to do with encouraging a fight. Dalliance is a little trickier, since it hints at a sort of illicit romance that fits well with Cindy's coy behavior with the boys, but it still does not have anything to do with actual fighting.

5. **(B)** Other   Difficulty: medium

This question fits the "other" category because the two blanks really have very little to do with each other. They share no relationship of direction, whether of contrast or a single, direct flow. Instead, each blank fits individually with its own part of the sentence. In this question, the first blank shares a direct relationship with the words "Ice Age," while the second blank must make the statement "ice and cold do not ---- appear out of nowhere" agree with the statement "ice ages develop gradually."

To answer this question correctly we must find a pair of words that can make each blank agree with its own part of the sentence. You can throw out grows . . swiftly and extends . . merely immediately, because grows and develops both carry a sense of increasing, and the temperatures most definitely do not increase when an ice age develops. You should also be able to discard lessen . . slowly and changes . . indirectly, because slowly and indirectly do not fit in the second blank: the statement "ice and cold do not slowly appear out of nowhere" means the opposite of the statement "ice ages develop gradually." Meanwhile, indirectly doesn't fit into the blank very well at all, since "ice and cold do not indirectly appear out of nowhere" doesn't really mean anything. That leaves us with decreases . . suddenly as the correct answer.

6. **(E)** Two Word Contrast   Difficulty: medium

The hinge word in this sentence is "while," which signals that we should look for words that will make the first two parts of the sentence contrast. In addition, the third clause of the sentence ("consolidating his power at the expense of his subjects' freedom") provides an important clue. Whatever word we choose for the second blank must describe the condition of consolidating power, and whatever word we choose for the first blank must contrast with that condition.

Free . . hero and salvage . . warrior can be discarded simply because of their second terms: neither a "hero" nor a "warrior" consolidates his own power at the expense of his subjects' freedom—a warrior might do such a thing, but it certainly is not part of the definition of a warrior. However, a "tyrant," a "thug," or a "despot" would all do such a thing, so we must consider each of the last three choices separately. Dominate . . tyrant can be eliminated because it fails to provide contrast. We can eliminate administrate . . thug because it fails to make sense when plugged into the sentence. The only answer choice that works is liberate . . despot: Napoleon hoped to be a liberator, but he quickly became a power-hungry ruler instead. This provides the necessary contrast and makes a coherent sentence.

7. **(B)** Two Word Contrast   Difficulty: medium

The hinge word in this sentence is "although," which indicates that the first two clauses of this sentence will be in contrast: *The New Yorker* is regarded as one thing, but it is actually something different. The third clause in this sentence ("with one of the largest circulations . . .") provides an additional clue: whatever word we select for the second blank, it must match the idea of *The New Yorker* having a large circulation.

Because most of the answer choices provide the contrast necessitated by the "although," the information provided by the third clause is extremely important to finding the right answer. The only one that is easy to discard is outdated . . superficial, which uses terms that have no clear relation to the ideas in the sentence. The other four choices each feature contrasting words, and without the third clause, any of them could work in the sentence. Since we know that the second term must imply a large readership, we can settle on elitist . . popular as the correct choice. Though *The New Yorker* is often seen as elitist or snobbish, it is actually very popular, and has a huge circulation. This choice provides the contrast necessitated by the "although," and matches the other information provided by the sentence.

8. **(B)** One Word Direct   Difficulty: high

In this question, the blank word describes "some ground sloths," and the comma introduces a second statement that gives meaning to the first. In other words, the two sides of the sentence provide information about one single idea. We must find the word that describes "some ground sloths" in such a way that those sloths, if accurately described, were "much larger than modern-day tree sloths."

Feral, which means "wild," amorphous, which means "without definite shape," and docile are all words that could apply to sloths, but none of these makes any reference to their size. On that basis, they should be eliminated. Anthropocentric means "looking at the world in terms of human perception and values." It clearly isn't the right answer once you know the definition, but if you don't know the definition, its length and difficulty might make you think it means huge. Hopefully, however, you know that gargantuan means "extremely big." If you do, then you should easily get this question right. If you do not, you should at least be able to eliminate those answer choices that you know do not apply to size, and guess from there.

9. **(B)** Two Word Direct   Difficulty: medium

Successful completion of this sentence depends on knowing the meaning of the word "erroneous"—something characterized by error. If you know that Louisa's statements were in error, then you know that Louisa's relation to historical matters must include some lack of skill or effort. With that in mind, you can eliminate all of the answers but ignorance . . epitomized and negligence . . eviscerated, since only those two have first words that define some sort of lack. If you plug in both of these choices, it should be clear that epitomized fits the sentence far better than eviscerated, which doesn't fit well in the sentence at all. If you didn't know the word eviscerated, you'd still be in a good position to guess between these two choices.

10. **(E)** One Word Contrast   Difficulty: high

The word "rather" is a hinge word—the sentence is looking for a verb that describes the opposite of presenting one's own views. This would be a simple question if it didn't contain such hard vocabulary. Promulgate means "make known by declaration," juxtapose means "contrast," enfranchise means "give the right to vote," and mitigate means "to lessen in force." All of these are wrong. Regurgitate literally means "to vomit," but it is often used metaphorically to mean "to repeat without thinking." Regurgitate is therefore the right answer. If you do not recognize some of these words, hopefully you can eliminate even one or two and guess on that basis.

Analogies

11. **(D)** Characteristic Use   Difficulty: low

"A BAKER typically uses an OVEN" is the best and most specific sentence for this stem pair. Similarly, scientists use microscopes. None of the other answer choices have this relation of a professional with a tool he or she uses. A teacher does use a desk, but the relation is not strong enough to make this a possible answer choice.

12. **(B)** Cause and Effect   Difficulty: low

FERTILIZER makes a PLANT grow larger in the same way that yeast makes dough grow larger. None of the other answer choices approximate this formula; some of them (root : harvest, leaf : canopy) reference ideas relating to plants, and some of them (candle : cake) reference ideas relating to baking, but in no case can one thing be added to another thing to produce growth. Only yeast : dough fits the same cause-effect pattern of FERTILIZER : PLANT.

13. **(B)** Relative Size and Degree   Difficulty: low

Something that is IMPOSSIBLE cannot happen, and something that is UNLIKELY will probably not happen. So IMPOSSIBLE is even more unlikely than UNLIKELY; similarly, hideous is even more ugly than ugly. The other answers are easy to eliminate; the only tricky choice is probable : doubtful, because those words relate to UNLIKELY and IMPOSSIBLE in terms of describing the chance of an event occurring. But whereas IMPOSSIBLE is a degree of meaning greater than UNLIKELY, probable and doubtful are antonyms.

14. **(A)** Other   Difficulty: low

A SECOND is a unit used to measure TIME, just as a foot is a unit used to measure height. This question is tricky first because you might read "foot" as referring to the body part, and while you were confused, you might get tempted by one of the two other answer choices that contain measurement words. However, each of these two answer pairs (minute : hour and pint : gallon) relates two measurements to each other, rather than a single measurement to the thing it measures. Finally, you should be able to discard velocity : speed since they are synonyms, and length : endurance because they don't have a good internal relation at all.

15. **(B)** Other   Difficulty: low

A good sentence for the stem pair would be: A NEGATIVE is the template from which a PHOTOGRAPH is made. Likewise, a pattern is the template from which a dress is made. A program determines a computer's function and output, but it is not the foundation upon which the computer itself is made. A plot can be thought of as the outline of a novel, but again, it is not a template from which the novel is created. Only dress : pattern has the same relationship as the stem pair.

16. **(C)** Other: Synonyms and Antonyms   Difficulty: medium

Something that is COVERT will de done SURREPTITIOUSLY, just as anyone who is sociable will act affably. Assuming you know the meaning of COVERT and SURREPTITIOUSLY, to pick this answer as the right one you also have to know the meaning of affably, which many people might not know. However, even if you weren't sure of the word affably, you could still work backwards. You should be able to discard passive : strongly and secret : obviously, and outdated : currently as possibilities, since all three pairs relate as antonyms, not synonyms. That leaves casual : remorsefully. If you know that remorsefully means "with great sadness", you should be able to see that the pair casual : remorsefully doesn't have much of an internal relation.

What if you didn't know the meaning of COVERT or SURREPTITIOUSLY? If you didn't know the words at all, you could still go through the answers and reject pairs with a weak internal relationship. You could then discard casual : remorsefully. And even by throwing out just that possibility you've put yourself in position to guess. You could also deduce that if two or more answers choices seem to have the same internal relation, then none of them can be the right answer (on what basis would one be better than the other?). That would allow you to discard passive : strongly, secret : obviously, and outdated : currently. Remember, even if you do not know the meaning of a word or even both words in an analogy, you can still put yourself into a good position to guess.

17. **(A)** Function   Difficulty: medium

"The function of an AMPLIFIER is to enhance SOUND" is the best and most specific sentence you could make with this stem pair. Similarly the function of binoculars is to enhance vision. A stereo is used to play music, while a screen is used to display a movie, and a museum is used to display art, but none of these pairs have the relation of one thing increasing the amplitude of another thing, as found in the stem pair. Only binoculars : vision has the same relationship as the stem pair.

18. **(D)** Characteristic Location   Difficulty: medium

A PAINTER typically works in a STUDIO. Similarly, a conductor typically works on a locomotive (a train). While a monkey might typically be found at a zoo and a violin will often be played in an auditorium, neither of these pairs include the idea of work that is so important to the relationship of PAINTER : STUDIO. A farmhouse exists within a landscape, but so does everything else in the world; it is not a good answer. A legislature might develop an amendment, but this relation has nothing to do with PAINTER : STUDIO.

19. **(D)** Part/Whole   Difficulty: medium

An ALBUM is made up of a series of SONGS just as a play is made up of a series of scenes. The other answer pairs do not relate a whole to its units or parts in the same way. Book : index is tricky, though, since an index can be part of a book. The problem with this pair is that a book is not composed of a series of indices (book : chapter, on the other hand, would have been correct). A freeway is a type of road and a compass provides direction, but neither is a part : whole relationship. Finally, fixture : animation has no relation at all. Even if you couldn't decide on an answer you should have been able to discard this choice.

20. **(A)** Relative Size and Degree   Difficulty: high

Someone who is EXULTANT has a great deal more joy than someone who is merely HAPPY, just as someone who is delirious has a great deal more bewilderment than someone who is merely confused. Notice that the term with the greater degree of meaning comes first. Of the other possible answers, only perspicacity : genius is really tricky, and only because perspicacity is a very hard vocabulary word. It means simply insight or intelligence and is therefore a degree of meaning less than genius, not greater. Considerate and disingenuous have no relation; repudiated and proved have an antonymic relationship; and wretched : horrendous have the same degree of meaning.

21. **(E)** Other   Difficulty: high

"To LUBRICATE something reduces FRICTION" is the best and most specific sentence you could make with this stem pair. Similarly, to illuminate something is to reduce darkness. To irrigate something is to increase, not decrease, hydration. It is possible that someone might venerate, or revere, a partisan (a person who fights for a particular cause), but that relation has nothing to do with LUBRICATE : FRICTION. Permeate, which means to spread throughout, has no good relation with dissonance, which means lack of harmony. Embellish, which means to decorate or to add fictitious details also has no real relation with enunciate, which means to pronounce deliberately. Illuminate : darkness is the only answer pair that, like LUBRICATE : FRICTION, has a relationship of diminishment.

22. **(B)** Description   Difficulty: high

"An extreme or excessive CRIME can be described as HEINOUS" is the best and most specific sentence you can make with this stem pair. Similarly an extreme or excessive decoration can be described as garish: the relationship here is one of extremity and excess. Tasty : food can be immediately eliminated since it offers a happy, positive relationship with which HEINOUS : CRIME obviously does not agree. Authentic : forgery is a relationship of opposites and can also be eliminated. Of the three remaining possibilities, hazardous and risk are nearly synonymous — a risk is always hazardous in some way. Garbled : larceny has no good relation (though larceny is related to the word CRIME, which might cause you confusion) This leaves garish : decoration as the correct answer.

23. **(A)** Attribute   Difficulty: high

A good sentence to use to connect these words is, "Anyone who acts with PERFIDY will not be STEADFAST." (PERFIDY means "treachery" or "betrayal," and STEADFAST means "loyal," so to have one quality, you must lack the other.) Similarly, anyone who acts with jubilance will not be melancholy. (Jubilance means "joy" or "celebration," and melancholy means "sad" or "depressed.") None of the other possible answers comes close to fitting the sentence, though you must have a grasp on the difficult vocabulary of this question to realize that quickly. Functionality and active have a roughly synonymous relationship, as do homestead and domestic, which clearly does not fit the sentence, as it is impossible to act "with homestead". Worthiness and penitent have no direct relationship, and neither do impudence and snubbed, though it would be very difficult to discount worthiness : penitent without knowing the meaning of penitent ("remorseful" or "repentant").

Reading Comprehension

24. **(B)** Specific Information   Difficulty: low

This is an easy question. The first sentence of the passage says that da Vinci was known during his age as an architect, engineer, artist, and scientist. It does not, however, make any mention of politics. Clearly, then, the correct answer is (B).

25. **(E)** Understanding Themes and Arguments   Difficulty: medium

You must go back to the passage to answer this question and look at the context. First, the passage states that da Vinci anticipated modern knowledge in the way that Plato anticipated modern philosophy (you can throw out answer (A) right there). The "knowledge" that the writer refers to must therefore be comparable to philosophy in some way: it must refer to a general field of understanding. The passage gives you a second clue as to the meaning of the phrase "modern knowledge" by claiming that da Vinci's work with flight was a particular example of his anticipation of modern knowledge. Now you know that "modern knowledge" refers to a field like philosophy, and includes a subject like analyzing the mechanics of flight. Of the remaining answer choices, only (E) would be a good general category for knowledge of human flight, so it is the correct answer.

26. **(A)** Understanding Themes and Arguments   Difficulty: medium
Most of these answers can be eliminated using common sense. By referring to "the life of the bird," da Vinci means the animating vitality that powers flight, which would be substituted for by the airplane's engine. The correct answer is (A).

27. **(B)** Words in Context   Difficulty: low
If you don't know the answer to this question, you can try to substitute each answer choice back into the passage, to see which makes the most sense in context. The passage gives a number of examples, and then states that those examples cannot begin to illustrate the entirety of da Vinci's knowledge or contributions. The only answer choice that fits is (B): the examples in the passage do not begin to cover the range of da Vinci's observations because there are so many that one could discuss.

28. **(E)** Implied Information   Difficulty: high
This question demands a subtle understanding of the argument being made. The lines in question refer to da Vinci's ideas as a "small thing" by today's standards, but the author then points out that da Vinci figured out these principles before today's standards existed. The writer is acknowledging that while da Vinci's insight might not seem incredible given the modern level of science, when the knowledge of his own time is taken into account his insight is incredible. Therefore, the writer is trying to defuse a reader's thoughts that da Vinci's ideas are simple and obvious. The correct answer is (E).

29. **(C)** Words in Context   Difficulty: medium
Again, the best way to approach this question if you don't immediately know the answer is to substitute the answer choices back into the passage. By doing this, you should immediately be able to throw out (A), since you can't use observation to demonstrate anything, and (B) and (D) because they make no sense in the context. (E) is a tempting choice because it has such a close meaning to "gathered" in normal circumstances, but you can't really "collect" anything from observations. The best answer is (C), which fits with the sentence, which states that da Vinci used observations to figure out specific aspects of the way a bird flies.

30. **(A)** Specific Information   Difficulty: low
This question just asks you to recall what you've read and to use a little common sense. Every incorrect answer choice is mentioned in the passage; not only is (A) not mentioned, the idea that birds should power flying machines is preposterous. Clearly, (A) is the correct answer.

31. **(D)** Author's Technique   Difficulty: high

The author uses this reference to demonstrate just how many of da Vinci's theories and ideas anticipated modern reality. The training of war pilots is not relevant to this passage or to the development of the airplane in general; however, this reference shows just how wide-ranging da Vinci's thoughts were. The correct answer is (D).

32. **(C)** Specific Information   Difficulty: low

This question just asks you to remember what you've read. The passage doesn't say anything about landing gear, so the correct answer is (C).

33. **(C)** Main Theme or Idea   Difficulty: medium

The second paragraph of the passage focuses specifically on a "student of the principles of flight" whose observations were "lengthy" and "original." The remainder of the passage seeks to demonstrate this idea. The emphasis on this passage is then obviously on da Vinci's powers of observation, making (C) the correct answer.

34. **(D)** Main Theme or Idea   Difficulty: high

Several of these answers—(C), (D), and (E)—look plausible. But you need to think carefully about the main aim of the passage and not get caught up either in specifics of the argument or in what was said in the preface to the passage. The author is interested in Leonardo's use of observation, but he does not make any claims about observation in general; therefore (C) is not the correct answer. While many of Leonardo's discoveries turned out to be principles used in modern aircraft design, Leonardo's treatise was not known to those inventing the airplane, as the passage notes; therefore (E) isn't the correct answer either. As the last paragraph of the passage says, the author seems to be mostly interested in Da Vinci's "genius": the correct answer is (D).

35. **(B)** Main Theme or Idea   Difficulty: low

This questions is just another way to test your general knowledge of the passage. Clearly, the main focus of this passage is da Vinci's struggle to understand the principles of flight and the possibilities for human flight. Only the title found in answer (B) describes this focus.

Math Section 3

1. **(D)** Arithmetic: Ratios and Proportions   Difficulty: low

We know that the 30 shaded windows represent $\frac{2}{5}$ of the total windows x; we can state that algebraically as $30 = \frac{2}{5}x$. We can solve for x by multiplying each side of the equation by $\frac{5}{2}$ to find that $x = 75$.

2.   **(D)**   Arithmetic: Divisibility and Remainders   Difficulty: medium

$28 \div 5 = 5 \, \frac{3}{5}$, which has a remainder of 3. Likewise, $30 \div 7 = 4 \, \frac{2}{7}$, which has a remainder of 2. When the remainders are multiplied the product is $3 \times 2 = 6$.

3.   **(B)**   Arithmetic: Rates   Difficulty: low

Hopefully you can immediately identify that twenty minutes is $\frac{1}{3}$ of an hour. Because the car can go 66 miles in an hour it can go $\frac{1}{3}$ that distance in twenty minutes. $66 \times \frac{1}{3} = 22$. More formally, you could have set up a proportion, $\frac{20}{60} = \frac{x}{66}$, and solved for x.

4.   **(D)**   Miscellaneous Math: Charts and Graphs   Difficulty: medium

The company faces a one-time fixed cost at the beginning of the cost function and then a constant cost for each box it makes. We can think about these events in terms of the standard equation of a line: $y = mx + b$. The initial cost represents b, the y intercept, or the cost of producing even 0 boxes. The unit cost is a constant additional cost associated with each incremental box and represents m, the slope. The correct answer will be graph with a positive y intercept and a constant positive slope.

5.   **(D)**   Algebra: Substitution   Difficulty: medium

Much of the solution to this problem rests on your ability to visualize the substitution of j for k and x for y. To further complicate the problem, some terms are written as j^2 while others are written as jj.

We can rewrite $k^2 y^2$ as $kkyy$. We can then rewrite each of the answer choices in terms of only k and y and without any exponents. By standardizing each of the terms, finding the solution will be as simple as matching the two identical terms.

   (A)   *ykkk*
   (B)   *kkkk*
   (C)   *kk + 2ky + yy*
   (D)   *kkyy*
   (E)   *yyyk*

Clearly, (D) matches exactly.

6.   **(C)**   Geometry: Triangles   Difficulty: medium

The segment $\overline{AD}$ divides the equilateral triangle ABC into two congruent 30-60-90 triangles. We know that in a 30-60-90 triangle, the ratio of longer leg to the hypotenuse is $\sqrt{3}/2 : 1$. In this case, we know that the longer leg of the triangle is 1, so the length of the hypotenuse is $\sqrt{3}/2/1 = 2/\sqrt{3}$.

7.   **(B)**   Arithmetic: Mean, Median, and Mode   Difficulty: medium

For purposes of calculating the new mean, we can consider both a and b to equal 10 and both c and d to equal 12. The sum of the five numbers is therefore $10 + 10 + 12 + 12 + 26 = 70$. The mean is calculated by dividing the sum of the terms by the number of terms: $70 \div 5 = 14$.

8.   **(C)**   Arithmetic: Basic   Difficulty: medium

To determine whether an answer choice is twice a palindrome, simply divide it by 2 and see if the quotient is a palindrome. 252 is the only answer that, when divided by 2, does not give a palindrome as an answer: half of 252 is 126 and $126 \neq 621$.

9.   **(A)**   Geometry: Polygons; Geometry: Circles   Difficulty: high

The area of the shaded region is equal to the area of triangle ABC minus the area of the segments of the circles that are created by angles A, B, and C. The area of the triangle is equal to one-half the base times the height. The base is 6, and we can draw in the height of the triangle which is a perpendicular bisector that divides the triangle into two 30-60-90 triangles. We can calculate the length of the height by using either the Pythagorean theorem or by using standard trigonometric ratios.

Using trigonometric ratios, the length of the side opposite the 30° angle is 3, and the hypotenuse is 6, so the length of the third leg, the height of triangle ABC, is $3\sqrt{3}$. Using the Pythagorean theorem:

$$h^2 + 3^2 = 6^2$$
$$h^2 = 27$$
$$h = \sqrt{27}$$
$$h = 3\sqrt{3}$$

The area of ABC is $\frac{1}{2} \times 6 \times 3\sqrt{3} = 9\sqrt{3}$.

Now to calculate the area of the circle segments created by the angles A, B, and C. Since ABC is an equilateral triangle, we know that each angle is 60° and that each angle intercepts an arc whose length is equal to $^{60°}\!/_{360°} = \frac{1}{6}$ of the length of the circumference. The area of three of these wedges is therefore equal to $3 \times \frac{1}{6} = \frac{1}{2}$ the area of the circle. We know that the radius of each circle is $6 \div 2 = 3$, so the area is $\pi r^2 = 3^2\pi = 9\pi$. The area of the three combined wedges is equal to $^{9\pi}\!/_2$. The area of the shaded region, therefore, is then equal to $9\sqrt{3} - {}^{9\pi}\!/_2$.

10. **(A)** Geometry: Angles and Lines   Difficulty: high

The easiest way to approach this problem is to draw a diagram. We know that A, B, and C are all on one line. We know that B and D are on a line perpendicular to the line $\overline{ABC}$. We know that C, E, and F are on a line parallel to line $\overline{BD}$. One possible diagram for this scenario is this one:

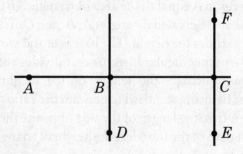

From this diagram, we see that the only lines which would be perpendicular to one another would be the lines $\overline{AB}$, and $\overline{CF}$, and so the answer must be (A).

Verbal Section 3

1. **(A)** Words in Context   Difficulty: low

Think of this question as a sentence-completion problem: insert each word and see which makes the most sense. Annulled means "cancelled," which has nothing to do with the word style. Eliminate it. But all the other choices *are* legitimate synonyms for "styled." However, whereas (B), (C), and (D) interpret the word literally, only (A) fits with the context and identifies correctly that "styled" is used metaphorically here to mean "deemed," or described as.

2. **(E)** Specific Information   Difficulty: low

This question is very straightforward. Whereas there is textual evidence in the first paragraph for the first four topics listed, "financial gain" is not mentioned in any capacity; the answer is therefore (E).

3. **(D)** Author's Technique   Difficulty: medium

In this part of the passage, the author is responding to the objection that baseball is a dangerous sport by pointing out potential dangers in sports that are generally considered safe. His goal is not to encourage or discourage people from participating in other sports, but to show that *any* sport can be defined as dangerous if examined too closely. This helps him make the claim that baseball is dangerous seem like an overreaction. Therefore, the correct answer is clearly (D).

4. **(A)** Author's Attitude or Tone   Difficulty: high

The author's patriotic editorializing is evidenced by his evocation of Americans' "inherent bravery" and "determination," both of which he presents as inarguable truths. The answer is therefore (A).

5. **(D)** Specific Information   Difficulty: low

In these lines the author clearly states that he sees the participation of high-level businessmen as adding stature to the game and "aiding" it to become the national pastime. The answer is therefore (D).

6. **(B)** Words in Context   Difficulty: medium

The best way to answer this question is to look at its context. The author identifies baseball as a game that helps "over-worked" clerks find relaxation. The "harassing" mental labor is part of this over-work, and so the best word to take the place of harassing is tiring, answer (B). This question is made more difficult because both "haranguing" and "molesting" are generally better synonyms for "harassing," but in the context of this passage they simply don't make sense.

7. **(B)** Main Theme or Idea   Difficulty: high

Try to answer this question through a process of elimination. First, you should note that there is no textual evidence in Passage 2 for (A), (C), or (D). Next, the author's assertion that his publication "[does] not share the opinion . . . that skill in our national pastime implies an exercise of the moral virtues" rules out (E). That leaves you with (B).

8. **(C)** Understanding Themes and Arguments   Difficulty: high

Though the question itself is not difficult, you might be tripped up by the vocabulary used in the answer choices. Noting that the author calls baseball both "dangerous" and "hazardous," we can assume that the correct response will be a synonym of one of these. (B) and (E) are easy to rule out, while "innocuous" ("harmless") and bellicose ("belligerent") don't seem to fit either. The correct response, "perilous," is a synonym for "dangerous."

9. **(C)** Specific Information   Difficulty: low

This question is quite easy, as the only one of the possible answer choices that seems appropriate in relation to the phrase "one of the best players . . . in a recent match" is (C).

10. **(D)** Author's Technique   Difficulty: medium

The word "best" is used ironically here to highlight the author's disdain for the undesirable impact that he claims baseball has had in breeding various forms of moral and financial corruption. The answer is therefore (D).

11. **(A)** Main Theme or Idea   Difficulty: high

With the exception of (E), all of the possible choices are mentioned somewhere in the two passages. However, only recreation is mentioned in both—see lines 10–11 in Passage 1 and line 22 in Passage 2. The answer is therefore (A).

12. **(E)** Specific Information   Difficulty: medium

In the second paragraph of Passage 1, the author admits that baseball is dangerous, but argues that this danger fosters bravery. The answer is therefore (E).

13. **(D)** Main Theme or Idea   Difficulty: medium

Although the author of Passage 1 mentions that business interests have been useful in the development of baseball (see line 45), neither author explicitly discusses the way in which the new sport is funded. The answer is therefore (D).

SAT Practice Test 2

SAT PRACTICE TEST 2 ANSWER SHEET

MATH SECTION 1	VERBAL SECTION 1	MATH SECTION 2	VERBAL SECTION 2
1. Ⓐ Ⓑ Ⓒ Ⓓ Ⓔ	8. Ⓐ Ⓑ Ⓒ Ⓓ Ⓔ	10. Ⓐ Ⓑ Ⓒ Ⓓ Ⓔ	22. Ⓐ Ⓑ Ⓒ Ⓓ Ⓔ
2. Ⓐ Ⓑ Ⓒ Ⓓ Ⓔ	9. Ⓐ Ⓑ Ⓒ Ⓓ Ⓔ	11. Ⓐ Ⓑ Ⓒ Ⓓ Ⓔ	23. Ⓐ Ⓑ Ⓒ Ⓓ Ⓔ
3. Ⓐ Ⓑ Ⓒ Ⓓ Ⓔ	10. Ⓐ Ⓑ Ⓒ Ⓓ Ⓔ	12. Ⓐ Ⓑ Ⓒ Ⓓ Ⓔ	24. Ⓐ Ⓑ Ⓒ Ⓓ Ⓔ
4. Ⓐ Ⓑ Ⓒ Ⓓ Ⓔ	11. Ⓐ Ⓑ Ⓒ Ⓓ Ⓔ	13. Ⓐ Ⓑ Ⓒ Ⓓ Ⓔ	25. Ⓐ Ⓑ Ⓒ Ⓓ Ⓔ
5. Ⓐ Ⓑ Ⓒ Ⓓ Ⓔ	12. Ⓐ Ⓑ Ⓒ Ⓓ Ⓔ	14. Ⓐ Ⓑ Ⓒ Ⓓ Ⓔ	26. Ⓐ Ⓑ Ⓒ Ⓓ Ⓔ
6. Ⓐ Ⓑ Ⓒ Ⓓ Ⓔ	13. Ⓐ Ⓑ Ⓒ Ⓓ Ⓔ	15. Ⓐ Ⓑ Ⓒ Ⓓ Ⓔ	27. Ⓐ Ⓑ Ⓒ Ⓓ Ⓔ
7. Ⓐ Ⓑ Ⓒ Ⓓ Ⓔ	14. Ⓐ Ⓑ Ⓒ Ⓓ Ⓔ	16. Ⓐ Ⓑ Ⓒ Ⓓ Ⓔ	28. Ⓐ Ⓑ Ⓒ Ⓓ Ⓔ
8. Ⓐ Ⓑ Ⓒ Ⓓ Ⓔ	15. Ⓐ Ⓑ Ⓒ Ⓓ Ⓔ	17. Ⓐ Ⓑ Ⓒ Ⓓ Ⓔ	29. Ⓐ Ⓑ Ⓒ Ⓓ Ⓔ
9. Ⓐ Ⓑ Ⓒ Ⓓ Ⓔ	16. Ⓐ Ⓑ Ⓒ Ⓓ Ⓔ	18. Ⓐ Ⓑ Ⓒ Ⓓ Ⓔ	30. Ⓐ Ⓑ Ⓒ Ⓓ Ⓔ
10. Ⓐ Ⓑ Ⓒ Ⓓ Ⓔ	17. Ⓐ Ⓑ Ⓒ Ⓓ Ⓔ	19. Ⓐ Ⓑ Ⓒ Ⓓ Ⓔ	31. Ⓐ Ⓑ Ⓒ Ⓓ Ⓔ
11. Ⓐ Ⓑ Ⓒ Ⓓ Ⓔ	18. Ⓐ Ⓑ Ⓒ Ⓓ Ⓔ	20. Ⓐ Ⓑ Ⓒ Ⓓ Ⓔ	32. Ⓐ Ⓑ Ⓒ Ⓓ Ⓔ
12. Ⓐ Ⓑ Ⓒ Ⓓ Ⓔ	19. Ⓐ Ⓑ Ⓒ Ⓓ Ⓔ	21. Ⓐ Ⓑ Ⓒ Ⓓ Ⓔ	33. Ⓐ Ⓑ Ⓒ Ⓓ Ⓔ
13. Ⓐ Ⓑ Ⓒ Ⓓ Ⓔ	20. Ⓐ Ⓑ Ⓒ Ⓓ Ⓔ	22. Ⓐ Ⓑ Ⓒ Ⓓ Ⓔ	34. Ⓐ Ⓑ Ⓒ Ⓓ Ⓔ
14. Ⓐ Ⓑ Ⓒ Ⓓ Ⓔ	21. Ⓐ Ⓑ Ⓒ Ⓓ Ⓔ	23. Ⓐ Ⓑ Ⓒ Ⓓ Ⓔ	35. Ⓐ Ⓑ Ⓒ Ⓓ Ⓔ
15. Ⓐ Ⓑ Ⓒ Ⓓ Ⓔ	22. Ⓐ Ⓑ Ⓒ Ⓓ Ⓔ	24. Ⓐ Ⓑ Ⓒ Ⓓ Ⓔ	**MATH SECTION 3**
16. Ⓐ Ⓑ Ⓒ Ⓓ Ⓔ	23. Ⓐ Ⓑ Ⓒ Ⓓ Ⓔ	25. Ⓐ Ⓑ Ⓒ Ⓓ Ⓔ	1. Ⓐ Ⓑ Ⓒ Ⓓ Ⓔ
17. Ⓐ Ⓑ Ⓒ Ⓓ Ⓔ	24. Ⓐ Ⓑ Ⓒ Ⓓ Ⓔ	**VERBAL SECTION 2**	2. Ⓐ Ⓑ Ⓒ Ⓓ Ⓔ
18. Ⓐ Ⓑ Ⓒ Ⓓ Ⓔ	25. Ⓐ Ⓑ Ⓒ Ⓓ Ⓔ	1. Ⓐ Ⓑ Ⓒ Ⓓ Ⓔ	3. Ⓐ Ⓑ Ⓒ Ⓓ Ⓔ
19. Ⓐ Ⓑ Ⓒ Ⓓ Ⓔ	26. Ⓐ Ⓑ Ⓒ Ⓓ Ⓔ	2. Ⓐ Ⓑ Ⓒ Ⓓ Ⓔ	4. Ⓐ Ⓑ Ⓒ Ⓓ Ⓔ
20. Ⓐ Ⓑ Ⓒ Ⓓ Ⓔ	27. Ⓐ Ⓑ Ⓒ Ⓓ Ⓔ	3. Ⓐ Ⓑ Ⓒ Ⓓ Ⓔ	5. Ⓐ Ⓑ Ⓒ Ⓓ Ⓔ
21. Ⓐ Ⓑ Ⓒ Ⓓ Ⓔ	28. Ⓐ Ⓑ Ⓒ Ⓓ Ⓔ	4. Ⓐ Ⓑ Ⓒ Ⓓ Ⓔ	6. Ⓐ Ⓑ Ⓒ Ⓓ Ⓔ
22. Ⓐ Ⓑ Ⓒ Ⓓ Ⓔ	29. Ⓐ Ⓑ Ⓒ Ⓓ Ⓔ	5. Ⓐ Ⓑ Ⓒ Ⓓ Ⓔ	7. Ⓐ Ⓑ Ⓒ Ⓓ Ⓔ
23. Ⓐ Ⓑ Ⓒ Ⓓ Ⓔ	30. Ⓐ Ⓑ Ⓒ Ⓓ Ⓔ	6. Ⓐ Ⓑ Ⓒ Ⓓ Ⓔ	8. Ⓐ Ⓑ Ⓒ Ⓓ Ⓔ
24. Ⓐ Ⓑ Ⓒ Ⓓ Ⓔ	31. Ⓐ Ⓑ Ⓒ Ⓓ Ⓔ	7. Ⓐ Ⓑ Ⓒ Ⓓ Ⓔ	9. Ⓐ Ⓑ Ⓒ Ⓓ Ⓔ
25. Ⓐ Ⓑ Ⓒ Ⓓ Ⓔ	32. Ⓐ Ⓑ Ⓒ Ⓓ Ⓔ	8. Ⓐ Ⓑ Ⓒ Ⓓ Ⓔ	10. Ⓐ Ⓑ Ⓒ Ⓓ Ⓔ
26. Ⓐ Ⓑ Ⓒ Ⓓ Ⓔ	33. Ⓐ Ⓑ Ⓒ Ⓓ Ⓔ	9. Ⓐ Ⓑ Ⓒ Ⓓ Ⓔ	**VERBAL SECTION 3**
27. Ⓐ Ⓑ Ⓒ Ⓓ Ⓔ	34. Ⓐ Ⓑ Ⓒ Ⓓ Ⓔ	10. Ⓐ Ⓑ Ⓒ Ⓓ Ⓔ	1. Ⓐ Ⓑ Ⓒ Ⓓ Ⓔ
28. Ⓐ Ⓑ Ⓒ Ⓓ Ⓔ	35. Ⓐ Ⓑ Ⓒ Ⓓ Ⓔ	11. Ⓐ Ⓑ Ⓒ Ⓓ Ⓔ	2. Ⓐ Ⓑ Ⓒ Ⓓ Ⓔ
29. Ⓐ Ⓑ Ⓒ Ⓓ Ⓔ	**MATH SECTION 2**	12. Ⓐ Ⓑ Ⓒ Ⓓ Ⓔ	3. Ⓐ Ⓑ Ⓒ Ⓓ Ⓔ
30. Ⓐ Ⓑ Ⓒ Ⓓ Ⓔ	1. Ⓐ Ⓑ Ⓒ Ⓓ Ⓔ	13. Ⓐ Ⓑ Ⓒ Ⓓ Ⓔ	4. Ⓐ Ⓑ Ⓒ Ⓓ Ⓔ
VERBAL SECTION 1	2. Ⓐ Ⓑ Ⓒ Ⓓ Ⓔ	14. Ⓐ Ⓑ Ⓒ Ⓓ Ⓔ	5. Ⓐ Ⓑ Ⓒ Ⓓ Ⓔ
1. Ⓐ Ⓑ Ⓒ Ⓓ Ⓔ	3. Ⓐ Ⓑ Ⓒ Ⓓ Ⓔ	15. Ⓐ Ⓑ Ⓒ Ⓓ Ⓔ	6. Ⓐ Ⓑ Ⓒ Ⓓ Ⓔ
2. Ⓐ Ⓑ Ⓒ Ⓓ Ⓔ	4. Ⓐ Ⓑ Ⓒ Ⓓ Ⓔ	16. Ⓐ Ⓑ Ⓒ Ⓓ Ⓔ	7. Ⓐ Ⓑ Ⓒ Ⓓ Ⓔ
3. Ⓐ Ⓑ Ⓒ Ⓓ Ⓔ	5. Ⓐ Ⓑ Ⓒ Ⓓ Ⓔ	17. Ⓐ Ⓑ Ⓒ Ⓓ Ⓔ	8. Ⓐ Ⓑ Ⓒ Ⓓ Ⓔ
4. Ⓐ Ⓑ Ⓒ Ⓓ Ⓔ	6. Ⓐ Ⓑ Ⓒ Ⓓ Ⓔ	18. Ⓐ Ⓑ Ⓒ Ⓓ Ⓔ	9. Ⓐ Ⓑ Ⓒ Ⓓ Ⓔ
5. Ⓐ Ⓑ Ⓒ Ⓓ Ⓔ	7. Ⓐ Ⓑ Ⓒ Ⓓ Ⓔ	19. Ⓐ Ⓑ Ⓒ Ⓓ Ⓔ	10. Ⓐ Ⓑ Ⓒ Ⓓ Ⓔ
6. Ⓐ Ⓑ Ⓒ Ⓓ Ⓔ	8. Ⓐ Ⓑ Ⓒ Ⓓ Ⓔ	20. Ⓐ Ⓑ Ⓒ Ⓓ Ⓔ	11. Ⓐ Ⓑ Ⓒ Ⓓ Ⓔ
7. Ⓐ Ⓑ Ⓒ Ⓓ Ⓔ	9. Ⓐ Ⓑ Ⓒ Ⓓ Ⓔ	21. Ⓐ Ⓑ Ⓒ Ⓓ Ⓔ	12. Ⓐ Ⓑ Ⓒ Ⓓ Ⓔ
			13. Ⓐ Ⓑ Ⓒ Ⓓ Ⓔ

SAT TEST

Time—30 Minutes 25 Questions	In this section solve each problem, using any available space on the page for scratchwork. Then decide which is the best of the choices given and fill in the corresponding oval on the answer sheet.

Notes:
1. The use of a calculator is permitted. All numbers used are real numbers.

2. Figures that accompany problems in this test are intended to provide information useful in solving the problems. They are drawn as accurately as possible EXCEPT when it is stated in a specific problem that the figure is not drawn to scale. All figures lie in a plane unless otherwise indicated.

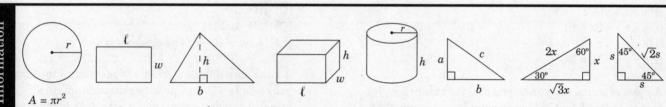
1. $a - b = 2b$ and $b = 2$. What is the value of $2a$?

   (A) 2
   (B) 3
   (C) 6
   (D) 12
   (E) 36

2. If $x = 3$ and $y = x$, what is the value of xy^2?

   (A) 27
   (B) 9
   (C) 6
   (D) 3
   (E) 1

3. In the figure above, if lines a and b are perpendicular, what is the value of x?

   (A) 36
   (B) 54
   (C) 64
   (D) 90
   (E) 180

GO ON TO THE NEXT PAGE

4. What is $\frac{4}{5}$ of $8\frac{1}{3}$?

   (A) $\frac{2}{5}$

   (B) $\frac{3}{4}$

   (C) 2

   (D) $6\frac{2}{3}$

   (E) $8\frac{4}{15}$

5. The sum of x and y is 10 more than 3 times z. Which of the following equations describes the relationship between x, y, and z?

   (A) $x + y = 3(z + 10)$
   (B) $3(x + y) = z$
   (C) $x + y = 3z + 10$
   (D) $x + y = z + 30$
   (E) $x + y + 10 = 3z$

6. A piece of string is x yards long. If it is cut into 5 equal pieces, each 1.5 feet in length, what is x? Assume that no string is left over. (Note: 3 feet = 1 yard.)

   (A) $\frac{1}{2}$

   (B) $\frac{7}{4}$

   (C) 2

   (D) $\frac{5}{2}$

   (E) $\frac{15}{2}$

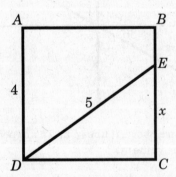

7. If $ABCD$ is a square, what is the value of x?

   (A) 1
   (B) 2
   (C) 3
   (D) 4
   (E) 5

8. For which of the following sets of numbers is the mode equal to the mean?

   (A) {1,2,2,7}
   (B) {1,1,3,7}
   (C) {3,4,4,5}
   (D) {0,1,1,6}
   (E) {-1,-1,3,7}

9. If $\frac{x}{2}$ is an integer, and $x \neq 0$, what must be true of $x^2 - \frac{x}{3}$?

   I.   It is an integer
   II. It is even
   III. It is positive

   (A) I only
   (B) II only
   (C) III only
   (D) I, II, and III
   (E) None of these is necessarily true

10. A gas pump pumps x gallons of gas every y minutes. If gas costs \$$z$ a gallon, and the pump automatically stops after dispensing gas for m minutes, how much does the dispensed gas cost?

   (A) \$ $\frac{mxz}{y}$

   (B) \$ $\frac{mx}{z}$

   (C) \$ $\frac{myz}{x}$

   (D) \$ $\frac{m}{xyz}$

   (E) \$ $\frac{xz}{my}$

11. If $x - y = -2$, what is $(x - y)^3$?

   (A) −8
   (B) −6
   (C) 6
   (D) 8
   (E) 12

GO ON TO THE NEXT PAGE →

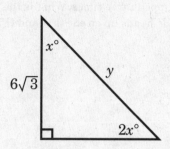

12. What is the value of y?

    (A) $3\sqrt{3}$
    (B) 6
    (C) $6\sqrt{3}$
    (D) 12
    (E) $12\sqrt{3}$

For questions 13–15, let $\bar{n}$ be the sum of the individual digits of n. For example, $\overline{134} = 1 + 3 + 4 = 8$.

13. What is $\dfrac{\overline{4371} - \overline{3441}}{\overline{231}}$?

    (A) 0.25
    (B) 0.5
    (C) 3
    (D) 7
    (E) 12

14. If $\leftarrow n$ means to reverse the order of the digits in n, then what is $\overline{1,234,533,234} - \overline{\leftarrow 1,234,533,234}$?

    (A) −2
    (B) −1
    (C) 0
    (D) 1
    (E) 2

15. If n is an integer and $10 < n < 90$, what is $\overline{(n + 1090)}$?

    (A) n
    (B) $\bar{n}$
    (C) $\overline{n-1}$
    (D) 100
    (E) $\bar{n} + 1$

16. If $x + 2y = 7$ and $x + y = 6$, what is x?

    (A) 1
    (B) 2
    (C) 5
    (D) 6
    (E) 7

17. A line with slope $\dfrac{3}{5}$ passes through $(h,0)$ and $(11h,6)$. What is h?

    (A) $\dfrac{3}{5}$
    (B) 1
    (C) $\dfrac{11}{15}$
    (D) $\dfrac{5}{3}$
    (E) $\dfrac{33}{5}$

18. How many whole numbers between 100 and 500 have a 9 as one or more of its digits?

    (A) 68
    (B) 76
    (C) 80
    (D) 95
    (E) 100

19. If $p < 0$ and $-1 < s < 1$, then what number value for ps^2 is not possible?

    (A) −5
    (B) −1
    (C) −.5
    (D) 0
    (E) .5

20. Two congruent triangles are joined to form a square. If the longest side of each triangle measures $5\sqrt{2}$, what is the area of the square?

    (A) 4
    (B) 5
    (C) 10
    (D) 25
    (E) 50

GO ON TO THE NEXT PAGE

21. John started reading his weekly textbook reading for his government class and finished half of his 120-page assignment in 3 hours. Then his friend showed up, and John became slightly less productive. If during the time his friend was there, he read 5 fewer pages per hour, then how many hours did John take to finish the remaining part of the assignment?

    (A) 2
    (B) 3
    (C) 4
    (D) 5
    (E) 12

22. If the diameter of a right cylinder is 6, and the height of the cylinder is 5, what is the surface area of the cylinder?

    (A) 18π
    (B) 30π
    (C) 38π
    (D) 48π
    (E) 78π

23. For which value of x is $xyz + 2$ equal to $4 - xyz$?

    (A) yz

    (B) $2yz$

    (C) $\dfrac{yz}{2}$

    (D) $\dfrac{1}{yz}$

    (E) $6 + 2yz$

24. A coin is flipped three times. What is the probability that it lands heads up on the first and third flips?

    (A) $\dfrac{1}{8}$

    (B) $\dfrac{1}{4}$

    (C) $\dfrac{1}{2}$

    (D) $\dfrac{3}{4}$

    (E) 1

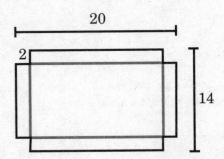

25. The figure above is produced by taking squares of length 2 out of the corners of a rectangle. The resulting figure is then folded along the gray lines in order to form an open box. What is the volume of the box?

    (A) 160
    (B) 280
    (C) 320
    (D) 560
    (E) 480

S T O P

IF YOU FINISH BEFORE TIME IS CALLED, YOU MAY CHECK YOUR WORK IN THIS SECTION ONLY.
DO NOT TURN TO ANY OTHER SECTION IN THE TEST.

SAT TEST

<table>
<tr><td>**Time—30 Minutes**
30 Questions</td><td>For each question in this section, select the best answer from among the choices given and fill in the corresponding oval on the answer sheet.</td></tr>
</table>

Each sentence below has one or two blanks, each blank indicating that something has been omitted. Beneath the sentence are five words or sets of words labeled A through E. Choose the word or set of words that, when inserted in the sentence, <u>best</u> fits the meaning of the sentence as a whole.

Example:
  Medieval kingdoms did not become constitutional republics overnight; on the contrary, the change was ----.

  (A) unpopular
  (B) unexpected
  (C) advantageous
  (D) sufficient
  (E) gradual

1. In *Moby-Dick,* the symbolic meaning of the color white is ----; some readers take it to represent death, some take it to represent divinity.

  (A) beautiful
  (B) ambiguous
  (C) benign
  (D) infinite
  (E) persuasive

2. He had lost money in the stock market before, but he was convinced that his new investments would bring him ----.

  (A) deficit
  (B) profit
  (C) shares
  (D) health
  (E) power

3. Thanks to his many ---- and friendly ----, Henri easily got the job at the new software company.

  (A) connections..evidence
  (B) achievements..demeanor
  (C) flaws..humor
  (D) talents..abandon
  (E) positions..appetite

4. Although Henrietta was quite ----, she was undisciplined and therefore often encountered academic ----.

  (A) intelligent..catastrophe
  (B) lazy..success
  (C) thoughtful..superiority
  (D) uninspired..prowess
  (E) irresponsible..failure

5. It caused a ---- at its premiere, but Stravinsky's "Rite of Spring" no longer seems so audaciously modern; in fact, it is actually quite ---- by the standards of avant-garde music today.

  (A) sensation..shocking
  (B) scandal..tame
  (C) stir..imposing
  (D) backlash..infuriating
  (E) riot..advanced

6. The ---- Supreme Court decision in *Roe v. Wade* for a woman's right to have an abortion continues to divide the United States; there is little common ground between the supporters and opponents of legalized abortion.

  (A) novel
  (B) oblique
  (C) untenable
  (D) controversial
  (E) figurative

GO ON TO THE NEXT PAGE ➔

7. In contrast to his ghost story *A Christmas Carol,* which is brief and tightly organized, Charles Dickens's *David Copperfield,* is ----.

   (A) jovial
   (B) reminiscent
   (C) dubious
   (D) implausible
   (E) sprawling

8. After espousing views inconsistent with official Christian religious doctrine, Joan of Arc was deemed a(n) ---- and subsequently burned at the stake.

   (A) perpetrator
   (B) populist
   (C) executioner
   (D) heretic
   (E) zealot

9. Though often ---- by literary critics, Rod McKuen was ---- by his readers, who made him the most popular poet of the 1960s.

   (A) emasculated..tarnished
   (B) redeemed..celebrated
   (C) denounced..ignored
   (D) derided..venerated
   (E) extolled..loathed

GO ON TO THE NEXT PAGE

Each question below consists of a related pair of words or phrases, followed by five pairs of words or phrases labeled A through E. Select the pair that <u>best</u> expresses a relationship similar to that expressed in the original pair.

Example:
CRUMB : BREAD ::

(A) ounce : unit
(B) splinter : wood
(C) water : bucket
(D) twine : rope
(E) cream : butter

10. DESK : WOOD ::

(A) scissors : metal
(B) balloon : string
(C) car : tires
(D) house : door
(E) paper : notebook

11. EXHAUSTION : SLEEP ::

(A) friendship : amusement
(B) charity : money
(C) power : influence
(D) hunger : food
(E) weariness : time

12. THERMOMETER : TEMPERATURE ::

(A) scale : weight
(B) prediction : weather
(C) ruler : inch
(D) book : pages
(E) clock : hour

13. INSIPID : CONVERSATION ::

(A) enthralling : performance
(B) ambivalent : sermon
(C) intimate : acquaintance
(D) banal : anecdote
(E) specific : example

14. EXPLANATION : CONCISE ::

(A) achievement : minimal
(B) novel : rotund
(C) statement : pithy
(D) manifesto : discomfited
(E) argument : rhetorical

15. REFUGEE : ASYLUM ::

(A) sojourner : haven
(B) recluse : government
(C) artist : portfolio
(D) poet : inspiration
(E) pariah : ostentation

GO ON TO THE NEXT PAGE

SAT TEST

The passage below is followed by questions based on its content. Answer the questions on the basis of what is <u>stated</u> or <u>implied</u> in the passage and in any introductory material that may be provided.

Questions 16–20 are based on the following passage.

In the following passage, the American writer Mark Twain discusses literature and art and the ways in which the two are perceived.

I wonder why some things are? For instance, Art is allowed as much indecent license today as in earlier times—but the privileges of Literature in this respect have been
Line sharply curtailed within the past eighty or ninety years.
5 Fielding and Smollett [*two English writers from the early-seventeenth century*] could portray the beastliness of their day in the beastliest language; we have plenty of foul subjects to deal with in our day, but we are not allowed to approach them very near, even with nice and guarded forms of speech.
10 But not so with Art. The brush may still deal freely with any subject, however revolting or indelicate. It makes a body ooze sarcasm at every pore, to go about Rome and Florence and see what this last generation has been doing with the statues. These works, which had stood in innocent nakedness
15 for ages, are all fig-leaved now. Yes, every one of them. Nobody noticed their nakedness before, perhaps; nobody can help noticing it now, the fig-leaf makes it so conspicuous. But the comical thing about it all, is that the fig leaf is confined to cold and pallid marble, which would be still cold and
20 unsuggestive without this sham and ostentatious symbol of modesty, whereas warm-blooded paintings which do really need it have in no case been furnished with it.
At the door of the Uffizi, in Florence, one is confronted by statues of a man and a woman, noseless, battered, black with
25 accumulated grime—they hardly suggest human beings—yet these ridiculous creatures have been thoughtfully and conscientiously fig-leafed by this fastidious generation. You enter, and proceed to that most-visited little gallery that exists in the world—the Tribune—and there, against the
30 wall, without obstructing rag or leaf, you may look your fill upon the foulest, the vilest, the obscenest picture the world possesses—Titian's *Venus*. It isn't that she is naked and stretched out on a bed—no, it is the attitude of one of her arms and hand. If I ventured to describe that attitude, there
35 would be a fine howl—but there the Venus lies, for anybody to gloat over that wants to—and there she has a right to lie, for she is a work of art, and Art has its privileges. I saw young girls stealing furtive glances at her; I saw young men gaze long and absorbedly at her; I saw aged,
40 infirm men hang upon her charms with a pathetic interest.

How I should like to describe her—just to see what a holy indignation I could stir up in the world—just to hear the
Line unreflecting average man deliver himself about my grossness
45 and coarseness, and all that. The world says that no worded description of a moving spectacle is a hundredth part as moving as the same spectacle seen with one's own eyes—yet the world is willing to let its son and its daughter and itself look at Titian's beast, but won't stand a description of it in
50 words. Which shows that the world is not as consistent as it might be.

16. In line 2, the word "license" is used to mean

(A) a document granting permission to perform a task
(B) immoral excess
(C) freedom from public objection or disapproval
(D) the badge of a bureaucrat
(E) censorship

17. When he describes the era of Fielding and Smollett (lines 5–9), what does Twain imply about the earlier attitude toward Literature?

(A) It was shocking; the earlier age had an immoral tolerance for literature about sin and vice.
(B) It was less advanced than the modern attitude, which protects impressionable children.
(C) It was a product of its time that could not be reproduced in the era in which Twain lived.
(D) It was better; Literature should be allowed to deal with the "foul subjects" of the day.
(E) In the past, people did not think much about morality when they thought about literature.

GO ON TO THE NEXT PAGE

18. In the first and second paragraphs, Twain uses the example of the fig leaves to illustrate

(A) modern society's limited understanding of ancient standards of dress
(B) a possible method for improving the appearance of ancient sculpture when it begins to deteriorate
(C) foods nomads are easily able to find in the desert
(D) different cultural standards with regard to morality and decency in art
(E) the absurd lengths to which people are willing to go to censor "indecent" sculpture

19. In lines 23–28, Twain writes that the statues in front of the Uffizi "hardly seem human" because

(A) they are so abstract
(B) they have deteriorated so much
(C) they are so poorly sculpted
(D) they are made of stone
(E) they are so gigantic

20. Why does Twain argue in lines 50–51 that the world's attitude toward Titian's painting of Venus is not "consistent"?

(A) The world pretends that erotic art is immoral, but then gazes on Titian's erotic painting with unabashed interest.
(B) The world objects to art that it should embrace.
(C) People who pretend to understand the painting are really quite ignorant about art.
(D) The world would censor a written description of the eroticism that it allows the painting to display openly, even though most people say that a picture is more powerful than a written description.
(E) Classical learning, for all its accomplishments, has failed to produce an adequate description of Venus's beauty.

GO ON TO THE NEXT PAGE

Questions 21–30 are based on the following passage.

In the following passage, the author discusses the difference between pure science and applied science, and the moral considerations that must be applied to each.

Pure science is a science of discovery, a science of figuring out the physical, chemical, and biological laws governing the universe. A scientist engaged in pure science gains knowledge of a limited sort. He or she may gain an understanding of the actions of particles under certain circumstances, or of the processes which make up the nitrogen cycle, but a researcher who discovers the why's and how's of scientific laws does not attempt to change those laws. Pure scientific research does not directly change the world and therefore does not impinge on the rights or privacy of particular individuals or communities.

Applied science, in contrast, by its definition involves an effort to harness the knowledge gained by pure science for the purpose of achieving specific ends. Applied science aims to change or affect the world. As a result of this aim, applied science holds the potential to greatly benefit humanity and ease humanity's existence in the world. Yet for precisely the same reason that applied science can be such a boon to mankind, because it attempts to affect or change the world in some way, it also holds the potential to cause great harm, whether that harm is explicit, such as the atomic bomb built specifically to destroy, or more subtle, such as the dangers inherent in nuclear reactors that were once trumpeted as the solution to the energy needs of the future. It is only when science becomes manifest in society through application that it can impinge on human rights.

Such an assertion seems to free pure scientists and pure science from any responsibility to individuals or society: since pure science seeks to map the laws of the universe rather than bend those laws to human will, there is no danger that the attempt might backfire. Of course, the assertion of such a strict separation between pure and applied science is itself open to criticism. But that distinction seems to hold up rather well for the sciences of matter: physics, chemistry, astronomy.

For example, even in the case of atomic physics, the discovery of which led to the development of the atomic bomb, there exists a marked contrast between the initial discovery of fission and the subsequent effort to develop the bomb during World War II. The scientists involved in building the atomic bomb for the United States justified their efforts in a variety of manners, many claiming a moral imperative to finish developing the bomb before fascist Germany. Whether those justifications ring hollow or true is not the issue (at least not here). Rather, the importance lies in the fact that the scientists saw their justifications as necessary at all; such a need for justification indicates the existence of a moral and ethical space around the bomb building process. J. Robert Oppenheimer, who coordinated the project to build the atomic bomb, powerfully referenced that moral dimension by resorting to biblical language, noting that "the physicists have known sin."

In contrast, no moral dimension surrounded the chemist Otto Hahn as he experimented with the idea of nuclear fission in 1938. Hahn, in fact, had created his experiments expressly to disprove the possibility of fission as a natural phenomenon. Hahn could have made no moral judgment about his work because he had no idea what he might find. Hahn was searching for the truth, whereas the scientists working on the bomb were after specific results whose ethical and moral implications could and should have been weighed.

21. The author's tone in this passage is best described as:

    (A) angry
    (B) concerned
    (C) disinterested
    (D) pleased
    (E) disappointed

22. Which of the following is *not* an example of applied science?

    (A) technology
    (B) engineering
    (C) product development
    (D) industrial design
    (E) experimentation

23. The phrase "becomes manifest" in line 25 means:

    (A) becomes obvious in
    (B) is introduced to
    (C) is fated to
    (D) becomes burdensome to
    (E) becomes revolutionary for

24. Lines 31–33 discuss challenges to the author's distinction between pure and applied science in order to:

    (A) weaken the overall argument
    (B) suggest other avenues of exploration
    (C) admit the author's ignorance
    (D) confuse the reader
    (E) preempt disagreement

GO ON TO THE NEXT PAGE

25. The reference to "fascist Germany" in line 43 suggests that:

    (A) applied science is always morally acceptable if it is used to fight fascism
    (B) the only acceptable justifications for applied science are religious ones
    (C) applied science is always appropriate in times of war
    (D) applied science can be vulnerable to political propaganda.
    (E) science should be patriotic

26. The author uses the parenthetical interjection "at least not here" in lines 44–45 to suggest that:

    (A) these particular justifications for building the atomic bomb should be questioned, though the author will not do so in this passage
    (B) any justifications are morally irrelevant
    (C) other essays on this subject concentrate on frivolous matters
    (D) scientists cannot evaluate their own moral reasoning
    (E) applied science needs no justification

27. Which of the following would this author consider an example of pure science?

    (A) researching ways to combat air pollution
    (B) cleaning up hazardous waste
    (C) discovering which rock formations are likely to bear gold
    (D) developing a technique to extract oil from small deposits
    (E) measuring the mass of the earth

28. How would this author feel about an experiment designed to measure the fission rates of various materials?

    (A) This experiment would be pure science and therefore always acceptable.
    (B) The author's feelings would depend on whether the experimenter is aware of potential human uses of fission.
    (C) It depends on the moral worth of the scientist involved.
    (D) This experiment is morally unacceptable.
    (E) The experiment probably would not work.

29. The term "truth" in line 59 means:

    (A) the best way to use scientific discoveries
    (B) the ethical context of scientific knowledge
    (C) the physical laws governing the universe
    (D) an understanding of the scientific method
    (E) the intentions of the scientist performing the experiment

30. Which of the following statements best reflects the author's feelings about applied science?

    (A) It is only objectionable if it involves producing weapons.
    (B) It is always objectionable.
    (C) It has no moral component.
    (D) It is potentially beneficial but its consequences need to be considered.
    (E) All scientific research is useful and desirable.

S T O P

IF YOU FINISH BEFORE TIME IS CALLED, YOU MAY CHECK YOUR WORK IN THIS SECTION ONLY.
DO NOT TURN TO ANY OTHER SECTION IN THE TEST.

SAT TEST

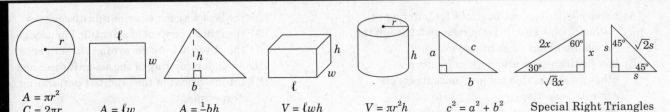
Directions for Quantitative Comparison Questions

Questions 1–15 each consist of two quantities in boxes, one in Column A and one in Column B.
You are to compare the two quantities and on the answer sheet fill in oval

A if the quantity in Column A is greater;
B if the quantity in Column B is greater;
C if the two quantities are equal;
D if the relationship cannot be determined from the information given.

AN E RESPONSE WILL NOT BE SCORED.

Notes:

1. In some questions, information is given about one or both of the quantities to be compared. In such cases, the given information is centered above the two columns and is not boxed.
2. In a given question, a symbol that appears in both columns represents the same thing in Column A as it does in Column B.
3. Letters such as x, n, and k stand for real numbers.

EXAMPLES

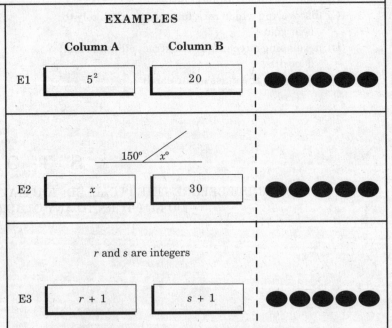

	Column A	Column B	
E1	5^2	20	●●●●●
E2	x	30	●●●●●
E3	$r + 1$	$s + 1$	●●●●●

150° $x°$

r and s are integers

<u>**Column A**</u> <u>**Column B**</u>

$x + 7 = 21$

1.
| x | 13 |

2.

$x = 45$

| x | y |

3.

$x + y = 2$ and $y = 3$

| x | 0 |

4.

$x, y > 3$ and $\frac{x}{y} = 0.75$

| x | y |

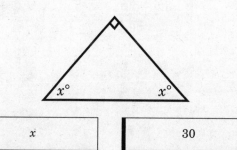

5.
| x | 30 |

<u>**Column A**</u> <u>**Column B**</u>

At a zoo, the number of female gorillas was fewer in 1998 than it was in 1999, but the total number of gorillas in the zoo remained constant.

6.
| The number of male gorillas in the zoo in 1998 | The number of male gorillas in the zoo in 1999 |

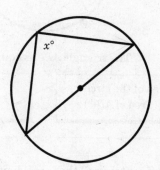

7.
| x | 90 |

$\frac{x}{z} = y$

8.
| $\frac{x}{2zy}$ | $\frac{yz}{4x}$ |

GO ON TO THE NEXT PAGE

Column A   **Column B**

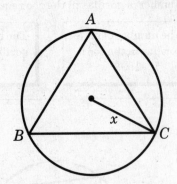

The triangle *ABC* is equilateral.

9. (area of the circle) − (area of *ABC*)   area of *ABC*

Set Z contains all the three-digit numbers that contain two and only two digits equal to 9.

10. The number of three-digit numbers in set Z   27

a, *b*, and *c* are positive numbers.

11. The mean of *a* and *b*   The mean of *a*, *b*, and *c*

Column A   **Column B**

$16 \le 5x + 7 \le 28$

12. *x*   5

27 cubes are stacked to form a large cube.

13. Number of cubes that share a face with the center cube   9

$x + y > 2, m > 1$

14. $(m^2)^{(x+y)}$ $m^2 \times m^{(x+y)}$

$x + y = 6$ and $x^2 - y^2 = 24$

15. $x - y$ 3

GO ON TO THE NEXT PAGE

SAT TEST

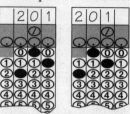
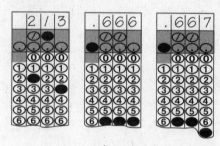
GO ON TO THE NEXT PAGE

16. If $2x + 3y = 0$, what is $6x + 9y - 2$?

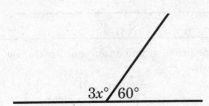

17. In the figure above, what is the value of x?

18. When x is divided by 4 the remainder is 3. When x^2 is divided by 4, what must the remainder be?

19. A publicity manager for a concert collects 3% commission on all ticket sales. If Gregory sells 300 tickets at $10 each, how much money does his publicity manager receive?

20. The mean of $a, b, c,$ and d is 24. The mean of $a, b,$ and c is 20. What is d?

21. What is the area of a square with vertices at $(-1, 3)$, $(2, 3), (2, 0),$ and $(-1, 0)$?

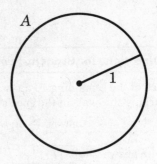

22. A cylinder has circle A as its two bases and a height of 5. What is the surface area of the cylinder?

23. If $\frac{1}{2}xy = \frac{2}{3}yz$, what is $\frac{x}{z}$? Assume that $y \neq 0$ and $z \neq 0$.

24. $(x^a)^b \times (x^2)^3 = x^9$ for any x. What is the value of ab?

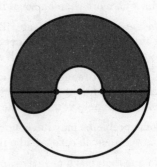

25. If the area of each of the small semicircles is 8π, what is the area of the shaded region divided by π?

S T O P

IF YOU FINISH BEFORE TIME IS CALLED, YOU MAY CHECK YOUR WORK IN THIS SECTION ONLY.
DO NOT TURN TO ANY OTHER SECTION IN THE TEST.

SAT TEST

**Time—30 Minutes
35 Questions**

For each question in this section, select the best answer from among the choices given and fill in the corresponding oval on the answer sheet.

Each sentence below has one or two blanks, each blank indicating that something has been omitted. Beneath the sentence are five words or sets of words labeled A through E. Choose the word or set of words that, when inserted in the sentence, <u>best</u> fits the meaning of the sentence as a whole.

Example:

Medieval kingdoms did not become constitutional republics overnight; on the contrary, the change was ----.

(A) unpopular
(B) unexpected
(C) advantageous
(D) sufficient
(E) gradual

---

1. In all her endeavors, Tamara was a(n) ---- employee: responsible, efficient, and, above all, courteous.

   (A) raucous
   (B) manipulative
   (C) irrelevant
   (D) exemplary
   (E) absorbing

2. The influence of the popular vote on the outcome of a presidential election is ----; it informs the Electoral College, which is the body that actually chooses the new president.

   (A) absolute
   (B) obscure
   (C) arbitrary
   (D) negligible
   (E) indirect

3. The jurors viewed the defendant's refusal to testify at her trial as a(n) ---- acknowledgement of her guilt.

   (A) impartial
   (B) tacit
   (C) undignified
   (D) magnanimous
   (E) tranquil

4. Instead of ---- for his pranks, the character Puck in Shakespeare's *A Midsummer's Night Dream* actually brags about them.

   (A) living
   (B) singing
   (C) striving
   (D) apologizing
   (E) fighting

5. In choosing a president, many Americans are less concerned about intelligence and more interested in ----, basing their votes on issues of character and morality.

   (A) temerity
   (B) exuberance
   (C) irreverence
   (D) gravity
   (E) integrity

6. Terrified of the prospect of war, the ambassador did everything he could to bring about ---- between the two nations.

   (A) ignorance
   (B) violence
   (C) nobility
   (D) prejudice
   (E) reconciliation

GO ON TO THE NEXT PAGE →

7. The author quickly lost sight of his original plan to write a ---- comedy, and instead penned a weighty ---- on a highly tragic theme.

(A) flippant..meditation
(B) maudlin..satire
(C) scintillating..farce
(D) banal..narrative
(E) wretched..proposition

8. The sales representative was expected to ---- the whole district, seeking orders from each new business.

(A) discern
(B) canvass
(C) validate
(D) incorporate
(E) castigate

9. Ignorant of the most basic social ----, Paul offended even the most forgiving host with his ---- table manners.

(A) conventions..refined
(B) graces..resplendent
(C) vicissitudes..deleterious
(D) precepts..atrocious
(E) expropriations..portentous

10. Many modern artists admire the delicate techniques Leonardo da Vinci employed in his paintings, but very few of them go so far as to ---- them in their own work.

(A) emulate
(B) inoculate
(C) rhapsodize
(D) vivify
(E) undermine

GO ON TO THE NEXT PAGE

Each question below consists of a related pair of words or phrases, followed by five pairs of words or phrases labeled A through E. Select the pair that best expresses a relationship similar to that expressed in the original pair.

Example:
CRUMB : BREAD ::

(A) ounce : unit
(B) splinter : wood
(C) water : bucket
(D) twine : rope
(E) cream : butter

11. SAW : WOOD ::

(A) pen : ink
(B) lamp : bulb
(C) scissors : paper
(D) sink : water
(E) keyboard : piano

12. COMMUTERS : SUBWAY ::

(A) water : reservoir
(B) airplane : passengers
(C) smoke : fire
(D) cargo : freighter
(E) tree : park

13. INTELLIGENCE : GENIUS ::

(A) talent : artist
(B) wealth : billionaire
(C) autocrat : power
(D) enemy : clash
(E) insurrection : rebelliousness

14. EULOGY : FUNERAL ::

(A) ceremony : wedding
(B) toast : celebration
(C) announcement : event
(D) birth : infant
(E) poem : lyric

15. ABRADE : SMOOTH ::

(A) endanger : hazardous
(B) map : navigable
(C) convince : persuasive
(D) desiccate : arid
(E) liquefy : solid

16. ENFRANCHISEMENT : VOTE ::

(A) verdict : appeal
(B) suffrage : women
(C) emancipation : liberty
(D) abolition : slavery
(E) protest : polemics

17. CALENDAR : MONTH ::

(A) day : afternoon
(B) team : player
(C) class : textbook
(D) police : chief
(E) watch : hand

18. FIRE : INFERNO ::

(A) pole : ice
(B) exigence : discipline
(C) fight : war
(D) drove : herd
(E) filter : cigarette

19. FRAUD : CRIME ::

(A) cruelty : tyranny
(B) psychosis : disorder
(C) desert : irrigate
(D) banishment : exile
(E) oscillate : indecision

20. PHILANTHROPIST : CHARITY ::

(A) hindsight : scholar
(B) landlord : business
(C) inoculation : disease
(D) farmer : horticulturalist
(E) guerilla : terrorism

21. PROTOTYPE : AUTOMOBILE ::

(A) photocopy : document
(B) blueprint : building
(C) fingerprint : individual
(D) frontispiece : volume
(E) hypothesis : experiment

GO ON TO THE NEXT PAGE

22. LETHARGY : RAMBUNCTIOUS ::

    (A) rumination : thoughtless
    (B) energy : excitable
    (C) exhaustion : sluggish
    (D) religion : saintly
    (E) blossom : floral

23. QUERULOUS : MEDIATE ::

    (A) assiduous : occupy
    (B) serpentine : uncoil
    (C) gregarious : socialize
    (D) sedate : invigorate
    (E) auspicious : commemorate

GO ON TO THE NEXT PAGE

SAT TEST

Questions 24–35 are based on the following passage.

The passage below is excerpted from an essay written by Theodore Roosevelt after he attended an art exhibit in New York. The essay was published in 1913.

The recent "International Exhibition of Modern Art" in New York was really noteworthy. Davies, Kuhn, Gregg, and their fellow members of the Association of American Painters and Sculptors did a work of very real value in securing such
Line
5 an exhibition of the works of both foreign and native painters and sculptors. Primarily their purpose was to give the public a chance to see what has recently been going on abroad. No similar collection of the works of European "moderns" has ever been exhibited in this country. The exhibitors were quite
10 right as to the need of showing our people in this manner the art forces which of late have been at work in Europe, forces which cannot be ignored.

This does not mean that I in the least accept the view that these men take of the European extremists whose
15 pictures were here exhibited. It is true, as the champions of these extremists say, that there can be no life without change, no development without change, and that to be afraid of what is different or unfamiliar is to be afraid of life. It is no less true, however, that change may mean death and
20 not life, and retrogression instead of development.

Probably we err in treating most of these pictures seriously. It is likely that many of them represent in the painters the astute appreciation of the power to make folly lucrative which the late P. T. Barnum [*P.T. Barnum was the*
25 *owner of Barnum and Bailey Circus*] showed with his fake mermaid. There are thousands of people who will pay small sums to look at a fake mermaid; and now and then one of this kind with enough money will buy a Cubist picture, or a picture of a misshapen nude woman, repellent from every
30 standpoint.

In some ways it is the work of the American painters and sculptors which is of most interest in this collection, and a glance at this work must convince anyone of the good that is coming out of the new movements, fantastic though many of
35 the developments of these new movements are. There was one note entirely absent from the exhibition, and that was the note of the commonplace. There was not a touch of simpering, self-satisfied conventionality anywhere in the exhibition. Any sculptor or painter who had in him
40 something to express and the power of expressing it found the field open to him. He did not have to be afraid because his work was not along ordinary lines. There was no stunting or

Line
45 dwarfing, no requirement that a man whose gift lay in new directions should measure up or down to stereotyped and fossilized standards.

For all of this there can be only hearty praise. But this does not in the least mean that the extremists whose paintings and pictures were represented are entitled to any
50 praise, save, perhaps, that they have helped to break fetters. Probably, in any reform movement, any progressive movement, in any field of life, the penalty for avoiding the commonplace is a liability to extravagance. It is vitally necessary to move forward and to shake off the dead hand,
55 often the fossilized dead hand, of the reactionaries; and yet we have to face the fact that there is apt to be a lunatic fringe among the devotees of any forward movement. In this recent art exhibition the lunatic fringe was fully in evidence, especially in the rooms devoted to the Cubists and the
60 Futurists, or Near-Impressionists. I am not entirely certain which of the two latter terms should be used in connection with some of the various pictures and representations of plastic art, and, frankly, it is not of the least consequence.

The Cubists are entitled to the serious attention of all
65 who find enjoyment in the colored puzzle-pictures of the Sunday newspapers. Of course there is no reason for choosing the cube as a symbol, except that it is probably less fitted than any other mathematical statement for any but the most formal decorative art. There is no reason why people should
70 not call themselves Cubists, or Octagonists, or Parallelopipedonists, or Knights of the Isosceles Triangle, or Brothers of the Cosine, if they so desire; as expressing anything serious and permanent, one term is as fatuous as another. Take the picture which for some reason is called "A
75 Naked Man Going Down Stairs." There is in my bathroom a really good Navajo rug which, on any proper interpretation of the Cubist theory, is a far more satisfactory and decorative picture. Now, if, for some inscrutable reason, it suited somebody to call this rug a picture of, say, "A Well-Dressed
80 Man Going Up a Ladder," the name would fit the facts just about as well as in the case of the Cubist picture of the "Naked Man Going Down Stairs." From the standpoint of terminology, each name would have whatever merit gleaned in a rather cheap straining for effect; and from the
85 standpoint of decorative value, of sincerity, and of artistic merit, the Navajo rug is infinitely ahead of the picture.

24. Which of the following statements best describes Roosevelt's attitude toward change as stated in the second paragraph of the passage?

    (A) Change is necessary but should be undertaken carefully.
    (B) Change is always positive.
    (C) Change is only good if it is reactionary.
    (D) Change is a European phenomenon.
    (E) Change is usually a bad thing.

25. By saying that "[p]robably we err in treating most of these pictures seriously" in lines 21–22 Roosevelt means that:

    (A) these paintings belong in museums and not private homes
    (B) the painters wanted to convey generally lighthearted messages through their paintings despite popular interpretation
    (C) people shouldn't pay too much for these paintings
    (D) these paintings are more important as examples of current artistic trends than as serious and timeless pieces of art
    (E) the people who put together the exhibition have bad taste

26. Roosevelt's references the legendary circus owner P.T. Barnum in the third paragraph to suggest that:

    (A) art has no commercial value
    (B) both art and circuses exploit women
    (C) low quality entertainment often sells quite well, so sales shouldn't be a factor in identifying great art
    (D) it is better to go to the circus than to buy these paintings
    (E) these paintings depict circus scenes

27. The author's tone in the third paragraph of the passage can best be described as:

    (A) optimistic
    (B) parodic
    (C) foreboding
    (D) confused
    (E) knowledgeable

28. Which of the following statements best describes the relationship between American and European artists?

    (A) European artists are more innovative than American artists.
    (B) American artists have better technical skills than European artists.
    (C) The work of both American and European artists breaks with convention.
    (D) Modern art is more successful commercially in Europe.
    (E) Europeans have been producing modern art for longer than Americans.

29. Which of the following best expresses the meaning of the word "fantastic" in line 34?

    (A) outrageous and excessive
    (B) wonderful and exciting
    (C) likely to appeal to new fans
    (D) based on fantasy
    (E) welcome and well-thought-out

30. Roosevelt uses the term "fossilized" in addition to the term "dead hand" in line 55 to do all of the following *except*:

    (A) Emphasize how long it has been since change has occurred.
    (B) Suggest that, although the old ways were once vital, renewal is necessary.
    (C) Suggest a connection to science.
    (D) Emphasize the weight of the past.
    (E) Reiterate that the bonds of the past, like stone, are difficult to shatter.

31. The author's tone in lines 64–74 can best be described as:

    (A) contemplative
    (B) suggestive
    (C) disappointed
    (D) bored
    (E) sarcastic

GO ON TO THE NEXT PAGE

32. Roosevelt uses the comparison in lines 75–86 between the Cubist painting and the Navajo rug primarily to:

    (A) illustrate the aesthetic qualities he values in art
    (B) belittle the Navajo rug
    (C) suggest all art should be utilitarian
    (D) claim that the painting should be walked on
    (E) argue about the definition of American art

33. In the final paragraph, Roosevelt's discussion of the painting's title implies primarily that:

    (A) the picture is wrongly titled
    (B) paintings shouldn't have titles
    (C) the Navajo rug looks more like the subject of the picture's title than the painting does
    (D) he believes that art should be realistic
    (E) the titles of pictures should be made up by viewers

34. Roosevelt finds the art exhibition noteworthy mainly for

    (A) the artistic talent on view
    (B) its inclusion of both American and European artists
    (C) its emphasis on Cubist art
    (D) its rejection of the commonplace
    (E) its convenient location in New York City

35. Roosevelt is primarily concerned with:

    (A) art
    (B) progress
    (C) the relationship between Europe and America
    (D) nomenclature
    (E) anthropology

S T O P

IF YOU FINISH BEFORE TIME IS CALLED, YOU MAY CHECK YOUR WORK IN THIS SECTION ONLY.
DO NOT TURN TO ANY OTHER SECTION IN THE TEST.

SAT TEST

**Time—15 Minutes
10 Questions**

In this section solve each problem, using any available space on the page for scratchwork. Then decide which is the best of the choices given and fill in the corresponding oval on the answer sheet.

Notes:
1. The use of a calculator is permitted. All numbers used are real numbers.

2. Figures that accompany problems in this test are intended to provide information useful in solving the problems. They are drawn as accurately as possible EXCEPT when it is stated in a specific problem that the figure is not drawn to scale. All figures lie in a plane unless otherwise indicated.

Reference Information

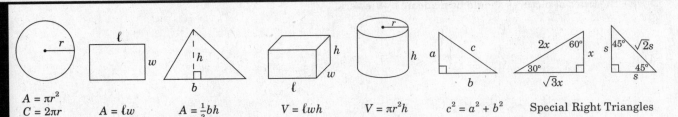

$A = \pi r^2$
$C = 2\pi r$ $A = \ell w$ $A = \frac{1}{2}bh$ $V = \ell w h$ $V = \pi r^2 h$ $c^2 = a^2 + b^2$ Special Right Triangles

The number of degrees of arc in a circle is 360.
The measure in degrees of a straight angle is 180.
The sum of the measures in degrees of the angles of a triangle is 180.

1. Britney pays a total of $18.50 for a compact disc and a book. If the price of the book is $5.50 less than the price of the compact disc, how much does the compact disc cost?

   (A) $11.00
   (B) $12.00
   (C) $12.50
   (D) $13.50
   (E) $14.00

2. If $\frac{t}{y} = t$, what is $3y$? Assume that $t \neq 0$.

   (A) 0
   (B) 1
   (C) 3
   (D) t
   (E) 3t

3. $\sqrt{xyz} = (xyz)^{2m}$. What is the value of m? Assume that x, y, and z are all positive.

   (A) $\frac{1}{16}$

   (B) $\frac{1}{4}$

   (C) $\frac{1}{2}$

   (D) 1

   (E) 4

GO ON TO THE NEXT PAGE

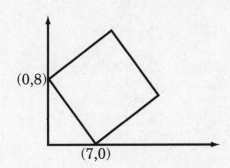

(0,8)

(7,0)

4. What is the area of the square pictured above?

(A) 49
(B) 56
(C) 64
(D) 112
(E) 113

Questions 5–6 refer to the following chart.

JOB PERFORMANCE RATINGS			
Worker	Period 1	Period 2	Period 3
Ray	△	△	△
Glenn	▽	☐	△
Sam	☐	△	△
Tim	▽	☐	△
Ervin	▽	☐	▽

Rating System: △ Excellent
                ☐ Fair
                ▽ Poor

5. Five workers, Ray, Glenn, Sam, Tim, and Ervin, have had their performance rated during three different time periods using the scale shown above. How many of these workers improved their performances between period one and period three?

(A) 0
(B) 1
(C) 2
(D) 3
(E) 4

6. Suppose a poor rating is worth one point, a fair rating is worth two points, and an excellent rating is worth three points. What is the average number of points scored by the five workers in period two?

(A) 0.8
(B) 2.2
(C) 2.4
(D) 2.6
(E) 12

1, 2, 4, 7, 13, ...

7. The first five terms of a sequence are shown above. After the third term, each term is equal to the sum of the three terms immediately preceding it. The difference between the eighth and seventh terms is equal to the difference between which two other terms?

(A) The ninth and eighth terms
(B) The thirteenth and tenth terms
(C) The twenty-first and fifteenth terms
(D) The seventh and fourth terms
(E) The sixth and second terms

8. If $x + y + z = 10$, $x + y = 3$, and $y + z = 8$, what is y?

(A) –5
(B) –1
(C) 1
(D) 2
(E) 5

9. The short side of the rectangle above is 16. The radius of each semicircle is half the length of the short side of the rectangle. What is the area of the shaded region?

(A) $32 – 16\pi$
(B) $128 – 16\pi$
(C) $512 – 128\pi$
(D) $32\pi – 16$
(E) $32\pi – 256$

GO ON TO THE NEXT PAGE →

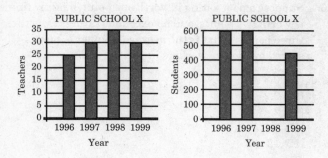

10. The two graphs above illustrate the teacher and student populations at Public School X from 1996 through 1999. The student population in 1998, however, is unknown. Suppose that the student-to-teacher ratio at Public School X dropped in each year from 1996 through 1999. Which of the following could be the 1998 student population?

(A) 400
(B) 500
(C) 600
(D) 700
(E) 800

S T O P

IF YOU FINISH BEFORE TIME IS CALLED, YOU MAY CHECK YOUR WORK IN THIS SECTION ONLY.
DO NOT TURN TO ANY OTHER SECTION IN THE TEST.

SAT TEST

**Time—15 Minutes
13 Questions**

For each question in this section, select the best answer from among the choices given and fill in the corresponding oval on the answer sheet.

The two passages below are followed by questions based on their content and on the relationship between the passages. Answer the questions on the basis of what is <u>stated</u> or <u>implied</u> in the passages and in any introductory material that may be provided.

Questions 1–13 are based on the following passages.

Hamlet, published in 1603, was written by William Shakespeare. The play tells the story of Hamlet, a prince of Denmark, whose father dies and whose mother quickly remarries her former husband's brother, Claudius. Soon after the marriage, Hamlet encounters his father's ghost, who claims to have been murdered by Claudius and demands that Hamlet take revenge. Yet Hamlet hesitates to take action. The passages below are adaptations of two essays that discuss Hamlet's psychology.

Passage 1

The death of Hamlet's father was a natural evil, and as such he endures it. That he is excluded by his mother's
Line marriage from succeeding immediately to the royalty that
5 belongs to him seems to affect him slightly; he seems above vehemence and vain ambition. He is moved by finer principles, by an exquisite sense of virtue and moral beauty. The impropriety of Gertrude's behavior, her ingratitude to the memory of her former husband, and the depravity she
10 displays in the choice of a successor afflict Hamlet's soul and cast him into utter agony. Here then is the principle and spring of all his actions.

The man whose sense of moral excellence is uncommonly exquisite will find it a source of pleasure and of pain in his
15 commerce with mankind. Susceptible to every moral impression, he delights at the display of virtuous actions, and the contrary excite uneasiness.

The triumph and inward joy of a son, on account of the fame and high desert of a parent, is by nature very sublime
20 and tender. His sorrow is no less acute and overwhelming if those connected to him by such intimate relations have acted unbecomingly and incurred disgrace. Such is the condition of Hamlet. Exquisitely sensible of moral beauty and deformity, he discerns depravity in Gertrude, his mother. Led by the
25 same moral principle to admire and glory in the high desert of his father, even this admiration contributes to his uneasiness. Aversion to his uncle, arising from the same origin, augments his anguish.

Agitated and overwhelmed with afflicting images, no
30 soothing, no exhilarating affection can have admission into his heart. His imagination is visited by no vision of happiness; and he wishes for deliverance from his afflictions, by being delivered from a painful existence.

Passage 2

Of all the characters of Shakespeare, that of Hamlet has been generally thought the most difficult to be reduced to any
Line fixed or settled principle. With the strongest purposes of
5 revenge, he is irresolute and inactive; amidst the gloom of deepest melancholy, he is gay and jocular; and while he is described as a passionate lover, he seems indifferent about the object of his affections. It may be worthwhile to inquire whether any leading idea can be found, upon which these
10 apparent contradictions may be reconciled. I will venture to lay before my readers some observations on this subject.

The basis of Hamlet's character seems to be an extreme sensibility of mind, apt to be strongly impressed by its situation, and overpowered by the feelings which that situation excites.
15 Naturally a virtuous man, Hamlet finds himself in circumstances which unhinge his noble principles of action, which, in another situation, would have delighted mankind, and made himself happy. That kind of distress which he suffered was, beyond all others, calculated to produce this effect. His
20 misfortunes were not the misfortunes of accident, which, though they may overwhelm at first, the mind will soon call up reflection to alleviate, and hopes to cheer: they were such as reflection only serves to irritate, such as rankle in the soul's tenderest part; they arose from an uncle's villainy, a mother's guilt, a father's murder!
25 Yet, amidst the gloom of melancholy, and the agitation of passion, in which his calamities involve him, there are occasional breakings-out of a mind richly endowed by nature. We perceive gentleness in his demeanor, wit in his conversation, taste in his amusements, and wisdom in his reflections.

30 That Hamlet's character, thus formed by nature, and thus modeled by situation, is often variable and uncertain, I am not disposed to deny. I will content myself with the supposition that this is the very character which Shakespeare meant to give Hamlet. Finding such a character
35 in real life, of a person endowed with feelings so delicate as to border on weakness, with sensibility too exquisite to allow for determined action, he has placed it where it could be best exhibited, in scenes of wonder, of terror, and of indignation, where its varying emotions might be most strongly marked
40 amidst the workings of imagination, and the war of passions.

This management of the character creates in us the most interest in his behalf. Had Shakespeare made Hamlet pursue his vengeance with a steady determined purpose, had he led him through difficulties arising from accidental causes, and not
45 from the doubts and hesitations of his own mind, the anxiety of the spectator might have been highly raised; but it would have been anxiety for the event, not for the person. As it is, we feel not only the virtues, but the weakness of Hamlet, as our own.

1. According to Passage 1, what is the general cause of Hamlet's unhappiness?

   (A) his psychological instability, which prevents him from being able to act
   (B) his intense jealousy that his uncle inherited the throne after his father died
   (C) his essential cowardice, combined with a powerful desire not to seem cowardly to those around him
   (D) his grief over his father's death
   (E) his acute moral sensitivity, aggravated by his reactions to the behavior of his parents and his uncle

2. According to the author of Passage 1, what exactly does Gertrude do to disturb Hamlet so greatly (lines 7–10)?

   (A) She knowingly marries the man who murdered his father.
   (B) She fails to honor his father's memory, and exhibits very poor judgment in choosing a new husband.
   (C) She demonstrates that it was only the example of his father that kept her behavior in check.
   (D) She begins to abuse her power over the common people.
   (E) She supports Claudius's attempt to take over the throne of Denmark.

3. What is the meaning of the word "commerce" in Passage 1, line 14?

   (A) economic activity
   (B) salesmanship
   (C) moral judgment
   (D) interaction with other people
   (E) emotional response

4. What is the logical implication of the author's observation about a child's reactions to his parents' behavior in Passage 1, lines 18–20?

   (A) A sensitive child will feel intense pride or shame based on the moral worth of his or her parents.
   (B) An intelligent child will realize that the behavior of parents does not always reflect on their child.
   (C) A child will be quick to seek revenge on anyone who insults or·injures a beloved parent.
   (D) Children always have strong feelings about their parents.
   (E) Parents do not always think of their children's feelings before they act.

5. How would you describe the author's tone in the final paragraph of Passage 1 (lines 28–32)?

   (A) defiant
   (B) dramatic and descriptive
   (C) measured and scholarly
   (D) resigned
   (E) confrontational

6. In Passage 2, line 5, what is "jocular" used to mean?

   (A) morbid, melancholy
   (B) violent, confrontational
   (C) giddy, happy
   (D) vengeful
   (E) confused, inactive

7. In the second paragraph of Passage 2 (lines 12–16), what two kinds of misfortune does the author compare?

   (A) misfortunes that one can remedy and misfortunes that one can do nothing about
   (B) misfortunes arising from accidental circumstance and misfortunes arising from the intentionally wicked behavior of others
   (C) misfortunes whose effect is detrimental to all concerned and misfortunes that harm some and benefit others
   (D) misfortunes that cause frustration and misfortunes that cause despair
   (E) misfortunes caused by others and misfortunes that one brings upon oneself

8. According to lines 34–40 in Passage 2, why might Shakespeare have chosen to make Hamlet's character so inconsistent and variable?

   (A) Shakespeare was attempting to portray his idea of psychological complexity, which involved self-contradiction.
   (B) The demands of the plot required the main character to act one way at one time, and another way at another time.
   (C) It was necessary to provide comic relief in the intensely disturbing story.
   (D) He wanted to make Hamlet puzzling and mysterious to his audience.
   (E) Shakespeare observed similar traits in real individuals and chose to examine them on the stage.

GO ON TO THE NEXT PAGE

9. According to the final paragraph of Passage 2 (lines 41–48), what does Shakespeare do to make us feel Hamlet's strengths and weaknesses "as our own"?

   (A) He makes Hamlet struggle against his own thoughts and feelings, rather than against outer events.
   (B) He makes all the characters around Hamlet seem suspect, so that Hamlet is the only person with whom the reader can identify.
   (C) He imbues Hamlet's personal struggles with deep truths common to all human experience.
   (D) He makes Hamlet the victim of fate rather than the victim of circumstance.
   (E) He portrays the moral universe of the play in very stark terms of good and evil, so that all viewers will be drawn to one side or the other.

10. According to Passage 2, what is the main cause of Hamlet's inability to act on his desire for revenge?

   (A) His moral awareness causes him to deliberate endlessly on the moral questions involved in killing Claudius.
   (B) Despite the pain she has caused him, he still loves his mother too much to kill her husband.
   (C) He worries that, in killing Claudius, he would lower himself to Claudius's level, and be no better than a common murderer.
   (D) He is acutely hurt by his family's traumatic situation, and his natural inconsistency to rise to the fore.
   (E) He is naturally fearful, and worries about the repercussions of killing the King of Denmark.

11. What aspect of Hamlet's character, very important to the author of Passage 2, does the author of Passage 1 fail to address?

   (A) Hamlet's violent temper
   (B) Hamlet's sensitivity to his family's behavior
   (C) Hamlet's variable, inconstant behavior
   (D) Hamlet's melancholy mood
   (E) Hamlet's temptation to sin

12. What do both passages indicate about Hamlet's mother?

   (A) She has been a moral example for Hamlet.
   (B) She is a beloved figure in Denmark.
   (C) She is innocent of Hamlet's father's death.
   (D) She deeply loves Claudius, her new husband.
   (E) She behaves immorally and inappropriately.

13. What is the main difference between the two passages' descriptions of Hamlet's sensitivity?

   (A) Passage 1 emphasizes Hamlet's sensitivity to the behavior of his mother, father, and uncle, while Passage 2 focuses on his sensitivity to his own feelings.
   (B) Passage 1 argues that Hamlet's sensitivity is a result of his basic nature, while Passage 2 claims that it is a result of the hardships he has suffered.
   (C) Passage 1 is concerned with Hamlet's sensitivity to beauty, while Passage 2 is concerned with his sensitivity to insults and injuries.
   (D) Passage 1 discusses Hamlet's sensitivity to moral behavior, while Passage 2 simply discusses Hamlet's sensitivity to events in general.
   (E) Passage 1 explores the effects of Hamlet's sensitivity, while Passage 2 explores its causes.

S T O P

IF YOU FINISH BEFORE TIME IS CALLED, YOU MAY CHECK YOUR WORK IN THIS SECTION ONLY.
DO NOT TURN TO ANY OTHER SECTION IN THE TEST.

SAT Practice Test 2 Explanations

Answers to SAT Practice Test 2

Test 2 Explanations

Question Number	Correct Answer	Right	Wrong
Math Section 1			
1.	D	——	——
2.	A	——	——
3.	B	——	——
4.	D	——	——
5.	C	——	——
6.	D	——	——
7.	C	——	——
8.	C	——	——
9.	C	——	——
10.	A	——	——
11.	A	——	——
12.	D	——	——
13.	B	——	——
14.	C	——	——
15.	E	——	——
16.	C	——	——
17.	B	——	——
18.	B	——	——
19.	E	——	——
20.	D	——	——
21.	C	——	——
22.	D	——	——
23.	D	——	——
24.	B	——	——
25.	C	——	——
Verbal Section 1			
1.	B	——	——
2.	B	——	——
3.	B	——	——
4.	A	——	——
5.	B	——	——
6.	D	——	——
7.	E	——	——
8.	D	——	——
9.	D	——	——
10.	A	——	——
11.	D	——	——
12.	A	——	——
13.	D	——	——
14.	C	——	——
15.	A	——	——
16.	C	——	——
17.	D	——	——
18.	E	——	——
19.	B	——	——
20.	D	——	——
21.	B	——	——
22.	E	——	——
23.	B	——	——

Question Number	Correct Answer	Right	Wrong
Verbal Section 1			
24.	E	——	——
25.	D	——	——
26.	A	——	——
27.	E	——	——
28.	B	——	——
29.	C	——	——
30.	D	——	——
Math Section 2			
1.	A	——	——
2.	C	——	——
3.	B	——	——
4.	B	——	——
5.	A	——	——
6.	A	——	——
7.	C	——	——
8.	A	——	——
9.	A	——	——
10.	B	——	——
11.	D	——	——
12.	B	——	——
13.	B	——	——
14.	A	——	——
15.	A	——	——
16.	−2	——	——
17.	40	——	——
18.	1	——	——
19.	90	——	——
20.	36	——	——
21.	9	——	——
22.	37.6	——	——
23.	4/3	——	——
24.	3	——	——
25.	80	——	——
Verbal Section 2			
1.	D	——	——
2.	E	——	——
3.	B	——	——
4.	D	——	——
5.	E	——	——
6.	E	——	——
7.	A	——	——
8.	B	——	——
9.	D	——	——
10.	A	——	——
11.	C	——	——
12.	D	——	——
13.	B	——	——

Question Number	Correct Answer	Right	Wrong
Verbal Section 2			
14.	B	——	——
15.	E	——	——
16.	C	——	——
17.	B	——	——
18.	C	——	——
19.	B	——	——
20.	E	——	——
21.	B	——	——
22.	A	——	——
23.	D	——	——
24.	A	——	——
25.	D	——	——
26.	C	——	——
27.	E	——	——
28.	C	——	——
29.	A	——	——
30.	C	——	——
31.	E	——	——
32.	A	——	——
33.	D	——	——
34.	D	——	——
35.	B	——	——
Math Section 3			
1.	B	——	——
2.	C	——	——
3.	B	——	——
4.	E	——	——
5.	D	——	——
6.	C	——	——
7.	D	——	——
8.	C	——	——
9.	C	——	——
10.	C	——	——
Verbal Section 3			
1.	E	——	——
2.	B	——	——
3.	D	——	——
4.	A	——	——
5.	B	——	——
6.	C	——	——
7.	B	——	——
8.	E	——	——
9.	A	——	——
10.	D	——	——
11.	C	——	——
12.	E	——	——
13.	D	——	——

Calculating Your SAT Score

Your raw score for SAT is a composite of your verbal and math raw scores. The raw scores of each section translate into a scaled score from 200 to 800. You can find your scaled scores for both verbal and math by checking the conversion table on page 350.

Your total SAT scaled score is the sum or your scaled math and verbal scores.

To Calculate Your Verbal Raw Score

The number of sentence completions, analogies, and reading comprehension questions you answered

$$\underset{\text{Correctly}}{\underline{\hspace{3cm}}} - (\frac{1}{4} \times \underset{\text{Incorrectly}}{\underline{\hspace{3cm}}}) = \underset{\text{A}}{\underline{\hspace{3cm}}}$$

Round the number in field A. This is your verbal raw score: $\underset{\text{B}}{\underline{\hspace{3cm}}}$

To Calculate Your Math Raw Score

The number of normal multiple-choice questions you answered

$$\underset{\text{Correctly}}{\underline{\hspace{3cm}}} - (\frac{1}{4} \times \underset{\text{Incorrectly}}{\underline{\hspace{3cm}}}) = \underset{\text{C}}{\underline{\hspace{3cm}}}$$

The number of quantitative comparisons you answered

$$\underset{\text{Correctly}}{\underline{\hspace{3cm}}} - (\frac{1}{4} \times \underset{\text{Incorrectly}}{\underline{\hspace{3cm}}}) = \underset{\text{D}}{\underline{\hspace{3cm}}}$$

The number of grid-ins you answered

$$\underset{\text{Correctly}}{\underline{\hspace{3cm}}} = \underset{\text{E}}{\underline{\hspace{3cm}}}$$

Add the numbers in fields C, D, and E = $\underset{\text{F}}{\underline{\hspace{3cm}}}$

Round the number in field F. This is your math raw score: $\underset{\text{G}}{\underline{\hspace{3cm}}}$

Math Section 1

1. **(D)** Algebra: Substitution   Difficulty: low

To solve this problem, first solve for a in terms of b and then substitute $b = 2$ to find a numeric value for a:

$$a - b = 2b$$
$$a = 3b$$
$$a = 3 \times 2$$
$$a = 6$$

From here, the solution is straightforward: $2a = 12$.

2. **(A)** Algebra: Substitution   Difficulty: low

Let's first replace all occurrences of y with x, since we have a value for x. We can rewrite the equation as follows:

$$xy^2 =$$
$$xx^2 =$$
$$x^3 =$$

Since we are given that $x = 3$, we can simply calculate that $3^3 = 27$.

3. **(B)** Geometry: Angles and Lines   Difficulty: low

Because a and b are perpendicular, the four angles formed by their intersection are right angles, or 90°. x is equal to the angle directly across from it (which we will call y), because x and y are opposite angles. Finally, we know that $y + 36 = 90$, because $\angle y$ and the 36° angle are complementary. We can see that $y = 54$ and therefore that x must also be equal to 54.

4. **(D)** Arithmetic: Fractions, Decimals, and Percents   Difficulty: low

To find the answer, you must first convert the mixed number $8\frac{1}{3}$ to an improper fraction by multiplying the denominator by the whole number and adding the numerator: $8\frac{1}{3} = (8 \times 3 + 1)/3$.

To find $\frac{4}{5}$ of $\frac{25}{3}$, we simply multiply the two fractions: $\frac{4}{5} \times \frac{25}{3}$. We can cancel terms to get $\frac{4}{1} \times \frac{5}{3} = \frac{20}{3}$. $\frac{20}{3}$ is not an answer choice, but we can convert this improper fraction to a mixed number by dividing 20 by 3 to get $6\frac{2}{3}$.

5. **(C)** Algebra: Building Expressions and Equations   Difficulty: low
This problem requires you to transform a mathematical description into an equation. The left side of the equation is "the sum of x and y," which can be written as $x + y$. The right side of the equation is "10 more than 3 times z," which can be written as $3z + 10$. The correct equation is $x + y = 3z + 10$.

6. **(D)** Arithmetic: Fractions, Decimals, and Percents   Difficulty: low
To figure out the length of the string, simply multiply the length of each piece by the number of equal pieces: $5 \times 1.5 = 7.5$ feet. Of course, the answer choices are in yards, so we need to convert 7.5 feet into yards by dividing by 3: $7.5 \div 3 = 2.5$ or $\frac{5}{2}$.

7. **(C)** Geometry: Polygons   Difficulty: medium
Because $ABCD$ is a square, we know that the length of side $\overline{CD}$ is equal to 4. ECD is a right triangle because all of the angles in a square are right angles. We also know that $\overline{ED}$, which equals 5, is the hypotenuse because it is the side opposite the right angle. With this information, we can use the Pythagorean Theorem to show that x must equal 3. You could have skipped the last step if you had recognized this as a 3:4:5 triangle.

8. **(C)** Arithmetic: Mean, Median, and Mode   Difficulty: low
The mean of a set of numbers is calculated by dividing the sum of the numbers by the number of elements in the set. The mode of a set of numbers is the element that occurs most frequently. Only in (C), where the mean and mode are 4, are they equal.

9. **(C)** Arithmetic: Definitions and Properties   Difficulty: medium
The first step in solving this problem is determining as much as possible about x. We can deduce that it is a non-zero even integer, though we do not know whether it is positive or negative. Now let's consider the three statements.

1. Is $x^2 - \frac{x}{3}$ an integer? x^2 is certainly an integer, but $\frac{x}{3}$ is not necessarily an integer, since not all even numbers are divisible by 3.

2. Is $x^2 - \frac{x}{3}$ even? Since all even numbers are integers, and we know that $x^2 - \frac{x}{3}$ is not always an integer, it certainly cannot always be even.

3. Is $x^2 - \frac{x}{3}$ positive? x^2 must be positive. We must now show that x^2 is greater than $\frac{x}{3}$ for all possible values of x. For all numbers whose absolute value is greater than 1, $x^2 > x$ and of course $x > \frac{x}{3}$. $x^2 - \frac{x}{3}$ is therefore always positive.

10. **(A)** Arithmetic: Rates   Difficulty: medium

Once we figure out how many gallons of gas were dispensed, we simply multiply that amount by \$$z$. Since we only know how much gas is pumped in intervals of y minutes, we can figure out how many of those intervals passed by dividing m by y. So, x gallons were pumped m/y times for a total of xm/y gallons of gas. At \$$z$ per gallon, the total cost of the dispensed gas is \$$xmz/y$.

11. **(A)** Algebra: Substitution   Difficulty: low

Substitute -2 in for $(x - y)$. $(-2)^3 = -2 \times -2 \times -2 = -8$.

12. **(D)** Geometry: Triangles   Difficulty: medium

To find y, we first need to find the measures of the angles in the triangle. We know that the sum of the angles in a triangle is equal to $180°$, so:

$$x + 2x + 90 = 180$$
$$3x + 90 = 180$$
$$3x = 90$$
$$x = 30$$

Now we know that the angles in the triangle are $30°$-$60°$-$90°$. The longer leg of a $30°$-$60°$-$90°$ triangle is related to the hypotenuse by the ratio $\sqrt{3}$:2. Multiplying both sides of this ratio by 6, we can see that when the longer side equals $6\sqrt{3}$, the hypotenuse must equal 12.

13. **(B)** Misc. Math: Unique Symbols; Arithmetic: Fractions   Difficulty: medium

To solve this problem, we first look at the numerator $\overline{4371} - \overline{3441}$. Note that $\overline{4371} = 4 + 3 + 7 + 1 = 15$ and $\overline{3441} = 3 + 4 + 4 + 1 = 12$. Therefore, the numerator is equal to $15 - 12 = 3$. The denominator is equal to $2 + 3 + 1 = 6$. The answer is $3/6 = 0.5$.

14. **(C)** Misc. Math: Unique Symbols; Algebra: Substitution   Difficulty: medium

The easiest way to solve this problem is to realize that $n = \overleftarrow{n}$. Naturally, when summing the digits of a number, it doesn't matter what order the digits are in.

Alternatively, you could have calculated $\overline{1234533234} = 1 + 2 + 3 + 4 + 5 + 3 + 3 + 2 + 3 + 4 = 30$ and $\overleftarrow{n} = 4323354321 = 4 + 3 + 2 + 3 + 3 + 5 + 4 + 3 + 2 + 1 = 30$ and $30 - 30 = 0$.

15. **(E)**   Misc. Math: Unique Symbols; Algebra: Substitution   Difficulty: high

There are two ways to approach this problem. Perhaps the faster way is to simply pick a value for n, calculate $\overline{n+1090}$, and see which one of the answer choices is correct. For example, let $n = 23$ and add it to 1090 to get 1113. $\overline{1113} = 1 + 1 + 1 + 3 = 6$. Because $\overline{23} = 2 + 3 = 5$, we find that $\bar{n} + 1 = 6$ is the only answer choice that works.

Alternatively, you could figure out the answer without substitution. When n is added to 1090, the resulting number is equivalent to $2000 + (n - 10)$. $\overline{n - 10}$ is one less than $\bar{n}$ and $\overline{2000} = 2$. So, $\overline{2000 + (n - 10)}$ is $2 - 1 = 1$ greater than $\bar{n}$, or $\bar{n} + 1$.

16. **(C)**   Algebra: Solving Systems of Equations   Difficulty: medium

Hopefully you can see that the only difference in the two equations is the addition of y to the left side and 1 to the right side, meaning that $y = 1$. If not, you can use one equation to solve for x in terms of y and then substitute that expression into the other equation. First,

$$x + y = 6$$
$$x = 6y$$

Then,

$$x + 2y = 7$$
$$6 - y + 2y = 7$$
$$6 + y = 7$$
$$y = 1$$

Now that you know that $y = 1$, x must equal 5 since $x + y = 6$.

17. **(B)**   Geometry: Slope   Difficulty: medium

The equation for the slope of the line in question is $\frac{6 - 0}{11h - h}$. We know that the slope equals $\frac{3}{5}$, so we can simply set up an equation and solve for h:

$$\frac{6 - 0}{11h - h} = \frac{3}{5}$$
$$\frac{6}{10h} = \frac{3}{5}$$
$$\frac{3}{5h} = \frac{3}{5}$$

At this point, you should be able to see that $h = 1$. If not, you can cross-multiply as usual when you have two equal fractions to see that $15h = 15$.

18. **(B)** Arithmetic: Basic Operations   Difficulty: medium

There are several ways to go about systematically counting numbers. The key is to make sure that you do so in an organized fashion. One way is to count how many numbers in each 100 numbers (e.g., 100 through 199) have a 9 as one of their digits. For every 100, there are 10 numbers with a 9 in the units place (i.e., 109, 119, 129, 139, 149, 159, 169, 179, 189, 199). There are also 10 numbers with a 9 in the tens place (i.e., 190, 191, 192, 193, 194, 195, 196, 197, 198, 199). We don't want to count 199 twice, so we only have 9 additional numbers. There are no possible numbers with a 9 in the hundreds place because such numbers are out not between 100 and 500. There are 19 numbers per 100, and 4 sets of 100 so there are 19 × 4 = 76 numbers that meet the stated criteria.

19. **(E)** Arithmetic: Positive and Negative Numbers   Difficulty: medium

Since p is always negative and s^2 is always positive or 0 (all squares are positive or 0), then ps^2 is always negative or 0. Thus, .5 is not a possible answer because it is a positive number.

20. **(D)** Geometry: Polygons   Difficulty: medium

Only two identical right isosceles triangles could fit together to form a square. They are joined at the hypotenuse, their longest side, so the legs of the triangles form the sides of the square. It might help you to jot down a picture of this problem, which would look like this:

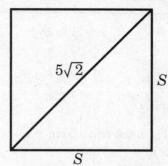

In order to find the area of the square, we need to know the length of the sides. Using the Pythagorean theorem, we can easily solve for s:

$$s^2 + s^2 = (5\sqrt{2})^2 = 50$$

So,

$$2s^2 = 50$$
$$s^2 = 25$$
$$s = 5$$

The area is $s^2 = 5^2 = 25$. The answer must be (D).

21. **(C)**   Arithmetic: Rates   Difficulty: high

Before John's friend showed up, John read 60 pages in 3 hours or $^{60}/_3 = 20$ pages per hour. After John's friend joined him, John's rate decreased from 20 to 15 pages per hour. Since John still had 60 pages to read, it would take $60 \div 15 = 4$ hours more to finish the assignment.

22. **(D)**   Geometry: Geometric Visualization; Solids   Difficulty: high

In order to find the surface area of a cylinder, we must find the area of the base as well as the area of the rectangle that wraps around the circular base. Start with the rectangle, whose height is that of the cylinder (5) and whose width is equal to the circumference of the base. The circumference is equal to πd or 6π and so the area of the rectangle is equal to $6\pi \times 5 = 30\pi$. The radius of the circles is equal to half the diameter, or 3. The area of each circular base is equal to $\pi \times 3^2 = 9\pi$. The surface area of the cylinder is therefore $30\pi + 9\pi + 9\pi = 48\pi$.

23. **(D)**   Algebra: Simplifying and Manipulating   Difficulty: high

To answer this question, we simply equate the two expressions given, and solve the resulting equation for x.

$$xyz + 2 = 4 - xyz$$
$$2xyz = 4 - 2$$
$$2xyz = 2$$
$$xyz = 1$$
$$x = \frac{1}{yz}$$

24. **(B)**   Arithmetic: Combinations and Probability   Difficulty: high

Each flip of the coin is independent of the other flips. The probability of a given flip landing heads up is ½. Thus, the probability of any two flips, in this case the first and the third, landing heads up is the product of each individual probability: ½ × ½ = ¼. The outcome of the second coin flip is irrelevant to this problem.

   Another way to approach this problem is to write out the possible outcomes for 3 flips of the coin. If we let H symbolize heads and T symbolize tails, then the possible outcomes are *HHH, HHT, HTH, HTT, THH, THT, TTH,* and *TTT.* Out of these 8 possibilities, only two have heads up on the first and third flips: *HHH* and *HTH.* Therefore, the probability is 2 times out of 8 or ¼.

25. **(C)**   Geometry: Solids   Difficulty: high

If the figure is folded as shown, we have a box with a rectangular base of width 16 and length 10. The height of the box is 2. Therefore, the volume of the box is simply $16 \times 10 \times 2 = 320$.

Verbal Section 1

Sentence Completions

1. **(B)** One Word Direct   Difficulty: low
In this question, the information after the semicolon expands on the earlier description of the meaning of white in the novel by suggesting that there are several possible interpretations. Our task, therefore, is to find the word that suggests multiple meanings. Beautiful, benign (which means "harmless"), and persuasive all fail to capture the idea that there could be different interpretations of white in the novel. All of these can be eliminated for that reason.

Ambiguous, which means "uncertain in meaning", certainly describes something that can be interpreted in various ways. This is the right answer. While there may well be additional symbolic interpretations for white, we have no reason believe that those interpretations are infinite. If you want to get really technical, you could argue that there are only as many meanings as readers, and, despite its tremendous popularity, *Moby-Dick* hasn't had an infinite number of them. While infinite might have some initial appeal and is certainly the second-best answer, ambiguous fits more precisely into the sentence.

2. **(B)** One Word Contrast   Difficulty: low
The hinge word in this sentence is "but," which implies that the direction of the sentence will change after the comma. Because of the "but," we know that the sentence is asking us to find a word that contrasts with the idea of losing money: the investor has lost money before, but now he thinks he will do the opposite. What we are really looking for, then, is a word that conveys the idea of *making* money.

Though several of the possible answer choices feature words associated with investment and finance (deficit, shares, and power), it is fairly easy to see that the answer is profit, which is the only word that conveys the idea of making money. Health is obviously wrong (the stock market can't bring you health), deficit conveys the idea of *losing* money, shares does not make sense in the sentence, and power fits too abstractly to be the correct choice. (If his new investments do bring him power, it will only be because they bring him profit first.)

3. **(B)** Two Word Direct   Difficulty: low
The word "thanks" that begins the sentence clearly implies that what happens to Henri in the second half of the sentence is dependent on the information given in the first. We know that Henri easily got the job, so the first half of the sentence must be very positive. We can therefore immediately throw out flaws .. humor, since if Henri had

many flaws he wouldn't get the job so easily. We can also throw out connections . . evidence, talents . . abandon, and positions . . appetite, since the second halves of these pairs do not fit in the sentence. That leaves us with the correct answer: achievements . . demeanor.

4. **(A)** Two Word Contrast   Difficulty: low

The hinge word "although" alerts us to be on the lookout for an opposition in this sentence, one which we need to be especially wary of as the two blanks are on different sides of the comma. In ascertaining the correct answer, we should first eliminate the choices wherein both words have either a negative or positive connotation, i.e., irresponsible . . failure. Next, we should think about the second half of the sentence: the blank describes what happens because Henrietta is undisciplined, so this is the half that should have a negative word. Therefore we can throw out lazy . . success, thoughtful . . superiority, uninspired . . prowess. Using these two strategies, we can conclude that the correct answer is intelligent . . catastrophe.

5. **(B)** Two Word Contrast   Difficulty: medium

Though this question is a Two-Word Contrast, its form is slightly unusual, in that the blanks do not fall in clauses on either side of the hinge word, "but"; instead, the second blank falls in the explanatory clause after the second part of the original statement. We know that whatever "Rite of Spring" caused at its premiere, it is something that matches the idea of audacious modernity, because we have been told that the piece no longer seems "so audaciously modern"; the second blank, which describes how the piece *does* seem today, must *contrast* with the idea of audacious modernity. Sensation . . shocking can be discarded because the second term reinforces rather than contrasts the idea of "audacious modernity." Stir . . imposing does not really make sense when plugged into the sentence, nor does backlash . . infuriating. The second term of riot . . advanced seems to reinforce the idea of modernity rather than contradict it. The only choice that fully makes sense is scandal . . tame: the piece was once scandalous, but today it seems tame.

6. **(D)** One Word Direct   Difficulty: medium

In this sentence, the missing word describes the Supreme Court decision, and the phrase after the semicolon expands upon this description. In other words, the two sides of the sentence are providing information about a single idea. We must find the word that describes the Supreme Court decision in such a way that it makes sense to say, "There is little common ground between the supporters and opponents."

Novel, meaning "curious because new" or "diverting," would be a strange, light-hearted way to describe a Supreme Court decision that has divided a nation. Because the *Roe v. Wade* decision has had a very *direct* effect on this country, as established in the second half of the question, oblique, which means "influencing indirectly," poorly fills the blank. If you described the decision as untenable, or "difficult or impossible to hold or implement," you would be asserting a pro-life opinion, rather than filling the blank with the word that makes the most sense. The latter, bear in mind, is what the SAT wants from you. Controversial, which means "giving rise to disagreement," is a good word to use to describe, neutrally, a deeply divisive issue. Figurative means "having a non-literal or non-practical meaning." By dividing the country, as the sentence makes clear that it does, the *Roe v. Wade* decision is hardly figurative.

You should note the form of this question: an initial simple statement that ends in a semicolon followed by a comma and a clarifying clause. In almost every circumstance, when the sentence follows this structure you will be dealing with a question in which some part or the whole of the second half of the sentence actually *defines* the blank word.

7. **(E)** One Word Contrast   Difficulty: medium

The hinge word in this sentence is actually a phrase, "in contrast to," which implies that the two books mentioned will be different in some way. *A Christmas Carol* is short and compact, but *David Copperfield* is just the opposite. Therefore, we know that the sentence is asking us to find a word that contrasts with the idea of brevity and organization, a word that implies an unruly, disorganized length.

Once you realize this, it's possible that you will immediately see the answer, sprawling, which means loose and unwieldy. However, if you don't immediately see the answer, you can always work backwards. Jovial and reminiscent have nothing to do with the sentence. Dubious, which means doubtful or improbable, also fails to relate concretely. Implausible is slightly tricky because we know that *A Christmas Carol* is a ghost story, and ghosts are rather implausible. But again, implausible fails to imply length and unruliness, and the word should describe *David Copperfield* anyway. The only word that fits is sprawling.

8. **(D)** One Word Direct   Difficulty: high

This question asks for a word that describes someone who goes against religious doctrine. In fact, there is a word among the answers that means exactly that: heretic. If you know the word *heretic*, then this question should be easy. If you don't, then you'll have to work backwards. *Perpetrator* means someone who is guilty of something; but a perpetrator has to be a perpetrator of some action (such as heresy). This is not the answer. *Populist* describes a political person whose most pressing concern is the common people; again, Joan might have been a populist, but she was killed for going against official religious doctrine and so the answer you choose must have some relation to religion. Populist does not. *Executioner* might be tempting because Joan was executed, as the question states, but she was not an executioner herself. Finally, *zealot* can refer to religion: a zealot is a person who believes fanatically in something, such as religion. But a zealot will not necessarily go against doctrine; some zealots believe fanatically in standard religious doctrine. Heretic is by far the best answer.

9. **(D)**   Two Word Contrast   Difficulty: high

The hinge word in this sentence is "though," which signals that the second half of the sentence will contrast with the first half: Rod McKuen's readers and his critics disagreed about his status. Apart from some difficult vocabulary (emasculated would imply that critics robbed McKuen of his manhood; extolled means "praised"), the most difficult problem posed by these answer choices is the question of contrast. Denounced . . ignored, derided . . venerated, and extolled . . loathed all offer enough contrast to work in the first two clauses of the sentence. Therefore, we must use the information provided in the third clause—the knowledge that McKuen was the most popular poet of the 1960s—to decide between the choices. Denounced . . ignored is easy to eliminate; if McKuen were "ignored" by his readers, he would not have been popular. Likewise, extolled . . loathed does not make sense: if critics loved him and readers hated him, he would not have sold so many books. Therefore, derided . . venerated is the only answer choice that makes sense in the sentence: the critical press mocked and disparaged him, but his readers glorified him by making him the most widely read poet of his time.

Analogies

10. **(A)**   Part / Whole   Difficulty: low

"A DESK is made from WOOD" is the best and most specific sentence you can make to relate this stem pair. The only answer pair that relates an object and the material from which it is made is scissors : metal. Paper : notebook is slightly tricky, since a notebook is made out of paper; however, the two items in paper : notebook are in the opposite order of the two in DESK : WOOD. While a desk is made out of wood, paper is not made out of a notebook. The other three answer choices clearly do not fit.

11. **(D)**   Lack   Difficulty: low

"EXHAUSTION results from a lack of SLEEP" is the best and most specific sentence you could make with this pair of stem words. Similarly, hunger results from a lack of food. None of the other answer pairs involve a relationship of lack, though weariness : time might catch your eye since the word weariness is so closely associated with SLEEP and EXHAUSTION.

12. **(A)**   Function   Difficulty: medium

"The function of a THERMOMETER is to measure TEMPERATURE" is the best and most specific sentence you could make with this stem pair. Similarly, the function of a scale is to measure weight. Ruler : inch and clock : hour might both have seemed appealing, since each also deals with measurement. However, whereas the stem pair involves a tool and the type of data it measures, ruler : inch and clock : hour both define a tool and the type of unit that tool measures. This is not the same relationship. You should be careful of this type of trick on the SAT; they often pull this on analogy questions dealing with measurement. Of the other answer choices, prediction : weather doesn't describe measurement, and book : pages is a whole:part relationship. Only scale : weight displays the same functional relationship as the stem pair.

13. **(D)** Description   Difficulty: high

"An INSIPID CONVERSATION is one of low quality and little interest" is the best and most specific sentence you could make with this stem pair. Likewise a banal anecdote is of low quality and little interest. Of the other choices, ambivalent : sermon has no clear relationship; intimate : acquaintance seem to go well together, but the pair does not suggest the state of low intelligence that the stem pair does; the words in specific : example also sound good together, but they also do not match the stem pair. That leaves enthralling : performance, which does involve a description that seems in line with the description in the stem pair. However, if you know that enthralling means, basically, "terrifically interesting or captivating," then you should see that the words in this pair actually share a relationship that is opposite that described in the stem pair. If you didn't know the word enthralling, you still should have been able to eliminate enough answer choices to guess.

14. **(C)** Description   Difficulty: high

"An EXPLANATION is CONCISE when it is as economical (as short and yet as complete) as possible" is the best and most specific sentence you can make with this stem pair. Similarly, an utterance is pithy when it too is economical; concise and pithy are almost synonyms. Novel : rotund makes no sense and can easily be eliminated. Achievement : minimal can be tricky: a minimal achievement is a small achievement and a concise explanation is a short explanation. However, a minimal achievement refers to the quality of an achievement and is a negative thing, while a concise explanation is one that contains all necessary information and is a good thing. Achievement : minimal is therefore not the answer. Manifesto : discomfited has no internal relation at all; the two words make no sense together. You can also eliminate argument : rhetorical, since "rhetorical" describes an argument that is not looking for a response, and "concise" holds no such connotation. This leaves utterance : pithy as the only choice for an answer.

   This question relied in large part on vocabulary. If you didn't know the meaning of "rhetorical" or "discomfited" it would be difficult to eliminate either of those answer choices. However, eliminating novel : rotund and achievement : minimal should not be so hard, and that puts you in position to guess.

15. **(A)** Characteristic Action   Difficulty: high

"A REFUGEE seeks ASYLUM as a safe shelter" is the best and most specific sentence you could make with this pair of stem words. Similarly, a sojourner, which is another word for a traveler, seeks haven as a safe place to rest or sleep. This is a tricky problem for a few reasons. Foremost, ASYLUM can have two meanings: an institution for the insane, or a place of safe haven (note that this use of a second, less popular meaning of word is a favorite SAT trick). If you were unsure of the word asylum, you could at least eliminate the answer pairs recluse : government and pariah : ostentation since neither one displays a clear relationship that can be stated simply. With respect to the other choices, artist : portfolio, does have a good internal relation, but a portfolio is a collection of an artist's work, not something that an artist seeks for shelter. Finally, poet : inspiration is the trickiest of the answer choices. A poet seeks or hopes for inspiration, so this might have been a good answer choice if there were not something clearly better. In this case, because ASYLUM and haven both connote shelter, and REFUGEE and sojourner both connote a displaced person who might need shelter, poet : inspiration is not the best answer choice.

The vocabulary in this question was very hard. If you didn't know the meaning of "pariah" or "asylum" or any of the other words, the question could be quite difficult to answer. Hopefully you would be able to eliminate at least those choices with poor internal relations. Otherwise, it might be best to skip this question.

Reading Comprehension

16. **(C)** Words-in-context   Difficulty: medium

This is a fairly simple question, as long as you check the answer choices against the text rather than simply trying to choose the correct definition of "license." Except for (E), each of the answer choices could represent a possible meaning for the word. So it is necessary to look at the passage, in which Twain says that Art is allowed as much license as it has had in the past, while the privileges of Literature have been curtailed, and literature is now censored. From this, it is fairly easy to discard (A) (this is obviously not the driver's license version of the word) and (D) (it is also not the bureaucratic version of the word). Because of the term "indecent" used before "license" in the text, (B) may seem to be a tempting answer. But a close reading of the passage will indicate that "indecent" refers to the freedom of art to portray indecent subjects, rather than to behave with "immoral excess." As a result, (C) is the only answer choice that fits: when it comes to portraying the indecent, Twain says, Art enjoys a freedom from public objection that is not granted to Literature.

17. **(D)** Implied Information   Difficulty: high

Because Twain uses words like "beastliness" and "foul," it may seem at first that he is critical of the era of Fielding and Smollett; this would make (A) and (B) seem like attractive answer choices. But a closer reading reveals that Twain seems to respect the openness of the earlier era: there were beastly subjects, and writers had the freedom and the power to tackle them with the beastly language that they required. In the current era, by contrast, there are foul subjects, but writers have lost the ability to tackle them with the same forcefulness. Once this understanding is reached (it is aided by absorbing the overall tone of the passage, which is consistently critical of attempts to censor art), it becomes obvious that (D) is the correct choice.

18. (E) Understanding Themes and Arguments   Difficulty: medium

If you have even scanned the passage by this point, it should be easy to discard (A) and (C): the passage has nothing to do with ancient standards of dress or nomads in the desert. The only way to choose among the remaining questions is to look at the passage and see how the fig-leaf example is developed. Twain describes several times the pointlessness of using fig leaves to cover the genitalia of sculptures, most of which are crumbling, and which are cold and unfeeling in any case, so the answer cannot be (B). Choice (D) might appear tempting, as it involves questions of morality and decency in art, which is the main subject of the passage, but Twain never mentions different cultural standards with regard to this subject; in fact, he presents the case as a universal condition, one shared by "the world." Therefore, (E) is the correct answer: Twain uses the fig leaf example to criticize the ridiculous decisions people will make in order to keep "indecent" sculpture from being scrutinized by the impressionable public.

19. (B) Specific Information   Difficulty: low

Twain writes that the figures before the Uffizi are "noseless, battered, black with accumulated grime." This indicates very clearly that they do not seem human because they have deteriorated so much with the passage of time (their noses have crumbled off, grime has accumulated, etc.). They are not abstract, poorly sculpted, or gigantic. They are simply ancient. As a result, (B) is the obvious answer choice.

20. (D) Specific Information   Difficulty: high

This question is designed to test your understanding of the specific meaning of the passage in question. The easiest way to work through the problem is to see how each answer choice matches the apparent meaning of the passage. In the passage, Twain criticizes the world's inconsistency for pretending that pictures are more powerful than words, but then censoring erotic writing while it allows erotic pictures to hang openly on display in the Uffizi gallery. Specifically, Twain says that if he were to describe Titian's painting of Venus, his description would outrage people, even though no one is outraged by the painting itself. With that in mind, it is fairly easy to see that the correct answer is (D).

What makes this question potentially difficult is that each of the answer choices except (E) describes an "inconsistency" that would be highly possible with respect to Titian's painting. However, if you return to the passage and look at the argument being made rather just look for key words, like "erotic" or "immoral," you should be able to resist any traps in the answer choices.

21. (B) Author's Attitude or Tone   Difficulty: low

This question is fairly simple. Answer (D) can be eliminated immediately, since it is obvious that the author is not pleased about the things he is describing. You can also eliminate (C), since the tone of the piece is not neutral: the author displays some feelings about the subject. However, those feelings are not terribly extreme: the author is neither angry nor disappointed, so you can throw out answers (A) and (E). That leaves you with answer (B), the correct answer. Another way to answer this question about the author's tone would be to ask yourself what the author is trying to do in this essay. Is the author denouncing scientists? No. The author is trying to point out some possibly dangerous trends. Therefore the author is concerned about what he sees going on in the world.

22. **(E)** Understanding Themes and Arguments   Difficulty: medium
The correct answer is (E). The way to answer this question is to consider the characteristics the author has associated with applied science and to then examine the possible answers. The most important characteristic of applied science, according to this author, is its connection to human needs. Answers (A), (B), (C), and (D) all refer to activities designed to produce products for human use. While experimentation may be a part of applied science, it in itself does not display the important characteristics that this author assigns to the discipline.

23. **(B)** Understanding Themes and Arguments   Difficulty: high
This is a difficult question. The correct answer is (B). Although all of these answers are in some sense possible meanings for the word "manifest," only one meaning is possible in this context. The surrounding sentences describe how science can only interfere with people's rights or well-being when it is created to have some sort of effect on that society. This science must then have a presence in that society, it must be introduced into that society. Only (B) completes this sense of the sentence.

24. **(E)** Author's Technique   Difficulty: high
This question asks you to think about some of the strategies this author may be using to persuade his or her reader. One good way to approach a question like this is by thinking about the effect the passage has on you as you read it. Do you remember the challenge discussed by the author in these lines when you finish reading the whole piece? Probably not, so you can eliminate answer (A), since this section seems to have little effect on the overall argument. You can also eliminate answers (C) and (D), since these are unlikely goals for the author of a passage like this. Of the remaining answers, the correct one is (E): the author acknowledges the reader's potential doubts so that the reader will set them aside for the time being. In other words, he or she anticipates possible criticisms and then defuses them.

25. **(D)** Understanding Themes and Arguments   Difficulty: medium
The correct answer is (D). The author is using the development of the atomic bomb as an example of more general precepts, and he or she does not mean that the specifics of this example have any particular importance. The author simply wants to show that scientists can be influenced by politics and other outside factors.

26. **(A)** Author's Technique   Difficulty: high

Answers (C), (D), and (E) can be eliminated immediately if you've read the passage carefully. These answers don't fit the ideas contained in the passage at all. To choose between the two remaining answers, it is helpful to identify this particular stylistic technique as an aside: something that is suggestive but outside the scope of the main argument. The author uses this parenthetical interjection to suggest that the history of justifications surrounding the atomic bomb is, indeed, worthy of examination, but that this is outside the scope of his or her current topic. The correct answer is (A).

27. **(E)** Implied Information   Difficulty: medium

This question tests your understanding of the author's distinction between pure and applied science. To this author, pure science is research that has no relation to human industry or other activities. Therefore the only answer that could be correct is (E).

28. **(B)** Implied Information   Difficulty: medium

The correct answer is (B). This author assigns moral considerations only to experiments designed to affect human life. If a scientist were experimenting with fissionable materials but the potentially destructive uses of such knowledge were unknown at the time, this experiment would fall under the category of pure science. However, if the scientist were aware that fission could be used to make weapons, then the experiment would have a moral component.

29. **(C)** Words-in-context   Difficulty: high

The correct answer is (C). In the context of this passage "truth" has a very specific meaning, which is tied in to the author's conception of "pure science" as the investigation of the objective state of affairs. Of the incorrect answers, (E) might be the most confusing, since the scientist's intention was to find the truth. But the question asks what "truth" means in this context, and it means the "why's and how's" of the world.

30. **(D)** Main Theme or Idea   Difficulty: low

The main point of this essay is that applied science can have profound effects on mankind. Although the author spends most of the essay discussing potential negative consequences, he or she also admits that applied science is often beneficial to mankind. Therefore the correct answer is (D).

Math Section 2

Quantitative Comparisons

1. **(A)**   Algebra: Solving Linear Equations   Difficulty: low
Simply solve for x in the given equation. Subtracting 7 from each side yields $x = 21 - 7 = 14$, which is greater than 13.

2. **(C)**   Geometry: Angles and Lines   Difficulty: low
Because $\overline{AB}$ is a line segment, the sum of the angles shown must equal 180°. This means that $2x + 2y = 180°$. Substituting 45 for x, the equation simplifies to $90 + 2y = 180°$. $2y = 90$ and $y = 45$. x and y are equal and the answer must be (C).

3. **(B)**   Algebra: Solving Linear Equations   Difficulty: low
Substituting $y = 3$ into the first equation yields $x + 3 = 2$. Subtracting 3 from both sides of this equation shows that $x = -1$, which is less than 0.

4. **(B)**   Arithmetic: Fractions, Decimals, and Percents   Difficulty: low
Because x/y is less than 1 and both x and y are positive, the numerator must be smaller than the denominator. It must be that $x < y$.

5. **(A)**   Geometry: Triangles   Difficulty: low
In an isosceles triangle, there is one right angle and two 45° angles, so $x = 45$, which is larger than 30.

6. **(A)**   Arithmetic: Sets   Difficulty: low
The total number of gorillas in a zoo is made up of the number of female gorillas plus the number of male gorillas. In other words, the set of all gorillas contains within it the set of female and the set of male gorillas. Therefore, if the number of female gorillas increased, in order for the total number of gorillas to remain the same there must have been some decrease in the number of male gorillas, making (A) correct. To make this question easier to visualize, you could plug in numbers. For example, if the total number of gorillas in the zoo remained 10 between 1998 and 1999, while the number of female gorillas rose from 5 to 6, you can see that the male population of gorillas had to fall from 5 to 4.

7. **(C)**   Geometry: Circles   Difficulty: low
Any inscribed triangle that includes a diameter is a right triangle, with the angle opposite the diameter having a value of 90°. The two columns must be equal.

8.   **(A)**   Algebra: Substitution   Difficulty: medium

The main thing you have to do here is substitute y for $\frac{x}{z}$ or vice versa. Making that substitution makes the comparison easier. In column A:

$$\frac{x}{2zy} =$$

$$\frac{y}{2y} = \frac{1}{2}$$

In column B:

$$\frac{yz}{4x} =$$

$$\frac{xz}{4xz} = \frac{1}{4}$$

Column A is greater than Column B.

9.   **(A)**   Geometry: Triangles   Difficulty: high

We need to find the area of the circle and the triangle. The area of the circle is straightforward: πx^2. Triangle ABC is equilateral, which means that the three angles are congruent and equal to 60°. We need to find a way to find the base and height of the triangle. Draw a line from the center that is perpendicular to the midpoint of a side adjacent to angle C. x bisects angle C so the resulting triangle is 30°-60°-90°. Because we know all of the angles and that the hypotenuse is equal to the radius, we can use the basic trigonometric functions to find the other two lengths.

Half of one side of the equilateral triangle is equal to $(\sqrt{3}/2)x$. The entire length of each side of the triangle is therefore $\sqrt{3}x$. Now that we know the length of each side (base) of the triangle, we need to find the height. If we extend x to the side opposite $\angle C$, we can create a 30°-60°-90° triangle where the hypotenuse is a side of the equilateral triangle, the shorter leg is half of a side of the equilateral triangle, and the longer leg is the height of the equilateral triangle. We can either use trigonometric functions to find the lengths of the triangle, or we can use the Pythagorean theorem, since we know two of the three sides.

$$\frac{\sqrt{3}x}{2}^2 + b^2 = \sqrt{3}x$$

$$\frac{3x^2}{4} + b^2 = 3x^2$$

$$b^2 = 3x^2 - \frac{3x^2}{4}$$

$$b^2 = \frac{12x^2}{4} - \frac{3x^2}{4}$$

$$b^2 = \frac{9x^2}{4}$$

$$b = \frac{3x}{2}$$

So, we can finally calculate the area of the equilateral triangle with base $\sqrt{3}x$ and height $3x/2$ by taking one half of their product:

$$A_{\text{triangle}} = \frac{1}{2} \times \sqrt{3}x \times \frac{3x}{2}$$

$$A_{\text{triangle}} = \frac{(\sqrt{3}x)3x}{(2)(2)}$$

$$A_{\text{triangle}} = \frac{3\sqrt{3}}{4}x^2$$

The question asks us to compare the difference in the areas to the area of the triangle. The difference in the areas is $\pi - (3\sqrt{3}/4)x^2$. The square root of 3 is about 1.7, and π is about 3.1, so the difference is about $1.8x^2$. This is greater than the area of the triangle, approximately $1.3x^2$.

10. **(B)** Arithmetic: Basic Operations　　　　　　　　　　　Difficulty: medium
First, count all the numbers that have the form $X99$, where X is any digit other than 9. There are eight possible numbers with this form (remember that 099 and 999 cannot be counted).

Second, count all the numbers that take on the form $99X$. There are nine possible numbers with this form (again, 999 must be excluded).

Finally, count all numbers of the form $9X9$. There are nine possible numbers with this form (again, exclude 999). In total, there are $8 + 9 + 9 = 26$ three-digit numbers that contain two and only two 9's. 27 is greater than 26.

11. **(D)** Arithmetic: Mean, Median, and Mode   Difficulty: medium

Remember that the mean of a set is not necessarily impacted by the number of elements in the set. For example, the mean of the first ten integers is certainly smaller than the mean of the set with the single element 1000. Depending on the value of c, the mean of the three numbers could be smaller, larger, or equal to the mean a and b alone.

12. **(B)** Arithmetic: Solving Inequalities   Difficulty: high

There are two ways to approach this problem. The quickest is to substitute the value in column B into the inequality. When $x = 5$ is substituted into the inequality, it no longer holds because $32 > 28$. In order to satisfy the inequality, $x < 5$, so column B must be greater than column A.

We could also algebraically manipulate the inequality by isolating x in the variable expression:

$$16 \leq 5x + 7 \leq 28$$
$$9 \leq 5x \leq 21$$
$$\frac{9}{5} \leq x \leq \frac{21}{5}$$

Now we have defined the possible values for x and can clearly see that $x < 5$.

13. **(B)** Geometry: Geometric Visualization   Difficulty: medium

A cube only has 6 faces, so it would be impossible to share 9 or more sides.

14. **(A)** Arithmetic: Exponents and Square Roots   Difficulty: high

Column A tests the following property of exponents: $(x^a)^b = x^{ab}$. In this case, $(m^2)^{x+y}$ can be rewritten as $m^{2(x+y)}$. Column B tests the following property of exponents: $x^a \times x^b = x^{a+b}$. Thus, $m^2 \times m^{x+y}$ can be rewritten as m^{2+x+y}. Now the quantities in both columns are expressed as the base m raised to a certain power. Because $m > 1$, we need only decide which power is greater to decide which quantity is greater. Given the condition that $x + y > 2$, we see that $2(x + y) > (2 + x + y)$, so the quantity is column A is greater than that in column B.

15. **(A)** Arithmetic: Solving Systems of Equations   Difficulty: high

There are several ways to find the values of x and y. Since the numbers are small, you could probably do well with trial and error. You can also factor the second equation to find a value for $(x - y)$.

$$x^2 - y^2 = 24$$
$$(x + y)(x - y) = 24$$
$$6(x - y) = 24$$
$$x - y = 4$$

Of course, you don't need to solve for x and y individually to see that $(x - y) > 3$.

Another method is to solve for one variable in the first equation and then plug that value into the second equation. From the first equation, we see that $x = 6 - y$. We can plug this expression for x into the second equation to get:

$$\begin{aligned} x^2 - y^2 &= (6-y)^2 - y^2 \\ &= (6-y)(6-y) - y^2 \\ &= 36 - 12y + y^2 - y^2 \\ &= 36 - 12y \end{aligned}$$

We know that $x^2 - y^2 = 24$ so we have $36 - 12y = 24$. We can solve this equation to see that $y = 1$. Because $x = 6 - y$ we know that $x = 5$. Therefore, the quantity $x - y$ is equal to $5 - 1 = 4$.

Grid-Ins

16. **−2**   Algebra: Simplifying and Manipulating Expressions   Difficulty: low
The key to solving this problem is realizing that $6x + 9y = 3(2x + 3y)$. Making this substitution, we have that $6x + 9y = 3(2x+3y) = 3(0) = 0$. Therefore, $(6x + 9y) - 2 = (0) - 2 = -2$. The algebra and arithmetic are very simple in this problem, but recognizing how to solve it may be difficult. Hopefully you noticed right away the linear equation $2x + 3y = 0$ can't be solved without more information since it has two variables. Faced with these circumstances, it requires some creativity to see that we don't in fact need to solve for x and y individually.

17. **40**   Geometry: Angles and Lines   Difficulty: low
Since the angles comprise a straight line, we know that their sum is 180°. Simply solve the equation $3x + 60 = 180$ to find that $x = 40$. Make sure that you solve for x, and not $3x$.

18. **1**   Arithmetic: Divisibility and Remainders   Difficulty: medium
The easiest way to answer this question is to pick a number for which the first statement applies, square it, and divide by 4. We only have to do this with one number because the question implies that this property holds for all numbers. Choosing small numbers that are 3 more than multiples of 4, such as 7 or 11, will make your work much easier. Squaring 7 gives us 49, which when divided by four is 12 with a remainder of 1.

To solve this problem algebraically, simply represent x as $4y + 3$ and x^2 as $(4y + 3)(4y + 3) = 16y^2 + 24y + 9$. The first two terms are multiples of 4 and have no remainder when divided by 4. 9 divided by 4 leaves a remainder of 1, which applies to any value of y. The remainder of any x^2 after dividing by 4 is 1 for any x that satisfies the initial condition.

19. **90**   Arithmetic: Fractions, Decimals, and Percents   Difficulty: low
Ticket sale revenues amount to $300 \times \$10 = \$3000$. If the publicity manager takes 3% of that, she will get $.03 \times \$3000 = \$90$.

20. **36**   Arithmetic: Mean, Median, and Mode   Difficulty: medium

In order for the mean of 4 numbers to be 24, their sum must be 96. Because the mean of a, b, and c is 20, their sum must be 60. In order for the sum of the 4 numbers to be 96, d must be equal to 36.

21. **9**   Geometry: Coordinate Geometry; Polygons   Difficulty: medium

If we plot the points out on a graph, we see that the length of one of the sides of the square is equal to the distance between $(-1,3)$, and $(2,3)$ which is 3. The area of the square is equal to the side squared, and so the area is 9.

22. **37.6**   Geometry: Polygons   Difficulty: medium

The surface area of a cylinder is the sum of its two bases, which are circles, and the rectangular piece that wraps around the circular bases. The rectangle has a height of 5 and a width equal to the circumference of the circle. The circumference of one circle is equal to $2\pi r$ or just 2π. The area of the rectangle is therefore equal to $(5)(2\pi) = 10\pi$. The area of each of bases is equal to $\pi r^2 = \pi(1)^2 = \pi$. The total surface area is $\pi + \pi + 10\pi = 12\pi$, which is roughly equal to 37.699 and can be filled in as either 37.6 or 37.7.

23. **4/3**   Algebra: Simplifying and Manipulating Expressions   Difficulty: high

We are given an equation relating x and z and our job is to manipulate it until we have an expression for x/z. Since we are given two equal fractions, we can cross-multiply to get two equal expressions:

$$\frac{1}{2}xy = \frac{2}{3}yz$$
$$3xy = 4yz$$

Now we just need to rearrange the terms of this equation to isolate the desired x/z term.

$$3xy = 4yz$$
$$3x = 4z$$
$$\frac{3x}{z} = 4$$
$$\frac{x}{z} = \frac{4}{3}$$

24. **3**   Arithmetic: Exponents and Square Roots   Difficulty: medium

The first step is to convert $(x^a)^b$ and $(x^2)^3$ to x^{ab} and x^6, respectively. This substitution follows from the exponential property that $(x^y)^z = x^{yz}$. We can then combine these two terms to get one that leads to the solution: $(x^{ab}) \times (x^6) = x^{ab+6}$. We know that $x^{ab+6} = x^9$ so $ab + 6 = 9$ and $ab = 3$.

25. **80**   Geometry: Circles   Difficulty: high

The shaded region is basically a half circle with 2 smaller half-circles added and one small half-circle subtracted. The area of the small semi-circles is given in the problem. Finding the area of the larger circle is a little more complicated, since we are not directly given any information about the radius of the larger circle. Notice that the diameters of the three smaller circles, lined up end-to-end, span the entire diameter of the larger circle. If we can determine the diameter of the smaller circles, we can also determine the diameter of the larger circle.

The area of the small semi-circle is 8π so the area of a full small circle is 16π. Working backwards, we can determine the radius of the small circles:

$$\pi r^2 = (\pi)(16)$$
$$r^2 = 16$$
$$r = 4$$

So the radius of each small semicircle is 4. There are three small diameters in the large diameter, so the large diameter is $8 \times 3 = 24$. Now we can find the area of the large half-circle is simply half of the area of a circle with a radius of 12: $12^2\pi/2 = 144\pi/2 = 72\pi$. So, the area of the shaded region is equal to the large semi-circle minus two small semi-circles plus one semi-circle: $72\pi + 16\pi - 8\pi = 80\pi$. Remember to divide by π to see that the answer is 80.

Verbal Section 2

Sentence Completions

1.   **(D)**   One Word Direct   Difficulty: low

The question asks for an adjective associated with someone who is "responsible, efficient, and . . . courteous" which are all positive qualities. Of the answer choices, only exemplary and absorbing could have positive connotations, and when we plug these into the sentence it is clear that exemplary is the correct answer.

2.   **(E)**   One Word Direct   Difficulty: low

In this question, the blank word characterizes "the influence of the popular vote on the outcome of a presidential election," and the semicolon introduces a second statement, which clarifies the process. Therefore, we must find the word that describes "the influence of the popular vote" in system in which the election of the president is one step removed from the popular vote.

The point of the sentence is to say that the popular vote only informs, rather than determines, the Electoral College; to say that the power of the popular vote is therefore absolute would be incorrect. Obscure and arbitrary are poor choices because they imply that the process is unclear or based on individual preferences. The sentence, however, clearly states that the process works in an understood, predictable way: the popular vote influences the Electors who vote for a candidate. We can also not say that the popular vote has a negligible effect, since it helps determine who will choose the president. The only answer choice, therefore, that captures the idea of the popular vote's influence mediated through the Electoral College is indirect. In fact, it is precisely this indirectness that is described in the second half of the sentence.

3.   **(B)**   One Word Direct   Difficulty: medium

The question describes a situation in which the jurors saw the defendant's silence as some sort of acknowledgement of guilt. It couldn't be an obvious or explicit admission of guilt, but rather something implicit and unspoken. Once you've realized this, the question becomes merely a quest for the proper vocabulary word. If you know that the word tacit fits the needed definition perfectly, then you're set. Otherwise, you should work backward. Impartial seems like a good word in a sentence about a trial, but it doesn't make sense to describe a defendant's silent admission of guilt as impartial, or without judgment. Further, there is no reason to surmise that the jury would see the defendant's admission as undignified or magnanimous. The jury might think either of these things, but the sentence itself does not suggest it. Finally, the idea of a "tranquil acknowledgement" just doesn't make sense, so you can eliminate that possibility as well. Even if you cannot eliminate every wrong answer, you should easily know that impartial, tranquil, and maybe even undignified must be wrong, which would put you in a great position to guess.

4.   **(D)**   One Word Contrast   Difficulty: low

Puck is the mischievous fairy in Shakespeare's play *A Midsummer Night's Dream*, but it is not necessary to know this in order to fill in this sentence correctly. Because of the hinge word "Instead," we know that the word that fills in the blank must contrast with Puck's actual attitude about his pranks. Because he brags about them, we know he is proud of them; what we are looking for, then, is a word that contrasts with the idea of pride, one that expresses an idea of shame or guilt.

   By this reasoning, the answer is "apologizing;" if he were to apologize for his pranks, Puck would express guilt about them, rather than the pride he expresses by bragging. Living, singing, striving, and fighting all make grammatical sense, but none of them match the meaning implied by the rest of the sentence. Singing obviously could not fit—how could someone sing for a prank? The others could conceivably work—one could live for pranks, strive for pranks, or fight for a prank—but none of those words would contrast sharply enough with the pride implied by Puck's bragging.

5.   **(E)**   One Word Direct   Difficulty: medium

In this sentence, the clause after the comma, specifically "character and morality," suggests the meaning of the word in the blank. We must find the word, therefore, that is strongly associated with these two qualities. If you know what the words mean, it is obvious that temerity, exuberance, and irreverence are poor choices. (They mean "boldness or audacity," "excitement or liveliness," and "lacking respect for something.") Gravity might seem like a more tempting choice because seriousness or thoughtfulness is often found in a person of good, moral character. The reason it does not work is that a thoughtful, dignified man can be completely immoral; there is nothing in the definition that actually suggests good morals. The best answer is integrity, a word that means strict adherence to a moral code.

6.   **(E)**   One Word Direct   Difficulty: medium

This sentence does not really use a hinge word; instead, it uses context clues to convey a sense of contrast. We know that the ambassador is "terrified" of war, so that he will want a result that is *different* from war. We know that he is an ambassador, and that the job of an ambassador is usually to negotiate peace through diplomacy. So even without a hinge word such as "but" or "though," we know we are looking for a word that contrasts with the idea of war or conflict.

   Ignorance obviously has no relation to the idea of war, and violence is the *same* idea—it would hardly make sense for an ambassador who was terrified of war to try to bring about violence. Nobility might seem to be a likely choice, because if the nations acted with nobility, they might be more likely to make peace. But nobility is not something an ambassador can bring about. Prejudice, like ignorance, does not directly relate to the idea of war, though it seems more likely to contribute to war than to avert it. An ambassador who wished to avoid war would not be wise to promote prejudice.

The only persuasive answer, then, is reconciliation, a word that implies forgiveness and the overcoming of differences. Reconciliation, unlike nobility, is something ambassadors can work for, and it is the only word that fits the shape of the sentence.

7.   **(A)**   Two Word Contrast   Difficulty: high

The hinge word in this sentence is "instead," which signals that the second half of the sentence will contrast with the first half: what the author originally intended to do differs from what he actually did. Further, from the context clues of the sentence, we know that the author's first intent was to write a comedy, but his actual work was both weighty and tragic. Therefore, we are looking for two contrasting words, the first implying a comedy, the second implying something weightier and more tragic.

Hackneyed . . satire, banal . . narrative, and wretched . . proposition can all be rejected because in each case the first word has a strongly negative connotation. No writer would want to write something trite or dull or very bad, so they cannot possibly work in the sentence. Scintillating . . farce can also be rejected because there is no such thing as a weighty farce (a farce is a kind of light comedy). The only choice that entirely fits the sentence is flippant . . meditation: the author meant to write a flippant (light and witty) comedy, but instead penned a weighty meditation on a tragic theme.

8.   **(B)**   One Word Direct   Difficulty: medium

In this question, the blank word describes an activity of a sales representative, and the comma introduces a clause that provides more information about this activity. We must find the word that describes what the sales representative was expected to do, in such a way that it means virtually the same thing as "seeking orders from each new business."

To discern means simply to detect with the eyes, or to notice. This idea is *necessary* to the meaning required by the blank, but is not *sufficient* to it. There needs to be more: a verb that includes not just seeing, but doing the activities described after the comma. Canvass is a tricky word. You probably have heard of the word "canvas," which is a type of fabric. You might look at this word and think of fabric and think "that doesn't fit at all." But canvass actually means "to solicit action from the residents of an area." With this meaning, it fits the sentence very well. Turning to the other incorrect choices, a salesperson might validate, or establish as valid, a region for future sales, but that's not the meaning the sentence requires. Finally, incorporate and castigate, which mean "bring together" and "criticize," respectively, simply make no sense in the context of the sentence.

9.　**(D)**　Two Word Direct　　　　　　　　　　　　　　　　Difficulty: high

This sentence features rather difficult vocabulary. Even so, as always, we should figure out what the sentence is looking for. We know that Paul "offended his host," meaning that his table manners must be bad, so the word that fills the second blank must have a negative connotation. Looking at the first blank, we know that Paul offends with his bad manners, so he must be ignorant of social rules or standards, so something that means "rules or standards" should fill the blank.

Because the vocabulary in the sentence is hard, you might have trouble eliminating answer pairs even with all this knowledge, but if you know even one word of a pair, you might be able to eliminate it. For example, refined and resplendent both have positive conotations, so you can eliminate conventions . . refined and graces . . replendent. From there, you might focus on either the first or the second term, as neither term in the remaining incorrect answers would fit in its respective blank. Specifically, vicissitudes means "changes," and portentous means "arrogant," so you can eliminate vicissitudes . . deleterious ("damaging") and expropriations ("things that are taken away") . . portentous. That leaves us with the right answer: precepts . . atrocious.

10.　**(A)**　One Word Contrast　　　　　　　　　　　　　　Difficulty: high

The hinge word in this sentence is "but," which implies that the direction of the sentence will change after the comma. Because of the "but," we know that the sentence is asking us to find a word that contrasts with the idea of admiration. Because of the phrase "go so far as," however, we can guess that the word will not contrast by being the *opposite* of admiration, but rather, by being greater in extent or degree. Because of the phrase "in their own work," we can guess that the import of the sentence is that many artists might admire Leonardo's techniques, but few artists go so far as to use them for their own paintings. So we are looking for a word that implies an artist using an old technique in his work.

Inoculate somehow sounds good in this sentence, but inoculate means to make something resistant to disease through injection; obviously, this is the wrong word. Rhapsodize means to think blissfully and dreamily about; again, not the right word for this sentence. Vivify, which means to give life to, does not relate to the sentence at all. Undermine also fails to fit; the artists admire da Vinci, so they would certainly never do something to detract from his reputation. The correct answer, therefore, must be emulate, which means to copy or mimic, and therefore fits extremely well into the contrast between the two halves of the sentence.

Analogies

11. (C) Function   Difficulty: low

"A SAW is used to cut WOOD" is the best and most specific sentence you could make with this stem pair. Similarly scissors are used to cut paper; scissors : paper is the correct answer. The key to answering this question is to make the sentence connecting the two words as specific as possible.

12. (D) Characteristic Location   Difficulty: low

"a SUBWAY carries COMMUTERS." Similarly, a freighter carries cargo. The relationship in airplane : passengers would be correct, except that the order has been reversed. Water : reservoir and tree: park both have object : location relationships, but neither also captures the idea of transportation.

13. (B) Attribute   Difficulty: medium

"A GENIUS possesses a great deal of INTELLIGENCE" in the same way that a billionaire possesses a great deal of wealth. Of the incorrect answer choices, the most potentially confusing are talent : artist and autocrat : power. An artist *may* possess a great deal of talent, but does not *necessarily* do so—a genius *necessarily* possess a great deal of intelligence. Autocrat : power is slightly confusing because autocrat is a relatively difficult word, and because an autocrat (meaning "dictator" or "ruler") does possess a great deal of power. But the word order invalidates this choice; in the analogy INTELLIGENCE : GENIUS, the attribute comes first, followed by the person who possesses that attribute.

14. (B) Function   Difficulty: medium

"A EULOGY functions to express the emotions at a FUNERAL" is the best and most specific sentence you could make with this stem pair. Similarly a toast functions to express the emotions surrounding a celebration. A ceremony is the functional part of a wedding, while an announcement is the notification of an event. The important thing here is to notice that eulogies and toasts are both types of speeches associated with certain events.

15. (E) Cause and Effect   Difficulty: medium

"If you ABRADE something, it is no longer SMOOTH," just as if you liquify something, it is no longer solid. Of the remaining answer choices, the most confusing is desiccate : arid, simply because of the difficult vocabulary involved. Desiccate means to remove the moisture of a thing, while arid means extremely dry—if you desiccate something, you do not make it less arid, and thus that choice does not fit our sentence. The other choices are faulty for similar reasons: to endanger something is not make it less hazardous, to map something is not to make it less navigable, and to convince someone is not to make them less persuasive.

16. **(C)** Function   Difficulty: high
"ENFRANCHISEMENT is the granting of the right to VOTE" is the best and most specific sentence you could make with this stem pair. Similarly, emancipation is the granting of liberty. Abolition is the repeal of slavery, an appeal is a reaction to a verdict, and the suffrage movement sought the right to vote for women. Protest : polemics has no easily stated relation. Only emancipation : liberty, like the stem pair, relates an action to its positive outcome (that is, the thing that it does or produces, rather than the thing that it repeals or cancels, which would be a negative outcome).

17. **(B)** Part / Whole   Difficulty: medium
"A CALENDAR is made up of a number of MONTHS" is the best and most specific sentence you could make with the stem pair. Similarly, a team is made up of a number of players: both players and months are the units that constitute a larger whole. An afternoon is part of a day, but a day is not a collection of afternoons. The other three answer choices are even more obviously wrong.

18. **(C)** Degree   Difficulty: medium
"An INFERNO is a much greater conflagration than a FIRE," just as a war is a much greater struggle than a fight. In both cases, the second term is a degree of meaning greater than the first term. The other answers are fairly easy to eliminate; though ice might relate confusingly to fire, the presence of pole as the first term of the pair clearly disqualifies that answer. Exigence (which means a kind of stringent discipline) is a degree of meaning greater than discipline, but the words occur in the wrong order to fit the terms of the question. Finally, drove and herd are virtually synonyms, and filter : cigarette has a part : whole relationship.

19. **(B)** Type   Difficulty: high
"FRAUD is a type of CRIME," just as psychosis is a type of disorder. None of the other word pairs match the "type of" relationship: cruelty is characteristic of tyranny; a desert needs irrigation to be habitable; banishment leads to exile; oscillate (meaning to move back and forth) can be used as a metaphorical synonym for indecision.

20. **(E)** Characteristic Action   Difficulty: high
"A PHILANTHROPIST engages in acts of CHARITY" is the best and most specific sentence you could make with this stem pair. Similarly, a guerilla engages in acts of terrorism. One way to approach this question if you did not know the definition of philanthropist would be to try to create sentences for the answer pairs, and then plug philanthropist and charity into the sentences you create; sometimes hearing a word in a sentence can jog your memory. You could also eliminate farmer : horticulturalist as an answer since, unlike the stem pair, that answer pair involves two people (you can infer this from the "ist" ending of horticulturalist). The pair hindsight : scholar also differs from the stem pair: the noun referring to a person appears second rather than

first. Landlord : business does not have an easily-stated relationship and could also be set aside. Making sentences with the remaining two possibilities then will hopefully point out the correct answer to you. If not, you've still gotten yourself into a good position to guess.

21. **(B)** Function   Difficulty: high
"A PROTOTYPE is the model for the production of an AUTOMOBILE" is the best and most specific sentence you could make with this stem pair. Likewise a blueprint is the model for the construction of a building. A photocopy is a reproduction of a document, not the template for it. A hypothesis is an assumption an experiment hopes to prove; while it may guide the design of the experiment, it does not serve as a template or model in the same way a blueprint or a prototype does. You may not know what a frontispiece (a façade) is, but it is hard to imagine what a template for sound would be, so you can eliminate frontispiece : sound as well. Finally, fingerprint : individual does not have a clear relationship, and it certainly is not related in the way that the stem pair is.

22. **(A)** Attribute   Difficulty: high
This question involves some difficult vocabulary. "A RAMBUNCTIOUS person does not display LETHARGY." There are two tricky answer choices whose words relate to LETHARGY and RAMBUNCTIOUS (energy : excitable and exhaustion : sluggish), but both of these pairs name something someone would have if he were the other. The same is true of religion : saintly. Floral : blossom does not fit the stem pair at all, leaving us only the correct answer, rumination : thoughtless: a thoughtless person does not display rumination.

23. **(D)** Characteristic Action   Difficulty: high
A good sentence to relate the stem pair would be that "a QUERULOUS person would not MEDIATE a situation." Similarly, a sedate person would not invigorate a situation. None of the other answer choices share this kind of relationship. If you did not know some of the vocabulary in the answer choices, this question could be very difficult. You would almost certainly know both words in at least one incorrect answer choice, and even that much would allow you to guess.

Reading Comprehension

24. **(A)** Understanding Themes and Arguments   Difficulty: medium
As indicated by the question, this question can be answered by referring back to the second paragraph of the passage. In that paragraph Roosevelt expresses his ambivalence about change, that it is necessary but not always good. Answer (A) is the only answer which reflects this ambivalence.

25. (D) Understanding Themes and Arguments   Difficulty: medium
Answering this question correctly requires having an understanding of the passage as a whole. While the paragraph in which this statement appears seems to focus on the exhibition and potential sale of these paintings, the statement in question actually concerns the more generalized importance of the works. In the first paragraph, Roosevelt praises the exhibit for exposing Americans to contemporary European art, but he goes on to criticize the quality of the works as pieces of art. The correct answer is (D).

26. (C) Author's Technique   Difficulty: high
Answers (B), (D), and (E) can be eliminated quickly. None of the three have anything to do with the passage. Since Roosevelt claims that people are foolish enough both to go to sideshows and to buy paintings of this sort, we can infer that the paintings must have some commercial value to someone, so (A) cannot be right. (C) is the correct answer because Roosevelt mentions Barnum to illustrate another time when people paid for something of no apparent value.

27. (E) Author's Attitude or Tone   Difficulty: medium
In the, paragraph Roosevelt adopts an almost paternal tone of authority; the answer choice that best describes this is (E). If this was not immediately apparent to you, you could check each answer choice individually; none of the other choices make much sense.

28. (C) Specific Information   Difficulty: medium
This question requires that you have a general understanding of the passage as a whole. Roosevelt does not make comparisons between American and European artists other than to say that he is more interested in American artists. The only answer that can possibly be correct, then, is (C), since it is the only one that does not make an explicit comparison between American and European artists. Indeed, Roosevelt notes that the entire exhibit lacked "the note of the commonplace."

29. (A) Words-in-context   Difficulty: medium
Without even looking at the context surrounding the word "fantastic," you should immediately be able to throw out answers (C) and (E). Once you look at the context, you should also be able to eliminate (B) and (D). "Based on fantasy" makes no sense at all given the context, and "wonderful and exciting" does not fit with the construction of the sentence, which clearly pits the "fantastic" work as working against the "good" that is coming from the exhibition. With the next sentence, that claims the exhibit is lacking in the commonplace, you should be able to see that (A) must be the right answer.

30. **(C)**   Author's Technique   Difficulty: medium

The use of the term "fossilized" is meant to evoke images of stone, time, and weight, and to suggest how difficult bonds with the past are to break. Additionally, fossilization suggests something that was once vital and alive, indicating that renewal is cyclical and necessary. The term as used has nothing to do with science. Answer (C) is the right answer.

31. **(E)**   Author's Attitude or Tone   Difficulty: low

Roosevelt is mocking Cubism by thinking of names for art movements that he thinks would be equally ridiculous. Only answer choice (E) captures the idea of making fun.

32. **(A)**   Author's Technique   Difficulty: medium

The comparison between the Cubist painting and the Navajo rug lets Roosevelt illustrate what he values in art: accurate representations of reality and "sincerity." The correct answer is therefore (A). You could also arrive at this by eliminating the other four answers, all of which are fairly obviously wrong.

33. **(D)**   Implied Information   Difficulty: high

Although many of the statements given as possible answers are suggestions that Roosevelt makes in this paragraph, his main point is to convey what he values in art, which seems to be some level of realism. He dislikes the painting because it does not look like what its title suggests. Importantly, Roosevelt is taking issue with the painting, not the title. Therefore (D) is the correct answer.

34. **(D)**   Main Theme or Idea   Difficulty: low

The correct answer is (D). Roosevelt praises the art in the exhibit for its thorough break with convention and little else. While he does mention that it is an important collection because it shows Americans what is happening in Europe, he does not mention the idea of New York City explicitly. If you have read the passage you should recognize that none of the other answer choices are really viable.

35. **(B)**   Main Theme or Idea   Difficulty: high

While the essay nominally discusses art, its author is primarily concerned with exploring how progress occurs in society. This is a subtle point and requires a good understanding of the passage. If this was not immediately apparent to you, you could at least start by eliminating answers (C), (D), and (E), which would at least give you a 50% chance of getting the correct answer.

Math Section 3

1.   **(B)**   Arithmetic: Solving Linear Equations   Difficulty: low

The first step to solving this problem is translating the word problem into equations. Let us use c to represent the cost of a compact disk and b to represent the cost of a book. We can express the cost of a CD and a book as $b + c = \$18.50$. We know that the book is \$5.50 less than the price of a CD: $b = c - 5.50$. Combining these two equations, we can solve for c:

$$\begin{aligned} c + b &= 18.50 \\ c + (c - 5.50) &= 18.50 \\ 2c - 5.50 &= 18.50 \\ 2c &= 24.00 \\ c &= 12.00 \end{aligned}$$

2.   **(C)**   Arithmetic: Basic Operations   Difficulty: low

Hopefully you can immediately see that y must equal **1**, because any other value would change the value of the numerator, t. If not, you could treat this equality like any other equation and solve for y and then multiply by 3:

$$\begin{aligned} \frac{t}{y} &= t \\ t &= yt \\ 1 &= y \\ 3y &= 3 \end{aligned}$$

3.   **(B)**   Arithmetic: Exponents and Square Roots   Difficulty: low

As long as you recognize that $\sqrt{x} = x^{1/2}$, you can see that $2m = \frac{1}{2}$. It's then easy to find the solution: $m = \frac{1}{4}$.

4.   **(E)**   Geometry: Coordinate Geometry   Difficulty: medium
The area of the square is the length of the side squared, so we must first find the length of side of the square. A right triangle is formed by the two axes and the square, so we can use the Pythagorean theorem to find the length of the hypotenuse.

$$s^2 = 7^2 + 8^2$$
$$s^2 = 49 + 64$$
$$s^2 = 113$$

At this point, we could solve for s, but don't forget that the area of the square is equal to s^2. By remembering what we're ultimately looking for, we can save ourselves the two steps of finding the square root and then squaring that quantity to find the area.

5.   **(D)**   Miscellaneous Math: Charts and Graphs   Difficulty: low
The three workers who improved their performance were Glenn, Sam, and Tim. Glenn improved from poor to excellent, Sam improved from fair to excellent, and Tim improved from poor to excellent. This answer is found by using the key, which tells us the meanings of the symbols.

6.   **(C)**   Miscellaneous Math: Charts and Graphs   Difficulty: medium
Translating the symbols in the chart to their corresponding point values, Ray scored 3 points, Glenn scored 2, Sam scored 3, Tim scored 2, and Ervin scored 2. The average is calculated by dividing the sum of the elements by the number of terms: $(3 + 2 + 3 + 2 + 2)/5 = 2.4$. This question is mostly a test of reading the table correctly, not of computation.

7.   **(D)**   Arithmetic: Series   Difficulty: high
The key to answering this question quickly and correctly is realizing that it is inefficient to determine each of the 21 terms in the sequence that the question refers to. Instead, consider the way each term is derived: by summing the three preceding terms, which we can write as $t_n = t_{n-1} + t_{n-2} + t_{n-3}$. The eighth term is the sum of the fifth, sixth, and seventh terms ($t_8 = t_7 + t_6 + t_5$), whereas the seventh term is the sum of the fourth, fifth, and sixth terms ($t_7 = t_6 + t_5 + t_4$). So, the difference between the eighth and seventh terms can be written algebraically:

$$t_8 - t_7 =$$
$$(t_7 + t_6 + t_5) - (t_6 + t_5 + t_4) =$$
$$t_7 + t_6 + t_5 - t_6 - t_5 - t_4 =$$
$$t_7 - t_4 =$$

Using only simple subtraction, the answer is evident.

8. **(C)**   Algebra: Solving Systems of Equations   Difficulty: high

By looking at the first two equations, we can see that the only difference between the two is the z term. Let's try subtracting the second equation from the first:

$$(x + y + z) - (x + y) = 10 - 3$$
$$x + y + z - x - y = 7$$
$$z = 7$$

Now that we've solved for z, we can substitute back into the third equation to see that $y = 1$.

9. **(C)**   Geometry: Circles   Difficulty: high

The area of the shaded region is simply the difference between the area of the rectangle and the area of the semicircles. There are 4 semicircles, which is the same as 2 full circles. Since the radius of each circle is 8 (½ of short side of the rectangle), the area of one circle is $8^2\pi = 64\pi$, and the area of the semicircles is $2 \times 64\pi = 128\pi$. From the figure, you can see that the long side of the rectangle is 4 times as long as the radius of each semicircle, or 32. The area of the rectangle is therefore $16 \times 32 = 512$ Since the area of the shaded area is simply the difference between the two areas, the answer is $512 - 128\pi$.

10. **(C)**   Misc. Math: Charts; Arithmetic: Ratios   Difficulty: high

We need to calculate the teacher to student ratios in 1997 and 1999 (note that we don't care about 1996). The 1997 teacher to student ratio is 30:600, or ¹⁄₂₀. The 1999 ratio is 30:450, or ¹⁄₁₅. Since the teacher to student ratio dropped in each year from 1996 through 1999, the 1998 teacher to student ratio must be between ¹⁄₂₀ and ¹⁄₁₅. We know that there were 35 teachers in 1998, so there must have been between 35×15 and 35×20 students in 1998 in order for our ratio to be in the correct range. Calculating these products, we see that the student population must be between 525 and 700. Thus, the only correct choice is 600. Note that if the student population were 700, the teacher to student ratio would have been ¹⁄₂₀, which would not have been a drop from the previous year.

Verbal Section 3

1. **(E)**   Main Theme or Idea   Difficulty: medium

This question essentially requires us to distill the main argument of the first passage into a general statement. Each of these answer choices might, on its own terms, be valid explanations for Hamlet's melancholy; it is necessary to read through the passage for both specific clues and a general sense of the author's argument. (B) can be immediately discarded, as the author specifically states that Hamlet did not feel jealousy over his uncle's ascension to the throne. After a bit more study, (E) emerges as the obvious answer choice—the passage makes no reference to Hamlet's cowardice or to his psychological instability, but it does refer several times to his "exquisite sense" of morality, to the importance that sense plays in his interaction with other human beings, and of the centrality of his parents' behavior in his own moral consciousness—as he loved and admired his father for his virtue, he comes to despise his mother for her vice.

2.   **(B)**   Specific Information   Difficulty: medium

A chief difficulty of this question, as with this passage generally, is simply deciphering the author's fairly complex prose; once this is done, however, this question becomes quite simple to answer. The lines referenced in the question say that Hamlet is troubled by Gertrude's "ingratitude to the memory of her former husband, and the depravity she displays in the choice of a successor." This makes (B) the only feasible answer choice: Gertrude dishonors the memory of her former husband, Hamlet's father, and displays "depravity" in choosing a new husband, Claudius.

3.   **(D)**   Words-in-context   Difficulty: low

The only tricky thing about this very simple question is that the word "commerce" usually has an economic overtone (it is the root of the word "commercial"). But in this case, a quick reading of the sentence in which the word is found makes it quite clear that (D) is the proper choice, and that the choices that do imply economic activity (A) and (B) are incorrect. Sometimes the best way to answer a vocabulary question is just read the sentence with the word taken out, and try to fill in the blank with each of the answer choices. If we read that "the man whose sense of moral excellence is uncommonly exquisite, will find it a source of pleasure and of pain in his _____ with mankind," the obvious word to plug in is "interaction." The context of this sentence has nothing to do with economics, and (D) is the correct choice.

4.   **(A)**   Understanding Themes and Arguments   Difficulty: high

Choice (C) may seem tempting because it involves a theme of revenge that is also central to *Hamlet,* and choices (D) and (E) may seem tempting because they are generally true to the spirit of passage, but a careful reading of the argument in lines 18–23 makes it clear that (A) is the most specific and appropriate answer choice. The writer says that a child will feel "joy" and "triumph" for morally worthy parents, and "acute" sorrow for unworthy parents—in other words, "intense pride or shame based on the moral worth of his or her parents." Apart from navigating through the answer choices, the main difficulty in this question lies in formulating the argument of the passage into a more general statement, but a close comparison of the passage with the possible answers should make it clear that (A) is the proper choice.

5.   **(B)**   Author's Attitude or Tone   Difficulty: high

This question requires the fairly difficult mental act of putting a word to the author's apparent attitude in the passage, the personality he seems to exhibit in his writing. It certainly seems that "defiant" and "confrontational" should be easy to eliminate, as the author never seems angry or hostile. By the same token, for the author to be "resigned" would imply that he is prepared to meet an unpleasant or unsatisfactory outcome, and no such outcome is suggested by this paragraph—there is apparently nothing for him to be resigned *to*. So the most compelling of the possible answer choices are (B) and (C)—the author is either dramatic or he is scholarly.

Because of the highly formal language the author uses in this paragraph, it may seem that he is intellectual or "scholarly." But reading the paragraph and trying to hear the way the words fit together in one's mind make it clear that the author is attempting to strike a dramatic effect rather than to be scholarly and measured. The author uses techniques such as colorful description ("Agitated and overwhelmed . . .") repetition ("no soothing, no exhilarating . . .") to present Hamlet's situation in suitably grand terms. (B) is the correct answer choice.

6.   **(C)**   Words-in-context   Difficulty: medium

The only difficulty that this fairly simple question poses is that each of the answer choices accurately describes one facet of Hamlet's behavior during the course of the play. They do not, however, all fit the definition of the word "jocular," and they do not all fit the context of the sentence in which the word is found. In the passage in question, the author lists several ways in which Hamlet's inner contradictions make him a difficult character to understand: he is committed to revenge, but fails to act; he is a passionate lover, yet seems uninterested in the woman he loves; and he is deeply melancholy, yet often acts in a "jocular" manner. In each case, Hamlet's behaviors seem to be directly self-contradictory; from that observation, we can assume that "jocular" means the opposite of melancholy or depressed. This is underscored by the fact that in the sentence, "jocular" is used along with the word "gay," meaning extremely happy. With that information in mind, (C) emerges as the obvious answer choice.

7.   **(B)**   Understanding Themes and Arguments   Difficulty: high

Each of the choices represents a complex, plausible possible answer to this relatively difficult question; in order to arrive at the correct answer, it is necessary to look at the passage indicated in the question. Unfortunately, this passage is fairly complicated itself, using formal language and a great deal of rhetoric. In general, the passage compares misfortunes that one can forget easily ("the mind will soon call up reflections to alleviate, and hopes to cheer") and misfortunes that linger in the mind (those that "reflection only serves to irritate"). The first, forgettable kind of misfortunes are categorized as "misfortunes of accident"; the second, memorable kind of misfortunes are not categorized, but only exemplified: "they arose from an uncle's villainy, a mother's guilt, a father's murder!"

Each of these seems to be an example of preconceived, intentional wrongdoing, which contrasts with the accidental circumstance at work in the first kind of misfortune. Thus the answer must be (B), which compares accidental misfortune to misfortune caused by the bad behavior of others. It is important to note that the main emphasis of the passage is on the memorableness of the misfortunes, not on their causes; since there is no answer choice relating to memorableness, it is necessary to read the passage very carefully in order to extract its description of the causes of misfortune and arrive at the correct answer choice.

8. **(E)** Specific Information   Difficulty: medium

To arrive at the correct explanation, it is necessary to compare the answer choices to the section of the text indicated in the question. Here, the author writes that Shakespeare might have encountered "such a character" in real life, and chosen to translate his attributes to the stage, where they could be observed through the workings of imagination and the conflict of the passions. (E) is therefore the obvious answer choice. The main difficulty in this question is navigating the plausible answer choices and deciphering the formal language of the passage; once the passage is read closely, however, the answer should be easily apparent. (If nothing else, the phrase "real life" in the passage should immediately suggest the right answer.)

9.   **(A)**   Understanding Themes and Arguments   Difficulty: medium

The passage says that Shakespeare makes the reader feel "anxiety for the person"—that is, for Hamlet—rather than "anxiety for the event," or suspense based on an uncertain outcome. He says that he does this by making Hamlet's difficulties arise from the thoughts and feelings of his own mind, rather than from accidental circumstance or a deliberate, focused attempt to achieve his goals. Because Hamlet's thoughts and feelings are the main focus of the play, the reader is able to feel Hamlet's struggles very personally, and even consider Hamlet's state of mind more important than the outward plot of the play. Thus, (A) is the only plausible choice—Hamlet becomes important to readers not because of his moral position or his outward situation, but because his inner situation is the main focus of the story and provides the play's major conflict.

10. **(D)** Main Theme or Idea   Difficulty: high

With the exception of (E) (Hamlet is never described as "naturally fearful"), each of these answer choices offers a viable (and partially true) explanation of Hamlet's inactivity. In order to find the correct answer, it is necessary to generalize largely about the passage as a whole—this question is essentially asking us to summarize the main theme of the passage in a single sentence. Looking over the passage briefly, we see that one paragraph of the passage discusses Hamlet's sensitivity to his surroundings and the pain his family has caused him, and that another paragraph describes Hamlet's natural inconsistency and variability.

With this in mind, it becomes clear that (D) is the most plausible answer choice. Though the others are tempting, they are not really relevant to the discussion in Passage 2. The author implies that Hamlet's sensitive and reflective nature is exacerbated by his situation, causing his erratic streak to emerge as he oscillates between commitment to revenge and helpless uncertainty.

11. **(C)**   Relating Two Passages;
           Understanding Themes and Arguments   Difficulty: high

This question is fairly difficult because it requires us to catalog the various aspects of Hamlet's character that each author discusses, and to compare our catalogs to see what the Passage 1 author leaves out that the Passage 2 author puts in. The easiest way to go about doing this is probably to run down the list of possible answers and try to find each of them in each passage. Approaching the question this way, we see that (A) and (E) are easy to eliminate, because neither passage mentions Hamlet's temper or his temptation to sin.

(B) and (D) can be eliminated for just the opposite reason: *both* passages discuss Hamlet's sensitivity to his family's behavior and his melancholy mood. The only answer choice that remains is (C), which, when we check the passages, is confirmed as the correct answer: the Passage 2 author explores the question of Hamlet's inconsistency at some length, while the Passage 1 author is more focused on the causes of his melancholy disposition.

12. **(E)**   Relating Two Passages; Main Theme or Idea   Difficulty: low

This question is extremely easy, as both passages are very simple and direct about Gertrude's behavior. Passage 1 describes the "impropriety" of her behavior in marrying Claudius so soon after her first husband's death, and says that Hamlet detects moral "depravity" in her actions. The second passage dramatically lists Hamlet's difficulties as including "an uncle's villainy, a mother's guilt, a father's murder!" If Hamlet's mother's "guilt" is involved in his uncle's villainy and his father's murder, it is quite easy to settle on (E) as the correct answer choice. Neither passage mentions her love for Claudius, her innocence in the matter of the murder, her popularity in Denmark, or her former role as a moral example for Hamlet. Each passage focuses solely on her current bad behavior and moral depravity; as a result, (E) is the best answer choice.

13. **(D)** Relating Two Passages; Specific Information   Difficulty: medium

Because of the long answer choices and wide variety of ideas they discuss, this simple question appears far more complicated than it really is. All we really need to do to find the correct answer is seek out the specific sections in both passages that discuss Hamlet's sensitivity, and then to compare them. Fairly early in both passages, we find descriptions of Hamlet's sensitivity. The Passage 1 author emphasizes Hamlet's acute moral feelings, saying that he responds to virtue and vice with extremely powerful reactions. The author of Passage 2 simply comments on Hamlet's general sensitivity, saying that he is "apt to be strongly impressed by his situation," and even "overpowered by the feelings which that situation excites."

With this in mind, it is quite clear that Passage 1 emphasizes Hamlet's moral sensitivity, while Passage 2 emphasizes his more general sensitivity to events, making (D) the only feasible answer choice. Though they reference a wide variety of ideas, many of which are important to the play, none of the other answer choices seems particularly relevant to the specific texts in question.

SAT Practice Test 3

SAT PRACTICE TEST 3 ANSWER SHEET

MATH SECTION 1	VERBAL SECTION 1	MATH SECTION 2	VERBAL SECTION 2
1. Ⓐ Ⓑ Ⓒ Ⓓ Ⓔ	8. Ⓐ Ⓑ Ⓒ Ⓓ Ⓔ	10. Ⓐ Ⓑ Ⓒ Ⓓ Ⓔ	22. Ⓐ Ⓑ Ⓒ Ⓓ Ⓔ
2. Ⓐ Ⓑ Ⓒ Ⓓ Ⓔ	9. Ⓐ Ⓑ Ⓒ Ⓓ Ⓔ	11. Ⓐ Ⓑ Ⓒ Ⓓ Ⓔ	23. Ⓐ Ⓑ Ⓒ Ⓓ Ⓔ
3. Ⓐ Ⓑ Ⓒ Ⓓ Ⓔ	10. Ⓐ Ⓑ Ⓒ Ⓓ Ⓔ	12. Ⓐ Ⓑ Ⓒ Ⓓ Ⓔ	24. Ⓐ Ⓑ Ⓒ Ⓓ Ⓔ
4. Ⓐ Ⓑ Ⓒ Ⓓ Ⓔ	11. Ⓐ Ⓑ Ⓒ Ⓓ Ⓔ	13. Ⓐ Ⓑ Ⓒ Ⓓ Ⓔ	25. Ⓐ Ⓑ Ⓒ Ⓓ Ⓔ
5. Ⓐ Ⓑ Ⓒ Ⓓ Ⓔ	12. Ⓐ Ⓑ Ⓒ Ⓓ Ⓔ	14. Ⓐ Ⓑ Ⓒ Ⓓ Ⓔ	26. Ⓐ Ⓑ Ⓒ Ⓓ Ⓔ
6. Ⓐ Ⓑ Ⓒ Ⓓ Ⓔ	13. Ⓐ Ⓑ Ⓒ Ⓓ Ⓔ	15. Ⓐ Ⓑ Ⓒ Ⓓ Ⓔ	27. Ⓐ Ⓑ Ⓒ Ⓓ Ⓔ
7. Ⓐ Ⓑ Ⓒ Ⓓ Ⓔ	14. Ⓐ Ⓑ Ⓒ Ⓓ Ⓔ	16. Ⓐ Ⓑ Ⓒ Ⓓ Ⓔ	28. Ⓐ Ⓑ Ⓒ Ⓓ Ⓔ
8. Ⓐ Ⓑ Ⓒ Ⓓ Ⓔ	15. Ⓐ Ⓑ Ⓒ Ⓓ Ⓔ	17. Ⓐ Ⓑ Ⓒ Ⓓ Ⓔ	29. Ⓐ Ⓑ Ⓒ Ⓓ Ⓔ
9. Ⓐ Ⓑ Ⓒ Ⓓ Ⓔ	16. Ⓐ Ⓑ Ⓒ Ⓓ Ⓔ	18. Ⓐ Ⓑ Ⓒ Ⓓ Ⓔ	30. Ⓐ Ⓑ Ⓒ Ⓓ Ⓔ
10. Ⓐ Ⓑ Ⓒ Ⓓ Ⓔ	17. Ⓐ Ⓑ Ⓒ Ⓓ Ⓔ	19. Ⓐ Ⓑ Ⓒ Ⓓ Ⓔ	31. Ⓐ Ⓑ Ⓒ Ⓓ Ⓔ
11. Ⓐ Ⓑ Ⓒ Ⓓ Ⓔ	18. Ⓐ Ⓑ Ⓒ Ⓓ Ⓔ	20. Ⓐ Ⓑ Ⓒ Ⓓ Ⓔ	32. Ⓐ Ⓑ Ⓒ Ⓓ Ⓔ
12. Ⓐ Ⓑ Ⓒ Ⓓ Ⓔ	19. Ⓐ Ⓑ Ⓒ Ⓓ Ⓔ	21. Ⓐ Ⓑ Ⓒ Ⓓ Ⓔ	33. Ⓐ Ⓑ Ⓒ Ⓓ Ⓔ
13. Ⓐ Ⓑ Ⓒ Ⓓ Ⓔ	20. Ⓐ Ⓑ Ⓒ Ⓓ Ⓔ	22. Ⓐ Ⓑ Ⓒ Ⓓ Ⓔ	34. Ⓐ Ⓑ Ⓒ Ⓓ Ⓔ
14. Ⓐ Ⓑ Ⓒ Ⓓ Ⓔ	21. Ⓐ Ⓑ Ⓒ Ⓓ Ⓔ	23. Ⓐ Ⓑ Ⓒ Ⓓ Ⓔ	35. Ⓐ Ⓑ Ⓒ Ⓓ Ⓔ
15. Ⓐ Ⓑ Ⓒ Ⓓ Ⓔ	22. Ⓐ Ⓑ Ⓒ Ⓓ Ⓔ	24. Ⓐ Ⓑ Ⓒ Ⓓ Ⓔ	**MATH SECTION 3**
16. Ⓐ Ⓑ Ⓒ Ⓓ Ⓔ	23. Ⓐ Ⓑ Ⓒ Ⓓ Ⓔ	25. Ⓐ Ⓑ Ⓒ Ⓓ Ⓔ	1. Ⓐ Ⓑ Ⓒ Ⓓ Ⓔ
17. Ⓐ Ⓑ Ⓒ Ⓓ Ⓔ	24. Ⓐ Ⓑ Ⓒ Ⓓ Ⓔ	**VERBAL SECTION 2**	2. Ⓐ Ⓑ Ⓒ Ⓓ Ⓔ
18. Ⓐ Ⓑ Ⓒ Ⓓ Ⓔ	25. Ⓐ Ⓑ Ⓒ Ⓓ Ⓔ	1. Ⓐ Ⓑ Ⓒ Ⓓ Ⓔ	3. Ⓐ Ⓑ Ⓒ Ⓓ Ⓔ
19. Ⓐ Ⓑ Ⓒ Ⓓ Ⓔ	26. Ⓐ Ⓑ Ⓒ Ⓓ Ⓔ	2. Ⓐ Ⓑ Ⓒ Ⓓ Ⓔ	4. Ⓐ Ⓑ Ⓒ Ⓓ Ⓔ
20. Ⓐ Ⓑ Ⓒ Ⓓ Ⓔ	27. Ⓐ Ⓑ Ⓒ Ⓓ Ⓔ	3. Ⓐ Ⓑ Ⓒ Ⓓ Ⓔ	5. Ⓐ Ⓑ Ⓒ Ⓓ Ⓔ
21. Ⓐ Ⓑ Ⓒ Ⓓ Ⓔ	28. Ⓐ Ⓑ Ⓒ Ⓓ Ⓔ	4. Ⓐ Ⓑ Ⓒ Ⓓ Ⓔ	6. Ⓐ Ⓑ Ⓒ Ⓓ Ⓔ
22. Ⓐ Ⓑ Ⓒ Ⓓ Ⓔ	29. Ⓐ Ⓑ Ⓒ Ⓓ Ⓔ	5. Ⓐ Ⓑ Ⓒ Ⓓ Ⓔ	7. Ⓐ Ⓑ Ⓒ Ⓓ Ⓔ
23. Ⓐ Ⓑ Ⓒ Ⓓ Ⓔ	30. Ⓐ Ⓑ Ⓒ Ⓓ Ⓔ	6. Ⓐ Ⓑ Ⓒ Ⓓ Ⓔ	8. Ⓐ Ⓑ Ⓒ Ⓓ Ⓔ
24. Ⓐ Ⓑ Ⓒ Ⓓ Ⓔ	31. Ⓐ Ⓑ Ⓒ Ⓓ Ⓔ	7. Ⓐ Ⓑ Ⓒ Ⓓ Ⓔ	9. Ⓐ Ⓑ Ⓒ Ⓓ Ⓔ
25. Ⓐ Ⓑ Ⓒ Ⓓ Ⓔ	32. Ⓐ Ⓑ Ⓒ Ⓓ Ⓔ	8. Ⓐ Ⓑ Ⓒ Ⓓ Ⓔ	10. Ⓐ Ⓑ Ⓒ Ⓓ Ⓔ
26. Ⓐ Ⓑ Ⓒ Ⓓ Ⓔ	33. Ⓐ Ⓑ Ⓒ Ⓓ Ⓔ	9. Ⓐ Ⓑ Ⓒ Ⓓ Ⓔ	**VERBAL SECTION 3**
27. Ⓐ Ⓑ Ⓒ Ⓓ Ⓔ	34. Ⓐ Ⓑ Ⓒ Ⓓ Ⓔ	10. Ⓐ Ⓑ Ⓒ Ⓓ Ⓔ	1. Ⓐ Ⓑ Ⓒ Ⓓ Ⓔ
28. Ⓐ Ⓑ Ⓒ Ⓓ Ⓔ	35. Ⓐ Ⓑ Ⓒ Ⓓ Ⓔ	11. Ⓐ Ⓑ Ⓒ Ⓓ Ⓔ	2. Ⓐ Ⓑ Ⓒ Ⓓ Ⓔ
29. Ⓐ Ⓑ Ⓒ Ⓓ Ⓔ	**MATH SECTION 2**	12. Ⓐ Ⓑ Ⓒ Ⓓ Ⓔ	3. Ⓐ Ⓑ Ⓒ Ⓓ Ⓔ
30. Ⓐ Ⓑ Ⓒ Ⓓ Ⓔ	1. Ⓐ Ⓑ Ⓒ Ⓓ Ⓔ	13. Ⓐ Ⓑ Ⓒ Ⓓ Ⓔ	4. Ⓐ Ⓑ Ⓒ Ⓓ Ⓔ
VERBAL SECTION 1	2. Ⓐ Ⓑ Ⓒ Ⓓ Ⓔ	14. Ⓐ Ⓑ Ⓒ Ⓓ Ⓔ	5. Ⓐ Ⓑ Ⓒ Ⓓ Ⓔ
1. Ⓐ Ⓑ Ⓒ Ⓓ Ⓔ	3. Ⓐ Ⓑ Ⓒ Ⓓ Ⓔ	15. Ⓐ Ⓑ Ⓒ Ⓓ Ⓔ	6. Ⓐ Ⓑ Ⓒ Ⓓ Ⓔ
2. Ⓐ Ⓑ Ⓒ Ⓓ Ⓔ	4. Ⓐ Ⓑ Ⓒ Ⓓ Ⓔ	16. Ⓐ Ⓑ Ⓒ Ⓓ Ⓔ	7. Ⓐ Ⓑ Ⓒ Ⓓ Ⓔ
3. Ⓐ Ⓑ Ⓒ Ⓓ Ⓔ	5. Ⓐ Ⓑ Ⓒ Ⓓ Ⓔ	17. Ⓐ Ⓑ Ⓒ Ⓓ Ⓔ	8. Ⓐ Ⓑ Ⓒ Ⓓ Ⓔ
4. Ⓐ Ⓑ Ⓒ Ⓓ Ⓔ	6. Ⓐ Ⓑ Ⓒ Ⓓ Ⓔ	18. Ⓐ Ⓑ Ⓒ Ⓓ Ⓔ	9. Ⓐ Ⓑ Ⓒ Ⓓ Ⓔ
5. Ⓐ Ⓑ Ⓒ Ⓓ Ⓔ	7. Ⓐ Ⓑ Ⓒ Ⓓ Ⓔ	19. Ⓐ Ⓑ Ⓒ Ⓓ Ⓔ	10. Ⓐ Ⓑ Ⓒ Ⓓ Ⓔ
6. Ⓐ Ⓑ Ⓒ Ⓓ Ⓔ	8. Ⓐ Ⓑ Ⓒ Ⓓ Ⓔ	20. Ⓐ Ⓑ Ⓒ Ⓓ Ⓔ	11. Ⓐ Ⓑ Ⓒ Ⓓ Ⓔ
7. Ⓐ Ⓑ Ⓒ Ⓓ Ⓔ	9. Ⓐ Ⓑ Ⓒ Ⓓ Ⓔ	21. Ⓐ Ⓑ Ⓒ Ⓓ Ⓔ	12. Ⓐ Ⓑ Ⓒ Ⓓ Ⓔ
			13. Ⓐ Ⓑ Ⓒ Ⓓ Ⓔ

SAT TEST

<table>
<tr><td>**Time—30 Minutes**
25 Questions</td><td>In this section solve each problem, using any available space on the page for scratchwork. Then decide which is the best of the choices given and fill in the corresponding oval on the answer sheet.</td></tr>
</table>

Notes:

1. The use of a calculator is permitted. All numbers used are real numbers.

2. Figures that accompany problems in this test are intended to provide information useful in solving the problems. They are drawn as accurately as possible EXCEPT when it is stated in a specific problem that the figure is not drawn to scale. All figures lie in a plane unless otherwise indicated.

  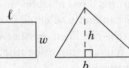
1. If $4x - y = 10$, and $2x = 6$, what is $2y$?

    (A) 0
    (B) 2
    (C) 4
    (D) 6
    (E) 8

2. What is $2\frac{3}{4} - 1\frac{1}{6}$?

    (A) $\frac{1}{2}$

    (B) -2

    (C) $\frac{11}{6}$

    (D) $\frac{13}{4}$

    (E) $\frac{19}{12}$

3. What number multiplied by 3 equals 4 less than 16?

    (A) 3
    (B) 4
    (C) 12
    (D) 36
    (E) 60

4. If $3x - 6 = 18$, what is $2x + 3$?

    (A) 4
    (B) 11
    (C) 13
    (D) 15
    (E) 19

GO ON TO THE NEXT PAGE

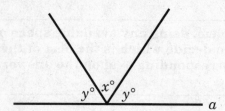

5. In the figure above, if *a* is a straight line, and the measure of angle *y* is 65°, what is the value of *x* in degrees?

    (A) 115
    (B) 57.5
    (C) 50
    (D) 40
    (E) 25

6. If $x/2$ is an integer, then which of the following values could possibly be equal to *x*?

    (A) −2
    (B) 1
    (C) 3
    (D) 4.5
    (E) 5

7. How many square kilometers is a rectangular field that measures 4000 meters by 5000 meters? (1 kilometer = 1000 meters)

    (A) 20,000,000
    (B) 1000
    (A) 200
    (D) 20
    (E) 9

8. A bus starts at point *A*, travels 30 miles due east to point *B*, turns north and drives 40 miles to point *C*, and then returns in a straight line back to point *A*. How many total miles has it traveled?

    (A) 70
    (B) 110
    (C) 115
    (D) 120
    (E) 140

9. In a bag of candies, the ratio of red to green to blue candies is 4:3:6, respectively. If there are a total of 65 candies in a bag, how many are green?

    (A) 3
    (B) 4
    (C) 5
    (D) 13
    (E) 15

10. $\sqrt{\dfrac{x+2}{y+2}} = 2\sqrt{\dfrac{1}{4}}$. Solve for *x* in terms of *y*.

    (A) $x = y + 2$
    (B) $x = 2y$
    (C) $x = y$
    (D) $x = y^2$
    (E) $x = 2\sqrt{y}$

11. A jar contains 3 red marbles and 6 white marbles. A marble is randomly selected from the jar. It is then put back into the jar. Then another marble is randomly selected. What is the probability that both marbles selected are white?

    (A) $\dfrac{1}{3}$

    (B) $\dfrac{4}{9}$

    (C) $\dfrac{1}{2}$

    (D) $\dfrac{2}{3}$

    (E) $\dfrac{4}{3}$

12. Let $x = y$. For what value of *a* is $(x + y)^2 = ax^2$?

    (A) x
    (B) y
    (C) 1
    (D) 2
    (E) 4

13. A cube has a volume of 64. What is the area of a circle whose radius is equal to the length of one of the edges of the cube?

    (A) 64π
    (B) 27π
    (C) 16π
    (D) 6π
    (E) (3/4)π

GO ON TO THE NEXT PAGE

14. If *m* is divided by 7, the remainder is 2. Which of the following CANNOT be a possible value of m?

   (A) 17
   (B) 23
   (C) 30
   (D) 51
   (E) 72

15. If $\dfrac{1}{abc} > \dfrac{1}{97}$ where *a*, *b*, and *c* are integers, and

   $a > b > c > 1$, what is the greatest possible value of *a*?

   (A) 2
   (B) 16
   (C) 17
   (D) 24
   (E) 96

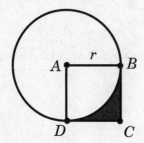

16. *A* is the center of circle *A*. *B* and *D* are points on the circle. *ABCD* is a square. What is the area of the shaded region in terms of radius r?

   (A) $\pi r^2 - r^2$

   (B) $\dfrac{3\pi r^2}{4}$

   (C) $r^2 - \dfrac{\pi r^2}{4}$

   (D) $\dfrac{\pi r^2}{4}$

   (E) $r^2 - \pi r^2$

17. $\dfrac{k^7}{k^x} = k$. $(k^2)^y = k^8$. What is the value of *xy*?

   (A) 10
   (B) 18
   (C) 21
   (D) 24
   (E) 28

Result	Flip 1	Flip 2	Flip 3	Flip 4	Flip 5
Heads	X				
Tails			X	X	

18. A fair coin is flipped five times. Three of the results are shown above in the chart. Which of the following could *not* be the percentage of heads after the five flips?

   (A) 20%
   (B) 40%
   (C) 60%
   (D) 80%
   (E) All of these percentages are possible.

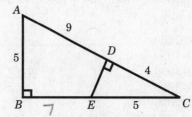

19. All lengths are integers. What is the ratio of the areas of *ABC*:*DEC*?

   (A) 2:1
   (B) 3:1
   (C) 4:1
   (D) 5:1
   (E) 6:1

20. Let $x \dagger y$ be equal to $xy - x + 3$. If $a \dagger b = 3$ and $a \neq 0$, what is the value of *b*?

   (A) −3
   (B) −2
   (C) 0
   (D) 1
   (E) 2

21. Let $\boxed{z} = z^2 + 1$. What is $\boxed{x+y} - \boxed{x-y}$?

   (A) 2*x*
   (B) 4*xy*
   (C) $4y^2$
   (D) x^2y^2
   (E) 8*xy*

GO ON TO THE NEXT PAGE

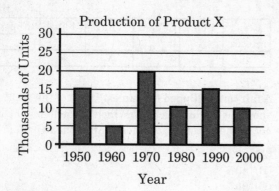

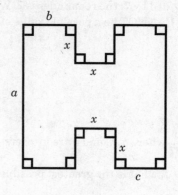

22. According to the graph above, in which ten-year period was the percentage decrease in production of Product X the greatest?

    (A) 1950–1960
    (B) 1960–1970
    (C) 1970–1980
    (D) 1980–1990
    (E) 1990–2000

23. Suppose the median of 5 numbers is n. Which of the following must be true?

    I. The largest number is at least 1 larger than the smallest number.
    II. One of the numbers is $n - 1$.
    III. The mode is also n.

    (A) I
    (B) II
    (C) III
    (D) I and III
    (E) None of these must be true

24. What is the perimeter of the figure above?

    (A) $2(a + b + c + 3x)$
    (B) $2(a + b + c) - 6x$
    (C) $2(a + b + c) - 3x$
    (D) $2a + b + c + 6x$
    (E) $2(a + b + c + x)$

25. If $a = bc$, which of the following must be equivalent to $\frac{b}{2}$?

    (A) $\frac{2a}{c}$

    (B) $\frac{a}{2c}$

    (C) $2ac$

    (D) $\frac{ac}{2}$

    (E) $\frac{c}{2a}$

S T O P

IF YOU FINISH BEFORE TIME IS CALLED, YOU MAY CHECK YOUR WORK IN THIS SECTION ONLY.
DO NOT TURN TO ANY OTHER SECTION IN THE TEST.

SAT TEST

Time—30 Minutes
30 Questions

For each question in this section, select the best answer from among the choices given and fill in the corresponding oval on the answer sheet.

Each sentence below has one or two blanks, each blank indicating that something has been omitted. Beneath the sentence are five words or sets of words labeled A through E. Choose the word or set of words that, when inserted in the sentence, <u>best</u> fits the meaning of the sentence as a whole.

Example:
  Medieval kingdoms did not become constitutional republics overnight; on the contrary, the change was ----.

(A) unpopular
(B) unexpected
(C) advantageous
(D) sufficient
(E) gradual   Ⓐ Ⓑ Ⓒ Ⓓ ●

1. Because it contained numerous unexplored ideas and uncalculated equations, many physicists considered string theory to be a(n) ---- field for research.

   (A) safe
   (B) unsatisfactory
   (C) promising
   (D) ancient
   (E) dubious

2. Antonio protested that he could not be ---- for a crime that he did not ----.

   (A) condemned..commit
   (B) regaled..pertain
   (C) adjourned..condone
   (D) convincted..commiserate
   (E) responsible..cauterize

3. Though his first experiment ended in disappointment, the chemist hoped his second try would bring ----.

   (A) collapse
   (B) hypothesis
   (C) success
   (D) renewal
   (E) skill

4. Although many people found him to be physically ----, Pee Wee Russell's clarinet playing was widely regarded as ----.

   (A) ugly..foul
   (B) pristine..dramatic
   (C) grotesque..beautiful
   (D) handsome..gentle
   (E) expressive..unique

5. Although Spartacus wished to ---- his army after vanquishing the Roman forces, his men insisted on remaining ---- and continuing to fight.

   (A) reward..affluent
   (B) execute..macabre
   (C) outfit..neutral
   (D) disband..together
   (E) encourage..immoral

6. Built on wooden stilts that had gradually rotted away over the years, the condition of Ting's seaside home became more ---- with every passing storm.

   (A) precarious
   (B) adventurous
   (C) absurd
   (D) seasonal
   (E) fruitful

GO ON TO THE NEXT PAGE

7. The Battle of Hastings in 1066 was a(n) ---- event in English History, for the Norman victory over the Saxons changed the future course of the nation.

   (A) irrelevant
   (B) seminal
   (C) disastrous
   (D) reputable
   (E) irrefutable

8. While her stepsisters set a new mark for grumpiness, Cinderella was ---- and lovely.

   (A) frosty
   (B) impeachable
   (C) endearing
   (D) flippant
   (E) uncouth

9. Despite having suffered through years of ---- rule, the people of Zambonia refused to forget the ---- traditions of their ancestors and continued to struggle for freedom.

   (A) benevolent..idiosyncratic
   (B) autocratic..egalitarian
   (C) destructive..despicable
   (D) idyllic..democratic
   (E) legislative..acrimonious

GO ON TO THE NEXT PAGE

Each question below consists of a related pair of words or phrases, followed by five pairs of words or phrases labeled A through E. Select the pair that <u>best</u> expresses a relationship similar to that expressed in the original pair.

Example:
CRUMB : BREAD ::

(A) ounce : unit
(B) splinter : wood
(C) water : bucket
(D) twine : rope
(E) cream : butter

10. MONUMENT : EVENT ::

(A) building : lifestyle
(B) syllabus : educate
(C) medal : bravery
(D) blueprint : construction
(E) analysis : summary

11. WRENCH : MECHANIC ::

(A) liquid : vial
(B) clinic : doctor
(C) needle : tailor
(D) apron : chef
(E) computer : disk

12. ZEALOT : FAITH

(A) candidate : politics
(B) person : gender
(C) conformist : rebellion
(D) partisan : faction
(E) panelist : forum

13. ONEROUS : TASK ::

(A) interminable : lecture
(B) gregarious : opponent
(C) assertive : hint
(D) intrepid : explorer
(E) superficial : statement

14. PASSION : PREDILECTION ::

(A) grudge : demise
(B) torrent : sprinkle
(C) fondness : spite
(D) imply : indicate
(E) hold : caress

15. UNDERSTATED : EXAGGERATION ::

(A) vociferous : volume
(B) indicative : random
(C) sane : lunacy
(D) positive : proof
(E) mischievous : rogue

GO ON TO THE NEXT PAGE ➤

SAT TEST

Questions 16–20 are based on the following passage.

The following passage is adapted from an essay written by W.E.B. Du Bois, a black leader and intellectual during the first half of the twentieth century. In the essay, Du Bois discusses the origins and complications of freedom for black Americans in the United States.

The problem of the twentieth century is the problem of the color line—the relation of the darker to the lighter races of men in Asia and Africa, in America and the islands of the

Line sea. It was a phase of this problem that caused the Civil War;
5 and however much they who marched South and North in 1861 may have fixed on the technical points of union and local autonomy, all nevertheless knew, as we know, that the question of slavery was the real cause of the conflict. No sooner had Northern armies touched Southern soil than this
10 old question, newly guised, sprang from the earth: What shall be done with Southern blacks? Peremptory military commands could not answer the query; the Emancipation Proclamation seemed but to broaden and intensify the difficulties; and the War Amendments created the problems
15 that now haunt the present.

It is the aim of this essay to study the period of history from 1861 to 1872 so far as it relates to the black Americans, and to study the attempts made by a great nation to grapple with vast problems of race and social condition.
20 No sooner had the Northern armies, both in East and West, penetrated Virginia and Tennessee than fugitive slaves appeared within their lines. They came at night, when the flickering camp-fires shone like vast unsteady stars along the black horizon: old men and thin, with gray and tufted hair;
25 women with frightened eyes, dragging whimpering hungry children; men and girls, stalwart and gaunt—a horde of starving vagabonds, homeless, helpless, and pitiable, in their dark distress.

Two methods of treating these newcomers seemed
30 equally logical to opposite sorts of minds. General Ben Butler, in Virginia, quickly declared slave property contraband of war, and put the fugitives to work; while General Fremont, in Missouri, declared the slaves free under martial law. Butler's action was approved, but Fremont's was hastily
35 countermanded, and his successor, Halleck, saw things differently. "Hereafter," he commanded, "no slaves should be allowed to come into your lines at all; if any come without your knowledge, when owners call for them deliver them." Such a policy was difficult to enforce; some of the black

40 refugees declared themselves freemen, others showed that their masters had deserted them, and still others were captured with forts and plantations.

Evidently, too, slaves were a source of strength to the Confederacy, and were being used as laborers and producers.
45 "They constitute a military resource," wrote Secretary Cameron, late in 1861, "and being such, that they should not be turned over to the enemy is too plain to discuss." So gradually the tone of the army chiefs changed; Congress forbade the return of fugitives to Southerners, and Butler's
50 "contrabands" were welcomed as military laborers.

This complicated rather than solved the problem, for now the scattering fugitives became a steady stream, which flowed faster as the armies marched. Northern generals began to ask the questions that would, after the war, become
55 crucial throughout the North: what must be done with all these men, women, and children, former slaves? Were they to be set free, penniless and starving as they were? How were they to be cared for, and who should do the caring?

16. The author asserts that the main cause of the Civil War was

   (A) slavery
   (B) the Emancipation Proclamation
   (C) the War Amendments
   (D) General Fremont
   (E) General Butler

17. In line 10, "guised" most closely means

   (A) dressed
   (B) disguised
   (C) excused
   (D) emasculated
   (E) shown

GO ON TO THE NEXT PAGE

18. The author's description of fugitive slaves (lines 22–28) is most likely aimed at evoking the reader's

    (A) condemnation
    (B) apathy
    (C) hatred
    (D) reticence
    (E) compassion

19. Compared to the policies of his predecessor, General Halleck's position on fugitive slaves described in lines 36–38,

    (A) did not represent a significant shift in policy
    (B) treated fugitive slaves more favorably
    (C) treated fugitive slaves less favorably
    (D) displayed greater understanding for the problems of slavery
    (E) indirectly led to the Union's victory in the Civil War

20. Du Bois claims that changes in the Union's policy on returning fugitive slaves came about because

    (A) slaves could be sent back as spies
    (B) Secretary Cameron owned many slaves
    (C) slave labor abetted the Confederate cause
    (D) fugitive slaves were the real enemies of the Union
    (E) slaves knowingly destroyed Southern crops

GO ON TO THE NEXT PAGE

SAT TEST

The passage below is followed by questions based on its content. Answer the questions on the basis of what is <u>stated</u> or <u>implied</u> in the passage and in any introductory material that may be provided.

Questions 21–35 are based on the following passage.

The following passage is adapted from an account of the invention of the first hot-air balloon.

It was a November night of the year 1782, in the little town of Annonay, near Lyons in France. Two young men, Stephen and Joseph Montgolfier, who worked as
Line representatives for a firm of paper makers, were sitting
5 together over their parlor fire. While watching the smoke curling up the chimney one propounded an idea by way of a sudden inspiration: "Why shouldn't smoke be made to raise bodies into the air?"
The world was waiting for this utterance, which, it would
10 seem, was on the tip of the tongue of many others. Cavendish[1] had already discovered what he designated "inflammable air," though no one had as yet given it its later title of hydrogen gas. By as many as fifteen years before 1782, Dr. Black of Edinburgh, Scotland had suggested that
15 "inflammable air" might be capable of raising a thin bladder in the air. With a shade more of good fortune, or maybe with a modicum more of leisure, the learned Doctor would have won the invention of the balloon for his own country. A man named Cavallo came even nearer, and, actually putting the
20 same idea into practice, had succeeded in the spring of 1782 in making soap bubbles blown with hydrogen gas float upwards. But he had accomplished no more when, as related, in the autumn of the same year the brothers Montgolfier conceived the notion of making bodies "levitate" by the
25 simpler expedient of filling them with smoke.
This was the crude idea, the application of which in their hands was soon marked with notable success. Their trade at the paper firm supplied ready and suitable materials for a first experiment, and, making an oblong bag of thin paper a
30 few feet in length, they proceeded to introduce a cloud of smoke into it by holding crumpled paper kindled in a chafing dish beneath the open mouth. What a subject is there here for an imaginative painter! As the smoky cloud formed within, the bag distended itself, became buoyant, and presently
35 floated to the ceiling. The simple trial proved a complete success, due, as it appeared to them, to the ascensive power of a cloud of smoke.
There is, however, an interesting and more detailed version of the story. While the experiment was in progress, a
40 neighbor of the Montgolfiers, the widow of a tradesman who had been connected in business with the firm, seeing smoke escaping into the room, entered and stood watching the

proceedings, which were not without difficulties. The bag, half inflated, was not easy to hold in position over the chafing dish,
45 and rapidly cooled and collapsed on being removed from it. The widow, noting this fact and the perplexity of the young men, suggested that they should tie the dish on at the bottom of the bag. This was the one thing wanted to secure success, and that good lady, whose very name is unhappily lost, deserves an
50 honored place in history. It was unquestionably the adoption of her idea which launched the first balloon into the air.
After the same experiment repeated in the open air proved a yet more pronounced success, more elaborate trials were quickly developed, and the infant balloon grew fast.
55 One worthy of the name, spherical in shape and of some 600 cubic feet capacity, was now made and treated as before, with the result that ere it was fully inflated it broke the strings that held it and sailed away hundreds of feet into the air. The infant was fast becoming a prodigy.
60 Encouraged by their fresh success, the inventors at once set about preparations for the construction of a much larger balloon some thirty-five feet in diameter (that is, of about 23,000 cubic feet capacity), to be made of linen lined with paper. This machine, launched on a favorable day in the
65 following spring, rose with great swiftness to fully a thousand feet, and traveled nearly a mile from its starting ground.

21. According to this passage, the Montgolfier brothers got the idea for their balloon from:

   (A) reading Dr. Black's essays on "inflammable air"
   (B) a childhood toy
   (C) watching smoke rise up their chimney
   (D) an engineer with whom they had worked
   (E) watching birds fly

22. Which of the following was *not* used in the construction or operation of early balloons?

   (A) Linen
   (B) Rubber
   (C) Paper
   (D) Chafing dish
   (E) Flame

GO ON TO THE NEXT PAGE

23. The discussion of smoke, "inflammable air," and hydrogen suggests that early balloon-makers felt which of the following was most important?

    (A) the substance used to inflate the balloon
    (B) the material used to make the balloon
    (C) the balloon's heat source
    (D) the size of the balloon
    (E) the material used to line the balloon

24. The comments regarding Dr. Black in lines 16–18 suggest that:

    (A) the Montgolfiers were smarter than their fellow inventors
    (B) nations were competing with one another to launch the first balloon
    (C) it takes a good deal of money to invent things
    (D) Dr. Black was too lazy to succeed
    (E) the Montgolfiers were helped by luck and circumstance

25. The term "crude" in line 26 means:

    (A) offensive and vulgar
    (B) preliminary and unrefined
    (C) poorly conceived
    (D) powered by oil
    (E) morally problematic

26. The reference to the suitability of the scene as material for a painter in lines 32–33 is used to suggest:

    (A) the dramatic quality of this scientific discovery
    (B) that there is something fictional about this version of events
    (C) that the Montgolfiers were good-looking young men
    (D) that science is frequently a good subject for art
    (E) that pictures would do the events more justice than words can

27. The phrase "as it appeared to them" in line 36 implies that:

    (A) the Montgolfiers couldn't see properly because of all the smoke
    (B) the Montgolfiers didn't have the proper equipment to make observations
    (C) common sense leads to the best explanations
    (D) the Montgolfiers didn't understand what made their balloon work
    (E) successful experiments always reveal why they work

28. The story of the widow is used to illustrate that:

    (A) women are frequently undervalued in the history of science
    (B) often more than one person is needed to successfully invent something
    (C) trial and error is the best method of experimentation
    (D) being a successful scientist requires a supportive community
    (E) often not everyone involved in an invention gets credit for it

29. The balloon that broke away from the Montgolfiers (line 55) was "worthy of the name" because:

    (A) it was the first to perform well
    (B) it was the first that the Montgolfiers called by the name "balloon"
    (C) it was the first to resemble in size and shape what we now call a balloon
    (D) it was the first of any significant size
    (E) it was spirited and broke away to freedom

30. The references to the balloon as an "infant" and then as a "prodigy" (lines 54 and 59) suggest that the author of this passage would likely agree with which of the following statements?

    (A) Inventing requires a childlike imagination.
    (B) Inventions usually require several stages of development.
    (C) Being a successful inventor depends on one's childhood education.
    (D) Even a child could have invented the balloon.
    (E) Though the idea behind the balloon now seems obvious, it wasn't then.

S T O P

SAT TEST

Directions for Quantitative Comparison Questions

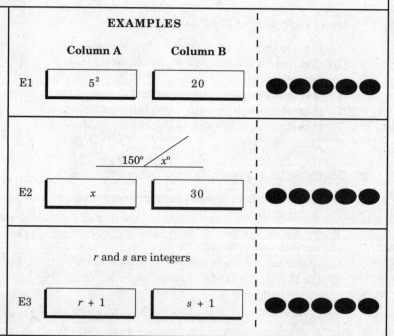

SAT—*Continued*

<table>
<tr><td colspan="2"><u>Column A</u></td><td colspan="2"><u>Column B</u></td></tr>
</table>

The number 724.793 is to be rounded
to the nearest hundredth.

1.
| The digit in the hundreds place of the rounded number | The digit in the tenths place of the rounded number |

$x \neq 0$

2.
| $-x^2$ | $(-x)^2$ |

3.
| $\frac{3}{4}$ of 60 | $\frac{5}{8}$ of 72 |

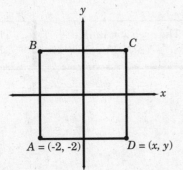

$A = (-2, -2)$ $D = (x, y)$

4.
| x | y |

5.
| Area of a circle with diameter of length 6 | Area of a square with side of length 5 |

6.
| $r(s + t)u$ | $rsu + rtu$ |

<u>Column A</u>   <u>Column B</u>

The sum of k, $k + 1$, and two times k is 21.

7.
| k | 4 |

$$\frac{1}{4} < k + \frac{1}{8} < \frac{1}{2}$$

8.
| k | $\frac{1}{8}$ |

9.
| The number of three-digit numbers with the ones digit equal to 4 | The number of three-digit numbers with the hundreds digit equal to 4 |

y is obtained by dividing x by $\frac{8}{3}$ and then
multiplying by $\frac{2}{9}$

10.
| $2x$ | $24y$ |

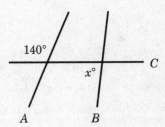

Lines A and B are parallel. Note: Figure not
drawn to scale.

11.
| $8x$ | 360 |

GO ON TO THE NEXT PAGE →

<u>**Column A**</u>   <u>**Column B**</u>   <u>**Column A**</u>   <u>**Column B**</u>

12. | x increased by 40% | | x decreased by 20% |

14. | The least prime number which is the sum of prime numbers | | (The number of factors of 42) − (the number of prime factors of 42) |

13. $\dfrac{\dfrac{320}{7} - \dfrac{240}{7}}{\dfrac{80}{7}}$ 2

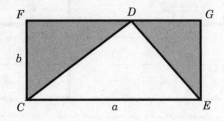

15. | The area of triangle $\triangle CDE$ | | The area of the shaded region |

GO ON TO THE NEXT PAGE ➤

SAT TEST

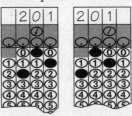
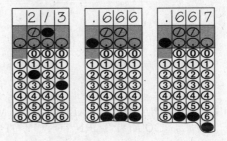
16. Seven apple trees in a grove are flowering. If there are 12 trees in total, what is the ratio of flowering to non-flowering trees? (Grid your ratio as a fraction.)

17. Let $x * y = x^2 - y^2$. What is $5 * 4$?

GO ON TO THE NEXT PAGE

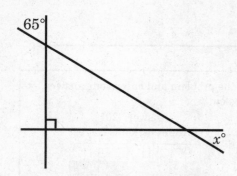

18. In the figure above, what is the value of x (in degrees)?

19. What is the sum of the mean and the median of the set {7, 6, 23}?

20. If $(4x + y)^2 = 49$, $2y^2 = 18$, and $x, y > 0$, what is x?

21. A rectangular solid has four faces which are 4 × 6 rectangles, and two faces which are squares with sides of length 4. What is the surface area of this solid?

22. What is the perimeter of the polygon shown below?

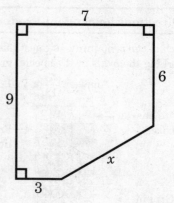

23. If $\dfrac{x}{y+2} \geq 16$ and $y \geq 3$, what is the least possible value of x?

24. Sequence A's first term is –6, and each term thereafter is 3 greater than the previous term. The nth term of sequence B is given by the formula $-5n + 25$. Note that the first term of sequence A is less than the first term of sequence B. What is the value of the term of sequence A that first exceeds the value of its corresponding term in sequence B?

25. What is the mean of the following set of numbers:

$$\{-50, -48, \ldots, 50, 52\}?$$

S T O P

**IF YOU FINISH BEFORE TIME IS CALLED, YOU MAY CHECK YOUR WORK IN THIS SECTION ONLY.
DO NOT TURN TO ANY OTHER SECTION IN THE TEST.**

SAT TEST

Time—30 Minutes
35 Questions

For each question in this section, select the best answer from among the choices given and fill in the corresponding oval on the answer sheet.

Each sentence below has one or two blanks, each blank indicating that something has been omitted. Beneath the sentence are five words or sets of words labeled A through E. Choose the word or set of words that, when inserted in the sentence, <u>best</u> fits the meaning of the sentence as a whole.

Example:
  Medieval kingdoms did not become constitutional republics overnight; on the contrary, the change was ----.

  (A) unpopular
  (B) unexpected
  (C) advantageous
  (D) sufficient
  (E) gradual

1. By mixing horror with farce, Alfred Hitchcock was known for making films at once ---- and hilarious.

    (A) gruesome
    (B) funny
    (C) staid
    (D) informational
    (E) moving

2. Ms. Gutierrez told her students that a good paper must be factually ---- and conform to all rules of proper ----.

    (A) obvious..explanations
    (B) negative..behavior
    (C) inconsistent..punctuation
    (D) correct..grammar
    (E) continuous..spelling

3. Because she was easily annoyed and constantly cutting people off, Sarah was not known for her ----.

    (A) abruptness
    (B) devotion
    (C) patience
    (D) hindsight
    (E) charity

4. Because he wasn't British, many members of the English Parliament saw Prince Albert as a meddler in English affairs and treated him with ---- after he married Queen Victoria in 1840 and gained great influence.

    (A) impatience
    (B) ecstasy
    (C) contempt
    (D) interest
    (E) sadness

5. T.S. Eliot's most famous poem, *The Waste Land,* is a verbal ----; images from many levels of language and experience jumble jarringly together in it.

    (A) symphony
    (B) hodgepodge
    (C) portrait
    (D) gesture
    (E) epilogue

6. Reindeer are often portrayed in American culture as merely ---- creatures, though in fact they are ---- to the survival of the people known as the Sami.

    (A) dim-witted..unnecessary
    (B) passive..instrumental
    (C) fanciful..crucial
    (D) Arctic..unhelpful
    (E) festive..detrimental

7. Though Byron's work "The Prisoner of Chillon" was intended to depict the ---- reality of life behind bars, the author himself was a ---- aristocrat with no firsthand experience of his subject.

    (A) brutal..criminal
    (B) unjust..fair-handed
    (C) chilling..common
    (D) harsh..privileged
    (E) luxurious..pampered

GO ON TO THE NEXT PAGE

8. The idea that Shakespearean plays are *only* serious and high-minded is false; many scenes from them are filled with ----.

   (A) brutality
   (B) harmony
   (C) tragedy
   (D) buffoonery
   (E) happiness

9. All of the costumes were ----, proving that the designer knew virtually nothing about the historical setting of the play.

   (A) empirical
   (B) archetypal
   (C) scrupulous
   (D) plausible
   (E) anachronistic

10. Popular interest in the trend was ----, vanishing as soon as the next trend came along.

   (A) indomitable
   (B) evanescent
   (C) vicarious
   (D) phlegmatic
   (E) unstinting

GO ON TO THE NEXT PAGE

Each question below consists of a related pair of words or phrases, followed by five pairs of words or phrases labeled A through E. Select the pair that <u>best</u> expresses a relationship similar to that expressed in the original pair.

Example:
CRUMB : BREAD ::

(A) ounce : unit
(B) splinter : wood
(C) water : bucket
(D) twine : rope
(E) cream : butter

Ⓐ ● Ⓒ Ⓓ Ⓔ

11. CARROT : VEGETABLE ::

(A) toilet : bathroom
(B) root : garden
(C) cabbage : soup
(D) vest : jacket
(E) silver : metal

12. CHIMNEY : BRICKS ::

(A) cabinet : shelf
(B) couch : cushion
(C) fire : wood
(D) hammer : nail
(E) word : letters

13. FOOD : REFRIGERATOR ::

(A) kitchen : cook
(B) dog : companionship
(C) book : shelf
(D) clothing : laundromat
(E) forest : berries

14. KILOMETER : DISTANCE ::

(A) barometer : pressure
(B) ounce : weight
(C) thermometer : temperature
(D) force : gravity
(E) power : battery

15. RAZOR : HAIR ::

(A) soap : shower
(B) pants : leg
(C) closet : clothing
(D) paper : notebook
(E) eraser : chalk

16. PAUPER : MONEY ::

(A) retiree : leisure
(B) professional : experience
(C) invalid : health
(D) student : learning
(E) author : text

17. BRILLIANT : CLEVER ::

(A) rough : abrasive
(B) manipulative : honest
(C) obvious : subtle
(D) striking : noticeable
(E) apparent : substantial

18. DIRECTOR : PLAY ::

(A) composer : song
(B) farmer : cattle
(C) waiter : meal
(D) climber : mountain
(E) conductor : symphony

19. DUCT : AIR ::

(A) ditch : dirt
(B) crane : materials
(C) canal : water
(D) pool : concrete
(E) pipe : wrench

20. PHOTOGRAPH : IMAGE ::

(A) text : newsprint
(B) drug : cure
(C) television : medium
(D) cement : brick
(E) computer : typewriter

21. VICIOUS : FEROCITY ::

(A) cruel : insult
(B) repulsive : masquerade
(C) joyful : desire
(D) cold : frigidity
(E) bland : excitement

GO ON TO THE NEXT PAGE

22. AMPLIFIER : SOUND ::

    (A) polish : sheen
    (B) magnifier : color
    (C) loathing : fear
    (D) conscientiousness : morality
    (E) metallurgy : platinum

23. THOROUGH : RESEARCH ::

    (A) exhaustive : investigation
    (B) content : sedative
    (C) illuminating : light
    (D) perverse : morality
    (E) wanton : supervisor

GO ON TO THE NEXT PAGE

The passage below is followed by questions based on its content. Answer the questions on the basis of what is <u>stated</u> or <u>implied</u> in the passage and in any introductory material that may be provided.

Questions 24–30 are based on the following passage.

In the following passage, the author discusses Herman Melville's novel Billy Budd. *The passage focuses on the importance and meaning of names, specifically in relation to the different subtitles that Melville considered for the novel.*

Because it went unpublished during Melville's lifetime, there has never been a clear consensus on the proper title for the work most commonly and concisely known as *Billy Budd.*
Line Melville had a passion for subtitling his work, and *Billy Budd*
5 stands as no exception. Though it is generally referred to simply as *Billy Budd,* in scanning the literature regarding the work, one is equally likely to come upon the titles *Billy Budd, Sailor* or *Billy Budd, Foretopman,* and always bound to notice a further subtitle, "An Inside Narrative." All of these additional
10 titles go further than the abbreviated version to illustrate one of Melville's major themes in the work: the constant dilemma of an individual forced to function in a society.

In the opening lines of *Moby-Dick, or The Whale,* Melville introduces his narrator in a rather curious and roundabout
15 way. He does not say, "I am Ishmael," or even, "My name is Ishmael," but rather, "Call me Ishmael." Thus, there is no way of knowing whether the narrator is really named Ishmael or not. All we know is that he wishes to be called Ishmael. All of this illustrates the point that a discrepancy
20 exists between an individual and his name. He may or may not be named Ishmael, and even if he is, at the essential core of his existence, he is more than just his name.

So, you are you. Beyond that you have your name, and then beyond that you have your title. In the case of Billy
25 Budd, he is a sailor or a foretopman. Because "foretopman" is a more specific title than "sailor," *Billy Budd, Foretopman* goes even further than *Billy Budd, Sailor* to illustrate the tensions inevitably elicited by an individual consciousness placed in a specific societal role. As a "sailor," Billy may still
30 be known as "Billy" more or less, but as a "foretopman," a more specific societal role with more specific duties and responsibilities, Billy will have a harder time resisting the infringements of his office on his person.

Example: As "James Corolla," I may have my own
35 impressions and opinions about *Billy Budd, Foretopman.* And these may change over time. But, once I decide to become "James Corolla, Writer," my impressions and opinions about *Billy Budd, Foretopman* take on a greater weight and assume a larger air of finality. Furthermore, if I
40 presume to be "James Corolla, Professor," my impressions

and opinions about *Billy Budd, Foretopman* become even more weighty. What I choose to say about *Billy Budd, Foretopman* can never again be simply something that I say
45 as "James Corolla," since I've already said it as "Professor," backed by all of the expectations and responsibilities associated with such a position. In this way, I exist as a "Professor" above and beyond my existence simply as "James Corolla," and my place as "Professor," in some sense, eclipses my place as "James Corolla," at least with reference to *Billy*
50 *Budd* and the other novels I choose to write about.

Thus, the moment that an individual enters into a society—and enter he must—he in some sense forfeits his rights to individual autonomy, whether as a sailor, a writer, or whatever he may be. However, the sense of individuality
55 remains and chafes against the constraints of the institution and its attendant laws. The clash between the individual and his society is one of the great themes of world literature, and, in *Billy Budd,* we have one of the finest modern explorations of man caught between his own specific conscience and his
60 broader sense of obligations to a just society.

As a self-described "Inside Narrative," *Billy Budd* places special emphasis on the interior consciousness of an individual, in an attempt to explore the private selves of men thrust into a social world. Melville's true concern in *Billy*
65 *Budd* is with this world behind a world. In each reader's attempt to get inside Melville's mind on the questions of morality, religion, and society, he or she will be sure to grapple fiercely with the interior narrative of his or her own ideas and values.

24. According to lines 1–5, why have scholars been unable to agree about the correct title of the novel?

(A) They have misread clues provided in the novel's text.
(B) Political disagreements have led to conflicting factions.
(C) Scholars never agree about anything.
(D) Melville never indicated the correct title.
(E) The novel was never published in Melville's lifetime, so a final title was never settled on.

GO ON TO THE NEXT PAGE

25. The author primarily lists all the subtitles associated with *Billy Budd* (lines 6–9) in order to

    (A) provide historical background information
    (B) give an early example of the way in which titles indicate social position
    (C) illustrate Melville's curious love of subtitles
    (D) explain why bookstores have such a hard time selling Melville's works
    (E) explain the differences between *Billy Budd* and *Moby-Dick*

26. The overall tone of this passage is

    (A) condescending
    (B) outraged
    (C) explanatory and objective
    (D) inquisitive
    (E) excited and enthusiastic

27. According to lines 13–22, what is unusual about the way Melville introduces his narrator in *Moby-Dick*?

    (A) He does not tell the reader whether "Ishmael" is the character's real name or not.
    (B) He does not give a physical description of the character.
    (C) He gives the narrator a highly unusual name.
    (D) He seems to imply that the narrator has a mysterious past.
    (E) He does not place the character in a social context, and therefore makes his name seem ambiguous.

28. The "discrepancy between an individual and his name" (lines 19–20) is best understood as

    (A) the difference between a person's name and his social position
    (B) the way some people's names do not suit them
    (C) the impossibility of knowing whether the name someone gives is his real name
    (D) the difference between a person's name and his inner identity
    (E) the psychological difficulty inherent in any attempt to label another human being

29. The word "foretopman" (line 25) refers to

    (A) the foreman of a factory or mill
    (B) a particular kind of sailor
    (C) the winner of a wrestling match
    (D) the sailor who keeps watch from the crow's nest
    (E) the assistant to a factory foreman

30. In lines 23–33, the author says that calling Billy a "sailor" would be different from calling him a "foretopman," because

    (A) being a foretopman involves a different kind of work
    (B) a sailor is expected to travel on the open sea, while a foretopman only deals with ships in port
    (C) sailors in general are considered socially undesirable, but foretopmen are an exception
    (D) being a foretopman implies having military expertise that the average sailor does not possess
    (E) the position of foretopman comes with a specific set of responsibilities and expectations, which will limit the social identity of anyone who is given the title

31. How does the author make use of his own name in the passage, in lines 34–50?

    (A) as an example of the various specializations available within a given field
    (B) as an example of the discrepancy between a given name and a person's inner identity
    (C) as an example of the constraints titles can place on an individual's social identity
    (D) to make *Billy Budd* seem less intimidating by providing a personal account of reading it
    (E) to indicate the importance of names in the way we think about other people

32. What is the meaning of the word "autonomy" in line 53?

    (A) freedom from the constraints of social expectation
    (B) the ability to choose one's own profession
    (C) freedom from religious or cultural oppression
    (D) a degree of choice in the amount of work one is expected to perform
    (E) the ability to go wherever one wishes to go

33. What is the meaning of the word "chafes" in line 55?

    (A) grows irritated
    (B) frays
    (C) limits
    (D) resists a limitation
    (E) breaks free

GO ON TO THE NEXT PAGE ➤

34. What does it mean that *Billy Budd* is an "inside narrative" (line 61)?

   (A) It portrays the "inside world" of a ship at sea.
   (B) The narrative focuses on the inner experience of the main character.
   (C) The novel is mostly concerned with social experiences that happen indoors, leaving the wilder outdoor world out of the story.
   (D) The novel is framed as a story-within-a-story, with the main plot functioning as an "inside" flashback within the "outer" plot.
   (E) The narrative openly talks about things such as storytelling technique and narrative devices, considerations that are usually left "outside" the words on the page.

35. What examples from *Billy Budd* itself does the author employ to justify his claim that the book contrasts the main character's "specific conscience" with his "broader sense of obligation" to society?

   (A) the novel's title and subtitles
   (B) the novel's title and several incidents from the narrative
   (C) the novel's title and several quotes from important characters
   (D) the novel's title and the personality of its main character
   (E) the opening and closing lines of the book

S T O P

IF YOU FINISH BEFORE TIME IS CALLED, YOU MAY CHECK YOUR WORK IN THIS SECTION ONLY.
DO NOT TURN TO ANY OTHER SECTION IN THE TEST.

SAT TEST

| Time—15 Minutes 10 Questions | In this section solve each problem, using any available space on the page for scratchwork. Then decide which is the best of the choices given and fill in the corresponding oval on the answer sheet. |

Notes:
1. The use of a calculator is permitted. All numbers used are real numbers.

2. Figures that accompany problems in this test are intended to provide information useful in solving the problems. They are drawn as accurately as possible EXCEPT when it is stated in a specific problem that the figure is not drawn to scale. All figures lie in a plane unless otherwise indicated.

Reference Information

$A = \pi r^2$
$C = 2\pi r$ $A = \ell w$ $A = \frac{1}{2}bh$ $V = \ell wh$ $V = \pi r^2 h$ $c^2 = a^2 + b^2$ Special Right Triangles

The number of degrees of arc in a circle is 360.
The measure in degrees of a straight angle is 180.
The sum of the measures in degrees of the angles of a triangle is 180.

1. John buys 4 boxes of apples that contain 20 apples each. If a box of apples costs 6 dollars, which of the following expressions gives the total price of the apples in dollars?

   (A) $4 \times 20 \times 6$

   (B) $\frac{20}{4} \times 6$

   (C) 4×6

   (D) 20×6

   (E) $\frac{6 \times 4}{20}$

2. There are two male singers in every choral quartet (a quartet is a group consisting of four singers). If a chorus is made of 50 quartets, how many male singers are there?

   (A) 2
   (B) 25
   (C) 50
   (D) 100
   (E) 200

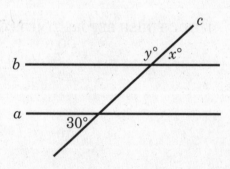

3. In the figure above, lines a and b are parallel, and intersected by line c. What is the value of $y - x$?

   (A) 180
   (B) 150
   (C) 120
   (D) 60
   (E) 30

GO ON TO THE NEXT PAGE

4. If Billy starts with n apples and after eating 8 there are 18 remaining, what is n?

(A) 8
(B) 10
(C) 18
(D) 26
(E) 36

5. Suppose there is a barrel filled with balls that are one of three colors: blue, red, or green. All blue balls have at least one star on them. All red balls have at least one dot on them. All balls with squares on them also have dots on them. No green balls have stars or dots on them. Given only these statements, which of the following statements cannot be true.

(A) Some blue balls have dots on them.
(B) All red balls have 3 dots on them.
(C) All balls with dots on them are red.
(D) All blue balls have squares on them.
(E) Some green balls have squares on them.

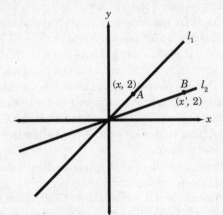

6. The slope of the line l_1 is $\frac{3}{2}$, and the slope of the line l_2 is $\frac{2}{3}$. What is the distance between A and B?

(A) 1

(B) $\frac{4}{3}$

(C) $\frac{3}{2}$

(D) $\frac{5}{3}$

(E) 4

7. If the mean of 11 consecutive numbers is 200 and you multiply each number by 2, what is the new mean?

(A) 50
(B) 100
(C) 200
(D) 400
(E) 800

8. The figure above is composed of three adjacent squares with diagonals of length $\sqrt{2}$. What is the area of the shaded regions?

(A) 12
(B) 6
(C) 3
(D) 1.5
(E) 1

9. Which pair of values of x and y is possible given the following equation?

$$\frac{1}{x} + \frac{1}{y} = \frac{3}{4}$$

(A) $x = 4, y = 8$
(B) $x = 3, y = 4$
(C) $x = 1, y = 2$
(D) $x = 4, y = 3$
(E) $x = 2, y = 4$

10. There are 300 people in John's graduating class. 40% of them went to the Senior Prom with another senior from the class, paying a joint price of $60 for a couple. Another 40% of the class brought a date from outside of the class; they were not allowed the buy the $60 couple tickets, so they had to pay separately for their tickets. 10% of the students came alone and 10% did not attend at all. All tickets sold individually were $35 for class members, and $40 for non-members. How much revenue did John's class bring in?

(A) $57
(B) $4,550
(C) $8,850
(D) $13,650
(E) $20,850

S T O P

IF YOU FINISH BEFORE TIME IS CALLED, YOU MAY CHECK YOUR WORK IN THIS SECTION ONLY.
DO NOT TURN TO ANY OTHER SECTION IN THE TEST.

SAT TEST

**Time—15 Minutes
13 Questions**

For each question in this section, select the best answer from among the choices given and fill in the corresponding oval on the answer sheet.

The passages below are followed by questions based on their content and the relationship between the passages. Answer the questions on the basis of what is <u>stated</u> or <u>implied</u> in the passages and in any introductory material that may be provided.

Questions 1–13 are based on the following passages.

In the mid-nineteenth century, the United States began to shift from being an agrarian nation whose population lived mostly on farms and in small towns to being a nation of major cities and industry. The following two passages, adapted from works written by the nineteenth-century American writers Henry David Thoreau and Walt Whitman, display two different views of the rise of cities and its effect on America.

Passage 1

When we walk, we naturally go to the fields and woods: what would become of us, if we walked only in a garden or a
Line
5 mall? Some sects of philosophers have even felt the necessity of importing the woods to themselves, since they did not go to the woods. Of course it is of no use to direct our steps to the woods, if they do not carry us there. I am alarmed when it happens that I have walked a mile into the woods bodily, without getting there in spirit. In my afternoon walk I would gladly forget all my
10 morning occupations and my obligations to Society. But it sometimes happens that I cannot easily shake off the village. The thought of some work will run in my head and I am not where my body is—I am out of my senses. In my walks I would like to return to my senses. What business have I in the woods, if
15 I am thinking of something out of the woods? I suspect myself, and cannot help a shudder when I find myself so implicated even in what are called good works.

My vicinity affords many good walks; and though for so many years I have walked almost every day, and sometimes for
20 several days together, I have not yet exhausted them. An absolutely new prospect is a great happiness, and I can still get this any afternoon. Two or three hours' walking will carry me to as strange a country as I expect ever to see. There is in fact a sort of harmony between the capabilities of the landscape within a
25 circle of ten miles' radius, or the limits of an afternoon walk, and the threescore years and ten of human life. Neither will ever become quite familiar to you.

Nowadays, almost all of man's improvements, so called, such as the building of houses and the cutting down of the forest
30 and of all large trees, simply deform the landscape, and make it more and more tame and cheap.

From my rural house I can easily walk ten, fifteen, twenty, any number of miles, commencing at my own door, without going by any house, without crossing a road except where the fox and
35 the mink do: first along by the river, and then the brook, and then the meadow and the woodside. There are square miles in my vicinity which have no inhabitant. From many a hill I can see civilization and the abodes of man afar. The farmers and

their works are scarcely more obvious than woodchucks and
40 their burrows. Man and his affairs, church and state and school, trade and commerce, and manufactures and agriculture—even politics, the most alarming of them all—I am pleased to see how little space they occupy in the landscape.

Passage 2

The general subjective view of New York and Brooklyn, these great seething oceanic populations, as I see them in this visit, are to me best of all. After an absence of many years (I went
Line
5 away at the outbreak of the secession war, and have never been back to stay since), again I resume with curiosity an interaction with the crowds and streets I knew so well. In Broadway, the ferries, the west side of the city, along the wharves, and in the perpetual travel of the horse-cars, or the crowded excursion
10 steamers, or in Wall and Nassau streets by day and in the places of amusement at night, there is a bubbling and whirling and moving. I have taken all this in for the last three weeks.

There is no need to specify minutely. It is enough to say that (making all allowances for the shadows and side-streaks of a massive city) the brief total of the impressions, the human
15 qualities, of these vast cities, is to me comforting, even heroic, and beyond statement.

Alertness, generally fine physique, clear eyes that look straight at you, a singular combination of reticence and self-possession mark the cities' inhabitants. Good nature and
20 friendliness, and a prevailing range of according manners, taste, and intellect, surely beyond any other place upon earth, are not only constantly visible here in these mighty channels of men, but they form the rule and average. In this city I find a palpable outcropping of the personal comradeship I look forward to as the
25 subtlest, strongest future hold of this United States.

Today, defiant of cynics and pessimists, and with a full knowledge of all their arguments and exceptions, I state my belief that an appreciative and perceptive study of the current humanity of New York gives the most direct proof yet of
30 successful Democracy. For in old age, lame and sick, and having pondered for years on doubts and danger for this Republic of ours, I find in this visit to New York, and the daily contact and rapport with its myriad people, the best, most effective medicine my soul has yet partaken. Manhattan Island and Brooklyn, the
35 grandest physical habitat and surroundings of land and water the globe affords, are cities of the most superb democracy, amid superb surroundings.

1. Thoreau's reference to "some sects of philosophers" in line 4 of Passage 1 suggests that this piece will most closely resemble:

   (A) an anti-intellectual creed.
   (B) a typical guidebook.
   (C) a philosophical essay.
   (D) a treatise on the aesthetics of nature.
   (E) a religious meditation.

2. What does Thoreau mean by saying he would "like to return to [his] senses" (line 14 of Passage 1)?

   (A) He wants to become fully aware and fully a part of his surroundings.
   (B) He wants to write more poetry.
   (C) He wants to get his daily tasks done so that he can relax.
   (D) He wants to listen more carefully for wildlife.
   (E) He wants to think more deeply.

3. The term "exhausted" in line 20 of Passage 1 refers to:

   (A) tired
   (B) bored
   (C) found
   (D) completed
   (E) breathed

4. According to the final paragraph of Passage 1, what does Thoreau appreciate most in human beings?

   (A) Rural values
   (B) Democratic thought
   (C) Outdoor skills
   (D) Social organizations such as villages
   (E) Their absence

5. Whitman's tone in Passage 2 can be best described as:

   (A) curious and enthusiastic
   (B) bitter and nostalgic
   (C) confused and frightened
   (D) relieved and excited
   (E) wry and optimistic

6. What does Whitman mean by the term "oceanic" (line 2)?

   (A) The population is mostly made up of immigrants.
   (B) His thoughts on the subject are deep and profound.
   (C) Most of the people of the city are sailors.
   (D) The population is spread out over a vast area of land.
   (E) The population is large, enduring, yet always changing.

7. What aspect of cities most interests the author of Passage 2?

   (A) Their geographical organization
   (B) The character of their inhabitants
   (C) Their transportation systems
   (D) The distribution of wealth
   (E) Their businesses

8. Lines 27–31 of Passage 2 suggest that Whitman thinks that his argument will be:

   (A) the subject of disagreement
   (B) received with enthusiasm
   (C) seen as a reflection of popular sentiment
   (D) largely ignored
   (E) dismissed as petty

9. How would Whitman react to Thoreau's assertion (line 42 in Passage 1) that politics are the "most alarming" of man's activities?

   (A) He would disagree and point to rural communities as examples of good political structures.
   (B) He would agree completely.
   (C) He would agree, but only where rural communities are concerned.
   (D) He wouldn't care; he doesn't seem to be interested in politics.
   (E) He would strongly disagree and would point to the city as democracy embodied.

10. How would Thoreau be most likely to react to Whitman's claim that the city can be "medicine for the soul" (lines 34–35 in Passage 2)?

    (A) He would wholeheartedly agree.
    (B) He would agree that a person's environment can affect his soul, but would disagree with Whitman's choice of the city.
    (C) He would argue that one's environment has nothing to do with the soul, and that one should lose oneself in deep thought.
    (D) He would agree, but only if one can avoid the city's politics.
    (E) He would argue that this is only the case for an older man like Whitman who is unable to walk in the woods.

GO ON TO THE NEXT PAGE ➤

11. Which of the following describes a primary distinction between the two authors?

 (A) Thoreau is interested in politics; Whitman is interested in philosophy.
 (B) Thoreau is interested in people; Whitman is interested in his surroundings.
 (C) Thoreau is interested in nature; Whitman is interested in people.
 (D) Thoreau is interested in the city; Whitman is interested in the country.
 (E) Thoreau is interested in thoughts; Whitman is interested in emotions.

12. The main point of both passages is to:

 (A) examine and comment upon a particular location and its effect on man
 (B) argue the aesthetic qualities of the country versus the city
 (C) look at what environments are best for democracy
 (D) prove the supremacy of the city as a method of social organization
 (E) describe the effects of old age on perception

13. How would Whitman most likely react if he were set down in the middle of Thoreau's woods?

 (A) He would explore enthusiastically.
 (B) He would be bored.
 (C) He would set to work building a house.
 (D) He would seek out the few settlements visible.
 (E) He would change his mind about cities.

S T O P

IF YOU FINISH BEFORE TIME IS CALLED, YOU MAY CHECK YOUR WORK IN THIS SECTION ONLY.
DO NOT TURN TO ANY OTHER SECTION IN THE TEST.

SAT Practice Test 3 Explanations

Answers to SAT Practice Test 1

Test 3 Explanations

Math Section 1

Question Number	Correct Answer	Right	Wrong
1.	C	——	——
2.	E	——	——
3.	B	——	——
4.	E	——	——
5.	C	——	——
6.	A	——	——
7.	D	——	——
8.	D	——	——
9.	E	——	——
10.	C	——	——
11.	B	——	——
12.	E	——	——
13.	C	——	——
14.	A	——	——
15.	B	——	——
16.	C	——	——
17.	D	——	——
18.	D	——	——
19.	D	——	——
20.	D	——	——
21.	B	——	——
22.	A	——	——
23.	E	——	——
24.	A	——	——
25.	B	——	——

Verbal Section 1

Question Number	Correct Answer	Right	Wrong
1.	C	——	——
2.	A	——	——
3.	C	——	——
4.	C	——	——
5.	D	——	——
6.	A	——	——
7.	B	——	——
8.	C	——	——
9.	B	——	——
10.	C	——	——
11.	C	——	——
12.	D	——	——
13.	A	——	——
14.	B	——	——
15.	C	——	——
16.	A	——	——
17.	B	——	——
18.	E	——	——
19.	C	——	——
20.	C	——	——
21.	C	——	——
22.	B	——	——
23.	A	——	——
24.	E	——	——
25.	B	——	——
26.	A	——	——
27.	D	——	——
28.	E	——	——
29.	C	——	——
30.	B	——	——

Math Section 2

Question Number	Correct Answer	Right	Wrong
1.	C	——	——
2.	B	——	——
3.	C	——	——
4.	A	——	——
5.	A	——	——
6.	C	——	——
7.	A	——	——
8.	A	——	——
9.	B	——	——
10.	C	——	——
11.	B	——	——
12.	D	——	——
13.	B	——	——
14.	C	——	——
15.	C	——	——
16.	7/5	——	——
17.	9	——	——
18.	25	——	——
19.	19	——	——
20.	1	——	——
21.	128	——	——
22.	30	——	——
23.	80	——	——
24.	6	——	——
25.	1	——	——

Verbal Section 2

Question Number	Correct Answer	Right	Wrong
1.	A	——	——
2.	D	——	——
3.	C	——	——
4.	C	——	——
5.	B	——	——
6.	C	——	——
7.	D	——	——
8.	D	——	——
9.	E	——	——
10.	B	——	——
11.	E	——	——
12.	E	——	——
13.	C	——	——
14.	B	——	——
15.	E	——	——
16.	C	——	——
17.	D	——	——
18.	E	——	——
19.	C	——	——
20.	C	——	——
21.	D	——	——
22.	A	——	——
23.	A	——	——
24.	E	——	——
25.	B	——	——
26.	C	——	——
27.	A	——	——
28.	D	——	——
29.	B	——	——
30.	E	——	——
31.	C	——	——
32.	A	——	——
33.	D	——	——
34.	B	——	——
35.	A	——	——

Math Section 3

Question Number	Correct Answer	Right	Wrong
1.	C	——	——
2.	D	——	——
3.	C	——	——
4.	D	——	——
5.	E	——	——
6.	D	——	——
7.	D	——	——
8.	A	——	——
9.	E	——	——
10.	D	——	——

Verbal Section 3

Question Number	Correct Answer	Right	Wrong
1.	C	——	——
2.	A	——	——
3.	D	——	——
4.	E	——	——
5.	A	——	——
6.	E	——	——
7.	B	——	——
8.	A	——	——
9.	E	——	——
10.	B	——	——
11.	C	——	——
12.	A	——	——
13.	D	——	——

Calculating Your SAT Score

Your raw score for SAT is a composite of your verbal and math raw scores. The raw scores of each section translate into a scaled score from 200 to 800. You can find your scaled scores for both verbal and math by checking the conversion table on page 350.

Your total SAT scaled score is the sum or your scaled math and verbal scores.

To Calculate Your Verbal Raw Score

The number of sentence completions, analogies, and reading comprehension questions you answered

$$\underline{\hspace{2cm}}_{\text{Correctly}} - (\frac{1}{4} \times \underline{\hspace{2cm}}_{\text{Incorrectly}}) = \underline{\hspace{2cm}}_{\text{A}}$$

Round the number in field A. This is your verbal raw score: $\underline{\hspace{2cm}}_{\text{B}}$

To Calculate Your Math Raw Score

The number of normal multiple-choice questions you answered

$$\underline{\hspace{2cm}}_{\text{Correctly}} - (\frac{1}{4} \times \underline{\hspace{2cm}}_{\text{Incorrectly}}) = \underline{\hspace{2cm}}_{\text{C}}$$

The number of quantitative comparisons you answered

$$\underline{\hspace{2cm}}_{\text{Correctly}} - (\frac{1}{4} \times \underline{\hspace{2cm}}_{\text{Incorrectly}}) = \underline{\hspace{2cm}}_{\text{D}}$$

The number of grid-ins you answered

$$\underline{\hspace{2cm}}_{\text{Correctly}} = \underline{\hspace{2cm}}_{\text{E}}$$

Add the numbers in fields C, D, and E = $\underline{\hspace{2cm}}_{\text{F}}$

Round the number in field F. This is your math raw score: $\underline{\hspace{2cm}}_{\text{G}}$

Math Section 1

1. **(C)** Algebra: Substitution   Difficulty: low

When you are given two equations, use one equation to find an expression for one variable and then substitute that expression into the other equation. We can easily solve for x in the second equation: $x = 3$. Substituting $x = 3$ into the first equation yields: $4 \times 3 - y = 10$. From there, $y = 12 - 10 = 2$ and $2y = 4$.

2. **(E)** Arithmetic: Fractions, Decimals and Percents   Difficulty: low

To solve the problem, we need to convert the two quantities into fractions with a common denominator. The first step is to convert the two mixed fractions to improper fractions: $2\frac{3}{4}$ = $^{11}\!/_4$ and $1\frac{1}{6}$ = $^7\!/_6$. Therefore, the problem can be restated as $^{11}\!/_4 - {}^7\!/_6$. Next we need to convert these fractions so that they have common denominators. The least common multiple of the denominators 4 and 6 is 12. We must multiply $^{11}\!/_4$ by 3 and $^7\!/_6$ by 2. Once we subtract the fractions with common denominators, we have solved the problem.

$$\frac{11}{4} - \frac{7}{6} =$$
$$\frac{33}{12} - \frac{14}{12} =$$
$$\frac{19}{12}$$

3. **(B)** Arithmetic: Basic Operations   Difficulty: low

This question is actually easy to convert into a mathematical equation. Notice that it has the word "equals" in it. On the left of that word is a "number multiplied by 3," or $3x$. On the right side of the "equals" is 4 less than 16, or $16 - 4$. So, $3x = 16 - 4$ or $3x = 12$. Simply dividing by 3, we see that $x = 4$.

4. **(E)** Algebra: Solving Linear Equations   Difficulty: low

We're given an equation with x in it and then asked to evaluate a second expression that depends on x. Solve for x in the first equation:

$$3x - 6 = 18$$
$$3x = 24$$
$$x = 8$$

Now simply substitute $x = 8$ into the second equation:

$$2x + 3 =$$
$$2(8) + 3 = 19$$

5.　**(C)**　Geometry: Angles and Lines　　　　　　　Difficulty: low

Because a is a straight line, we know that it measures 180°, so $x° + y° + y° = 180°$. We are told that $y = 65°$, so we can make that substitution to get that $x° + 65° + 65° = 180°$. Solving for x, we get $x = 50$.

6.　**(A)**　Arithmetic: Odd and Even Numbers　　　　Difficulty: low

Because $x/2$ is an integer, then x must be a multiple of 2. In other words, it must be even. You could show this mathematically by first writing that $y = x/2$ and then solving for x: $x = 2y$. The only answer choice that is an even number is –2. Of course, if this isn't apparent right away, you could test all five answers fairly quickly.

7.　**(D)**　Geometry: Polygons　　　　　　　　　　Difficulty: low

Calculating the area of the rectangle is the easy part. Remembering to convert meters to kilometers might slip past you, though. The area of the field in square kilometers is the product of its length and width in kilometers. First we should convert the measurements from meters to kilometers. 4000 meters is equal to 4 kilometers, and 5000 meters is equal to 5 kilometers. To find the area of the field, we multiply the two lengths and we find that the area equals $4 \times 5 = 20$ square kilometers.

8.　**(D)**　Geometry: Triangles　　　　　　　　　Difficulty: medium

It probably helps to sketch a quick diagram in your workbook. Following the path of the bus, you would have a right triangle with legs of length 30 and 40. We have to find the length of the hypotenuse of this triangle, after which finding the perimeter should be simple. To find the length of the hypotenuse, c, we use the Pythagorean theorem:

$$30^2 + 40^2 = c^2$$
$$900 + 1600 = c^2$$
$$2500 = c^2$$
$$c = 50$$

The total distance traveled is equal to the perimeter of the triangle, which is simply the sum of the lengths of the three sides: $30 + 40 + 50 = 120$ miles.

　　You might have noticed immediately that this was a 30:40:50 right triangle. We're not suggesting that you memorize every possible combination, but you should be on the lookout for the three most common and multiples thereof: 3:4:5, 5:12:13, and 8:15:17.

9. **(E)** Arithmetic: Ratios and Proportions   Difficulty: medium

Remember that a ratio can be written as a fraction. For every 3 green candies in the bag there are 4 red ones and 6 blue ones, in other words, $3/13$ of the candies are green. To find the total number of green candies in the bag, simply calculate $3/13 \times 65 = 15$.

10. **(C)** Arithmetic: Exponents and Square Roots   Difficulty: medium

The easiest way to solve this problem is to square both sides of the equation. After doing so, we see that $^{x+2}/_{y+2} = 4 \times 1/4 = 1$. Therefore, $x + 2 = y + 2$, and $x = y$.

11. **(B)** Arithmetic: Combinations and Probability   Difficulty: low

There are 6 white marbles out of a total of 9 marbles, so the probability of selecting a white marble in a single drawing is $2/3$. Because the first drawing is independent of the second, the probability of both events occurring is simply the product of their individual probabilities, which is $2/3 \times 2/3 = 4/9$. Make sure you know that the probability of independent events occurring is simply the product of their respective probabilities.

   Even if you didn't see how to solve this problem, you should have been able to recognize that $4/3$ is not a valid probability. The probability of an event is always zero, one, or some value within these bounds.

12. **(E)** Arithmetic: Exponents and Square Roots   Difficulty: medium

Since $x = y$, we can rewrite the left side of the equation as $(2x)^2$. Then, making use of the exponential property that $(ab)^c = a^c \times b^c$, we see that $(2x)^2 = 4x^2$ and that $a = 4$.

13. **(C)** Geometry: Solids   Difficulty: medium

The volume of a cube is equal to s^3, where s is the length of each edge. To determine the length of an edge given the volume of a cube, simply take the cube root of the volume. In this case, we take the cube root of 64 to find that an edge of the cube has length 4.

   The length of an edge is equal to the radius of the circle whose area we need to find. By substituting 4 into the equation for the area of a circle ($A = \pi r^2$), we see that $A = (4^2)\pi = 16\pi$.

14. **(A)** Arithmetic: Divisibility and Remainders   Difficulty: medium

For the remainder of $m \div 7$ to be 2, m has to be 2 more than a multiple of 7 or $m = 7x + 2$. The correct answer is the one, which after subtracting 2, is not a multiply of 7. Simply subtract 2 from each answer choice to find the one that is not a multiple of 7. 17 satisfies the condition since $17 - 2 = 15$ is not a multiple of 7.

   Alternatively, you could try dividing each answer by 7 and finding the remainder for each answer. Either way, you would find that (A) is the only one that, when divided by 7, does not yield a remainder of 2 (the remainder of $17 \div 7$ is $17 - (2 \times 7) = 3$).

15. **(B)** Arithmetic: Basic Operations   Difficulty: medium

There are really two pieces to this problem. The first is understanding what values of abc allow $\frac{1}{abc} > \frac{1}{97}$ to hold. The second is understading what values a, b, and c may take.

In order for $\frac{1}{abc}$ to be greater than $\frac{1}{97}$, abc must be less than 97. And because we know that a, b, and c are integers, their product must be an integer as well, so we can be a little more precise and conclude that $abc \leq 96$. In order to maximize a, both b and c must be minimized. Since we know that $b > c > 1$, and a, b, and c are integers, the smallest value for c is 2 and for b is 3. We found earlier that $abc \leq 96$, meaning that $(3)(2)(a) \leq 96$. Dividing each side of the equation by 6, we see that $a \leq 16$, so **16** is the largest integer value of a that satisfies the problem.

16. **(C)** Geometry: Polygons; circles   Difficulty: high

It is easy to see that the area of the shaded region is equal to the area of the square minus the area of a quarter-circle. The area of the square is simply r^2 and the area of the quarter-circle is $\frac{1}{4}\pi r^2$. The area of the shaded region is therefore equal to $r^2 - \frac{1}{4}\pi r^2$.

17. **(D)** Arithmetic: Exponents and Square Roots   Difficulty: medium

There are two properties of exponents that will lead us to the solution. First, we'll need to know that $x^a / x^b = x^{(a-b)}$. Using this property, we can solve for x:

$$\frac{k^7}{k^x} = k$$
$$\frac{k^7}{k^x} = k^1$$
$$7 - x = 1$$
$$x = 6$$

The second property of exponents we need is that $(x^a)^b = x^{ab}$. This property will allow us to solve for y:

$$(k^2)^y = k^8$$
$$k^{(2y)} = k^8$$
$$2y = 8$$
$$y = 4$$

Now that we've solved for x and y, finding their product is the easy part: $xy = 6 \times 4 = 24$.

18. **(D)** Miscellaneous Math: Charts and Graphs; Logic;
 Arithmetic: Fractions, Decimals, Percents   Difficulty: high

We know the outcomes of 3 of the 5 coin flips. In the other two tries, the coin could land heads either 0, 1, or 2 times. In addition to the 1 head listed in the chart, the total number of heads generated in all 5 flips could be 1, 2, or 3. Stated as percentages, ⅕, ⅖, and ⅗ are equivalent to 20%, 40%, and 60%, respectively. Of the answer choices, only 80% is an impossible outcome.

19. **(D)** Geometry: Triangles, arithmetic: ratios   Difficulty: high

We need to find the ratio of the areas of two right triangles. To do so, we must find the area of each triangle. Let's find the area of triangle *ABC* first. The hypotenuse is 13 and one side is 5. Using the Pythagorean theorem:

$$5^2 + \overline{BC}^2 = 13^2$$
$$25 + \overline{BC}^2 = 169$$
$$\overline{BC}^2 = 144$$
$$\sqrt{\overline{BC}^2} = \sqrt{144}$$
$$\overline{BC} = 12$$

Now we can find the area of *ABC*: (½)($\overline{BC}$)($\overline{AB}$) = (½)(12)(5) = 30. We can also find the area of *DEC* using the Pythagorean theorem:

$$4^2 + \overline{DE}^2 = 5^2$$
$$16 + \overline{DE}^2 = 25$$
$$\overline{DE}^2 = 9$$
$$\sqrt{\overline{DE}^2} = \sqrt{9}$$
$$\overline{DE} = 3$$

The area of *DEC*, then, is (½)($\overline{DE}$)($\overline{DC}$) = (½)(3)(4) = 6. So the ratio of the area of *ABC*:*DEC* = 30:6 = 5:1.

20. **(D)** Miscellaneous Math: Problems with Unique Symbols;
 Algebra: Substitution   Difficulty: high

All we need to do is to apply the † function:

$$a \dagger b = 3$$
$$ab - a + 3 = 3$$
$$ab = a$$
$$b = 1$$

21. **(B)** Misc. Math: Unique Symbols;
        Algebra: Simplifying Expressions   Difficulty: high

While this question introduces a new function, the algebra that it requires is not that difficult. In this case we simply replace $\boxed{z}$ by $x + y$ and then by $x - y$:

$$\boxed{x + y} = (x + y)^2 + 1$$
$$\boxed{x - y} = (x - y)^2 + 1$$

Once you create these expressions, the rest is algebra.

$$(x + y)^2 + 1 - ((x - y)^2 + 1) = \boxed{z}$$
$$x^2 + 2xy + y^2 + 1 - (x^2 - 2xy + y^2 + 1) = \boxed{z}$$
$$x^2 + 2xy + y^2 + 1 - x^2 + 2xy - y^2 - 1 = \boxed{z}$$
$$x^2 - x^2 + y^2 - y^2 + 1 - 1 + 2xy + 2xy = \boxed{z}$$
$$4xy = \boxed{z}$$

22. **(A)** Misc Math: Charts; Arithmetic: Fractions   Difficulty: medium

Note first that there are only three ten-year periods in which the production of Product X decreased at all: 1950–1960, 1970–1980, and 1990–2000. We just have to calculate which ten-year period saw the greatest percentage decrease. The percentage decrease is calculated by taking the decrease in production and dividing it by the initial production. So, for the ten-year period from 1950–1960, production dropped from 15,000 units to 5,000 units. The percentage decrease is therefore $^{15,000 - 5,000}/_{15,000} =$ $^{10,000}/_{15,000} \approx 0.67$ or 67%. Calculating the other two percentage decreases the same way, we see decreases of 50% and 33%, so the 67% decrease from 1950–1960 was indeed the greatest of all the ten-year periods on the chart.

23. **(E)** Arithmetic: Mean, Median, and Mode   Difficulty: high

The only one of these statements that you should recognize immediately is statement III, which claims that the median is always equal to the mode. You should immediately know that statement to be false, eliminating (C) and (D). In order to evaluate I and II, it's a good idea to try to come up with a sample set of numbers to test the statements on. A couple obvious sets come to mind: $\{n - 2, n - 1, n, n + 1, n + 2\}$ and $\{n, n, n, n, n\}$. From the first set, we see that both statements I and II appear to hold true. The second set, however, disproves both statements.

   Of course, you do not have to think of a particular set. If you really understand the definitions of "median" and "mode," you can see that there is no conceptual reason why any of the statements must be true. Constructing a sample set is really just a way to assure yourself that you're right.

24. **(A)**   Geometry: Polygons   Difficulty: high

Because all of the angles are right angles, we know that corresponding sides of the polygon are identical, so we can label each side in the following way:

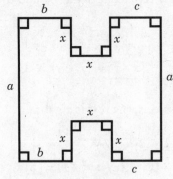

We can now solve for the perimeter, p, by adding the values of the lengths of the sides and simplifying:

$$p = a + b + x + x + x + c + a + c + x + x + x + b$$
$$p = 2a + 2b + 2c + 6x$$
$$p = 2(a + b + c + 3x)$$

25. **(B)**   Algebra: Simplifying and Manipulating Expressions   Difficulty: high

There are two ways to go about solving this problem. One way is to solve for b directly and then divide that quantity by 2 to generate an expression for $b/2$. Another way is to create a new variable and insert it into the original equation. Of course, they're really the same process, one is just more direct than the other.

First, let's solve for b:

$$a = bc$$
$$\frac{a}{c} = b$$

To find the value of $b/2$, simply divide a/c by 2, to see that $b/2 = a/2c$.

This second approach is probably unnecessary for this particular problem, but it's useful to know in case a future problem is a little more complex. First, create a new variable that is equal to the value we're trying to solve for: $d = b/2$. Solving for b in terms of d, we see that $b = 2d$. Substituting this expression into the original equation, we get $a = 2dc$. Remember that we're now solving for d, which is achieved by simply dividing each side by 2c: $d = a/2c$.

Verbal Section 1

Sentence Completions

1. (C) One Word Direct   Difficulty: low

In this question, we know from the structure of the sentence that we are looking for a word whose meaning is "containing numerous unexplored ideas and uncalculated equations." It is safe to assume that researchers would be excited by a field in which very little is understood; the less that is known, the more there is to be researched. Therefore, the blank word that describes the field of string theory should be a positive word, meaning "abundant" or "likely to yield a good amount of research." Taking the answers in turn, safe is a positive word, but it does not describe the field as something full of possibility. Unsatisfactory is a negative word, so it won't work. Promising seems like a good fit, since this word is positive and describes the field as full of possibility. Dubious is a rather negative word that characterizes the field as either past its prime or of questionable value, so it won't do. Ancient simply fails to relate to the sentence at all.

2. (A) Two Word Direct   Difficulty: low

Using your own intuition, it's pretty easy to fill in the blanks here—but the question tries to trip you up with a lot of options that sound similar to one another. While condemned, convicted, and responsible are all appropriate options in this context, of their counterparts only commit is equally relevant. Commiserate is a synonym of "empathize," and cauterize means "to make insensible," neither of which makes any sense in reference to a man protesting his innocence. The answer is therefore condemned . . commit.

3. (C) One Word Contrast   Difficulty: low

Because of the hinge word "though," we know that the sentence is asking us to find a word that contrasts with "disappointment": the chemist hopes that his next try will produce a result that is *not* a disappointment.

We can eliminate collapse because any chemistry experiment that resulted in collapse would probably be thought of as a disappointment or worse. Hypothesis might seem likely for a moment, simply because it is a word often used in conjunction with scientific experiments, but when plugged into the sentence, it does not make sense. No experiment could "bring hypothesis"—hypothesis, unlike disappointment, is not a state of being. Renewal is another tricky word. In a way, it contrasts with the very general sense of "disappointment." But when put into the sentence, it does not really make sense; its relation to "disappointment" is much too vague to fit the narrow requirements of this sentence. In the same sense, skill might seem a good choice, because if the chemist had skill, he might conduct a less disappointing experiment. But his second try could not *bring* him skill; he would have to have skill before he began. The only answer choice that fits, then, is success. An experiment that brought success would not be a disappointment.

4. **(C)** Two Word Contrast   Difficulty: low

The hinge word, "although," signals that we should be looking for two contrasting words to describe the difference between Pee Wee Russell's face and his clarinet playing. Ugly . . foul can be immediately discarded, as those words do not contrast with one another. Pristine . . dramatic might be words that could be used to describe clarinet playing, but neither of them can really be applied to a face, and in any case they do not contrast directly enough to warrant the "although." The same is true of handsome . . gentle and expressive . . unique. The only answer that fits the sentence, then, is grotesque . . beautiful. Despite his ugly face, Pee Wee Russell played the clarinet beautifully. This answer choice offers contrast, and it successfully describes the difference between Russell's face and his style of musicianship.

5. **(D)** Two Word Contrast   Difficulty: medium

The hinge word in this sentence is "although," which indicates that we should be looking for words that will make the two parts of this sentence contrast with one another. Whatever Spartacus wished to do to his army, it contrasted with his men's desire to continue fighting. So we can immediately discard reward . . affluent, as the words do not contrast, and do not make sense when inserted into the sentence. Execute . . macabre does not have any definite relation, and outfit . . neutral makes the sentence nonsensical. Encourage . . immoral are closer, but when plugged into the sentence, they still fail to make sense — why would Spartacus need to encourage an immoral army that wanted to go on fighting? The only choice that makes sense is disband . . together: Spartacus wished to disband his army after it defeated the Romans, but the soldiers wished to stay together and continue fighting. This answer choice immediately makes sense and fits the requirement for contrast created by the "although."

6. **(A)** One Word Direct   Difficulty: medium

From the information provided in the sentence that the supports of the house had rotted away, we can assume that Ting's house is in danger of collapsing. The word that fills the blank must somehow make sense in reference to a collapsing seaside house. Seasonal clearly does not describe the condition of a collapsing house. Living in the house might be adventurous, but the house itself is not adventurous, so that answer can be thrown out. Same with absurd. Is it absurd that the house might fall? No, it makes perfect sense. Fruitful is the hardest word of the bunch, but if you know that it's a positive word (since it means profitable), then you know it doesn't fit in a sentence describing a collapsing house. That leaves precarious, which is the only answer that describes a situation characterized by a lack of stability or security.

7. **(B)** One Word Direct   Difficulty: high

The hinge word in this sentence is "since," but it is a hinge word that calls for the sentence to continue on a single flow of meaning. When you see the word since, you should immediately recognize that the second half of the sentence and the first half of the sentence will fit together: what happens in the second half of the sentence will define what type of "event in English History" the Battle of Hastings was. So, if a battle "changed the future course of a nation," what kind of battle was it? The word that should come to mind is "important" or "significant."

You should immediately be able to eliminate irrelevant as a possibility, since it means the opposite of what we are looking for. Similarly, you should be able to throw out disastrous, since the sentence doesn't claim that the outcome of the battle changed the future of the nation for the worse. That leaves us with the possibilities of seminal, reputable, and irrefutable. Reputable means "of good reputation," which makes little sense in reference to the sentence. Irrefutable means "impossible to disprove." This word is a little tricky, because if something is "impossible to disprove" it seems as if that thing would be important. But let's say you just ate a sandwich and took a picture of yourself eating the sandwich, then that sandwich eating would be an irrefutable fact of history. So irrefutable doesn't actually mean important. Seminal, however, does mean important, and so it is your answer.

8. **(C)** One Word Contrast   Difficulty: high

The hinge word in this sentence is "while," which implies that the direction of the sentence will change after the comma. Because of the "while," we know that the sentence is asking us to find a word that contrasts with the idea of grumpiness: Cinderella's stepsisters are grumpy, but she is different. In other words, we are seeking a word that implies cheerfulness and pleasantness.

Frosty implies coldness and chilliness and is not generally used to describe a person, so we can throw it out. Impeachable implies that one can be called to account for one's flaws, a state that has no direct relationship to being grumpy. (If one is grumpy, perhaps, one is impeachable—but the words are certainly not contrasting.) Flippant means talkative and witty, which may be pleasant to some people, but does not directly mean "pleasant"—one can be both flippant and grumpy, in any case. Uncouth implies rudeness and poor manners, so it is obviously not the word for this sentence. The only word remaining is endearing, which can imply either physical beauty or a pleasant attitude. Of course, endearing is the correct answer.

9. **(B)** Two Word Contrast   Difficulty: high

The hinge word "despite" clues us in to a reversal in the flow of the sentence. A close reading of this sentence reveals that the type of rule now in place in Zambonia is at odds with the kind of government that has characterized it historically. We should therefore be on the lookout for a pair of words with conflicting meanings. The word "suffered" also alerts us to keep an eye out for a word in the first blank with negative connotations.

Knowing that the first blank will be negative, you can immediately throw out benevolent . . idiosyncratic, idyllic . . democratic, and legislative . . acrimonious, since both benevolent and idyllic are clearly positive words, and legislative is neutral at worst. You should also be able to eliminate destructive . . despicable because the sentence describes the people of Zambonia in a heroic way, and what's heroic about refusing to forget despicable traditions? That leaves autocratic . . egalitarian, which makes perfect sense in the sentence, as the correct answer.

Analogies

10. **(C)** Function   Difficulty: medium
"The function of a MONUMENT is to celebrate or commemorate an EVENT." Similarly, a medal is awarded to someone to celebrate and commemorate his or her bravery. Of the other answer pairs, none come very close to approximating the sense of remembrance and celebration embodied in the stem pair. An analysis explains a summary, a blueprint is a model for construction, a syllabus describes what a teacher will teach, while building : lifestyle doesn't share a very good relation at all (even if you were not sure what the relation between MONUMENT and EVENT was, you should still have been able to eliminate building: lifestyle).

11. **(C)** Characteristic Use   Difficulty: low
"A WRENCH is a tool used by a MECHANIC" is the best sentence you could make using this stem pair. Similarly, a needle is a tool used by a tailor. A clinic is the place where a doctor works, and an apron is part of a chef's clothing: neither of these have the same relationship as the stem pair. This question is slightly tricky because you could make the sentence, "A computer uses disks," but a computer doesn't use disks as tools in the same way that a MECHANIC uses a WRENCH.

12. **(D)** Type   Difficulty: high
A ZEALOT is a fervent follower of a FAITH is the best and most complete sentence you could make with this stem pair. Likewise, a partisan is a fervent follower of a faction, usually a political one. Some of the other answers might be a little tricky, since the relationship between their pairs is rather strong: a candidate is heavily involved in politics, just as a panelist is a very important part of a forum. But neither of these pairs describes the relation of blind, even violent, adherence that exists between ZEALOT and FAITH. The relation of conformist : rebellion is opposite that of ZEALOT : FAITH, since a conformist is very unlikely to engage in any rebellion at all. Person : gender doesn't fit the stem pair because while a person has a certain gender, in no sense does that person believe strongly in their gender. Partisan : faction is the only possible answer pair.

13. **(A)** Description   Difficulty: high

An ONEROUS TASK is one that is unpleasant and difficult to bear, just as an interminable lecture is one that is unpleasant, long, and dull. Superficial : statement implies a similarly negative relationship, suggesting a statement that is poorly thought out, but "superficial" does not denote tedious or dull, as "onerous" and "interminable" both do. Gregarious : opponent and assertive : hint have no easily articulated relationships. Intrepid : explorer has a positive relationship (an explorer must be intrepid, i.e., strong and fearless, in order to succeed) whereas the onerous : task relation is clearly negative. That leaves interminable : lecture as the correct answer.

14. **(B)** Relative Size and Degree   Difficulty: high

This question is difficult mainly because of two hard words, one in the question and one in the correct answer: PREDILECTION (which means a fondness for something) and torrent (a pouring rain). If one has a PASSION for something, one loves it far more than if one has a PREDILECTION for it. Similarly, if the rain comes down in a torrent, it comes down far harder than it does as a sprinkle. In each case, the words are almost synonyms, but the word with the stronger connotation appears first. Of the other choices, imply : indicate feature words of about the same degree; fondness and spite are antonyms; and hold : caress and grudge : demise feature words that are not synonyms at all. Therefore, even if you were unsure of the relation between PASSION and PREDILECTION, you still should have been able to eliminate hold : caress and grudge : demise.

15. **(C)** Attribute   Difficulty: high

Something that is UNDERSTATED is not marked by EXAGGERATION, just as someone who is sane is not marked by lunacy. The relation between the words is negative. Of the remaining answer choices, three have the positive relationships (vociferous : volume, positive : proof, and mischievous : rogue), while one pair does not relate in any concrete way (indicative : random). The hardest thing about this particular question is the vocabulary—vociferous means "loud" or "vocal" and a rogue is a person who is unprincipled or mischievous.

Reading Comprehension

16. **(A)** Main Theme or Idea   Difficulty: low

The author states the answer to this question plainly in the first passage: "... however much they who marched South and North in 1861 may have fixed on the technical points of union and local autonomy, all nevertheless knew, as we know, that the question of slavery was the real cause of the conflict" (lines 5–8). You should not have had to go back to the passage to answer this question. The answer is (A).

17. (B) Words-in-context   Difficulty: medium

The full sentence reads: "No sooner had Northern armies touched Southern soil than this old question, newly guised, sprang from the earth: What shall be done with Southern blacks?" Viewed in context, we see that "guised" refers to the "old question" mentioned previously. And keeping in mind Du Bois' assertion in the previous paragraph that "however much they . . . may have fixed on the technical points of union and local autonomy, all nevertheless knew . . . that the question of slavery was the real cause of the conflict" (lines 5–8), we can see that these new conflicts are acting as mere cloaks, or disguises, for an underlying problem. The answer is therefore (B).

18. (E) Author's Attitude and Tone   Difficulty: medium

Du Bois' tone throughout this section is aimed at making the reader feel pity for the subject that he is describing, as revealed by the use of phrases such as "whimpering hungry children" and, most explicitly, "starving vagabonds, homeless, helpless, and pitiable." The answer is therefore (E).

19. (C) Specific Information   Difficulty: medium

In lines 32–33, we learn that Fremont "declared the slaves free under martial law." Halleck, by contrast, ordered that fugitive slaves be returned to their owners (lines 36–38). Based on these two pieces of information it is clear that slaves fared worse under Halleck; the answer is therefore (C).

20. (C) Understanding Themes and Arguments   Difficulty: high

In the second to last paragraph, Du Bois prefaces the changes that Cameron instituted regarding the Union's policy on fugitive slaves by noting that "[e]vidently, . . . slaves were a source of strength to the Confederacy, and were being used as laborers and producers" (lines 43–44). As such, returned fugitives assisted the Confederacy inasmuch as they kept its economy going. The answer is therefore (C).

21. (C) Specific Information   Difficulty: low

This is a simple question, since the answer it seeks was stated explicitly in the first paragraph of the passage: "While watching the smoke curling up the chimney one propounded an idea by way of a sudden inspiration: 'Why shouldn't smoke be made to raise bodies into the air?'" The correct answer is (C).

22. (B) Specific Information   Difficulty: low

This question asks you to recall what you've read. Rubber is never mentioned in this passage, but every other answer choice is; therefore the correct answer is (B).

23. **(A)**   Implied Information   Difficulty: medium
Each of the answer choices is an important element in the making of a balloon, but the focus in the passage (and in the question) on the gasses that fill the balloon suggests that what was inside the balloon presented the biggest challenge to potential inventors. Therefore the correct answer is (A).

24. **(E)**   Understanding Themes and Arguments   Difficulty: high
These lines state that Dr. Black might have invented the balloon first, had he been blessed with better fortune and more leisure time. Noting that "fortune" is used here to mean luck, not money, we see that the Montgolfier's were only the first to design a working balloon because others capable of beating them had bad luck and were busy. The latter part of the sentence might tempt you into thinking that (B) is the correct answer, but keep in mind that only a handful of people had even conceived of a balloon, so international competition over a balloon launch would have been impossible. The correct answer, therefore, is (E).

25. **(B)**   Words-in-context   Difficulty: medium
The sentence is referring to the Montgolfiers' first design, which was simple and not nearly as sophisticated as what they later built. The correct answer is therefore (B). If, however, the answer was not immediately obvious to you, you could eliminate several of the answers. The invention of the balloon is not discussed in moral terms, so you could eliminate answers (A) and (E). There is no mention of oil in the passage either, so you could eliminate (D) as well. Of the two remaining answers, you could eliminate answer (C) by remembering that the invention in fact worked, so it was probably not poorly conceived. This process of elimination will leave you with the correct answer.

26. **(A)**   Author's Technique   Difficulty: high
This kind of question can be difficult because you cannot refer to the text for the answer; you have to intuit the author's intentions for writing as he does. If you cannot immediately recognize (A) as the correct answer, you could almost certainly eliminate (B), (C), and (D) just because they do not make much sense in the context. Hopefully, you could then see that the author uses this interjection to reinforce the dramatic nature of the events rather than comment on some inadequacy of his own narration.

27. **(D)**   Understanding Themes and Arguments   Difficulty: medium
The phrase in question serves to create a little shadow of doubt. The Montgolfiers believed that it was the smoke that was making their balloon rise, while we, with a more modern understanding of physics, understand that it is the temperature difference between smoke and normal air that made the balloon rise. The phrase serves to reinforce the idea that the Montgolfiers may have developed the balloon but that they didn't necessarily have the scientific knowledge to fully understand their own invention. The correct answer is (D).

28. (E)   Understanding Themes and Arguments   Difficulty: medium

The correct answer is (E). One way to approach this question would be to notice that the passage as a whole tells the story of the invention of the balloon, carefully giving credit to those who conceived of the idea of the balloon and those who helped the Montgolfiers in their discovery. The story of the widow is not part of the lore of the discovery of the balloon the way the others are, and the author goes to special effort to note that her name has been "unhappily lost" despite her contributions.

29. (C)   Words-in-context   Difficulty: medium

Answers (B) and (E) can be quickly eliminated. Of the remaining answers, a careful reading of the lines will show you that (C) is the correct one. The passage mentions that this balloon was both spherical and large: in short, it resembled a modern balloon.

30. (B)   Author's Technique   Difficulty: high

This question is a little tricky because several of these statements are ones that the author would potentially agree with, based on other parts of the passage. However, only one of them is implied by the use of these words to describe the balloon. The balloon itself is described like a child growing up, which implies that inventions take several stages of development to reach their final state. The correct answer, therefore, is (B).

Math Section 2

Quantitative Comparisons

1. (C)   Arithmetic: Basic Operations   Difficulty: low

When you round 724.793 to the nearest hundredth, you get 724.79. In this rounded number, the digit in the hundreds place is 7 and the digit in the tenths place is 7, so the quantities are equal.

2. (B)   Arithmetic: Exponents and Square Roots   Difficulty: low

It might be helpful to insert parentheses in the quantity in column A so that it is easier to compare to other quantity: $-(x^2)$. We know that a squared quantity can never be negative. This helps us see that column A is negative and that column B is positive (remember that $x \neq 0$). Therefore, the quantity in column B is necessarily larger.

3. (C)   Arithmetic: Fractions, Decimals, and Percents   Difficulty: low

This question is a matter of simple computation. $\frac{3}{4} \times 60 = 45$ and $\frac{5}{8} \times 72 = 45$. The quantities are equal.

4.   **(A)**   Geometry: Coordinate Geometry   Difficulty: low

Point D is in quadrant IV, which is on the positive side (to the right) of the x-axis and on the negative side (below) of the y-axis. There is no need to calculate the exact values because x must be positive and y must be negative, so x must be greater than y.

5.   **(A)**   Geometry: Circles   Difficulty: low

The area of a circle with diameter 6 (or radius 3) is: $3^2\pi = 9\pi$. The area of a square with sides of length 5 is $5^2 = 25$. You could find the value of 9π ($9 \times 3.14 = 28.26$), but that's not necessary. As long as you know that $9 \times 3 = 7$, you should be able to determine immediately that $9\pi > 25$ and that the area of the circle is greater than the area of the square.

6.   **(C)**   Arithmetic: Solving Linear Equations   Difficulty: medium

There are two ways to approach this problem, depending on whether you are more comfortable factoring or multiplying. First, let's try factoring the quantity in column B to see how it compares to the quantity in column A. The r and u are common to both terms, so they can be factored out: $ru(s + t)$. You can see right away that columns A and B are equal.

We can also use the distributive property to expand the expression in column A: $rus + rut$. Again, columns A and B are equal.

7.   **(A)**   Arithmetic: Solving Linear Equations   Difficulty: medium

To solve for k, simply write the given information in equation form as: $k + k + 1 + 2k = 21$ or $4k + 1 = 21$. Subtracting 1 and dividing by 4, we see that $k = 5$ and that the quantity in column A is greater than 4.

8.   **(A)**   Arithmetic: Fractions, Decimals, and Percents   Difficulty: medium

We should begin by trying to isolate k in the inequality. To do so, simply subtract $\frac{1}{8}$ from each term. If you're not comfortable with halves, fourths, and eighths, you may want to change all of the terms into common denominators ($\frac{1}{4} = \frac{2}{8}$ and $\frac{1}{2} = \frac{4}{8}$). Subtracting $\frac{1}{8}$ from each term, we get the simplified inequality: $\frac{1}{8} < k < \frac{3}{8}$. It's clear that $\frac{1}{8} < k$, so column A is larger.

9.   **(B)**   Arithmetic: Basic Operations   Difficulty: medium

The number of three-digit numbers with the ones digit equal to 4 is 90. You can figure this out by noting that there are 10 numbers that end in 4 in every set of 100 (e.g. For 100 through 199, you should count 104, 114, 124, 134, 144, 154, 164, 174, 184, and 194). Since there are 9 sets of 100 from 100–999, you multiply

$$(10 \text{ numbers in each set}) \times (9 \text{ sets}) = 90 \text{ numbers}$$

The number of three-digit numbers with the hundreds digit equal to 4 is 100, counting all numbers between 400 and 499. 100 is greater than 90, so the answer is (B).

10. **(C)**   Arithmetic: Fractions, Decimals, and Percents   Difficulty: medium
Converting the statement into an equation, we get $y = (x \div \text{⅛}) \times \text{⅖}$. Note that to divide x by ⅛, we need to multiply x by the reciprocal of ⅛, or ⅜.

$$y = x \div \frac{8}{3} \times \frac{2}{9} =$$
$$y = x \times \frac{3}{8} \times \frac{2}{9} =$$
$$y = \frac{6x}{72}$$
$$y = \frac{x}{12}$$

The two quantities are equal.

11. **(B)**   Geometry: Angles and Lines   Difficulty: medium
Don't be distracted by the figure, which isn't drawn to scale. Using the rules that govern intersecting lines, you should know that supplementary angles always sum to 180°. The supplementary angle of a 140° angle is 40°. Also, you should see that $\angle X$ is equivalent to the supplementary angle of the 140° angle. This means that $x = 40$, and $8x = 320$. Since 320 is less than 360, the correct answer must be (B).

12. **(D)**   Arithmetic: Fractions, Decimals, and Percents   Difficulty: high
At first glance this questions seems simple: of course a number increased by 40% would be greater than that same number decreased by 20%. However, no domain for x is specified, meaning that x could be positive, negative, or zero. If x is negative, then decreasing x by 20% ($.8x$) would produce a number greater (less negative) than $1.4x$ (the result of increasing x by 40%). If x is positive, then increasing x by 40% would produce the larger number. If $x = 0$, multiplying it by .4 or .2 produce the same answer, 0. The answer, therefore, must be (D).

13. **(B)**   Arithmetic: Fractions, Decimals, and Percents   Difficulty: high
Since dividing by ⁸⁰⁄₇ is the same as multiplying by its reciprocal, ⁷⁄₈₀, we can manipulate the quantity in column A:

$$\left(\frac{320}{7} - \frac{240}{7}\right) \times \frac{7}{80} =$$
$$\frac{80}{7} \times \frac{7}{80} = 1$$

Because 1 is less than 2, the answer must be (B).

14. (C) Arithmetic: Multiples, Factors, and Primes   Difficulty: high

To identify the quantity in column A, we're looking for a small prime number that can be expressed as the sum of other (smaller) prime numbers. It's a good idea to list the first few prime numbers: 2, 3, 5, 7, 11, and 13. Let's attack the quantity in column A first. We're looking for a prime number that is the sum of two other prime numbers, and we want it to as small as possible. Let's see if any of the first few prime numbers can be expressed as the sum of two other prime numbers. 2 is the smallest prime number, so it can't be expressed as the sum of two other primes. 3 can't be expressed as the sum of two primes either. 5, the next lowest prime, is the sum of 2 and 3, so it is the smallest prime number that is the sum of two other prime numbers.

Next we must turn to the quantity in column B. What are the factors of 42? They are {1, 2, 3, 6, 7, 14, 21, 42}. There are 8 factors. Of those factors, three are prime: 2, 3, and 7. Thus, the quantity in column B is $8 - 3 = 5$. The two quantities are equal.

15. (C) Geometry: Triangles   Difficulty: high

The whole area of the rectangle is comprised of the triangle and the shaded area. The area of the rectangle is simply the length times the width or ab. The area of the triangle is one half the product of its base (a) and its height (b) or $\frac{1}{2}(ab)$. The area of the shaded region is simply equal to the difference in the areas of the rectangle and the triangle: $ab - \frac{1}{2}(ab) = \frac{1}{2}(ab)$. The shaded region is equal to the area of the triangle. Alternately, by simply drawing a vertical line through point D, it should be obvious that half of the area is shaded.

Grid-Ins

16. 7/5 Arithmetic: Ratios   Difficulty: low

Since there are 7 flowering trees we know that there are $12 - 7 = 5$ non-flowering trees. This makes the ratio of flowering:non-flowering 7:5, or $\frac{7}{5}$.

17. 9 Misc. Math: Unique Symbols; Algebra: Substitution   Difficulty: low

Simply substitute 5 for x and 4 for y. The expression $x * y = x^2 - y^2$ becomes $5 * 4 = 5^2 - 4^2 = 25 - 16 = 9$.

18. 25 Geometry: Angles and Lines   Difficulty: low

In the intersection of two lines, opposite angles are always equal. We know that the top angle in the triangle is 65° and the right angle is 90°. Since the sum of the interior angles of a triangle is 180°, we know that $x + 65 + 90 = 180$, and $x = 25$.

19. **19**   Arithmetic: Mean, Median, and Mode   Difficulty: low

Recall that the median is the middle number of a set whose numbers are arranged in increasing order. For this set, the median is 7. The mean is calculated by dividing the sum of the elements by the number of elements in the set. In this case: $^{7 + 6 + 23}/_3 = {}^{36}/_3 = 12$. Therefore, the sum of the mean and the median is $7 + 12 = 19$.

20. **1**   Arithmetic: Exponents and Square Roots;
         Algebra: Simplifying and Manipulating Expressions   Difficulty: medium

We can simplify each of the equations by eliminating the exponents. The square roots of 49 are 7 and −7. Since $v, y > 0$, we know that we'll be dealing with positive quantities. Taking the square root of each side, we can simplify the first equation to $(4x + y) = 7$. We can solve for y in the second equation:

$$2y^2 = 18$$
$$y^2 = 9$$
$$y = 3$$

Remember that we can disregard the possibility that $y = -3$ because the problem states that $y > 0$. Plugging $y = 3$ into the first equation:

$$4x + 3 = 7$$
$$4x = 4$$
$$x = 1$$

21. **128**   Geometry: Polygons   Difficulty: medium

To find the surface area of a rectangular solid, simply sum the areas of its six faces. Because four of the faces are 4×6 rectangles, the area of each one is $4 \times 6 = 24$. The other two faces are squares with sides of length 4, so their areas are $4 \times 4 = 16$. Summing the areas of all six faces, we find that the surface area of the solid is $(4 \times 24) + (2 \times 16) = 96 + 32 = 128$.

22. **30**   Geometry: Polygons   Difficulty: medium

The perimeter of the figure is $7 + 6 + 9 + 3 + x = 25 + x$. The easiest way to find x is to create a right triangle in which x is the hypotenuse. To do so, imagine extending the sides of lengths 6 and 3 to form a larger rectangle in which there is a right triangle in the corner. The legs of such a triangle have lengths $9 - 6 = 3$ and $7 - 3 = 4$. We can find from the Pythagorean Theorem that the hypotenuse has length $\sqrt{3^2 + 4^2} = \sqrt{9 + 16} = \sqrt{25} = 5$. So the perimeter of the figure is $25 + 5 = 30$.

23. **80** Algebra: Solving Inequalities   Difficulty: medium

It is important to determine whether $y + 2$ is positive or negative, since that will determine whether we need to reverse the inequality when we multiply by $(y + 2)$. Because $y \geq 3$, we know that $y + 2 \geq 5$. Since $y + 2$ is guaranteed to be a positive number, we can multiply both sides of the first inequality by $y + 2$ and the inequality will still hold. This leads to $x \geq 16(y + 2)$ or $x \geq 16y + 32$. From this inequality, we see that the smallest value of x will occur when y is equal to its smallest possible value, 3. Therefore, $x \geq 16(3) + 32$ or $x \geq 80$.

24. **6** Arithmetic: Series   Difficulty: high

The first thing to do in this problem is to list the first few terms of each sequence to familiarize yourself with them. Look at these few terms and decide if you can arrive at a solution by continuing to list terms, or if you must try to find some pattern or shortcut to solve the problem: $A = \{-6, -3, 0, 3 \ldots\}$ and $B = \{20, 15, 10, 5 \ldots\}$. By looking at the first four terms it should be apparent that soon after the fourth term, the value of a given term in A should exceed the value of the corresponding term in B since they are converging so quickly.

When you calculate just one more term in each sequence, you see that the fifth term of A, 6, is greater than the fifth term of B, 0. Therefore the value of the term in sequence A that first exceeds the value of the corresponding term in sequence B is 6. It's usually a safe bet to list three or four terms in a sequence if you don't know how to start solving a given problem involving sequences. This will often allow you to understand more about the sequence than you could at first glance.

25. **1** Arithmetic: Mean, Median, and Mode   Difficulty: high

Hopefully, your test-taking intuition will tell you that summing the terms is not the best way to solve this problem. There are a variety of shortcuts to solving this problem. You could notice that every negative term has a corresponding negative term (summing to 0), leaving only the 0 and 52 terms unaccounted for. You could then determine that the sum of all 52 terms is 52, yielding a mean of 1.

Also, for any set where all elements differ by a constant term (in this case 2), the average of the outermost pair is the same as the average of the entire set. So, to find the average of the entire set, simply find the average of -50 and 52, which is $^{(-50\, +\, 52)}\!/_{2} = 1$.

Verbal Section 2

Sentence Completions

1. **(A)**   One Word Direct   Difficulty: low

Since the first part of the sentence says that Hitchcock's films blended "horror and farce," the two adjectives describing his films must touch on both of these two ideas. In the second half of the sentence, "hilarious" already captures the idea of farce, so the missing word must have some strong association with horror. Gruesome has such an association, so it is the correct answer.

Of the remaining answer choices, funny is so close in meaning to "hilarious" that we know immediately that it is a poor choice for the blank. Staid means "reserved" or "refraining from intensity," which has no relationship to anything in the sentence. Horror might be considered either informational or moving, but either choice requires you to move beyond the scope of the question and introduce your own opinion, something that should never happen on the SAT.

2. **(D)**   Two Word Direct   Difficulty: low

Since we are told that the teacher is instructing her students on how to write a good paper, we know to look for words that will create a positive description of the paper. Once we realize this, we can immediately throw out inconsistent . . punctuation, since a paper that is "factually inconsistent" could never be a good paper. We can also discard continuous . . spelling and negative . . behavior, since "factually continuous" and "factually negative" don't really mean anything. Finally, we can eliminate obvious . . explanations as an answer since it makes the sentence refer to "proper rules of explanations," which makes no sense. That leaves you with the correct answer, correct . . grammar.

3. **(C)**   One Word Direct   Difficulty: low

In this question, the blank word describes a quality associated with being "annoyed" and "cutting people off." However, because we also know that Sarah was *not* known for this quality, the sentence is asking you to find a quality that is associated with the *opposite* characteristics of those listed. The only logical answer, therefore, is patience. Think of it this way: someone who *is* known for their patience is usually *not* easily annoyed and does not usually cut people off.

4. **(C)** One Word Direct   Difficulty: low

The sentence tells us that many members of Parliament saw Albert as a meddler in English affairs, so we know that they did not like him. We also know that he had some power as Victoria's husband. We must find a word that describes how Parliament might describe a man it saw as a "meddler with power."

Ecstasy and interest both have a positive connotation inappropriate for this sentence, so we can eliminate them. Sadness does have a negative connotation, but when plugged into the sentence, it yields the phrase, "treated him with sadness," which makes no sense, so we can throw it out too. Impatience implies a frustration with or general condescension towards someone or something. While it is possible, even likely, to be impatient with someone you do not like, it isn't that likely that you would act impatiently with someone who held a great deal of power and influence. Contempt, which means "derisive feeling" is the best answer because it resonates with the information given in the statement. These Lords and Commoners were not happy with Prince Albert.

5. **(B)** One Word Direct   Difficulty: medium

In this question, the information after the semi-colon elaborates on the description of *The Waste Land* provided before the semi-colon. We must find the word that describes the poem as "images from many levels of language and experience jumbling jarringly together."

The conventional conception of a symphony is something harmonious, not something "jumbling jarringly together." Although symphony captures the idea of multiple voices mixing together, its connotation is too imprecise. Since a hodgepodge is a mix of disparate elements, this word follows the cues of the sentence and accurately describes the levels of language and experience that make up *The Waste Land*. The remaining answer choices all fail to imply a diversity of elements. In particular, portrait suggests a unity of subject, while epilogue refers to something that appears at the end of a book, not an entire poem.

6. **(C)** Two Word Contrast   Difficulty: medium

The hinge word in this sentence is "though," which indicates that we are looking for words that will make the two parts of the sentence contrast: whatever American culture thinks of reindeer, it does not match their role in the lives of the Sami. The answer choices are each slightly confusing in that the first term of each choice actually could apply to the perception of reindeer in American culture (dim-witted, passive, fanciful, Arctic, festive), while the second term could at least make grammatical sense in the second blank. So it is necessary to look over each of these choices. Most of them can be discarded for failing to contrast: dim-witted . . unnecessary, arctic . . unhelpful, and festive . . detrimental.

Of the remaining two choices, each seems to offer the necessary contrast, but passive . . instrumental does not seem to offer it in a way that makes sense in the context of the sentence. If reindeer are instrumental to the lives of the Lapps, they probably are not instrumental solely because they are not passive, as the sentence would imply with those words plugged into it. Fanciful . . crucial makes better sense—Americans tend to associate reindeer with Santa Claus and flying sleighs, while to the Lapps they are a vital part of existence.

7.   **(D)**   Two Word Contrast   Difficulty: medium

The hinge word in this sentence is "though," which signals us to look for words that will make the two parts of the sentence contrast. Whatever Byron intended to convey about prison life in his poem fails in some way to match Byron's actual experience, so whatever word we choose for the second blank must reinforce the idea that Byron had "no firsthand experience of his subject." We can discard brutal . . criminal immediately for that reason. Chilling . . common is also easy to eliminate, simply because the idea of a "common aristocrat" is nonsensical. Luxurious . . pampered can be discarded because it fails to provide the necessary contrast, making it seem as though life in prison and Byron's life are more alike than different. Moreover, life in prison is hardly "luxurious." Unjust . . fair-handed looks like a good choice—it provides the necessary contrast, at least—until it is plugged into the sentence; when we put the words in the blanks, we can see that fair-handed fails to match the idea that Byron had "no firsthand experience of his subject."

The only choice that implies he had no first-hand experience with his subject while also providing the necessary contrast for the sentence is harsh . . privileged: Byron tried to depict the unpleasant life of a prisoner, though his own life was one of wealth and privilege.

8.   **(D)**   One Word Direct   Difficulty: medium

In this sentence, the phrase after the semi-colon elaborates on what has come before. If Shakespeare's plays are not totally serious, the word in the blank must be strongly associated with "lightheartedness" or "comedy."

Brutality and tragedy can be immediately eliminated because they are antithetical to the idea of comedy or lightheartedness. Harmony, too, is a poor choice of an opposite to the high-minded and the serious. Harmony is traditionally associated with high-minded activities such as art and music.

Buffoonery, that is, "foolish or playful behavior or practice," is exactly the contrast we are looking for: the opposite of high-minded and serious. Because what is serious and high-minded is likely to be more somber than happy, happiness might not be a terrible answer. However, happiness is less specifically opposed to high-mindedness than is buffoonery.

9.   **(E)**   One Word Direct   Difficulty: high

In this question, what comes after the comma implies that the costumes were inappropriate for the time period in which the play was set. We are looking for a word, therefore, that suggests that the costumes were out of context.

Empirical means "originating or based in real experience," and archetypal means "of or related to archetypes," which are the original patterns or prototypes or ideas behind all things. We would never call costumes empirical or archetypal, so we can eliminate these answer choices. Scrupulous and plausible would each suggest that the costumes were carefully made or appropriate. Given the second half of the sentence, however, we should be looking for a word that would point out a problem with the costume, not one that praises them. Anachronistic means "of or relating to a chronological misplacing." This word is perfect in the sentence.

10. **(B)** One Word Direct   Difficulty: high

In this question, a comma links the two parts of the sentence and implies that the second half will elaborate on the first. The blank word, therefore, must suggest that interest in the trend was fleeting.

If popular interest were indomitable, "incapable of being dominated," it would probably not vanish so quickly. Evanescent means "vanishing like smoke or vapor," which is a good way to describe quickly shifting popular trends. Vicarious, which means "experienced through another person," makes no sense in the sentence. The best synonym for phlegmatic is "sluggish," and it would be counterintuitive to describe as sluggish a kind of popular interest that vanishes quickly. So phlegmatic is out. If popular interest is unstinting, or "all-out," there is no reason to think that it would disappear quickly.

Analogies

11. **(E)** Type   Difficulty: low

"A CARROT is a kind of VEGETABLE." Applying this relationship to the possible answers, the only pair that fits is silver : metal; silver is a kind of metal. Root : garden and cabbage : soup have some relation to the word VEGETABLE and therefore might have distracted you, but the relations between both of these pairs is not that of specific example to general type.

12. **(E)** Part / Whole   Difficulty: low

"A CHIMNEY is made of BRICKS" is the best and most specific sentence you could make with this pair of stem words. The only answer pair that relates an object and the material from which it is made is word : letters. This is slightly tricky because words and letters are not physical objects; the key to this question lies in paying attention to the relationship and not the components of the answer.

13. **(C)** Characteristic Location   Difficulty: low

"FOOD is usually stored in a REFRIGERATOR." Likewise, a book is generally kept on a shelf. While you would find clothing in a laundromat, you would not store it there, so that relationship is not as good as it needs to be.

14. **(B)** Type   Difficulty: low

"A KILOMETER is the unit of measurement for DISTANCE" is the best and most specific sentence you could make with this stem pair. Similarly, ounce is a unit of measurement for weight. The key to answering this question lies in making a specific sentence: simply saying that coloumbs are used to measure charges would mean that barometer : pressure and thermometer : temperature could also be answers. However, those two pairs refer to the instrument used to measure, while the stem pair and correct answer both refer to the unit of measurement.

15. **(E)** Function   Difficulty: low

"The function of a RAZOR is to remove HAIR" is the best and most specific sentence you could make with this stem pair. Similarly, an eraser is used to remove chalk. Soap : shower and closet : clothing are both relationships of location, while pants : leg and paper : notebook are part : whole relationships. Only eraser : chalk has a functional relationship, so we know it must be the correct answer.

16. **(C)** Lack   Difficulty: medium

"A PAUPER lacks MONEY" is the best and most specific sentence you can make to relate this stem pair. Similarly, an invalid lacks health. None of the other answer pairs necessarily involve a relationship of lack. In particular, a retiree has lots of leisure time, precisely the opposite of the relation you should be looking for.

17. **(D)** Relative Size and Degree   Difficulty: medium

"Someone who is BRILLIANT is more intelligent than someone who is merely CLEVER;" BRILLIANT is a degree of meaning greater than CLEVER. By the same token, something that is striking is more attention-grabbing than something that is merely noticeable. The other answer choices are fairly easy to weed out. Manipulative : honest and obvious : subtle are antonyms, not relations of degree, and apparent : substantial seems to have no direct relationship at all. Rough and abrasive have almost the same meaning, but if anything, abrasive is stronger than rough, so the words would be out of order.

18. **(E)** Characteristic Action   Difficulty: medium

"A DIRECTOR oversees the production of a PLAY" just as a conductor oversees the performance of a symphony. This question is of moderate difficulty because of the complexity of this relationship. A composer writes a song, while a farmer raises cattle. Both of these answers may seem correct because they involve the creation of something, which you might think directing a play does, but whereas directing a play involves coordinating a large group, songwriting and cattle-raising do not. A waiter merely delivers a meal, and a climber ascends a mountain. In neither of these options is there a sense of the first word changing or shaping the other, so they are obviously wrong. At the least, you should have been able to eliminate these last two and then guessed.

19. **(C)** Function   Difficulty: medium

"A DUCT is something that AIR moves through" is the clearest and most specific sentence you could make with this stem pair. Likewise, a canal is a conduit for the movement of water. Ditch : dirt and pool : concrete both describe types of conduits or receptacles, but the answer pairs relate them to the materials out of which they are made. Crane : materials describes a machine and something that machine might lift. Finally, a wrench is used to fix a pipe; even if you don't know what a DUCT is, it is safe to assume that AIR is not used to fix it, so you can certainly throw out wrench : pipe.

20. **(C)** Type   Difficulty: medium

"A PHOTOGRAPH is a type of IMAGE." The only answer pair that has a similar relationship is television : medium, since television is a type of medium. You might have been tricked by text : newsprint, since newsprint is a type of text. Note, however, that in this pair the word order is backward.

21. **(D)** Attribute   Difficulty: medium

"A VICIOUS person is marked by his or her FEROCITY." Similarly, a cold person is marked by his or her frigidity. Of the other possible choices, two seem not to have a direct relationship (repulsive : masquerade and joyful : desire), cruel : insult has the wrong relationship, and bland : excitement has exactly the opposite relation of what we want: a bland person is not characterized by excitement. The only tricky possibility is cruel : insult. Because insults and cruelty are such negative things, these words might seem vaguely to relate to VICIOUS and FEROCITY. Nevertheless, it cannot be said that insult is an attribute of a cruel person, so this pair cannot be the answer.

22. **(A)** Cause and Effect   Difficulty: medium

This question is fairly difficult, as the relation between AMPLIFIER and SOUND may seem somewhat more abstract and somewhat less material than that between polish and sheen. Nevertheless, "an AMPLIFIER is meant to increase SOUND," just as polish is meant to increase sheen—that is, to make something shinier. Of the other answer choices, magnifier : color is the most confusing, as magnifier seems to go with AMPLIFIER; but a magnifier does not increase or intensify color, it only increases the size of an image. Loathing : fear has no clear internal relationship, conscientiousness : morality does not have a cause-effect relationship, and metallurgy (the study of metals) is obviously not meant to increase platinum.

23. **(A)** Description   Difficulty: high

"THOROUGH RESEARCH is extremely meticulous research." Similarly, an exhaustive investigation is one that is meticulous and covers all possible angles.

    This question relies in some measure on your vocabulary. If you knew the word exhaustive, then the question was probably not that hard. However, if you were unsure of exhaustive, or if you took it to mean "exhausting" (as in something that makes one tired), then the answer might have been difficult to find. In that case, you could go through the answer choices to eliminate obviously wrong answers. Content : sedative does not have a good relation; a sedative makes someone calm, but it will not necessarily make him content. That answer can easily be eliminated. Wanton : supervisor can similarly be eliminated since the words do not seem to have any clear relation. Perverse and morality have a rather strong relationship as antonyms; illuminating : light also has a strong internal relation. If you didn't know the stem words, these two answers would be difficult to eliminate. However, if you did know the stem pair and could figure out its relation, then it's fairly obvious that neither perverse : morality nor illuminating : light have anything in common with THOROUGH : RESEARCH.

Reading Comprehension

24. **(E)** Specific Information   Difficulty: medium
Provided one consults the lines referenced in the question, finding the correct answer is fairly easy. But it is important to look back, rather than to try to find an answer based on one's sense of the passage as a whole. This is because each of the answer choices could easily be true of the general question, "Why have scholars been unable to agree about the correct title of the novel?" But the question requires that we answer that question according to the information in lines 1–3, which indicate that the novel's name has been in doubt because the novel was not published in Melville's lifetime. (E) is the only feasible answer.

25. **(B)** Understanding Themes and Arguments   Difficulty: medium
This question is fairly simple, but in order to answer it, it is necessary to think about the small part of the passage indicated in the question within the context of the passage as a whole. After the author describes all the subtitles *Billy Budd* has had, he goes on to explain how those subtitles indicate the novel's take on the conflict between the individual and society. He then describes how that conflict can be represented by the idea of personal titles, such as "writer," "sailor," "professor," or "foretopman." Because the main subtitles in *Billy Budd* ascribe various personal titles to the main character, the main function of the subtitles in this passage is to illustrate the author's idea about personal titles and the way they indicate social position. Thus (B) is the best answer choice.

26. **(C)** Author's Attitude and Tone   Difficulty: medium
The only way to answer a question such as this is to think about your general impression of the author's attitude in this passage, and then give your impression a word. In this case, the author seems calm, instructive, and dispassionate. His main goal seems to be to teach his readers about his subject; he does not advocate any particular argument, and does not use rhetoric to persuade other people that his position is correct. He is certainly not "condescending" or "outraged." He seems like an

"inquisitive" person, but this passage is designed to answer questions rather than to ask them. Because of his calm demeanor, he cannot be said to be "excited and enthusiastic." "Explanatory and objective" is a much better fit: he is explaining his idea about *Billy Budd* in a comprehensive way. (C) is clearly the correct answer choice.

27.   **(A)**   Specific Information   Difficulty: low

This question is extremely easy if you remember to look back at the lines referenced in the question. In these lines, the author clearly states that Melville's introduction of Ishmael, using the words "Call me Ishmael," is "curious" because he does not tell us whether Ishmael is the narrator's real name. So (A) is the obvious answer choice. The only confusion presented by the other possible choices is that some of them also refer to the ambiguity of the character's name. But the author never says that "Ishmael" is an unusual name, as (C) implies, or that the name is ambiguous because of social context, as (E) implies.

28.   **(D)**   Understanding Themes and Arguments   Difficulty: high

This question is somewhat difficult, as each of the answer choices indicates a fairly sophisticated and complex way of interpreting the question. To answer the question correctly, it is necessary not just to find a plausible definition for "the discrepancy between an individual and his name," but also to find the definition that best describes the *author*'s idea of the discrepancy. To find this definition, we must look at the passage as a whole, both for specific clues and for a general sense of how the author thinks about identity. Once we do this, it becomes clear fairly quickly that (D) is the best answer choice. The passage in general is concerned with the conflict between exterior labels, such as names and titles, and a person's inner conception of himself. Further, there are specific clues, passages such as "at the essential core of his existence, he is more than just his name" and "you are you. Beyond that you have your name…" These passages both seem to indicate that a person's name is not the essence of a person's inner identity; as a result, the answer reading "the difference between a person's name and his inner identity" is clearly the right choice.

29.   **(B)**   Words-in-context   Difficulty: medium

The passage does not provide a specific definition of "foretopman," but it does provide a general definition, stating that a foretopman is a particular kind of sailor ("*Billy Budd, Foretopman* goes even further than *Billy Budd, Sailor*"). Three of the answer choices, (A), (C), and (E), can immediately be discarded, as they contradict the notion of a foretopman as a sailor. (The only difficulty these choices present is that they involve some of the notions implied by the word "fore-top-man"—the foreman of a factory or the man who comes out on top in a wrestling match. If you are careful, you will not be fooled by such tricks.) (D) does define the foretopman as a specific kind of sailor, but it makes the definition *too* specific—the text never indicates that a foretopman keeps watch from the crow's nest. For that reason, (B) is the correct answer choice.

30. **(E)** Specific Information   Difficulty: high

This question is fairly difficult, because to answer it, one needs not only to consult the lines referenced in the question, but also to have come to the right conclusion about the passage's definition of the unfamiliar word "foretopman." The lines referenced in the question tell us that being a sailor is different from being a foretopman, because "sailor" is a general category, while "foretopman" comes with specific duties and responsibilities. The question then becomes whether the passage describes what those duties and responsibilities are—if it says that a foretopman is a military sailor, then the correct answer is (D); if it says that a foretopman is a port inspector, then the correct answer is (B). Of course, the passage does not specifically define the role of a foretopman, but only implies that a foretopman is a particular kind of sailor.

With that in mind, we can limit the possible answer choices to (A) and (E). (A) is on the right track, but it is an incomplete answer—being a foretopman does not exactly imply a *different kind* of work, only a specific set of duties within the general work of being a sailor. Further, (A) does not take into account the thematic importance of the distinction, which is one of the main themes of the passage. Having a more specific role necessarily limits one's social identity, even if one's inner identity is unchanged. Thus, (E) is the best of all the answer choices.

31. **(C)** Author's Technique   Difficulty: high

This is a fairly challenging question, because it requires us to think about the author's larger intent in framing his argument as he does—why does he choose to make his argument this way, instead of in a different way? To understand that, it is necessary to have a thorough understanding of the themes at work in the passage generally. Further, several of the incorrect answer choices might seem very appealing, because they involve some of those same themes, though they apply them incorrectly. Generally speaking, the author uses his own name, "James Corolla," to illustrate his point about the ways in which titles can limit social identity. He does this by affixing various titles ("writer," "professor") to his name, and describing how his arguments about *Billy Budd* take on different implications depending on his title. If he is a professor, for instance, his arguments are more weighty and authoritative than if he is a writer, but he has less freedom to change his mind. So the correct answer choice is (C)—he uses his own as an example of the constraints titles can place on social identity.

To arrive at this answer, it is also necessary to discard the incorrect answer choices, some of which are fairly tricky. (A) is one of the choices that is close to correct: the author does use his name as an example of the specializations that are available in a given field (such as writer/professor or sailor/foretopman). But that is certainly not the main point of the passage, or the main point of this particular section of it. (B) is tricky because it references an earlier moment of the passage, the section that discussed the discrepancy between a person's name and his inner identity. But this section is not so concerned with that discrepancy—it uses the name for a different purpose than explaining how it is different from the writer's inner self.

(D) is the easiest choice to eliminate—the writer never offers a personal account of reading *Billy Budd*. (E) is so general that it might seem tempting, but the passage really never discusses the importance of *names* in the way we think about other people, only the importance of *titles* in the way we think about other people. We do not think of James Corolla differently because he is named James Corolla; we think of him differently because he is a writer or a professor.

32. (A) Words-in-context   Difficulty: medium

This question is fairly simple; the only complication is that each of the answer choices represents a plausible possible meaning for the word "autonomy." Nonetheless, it only takes a very basic understanding of the themes explained several times in this passage to arrive at the correct choice. The passage as a whole involves the theme of the constraints of social expectation: once a person "enters society," one receives a label such as "writer" or "sailor," and one is then expected to perform a set of actions based on that label. As a result, the meaning of "autonomy" in this passage is clearly best represented by (A). The other answer choices could define autonomy in a different context, but they have very little to do with the context established by this passage.

33. (D) Words-in-context   Difficulty: low

This is a very simple question, requiring little more than knowledge of the definition of the word "chafe." The line in question describes the way a person's individuality "chafes against" exterior social limitations. Society attempts to limit a person's role, and the person's sense of individuality resists the limitation. (D) is obviously the correct answer.

The only other tempting answer choice might be (A), since a literal meaning of "chafe" is the way one's skin grows irritated or sore from rubbing against a confinement, such as a rope. But this passage uses "chafe" in a metaphorical sense rather than a literal sense. There is no actual rope present, and so "grows irritated" fails to capture the connotation of the word as used in the passage.

34. (B) Specific Information   Difficulty: medium

Without referencing the text, this question would be almost impossible to answer, because each of the answer choices presents a plausible and convincing explanation for what the implications of an "inside narrative" might be. Fortunately, even a perfunctory examination of the passage makes it fairly easy to pick out the right choice. As the passage says, an "inside narrative . . . places special emphasis on the interior consciousness of an individual, in an attempt to explore the private selves of men thrust into a social world." Thus, no matter how persuasive the other answer choices may be on their own terms, there is no doubt that (B) is the only viable choice: an "inside narrative" takes you inside the mind of a character, to show how his inner experience compares with his "outside" experience of human society.

35. **(A)**   Understanding Themes and Arguments   Difficulty: low
This question requires us to think about the passage as a whole rather than to look at one particular part of it, but it is still a relatively simple question to answer. Interestingly, this passage (which is possibly part of a larger work) draws some very detailed conclusions based only on the novel's titles (*Billy Budd, Sailor* or *Billy Budd, Foretopman*) and subtitles ("An Inside Narrative"), which are laid out in the first paragraph. The other examples used to develop the argument—the opening of *Moby-Dick*, the author's own name and personal titles—are taken from outside the book itself. The only way to answer this question is to look through the passage and see what examples it uses. When this is done, all the other answer choices can easily be discarded, and (A) emerges as the clear choice.

Math Section 3

1. **(C)**   Arithmetic: Basic Operations   Difficulty: low
The number of apples in each box is irrelevant to the solution. We know the price per box of apples and the number of boxes that was purchased, so we can simply take their product. The total price that John paid is 4×6 dollars.

2. **(D)**   Arithmetic: Ratios and Proportions   Difficulty: low
In every quartet, 2 of the singers are male. Therefore, if there are 50 quartets, then there are $2 \times 50 = 100$ male singers. Although we could solve this problem by finding the total number of singers and then dividing by 2 since half of the singers are male, that method takes more time and increases the likelihood of an error.

3. **(C)**   Geometry: Angles and Lines   Difficulty: low
Since a and b are parallel, we know that x equals 30°, because the transversal c creates congruent alternate exterior angles. We also know that $(x + y) = 180°$, because x and y are supplementary angles. Therefore, $(30 + y) = 180$, and $y = 150°$. To solve for $(y - x)$, just plug in the values for y and x: $(150 - 30) = 120$.

4. **(D)**   Algebra: Solving Linear Equations   Difficulty: low
Billy starts with n apples. After eating (subtracting) 8 apples, there are 18 remaining. This is expressed by the equation $n - 8 = 18$. Adding 8 to both sides yields $n = 26$.

5. **(E)**   Miscellaneous Math: Logic   Difficulty: medium
We will solve this problem by examining each of the possible choices. The first choice is "some blue balls have dots on them." In the problem, we are told that all blue balls have at least one star on them. However, we are not told what other markings might appear on blue balls. Therefore, some blue balls could have dots on them, and we can eliminate (A). The second choice is "all red balls have 3 dots on them." We know that all

red balls have at least one dot on them, so it is entirely possible that all red dots could have 3 dots on them. Since this statement could be true, we can eliminate (B). The third choice is "all balls with dots on them are red." Again, we know that all red balls must have at least one dot on them, and it is entirely possible that no other colored balls have dots on them. Therefore, this statement could be true, and (C) is not the correct answer. The fourth choice is "all blue balls have squares on them." We know that all blue balls have at least one star on them. We also know that all balls with squares on them also have dots on them. However, these statements do not preclude the possibility that all blue balls have squares on them. Therefore, choice (D) could be true, and so we can eliminate it. This leaves choice (E), "some green balls have squares on them." This can never hold because all balls with squares on them also have dots on them, and we know that no green balls have stars or dots on them. Therefore, if any green balls did have squares on them, they would also have to have dots, which is a contradiction of the statement "no green balls have stars or dots on them." Therefore, choice (E) can never be true and is therefore the correct answer.

6. **(D)**   Geometry: Slope   Difficulty: medium
The first step is to write the equations of the two lines. This is easy because both lines pass through (0,0), which makes the slope-intercept form of the equation of the line simply $y = mx$, where m is the slope. The equation of l_1 is simply $y_1 = 3/(2x_1)$ and $1L_2$ is $y_2 = 2/(3x_2)$. Both points A and B have $y = 2$, so the distance between them is just the difference in the x-coordinate. Substituting $y = 2$ into the first equation, we see that $x = \frac{4}{3}$. Substituting $y = 2$ into the second equation, we see that $x = 3$. So the distance between the two points is $(3 - \frac{4}{3}) = \frac{5}{3}$.

7. **(D)**   Arithmetic: Mean, Median, and Mode   Difficulty: medium
To answer this question, you could figure out the value of each number in the set, multiply them by 2 and recalculate the mean, but that would take a lot of time and is completely unnecessary. When you double the value of every member of a set of numbers, the mean of that set will double as well, so since the average was 200, it must now be 400.

This rule holds for any basic linear operations (not squaring) performed on all numbers of a set. If you do the same thing to every number, you can find the new mean by performing that same operation on the previous mean.

8.   **(D)**   Geometry: Triangles; Polygons   Difficulty: high
Because we know that the length of the diagonals is $\sqrt{2}$, we can find an equation for the length of the sides s of the squares. Using the Pythagorean theorem we can solve for s:

$$s^2 + s^2 = \sqrt{2}^2$$
$$2s^2 = 2$$
$$s^2 = 1$$
$$s = 1$$

The entire figure is a rectangle with a length equal to 3, a height of 1, and an area of $3 \times 1 = 3$. The shaded region comprises one-half of the total area or $\frac{1}{2} \times 3 = 1.5$.

9.   **(E)**   Arithmetic: Fractions, Decimals, and Percents   Difficulty: high
The best way to attack this problem is to test each answer choice. Simply substitute each pair of values into the given equation.

(A) $\frac{1}{4} + \frac{1}{8} = \frac{2}{8} + \frac{1}{8} = \frac{3}{8}$
(B) $\frac{1}{3} + \frac{1}{4} = \frac{4}{12} + \frac{3}{12} = \frac{7}{12}$
(C) $\frac{1}{1} + \frac{1}{2} = \frac{2}{2} + \frac{1}{2} = \frac{3}{2}$
(D) $\frac{1}{4} + \frac{1}{3} = \frac{3}{12} + \frac{4}{12} = \frac{7}{12}$
(E) $\frac{1}{2} + \frac{1}{4} = \frac{2}{4} + \frac{1}{4} = \frac{3}{4}$

By inspection, we can determine that the correct answer is (E).

10.   **(D)**   Arithmetic: Fractions, Decimals, and Percents   Difficulty: high
The best way to solve this problem is to calculate how much the class made off of each group of students. The senior-senior couples make up 40% of the class of 300, or 120 people. Since couples pay per couple rather than per person, 60 couples bought their tickets to the prom for $60 generating $60 \times \$60 = \$3600$.

There are $40\% \times 300 = 120$ students who took dates from outside the class. For those students and their dates to attend prom, they must purchase one $40 ticket and one $35 ticket. So, there are 120 couples who paid $75 for their tickets, for a total of $120 \times \$75 = \$9000$.

10% of the class came to the prom by themselves, meaning that 30 people purchased individual tickets. Their tickets generated $30 \times \$35 = \$1050$. Adding all these amounts together, we arrive at the correct answer of $13,650.

Verbal Section 3

1. **(C)**   Main Theme or Idea   Difficulty: medium

This reference is part of the first paragraph of his passage, in which Thoreau begins to ponder the effect of the woods on the human psyche. The philosophers in question value the woods in the same way that Thoreau does—for their serenity and ability to allow one to contemplate, though not necessarily on religious themes. Thus answer (C) is the correct one.

2. **(A)**   Understanding Themes and Arguments   Difficulty: low

For Thoreau, as he describes it in this passage, the problem with civilized life is that man often ends up outside of himself, lost in thought and concentrating on the tasks of the day. The benefit of being in the woods is that one can become reintegrated into the surrounding world by becoming more fully conscious of it. The correct answer is therefore (A).

3. **(D)**   Words-in-context   Difficulty: low

In the surrounding context, Thoreau states that he has been walking on the paths near his home for many years, but he still finds new walks and views. This should clue you in to what the meaning of "exhausted" could be. If he has been walking on the paths for many years, you might expect that he would have taken all the walks, but his statements make it clear that he hasn't taken, or completed, every possible walk. This interpretation is further supported by the following sentence, in which Thoreau comments on the joys of things that are new, unexperienced, unexhausted. With this context in mind, you should be able to pick (D) as the right answer, even though (A) is the more common definition of exhausted.

4. **(E)**   Specific Information   Difficulty: medium

This is a bit of a trick question, for, as the passage reveals, Thoreau doesn't appreciate much about people at all. In fact, what he seeks is their absence from the scene; therefore the correct answer is (E).

5. **(A)**   Author's Attitude and Tone   Difficulty: medium

To answer this question you must read the answer pairs carefully. In some of them, particularly answers (D) and (E), one of the terms in the answer is correct, but the other is not. He is excited but not relieved, optimistic but not wry. Answers (B) and (C) don't capture Whitman's tone at all and should be immediately discarded. That leaves answer answer (A), the only answer that contains two terms both of which describe Whitman's tone.

6. **(E)** Words-in-context   Difficulty: high

This is a fairly difficult question, particularly since Whitman, the author of this passage, is known for using words in obscure and idiosyncratic ways. The key to answering this question is to look at the passage carefully. The two adjectives that accompany the word "oceanic" are "great" and "seething," suggesting something that is large and in tumult. Therefore the correct answer is (E).

7. **(B)** Specific Information   Difficulty: low

If you've read the passage you should be able to get this one with no problem, but look in particular at the second-to-last paragraph. Even if you weren't able to pick the right answer straight off, you should be able to eliminate all the wrong answers pretty easily. In this passage, Whitman very clearly is not interested in the distribution of wealth or in businesses. Though he mentions some means of transportation they are not his focus. Neither is geography. Whitman claims that he is studying humanity in New York, and one can only do that by studying the people of New York. The correct answer is (B).

8. **(A)** Understanding Themes and Arguments   Difficulty: low

Whitman is enthusiastic about American democracy, but he knows that "critics and pessimists" will disagree with him. The answer, then, is (A).

9. **(E)** Relating Two Passages   Difficulty: medium

This question first requires that you decide whether Whitman thinks politics are a good thing or not. The tone of his piece suggests that he finds politics a positive force, so you can eliminate the answers that have him either agreeing with or indifferent to Thoreau's claim. The two remaining answers offer a choice of either the city or the country as a political ideal for Whitman. Choosing between these two should be easy; he admires the city as "the most direct proof yet of successful Democracy," so the correct answer must be (E).

10. **(B)** Relating Two Passages   Difficulty: medium

The correct answer is (B). Whitman and Thoreau are both interested in the influence of environment upon the soul, but they differ in their choice of environment: Whitman prefers the city, while Thoreau chooses the woods.

11. **(C)** Relating Two Passages   Difficulty: high

The correct answer is (C). Thoreau writes about the serenity of the woods, and Whitman focuses on the character that the people of New York give to the city.

12. **(A)** Relating Two Passages   Difficulty: high

Although they make very different arguments, the conceptual aim of both passages is to look at the relationship between man and his environment. Therefore the correct answer is (A).

13. **(D)** Relating Two Passages   Difficulty: high
This question requires that you have a good sense of the second passage as a whole. Whitman is marked by his enthusiasm and his curiosity about human institutions. Therefore it is most likely that, of these alternatives, he would seek out rural settlements to meet the people who live there. The correct answer is therefore (D).

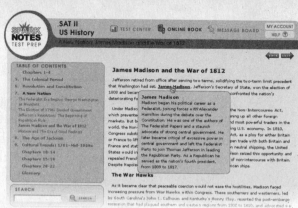
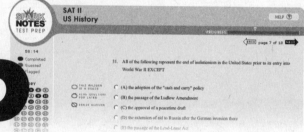

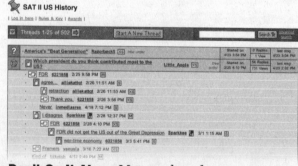